SILENT VIOLENCE

Geographies of Justice and Social Transformation

SERIES EDITORS

Deborah Cowen, University of Toronto
Nik Heynen, University of Georgia
Melissa W. Wright, Pennsylvania State University

ADVISORY BOARD

Sharad Chari, London School of Economics
Bradon Ellem, University of Sydney
Gillian Hart, University of California, Berkeley
Andrew Herod, University of Georgia
Jennifer Hyndman, York University
Larry Knopp, University of Washington, Tacoma
Heidi Nast, DePaul University
Jamie Peck, University of British Columbia
Frances Fox Piven, City University of New York
Laura Pulido, University of Southern California
Paul Routledge, University of Glasgow
Neil Smith, City University of New York
Bobby Wilson, University of Alabama

SILENT VIOLENCE

Food, Famine, and Peasantry in Northern Nigeria

With a new introduction

Michael J. Watts

University of Georgia Press
Athens and London

Paperback edition published in 2013 by
The University of Georgia Press
Athens, Georgia 30602
www.ugapress.org
© 1983 by the Regents of the University of California
"Preface to the New Edition" and "Bare Life and the Long Interregnum:
Introduction to the New Edition" © 2013 by Michael J. Watts

Printed digitally in the United States of America

Library of Congress Cataloging-in-Publication Data

Watts, Michael, 1951–
    Silent violence : food, famine, and peasantry in northern Nigeria :
with a new introduction / Michael J. Watts.
        p. cm. — (Geographies of justice and social transformation)
    "Silent violence: food, famine, and peasantry in northern Nigeria was
previously published in 1983 by the University of California Press."
    Includes bibliographical references and index.
    ISBN 978-0-8203-4445-4 (pbk. : alk. paper)
    1. Famines—Nigeria, Northern. 2. Food supply—Nigeria, Northern.
3. Peasants—Nigeria, Northern. I. Title.
    HC1055.Z7N679 2013
    338.19669–dc23   2012020887

British Library Cataloging-in-Publication Data available

Frontispiece: A man carrying a sack en route to Sokoto market, Sokoto
State. Irene Becker, Budapest, Hungary.

Silent Violence: Food, Famine, and Peasantry in Northern Nigeria was previously
published in 1983 by the University of California Press.

This book is dedicated to
Gunnar Olsson,
teacher and friend.

CONTENTS

PREFACE TO THE NEW EDITION

It remains an indelible image. Flying low over Kano city, preparing to land, I was taken aback by what appeared to be a farmer and a donkey crossing the runway. As we took our final approach, I saw that it was, in fact, man and beast. It was late August 1972, and it seemed I was entering a world unlike any other I had ever encountered. It turned out to be true. Indeed, that landing had a strange echo several years later when I was driving my trusty motorcycle from Katsina, where I was then living, to Kano. Along the perimeter of the Kano airport, I turned a corner to find the still burning fuselage of a wrecked plane in the middle of the road. Nigeria has always seemed to conjure up a heady mix of the fantastic (or perhaps I should say of magical realism), of a high-octane humanity, and prophesies of the coming catastrophy. As I write, the front page of the April 15, 2012, *New York Times* carries a story of Nigerian population growth—"a preview of a global problem"—and the nightmarish living conditions of the Lagosian slum world, perhaps twenty million people strong, many of whom live with their families in the locally named "face me, face you" rooms, barely eighty square feet and without water and sanitation.

If Nigeria has a reputation—perhaps infamy is a better word—in the contemporary world of development, it is one of oil-fueled corruption, a chronically failed secular postcolonial project with little to show for the $700 billion dollars of oil revenues captured by the state over the last half century. I conducted the research for *Silent Violence* during the first oil boom of the 1970s, a period of overheated resource-nationalism in which the Nigerian postcolonial state was refashioning itself. Oil provided a backdrop for my study of food security and famine in the country's drought-prone north, a heavily settled and deeply commercialized Muslim region of largely peasant producers. Three decades later, climate threats are front and center once again. This time operating under the sign of global climate change, they are now framed by a political economy in which oil has seeped into virtually every cultural, social, and political crease and pore of the country. The great tragedy is that in many respects the picture I painted of rural poverty and chronic food insecurity in the Sahelian zones of the north remains largely the same and in some respects is even worse. In any event, in an oil-rich state conditions are deplorable and can only be regarded as a massive political failure.

In part because of the influx of oil revenues since the 1970s, the social and political forcefield of the north—indeed the whole country—has been transformed. The northern states have witnessed a perfect storm of simultaneous economic stagnation, demographic growth (and a massive youth bulge), and the splintering of the Muslim community. That storm is given vivid expression in the rise of a popular Islamist insurrectionary movement with the Hausa nickname Boko Haram and officially known in Arabic as *Jama'atu Ahlis Sunna Lidda'awati Wal-Jihad* (People Committed to the Propagation of the Prophet's Teachings and Jihad). Over the last year or so Boko Haram's militants have carried out audacious attacks, assassinations, and suicide bombings targeting representatives of the state they believe have cheated or failed them. The movement's propulsive energy arises from the deep contradictions of a failed oil-development project that has left the rural and urban poor materially deprived and politically frustrated.

Long before the Occupy Movement forced economic and class inequality onto the political agenda in the United States, Nigeria had its own "we are the 99 percent" rallying cry. According to the World Bank, over 80 percent of the vast oil revenues flowing into the Nigerian exchequer—$59 billion in 2010—were captured by 1 percent of the population. The Nigerian political, military, and commercial elites' furious and bloody struggle to capture oil wealth highlights the deep rupture between rulers and ruled in a rowdy country destined to have a population of over 400 million by 2050. On the larger canvas of failed oil development and desolation in the rural and urban slum worlds, it is perhaps no surprise that President Goodluck Jonathan's rash and abrupt decision on January 1, 2012, to abolish petroleum subsidies in the wake of a visit by IMF director Christine Lagarde should have triggered an explosive reaction on the streets. The removal of the subsidy—by the government's account, fuel subsidies cost $8 billion a year, more than a quarter of the total government budget—caused an immediate doubling of oil and food prices. In turn, five days of strikes and protests brought the country to its knees, costing the government over $1.2 billion.

All of this makes the appearance of the second edition of *Silent Violence* both sadly relevant and deeply tragic. In the years since the book's initial publication, I increasingly turned my attention to another part of Nigeria, the oil-producing Niger delta. Yet ironically both of the stories I have charted over these last decades end up in the same place: a militant insurgency and extraordinary violence. Boko Haram and the Movement for the Emancipation of the Niger Delta, while seemingly markedly different on their face, share some striking family resemblances.

Working in Nigeria for almost forty years has been energizing, exciting, and enriching. At the same time it has been one of the most dispiriting of experiences. Any country in which hundreds of billions of dollars have not added anything to the standard of living of millions of average citizens is in deep trouble. The life chances of those with whom I lived in northern Nigeria in 1976 don't appear to be much better in 2012. At the same time, the country has always seemed to pull itself back from the brink and, on occasion, produce something of a political miracle (the rejection of President Obasanjo's sinister effort to run for a third term in 2006, for example). My continuing faith in the country, evidence to the contrary, may be wildly optimistic but is not entirely myopic.

San Francisco, April 23, 2012

ERRATA

A number of errors appeared in the first edition, and I would like to correct several important ones here.

Page xxx. Line 7 of the third paragraph should read: I have chosen to ground this geographic content . . .

Page 222. The subhead should read: Grains Trade, Domestic Storage, and the Minefields.

Pages 453–54. This discussion is taken from the pathbreaking research of Paul Ross. In addition to the unpublished paper referred to in the bibliography, the reader should read his chapter, based on his doctoral research, in M. Watts, editor, *State, Oil, and Agriculture in Nigeria* (Berkeley: Institute of International Studies Press, University of California, 1987).

Pages 508–9. The discussion of the Yan Tatsine rebellion is taken from discussions with my fellow Hausa scholar Paul Lubeck. His foundational analysis was published subsequently as "Islamic Protest under Semi-industrial Capitalism: Yan Tatsine Explained," *Africa* 55 (1985): 369–89.

PREFACE TO THE 1983 EDITION

The crisis consists precisely in the fact that the old is dying and the new cannot be born; in this interregnum a great variety of morbid symptoms appear.

                             Antonio Gramsci, Prison Notebooks

                            Most of sub-Saharan Africa is in the midst of a massive food crisis. Domestic production has stagnated, imported staple foodstuffs continue to grow alarmingly, and the threat of famine is omnipresent. Africa remains in large measure a continent of peasant producers, strapped by simple agrarian technologies and vulnerable to the vicissitudes of nature, especially drought in rainfed agricultural systems. Why has this crisis arisen, what are its historic origins, and why do food systems periodically break down completely? Why, in other words, do famines occur and how have their genesis and effects changed through time? In this study, I attempt to trace the changing character of food systems in northern Nigeria among Hausa peasant farmers and examine the record of food crises. In desert-edge environments, drought and extreme climatic variability constitute critical threats to sustained food production. I attempt to assess how peasants cope with these climatic risks, how food systems may collapse, and how the capability of rural producers to accommodate risk and food shortage can be progressively eroded. Using archival sources and a fifteen-month village study in northern Katsina, I argue that the history of peasant food supply and famine is relevant for an understanding not only of the current food crisis in Nigeria but also to grasp the essentials of the agrarian question in the Third World.

In the widest sense, then, this book examines the complex and changing relationships between nature and society. More specifically, I attempt to trace some of the significant changes that have occurred in peasant subsistence and consumption in northern Nigeria, roughly between the middle of the nineteenth century and the present, in a region subject to recurrent drought and considerable climatic irregularity. My concern with food, environmental perturbations, and complex social systems strikes to the very core of contemporary geography, whose intellectual lineages are closely bound to the study of the changing forms of the human appropriation of nature. The brilliant Brazilian geographer Josué de Castro for example spent much of his academic life wrestling with these same concerns, freeing the discussion of Third World peasant food supply from its Malthusian shackles and situating it within the context of the political economy of underdevelopment. The early French geographers, writing on similar subject matters, exerted a seminal influence on the *Annales* school of historiography, and specifically on the epochal contributions of Braudel and Le Roy Ladurie on climate and society in Western Europe. Climate has, of course, been held responsible for the genesis and demise of civilization, the origin of the state, and doubtless much more. There is a tendency, however, to take climate as a given in view of its obvious biological importance and to view society "as a passive receptor of the impact of climate" (Garcia 1981, p. xi). Rather than adopt these simple notions of causality and effect, I concentrate on the social dimensions of drought and, as a corollary, on the social production of famine. All climatic phenomena have social referents which are historically specific forms of society.

I am particularly interested in one moment in the dialogue between society and its physical environment—the moment when the cycle of household reproduction among smallholders is thrown into jeopardy; that is to say, when food systems fail and famine develops. These crises are preeminently social and should not be posed as simple technical or demographic failures or as the inevitable consequence of a predatory climate. In colonial and postcolonial Africa, I argue, famines were and are organically linked to the rupture of the balance between peasant subsistence and consumption precipitated by the development and intensification of commodity production. More concretely, a historical study of subsistence crises in Nigerian Hausaland must be grounded in the unfolding of capitalism in Nigeria, and in what Perry Anderson calls "the jagged temporal rhythms and breaks and the uneven spatial distributions and displacements of capital accumulation" (1980, pp. 33, 34).

In spite of the current concern with food and hunger in the Third World periphery, perhaps thrown into starkest relief by the massive Sahelian famine of the early 1970s, famine is neither new nor unprecedented. It has been a doggedly recursive phenomenon throughout human history. In this work, then, I adopt a self-consciously historical perspective because famines did not surface for the first time in 1972; neither are subsistence crises in themselves of spellbinding academic significance. But in the nineteenth century, the Sokoto Caliphate exhibited a remarkable resiliency to climatic stress. The normal risks of agricultural production could be accommodated through the essential strengths of the social relations of production. Subsistence security resided in a type of moral economy which is to be understood, as Edward Thompson suggested, as an outgrowth of the particular social relations of production, of the relative strengths and weaknesses of peasants and state. In this period famines were typically precapitalist crises, reflecting the obvious technical limitations of the productive system. The effect of the particular form of capitalist development in northern Nigeria was to rupture the cycle of peasant production, to expand commodity production and to individuate peasant society. Peasants were subject to the horrors and moodiness of the market without the benefits of transformed forces of production. The tissues of the moral economy were stripped away, making peasants vulnerable to both market crises and a capricious climate. The mode of capital accumulation in northern Nigeria expanded the role of the market yet blocked social development along other lines. Colonial famines were not crises of the old type but reflected the essential strengths and weaknesses of a retarded capitalism. The colonial state was incapable of regularizing the conditions of production in northern Nigeria and often contributed directly to the vulnerability of peasants upon whom it ultimately depended. This contradiction can only be understood in relation to the class forces operating within colonial Nigeria. As a result, colonial famines were not natural, drought-induced disasters but in a real sense socially produced. The food crisis and famine of the 1970s is a historical continuation of these processes compounded by the expanded role of the Nigerian state in the oil boom era. I attempt to analyze the current situation among rural producers through a village study, paying particular attention to the adaptive flexibility of farmers in the face of drought and the constraints and vulnerabilities imposed by the prevailing social relations of production. I conclude with an examination of the state responses to the current food crisis in Nigeria and the implications of the new Green Revolution strategy for the continuity of small-scale commodity production.

This is a study of the political economy of food production. It offers insights into three broad areas. First is the manner in which capital relations spawned hybrid and contradictory forms of production in rural Nigeria and the unique mode of capital accumulation that transpired. Second covers the implications of expanded commodity production for food security among peasant producers; in particular why food systems collapse, what are the effects of famine on social differentiation, what are characteristic patterns of famine behavior, and how do food crises possess a logical structure? And third, policy implications for agrarian transformation; the role of the state in the countryside, peasant communities as repositories of agricultural knowledge, the detail of national and local food security and famine relief systems and the manner in which rural productivity can be raised among small-scale producers. This is also of

some consequence in understanding how rural producers have historically carried the burden of so-called development and how they have
resisted, and continue to resist, state predation and capitalist expropriation.

In writing *Silent Violence* I have been profoundly influenced by the
sustained theoretical and political writing of British social historians, most
notably E. P. Thompson, Eric Hobsbawm, and Raphael Samuel. A great
strength of such work is that it is a "people's history," a history from below.
This corpus of writing represents not only an attempt to broaden the basis
of its subject but to take seriously the need for a real life history of the
oppressed. Such an agenda legitimately returns empirical work to the
center of the theoretical stage, and yet demands an understanding of the
totality of social relations. This book is specifically about the lives and
social relations of peasants and smallholders in northern Nigeria. As John
Berger says, "peasant life is a life committed completely to survival." But it
is a survival inseparable from the webs of often oppressive and asym-
metrical social relations in which peasants find themselves. To hint,
however, that Hausa farmers have been and continue to be exploited and
marginalized, is hardly the stuff of intellectual originality. Even the most
Panglossian writings by neoclassical economists desultorily confess as
much. But I argue that in a sense we have only incompletely identified the
Tolstoyan burden that rural producers in northern Nigeria have borne
since 1900. This underestimation can, in my opinion, be rectified—and
its political consequences assessed—by an analysis of changing patterns of
food supply and material deprivation. My belief is that because of the
outwardly static appearance of the form of subsistence production and
household reproduction in northern Nigeria over the last century, some
highly significant changes in the conditions of peasant survival have been
obscured. Yet between 1900 and 1980, there has been an extraordinary
sequence of famines in Nigeria—and of course over much of Africa—in
which those who produced were also those who starved. Furthermore,
this suffering is almost unassessable, especially in the colonial period
when famine relief proved frequently ineffective for the task at hand, or
was neglected altogether. A good deal of peasant hardship went unnoticed and unrecorded. The contradiction of colonial rule in Nigeria
was that while the success of metropolitan capital depended upon expanded commodity production by households who subsidized the reproduction of their own labor power, the demands of capital and the effects
of commodity production simultaneously undermined (and occasionally
threatened) the survival of those upon whom it ultimately depended.
There is, then, a structural relationship between famine and the political
economy of colonialism that legitimately warrants the use of the term
"violence." This structural causality and the absences and neglect that

mark the history of famine in northern Nigeria, in spite of the cognitive significance of food crises among Hausa farmers themselves, is the "silent violence" to which the title of this book refers.

In the course of conducting my research, I became painfully aware that peasant food supply had to be grounded in the wider processes of social change and the effects of the insertion of Nigerian producers into a global division of labor. More especially, the genesis of famine afforded an insight into, and indeed could only be fully comprehended through, the specific social dynamics of the society so affected. Because food raised the issue of the reproduction of households which were the material basis of the colonial state and the extended reproduction of metropolitan capital, I logically had to account for the historical unfolding of capitalism in northern Nigeria. As a consequence I found myself in a hall of mirrors; famine and subsistence were in some way constitutive of colonial political economy but the peculiar form of capitalist development in Nigeria necessarily informed the study of food crises.

Though the development of household commodity production in northern Nigeria progressed by an articulation of precapitalist production systems with international capital under the aegis of the colonial state, the development of capitalism and commodity production was not, and probably never has been, uniform and uninterrupted. Rather this syncretic articulation produced "hybrid and contradictory forms of capital [which] set limits to capitalist accumulation" (Murray 1981, p. x). The contours of this process, moreover, were critically shaped and forged not only by the demands of a hegemonic capitalism but also by the dynamics and class constitution of precapitalist societies, in this case the Sokoto Caliphate. In short, I required a theoretical capability to accommodate the complex and prismatic forms of class formation and the untidy, kaleidoscopic expressions of conflict, struggle and change that accompanied the contradictory conjoining of capitalist and noncapitalist production processes in northern Nigeria. Only in this fashion, for example, could one begin to appreciate that expanded commodity production did not always imply material impoverishment or heightened vulnerability to food shortage, that some peasants could thrive sometimes and that a Bonapartist colonial state was not only an unconvincing instrument of capital logic but was equally incapable of keeping alive those producers upon whom it, and a good many other representatives of capital, ultimately depended.

And so this work is theoretically informed in a way that reflects my confrontation with theory at every turn. I have, therefore, tried to avoid a massive theoretical exegesis at the beginning but have tried to weave theory and history into each chapter. This is meant partly as an apology for those who expect and enjoy a theoretical catharsis early on in their reading, but also as an explicit recognition of the manner in which this book evolved and was ultimately written. Of course, theory is not something ready-made or God given but has its own material and ideological conditions of existence. And for this reason it has become clear to me that theoretical advances will emerge less from continual conceptual refinement than "from the different and unanswered questions thrown up by political practice" (Raphael Samuel 1981, p. 2). People's history and the debate on African underdevelopment are both inseparable from these political agendas.

ACKNOWLEDGMENTS

         This book has been a long time coming. It is also very long. As a result, I feel somewhat justified in grasping this unbridled opportunity for self-indulgence and to provide some sort of an explanation of its gestation. In explaining why *Silent Violence* came to be written, and ultimately rewritten, in its present form is to simultaneously identify and acknowledge those who entered into its coproduction. The intellectual lineaments represented in this work centrally affirm to me how much of a genuinely collective effort its production has actually been. I also have an irrepressible belief, moreover, that such an exercise is far more than an inventory of academic acquaintances (as important and laudable as this may be). It is a suspicion lent much credence by the fact that the passage of my doctoral dissertation, on which this book is loosely based was blocked until such time as the acknowledgments were specifically altered. They were, in the words of my chief protagonist and erstwhile censor, "like a little bit of disco in la Bohème."

    Silent Violence began as an attempt to understand how farmers perceived their (hazardous) environment. This concern was nourished, in quite complex ways, in the context of my first visit to Northwest State Nigeria during the worst drought in over half a century. That such an agenda did not come to much at the time is owing in large measure to the fortuitous interventions of Kent Flannery, Bill Durham, Barney Nietschmann and, especially, Skip Rappaport (who introduced me to the work of Gregory Bateson)—all of whom gave me much cause to rethink human ecology, hazards research, and the nature of adaptation. At about the same time I ploddingly came to the conclusion that Hausa farmers fell into one of the largest and most amorphous class categories known to the modern world, namely "peasants" (the other, of course, being the "petite bourgeoisie"), and Marshall Sahlins and Mick Taussig showed me that this raised certain knotty theoretical problems for the prismatic nature of class formation. Maxwell Owusu, Jim Clarkson, and Aram Yengoyam posed all of these abstractions in the context of doing fieldwork—an even more prismatic process—and of taking seriously the epistemological difficulties contained therein. Gunnar Olsson suggested that I simply could not do anything until I had read Marx and Wittgenstein.

I arrived in Nigeria—in many respects embarrassingly underprepared—in an equally ill-prepared Land Rover having driven there from Britain, which does necessitate some sort of negotiation with the Sahara Desert. What is perhaps more surprising than the manner in which this was accomplished is that I persuaded my father to be part of the negotiation. But that's another story.

In Northern Nigeria, and in Zaria in particular, I was forced to confront the shallowness of my agenda. This took the form of reading the extraordinary historical and political writings of Yusufu Bala Usman and confronting the demanding, if not formidable, intellects of Richard Palmer-Jones, Paul Clough, Louise Lennihan, Jan van Appeldorn, George Kwanashi, George Abalu, Pat Benoit, Tina Wallace, Sam and Jay Jackson, Bjorn Beckmann, Michael Mortimore, and a bevy of Nigerian graduate students. Not least, Bob Shenton and Bill Freund convinced me of the absolute imperative of both a subtle historical analysis and of explicitly theorizing the form of capitalist development in Northern Nigeria. This sent me scuttling off to the archives for five months—in which Maxwell Owusu had an unparalleled role—and precipitated a still unresolved engagement with the "peasant differentiation problem."

That the organized anarchy of village research did not entirely degenerate was owing in large measure to the intellectual and personal support of individuals in Zaria and also to the work of four Hausa hands: Polly Hill, M. G. Smith, Guy Nicolas, and George Bargery. I have almost constantly returned to Hill's brilliant writing as the critical reference point for much of my own work, though I have some profound theoretical disagreements with her. The broad corpus of empirical work by Smith and Nicolas is, of course, almost unmatched anywhere in Africa; Bargery's dictionary of the Hausa language is quite simply an ethnographic gold mine and a fieldworker's lifeline.

While so many visitors and residents bemoan the logistical hardships of life and research in Nigeria, my own sojourn in Katsina and Kaita was an extraordinary delight. I would especially like to thank the Magajin Gari of Katsina, Alhaji Usman Kabir, his assistant Alhaji Gambewa and the four Wakili. Mallam Sadoki and Jay Patel became close friends, as did the Max Lock crew, Sani Abubakar, Alhaji Garba Jibiya, Sarkin Dankama, and Abdullahi Saulawa. The chairman of Katsina local government, Isa Katsina, was always supportive of my work and ensured that I received cooperation at every turn. Sarkin Sullubawa Hussaini allowed me to work and live in Kaita village. His graciousness and generosity were unfailing. Sarkin Dogarai, Sarkin Zango, Jarici, and the district scribe were always around to tactfully point out when I was asking particularly absurd questions. Mohammed Sokoto was an indifferent assistant, but a great friend who taught me more about illicit trade than I care to think about. Mallam Abdu Kaita was a true *mutum kirki*. Should any of these individuals come to study my village of Berkeley I should be hard put to match their generosity, patience, and largesse. The department of geography at the University of Ibadan provided me with research associateship and I am especially grateful to Reuben Udo, Akin Mabogunje, and Julius Oguntoyinbo for the welcome they gave me, even though I was only an occasional resident.

Since arriving at Berkeley I have had the opportunity to rework and rethink the field material and to specifically benefit from the sustained criticisms of Michael Burawoy, Dick Walker, Alain de Janvry, Judith Tendler and, in particular, Paul Lubeck whose own work on class formation in Kano I have drawn on extensively. The geography department has also provided a supportive intellectual environment in which to work and I would like to acknowledge the constant theoretical challenges and proddings provided by Tom Bassett, Susan Christopherson, Abdi Samatar, Michael Storper, Michael Heiman, Mary Beth Pudup, Allan Pred, Elna Brunckhorst, Doug Greenberg, Eric Ingersoll, Bob Argenbright, Judy Carney, and John Simon. The following individuals scattered around the world have also made various critical contributions to various parts of the text, though in many cases I have not been able to respond adequately to their criticisms: Gavin Williams, Sam Popkin, Keith Hart, Bob Kates, Larry Grossman, Sara Berry, Alan Richards, Rhoda Howard, Jean Copans, Marie-Hélène Collion, Neil Skinner, Phil Porter, Paul Ross, and Steve Baier.

Toward the end of the project I came to rely heavily on the cartographic skills of Cathy Grant and Adrienne Morgan, on the typing wizardry and patience of Natalia Vonnegut, the proofreading and editing talents of Mary Beth Pudup and, not least, the editorial support of Shirley Warren, and Stanley Holwitz of the University of California Press. The entire enterprise has been funded by the Social Science Research Council (American Council of Learned Societies), the National Science Foundation, Resources for the Future, the Wenner-Gren Foundation for Anthropological Research, the Rackham Graduate School of the University of Michigan, and the University of California at Berkeley. Which all goes to show, as someone else once observed, that there is no simple relationship between base and superstructure.

As with most endeavors of this sort, I would like to single out the very special contributions of Bob Shenton, John Sutter and Katharyn Davies. I have drawn unashamedly from Bob Shenton's important forthcoming book (*The Development of Capitalism in Northern Nigeria*) and in particular from his penetrating analysis of the colonial state. John Sutter and I have labored so long over the differentiation question—and a good deal else—that I cannot disassociate any of my ideas from his. And my wife, Katharyn Davies, has been part of the project and my life from the beginning almost to the end; her support, sustenance, and sacrifices are simply unassessable.

A good deal of the text was written under personal duress. That it happened at all is owing in large measure to the support of Tom Trimbur, John and Joan Watts, L. Reed, John Broughton, John Coltrane, Art Blakey, Don and Bunny, Mick and Ned and Peter and Shadi. And not least, I cannot neglect my pet monkey who slowly demolished a small neighborhood in Katsina centered on my compound. He was a deviant of massive proportions, capable of willful destruction, premeditated aggression and sick humor, all executed with sublime neglect of our material welfare and social standing. He was incapable of, or perhaps thoroughly disinterested in, any form of learning. Had Pavlov used this monkey, the history of behavior psychology might have been very different. It is, then, somewhat ironic that this bisexual leviathan should have been passed on upon our departure to a friend in the village of Batagarawa, the very community where Polly Hill conducted her seminal research on rural Hausaland.

And finally for those dissenting voices (not least is my own department) who ask whether this is indeed geography at all—or like one of my anonymous reviewers that *Silent Violence*, like all geography, was "generalist"—I believe that this book strikes to the very intellectual heartland of the discipline; to the complexities of the relations between society and nature; to the agenda of the likes of Carl Sauer, Clarence Glacken, and Ellen Semple. I have chosen to ground this geographic content in an embracing political economy—in the same manner that a sociologist might embed race relations in the context of unequal access to resources—that presupposes a theory of capitalist development. I have accordingly been deeply influenced by the Marxist-inspired work of Henry Bernstein, Perry Anderson, Edward Thompson, John Berger, and Samir Amin. At the same time, to uncritically accept Marxism is to simultaneously impoverish it. Marxism without critique is contemptible and this must be the starting point of any critical elaboration, including geography. At any rate, I believe like Edward Said that we must take seriously Vico's observation that we make our own history, that what we can know is what we have made, and to extend it to geography.

M. W.

Mendocino, California
October 6, 1982

ABBREVIATIONS AND CONVENTIONS

BCGA	British Cotton Growing Association
COLA	Cost of Living Allowance
CNRS	Centre National de la Recherche Scientifique, Paris
CSER	Center for Social and Economic Research, Ahmadu Bello University
CSZ	Close Settled Zones, especially Kano, Katsina, and Sokoto
FADP	Funtua Agricultural Development Project
FAO	Food and Agricultural Organization of the United Nations
GDP	Gross Domestic Product
HMSO	Her Majesty's Stationery Office
HYV	High Yield Varieties
ICRISAT	International Centre for Research in the Semiarid Tropics, Hyderabad
IBRD	International Bank for Reconstruction and Development
IDEP	International Development and Environment Program
IDS	Institute of Development Studies, Sussex University
IFPRI	International Food Policy Research Institute, Washington, D.C.
ILO	International Labor Office, Geneva
IRDP	Integrated Rural Development Project
ISS	Institute of Social Studies, the Hague
ITCZ	Inter-Tropical Convergence Zone

KCO	Archives, Katsina Central Office
KDO	Archives, Katsina Divisional Office
KM	Archives, Katsina Museum
LBA	Licensed Buying Agent
NA	Native Authority
NAFPP	National Accelerated Food Production Program
NAI	Archives, National Archives Ibadan
NAK	Archives, National Archives Kaduna
NGB	National Grains Board
NGPC	National Grain Production Company
NISER	Nigerian Institute for Social and Economic Research, Ibadan
OFN	Operation Feed the Nation
PRO	Archives, Public Records Office, London
PRP	People's Redemption Party
SOAS	School of Oriental and African Studies, University of London
UAC	United Africa Company
UNRISD	United Nations Research Institute for Social Development, Geneva
USAID	United States Agency for International Development
USDA	United States Department of Agriculture
WAFF	West Africa Fighting Force

Currency: Throughout the colonial period and up to 1972, the Nigerian currency was pounds, shillings, and pence. Since then the monetary unit has been the naira, consisting of one hundred kobo. The rate of exchange was N1 = £ 1.15 = US \$0.64 in 1982 and N1 = US \$0.006 in 2012. At the time the British arrived in northern Nigeria in 1900, cowry currency was widespread, suitable for both local and long-distance commercial transactions. *Kudin kassa* was in fact still partially collected in cowries in 1911 in some of the northern provinces. The rate of exchange in 1910 was roughly 1300 cowries per six English pence.

Statistical matters: I have rounded the majority of percentages, particularly those pertaining to fieldwork measurement, to the nearest integer with the result that they do not always total 100. To do otherwise would have lent a spurious accuracy to data, in which occasionally I have little confidence.

Farm terminology: In keeping with Polly Hill's seminal work (*Rural Hausa: A Village and a Setting*, [London: Cambridge University Press, 1972]) the word "farm" corresponds to the Hausa word "*gona*" meaning a field or discrete area cultivated by a farmer. A holding or farm holding comprises all the separate farms owned by an individual. The small lowland (*fadama*) farms used for dry season irrigation (*lambu*) are referred to as plots (*garka*), and within each plot the minute irrigated gardens are referred to as beds (*fangali*).

GLOSSARY

The following Hausa words are those employed most frequently in the text.

Throughout this book I use conventional Hausa orthography (see G. Bargery, *A Hausa-English Dictionary*, London: Oxford University Press, 1934) rather than English in the spelling of names and substantive vocabulary words. With regard to transliteration, there are no diacritical marks other than the apostrophe, but there are glottalized consonants (hooked letters b, d, and k), which I have not employed since there is little possibility of misunderstanding. Plurals are given in parentheses.

Aro: a loan of something that is to be returned (e.g., a farm)

Arziki: wealth; mai arziki (masu arziki) is a wealthy person

Bamugaje (maguzawa): non-Muslim Hausa

Bara (barori): a servant, client, or retainer

Baranda: buying goods for resale

Barantaka: the institution of Hausa clientage

Bashi (basusuwa): a general term for a loan or debt

Bawa (bayi): slave

Biki (bukuwa): a contribution system linking partners

Binne, bizne: dry planting prior to the rains

Birni (birane): a city; the seat of an emir

Bori: Hausa spirit cult

Bushi (also fari): drought

Chaffa, cheppa, chappa: allegiance, a variant of clientage

Cin rani: dry season migration

Daji: bush land

Damana: wet season

Dankali: sweet potatoes

Dawa (dawoyi): sorghum, guinea corn

Demi (dammuna): a bundle

Dillali (dillalai): a broker

Dubu: the ceremony of investiture of a sarkin noma

Fadama (fadamu): low lying seasonally wet or inundated area

Falle: a loan, usually referring to borrowing of grain

Fangali: irrigated beds

Fartanya (faretani): small hoe

Fatauci: long distance trading

Filanin gawo (sometimes called bororo): nomadic cattle Fulani

Filanin gida: settled nomadic Fulani who are mixed farmers

Fuloti: a buying station for the marketing boards

Gado: inherited item

Galma (galmuna): hand plough

Gandu (gandaye): can refer to the complex farming unit (a father plus his married sons), a slave estate, or a large farm

Gayauna (gayauni): a private farm belonging to a gandu member

Gayya: a communal work party

Gero: millet

Gida (gidaje): a house or compound

Gona (gonaki): a farm or field; they are to be distinguished from holdings (i.e., the total of all household fields)

Goro (gwarra): kola nut

Gulbi (gulabe): river

Gyada: groundnuts

Hakimi (hakimai): district head

Haraji: local community tax

Hatsi: grain

Huri: first weeding

Iri: seed, seedlings

Iyali (iyalai): nuclear family

Jangali: cattle tax

Jekada (jekadu): precolonial administrator, tax collector

Jigawa: sandy, upland soil

Jihad: a holy struggle or conflict

Jingina: pledge or pawn

Kaka: harvest

Korama: irrigation channel

Kudi: money

Kudin kassa: land money (i.e., the land tax)

Kulle: wife seclusion, purdah

Kutara: shaduf

Kwadago: work done for wages; yan kwadago refers to wage laborers

Kwando (kwanduna): a large basket

Kwarami: trading in grains; yan kwarami means grain trader

Kyauta (kyautayi): a gift

Laka: a lowland soil

Lalle: henna

Lambu (lambuna): an irrigated farm

Magaji (magadai): an official position, often a village head (dagaci)

Mai arziki (masu arziki): a wealthy person

Mai gari (masu garuwa): a village head or town head

Mai gida (masu gidaje): household head

Mai sarauta (masu sarauta): an office holder

Malami (malamai): Koranic teacher

Mangala (mangaloli): a leather or woven donkey panier

Manyan noma: large farmer

Matalauta: poor persons

Mudu (mudaye): a measuring bowl, roughly four handfuls of grain

Noma: farming; noman rani is dry season farming

Rance: short-term borrowing

Rani: dry season

Rogo: cassava

Rumbu (rumbuna): granary

Ruwa (ruwaye): rain, water

Sadaka (sadakoki): alms

Sadaki: marriage expenses

Sana'a (sana'oi): occupation, trade

Sarki (sarakuna): any chief, emir

Sarkin noma (sarakunan noma): king of farming, a ritual official, and large farmer; nowadays largely honorific

Shinkafa: rice

Shuka: sowing of grains

Taba: tobacco

Tabki: lake

Taki: manure, pace; also refers to a colonial taxation system

Talaka (talakawa): peasant, common person

Talauci: extreme poverty

Tiya: a standard measure, roughly six pounds of millet

Tudu: upland

Uban daki: patron

Ulema: Islamic scholars

Unguwa (unguwoyi): a hamlet, ward,or administrative area

Uwar gida: senior wife

Wake (wakaikai): cowpeas

Yunwa: hunger, famine

Zakka, zakkat: grain tithe

BARE LIFE AND THE
LONG INTERREGNUM
Introduction to the New Edition

[No] society breaks down and can be replaced until it has developed all the forms of life which are implicit in its internal relations. . . .

Caesarism can be said to express a situation in which the forces in conflict balance each other in a catastrophic manner. . . . they balance each other in a way that the continuation of the conflict can only terminate in their reciprocal destruction.

—Antonio Gramsci, *The Prison Notebooks*, 1916–35

It does bear repeating. Close to one billion people in the world go to bed hungry each night.[1] In historical terms, it is, of course, quite true that the proportion of the global population who are undernourished has fallen since the late 1960s; according to the United Nations World Food Programme, hunger prevalence fell from 33 percent in 1969–71 to 16 percent in 2011. In practice a disproportionately large share of this impressive decline is accounted for by the explosive performance of the East Asia growth machine and its remarkable success in reducing poverty and improving life chances. Low-income states, however, have seen an overall increase in the number of hungry people from 827 million in 1990–92 to 906 million in 2010. Historically speaking, hunger has proven to be exceptionally durable. The world, as the *Economist* (February 18, 2012) recently put it, has not been terribly good at fighting hunger. Since the 1960s, the global hunger headcount has remained largely unchanged at roughly 0.9 billion. To compound this failure, another billion are malnourished in that they have a micronutrient deficiency, and yet a further billion are malnourished because they eat too much and are obese. A new report by Save the Children titled *A Life Free from Hunger* claims that malnutrition alone accounts for 2.6 million deaths each year, one-third of the global total.[2] One in four of the world's children is stunted, and global progress on reducing malnutrition has been pitifully slow for the last twenty years, with numbers falling an average of only 0.65 percent per year since 1990.[3] When all is said and done, it is a damning record on virtually every front.

The sheer tenacity in the world hunger picture should not imply that little has changed over the last fifty years in the West African Sahel or, for that matter, in the circumstances in which poor people across the global south find themselves as net buyers or sellers of food.[4] The dynamics of food provisioning *have* changed, and the centrality of grain markets and their operations in the lives of the poor has deepened. Take, for example, the enduring political question of the price of bread and John Stuart Mill's observation long ago that "men might as well be imprisoned, as excluded from the means of earning their bread." Real and nominal prices of staple foods have actually declined steadily since the global food crisis of the early 1970s. They remained relatively low and stable between 1990 and 2006 but then surged forward between late 2006 and mid-2008, driven by the financial crisis and rising fuel costs. By some estimates another one hundred million worldwide were pushed into poverty while the frontier of under-nourishment in sub-Saharan Africa was extended still further. Between 2005 and 2009 the number of the world's hungry probably grew from roughly 850,000 to slightly over one million. Price volatility and the turbulence of global food markets reverberated across the globe among the rural and urban poor with catastrophic consequences for food-insecure households.[5] Food prices had fallen sharply by mid-2008, but ominously two years later, prices began a sharp ascent once more, and through 2011 they were running above the high point of prices in 2008.[6] What is new, in other words, is not the return of the Malthusian specter (demographic growth) or the challenges of low agricultural productivity (the purported end of the Green Revolution). Rather what is on offer is a reconfiguration of the landscape of global food provisioning and what Ghosh calls an unnatural coupling of food, fuel, and global finance.[7]

Nowhere has the stubbornness of hunger revealed itself with more drama than in sub-Saharan Africa. Almost a quarter of a billion Africans suffer from hunger and malnutrition; moderate and severe stunting stands at 38 percent, while the number of undernourished exploded from 170 million in 1990 to 223 million in 2006–8 (the proportion of undernourished has stalled, only shifting from 26 percent to 23 percent over the previous decade and a half).[8] Nobody seriously expects that the Millennium Development Goal (MDG) of halving the number of hungry people between 1990 and 2015 will be met in Africa or, indeed, globally.[9] The incidence of famine and famine mortalities has seemingly declined since the 1960s,[10] leading some observers, like Cormac O'Grada in *Famine: A Short History*, to refer to contemporary food crises as "small-scale famines."[11] Yet Africa remains a striking outlier.[12] In 2011 some ten million people were drawn into the clutches of the terrible food crisis in Somalia, Kenya, and Ethiopia.[13] As I write, the UN is calling for a massive food-aid mobilization in view of a looming subsistence crisis in the Sahel; in the wake of the poor 2011 rains, over eight million people will require "life-saving food assistance," according to the World Food Programme.[14] The Sahel, broadly construed, has also emerged as a new front in the prosecution of a counterinsurgency against radical Islam. It is also one of the regions on which, according to the Intergovernmental Panel on Climate Change, the deadweight of global warming is about to fall. In some quarters—Christian Parenti from the left, the United States Department of Defense on the right[15]—this new conjuncture of violence, poverty, and climate change defines the coming apocalypse—the "tropic of chaos," as Parenti calls it.

To speak of famines writ small or large as discrete or hermetically sealed events characterized by mass mortality and starvation is in any case open to question. Famines are, as I try to make clear in this book, social processes, and complex social processes at that. One of the signal lessons to have been learned from the serial failures to improve food security and life chances in the arid-lands of West Africa[16] is that the boundary lines between mass starvation and the *longue durée* of permanent hunger and undernourishment are porous and flimsy.[17] Existentially, what we are witnessing is something close to a condition of slow death, a death by attrition: "The phrase *slow death* refers to the physical wearing out of a population and the deterioration of people in that population that is very nearly a defining condition of their experience and historical existence."[18] Put somewhat differently, what I have called silent violence, which conveys the permanency and normalization of hunger, is in fact the necessary ether from which famines and mass starvation draw their ignition and fuel. At the same time this violence represents a radical reduction of human existence to what Agamben calls bare life.[19] Famine and hunger are inextricably intertwined, the deepest expressions of what Mike Davis in *Late Victorian Holocausts*[20] properly called the war over the right to existence.

I wish to inquire
Into the whereabouts of the dead.

—W. G. Sebald, *Across the Land and the Water*, 2011

Every author of a book on famine harbors a secret, contrarian wish that a second edition should never see the light of day. Scholars of subsistence crises ideally would only look backward to the past. As *historians* of famine they would be the documentarians of terrible cataclysmic events that happened "back then" in Bengal in 1943, in China during the Great Leap Forward, in the Ukraine in 1932–34, and so on. This historical inventory is no small task, of course. More than seventy million people died as famine victims—excess mortalities is the term of art—in the course of the twentieth century and perhaps almost as many again in the last quarter of the nineteenth century if Mike Davis's estimates hold water. But the stark reality is that famines are still with us and hunger remains a stain on the modern world. Sadly, the study of famine has become something of a growth industry, and I suppose this book is a testament to it.

Silent Violence was written against the backdrop of, and in some measure as a direct response to, the great Sahelian famine that struck West Africa and the Horn of Africa between 1969 and 1974 (I was an erstwhile resident living in the region in the early 1970s). Over half a million people perished, perhaps many more. In its wake came devastating famines in Bangladesh, Mozambique, Sudan, Korea, and Uganda. Large swaths of Africa, one can plausibly claim, suffer from something close to "permanent famine," serial crises that have become, in effect, the new normal. It is a life of what Paul Farmer calls extreme suffering.[21] I arrived in northern Nigeria in 1976 to study a set of paradoxes: namely, why were hunger and starvation not accompanied by absolute scarcity (there was always food in the market); why were those who perished typically always those who grew food; and why would farmers sensitive to the vagaries of rainfall in a drought-prone and high-risk environment resign themselves to starvation in the face of drought? My brief was to understand the prismatic relations between drought and food in a region that had experienced, all too regularly, the deadweight of famine (this much I knew since the great 1913–14 and 1927 famines had been documented, if not fulsomely so) and extreme food shortage (most recently in the early 1970s). One part of my quest took me into dusty and termite-ridden archives (and to conversations with older heads who could recall the terrible famines of the past). Another part carried me to Kaita village, a district center in the Sahelian belt of northern Nigeria, northwest of Katsina town, and formerly part of the old Katsina emirate, a distinguished member of the nineteenth-century Sokoto Caliphate.[22]

With the powers of hindsight, it can be said that Nigeria has not suffered a major famine since the Biafran war (1967–70), when a million and more people starved in the old eastern region, many as a result of the war-induced disruption of the harvest and a massive displacement of Ibo refugees fleeing the war front. By 1968 it was estimated that perhaps two hundred thousand people were dying monthly. Biafra turned out to be one of the first televised famines, and it was also archived in images through the extraordinary war pictures of photographers such as Don McCullin. Biafra in fact helped give birth to what one might call the humanitarian international. But this sort of famine *is* a thing of the past in Nigeria. The drought years and harvest failures of the early 1970s did, most assuredly, produce food shortage, massive livestock depletion, and much suffering across the northern states, but conditions did not rise to the level of severe famine.[23] But food shortage, food insecurity, and food vulnerability are other matters entirely. Here the picture is frighteningly, and instantly, recognizable. Not unexpectedly, erratic rainfall and periodic drought continue to haunt the region. According to geographer Michael Mortimore there were nine extreme or severe drought events between 1942 and 1990 in Katsina.[24] In the period after I left Kaita village, drought years (and price hikes) were particularly dramatic in 1984, 1985, and 1987. The 1990s proved to be no better (the mean decadal rainfall was almost 40 percent lower than in the 1970s[25]); drought and poor harvests marked the 2005 and 2010 growing seasons, too.

The larger food picture provides no relief either. Land scarcity, endemic poverty, the annual preharvest food scarcity, food price volatility, periodic bouts of asset liquidation as farmers desperately purchased grains, harvest fluctuations, declining food output, and stagnant yields were all part and parcel of the larger picture of deepening commercialization of the food sector. The area harvested in Katsina State between 1990 and 2000 reveals a secular decline for most all staple foodstuffs; yields over the same period did not budge (except for cowpeas maize, which fell dramatically, and cotton, which increased). Significantly, average annual staple prices revealed a slow downward trend over the same period, suggesting that cross-border trade and massive imports were compensating for the slump in domestic output[26]—something to which I shall turn shortly. Since 2003 the staple food price index has risen inexorably from 100 in January 2003 to 260 in January 2011.[27] As if to drive home the sense of a food system on the brink, lurching from one bout of vulnerability to the next, the Katsina State government was compelled to release grains for sale at a 50 percent discount in February 2012 in the face of unsustainably high local prices. The release was aimed at "alleviating the suffering of the people."[28] In some respects it all seems the same, but worse.[29]

None of this should imply a regional economy locked in the prison house of rural stagnation and decay. The last three decades and more have witnessed an extraordinary transformation—or, rather, a raft of transformations—in rural and urban livelihoods in Nigeria. What is now on offer is a fully fledged oil nation, a petro-state, whose broad lineaments were partially visible in the mid-1970s.[30] Suffice it to say, at one level, that the explosive genesis of an oil economy and unimaginable petro-wealth have reverberated throughout the Katsina region. Kaita, the small community in which I conducted my field research, certainly bears the marks of these changes. Politically, Nigeria's federal structure changed with the creation of new states in 1987, 1991, and 1996, almost doubling the number of states within the federation since I completed my field research in 1978.[31] Katsina State came into existence on September 23, 1987, covering the same area as the former Katsina Province of the defunct Northern Region. Its creation along with Akwa Ibom State raised the number of states from nineteen to twenty-one, which was expanded still further in 1991 and again in 1996 to bring the total to thirty-six (figure 1). In August 2000, Katsina became one of the first

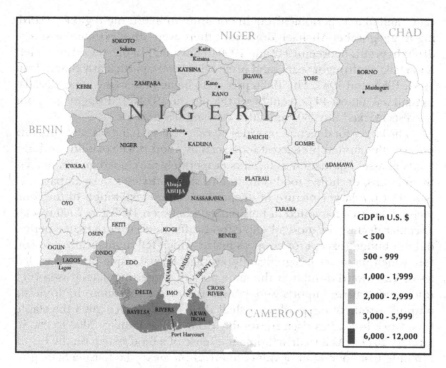

Figure 1. Nigeria: per capita income ($PPP) by state. Drawn and designed by Darin Jensen,
           Department of Geography, University of California, Berkeley.

northern Nigerian states to adopt Islamic sharia law. Alhaji Umaru Musa
Yar'adua was elected in May 1999 as the state's first civilian governor after
the demise of the military dictatorship that had held power since 1983. Hail-
ing from a distinguished Katsina family, he became the country's president
eight years later in 2007.

Currently, Katsina State has a population of 6.483 million—an average
population density of 160 per square kilometer[32]—and contains thirty-four
local government areas (LGAs), each presided over by a local government
council (LGC). In the extraordinary multiplication of LGAs since the 1970s
(nationally the number of LGAs exploded from 301 in 1976 to 774 in 1999),
Kaita, a former district center, became the local government center for a
new Kaita LGA. Its elevation to a government center in part explains the
sizeable growth of the community since my field research and an expanded
infrastructure (a raft of new local government buildings and offices, a tarred
road connecting Katsina with the Niger border, a larger school, and so on).
Kaita LGA covers 925 square kilometers and contained a population in 2006
of 184,401. It remains very densely settled (over 200 per square kilometer),
comparable to the exceptionally high settlement densities in the so-called

Kano close-settled zone (Danbatta LGA in Kano State, for example, has a comparable density of 284 per square kilometer). The population of the Kaita LGA almost doubled between 1991 and 2006; some portion of the increase doubtless reflected cross-border migration from Niger as rural conditions (and food insecurity) in that country deteriorated.

Katsina, in sum, was a beneficiary, and a product, of the remarkable multiplication of the Nigerian postcolonial political infrastructure—namely, states and local governments. This new political machinery, which Michael Mann calls infrastructural power,[33] was the product of the oil boom and the ability of the Nigerian state to capture oil rents. All petro-states have a mechanism for the distribution of oil revenues; in Nigeria it is the revenue allocation and mobilization process, which is in effect a formula, a political formula, by which the state apportions oil revenues to the federal government, the states, and local governments.[34] By 2005, Katsina State was receiving over ₦1.8 billion (US $1.1 billion) per month from the statutory revenue allocation. The following year it received in total almost a quarter of a billion US dollars ($235 million) from the federation account; the thirty-four Katsina LGAs collectively pocketed another $237 million (in aggregate terms it amounts to $73 per capita or $250 per household per year). Kaita LGA was allocated $0.5 million per month, equivalent to roughly $150 per household per year (i.e., 2 percent of total average household income). Katsina State's gross allocation places it in the top third of all states—considerably less than the oil producing states that benefit from the derivation principle—but roughly similar in gross dollars to the thirty non-delta states. On a per capita basis, the picture is different: Katsina, like Kaduna and Kano States, receives a disproportionately small share of gross allocations (Katsina has 4.13 percent of the federation's population but receives only 2.66 percent of federation account revenues).[35]

The launching of the oil boom during the 1970s radically deepened and extended the rentier character of the Nigerian state (ironically my sojourn in Katsina, between the first tripling of oil prices in 1973 and the doubling of prices in 1978–79, corresponded to the price slump between the twin booms). Since 1970, the Nigerian exchequer has captured perhaps $700–800 billion in oil revenues, rents that, by fair means or foul, have been integral to the operations of the federal system. Oil revenues come and go, of course, and are notoriously volatile, but the indisputable fact is that Nigeria was, when I resided in Kaita, and remains awash in money. Petrodollars course through the state, federal, and local government systems.

What Katsina has to show for all of this oil wealth is precious little and might lead one to conclude that oil has placed a curse upon the country, the "devil's excrement," as a former Venezuelan president famously described petroleum wealth. The Nigerian Bureau of Statistics estimates that the poverty rate for the northwest zone[36] (including Katsina State) grew from

52 percent in 1985 to 71 percent two decades later (the comparable figure in the so-called South South region for 2005 is 35 percent). Nearly three-quarters of northerners currently live on less than $200 a year, far below any poverty line (*Economist,* January 14, 2012). In Katsina State the poverty head count grew from 54.7 percent to 60.9 percent between 2004 and 2010.[37] After four decades of oil development, the social and human development indices for the state remain shockingly low even by Nigerian standards. Among a population of 6.4 million, 1.83 million have never attended school; 68.3 percent of people reside in mud or thatch dwellings; almost half of the population obtains water from lakes, streams, and unprotected wells; and nearly two-thirds are without electricity.[38] The *official* unemployment rate—admittedly a meaningless figure—is 37.8 percent. Katsina is certainly not the poorest state in the federation (figure 1). Yet incontestably it is part of a great swath of the northern region, a Muslim bloc comparable in size and complexity to Egypt or Turkey, mired in abject poverty (table 1 and table 2).

A gloss of rural conditions in the state can be gleaned from a UN International Fund for Agricultural Development (IFAD) baseline study of farmers in three Katsina LGAs conducted in 2004.[39] It reveals an utterly miserable profile of rural poverty in the state.[40] Two-thirds of the sample never attended school, and 0.4 percent had higher education. About 90 percent of the respondents had never taken the hadj (an indication of economic well-being). Among respondents, 91.7 percent owned wood or mud thatched-roof buildings, and only 0.2 percent owned modern cement/brick zinc-roofed dwellings. The survey revealed that 71.4 percent acquired water from a well and 2.3 percent from rain water; 90 percent used firewood as fuel. Household income derived from the last season's crop sales

TABLE 1.
NIGERIA: POVERTY RATES BY ZONE (US$ PER DAY BASED
ON ADJUSTED PURCHASING POWER PARITY).

Sector/Region	Poor	Nonpoor
National	51.55	48.45
Urban	40.11	59.89
Rural	60.58	39.42
South South	47.56	52.44
South East	31.24	68.76
South West	40.2	59.8
North Central	58.64	41.36
North East	64.82	35.18
North West	61.23	38.77

SOURCE: United Nations Development Program, *Human Development Report, Nigeria 2008–2009* (Abuja: UNDP, 2009), 150.

TABLE 2.
Nigeria: Human development indices and income Gini coefficients by zone.

Zone	Human development index (HDI) value	Human poverty index (HPI)	Gender development measure (GDM)	Gender empowerment measure (GEM)	Inequality measure (INQ)	Ranking by population	Ranking by per capita income	Gini coefficient
North Central	0.49	34.65	0.478	0.244	0.49	6	2	0.3934
North West	0.42	44.15	0.376	0.117	0.44	1	3	0.3711
North East	0.332	48.9	0.25	0.118	0.42	5	5	0.4591
South West	0.523	21.5	0.507	0.285	0.48	2	4	0.5538
South East	0.471	26.07	0.455	0.315	0.38	4	6	0.4494
South South	0.573	26.61	0.575	0.251	0.41	3	1	0.5072

SOURCE: United Nations Development Program, *Human Development Report, Nigeria 2008–2009* (Abuja: UNDP, 2009), 93, 194.

revealed that about 67.4 percent of the respondents received ₦15,000 or less (US$115). Over 81 percent of the respondents held less than one hectare of land, and 61.8 percent of households purchased food (14 percent daily, 35 percent weekly). Three-quarters of respondents indicated they had coped with food shortage by borrowing money (27.5 percent), borrowing food (23.5 percent), and selling assets (20.3 percent) (IFAD, "Country Evaluation Programme," 30). A subsequent March–April 2007 USAID survey in Bulungudi, Zango LGA, to the east of Kaita, sketched a similar pattern. Almost 40 percent of the households were poor (owning less than than two hectares); 80 percent of household staples were purchased, and 65 percent of household income was derived from casual work and remittances.[41]

Enduring structural weaknesses within northern Nigeria's food provisioning system are inseparable from the transformative impact of oil revenues on the politics and economics of the country since the 1960s. Oil wealth, on the one hand, confers upon the state the capability to fall back on the global marketplace. Over the last fifteen years the Nigerian food import bill has assumed truly gargantuan proportions. In 1994 Nigerian food imports amounted to 0.67 million metric tons (US$0.75 billion); by 2001 it was almost 7 million metric tons (US$2 billion).[42] There were two key moments in the transformation of food and live animal imports. In the early 1990s in the wake of the 1986 structural adjustment reforms,[43] food imports (by value) increased by almost 500 percent between 1994 and 1995 alone after the lifting of a ban on maize and rice imports. Food imports rose again after 2000 amid considerable confusion and instability over input subsidies by the Obasanjo government. Staples in the 1980s constituted over 15 percent of merchandise imports and rose to an astonishing 27 percent in 2000. More recently (2008–11), food imports have been running at between 9 percent and 11 percent of merchandise imports, costing over $3 billion annually.

The costs of a deep dependence on the global food market became especially vivid in the global oil-fuel crisis in 2008. From the beginning of 2007, the prices of some of the most basic food commodities increased dramatically on international markets. The traded market price of wheat doubled from February 2007 to February 2008, hitting a record high of over US$10 a bushel. Rice prices also reached ten-year highs. A rapid run-up in fuel (and fertilizer) prices, coupled with crop substitutions from food to biofuels and speculation by traders in commodity futures following the collapse of the financial derivatives, drove up prices sharply.[44] In Nigeria, food-price inflation rose from 8.2 percent in December 2007 to 18.1 percent in June 2008. Given that food accounts for about 63.3 percent of household consumption expenditure (64 percent and 62.6 percent for rural and urban areas respectively), Nigeria's import dependence in a turbulent and unpredictable grains market was exceptionally worrisome.[45] In August 2011, the minister of agriculture solemnly announced that Nigeria was one of the largest food importers in the world. Nigeria's food import bill in 2007–10 was a staggering ₦98 trillion (almost $8 billion). In 2010 alone, Nigeria spent ₦635 billion on the import of wheat, ₦356 billion on rice, and ₦217 billion on sugar—all commodities cultivated in Nigeria, for which the country purportedly possesses a comparative advantage.[46]

In truth the Nigerian structural food deficit must be situated on the larger canvas of an agrarian crisis superintended by a postcolonial state enamored with, and beholden to, the lure of oil wealth. When I arrived in Katsina in 1976, national agriculture had already begun its calamitous descent. Between 1970 at the end of the civil war and 1978 (when I left Nigeria), the volume of agricultural output had fallen by 60 percent and the index of agricultural production by one third.[47] In some measure this decline reflected what I was, in fact, studying, namely a run of drought years and poor harvests. But it was clear that the impact of oil, changing terms of trade for agricultural commodities, the rapid appreciation of the naira, and a cost-of-production squeeze in an inflationary economy were all taking their toll. Nowhere was this more clear than in the export sector. Since the 1960s, the Nigerian agricultural export sector has been utterly pulverized. Its historically dominant position in the export of key crops such as palm oil, groundnut, and cocoa—the country controlled 60, 30, and 15 percent of global exports respectively in the 1960s—vanished and has never been reclaimed. Between 1970 and 1985 the index of agricultural export production fell from 126 to 100, and the volume of exports fell by an astonishing 85 percent (from just over one million tons to 166,000 tons) (figure 2).[48]

The larger agrarian picture instills no greater confidence. Since 1960, when Nigeria achieved independence, the performance of the nation's agricultural sector has been at best "inconsistent."[49] Between 1960 and the late 1980s, real agricultural growth per capita fluctuated between –19 percent and +15 percent per year due to year-to-year production swings and instability in international commodity prices.[50] Nationally, real agricultural growth was 4.5 percent in the 1980s, 3.4 percent in the 1990s, and 5.6 percent from 2000 through 2007. In reality, however, the upsurge in agricultural GDP growth has been driven mainly by the expansion in area planted to staple crops and has a strong class dimension (large growers account for a disproportionate share of the output). Productivity conversely has remained flat, and yields of most crops have actually declined over the past two decades.[51]

In a country whose economic trajectory has been defined by the growth of oil revenues, it is no surprise that the agricultural sector in Nigeria has declined in importance over time. The decline was precipitous during the first two decades after independence, when the GDP share of agricultural value added dropped from 60 percent to 20 percent (figure 3). More recently it has started to rise again as a result of growth in the sector, combined with a

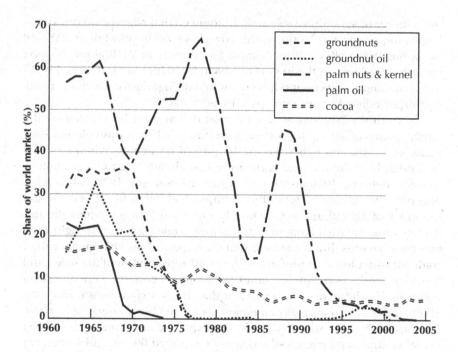

Source: Walkenhorst (2007). From: UN Comtrade database (using mirror data).

Figure 2. Nigeria: world share of major export crops; three-year moving average percentage
(1960–2005). Tewodaj Mogues et al., "Agricultural Spending in Nigeria" (IFPRI
Discussion Paper 00789, International Food Policy Research Institute, Washington,
D.C., 2008), 6.

contraction in oil revenues. Agriculture's share of GDP rose from 30 percent
in 1981 to about 36 percent in 2000 and 42 percent in 2007.[52] But it remains
a strikingly declensionist narrative; the share of the population residing in
rural areas, the share of the labor force employed in agriculture, and the
share of the nation's export earnings derived from agricultural commodities have all fallen (figure 4).

The federal commitment to—or more properly abdication of—the agricultural sector has been a crucial component of the tragic stagnation in
rural livelihoods. As a proportion of total federal expenditures, agriculture
represented 7 percent over the period 1962–68, 6.3 percent in 1970–74,
and 4.8 percent in 1975–80.[53] By 2000 it had fallen vertiginously to 1.94
percent (it was, in fact, running at barely 2 percent across the 1990s). In
2005 actual expenditures were 1.67 percent of the federal capital budget,
far lower than spending in other key sectors such as education, health,

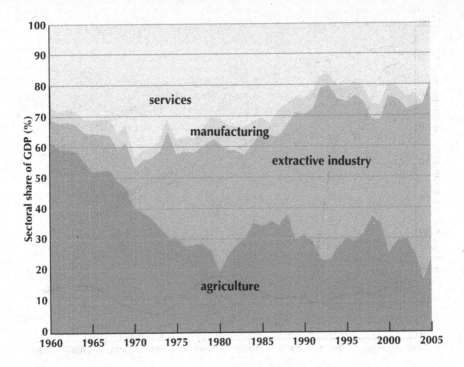

Source: WDI (2007).

Figure 3. Nigeria: sectoral value added as percentage of GDP (1960–2005). Tewodaj Mogues
        et al., "Agricultural Spending in Nigeria" (IFPRI Discussion Paper 00789, Interna-
        tional Food Policy Research Institute, Washington, D.C., 2008), 8.

and water.[54] To put this in some perspective, this ratio of federal spending is radically disproportionate to the sector's importance in the Nigerian
economy and to the Nigerian government's policy emphasis on diversifying
away from oil. Eighty-one percent of federal spending on agriculture is accounted for by only 3 of the government's 179 programs; three-quarters of
this trio's spending is devoted solely to government purchase of agricultural
inputs and agricultural outputs, which have historically served as a major
sump of political rents.[55] Furthermore, budget execution is a shambles. The
Public Expenditure and Financial Accountability (PEFA) best-practice standard for budget execution is no more than 3 percent discrepancy between
budgeted and actual expenditures. In the IFPRI study, the Nigerian federal
budget execution averaged only 79 percent, meaning 21 percent of the
approved budget was never spent. Budget execution at the state and local
levels was worse still, ranging from 71 percent to 44 percent.

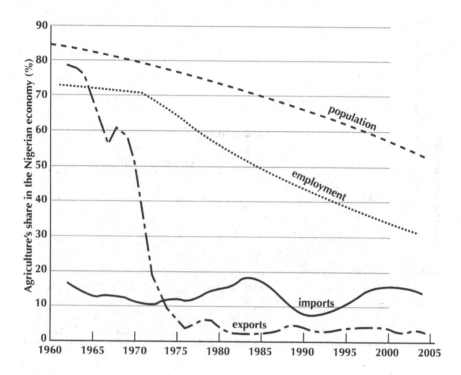

Source: Walkenhorst (2007).

Figure 4. Nigeria: share of agriculture in the Nigerian economy (1960–2005). Tewodaj
       Mogues et al., "Agricultural Spending in Nigeria" (IFPRI Discussion Paper 00789,
       International Food Policy Research Institute, Washington, D.C., 2008), 9.

Underinvestment in agriculture is gradually shifting.[56] The allocation
of funding to agriculture and rural development proposed in the official
papers of the federal government budget for 2006 was set at ₦30.8 billion
(US$240 million), equivalent to 2 percent of the total government recur-
rent and capital budget allocations. In 2007, the corresponding allocation
was reported to be ₦38 billion (US$304 million), representing 4 percent of
the total. President Musa Yar'Adua (a Katsina man) assumed power in May
2007 and immediately placed agriculture at the forefront of funding priorities for 2008, with a reported ₦121 billion (US$1 billion) being devoted to
the sector. Yar'Adua's illness and eventual death, and the twin crises that
followed the appointment of President Goodluck Jonathan in May 2010—
namely the violence in the Niger delta and the growing Islamist insurgency
in the north—dashed any prospect of a dramatic change in agriculture's
prospects.

These statistical assessments of Nigeria's agricultural performance are aggregate, "big-picture" narratives often based on data of suspicious quality. Agrarian dynamics are, at the end of the day, local, and even within the arid north, the patterns of rural accumulation and agrarian practice, to say nothing of the operations of local food markets, are heterogeneous and varied. Without question export volumes in northern Nigeria groundnuts and cotton collapsed during the 1970s oil boom. But this is not to suggest that rural food production collapsed too. Quite the contrary. Food crops became increasingly profitable, largely as demand for food expanded among urban beneficiaries of the oil rents and as inflation (also oil-driven) drove up food prices in Nigeria. Public-sector wages were doubled in 1974, further stimulating demand against a backdrop of diminished state control of producer prices.[57] As I discovered in Kaita, and as Meagher and Mustapha also discovered in their research of rural Kano in the 1980s, millet, sorghum, and cowpeas were becoming the new cash crops. Oil fueled the deepening commercialization of the rural economy across the north, but not all farmers could benefit equally from higher producer prices for grain, and many land-poor farmers were compelled to buy grain when prices were at their highest prior to harvest. In sum, the 1970s signaled a double movement: a reorientation toward the internal market and a simultaneous reorientation toward an expanding parallel market trade with Niger Republic to the north. The Katsina region has become, as a result, ever more integrated into a vast regional (and transnational) commercialized food network, what has been dubbed the "Kano-Katsina-Maradi K^2M Corridor."[58] The deepening of domestic food commercialization in northern Nigeria paints a forbidding picture of limited productivity gains, the extension of the cultivation frontier, and rural impoverishment.

The commodification of foodstuffs and the reorganization of the regional grains trade are particularly significant in respect to the rural differentiation of Hausa peasant communities. That is to say, patterns of landholding, livestock and other assets, household self-sufficiency in staples (whether households are grain deficit or grain surplus), and the ecological capital of farming families. As *Silent Violence* shows, these processes give a different complexion to the agrarian transformation of the 1970s. In Kaita a significant proportion of households were already in grain deficit by 1976. Matlon's study roughly concurrent with my own in a grain-surplus region of southern Kano State indicates that high grain prices constituted serious threats to the 20 percent of households that were grain deficit producers.[59] As Mustapha and Meagher properly note, in the far north the grain-deficit situation was an even more serious impediment to smallholders' ability to

benefit from rising grain prices: "while in the early 1960s deficit grain production in this region was largely a product of a concentration on groundnut production, by the late 1970s, declining annual rainfall, accelerating soil
exhaustion, and limited access to inputs combined to intensify deficit grain
production among smallholders, even after the collapse of the groundnut
economy."[60]

After structural adjustment in the mid-1980s, the impact of increases
in production and reproduction costs compounded the vulnerability of
grain-deficit families. Rising prices of agricultural inputs and food compelled households to shift to off-farm occupations, especially wage labor,
at the same time that the use of fertilizers and the planting of the hybrid
varieties introduced earlier decreased substantially. Mustapha and Meagher estimate in their rural Kano study that the proportion of grain-deficit
families increased by almost 20 percent among small farmers (and by almost as much among medium farmers) between 1989 and 1993.[61] Over
the longer term the pattern in the north seems as follows: the cultivable
area has expanded, but average household landholdings have declined,
and the degree of landlessness has increased. Where ecologically possible,
irrigated (*fadama*) agriculture has expanded considerably. Kaita is a case
in point, but access to these limited biomes is unevenly distributed among
farming households. Food deficit families in the close-settled zones are now
endemic in a food market that is regional, volatile, and subject to the ever-
present vagaries of rainfall. These climatic perturbations are compounded
by the downward trend in average rainfall and the looming uncertainties of
global climate change.

New research that makes effective use of an earlier survey by Chris
Udry of Yale University comparing agrarian change over a twenty-year period (1988–2008) among four communities near Zaria (in Kaduna State)
is suggestive in this regard.[62] The increase in total land cultivated is consistent across villages, but landless households increased by 40 percent.
Household land holdings decreased by almost three hectares over the
twenty-year period, while the number of plots cultivated per household
also decreased. Plot sizes and total land cultivated decreased, but access to
lowland, fadama plots remained constant across households between the
two survey years. Land rentals, almost nonexistent in 1988, are now widespread. Fallowing had in effect disappeared entirely, and farmers widely
endorsed the view that soil fertility was declining. Total real crop value
increased by 44.8 percent between 1988 and 2008, while crop value per
hectare increased by 66 percent. The increase in crop value correlated
with higher input utilization of seed, fertilizer and pesticides, agricultural
capital, and hired labor on household plots. Household livestock holdings
increased at a higher rate than utilization of hired inputs, either tractor or
ox-plough hire, but livestock assets and real crop values varied widely across

rural classes. In sum, the simultaneous commodification of food, land, and labor—not agrarian stagnation—defines the great arc of Nigerian petro-agriculture.

Oil creates the illusion of a completely changed life, life without work, life for free. . . . In this sense oil is a fairy tale and like every fairy tale a bit of a lie.

—Ryszard Kapuściński, *Shah of Shahs*, 1982

Since my first visit there almost exactly forty years ago, Nigeria has become an archetypical oil nation. According to the consultancy group PFC Energy, it is entirely possible that between now and 2020 Nigeria might pocket over half a trillion dollars in oil revenues. Nigeria is the eleventh-largest producer and the eighth-largest exporter of crude oil in the world, and oil production (crude production and natural-gas liquids) is currently running at roughly 2.45 million barrels per day.[63] Roughly two-thirds of production is on shore; the remainder is derived off shore from the continental shelf in both shallow and deep water.[64] Like other OPEC countries, in an era of high oil prices Nigeria is and has been over much of the last decade awash in petrodollars. It is an oil-state, driven by two cardinal principles: capture oil rents and sow oil revenues. Oil has seeped deeply and indelibly into the political, economic, and social lifeblood of Nigeria. In 2011 over 87 percent of government revenues, 90 percent of foreign exchange earnings, 96 percent of export revenues, and almost half of gross domestic product (GDP) is accounted for by just one commodity: oil. With oil prices now over $100 a barrel, oil rents—what economists call unearned income—will provide the Nigerian exchequer with at least $70 billion annually. What this oil wealth has wrought, and is likely to bring, is another question entirely.

Nigeria is certainly no El Dorado. To compile an inventory of the achievements of Nigerian petro-development is a dismal exercise: 85 percent of oil revenues accrue to 1 percent of the population; between 1985 and 2004, income inequality Gini coefficients in Nigeria deteriorated (rising from 0.43 to 0.49), placing the country among those with the highest inequality levels in the world. The total poverty head count rose from 27.2 percent in 1980 to 65.6 percent in 1996, an annual average increase of 8.83 percent over sixteen years.[65] Between 1996 and 2004, the poverty head count actually declined to 54.4 percent, which I suppose makes a grim picture marginally better (table 3), except that over the same period, the percentage of the population in the core poor category rose from 6.2 to 29.3 before declining to 22.0 in 2004. Human development rose to 0.456 in 1995, 0.486 in 2003, and 0.499 in 2006, which were the highest marks the country had recorded in the past two and one-half decades (table 4). But these figures signify only that after a half century of oil wealth, Nigeria ranks

TABLE 3.
NIGERIA: POVERTY RATES BY STATE ZONE (US$ PER DAY BASED ON
ADJUSTED PURCHASING POWER PARITY).

State	Poor	Nonpoor
National	51.55	48.45
Abia	28.01	71.99
Adamawa	68.91	31.09
Akwa Ibom	46.04	53.96
Anambra	30.36	69.64
Bauchi	76.51	23.49
Bayelsa	26.29	73.71
Benue	42.84	57.16
Borno	48.65	51.35
Cross Rivers	51.64	48.36
Delta	62.28	37.72
Ebonyi	46.06	53.94
Edo	44.31	55.69
Ekiti	35.51	64.49
Enugu	33.89	66.11
Gombe	66.34	33.66
Imo	26.46	73.54
Jigawa	89.54	10.46
Kaduna	37.72	62.28
Kano	46.7	53.3
Katsina	60.42	39.58
Kebbi	86.2	13.8
Kogi	87.46	12.54
Kwara	79.85	20.15
Lagos	64.05	35.95
Nasarawa	48.17	51.83
Niger	56.01	43.99
Ogun	29.84	70.16
Ondo	41.47	58.53
Osun	22.66	77.34
Oyo	19.28	80.72
Plateau	46.78	53.22
Rivers	43.12	56.88
Sokoto	70.54	29.46
Taraba	54.07	45.93
Yobe	74.12	25.88
Zamfara	73.38	26.62
FCT	46.98	53.02

SOURCE: United Nations Development Program, *Human Development Report, Nigeria 2008–2009* (Abuja: UNDP, 2009), 150.

TABLE 4.
NIGERIA: HUMAN DEVELOPMENT INDICES BY STATE.

States	Human development index (HDI) value	Human poverty index	Gender development measure	Gender empowerment measure	Inequality measure
Abia	0.516	21.9	0.527	0.383	0.3
Adamawa	0.372	42.4	0.287	0.285	0.33
Akwa Ibom	0.616	27.1	0.622	0.31	0.34
Anambra	0.427	22.8	0.437	0.414	0.4
Bauchi	0.291	48.8	0.07	0.129	0.4
Bayelsa	0.593	32.5	0.6	0.219	0.4
Benue	0.532	36	0.508	0.204	0.4
Borno	0.345	55.9	0.25	0.033	0.4
Cross River	0.539	31.9	0.544	0.148	0.4
Delta	0.592	23.6	0.591	0.316	0.4
Ebonyi	0.401	34.3	0.398	0.284	0.4
Edo	0.465	21.7	0.475	0.148	0.4
Ekiti	0.523	22.1	0.519	0.38	0.4
Enugu	0.502	28.6	0.494	0.192	0.4
Gombe	0.353	45	0.076	0.057	0.4
Imo	0.51	22.7	0.418	0.303	0.4
Jigawa	0.362	48.4	0.303	0.055	0.4
Kaduna	0.448	34.3	0.422	0.213	0.4
Kano	0.436	43	0.333	0.092	0.4
Katsina	0.410	49.9	0.383	0.129	0.44
Kebbi	0.377	50.2	0.383	0.175	0.46
Kogi	0.411	34.4	0.359	0.069	0.46
Kwara	0.429	33.3	0.47	0.482	0.47
Lagos	0.607	14.5	0.548	0.357	0.48
Nasarawa	0.488	38.5	0.465	0.236	0.48
Niger	0.463	42.8	0.474	0.244	0.48
Ogun	0.465	24.5	0.466	0.247	0.5
Ondo	0.592	23.9	0.586	0.181	0.5
Osun	0.475	22.1	0.475	0.234	0.5
Oyo	0.478	21.9	0.447	0.311	0.5
Plateau	0.392	36.5	0.393	0.415	0.5
Rivers	0.633	22.8	0.616	0.367	0.5
Sokoto	0.475	40.5	0.385	0.099	0.5
Taraba	0.351	43.4	0.651	0.032	0.5
Yobe	0.278	58	0.166	0.172	0.5
Zamfara	0.434	42.6	0.422	0.056	0.51
FCT Abuja	0.717	21	0.68	0.062	0.64

SOURCE: United Nations Development Program, *Human Development Report, Nigeria 2008–2009* (Abuja: UNDP, 2009), 92.

156th of 187 countries, slightly below the sub-Saharan Africa average and roughly on par with Haiti. The inequality-adjusted HDI index places Nigeria below Ethiopia (ranked 174th on the Human Development Index). It is hard to see how these rankings might constitute an achievement.

According to former World Bank President Paul Wolfowitz, at least $400 billion of the $700 billion in oil revenues accrued since 1960 have simply "gone missing."[66] Nigerian anticorruption czar Nuhu Ribadu claimed that in 2003 70 percent of the country's oil wealth was stolen or wasted; by 2005 the figure was "only" 40 percent. By the most conservative estimates almost $130 billion was lost in capital flight between 1970 and 1996. Nigeria appears close to the top of virtually everyone's global rankings of corruption, business risk, lack of transparency, fraud, and illicit activity. If readers of this book have any association with Nigeria, it is probably through email fraud: "Dear Sir: I am a former oil minister and I have the privilege of requesting your assistance in transferring $47 million"—what are called 419 scams in Nigeria. Nigerian fraud has its own FBI website. Nuhu Ribadu, then the head of the Economic and Financial Crimes Commission (EFCC), expressed the matter with great precision: the government is "not even corruption. It is organized crime" (*Economist*, April 28, 2007, 56). Nigeria has become a model failure.

The most recent Millennium Development Goals report not unexpectedly reveals a very mixed performance, too (even if the language of the report is upbeat).[67] There certainly is some good news. Maternal mortality fell by 32 percent, from 800 deaths per 100,000 live births in 2003 (at the time one of the highest maternal mortality rates in the world) to 545 deaths per 100,000 live births in 2008. Under-five mortality has fallen by over a fifth in five years, from 201 deaths per 1,000 live births in 2003 to 157 deaths per 1,000 live births in 2008 (these levels remain frighteningly high). In the same period, the infant mortality rate fell even faster, from 100 to 75 deaths per 1,000 live births. Recent economic growth, particularly in agriculture, has markedly reduced the proportion of underweight children, from 35.7 percent in 1990 to 23.1 percent in 2008. In a major step forward, nearly nine out of ten children, 88.8 percent, are now enrolled in school.[68] Yet it remains, as the MDG report points out, that 60 percent of the population was living in relative poverty in the year 2000. This figure is expected to fall to 21.35 percent in 2015, in line with the MDG 1 target. But in 2007, the midpoint for implementation of the relevant MDG programs in Nigeria, the percentage of the population living in extreme poverty should have fallen to 28.78 to meet the MDG target. The only data currently available (2004) shows that 54.4 percent of the population lives in relative poverty, and the incidence of "core poor" remains unacceptably high (table 5). New data from the Nigerian National Bureau of Statistics indicates that 61 percent of all Nigerians—nearly 100 million (97.6 million)—made less than one dollar a day in 2010, 10 per-

TABLE 5.
NIGERIA: INCIDENCE OF CORE POVERTY BY SECTOR AND ZONE, 1980–2004.

State/region/sector	Percent	1980	1985	1992	1996	2004
National	Total poor	28.1	46.3	42.7	65.6	54.4
	Core poor	6.2	12.1	13.9	29.3	22
Urban	Total poor	17.2	37.8	37.5	58.2	43.2
	Core poor	3	7.5	10.7	25.2	15.7
Rural	Total poor	28.3	51.4	66	69.3	63.3
	Core poor	6.5	14.8	15.8	31.6	27.1
South South	Total poor	13.2	45.7	40.8	58.2	35.1
	Core poor	3.3	9.3	13	23.4	17
South East	Total poor	12.9	30.4	41	53.5	26.7
	Core poor	2.4	9	15.7	18.2	7.8
South West	Total poor	13.4	38.6	43.1	60.9	43
	Core poor	2.1	9	15.7	27.5	18.9
North Central	Total poor	32.2	50.8	46	64.7	67
	Core poor	5.7	16.4	14.8	28	29.8
North East	Total poor	35.6	54.9	54	70.1	71.2
	Core poor	11.8	16.4	18.5	34.4	27.9
North West	Total poor	37.7	52.1	36.5	77.2	71.2
	Core poor	8.3	14.2	9	37.3	26.8
Population in poverty (million)		17.7	34.7	39.2	67.1	68.7

SOURCE: United Nations Development Program, *Human Development Report, Nigeria 2008–2009* (Abuja: UNDP, 2009), 64.

cent higher than the previous poverty study in 2004. The report notes that income inequality also has increased over the same period.[69]

If there is indeed limited progress, it is hard to see beyond the brute facts: namely, an astonishing degree of poverty in a country with a GNP per capita (PPP) of $2,170 and two homegrown insurgencies—one, a radical Islamist faction launched in the name of Boko Haram in the cities of the Muslim north; the other, under the sign of MEND (the Movement for the Emancipation of the Niger Delta), blowing onto the Nigerian stage in late 2005 and bringing the oil industry to its knees.[70] The grim reality is that for the majority of the MDG goals progress remains "weak or average." In my estimation, the MDG prospects for 2015 are hopeless.

What is on offer in the name of oil development is the catastrophic failure of secular nationalist development. It is not simply that Nigeria is a sort of Potemkin economy; it is, of course. The cruel fact is that the country has become a perfect storm of waste, corruption, venality, and missed opportunity. Nigeria is still as much a profession as it is a country. Life chances of those with whom I lived in 1976 don't appear much better in 2012 (table 6).

It all seems on its face to be a stellar—perhaps a textbook—case of a resource curse, to quote the title of Michael L. Ross's new book *The Oil Curse.*[71] The great Polish journalist Ryszard Kapuściński, who was witness to

TABLE 6.
NIGERIA: HUMAN POVERTY INDICES BY STATE.

State	Probability at birth of not surviving to age 40 (Percent of cohort)	Illiteracy rate (Percent aged 15 and above)	Population not using improved water sources	Underweight children under age five	Unweighted average of population not using an improved water source and children underweight for age	Human poverty index
Nigeria	0.313	35.8	50.9	25.3	38.1	32.3
Abia	0.306	20.8	36.4	20.1	28.3	21.9
Adamawa	0.325	45.4	81	21.7	51.3	42.4
Akwa Ibom	0.3	20	46.7	27.8	37.2	27.1
Anambra	0.358	23	42.6	14.8	28.7	22.8
Bauchi	0.271	61.3	64.8	33.1	49	48.8
Bayelsa	0.3	35.7	63.4	14	38.7	32.5
Benue	0.314	34.6	75.9	16.6	64.2	36
Borno	0.265	73.1	70	32.1	51.1	55.9
Cross River	0.24	25.4	69.1	17.5	43.3	31.9
Delta	0.305	27.1	34.4	19.6	27	23.6
Ebonyi	0.36	43.4	48.8	19	33.9	34.3
Edo	0.355	23.8	39.3	12.4	25.9	21.7
Ekiti	0.272	25.6	32.6	17.2	24.9	22.2
Enugu	0.299	25.4	62.2	13.4	37.8	28.6
Gombe	0.274	48.3	81.8	26.9	54.3	45
Imo	0.323	24.6	37.4	17	27.2	22.7
Jigawa	0.342	61.3	44	51.5	47.7	48.4

Kaduna	0.316	37.7	51.1	30.3	40.7	34.3
Kano	0.296	42.5	60.2	48.8	54.5	43
Katsina	0.306	63.5	57.1	40.7	48.9	49.9
Kebbi	0.303	51.4	80.1	45.1	62.6	50.2
Kogi	0.364	36.5	63.8	20.1	42	34.4
Kwara	0.327	44.4	29.1	27.6	28.3	33.3
Lagos	0.324	10.6	24.4	15.6	20	14.5
Nasarawa	0.279	48.9	55.3	20.5	37.9	38.5
Niger	0.241	58.3	38.9	28	33.4	42.8
Ogun	0.33	31.5	26.1	20.6	24.4	24.5
Ondo	0.323	24.2	42.8	17	29.9	23.9
Osun	0.295	26.2	31.4	17.4	24.4	22.1
Oyo	0.309	27.4	20.5	24.3	22.4	21.9
Plateau	0.347	39.4	68.7	19.1	43.9	36.5
Rivers	0.361	19.5	39	21.8	30.4	22.8
Sokoto	0.305	32.6	70.7	38.9	54.8	40.5

SOURCE: United Nations Development Program, *Human Development Report, Nigeria 2008–2009* (Abuja: UNDP, 2009), 146.

the spectacular oil boom in West Asia during the 1970s, says oil "is a filthy, foul-smelling liquid that squirts obligingly up into the air and falls back to earth as a rustling shower of money."[72] It is, he said, a resource that anesthetizes thought, blurs vision, and is above all a source of great temptation. Oil has always been vested with enormous, often magical, powers. It has been called a resource curse, the devil's excrement, the source of the Dutch Disease. Oil distorts the organic, natural course of development. Oil wealth ushers in an economy of hyperconsumption and spectacular excess: bloated shopping malls in Dubai or corrupt Russian "oilygarchs." There is even a psychological appellation to describe the condition: the Gillette syndrome. ElDean Kohrs studied the booming coal town of Gillette, Wyoming, in the 1970s and was witness to how a commodity boom brought a corresponding wave of crime, drugs, violence, and inflation. The syndrome would afflict new gas fields of Wyoming, indigenous oil communities of Ecuador, and the rough and tumble Russian oilfields of Siberia.

There is inevitably an economic and political form of the Gillette syndrome.[73] Nigeria figures quite centrally in Oxford University economist Paul Collier's hugely influential book on the resource curse, *The Bottom Billion.*[74] Big Oil engenders Big Patronage, says Collier: the law of the political jungle produces what he wittily calls "the survival of the fattest." Oil wealth relaxes political constraints most obviously by obviating the need to tax (no tax—no restraint). The sort of democracy that resource-rich states get is dysfunctional for economic development, especially if they are low income and ethnically diverse. To round out the story, the combustible mix of the law of the survival of the fattest under the dispensation of oil provides ideal grounds for resource predation and the illicit economy of rebellion (the economic basis of civil war[75]). Others like Michael Ross argue that "oil hinders democracy" (as if copper might promote constitutionalism): its revenues permit low taxes and encourage patronage (thereby dampening pressures for democracy); it endorses despotic rule through bloated militaries; and it creates a class of state-dependents employed in modern industrial and service sectors who are less likely to push for democracy. *New York Times* columnist Thomas Friedmann has even identified a First Law of Petropolitics: the higher the average global crude price of oil, the more free speech, free press, fair elections, an independent judiciary, the rule of law, and independent political parties are eroded. Hugo Chavez is, of course, the law's most devious exponent.

There is a ring of truth here. Oil wealth can be, and often is, ill-managed. Oil-producing states are among the most corrupt and venal anywhere. The world of oil-rents is one of spectacular consumption pushed to its limits. But the language of curse invokes a merciless force for adversity, a sort of ineluctable commodity determinism vesting oil with capabilities it can neither possess nor dispense. The danger is that the curse substitutes the commodity for the larger truths of capitalism, markets, and politics. Is Nigeria cursed by oil or capitalism; by petroleum or politics; by hydrocarbons or ethnicity? The answer is surely both. It is what I have called the oil assemblage,[76] which draws together oil as commodity and as capital with the specific political economy of Nigerian capitalism into which petroleum was inserted fifty years ago. The operations of this assemblage can help us grasp the devastating indictment by the IMF that Nigeria's capture of over $700 billion dollars of oil revenue has "not significantly added to the standard of living of the average Nigerian."[77]

Fifty years after the discovery of commercial quantities of oil, the Nigerian economy remains as dependent upon oil revenues as it ever was, and the logic of politics remains a vicious, take-no-prisoners struggle for access to oil revenues by powerful regional (and ethnic) constituencies. What one can say is that the power of the federal center has seen a devolution of both power and money to the states and a concomitant rise of what are called regional godfathers. If there has been a decentralization of power, there has also been a decentralization of state corruption to the local level as oil revenues now cascade through the state and local governments, especially in the oil-producing regions. Moreover, there has been a decentralization of violence. Over the last decade militants in the name of revolutionary Islam and resource control have wreaked devastation in the oilfields of the Niger delta and in the cities of the Muslim *umma* in the north. In hindsight one can see how the incubus of these insurgencies was being put in place during my sojourn in Katsina.

Large related bodies of thought appear, at first like distant riders stirring up modest dust clouds, who, when they arrive, reproach one for his slowness in recognizing their numbers, strength and vitality.

—Clarence J. Glacken, *Traces on the Rhodian Shore,* 1967

My own interests in Nigeria were nurtured in the late 1960s when I was an undergraduate in London, but they took form in, and were shaped by, the great political, economic, and social firmament of the 1970s. With the powers of hindsight one can see what an extraordinary decade it was and how it necessarily framed research programs, both in geography and in the social sciences more generally. The events of that decade bear recapping: an imperialist war in Southeast Asia; a troubled American Fordism feeling the pressures of global competition; deepening class struggles over the future of embedded liberalism; the Nixon dollar devaluation and the turn to global financialization; massive volatility in commodities markets, especially food and oil; a robust Third World nationalism and a raft of successful revolutionary movements ultimately hobbled by balance of payments deficits;

massive public-sector debt and Cold War "low-intensity conflict" and proxy wars; popular energies unleashed by a global environmental movement; and not least, the first stirrings of what was to become the global neoliberal counterrevolution. The 1970s actually became the high-water mark for radical theorizing, enriched by exciting (and not so exciting) political experiments, not the least of which were the various African socialisms in the former Portuguese colonies (Guinea-Bissau, Angola, Mozambique) and in Zimbabwe, Ethiopia, Tanzania, and elsewhere. Some locations—one thinks in particular of Dar es Saalam, Zaria, Dakar, Nairobi—became centers of great intellectual vitality.

In other words, I arrived in Zaria (at Ahmadu Bello University [ABU]) and later in Katsina in the white heat of Third World nationalism. Nigeria had become a major oil producer by 1970 and reaped the benefits of the oil crisis and OPEC assertiveness in 1973 and 1979 when oil prices skyrocketed; a raft of authoritarian military governments aggressively promoted import substitution, partial nationalizations, and a robust antipathy to both former colonial powers and the growing significance of Cold War polarization. I had some familiarity with northern Nigeria, having lived previously in the provincial towns of Sokoto and Birnin Kebbi, but was immediately inserted into the firmament of a deeply politicized ABU, then the primary research institution in the Muslim north of country. The state military government at the time was loathe to give me research permission for a long-term rural residence even though I was formally affiliated with the Department of Geography at Ibadan University in the south of the country. Soldiering on, I waited six long months before permission was granted, but in a curious way this had huge payoffs (and it needs to be said a downside—living in the back of an old Land Rover that I drove across the Sahara desert from the UK, but that is another story).

One upside of the delay was the exploration of the rich historical and archival sources available in Zaria, Ibadan, and Kaduna that allowed me to reconstruct a long-twentieth-century history of droughts and famines in the region and to explore the relations between agrarian commercialization, colonial tax policy, and household food security. On the one hand I became a historical geographer (of sorts), and on the other, I was immersed in the intellectual hothouse of ABU. The campus and the students had been animated by a number of charismatic Nigerian scholars (most obviously Yusufu Bala Usman, the great Katsina historian of the Hausa states and the Sokoto Caliphate, and sociologist Ibrahim Tahir, whose brilliant PhD at Cambridge University on capitalism in Kano was exceptionally generative) and by a large constituency of Left-leaning expatriate faculty (Bjorn Beckman, Bill Freund, Patrick Wilmott, among others) and a posse of British, Canadian, and American graduate students (Louise Lennihan, now of CUNY; Bob Shenton, now of Queen's; Paul Clough, now of the University of Malta;

and Sam Jackson and Richard Palmer-Jones, both now of the University of East Anglia).[78] It was an extraordinary group who were in different ways challenging the orthodox accounts of northern Nigerian history (the so-called vent-for-surplus model and related anodyne accounts of the impact of European mercantile activity and colonial state practice), using the tools of Marxian political economy.

At the heart of this revisionist history was a rethinking of the agrarian question. Agriculture and the environment had a particular salience because ABU was home to the Institute for Agricultural Research (IAR), one of the most distinguished schools of agricultural economics (and agricultural science) on the continent, and had—with considerable support from the US land grant colleges and USAID—generated a mountain of survey data on farming systems and provided a large body of neoclassical analysis of the northern agrarian systems emphasizing market efficiency and smallholder productivity. There were other foundations, too. Jamaican anthropologist M. G. Smith had provided a provocative interpretation of the Hausa states and of rural livelihoods in *kasar* Hausa[79]; Murray Last's exploration of the *longue durée* of the Hausa states was without peer[80]; and not least the brilliant economic anthropologist Polly Hill of Cambridge University—niece of John Maynard Keynes—had offered a detailed and compelling account of a rural Hausa community near Katsina.[81] Hill's monograph—*Rural Hausa*—remains a classic text, a prescient mix of ethnography and survey analysis focusing specifically on questions of economic inequality and patterns of stratification and mobility in a commercial farming community in the northern savannas. The presence of similar work being conducted in Nigerien Hausaland, just across the border, by French geographers and anthropologists such as Claude Raynault, Guy Nicolas, and Emmanuel Gregoire, added a further frisson to the entire enterprise.[82]

The combination of Hill's foundational work—an essentially Chayanovian account of rural inequality—and IAR's extensive if often uncritical survey work provided the touchstone for my and others' revisionist treatment of Nigeria's agrarian question. Without this platform of high-quality scholarship to respond to, my own education, and indeed the quality of the scholarly work on northern Nigeria in general, would have been much the worse. Polly Hill's corpus provided a rigorous and synoptic account with which any serious student of northern Nigeria had to engage. At the time, a small army of faculty and graduate students were conducting field research on everything from the role of merchants' activities and money lending in household reproduction to gender and economic inequities associated with new, large, state-funded irrigation systems; to the impact of state marketing policies on class formation and agrarian politics; and in my own case, to the relations between drought and food security. At the center of all of this work was a rereading of the historical dynamics of capitalist development in northern Nigeria from 1900, through careful village- and household-based ethnographies and fieldwork, and a sort of methodological engagement with basic questions of political economy (how might exploitation or "surplus" be quantified; how could money lending and seasonal crop loans be accurately documented; how could landholding and landed inequality be measured; and so on). It was all very heady.

Not least, this focus on agrarian issues was part of, and was animated by, two other broad intellectual vectors of the time. The first was the "peasant studies boom" of the 1970s (one thinks of the *Journal of Peasant Studies* group at the University of London, the central contributions by figures such as Eric Wolf, Terry Byres, Claude Meillassoux, and Teodor Shanin, and the growing interest in questions of peasant politics and peasant resistance associated with James Scott, Sam Popkin, and others). The second was the debate within and over Marxism, not least the operations of the great Althusserian reactor and how this might be squared with the so-called cultural Marxism of an Edward Thompson or the Trotskyism of a Perry Anderson.[83] My own research program was explicitly framed by these engagements.[84]

Silent Violence, like any book, is an artifact of its time. Inevitably it is, in historical and conceptual terms, a "rough draft." The book appeared in 1983, significantly two years after the publication of Amartya Sen's foundational book on famine, *Poverty and Famines*—when debates about cultural and structural Marxism were at full throttle and when poststructuralism (and the cultural turn) was reshaping the social sciences. In part because of changing theoretical fashion or disposition and in part because of new historical and empirical field research, some of the subsequent scholarship on northern Nigeria has inevitably challenged some of what *Silent Violence* had to say.[85] Mohammed Salau's important book on a late nineteenth-century slave plantation near Kano city provided evidence that slave-based production not only was extensive but was key to the vaunted groundnut revolution of the early twentieth century.[86] Stephen Pierce, adopting a broadly Fouacauldian rubric, provided an innovative rereading of land tenure in colonial (and postcolonial) Kano turning on the colonial state's misreading and simultaneous fetishization of land tenure, which is installed at the heart of government.[87] And not surprisingly, a group of young scholars deepened our understanding of rural accumulation and agrarian dynamics in the 1980s and 1990s, focusing in particular on the relation between polygamous farming households, economic mobility and accumulation, the organization of the grains trade, new centers of state-sponsored irrigated production, and the impact of neoliberal reforms on the rural poor.[88]

Much of this is especially relevant in charting the changing contours of the regional food system and the circuits of rural accumulation during the reform period. Very little of this work, however, offered a radically new view of northern Nigeria's agrarian question,[89] and I am not entirely convinced that it provides grounds for rejecting my principal claims about food crises and famine. A number of monographs specifically addressed drought and food in the Sahelian zone, most notably Michael Mortimore's *Adapting to Drought* and his book coauthored with William Adams, *Working the Sahel*[90]— conducting research in differing parts of the north (Kano and the north-east) but covering similar ground as *Silent Violence* (cropping strategies, labor flexibility, responses to food shortage, and so on). Careful, longer-term empirical research of this sort is especially needed, but these books suffer in at least two profound respects. On the one hand, this work emphasized, to quote Mortimore, the "adaptability" of the farming system and the ingenuity and arduousness of the peasantry (in contradistinction to what he saw as the "determinism" of other approaches). Doubtless this praise-singing of the virtues of the peasantry is justified—I, too, cover similar ground—but it has little to say about the *limits* of adaptability and how the social relations of production impose constraints, rigidities, and inflexibilities. On the other hand, concerning the operations of the market and the deepening commercialization of the countryside during the crucible of neoliberalism in Nigeria, the authors are silent.[91]

Sadly, however, one of the striking aspects of research on Nigerian Hausaland over the last few decades is the relative demise of what has been one of the region's distinctive strengths, namely field-based rural studies of virtually any stripe. This has been the case especially over the last decade, when, for different reasons, the work of the Institute of Agricultural Research at Ahmadu Bello University and of the younger generation of Euro-American and Nigerian scholars has not continued to contribute to the illustrious tradition of studies in agrarian political economy.[92] What, after all, do we know about the purported turnaround, much praised by the World Bank, in agrarian production since 2000? If we mean serious field and case studies, the answer is precious little. The intellectual energy on both sides of the Atlantic now resides elsewhere, in a revisionist history of Islam and an inquiry into the radical transformation of the political sociology of northern Nigerian Islam,[93] prerequisites in fact for any understanding of not only the rapid adoption of sharia across the twelve northern states after 1999 but also the emergent militant strains of radical neo-Salafist Islam that, as I write, threaten the very stability of the country itself. Here too, however, Islamism in its various forms is often an urban story, and in what manner and ways the millions of Hausa and Fulani peasants are being swept up into its vortex remains an open (and largely understudied) question.

Finally, there is the now substantial corpus of work on famines that has appeared in the nearly three decades since *Silent Violence* appeared. One line of engagement stimulating a substantial amount of debate is derived, not unexpectedly, from Amartya Sen's work on entitlements.[94] In their important book *Hunger and Public Action*, Sen and his collaborator Jean Drèze address the poverty-hunger equation primarily in economic terms through forms of command over food.[95] Famine and hunger are defined by entitlement collapse and are expressed through the socially circumscribed distribution of entitlements over basic necessities. Entitlement-based theories of vulnerability have the great merit of highlighting the specific social, economic, and institutional relations between food and people (in contradistinction to an emphasis on supply-side dynamics). They further help to explain why some social classes are affected by hunger and others hardly touched. There remains, however, the question of what sort of explanation (if any) entitlements actually provide.[96] While Drèze and Sen broadly see entitlements as embracing not only food intake (biology) but also access to health care and education (the social environment)—that is to say the broader domain of well-being and advantage—they have less to say about what they call "capability" and the "totality of rights," which secure basic needs. First, entitlement as commodity bundle provides a "conjunctural" analysis, highlighting the immediate, triggering, or proximate mechanisms (price movements, speculation, drought) that precipitate a shift in entitlements. It has much less to say about the long-term structural and historical processes by which specific patterns of entitlements and property rights come to be distributed or shift temporally—in other words, political economy. In failing to elaborate structural and often contradictory political, economic, and social determinants that mark the onset of the famine process, entitlement misses an important opportunity to link crisis theory with the longer term processes that allocate and deprive households and individuals of assets and endowments. Second, the entitlement approach also fails to take into account the central dimensions of famine consequence and recovery.[97] It explains neither what transpires in the wake of mass starvation nor the lineaments linking a single famine to earlier or later crises. In this sense, entitlement—especially when read in a narrow legal or market sense—runs the grave danger of neglecting historical processes and, to invoke Gramsci, the situations and conjunctures producing such calamitous outcomes. Finally, entitlements have often been construed much too narrowly, thus constraining the variety of social domains in which claims over food and security can be exercised. Concerns with gender, generation and age, and caste and ethnicity, for example, have received less attention than occupational status, property, and the market.[98]

In my view, entitlements have to be radically extended not simply in a social or class sense but politically and structurally. In other words, an analysis of famine and hunger based on entitlements must account for the particular distribution of entitlements and how they are reproduced in specific circumstances, the larger canvas of rights by which entitlements are defined, fought over, contested, and won and lost (that is, empowerment or enfranchisement), and the structural properties (what I have called crisis proneness) of the political economy that precipitates entitlement crises. To encompass these questions, entitlements would need to be deposited in what Sen himself calls—but does not explore—the mode of production.[99]

Another body of work has an even more restrictive economic account because it limits the purview of famine to the functioning of markets.[100] More precisely, it considers famine a function of imperfect markets that are weak, unintegrated, and possibly driven by speculative or hoarding behavior. Collectively these market pathologies drive up food prices beyond the capacity (of some) to buy. The International Food and Policy Research Institute's (IFPRI) synthetic work on African famines is a case in point.[101] Famine is largely seen in technocratic terms as a function of institutional, organizational, and policy failures, which is to say that famine is a poverty problem rooted in poor economic performance and failed or weak states. Policy failures are never construed as political or military, both of which are simply seen as derivative of, and secondary to, low productivity of the poor and an anodyne sense of "policy failure." Yet paradoxically, much of the famine corpus of the last two decades necessarily focused on Africa, where it was glaringly clear that famines could *only* be understood in relation to politics, civil wars, militarism, and Cold War conflict.

The politics of famine points to the third strand of research, which precisely starts from the presumption that famines are crises of political accountability, both national and international.[102] In this accounting famines are "complex emergencies"—humanitarian crises linked to large-scale violent conflict in which violence is the hand-maiden of food distribution.[103] Compelling analyses of the food crises in Sudan and the Horn of Africa raise the prospect of what Devereux calls "new famines."[104] Starvation reflects not simply the absence of a political contract—the notion that crises are deterred by antifamine contracts between rulers and ruled—but also of the failures by humanitarian agencies and international governments to shape how and whether food relief—the central requirement in alleviating failed entitlements—is effective.[105] Food and food aid are, and have been, regularly deployed as weapons, but the larger point is that food entitlements and food delivery are themselves political. Some of the most compelling work on famine of late extends politics beyond the boundaries of African civil war and conflict and locates the crises of accountability within the vortices of state power. Mukerjee's analysis of Churchill's secret war on India, Frank Dikotter's and Yang Jisheng's extraordinary accountings of the internal political struggles surrounding the Great Leap Forward and the devastating Chinese famine (1958–62), and not least, Lizzie Coolingham's brilliant examination of the global reverberations of the Second World War that resulted in the starvation of over twenty million people (including, of course, the Great Bengal famine) are outstanding exemplars of the genre.[106] Each of these studies can perhaps best be seen as complementary to Mike

Davis's remarkable—and devastating—picture of the last quarter of the nineteenth century as the great forcing house of starvation. The holocaust was produced by the intersection of two global processes: telekinetic activity in the world's climate cells through El Niño Southern Oscilliations (ENSO) and late nineteenth-century imperialism, which Hanna Arendt called the political emancipation of the bourgeoisie.[107] Violent primitive accumulation (draped in the ideology of late Victorian capitalism) running headlong into global climate perturbation took the lives of some sixty million.[108]

The circumstances of hunger and starvation depicted in *Silent Violence* were not animated by war and civil conflict though, of course, the Biafran war in Nigeria and, indeed, much of the colonial hardship I describe were not unrelated to the global conflagrations in Europe. But politics *is* central to my story. The failure of the antiscarcity contract in colonial and postcolonial Nigeria is a political story. But as I hope to show, it is a political story inseparable from the rhythms and turbulence of colonial and postcolonial capitalism, the forms of surplus extraction, and the prismatic ways in which labor, land, and food are commodified. It is a political ecology of famine that I have to offer, and to this extent my book is a local account (albeit cast in global terms) of the planetary holocaust depicted in *Late Victorian Holocausts*.

––––––––

> Foucault focuses on biopower's attempt to manage what he calls "endemics," which, unlike epidemics, are "permanent factors . . . [that] sapped the population's strength, shortened the working week," and "cost money." In this shift Foucault dissolves the attention to scenes of *control* over individual life and death under sovereign regimes and refocuses on the dispersed *management* of the biological threat posed by certain populations to the reproduction of the normatively framed general good life of a society. Slow death occupies the temporalities of the endemic.
>
> —Lauren Berlant, *Slow Death*, 2007

The colonies were always much more than a canvas on which Europe painted a modern picture of itself. Provincializing Europe entails not only recognizing that European imperial projects were compromised in what they could achieve in political and economic terms but also in acknowledging that the colonies became centers of experimentation and agency, the laboratories of modernity. As Helen Tilley notes in her important book *Africa as a Living Laboratory*, the colonies provided the bricks and mortar of disciplines, theories, and institutions.[109] Ecological rationalities of government were framed not only by deforestation and pollution in Europe but were also forged within the crucible of colonial rule.

Formal colonial rule brought forth armies of scientists, research centers, commissions, and field expeditions and at the same time had the effect of Africanizing science—that is to say, it converted Africa, in key domains, into an object of scientific scrutiny, on the one hand, and drew Africans and African knowledge into a constitutive process of what Tilley calls "vernacular science," on the other. Africa's laboratories were many and multifaceted,[110] and they were achieved through institutions, networks, and the circulation of ideas—and importantly an interplay between field and laboratory sciences—that were often at the heart of imperial government broadly construed. The disciplines of ecology, geography, and anthropology were central to the vernacularization of scientific knowledge. In other words, the localization of scientific knowledge (that is to say, a clear distinction between what was universal and what was site specific) had a way of entering into the archive of global science even if Africans themselves were rarely at the helm of decision-making.[111]

Silent Violence was able to show that northern Nigeria proved to be an African laboratory, too, of smallholder agriculture, of conservation and afforestation, and of rights to subsistence. The market, new crops and new farming practices, the role of colonial scientific practitioners, and an array of African actors collectively constituted the mix within which both ecological and conservation ideas and practices were debated as parts of the wider challenges to colonial rule. One issue that I documented was the nature of climatic and rainfall variation and the ability of peasants to adapt to such perturbations. Another, dating to the Great Depression of the 1930s, was the incubation of thinking about what the colonial office in western and southern Africa saw as a debilitating intersection of overpopulation (by humans and animals), soil erosion ("desertification"), and deforestation.[112] The big push toward colonial conservation—and various patterns of resistance to conservation measures—became part of a wide-ranging discussion, with connections to the Dust Bowl debates in the United States, that animated scientific and colonial-administrator constituencies across the French and British colonial empires in the 1930s. African agency was obviously constitutive of this vernacular ecology and emergent conservationist practice. Early in the twentieth century, agricultural officers in northern Nigeria could be heard singing the praises of peasant farmers and their local knowledge. On the other side stood a number of Africans (typically not scientifically trained) who worked closely with the colonial research apparatus and in this sense approximated what in a different setting Steven Shapin has called invisible technicians.[113] The green current running across colonial rule in Africa was deeply dialectical, emerging from the local and the global, the universal and the vernacular, the cosmopolitan and the parochial.

By the 1970s West Africa was proving to be a different sort of laboratory. The period between the late 1960s through the early 1980s was a long decade of economic and political turbulence driven by the oil boom and bust, by financial liberalization and the launching of structural adjustment programs, and by the massive human ecological crisis triggered by the drought-famines that extended across the Sahel. At base, this was a crisis of the agrarian and pastoral economies—comprising peasants and herders for the most part—that occupied the great swaths of the semiarid savannas, which is to say the ecological heart of the continent. The great drought-famines of the 1970s were framed by two important events: the first was the UN Conference on the Human Environment held in Stockholm in 1972, and the second was the release of the Club of Rome's report *Limits to Growth* in the same year. Both were foundational to the rise of a sort of "international environmentalism" addressing what were later to be understood as the challenges of "sustainable development." Both were fundamentally shaped by a robust Malthusianism. For the Club of Rome, founded as a global think tank in 1968 by an Italian industrialist and a Scottish international scientific civil servant (respectively, Aurelio Peccei and Alexander King), the oil crisis was a harbinger of a larger structural problem of resource scarcity, population pressure, and ecological degradation. Methodologically, the Club outsourced its study to the MIT Systems Dynamics Group, a team made up of seventeen researchers from a wide range of disciplines and countries and led by Dennis Meadows.[114] They assembled vast quantities of data from around the world to feed into the model, focusing on five main variables: investment, population, pollution, natural resources, and food. Calibrated to examine the interactions among these variables and the trends in the system as a whole over the next ten, twenty, and fifty years assuming extant growth rates, the model's scenarios predicted various sorts of system collapse or system unsustainability. In all, twelve million copies of the book have been sold, and it has been translated into thirty-seven languages.[115]

Peter Taylor has referred to the prevailing *Limits to Growth* discourse as "neo-Malthusian environmentalism" and interestingly made use of, as a historian of science and an ecologist, the influential studies of agro-pastoral systems in the West African Sahel conducted by the MIT Systems Dynamics team in the wake of the 1970s crisis.[116] By 1973, the semiarid Sahel region had experienced five years of drought and developing crisis. Many pastoralists (livestock herders) and farmers were in refugee camps, their herds decimated and their crops having failed again. Prevailing analysis at the time focused not only on famine relief but on the causes of the crisis and on prospects for the region's future, a view that heralded drought and famine as a forerunner of future demographically driven scarcity and shortage (through human population growth and settlement into increasingly marginal and overexploited environments, and animal overstocking on open ranges): in short, a Malthusian dystopia. The consensus was that the ecological resource base of the Sahel region had been seriously damaged. Once emergency relief was under way, discussion turned to longer-term measures needed for recovery and for prevention of future disasters. The US Agency for International Development (USAID) funded a one-year, $1 million project at MIT to evaluate long-term development strategies for the Sahel and the bordering "Sudan" region. The computer model (in a sense, a regional variant of the Club of Rome's global models) included a capacious menu of factors and mathematical relationships, all converted into a systems analysis anchored in (and confirmatory of) the "tragedy of the commons."[117] As calibrated, the model determined that overstocking and overgrazing were inevitable. Soil degradation and eventual desertification could be avoided only if all the pastoralists replaced their individual self-interest (and outdated forms of communal property) with "long-term preservation of the resource base as their first priority," perhaps requiring them to enter ranching schemes that privatized or strictly supervised access to pasture.[118] *Silent Violence* was written in response to, and against, precisely this conventional wisdom (see Figure 5).

The environmental and related agrarian crisis of the 1970s proved to be a veritable laboratory for economic ideas. Ecology, food, and climate fed into arguably one of *the* founding documents in the rise and consolidation of neoliberal development and the rise of the Washington Consensus, namely, the Berg Report (named after Michigan economist Elliot Berg), released as *Accelerated Development in Sub-Saharan Africa* by the World Bank in 1981.[119] At the core of Africa's crisis was "domestic policy" and a poor export performance in basic commodities in which the continent had a comparative advantage. Distorted markets and state marketing boards became the conceptual frontlines in a ferocious assault on the African state, a critique

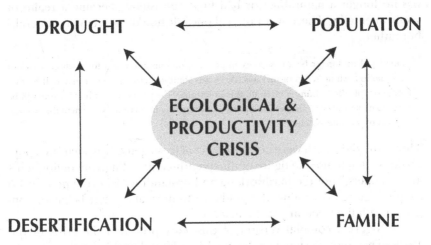

Figure 5. The neo-Malthusian model: the Sahelian crisis in the 1970s. Designed by Michael Watts and drawn by Darin Jensen, Department of Geography, University of California, Berkeley.

backed up with the prescriptive heavy artillery of structural adjustment and stabilization. The solutions to the environment-development crisis resided in a technical fix (bringing the green revolution and irrigation, and improved transportation, to the continent) and in exploiting export markets by releasing peasant innovativeness from the yoke of the state. The African peasant emerged, in this account at least, as one part indigenous ecologist and one part diminutive capitalist (and rational economic agent).

If *Silent Violence* was in conversation with this drought-population-subsistence-markets narrative and ultimately rejected it,[120] it is useful to reflect upon what sort of ecological and governmental rationalities lay behind the African food-climate-ecology crisis of the late 1960s and 1970s. It is worth recalling that a European version of the politics of food was central to Foucault's account of the rise of biopower, in which the "old power of death" was not abandoned but justified through the "calculated management of life" and appeals to the improvement of and the control over populations.[121] Central to this shift was the rise of apparatuses of security—what Foucault called the spaces of security, the management of uncertainty, mechanisms of normalization, and the population as a realm of conduct—around the problem of scarcity (*la disette*) as a crisis of government. Food and famine now, as a government matter, turned on questions of subsistence rights, the trade in grains, the management of droughts, and the control of food riots. The "antiscarcity" system of the ancien régime—the customary entitlements of the Elizabethan period in England, for example, famously described by Karl Polanyi[122]—was gradually displaced by the logic of the market and by concerns with agro-ecology, transportation, and farming practice. Famine was no longer a natural act or bad luck: subsistence became a realm of governmentality. There was not, as Foucault noted, "scarcity in general," but rather,

> There will no longer be any scarcity in general, on condition that for a whole series of people, in a whole series of markets, there was some scarcity, . . . and it may well be that some people die of hunger after all. But by letting these people die of hunger one will be able to make scarcity a chimera and prevent it occurring in this massive form of the scourge typical of previous systems.[123]

Those who did perish were not the object of management as such (i.e., populations) but, to use the figure of nineteenth-century England, delinquents and "paupers," not the hardworking and upstanding "laboring poor," who simply required discipline and guidance to normalize their behavior congruent with the freedoms of the market.[124]

A Nigerian colonial version of this story preceded the crisis of the 1970s. The colonial state was engaged in a biopolitical balancing act. On the one hand, the old indigenous antiscarcity system—the moral economy of subsistence—was eroding, often quickly and under force, while on the other hand, the effects of commercialization and states' exactions vastly expanded the likelihood of famine, which raised the possibility of millions perishing. British imperialists reluctantly and ineffectively institutionalized a minimalist antifamine policy (colonial welfare) for the indigent and invoked, with varying degrees of commitment, the "will to improve" colonial subjects who suffered from various indigenous deficits (recalcitrance, foot dragging, economic irrationality) and incompetencies. The food and ecological crisis of the 1970s represented a formalization of this emerging food-environment-security nexus. Not unlike geographer David Nally's stimulating account of "colonial biopolitics" in the Irish famine,[125] development practice focused on agricultural (and pastoral) rationalization, population control or resettlement, and state discipline.

While African starvation—whether in Ethiopia or Burkina Faso—loomed large in the media in the 1970s, at base the emaciated famine victim was always draped in the sackcloth of Malthusian overpopulation. Garrett Hardin, after all, raised the specter of the "lifeboat ethic"—letting die, in Foucault's terms—as the cost associated with the implacable logic of overpopulation, overgrazing, resource scarcity, and inadequate property rights displayed in the Club of Rome report. The commons stood in as a metaphor for the old antiscarcity system, which, as Malthus and others predicted in the early nineteenth century, would compound the problem of food security, improvement, and growth. Climate, environment, and populations needed to be managed: improvement, market forces, and property rights were its modalities. It was the vision of John Stuart Mill and Adam Smith, confirmed by the raft of market studies conducted in the wake of the famine by, perhaps appropriately, Elliot Berg and his associates at the University of Michigan, who confirmed that markets were efficient and "nonmonopolistic" but required investments in transportation and credit to realize their potential.[126] Africa, if overpopulated and crippled by state corruption and poor weather, was at least inhabited by some form of *homo economicus*.

Eventually the neo-Malthusian model, its technicist beliefs and assumptions, and the incomplete or distorted market (neoclassical) account were increasingly questioned by a new wave of social science research rooted in careful ethnographic and local studies of human ecological dynamics and the intersection of social and ecological relations of production among rural producers (which in a statistical sense represented the majority of Africans).[127] The challenges came from several fronts, and *Silent Violence* represented one small part. Amartya Sen's pivotal book *Poverty and Famines* decisively broke the purportedly causal connection between drought and famine.[128] Food crises and starvation bore no necessary relation to absolute food decline, and the effects of drought were typically mediated by farming practice and the market (in the latter case compounded by the deleterious effects of price increases and entitlement declines). Second, a body of work operating under the sign of peasant studies saw African communities as less composed of self-interested individuals (*contra* Hardin) than enmeshed in processes of commodification and social relations of production that rendered significant proportions of the rural populace vulnerable to all manner of ecological events even in "normal" times. The effects of climate and of ecological conditions were, in other words, experienced differentially in relation to class, asset holding, and the operations of the market. The sense in which indigenous knowledge and vernacular peasant practice could be captured and deployed was sharply constrained by the social relations of production in farming communities. The adaptive capacity much praised by geographers, anthropologists, and rural sociologists could be, and often was, undercut, eroded, or destroyed by the operations of the market. This was the heart of James Scott's influential book[129] on the moral economy of the peasantry, after all, and this was the center of what I tried to argue in *Silent Violence*. This realization had direct implications regarding who was vulnerable, how ecological processes were experienced, and in turn, how people and land might recover. Finally, Melissa Leach, Jeremy Swift, and others led a turn toward discursive analysis, pointing to what they called dominant models or narratives of environmental crisis that reflected particular readings or constructions of local African conditions. In part, the framing of particular environmental problems—for example, desertification and the deterioration of rangelands—was also questioned by the rise of a "new ecology" that focused on disequilibrium and a rethinking of the old static systems models of tropical ecology.[130] By the 1980s and into the 1990s, these intellectual developments—rooted partly in the field of political ecology, partly in ecological science and science studies, and partly in anthropological critiques of development—represented a fundamental challenge to the legitimacy and standing of the conventional narratives of Africa's environmental conditions, its actors, and its agents.

In the twenty-first century the African laboratory has conjured up a new ecological rationality, a new form of governmentality. Since I left Kaita in 1978, the centrality of global climate change has become the vehicle for a new laboratorial offering. Global climate change became, hot on the heels of structural adjustment, a theater for "governance through markets": government provides incentives and subsidies, and corporations establish their own (voluntary) standards.[131] In the current neoliberal order, the short-term future depends on a precise costing of climatic impacts and on getting the prices right.[132]

In a discursive sense, then, climate change as a planetary emergency mobilizes powerful actors around the threat of massive risks and uncertainties to the notion that the world (the Sahel let's say) must now be "attuned to uncertain and multiple potential futures that do not operate according to statistical, probabilistic or epidemiological rules."[133] But it also returns us to the expanded sense of security implied by Foucault in his lectures on security and territory. As he put it, "New elements are constantly being integrated: production, psychology, behavior, the ways of doing things of producers, buyers, consumers, importers, and exporters, and the world market. Security therefore involves organizing, or anyway allowing the development of ever-wider circuits."[134] Nowhere is this clearer than in the ways in which climate change and environmental security are now seen as a path to climate-proofing semiarid Africa. The West African Sahel, according to the Intergovernmental Panel of Climate Change, potentially will be devastated by the transformation of rainfall dynamics due to continued global warming,[135] and it is to be saved by building adaptive capacity and resiliency.[136] Gone is the language of overpopulation, incomplete markets, poor transportation, and local management deficits; gone too is any lingering sense of state welfare. There is now an assemblage of ecological rationalities, not all of which have the state as their guarantor and the nation as their locus of operation, that collectively expand the sense of security and securitization. The very uncertainty of the effects of global climate change (global climate-change models are robust on system dynamics but weak on regional and local predictions) is antithetical to the sort of predictive modeling exercises practiced by the Club of Rome. The securitization of the environment—which not only embraces the threats to food and water systems but now encompasses the likelihood of conflict and violence around access to scarce resources[137]—requires not so much a strong or disciplinary state operating within closed spaces of institutions but something consistent with the global and multiple planes of movements of persons, information, and commodities and with an environment construed as a supplier of "ecosystem services."

The old modes of calculation—the insurance-based logic of calculable risks assessed through probabilities—are replaced with modalities that can still render the uncertain future thinkable and something that can be prepared for and remediated. It is at this point that culture—especially institutions many of which are indigenous or hybrids of local custom and the modern—meets the so-called resiliency school and theories of "complex adaptive systems."[138] Its function is to incorporate social and economic systems in an overarching complex science of "socioecological resilience" rooted in civil society (the community looms very large here). The scope and scale (and institutionalization) of resiliency thinking are now vast, encompassing most fields of expertise that address security in the broadest sense (from the IMF to Homeland Security). It is an enormous industry that encompasses great swaths of the social, economic, and political landscape; its origins, however—and its great strength—remain in the area of green governance and the linking of social and environmental systems. Local knowledge and practice, notions of vulnerability and exposure—in other words the critical responses to the neo-Malthusian approach—have been grafted onto a new turbocharged systems theory derived in particular from the work of ecologist C. S. Holling and his associates, and they have been brought together in a highly influential think tank called the Stockholm Resilience Centre.[139] Sahelian communities can now be fine-tuned—paradoxically building on their traditional strengths (for example, the social capital of village communities) yet supplemented by the expertise of development and state practitioners. The echo of Foucault's account of civil society in a neoliberal order is loud and clear:

> Civil society, therefore is an element of transactional reality in the history of governmental technologies, a transactional reality which seems to me to be absolutely correlative to the form of governmental technology we call liberalism, that is to say, a technology of government whose objective is its own self-limitation insofar as it is pegged to the specificity of economic process.[140]

The new ecology of rule, if we can return to the Sahel, is the language of adaptation to climate change and the resiliency of socioecological systems, what Rose in another setting has called "government through community."[141] Geographers, ecologists, and political scientists have been its central theoreticians, addressing the question of how the possible burdens of climatic change, sea-level rise, and potential catastrophic events are to be distributed geographically and in social and class terms. The West African Sahel once again becomes a major knowledge laboratory because it is already clear that the burden of climate change will fall heavily in Africa and on the West African semiarid tropics in particular.

The origins of the resiliency work lay in the 1970s with the ideas of Holling, who attempted to locate the equilibrium-centered work of systems ecology on the larger landscape of the biosphere as a self-organizing and nonlinear complex system. Complexity science—the hallmark of contemporary systems ecology—represents a meeting point of several multidisciplinary strands of science, including computational theory, nonequilibrium thermodynamics, evolutionary theory, and earth systems science. At the heart of Holling's early work was an analysis of how systems retain cohesiveness under stress or radical perturbations (such as climate variation). Resilience determined the persistence of relations in a system. A key policy document, *The Roots of Resilience*—bearing the imprimatur of UNEP, the World Bank, and the World Resources Institute—reads,

> Resilience is the capacity to adapt and to thrive in the face of challenge. This report contends that when the poor successfully (and sustainably) scale-up ecosystem-based enterprises, their resilience can increase in three dimensions. They can become more economically resilient—better able to face economic risks. They—and their communities—can become more socially resilient—better able to work together for mutual benefit. And the ecosystems they live in can become more biologically resilient—more productive and stable.[142]

Through his Resilience Alliance and later the Resilience Center, Holling's adaptive systems thinking was pushed far beyond ecology to encompass a coevolutionary theory of societies and ecosystems as a single science ("panarchy"). Holling extended his view of resiliency by suggesting that all living systems evolved through disequilibrium, that instability was the source of creativity: crisis tendencies were constitutive of complex adaptive systems. What linked the social, economic, and ecological was the idea of capital as the inherent potential of a system available for change.[143] What began as a study of the local ended as an abstract theory of just about everything, a system marked by episodic change, turbulence, and a lack of predictability. What is striking in such an integrated field theory is that there is no point of intersection between system resiliency and virtually any contemporary account of social power or, for that matter, of the contradictory dynamics of capitalist accumulation or the social relations of production operating in Sahelian peasant communities.

At the time that Holling was laying out his first ideas (and in the midst of the Sahelian famine in Africa), Friedrich Hayek delivered his Nobel Prize speech, which, as M. Cooper and J. Walker brilliantly show, has an elective affinity with Holling's ideas.[144] Hayek was moving toward his mature theorization of capitalism as an exemplar of the biological sciences: the extended market order is "perfectly natural . . . like biological phenomena, evolved in the course of natural selection."[145] In his Nobel lecture, he returned to the epistemology of limited knowledge and uncertain future, a position that led him to explicitly reject and denounce the Club of Rome *Limits to Growth* report.[146] To provide the guide for his "spontaneous market order" of capitalism, he turned to biological systems and complex, adaptive, and nonlinear dynamics. Both endorse the view of limited knowledge, unpredictable environments, and order through survival. As Cooper and Walker note, resiliency is the form of governmentality appropriate to *any* form of perturbation and uncertainty: extreme weather events are analogous to coping with recurrent financial shocks, and both are subject to the calculus of a form of neoliberal governmentality through which economic and social resilience is to be achieved.

The notion of adaptive capacity and government through communities does, of course, rest on a substantial body of research that demonstrates how rural communities in Africa (and elsewhere) adapt to climate change through mobility, storage, diversification, communal pooling, and exchange by drawing on social networks and their access to resources.[147] Yet what is on offer in the new post-Washington Consensus is even more consistent with Hayek's mature vision of the market order than its earlier raw and crude neoliberal version. *Roots of Resilience* proposes to scale up "nature based income and culturing resilience," which require ownership, capacity, and connection. Ecosystem-based enterprises, rooted in community resource management, will entail local-state and private-civic partnerships and enterprise networking. Markets in ecosystem services, and delegation of responsibility to communities and households as self-organizing productive units, will constitute the basis for survival in biophysical, political, economic, and financial worlds defined by turbulence, risk, and unpredictability. Some will be suitably resilient, but others will be either too resilient or not resilient enough.

Resiliency offers a of tipping points, thresholds, and maladaptation. Ecological resiliency is the calculative metric for a brave new world of turbulent capitalism and global climate change: a new ecology of rule. Africa's bottom billion provides a laboratory in which the poor will be tested, and tested whether they can survive in the new global order. To return to Foucault and his notion of an expanded sense of ecosecurity, resiliency is an apparatus of security that will determine the process of "letting die." Africa, once again, is the testing ground for a vision of security and care in which life is nothing more than permanent readiness and flexible adaptiveness. It is a deeply Hayekian project—an expression of the neoliberal thought collective—in which the idea of a spontaneous market order has become, ironically, a form of sustainable development. The challenges of adapting to the radical uncertainties and perturbations of global climate change produce a new sense of *homo economicus*. The West African peasant, as Foucault says, becomes "an entrepreneur of himself,"[148] a sort of hedge-fund manager for his own impoverished life.

I stood on a hill and I saw the Old approaching, but it came as the New.

It hobbled up on new crutches which no one had ever seen before and stank of new smells of decay which no one had ever smelt . . .

So the Old strode in disguised as the New, but it brought the New with it in its triumphal procession and presented it as the Old.

The New went fettered and in rags. They revealed its splendid limbs.

—Bertolt Brecht, *Parade of the New*, 1938

How different a country is contemporary Nigeria from the place where I lived during the 1970s? A decade and more of civilian rule and a presidency occupied by an ethnic minority from the Niger delta certainly suggests a tectonic shift. President Goodluck Jonathan, a bookish, modest leader from the oil-producing Niger delta came to power in May 2010 on the back of considerable controversy following the death of then president Umaru Yar'Adua after only three years in office. Politicians in the Muslim north invoking a rotation principle insisted that their region be allowed to present a candidate. A bitter and acrimonious battle ensued, and the north lost. Shortly after his incongruous ascent to power—several years earlier, Jonathan was a little-known politician in Bayelsa State—the new president presided over the fiftieth anniversary of Nigeria's independence on October 1, 2010, in Abuja. There was little to celebrate: the oil-producing region had sunk into a guerilla insurgency; a radical Islamist group that had appeared in 2002 launched deadly attacks on military and security forces in Borno and Bauchi; and horrific sectarian violence near Jos in January and May 2010 between Muslim and Christian communities resulted in the slaughter of over one thousand people. The celebrations were marked, in any case, by a massive explosion in the capital city of Abuja, allegedly caused by militants from President Goodluck Jonathan's own oil-producing region. It all added up to what Nigerian journalist Ike Okonta has described as Nigeria's "boiling cauldron."[149]

No matter how one reads the elections, the challenges facing the new administration in 2012 remain truly daunting. Nigeria is held up as the worst exemplar of virtually every species of developmental failure: rampant official corruption, corporate bribery, decaying social and physical infrastructure, military indiscipline, ethnic and religious insurgencies, to say little of its criminal economy, industrial and agricultural decay, and deplorable health indicators (3.3 million people are infected with HIV/AIDS—10 percent of the world's total). Nigeria's demonstrated failure to effectively revive its manufacturing sector and even to produce electric power is devastating: the seventh-most populous country in the world has roughly as much grid power as Stockton, California. And the well of corruption remains deep.

Jonathan had to immediately confront two home-grown insurgencies, both driven by a rising and deeply frustrated population of youth confronting limited job prospects and a profoundly insecure future. The oil fields have been crippled by the gradual emergence of a welter of militant groups operating under the sign of the Movement for the Emancipation of the Niger Delta (MEND), an insurgent group that dramatically appeared in late 2005 proclaiming resource control, self-determination, and a desire to lock in oil production.[150] As oil output collapsed by over half, a counterinsurgency by federal military forces in May 2009 led to a negotiated truce and an amnesty accepted by over 25,000 militants. In the last year the political temperature in the creeks has been reduced largely because huge quantities of money are flowing through the amnesty program attempting to purchase a degree of acquiescence among the demobilized but angry insurgents. This year's government budget will include $458 million for sustaining the amnesty—more than is given to the Universal Basic Education Commission. Dispensing money may buy time but little else. The situation remains tense and volatile.

In the Muslim north, rising inequality and poor governance has nurtured a popular Islamist insurrection labeled Boko Haram, which is the

Hausa nickname for the group officially known in Arabic as *Jama'atu Ahlis Sunna Lidda'awati Wal-Jihad*—the People Committed to the Propagation of the Prophet's Teachings and Jihad. The name Boko Haram translates loosely as "Western education is forbidden" and is derived from one of the chief tenets of the teachings of Muhammad Yusuf, the group's early leader. Salafist in orientation, Boko Haram, by drawing on historical traditions of popular justice, has become more brazen, better organized, and more technically proficient in launching assaults against security forces. Assassinations carried out by motorcycle riders target representatives of the state they believe has cheated or failed them: politicians, officials, rival religious scholars, and especially representatives of the dreaded police and security forces who routinely engage in extrajudicial killings according to international human rights groups. Paul Lubeck's brilliant analysis[151] shows how Boko Haram's carefully executed jail breaks or calls for imposing sharia law throughout Nigeria garner most of the media attention. But the movement's greatest power arises from energy generated by the demographic time bomb ticking within the region, coupled with social and economic collapse, a low adult literacy rate, and the implosion of the textile sector (once the region's largest industrial employer). Impoverished and uneducated, the rural poor flee to the northern cities, often assuming the guise of Quranic students who share a common urban religious space with unemployed secondary and university graduates. This convergence, according to Lubeck, is critical because school leavers have learned to use the digital tools of Islamist insurrectionary tactics now downloadable from accessible global media sources.[152] Over the last three years Boko Haram has killed almost one thousand people across the north, including a devastating attack on a United Nations compound in the capital city of Abuja. On January 20, 2012, following afternoon prayers, twenty coordinated bomb attacks occurred in Kano city, launched by Boko Haram. Close to two hundred persons were reported dead; the city—the commercial center of the north—was placed under curfew. Other reports indicated that at least five of the detonations were perpetrated by suicide bombers, and many other undetonated bombs were discovered around the city. All of this mayhem pointed to the obvious fact that northern Nigeria is in a full-fledged state of emergency.[153]

Boko Haram can only be understood within the circumference of the larger movement of the adoption of sharia law in the twelve northern states of Nigeria, a trend in which Katsina State played a leading role. But the complex social and political fragmentation of Islam in northern Nigeria, the weakening of the Sufi brotherhoods, and the rise of neo-Salafist reform movements are closely bound to the corrupt oil oligarchies and the moral decay of the state from which the deep and longstanding strains of Muslim populism drew strength. The more militant Shiite and radical groups like Boko Haram opposed partial restoration at the state level and insisted that

Nigeria should be transformed into a true Islamic state with full adoption and implementation of sharia.

Perhaps more than any other change, this new political sociology of Islam points to a sharp contrast to the Katsina I left thirty-five years ago. Many Katsina Muslims, while certainly not endorsing the violence of Boko Haram, nevertheless echo the conclusion reached by Tijjani Naniya, a historian who is Kano State's commissioner for information and culture. Naniya makes the point that against the backdrop of forty years of corruption and military rule the return to civilian rule in 1999 was seen as a great opportunity. While the solutions proposed ranged from a redefinition of Nigeria federation to regional autonomy and resource control, some northern Nigerians, he noted, were opting for a return to sharia: "To these states, the strategies for social transformation and economic development induced by the West have failed. The alternative for them is for a return to their religio-cultural heritage represented by the Shari'a."[154] Paul Lubeck makes the point powerfully: "Today, there are quotes from the Qur'an in English and Arabic posted on road signs throughout Kano City as well as billboards exhorting the *ummah* to realize a 'republic of virtue' by fulfilling the ideals of *dar al-Islam*. . . . the shari'a movement has introduced a new form of citizenship, that of the *ummah*, one which is both regional and global, to complement Nigerian citizenship."[155]

Any long-term resolution of the problems driving these insurgencies can only be reached if Nigeria drastically restructures economic and social policies. Boosted by oil and gas prices, the economy currently grows at about 7 percent per annum. But this figure masks deep stagnation within the agricultural, manufacturing, and small-scale industrial sectors. Industrial employment alone has shrunk by 90 percent over the last decade. What is needed is an alliance of oil and maize in which each region develops linkage industries from its regionally based resources. Agriculture, needless to say, looms large in any vision for real and meaningful development.

———

The promise is that again and again, from the garbage, the scattered feathers, the ashes and the broken bodies, something new and beautiful may be born.

—John Berger, *Rumor*, 1993

Staring down at me from a picture frame hanging above my desk is a letter written to me by John Berger. I had mailed him a copy of *Silent Violence* in late 1984 because I had so admired his writing on the lives of peasants and much else. If nothing else he could, I suggested, use the book as a door-stop in his French country home in Haute Savoie. Sometime later—on January 18, 1985, to be precise—he wrote back to me saying that the book touched him because of the silence of history: "what is talked about in our world normally covers so little of what is being lived in the world that surrounds ours." Writing books is narcissistic, yet Berger made the point that it is political, too, because, as he went on to explain, "from this silence and this ignoring comes so much evil." Remembering surely stands at the center of what a critical intellectualism must strive for. *Silent Violence*, I hope, is in some small way a memorial to famines and politics, exhorting us not to forget the famine victims and the holocausts of the past and showing how each can be made to speak to what is being lived in the present.

NOTES

I am grateful to Derek Krissoff for shepherding this book through the publication process; to Darin Jensen for his cartography; to my unflagging undergraduate research assistants at Berkeley, Josh Netter and Lexi Gelb; and to two photographers, Pascal Maitre and Irene Becker, whose images grace the book cover and frontispiece.

1. Two-thirds of the hungry live in just seven countries (Bangladesh, China, the Democratic Republic of the Congo, Ethiopia, India, Indonesia, and Pakistan), and over 40 percent live in China and India alone. World Food Programme, *Global Hunger Declining but Still Unacceptably High* (Rome: UNFAO, September 2010), http://www.fao.org/docrep/012/al390e/al390e00.pdf.

2. Save the Children, *A Life Free from Hunger: Tackling Child Malnutrition* (London: Save the Children, 2012).

3. The report concludes that if current trends continue 11.7 million more children will be stunted in sub-Saharan Africa in 2025 than in 2010, and the lives of more than 450 million children globally will be affected by stunting in the next fifteen years (Save the Children, *Life Free from Hunger*, xiii). In January 2008, *The Lancet*—one of the most respected medical journals in the world—published a five-part series on the irreversible effects of early childhood malnutrition. Bread for the World, *Our Common Interest* (Washington, D.C.: Bread for the World, 2011).

4. In terms of food, any particular household is located by subtracting the value of food consumed, including from its own production, from the value of food produced, taking into account marketing costs and seasonality by valuing production at farmgate prices and consumption at retail prices. UNFAO, *The State of Food Insecurity 2011* (Rome: UNFAO, 2011). As I document in this book, a household may be a net seller of food during harvest time and a net buyer at other times. As the UNFAO report points out, "on an annual basis a household might actually produce more than it consumes in quantity terms but it could still be a net food buyer if it sells the entire crop at harvest and buys back from the market later because retail prices are higher than farmgate prices." UNFAO, State of Food Insecurity 2011, 15.

5. While the average income of net food buyers is higher than that of net food sellers in most developing countries, "high food prices hurt the poor, and in more ways than just pushing them below the poverty line. Generally speaking, energy intake is less affected than dietary diversity and consumption of protein and micronutrients." UNFAO, *State of Food Insecurity 2011*, 16.

6. The astonishing volatility in food prices over the last five years can be seen graphically on the UNFAO website, http://www.fao.org/worldfoodsituation/wfs-home/foodpricesindex/en/.

7. See the "Symposium: The 2007–8 World Food Crisis," special issue, *Journal of Agrarian Change* 10, no. 1 (2010), especially Jayati Ghosh, "The Unnatural Coupling: Food and Global Finance," 72–86.

8. UNFAO, *State of Food Insecurity 2011*, 44–45. According to Save the Children, there are now 15 million *more* stunted children in Africa than in 1990, 60 million in total. Essentially, there has been little progress on nutrition in Africa in a generation. The number of African children who are stunted is predicted to continue growing. By 2020 it will be 8.5 million higher than today, and by 2025 this figure will have risen to 11.7 million. *Life Free from Hunger*, 14.

9. United Nations, *Millennium Development Goals Report 2012* (New York: United Nations, 2012).

10. Devereux estimates that famine mortalities increased decennially since the 1930s to peak in the 1960s; they fell sharply thereafter, with a small upward trend during the 1990s. He estimates that over seventy million people died from famine during the twentieth century. Stephen Devereux, "Famine in the Twentieth Century" (Working Paper 105, Institute of Development Studies, University of Sussex, 2000), 7.

11. Cormac O'Grada, *Famine: A Short History* (Princeton, N.J.: Princeton University Press, 2009), 278.

12. The numbers in Sudan, Ethiopia, and Somalia alone probably total over three million; if one were to include the "famine" victims of the continent's central African conflagration in which five to six million have died in the greater Congo, then the numbers would rise still further.

13. The worst drought in sixty years coupled with the bloodletting in the Somali civil war led the United Nations to formally declare a famine in July 2011; conditions deteriorated over the following months as the Al-Shabab Islamists blocked food-aid distribution. Thousands died, with some estimates running as high as five hundred thousand. See http://www.nytimes .com/2011/07/21/world/africa/21somalia.html and http://topics.nytimes.com/topics/ reference/timestopics/subjects/f/famine/index.html.

14. World Food Programme, "Fighting Hunger in the Sahel," press release, February 12, 2012, http://documents.wfp.org/stellent/groups/public/documents/communications/ wfp244897.pdf. The World Food Programme notes that while the earlier food crises of 2005 and 2010 were severe in Chad and Niger, the currently looming crisis is affecting a "broad swathe of countries across the region." Output is down by at least a third; food prices are considerably higher than 2010; and many households have not recovered from the food shortage and high prices of the previous year. In Niger and Chad alone there are almost eight million "severely food insecure people."

15. Christian Parenti, *Tropic of Chaos: Climate Change and the New Geography of Violence* (New York: Nation Books, 2011); United States Department of Defense, *Trends and Implications of Climate Change for National and International Security* (Washington, D.C.: United States Department of Defense, 2011), http://www.acq.osd.mil/dsb/reports/ADA552760.pdf.

16. Here is the assessment of the Sahel forty years after I first saw famine refugee camps and terrible hardship in the region: "The 2009–10 food crisis highlighted a host of long term policy failures, including adapting to climate change and controlling volatile prices of food in the markets . . . linked to state fragility and governance, and the ineffectiveness of aid. The 2010 crisis made visible the deep structural food and nutrition security problems that have persisted for decades. Most strikingly, the severe food deficit situation of households, combined with structural factors such as gender inequality and poor access to healthcare, have been generating catastrophic rates of child under-nutrition in the Sahelian zone of Chad for many years." Peter Gubbels, *Escaping the Hunger Cycle: Pathways to Resilience in the Sahel* (N.p.: Sahel Working Group, Groundswell International, 2011), http://www.oxfam.org/en/policy/ escaping-hunger-cycle. See also Action Against Hunger, *Sahel Food Crisis: A Race Against Time* (London: Action Against Hunger, 2011), http://www.actionagainsthunger.org.uk/fileadmin/

contribution/0_accueil/pdf/Sahel%20Food%20Crisis_LR_01.pdf; on the 2005 crisis in Niger, Frederic Moussaeu and Anuradha Miital, *Sahel: Prisoner of Starvation* (Oakland, Calif.: The Oakland Institute, 2006); on the current crisis see the OXFAM report, "Oxfam Reactive to WFP Emergency High-Level Meeting of the Sahel Food Crisis," February 15, 2012, http://www.oxfam.org/en/grow/pressroom/reactions/oxfam-reactive-wfp-emergency-high-level-meeting-sahel-food-crisis.

17. Alex de Waal's informants in the Sudan reminded him that there are famines that kill and famines that cause hunger. Alex de Waal, *Famine That Kills: Darfur, Sudan, 1984–1985* (Oxford: Clarendon Press, 1989).

18. Lauren Berlant, "Slow Death," *Critical Inquiry* 33 (Summer, 2007): 754–76. See also Rob Nixon, *Slow Death and the Environmentalism of the Poor* (Cambridge, Mass.: Harvard University Press, 2011).

19. Giorgio Agamben, *Homo Sacer: Sovereign Power and Bare Life* (Stanford, Calif.: Stanford University Press, 1998). See also Akhil Gupta, *Red Tape: Bureaucracy, Structural Violence, and Poverty in India* (Durham, N.C.: Duke University Press, 2012).

20. Mike Davis, *Late Victorian Holocausts: El Niño Famines and the Making of the Third World* (London: Verso, 2000).

21. Paul Farmer, *Pathologies of Power: Health, Human Rights, and the New War on the Poor* (Berkeley: University of California Press, 2003).

22. Although I have revisited Kaita in the years since 1978, I have not had an opportunity to conduct a systematic restudy, in part because my interests in Nigeria took me subsequently to another part of the country, the Niger delta.

23. This immediately, of course, raises the thorny question of how precisely one defines famine. Since I wrote *Silent Violence*, and in some small way because of it, much subsequent research has given cause to rethink famine as starvation-induced mass mortality. Famines, as I have suggested, are less aberrant events than extensions of the normal; behaviorally, many famine victims do not regard excess mortality as the defining quality of famine; many famine mortalities are a function of disease rather than absolute food scarcity. De Waal, *Famine That Kills*, and David Nally, *Human Encumbrances* (Notre Dame, Ind.: University of Notre Dame Press, 2011). Some famines are ordinary, some are catastrophic and deadly. As Devereux points out, "mass starvation is one possible outcome of the famine process." *Famine in the Twentieth Century*, 4.

24. Michael Mortimore, "Profile of Rainfall Change and Variability in the Kano-Maradi Region, 1960–2000" (Working Paper 25, Drylands Research, Crewkerne, Somerset, UK, 2000).

25. Emeka Obioha, "Climate Variability, Environmental Change and the Food Nexus in Nigeria," *Journal of Human Ecology* 26, no. 2 (2009): 113.

26. J. Ayodele Ariyo, J. Voh, and B. Ahmed, *Long-Term Change and Food Provisioning in the Kano Region, 1960–2000* (Working Paper 34, Drylands Research, Crewkerne, Somerset, UK, 2001).

27. This data comes from F. Samuels, Maja Gavrilovic, Caroline Harper, and M. Nino-Zarazua, *Food, Fuel and Finance: The Impacts of the Triple F Crisis in Nigeria* (background paper, Overseas Development Institute, London, October 2011). They conclude Nigeria displayed considerable resilience during the 2007–8 global food price hikes and avoided a national food crisis. A number of factors cushioned the country against food crisis, "such as relatively good harvests, household dependence on own food production, the diversity of staple crops and increased government investment in the agriculture sector. However, . . . analysis suggests that the short-term variability has affected the welfare status of certain communities and households, as well as their access to food, with poor net food buyers facing disproportionate difficulties in managing these shocks." *Food, Fuel and Finance*, 213.

28. Segun Olaniyan, "Katsina Releases Grains for Sale," *Nigerian Tribune*, February 6, 2012, http://tribune.com.ng/index.php/community-news/35454-katsina-releases-grains-for-sale. Compounding the food shortage/market volatility problem is the incoherence in the government's policy and implementation strategies for the food sector. For example, as a response to the recent food crisis, Nigeria's Federal Ministry of Agriculture (FMA) facilitated the development of a National Food Crisis Response Program (NFCRP). The Food Security Thematic Group (FSTG) was also established (2009), and the Food and Agricultural Organization (FAO) was invited to provide guidance. Since those agencies' establishment, nothing of substance or in the way of coordination or consolidation has happened. In theory, Nigeria could cope with a food emergency—the government is supposed to have the capacity to hold three hundred thousand metric tons of grain in reserve. But in practice, many of the silos for these grains have not yet been built, and those that have been built stand empty or are half full. According to David Hecht, "At best, the government's capacity is 300,000 metric tons and that capacity is only being half-utilized. . . . Guido Firetti, a silo contractor . . . recently took over the job of completing a 25,000-ton silo that has been under construction for more than 15 years." http://pulitzercenter.org/articles/little-keeps-nigeria-crisis-hunger.

29. The connections between dwindling food production capacity, rising food prices, and dependency on food importation were clearly demonstrated in the 2010 Sahel food crisis, which also affected many of the eleven northern states of Nigeria. The Nigerian National Emergencies Management Agency (NEMA) says roughly 30 percent of the population—about fifteen million people—in this region is food insecure.

30. See Andrew Apter, *The Pan African Nation: Oil and the Spectacle of Culture in Nigeria* (Chicago: University of Chicago Press, 2005); Peter M. Lewis, *Growing Apart: Oil, Politics, and Economic Change in Indonesia and Nigeria* (Ann Arbor: University of Michigan Press, 2007); Ricardo Soares de Oliveira, *Oil and Politics in the Gulf of Guinea* (New York: Columbia University Press, 2007); Michael Watts and Ed Kashi, *Curse of the Black Gold: 50 Years of Oil in the Niger Delta* (Brooklyn: PowerHouse Books, 2010).

31. After the British colonial conquest in 1903, Katsina and Daura emirates became Katsina Province in the former Northern Region. Subsequently Katsina and Zaria Provinces were amalgamated to form the North Central State under the Gowon regime's twelve-state structure in 1967; North Central State was left intact in 1976 when the number of states was further expanded to nineteen, but it was renamed Kaduna State.

32. The state's current rural population density is also very high, roughly 178 per square kilometer, reflecting the substantial growth in population of the emirate from 925,848 in 1931 to over six million today (a sixfold increase in eighty years and a staggering annual growth rate of 7.5 percent). Mary Tiffen, "Profile of Demographic Change in the Kano-Maradi Region" (Working Paper 24, Drylands Research, Crewkerne, Somerset, UK, 2001). The average household size for the state is 7.2 persons (Nigerian National Bureau of Statistics data from 2005).

33. Michael Mann, *The Sources of Social Power*, vol. 2, *The Rise of Classes and Nation States, 1760–1914* (Cambridge: Cambridge University Press, 1993).

34. This is not the place to review the revenue system (see R. Suberu, *Federalism and Ethnic Conflict in Nigeria* [Washington, D.C.: United States Institute for Peace, 2001]) and the complexities of fiscal federalism, which can be plausibly said to condense the entire political history of the country. Suffice it to say that the sources of public revenue in Nigeria are proceeds from the sale of crude oil, taxes, levies, fines, tolls, and penalties and accrue in general to the federation account. The federation account excludes the derivation account by which a percentage (currently 13 percent) of revenues from resources flows directly to its state of origin, which

necessarily benefits the oil-producing states. The balance of the total federally collected revenues is paid into the federation account, which is currently roughly 60 percent of the total, down from over 90 percent in 1970. Oil revenues are the main source of public revenue, accounting for about 80–85 percent of the total. In the period 2001–9, oil revenues averaged 27 percent of GDP, while tax revenues averaged 6.4 percent. In 1992 the vertical allocation system—the proportion of revenues allocated to differing tiers of government—was changed to 48.5 percent, 24 percent, and 20 percent for federal, state, and local governments respectively. The current vertical allocation, adopted by then minister of finance Dr. Ngozi Okonjo-Iweala in March 2004, is 52.68 percent, 26.72 percent, and 20.60 percent for the federal, state, and local governments respectively. Adekele Salami, "Taxation, Revenue Allocation and Fiscal Federalism in Nigeria," *Economic Annals* 189 (June 2011): 27–50. Local governments and states rely overwhelmingly (over 70 percent for local governments, over 50 percent for the states) for their revenues on the federation account; that is to say, centralized oil revenues have come at the expense of other forms of internal revenue generation.

35. Siri Rustad, *Power-Sharing and Conflict in Nigeria* (working paper, Center for the Study of Civil War, Peace Research Institute, Oslo, 2008).

36. The Nigerian zonal (or regional) system is as follows: North West (Kaduna, Kano, Katsina, Kebbi, Jigawa, Sokoto, and Zamfara); North Central (Benue Abuja, Kogi, Kwara, Nassarawa, Niger, Plateau); North East (Adamawa, Bauchi, Borno, Gome, Taraba, Yobe); South West (Ekiti, Lagos, Ogun, Ondo, Osun, Oyo); South East (Abia, Anambra, Ebonyi, Enugu, Imo); South South (Akwa Ibom, Bayelsa, Delta, Rivers, Cross River).

37. An International Institute of Tropical Agriculture (IITA) study conducted in 2001 estimated that household daily income in Kaita was ₦260 (US$2.5). The survey, devoted largely to undernourishment issues, determined that rates of vitamin-A deficiency and iodine deficiency were exceptionally high. Christopher Legg, Patrick Kormawa, Bussie Maziya-Dixon, Richardson Okechukwu, Sam Ofodile, and Tunrayo Alabi, "A Report on Mapping Livelihoods and Nutrition in Nigeria Using Data from the National Rural Livelihoods Survey and the National Food Consumption and Nutrition Survey" (IITA study, Ibadan, Nigeria, n.d.), http://gisweb.ciat.cgiar.org/povertymapping/download/Nigeria.pdf.

38. National Bureau of Statistics, *Social Statistics in Nigeria* (Abuja: Federal Government of Nigeria, 2009.

39. IFAD, "Country Evaluation Programme: Federal Republic of Nigeria" (Office of Evaluation study, IFAD, Rome, 2009); IFAD, "Katsina State Household Baseline Survey," March 2004, http://www.fidafrique.net/article936.html.

40. The study was based on a sample of two hundred farmers randomly drawn from three local government areas of Katsina State (communities in parenthesis): Danja (Kahutu), Musawa-Jikamshi (Garu), and Kurfi (Tsauri). IFAD, "Katsina State Household Baseline Survey."

41. USAID, "Preliminary Livelihoods Zoning: Northern Nigeria" (special report, United States Agency for International Development, Washington, D.C., March 2007), http://pdf.usaid.gov/pdf_docs/PNADL380.pdf.

42. The confidence level in much of this national and FAO aggregate data is probably low. I have generally made use of the UNFAO data sources, http://www.fao.org/tc/tca/work05/Nigeriappt.pdf.

43. In June 1986, the Structural Adjustment Program (SAP) was launched. It aimed to eliminate administrative price distortions within the economy and reallocate resources in favor of smallholder agriculture. The main policy initiatives, as Mustapha and Meagher note, were initially efforts to reduce public sector deficits and tighten monetary supply, to combat infla-

tion. A. R. Mustapha and K. Meagher, "Agrarian Production, Public Policy and the State in the Kano Region, 1900–2000" (Working Paper 35, Drylands Research, Crewkerne, Somerset, UK, 2000), 45. In addition the Naira was floated in June 1986; six commodity marketing boards were suspended; and the government offered a commitment to liberalize agricultural input markets and to remove input subsidies.

44. "Desperate for quick returns, dealers are taking trillions of dollars out of equities and mortgage bonds and ploughing them into food and raw materials. It's called the 'commodities super-cycle' on Wall Street, and it is likely to cause starvation on an epic scale." Iain Mcwhirter, "The Trading Frenzy That Sent Prices Soaring," *New Statesman*, April 17, 2008, http://www.newstatesman.com/world-affairs/2008/04/haiti-food-price-commodities.

45. According to the MDG 2010 report, "For Nigeria, the impact of the 2007–2008 food crisis on the poor is debatable. Nigeria has experienced episodes in the past when food price inflation was higher than that experienced in 2007–2008. For example, food price inflation peaked at 38 per cent in 2005, Nigeria's worst food crisis of the decade, though it did not receive world attention." *Nigeria Millennium Development Goals: Report 2010* (FGN report, Abuja, 2010), 56, http://www.mdgs.gov.ng/mdg-report-2010.

46. "Nigeria: Our Food Import Bill," editorial, *Daily Champion*, August 31, 2011, http://allafrica.com/stories/201108310782.html.

47. Tewodaj Mogues, Michael Morris, Lev Freinkman, Abimbola Adubi, and Simeon Ehui, "Agricultural Public Spending in Nigeria" (IFPRI Discussion Paper 00789, International Food Policy Research Institute, Washington D.C., 2008).

48. By 2005 the index had recovered to 186 (representing a miserable 35 percent increase in output over twenty-five years); export volumes had risen to 456,000 tons, but this represented an overall *decline* of more than 50 percent since 1970).

49. Adebiyi Daramola, Simeon Ehui, Emmanuel Ukeje, and John McIntire, "Agricultural Export Potential in Nigeria," in *Economic Policy Options for a Prosperous Nigeria*, ed. Paul Collier, C. C. Soludo, and Catherine Pattillo (London: Palgrave, 2008).

50. National data suggests that the index of agricultural production doubled over three decades (1970–2000). http://earthtrends.wri.org/pdf_library/country_profiles/agr_cou_566.pdf.

51. The roots and tubers subsector offers a stark example. The area planted to roots and tubers has quadrupled since the mid-1980s, yet yields have dropped by more than 40 percent. Yield trends are qualitatively similar, although less pronounced, in the cereals and oilseeds subsectors.

52. Evidence suggests that the agricultural sector has shown more dynamism since the early 2000s, and according to the UNDP the declining share of agriculture in GDP since the 1970s has been reversed since 1999. United Nations Development Program, *Human Development Report, Nigeria 2008–2009* (Abuja: UNDP, 2009), 10. The share of crop production within the agriculture sector has grown at over 7 percent annually since 2003.

53. Mogues et al., "Agricultural Public Spending in Nigeria."

54. A. Anete and T. Amusa, "Challenges of Agricultural Adaptation to Climate Change in Nigeria: A Synthesis from the Literature," *Field Actions Science Reports* 4 (2010): 20, http://factsreports.revues.org/678.

55. Mogues et al., "Agricultural Public Spending in Nigeria."

56. The guiding instrument of the Government's policy and strategy for rural and regional development to promote economic growth and to combat poverty and income disparity is the National Economic Empowerment and Development Strategy (NEEDS) of 2005 and the

complementary state and local empowerment and economic development strategies (SEEDS and LEEDS). NEEDS was the government's strategic blueprint to address the country's development challenges.

57. Mustapha and Meagher, "Agrarian Production, Public Policy and the State."

58. Sahel and West Africa Club, "Food Security and Cross Border Trade in the Kano-Katsina-Maradi (K2M) Corridor" (joint mission report, Sahel and West Africa Club, Paris, 2006), http://www.oecd.org/dataoecd/0/49/38490617.pdf.

59. P. Matlon, "The Size Distribution, Structure, and Determinants of Personal Income among Farmers in the North of Nigeria" (PhD thesis, Cornell University, 1977), 243.

60. Mustapha and Meagher, "Agrarian Production, Public Policy and the State," 45.

61. Ibid.

62. Andrew Dillon and Esteban Quinones, "Asset Dynamics in Northern Nigeria" (IFPRI Discussion Paper 01049, International Food Policy Research Institute (IFPRI), Washington, D.C., December 2010); Andrew Dillon and Esteban Quinones, "Gender Differentiated Asset Dynamics in Northern Nigeria" (ESA Working Paper #11–06, UNFAO, Agricultural Economics Division, Rome, March 2011).

63. The Nigerian government expects proven reserves (in 2007 estimated to be 36.2 billion barrels) to grow to 40 billion by 2010. Nigeria contains the largest natural gas reserves in Africa (176 trillion cubic feet) and is a global player in the production of liquefied natural gas.

64. The heart of the oil infrastructure resides in the oilfields of the Niger delta in the southeast of the country, far from Katsina. Virtually every inch of the region has been touched by the industry directly through its operations or indirectly through neglect. Over 6,000 wells have been sunk, roughly one well for every 10-square-kilometer quadrant in the core oil states. There are 606 oilfields (355 on shore) and 1,500 "host communities" with some sort of oil or gas facility or infrastructure. There are 7,000 kilometers of pipelines, 275 flow stations, 10 gas plants, 14 export terminals (5 on shore at Qua Iboe, Pennington, Forcados, Ecravos, Brass and Bonny, and 9 FPSOs), 4 refineries, and a massive LNG and gas supply complex.

65. United Nations Development Program, *Human Development Report Nigeria 2008–2009* (Abuja: UNDP, 2009), 11. All data in this section is derived from the report. Between 1970 and 2000, the number of people subsisting on less than one dollar a day in Nigeria grew from 36 percent to more than 70 percent, from 19 million to a staggering 90 million.

66. Address to the National Press Club, Washington, D.C., December 7, 2005, http://web.worldbank.org/WBSITE/EXTERNAL/EXTABOUTUS/ORGANIZATION/EXTPRESIDENT2007/EXTPASTPRESIDENTS/EXTOFFICEPRESIDENT/0,,contentMDK:20747792~menuPK:64343271~pagePK:51174171~piPK:64258873~theSitePK:1014541,00.html.

67. *Nigeria Millennium Development Goals: Report 2010.*

68. This does not square with a recent UNDP report: "A recent national child labour survey in Nigeria found that of the 38,061,333 children aged 5–17 years covered in the survey, 39.4 per cent were outside the school system. Of this figure, 13.1 engaged in economic activities and 26.3 per cent were domestic helps. Only 57.5 per cent concentrated on their schooling alone." United Nations Development Program, *Human Development Report Nigeria 2008–2009, Achieving Growth with Equity* (Abuja: UNDP, 2009), 70.

69. Mary Alice Salinas, "More Nigerians Slip into Poverty, Particularly in North," Voice of America, March 1, 2012, http://www.voanews.com/english/news/africa/west/More-Nigerians-Slip-Into-Poverty-Particularly-in-North-141069863.html.

70. Michael Watts, "Petro-Insurgency or Criminal Syndicate?," *Review of African Political Economy*, no. 114 (2008): 637–60.

71. Michael L. Ross, *The Oil Curse: How Petroleum Wealth Shapes the Development of Nations* (Princeton: Princeton University Press, 2012).

72. Ryszard Kapuściński, *Shah of Shahs* (New York: Knopf, 1982), 82.

73. For reviews of this literature see C. Brunnschweller and E. Bulte, "Linking Natural Resources to Slow Growth and More Conflict," *Science,* May 2, 2008, 616–17; A. Rosser, "Escaping the Resource Curse," *New Political Economy* 11, no. 4 (2006): 557–69.

74. Paul Collier, *The Bottom Billion* (London: Oxford University Press, 2007).

75. Nigeria and its oil-producing Niger delta are, in Collier's accounting, a textbook case of why rebellions have much less to do with what rebel leaders have to say about their political project (liberation, justice, etc.) and much more to do with organized crime and the readiness with which the resource upon which the fattest depend can be looted and predated.

76. Michael Watts, "Blood Oil," in *Crude Domination: An Anthropology of Oil,* ed. Stephen Reyna and Andrea Behrends (Oxford: Berghahn, 2011), 49–80.

77. Xavier Sala-i-Martin and Arvind Subramanian, "Addressing the Resource Curse: An Illustration from Nigeria" (working paper, International Monetary Fund, Washington, D.C., 2003), 4.

78. Two other individuals, both geographers, were also major voices in the study of rural Hausaland. Michael Mortimore, who taught at ABU between 1962 and 1979, conducted pathbreaking research on the Kano close-settled zone, and Paul Richards (recently retired from the University of Wageningen) taught at the University of Ibadan and had written on drought and agrarian flexibility in northern Nigeria, which became central to his hugely influential corpus on African agriculture.

79. In 1949–50, 1958–59, 1972, and 1977–78, Smith studied the Hausa, Kagoro, and Kadara in Northern Nigeria, and his three monographs—*Government in Zazzau, 1800–1950* (London: Oxford University Press, 1960); *The Affairs of Daura* (Berkeley: University of California Press, 1978); and *Government in Kano, 1350–1950* (Boulder, Colo.: Westview Press, 1997)— remain indispensable sourceworks for the scholar of northern Nigeria.

80. Murray Last, *The Sokoto Caliphate,* Ibadan History Series (London: Longmans, Green and Co. Ltd., 1967).

81. Polly Hill, *Rural Hausa: A Village and a Setting* (London: Cambridge University Press, 1972), and Polly Hill, *Population, Prosperity and Poverty: Rural Kano 1900 and 1970* (London: Cambridge University Press, 1977).

82. Much of this long-term research project on the changing political economy and ecology of the Maradi region under the auspices of the University of Bordeaux II has been brought together in Claude Raynault et al., *Societies and Nature in the Sahel* (London: Routledge, 1997). Continuing in these footsteps, the French-influenced research has been extended in the exemplary work of the West African Borders and Integration project. Sahel and West Africa Club, "Food Security and Cross Border Trade in the Kano-Katsina-Maradi (K2M) Corridor." The reader interested in the work of Guy Nicholas and other French students of Nigerien Hausaland can find the work referenced in the bibliography.

83. The canonical texts are E. P. Thompson, *The Poverty of Theory* (New York: Monthly Review Press, 1978), and Perry Anderson, *Arguments within English Marxism* (London: Verso, 1980).

84. Africa, and not just Nigeria, emerged in the 1970s, and especially the 1980s, as the laboratory for some of the most exciting geographical and critical social science work on development. Agrarian studies and political ecology broadly construed were central to this excitement. Much of the so-called household debate—opening upon the black box of the farming

household to appreciate how gender, age, and social status shaped the process of access to and control over resources—was pushed forward by geographers and anthropologists working on the continent (one thinks of Gillian Hart, Jane Guyer, Pauline Peters). No less the case was the work on agrarian dynamics and the relations between social structure, culture, ecology, and agrarian commercialization (the work of geographer Paul Richards was absolutely indispensable, as was later research by geographers Tom Bassett, Matt Turner, Abdi Samatar, Judith Carney, Jesse Ribot, Rod Neumann, and Richard Schroeder). All of which is to say that there was a deep geographical tradition of fieldwork on the continent that contributed to the generative debate and theoretical production surrounding questions of African nature, culture, and political economy.

85. I should add here that my good friend Paul Lubeck's brilliant book, *Islam and Urban Labor in Northern Nigeria* (London: Cambridge University Press) appeared in 1985.

86. Mohammed Salau, *The West African Slave Plantation* (London: Palgrave, 2011). Salau was able to provide evidence on the extent of slave-based production, confirming what Paul Lovejoy and Jan Hogendorn in *Slow Death for Slavery: The Course of Abolition in Northern Nigeria* (London: Cambridge University Press, 1993) suspected but were utterly unable to demonstrate.

87. Stephen Pierce, *Farmers and the State in Colonial Kano: Land Tenure and Legal Imagination* (Bloomington: Indiana University Press, 2005).

88. A. R. Mustapha, "Peasant Differentiation and Politics in Rural Kano: 1900–1987" (DPhil thesis, Oxford University, 1990); K. Meagher, "A Vent for Shortage: The Development of Parallel Trade in Northern Nigeria" (MPhil thesis, University of Sussex, 1990); K. Meagher, "Veiled Conflicts: Peasant Differentiation, Gender and Structural Adjustment in Nigerian Hausaland," in *Disappearing Peasantries? Rural Labour in Africa, Asia and Latin America*, ed. D. Bryceson, C. Kay, and J. Mooij (London: Intermediate Technology Publications, 2000); P. Clough, "The Economy and Culture of the Talakawa of Marmara" (DPhil thesis, University of Oxford, 1996); M. Karaye, "Hausa Peasants and Capitalism" (PhD dissertation, University of Wisconsin, Madison, 1990).

89. An important exception is Paul Clough's extraordinary work in Marmara, southern Katina, covering almost three decades, and his use of Marx and Weber to show how rural accumulation and the appearance of very large farms is structured by polygyny and clientage. Paul Clough, "Polygyny and Rural Accumulation of Capital," *Etnofoor* 16, no. 1 (2003): 5–29.

90. Michael Mortimore, *Adapting to Drought: Farmers, Famines and Desertification in West Africa* (London: Cambridge University Press, 1989); Michael Mortimore and William Adams, *Working the Sahel* (London: Routledge, 1999). See also Roy Maconachie, *Urban Growth and Land Degradation in Developing Countries: Change and Challenges in Kano, Nigeria* (Aldershot, UK: Ashgate, 2007).

91. The emphasis on flexibility and adaptability has an intriguing parallel in the debates between Pauline Peters and Sara Berry over the negotiability of property rights in African land law during periods of rapid commercialization and capitalist accumulation. See Pauline Peters, "Inequality and Social Conflict Over Land in Africa," *Journal of Agrarian Change* 4, no. 3 (2004): 269–314. Mortimore in *Adapting to Drought* concludes with the conundrum of human (peasant) capabilities and adaptive responses in the face of the modern pessimism (229–30). In *Working the Sahel*, he and Adams say that wealth or poverty must be "embedded in a large economic system" (187), but they have little to say about the dynamics of this embeddedness or how to theorize it.

92. One notable exception is the continuing work of geographer Michael Mortimore, whose projects at Cambridge University on adaptation to environmental change and livelihoods in northeast Nigeria during the 1990s and more recently his hugely important institute, Drylands Research (http://www.drylandsresearch.org.uk/), have continued to make research available on rural northern Nigeria. Much of this recent work, however, does not rely on new field-based studies.

93. Ousmane Kane, *Muslim Modernity in Postcolonial Nigeria: A Study of the Society for the Removal of Innovation and Reinstatement of Tradition* (Leiden: Brill, 2003); Roman Loimeier, *Islamic Reform and Political Change in Northern Nigeria* (Evanston, Ill.: Northwestern University Press, 1996); Muhammad S. Umar, *Islam and Colonialism: Intellectual Responses of Muslims of Northern Nigeria to British Colonial Rule* (Leiden: Brill, 2006); Tijjani Muhammad Naniya, "History of the Shari'a in Some States of Northern Nigeria to Circa 2000," *Journal of Islamic Studies* 13, no. 1 (2002): 14–31; Tahir Haliru Gwarzo, "Islamic Civil Society Organizations and the State: A Kano Case Study" (PhD dissertation, Bayero University, 2006); Ricardo René Larémont, *Islamic Law and Politics in Northern Nigeria* (Trenton, N.J.: Africa World Press, 2011); John Paden, *Muslim Civic Cultures and Conflict Resolution* (Washington, D.C.: Brookings Institution Press, 2005); Johannes Harnischfeger, *Democratization and Islamic Law: The Shari'a Conflict in Nigeria* (Frankfurt: Campus Verlag, 2008).

94. See, for example, B. Fine, "Entitlement Failure?," *Development and Change* 28 (1997): 617–47; C. Gore, "Entitlement Relations and 'Unruly' Social Practices: A Comment on the Work of Amartya Sen," *Journal of Development Studies* 29 (1993): 429–60; P. Nolan, "The Causation and Prevention of Famines: A Critique of A. K. Sen," *Journal of Peasant Studies* 21 (1993): 1–28; M. Watts, "Entitlements or Empowerment?: Famine and Starvation in Africa," *Review of African Political Economy* 18, no. 51 (1991): 9–26.

95. J. Drèze and A. K. Sen, *Hunger and Public Action* (New York: Oxford University Press, 1989; J. Drèze and A. Sen, eds., *The Political Economy of Hunger*, 3 vols. (New York: Oxford University Press, 1990).

96. In the 1980s and 1990s, I laid out my own critique: Michael Watts and Hans-Georg Bohle, "The Space of Vulnerability: A Realist Theory of Famine and Hunger," *Progress in Human Geography* 17, no. 1 (1993): 43–67; M. Watts, "The Great Tablecloth: Bread and Butter Politics, and the Political Economy of Food and Poverty," in *The Oxford Handbook of Economic Geography*, ed. G. Clark, M. Gertler, and M. Feldman (London: Oxford University Press, 2000), 195–215; M. Watts, "Entitlement or Empowerment?," 9–26; and M. Watts and H. Bohle, "Hunger, Famine and the Space of Vulnerability," *GeoJournal* 30, no. 2 (1993): 117–25.

97. See, for example, J. Corbett, "Famine and Household Coping Strategies," *World Development* 16, no. 9 (1988): 1099–112; see also Rebecca Solnit, *A Paradise Built in Hell: The Extraordinary Communities That Arise in Disaster* (New York: Viking, 2009).

98. Only relatively recently have entitlement analyses begun to link different levels of investigation, focusing, for example, on household entitlements and the state, regions vis-à-vis nations, and national entitlements in relation to global food security; see S. Devereux, *Theories of Famine* (London: Harvester Wheatsheaf, 1993); J.-P. Platteau, "Traditional Systems of Social Security and Hunger Insurance: Past Achievements and Modern Challenges," in *Social Security in Developing Countries*, ed. E. Ahmad, J. Dréze, J. Hills, and A. Sen (Oxford: Clarendon Press, 1991).

99. Amartya Sen, *Poverty and Famines: An Essay on Entitlement and Deprivation* (Oxford: Clarendon, 1981), 180.

100. M. Ravallion, *Markets and Famines* (Oxford: Oxford University Press, 1987); M. Ravallion, "Famines and Economics" (Policy Research Working Paper 1693, World Bank, Washington, D.C., 1996).

101. J. von Braun, T. Teklu, and P. Webb, *Famine in Africa: Causes, Responses, and Prevention* (Baltimore: Johns Hopkins University Press, 1998).

102. A. de Waal, *Famine That Kills*; A. de Waal, *Famine Crimes: Politics and the Disaster Relief Industry in Africa* (Bloomington: Indiana University Press, 2009); D. Keen, *The Benefits of Famine: A Political Economy of Famine and Relief in Southwestern Sudan, 1983–1989* (Princeton, N.J.: Princeton University Press, 1994); Thomas Kenally, *Three Famines: Starvation and Politics* (New York: Perseus Books, 2011).

103. David Keen, *Complex Emergencies* (Cambridge: Polity Press, 2008).

104. Stephen Devereux, "From 'Old Famines' to 'New Famines,'" introduction to *The New Famines*, ed. Stephen Devereux (London: Routledge, 2007).

105. See A. de Waal, *Famine Crimes*; as a case study see Jennifer Clapp, *Hunger in the Balance: The New Politics of International Food Aid* (Ithaca, N.Y.: Cornell University Press, 2011).

106. M. Mukerjee, *Churchill's Secret War: The British Empire and the Ravaging of India during the Second World War* (New York: Basic Books, 2010); Frank Dikotter, *Mao's Great Famine* (New York: Walker, 2011); Yang Jishen's book *Mubei* has not been translated and is reviewed by Perry Link, "China: From Famine to Oslo," *New York Review of Books*, January 13, 2011, 52–53; Lizzie Collingham, *The Taste of War: World War Two and the Battle for Food* (London: Allen Lane, 2011).

107. Hanna Arendt, *Imperialism* (New York: Harcourt Brace, 1948).

108. In the interests of full disclosure, Davis makes extensive use of my approach, though I have taken issue with some aspects of his analysis. Michael Watts, "Black Acts," *New Left Review* 9 (2001): 125–40.

109. H. Tilley, *Africa as a Living Laboratory: Empire, Development, and the Problem of Scientific Knowledge, 1860–1960* (Chicago: University of Chicago Press, 2010).

110. See, for example, P. Rabinow, *French Modern* (Cambridge, Mass.: MIT Press, 1989), and R. Grove, *Green Imperialism: Colonial Expansion, Tropical Island Edens and the Origins of Environmentalism, 1600–1800* (Cambridge: Cambridge University Press, 1995).

111. Tilley, *Africa as a Living Laboratory*.

112. W. Beinart and L. Hughes, *Environment and Empire* (Cambridge: Cambridge University Press, 2007).

113. S. Shapin, *The Social History of Truth* (Chicago: University of Chicago Press, 1994).

114. D. Meadows, J. Randers, and W. Behrens, *The Limits to Growth: A Report on the Predicament of Mankind* (London: Earth Island, 1972).

115. *Limits to Growth* became a touchstone for the global modeling of human ecological problems (in a sense a forerunner of the IPCC) and provided a compelling narrative of global catastrophism that came to stimulate a debate over what King, then at the OECD, called "the temple of growth," but it linked the "predicament of mankind" to questions of global inequality and called for a New International Economic Order.

116. P. Taylor, "What Can Agents Do?," in *Advances in Human Ecology*, vol. 8, ed. L. Fresse, 125–56 (Greenwich, Conn.: JAI, 1999); A. C. Picardi, "A Systems Analysis of Pastoralism in the West African Sahel," in *A Framework for Evaluating Long-Term Strategies for the Development of the Sahel-Sudan Region*, ed. W. W. Seifert and N. Kamrany (Cambridge, Mass.: MIT Press, 1974).

117. G. Hardin, "The Tragedy of the Commons," *Science* 162 (1968): 1243–48.

118. The contours of the crisis were an echo of similar debates conducted within the ranks of the British and French colonial offices during the 1930s. West Africa had its own Dust Bowl

experience in which advancing deserts, rapid deforestation, and declining soil productivity were driven by the poor land-use practices of African peasants and the dead hand of population pressure. Colonial scientists, nonetheless, were deeply divided in the 1930s as to whether and how fast desertification may have been taking place in the West African Sahel.

119. The World Bank, *Accelerated Development in Sub-Saharan Africa* (Washington, D.C.: The World Bank, 1981).

120. Part of my inspiration here was the French Marxist writing on the Sahelian famine, although I came to believe that its emphasis on crop substitution (cotton for food) and the commercialization of food circuits was too blunt and mechanistic. See Comité Information Sahel, *Qui se nourrit de la famine en Afrique?*, (Paris: Maspero, 1974), and *Sécheresse et famines du Sahel*, ed. Jean Copans, 2 vols. (Paris: Maspero, 1975).

121. See Michel Foucault, *Security, Territory, Population: Lectures at the College de France 1977–1978* (New York: Palgrave, 2007); see also D. Nally, "That Coming Storm," *Annals of the Association of American Geographers* 98, no. 3 (2008): 714–41.

122. K. Polanyi, *The Great Transformation* (Boston: Beacon, 1947).

123. Foucault, *Security, Territory, Population*, 41–42.

124. M. Dean, *Governmentality* (London: Sage, 1999); J. Vernon, *Hunger* (Cambridge: Harvard University Press, 2007).

125. David Nally, *Human Encumbrances* (Notre Dame, Ind.: University of Notre Dame Press, 2011).

126. E. Berg, *Marketing, Price Policy and Storage of Food Grains in the Sahel*, vol. 2 (Ann Arbor: CRED/University of Michigan, 1977). Ironically, I was a student at the University of Michigan when Berg's influential Sahel work was being conducted.

127. P. Richards, *Indigenous Agricultural Revolution: Ecology and Food Production in West Africa* (London: Unwin, 1985).

128. Sen, *Poverty and Famines*; Amartya Sen, "Property and Hunger," *Economics and Philosophy* 4, no. 1 (1988): 57–68; and Amartya Sen, "Food, Economics, and Entitlements," in *The Political Economy of Hunger*, vol. 1, ed. J. Drèze and A. K. Sen (London: Clarendon, 1990), 34–50.

129. James Scott, *The Moral Economy of the Peasantry* (New Haven, Conn.: Yale University Press, 1977).

130. See M. Leach and R. Mearns, *The Lie of the Land: Challenging Received Wisdom on the African Environment* (Portsmouth, N.H.: Heinemann, 1996). Melissa Leach and James Fairhead showed how in Guinea French colonial officials and a cadre of experts interpreted the patches of forest in the savanna zone as evidence of deforestation and framed their policies accordingly. Leach and Fairhead argued that locals provided a different "reading" of the forest landscape. Forest islands were not the residuum of destructive farming practice but were self-consciously formed by farmers themselves. J. Fairhead and M. Leach, *Misreading the African Landscape: Society and Ecology in a Forest-Savanna Mosaic* (Cambridge: Cambridge University Press, 1996).

131. N. Klein, *Shock Doctrine* (New York: Picador, 2007); G. Monbiot, *Heat* (Toronto: Doubleday, 2006).

132. The EU's Emissions Trading Scheme (ETS), which started in 2005, is the only large-scale attempt to set a carbon price (EU countries receive national allocations parceled out to firms in five dirty industries). The ETS makes up the lion's share of the global market, at $122 billion, but the price ($22 per ton) does not encourage much of an energy transition. The US Congress is proposing $12 a ton, which will not encourage any investment. Most experts believe that onshore wind energy and solar cells need carbon prices of $38 and $196 per ton, respectively.

Bare Life and the Long Interregnum

133. F. Lentzos and N. Rose, "Governing Insecurity," *Economy and Society* 38, no. 2 (2009): 236.

134. Foucault, *Security, Territory, Population*, 45.

135. C. Toulmin, *Climate Change in Africa* (London: Zed Books, 2010); Intergovernmental Panel on Climate Change, *IPCC Fourth Assessment Report: Climate Change 2007* (Geneva: Intergovernmental Panel on Climate Change, 2007). This is partly why the African delegations were so demonstrative at the Copenhagen COP15 meetings about resources being made available in order to honor their commitments to a problem they did little to create.

136. World Resources Institute, *Roots of Resilience* (Washington, D.C.: World Resources Institute, 2008); Peter Gubbels, *Escaping the Hunger Cycle: Pathways to Resilience in the Sahel* (Washington, D.C.: Sahel Working Group, Groundswell International, 2011), http://www.oxfam.org/en/policy/escaping-hunger-cycle; J. Sendzimir, C. P. Reij, and P. Magnuszewski, "Rebuilding Resilience in the Sahel: Regreening in the Maradi and Zinder Regions of Niger, *Ecology and Society* 16, no. 3 (2011): 1, http://dx.doi.org/10.5751/ES-04198-160301; Matt Turner, "Climate Change and Social Resilience: Adaptive Conflict in the Sahel," Environmental Politics Workshop, University of California, 2009, http://globetrotter.berkeley.edu/bwep/colloquium/papers/Turner_ClimateChangeAndSocialResilience.pdf.

137. See "Climate Change and Conflict," ed. Nils Petter Gleditsch, special issue, *Journal of Peace Research* 49, no. 1 (2012); Simon Mason and Adrian Muller, *Linking Environment and Conflict Prevention* (Zurich: Center for Security Studies, ETH, 2008); United States Department of Defense, *Trends and Implications of Climate Change*.

138. N. Adger, I. Lorenzoni, and K. O'Brien, eds., *Adapting to Climate Change* (Cambridge: Cambridge University Press, 2009).

139. C. S. Holling, "Resilience of Ecosystems: Local Surprise and Global Change," in *Sustainable Development of the Biosphere*, ed. W. C. Clark and R. E. Munn, 292–317 (Cambridge: Cambridge University Press, 1986); C. S. Holling, "Understanding the Complexity of Economic, Ecological and Social Systems," *Ecosystems* 4 (2001): 390–405. The Stockholm Resilience Centre can be located at http://www.stockholmresilience.org/.

140. M. Foucault, *Security, Territory, Population*, 297.

141. N. Rose, *Powers of Freedom* (Cambridge: Cambridge University Press, 1999).

142. World Resources Institute, *Roots of Resilience*, ix.

143. C. S. Holling, "Understanding the Complexity of Economic, Ecological and Social Systems," *Ecosystems* 4 (2001): 390–405; see L. Gunderson and C. S. Holling, eds., *Panarchy: Understanding Transformations in Human and Natural Systems* (Washington, D.C.: Island, 2002).

144. Jeremy Walker and Melinda Cooper, "Genealogies of Resilience," *Security Dialogue* 42, no. 2 (2011): 143–60.

145. *The Collected Works of F. A. Hayek*, ed. W. W. Bartley III, vol. 1, *The Fatal Conceit: The Errors of Socialism* (London: Routledge, 1988); Cooper and Walker, "Genealogies of Resilience," 143.

146. See P. Mirowski and D. Plehwe, eds., *The Road to Mont Pèlerin: The Making of the Neoliberal Thought Collective* (Cambridge: Harvard University Press, 2009).

147. See for example the work of Michael Mortimore, op. cit., and R. Behnke, Natural Resource Management in Pastoral Africa, *Development Policy Review* 12, no. 1 (1994): 5–27.

148. Michel Foucault, *The Birth of Biopolitics* (London: Palgrave, 2008), 226.

149. On this pessimistic canvas, the April 2011 presidential, national assembly, and gubernatorial elections in which Jonathan ran for the presidency as the incumbent—did represent

something of a milestone. For the first time in Nigerian history a southern minority was declared the president. Inevitably there were some irregularities, but nonetheless, the US-based National Democratic Institute properly called the electoral process a major step forward.

150. See my "Blood Oil," and my "Economies of Violence: More Blood, More Oil," in *Contested Grounds: Essays on Nature, Culture and Power*, ed. A. Baviskar, 106–36 (New Delhi: Oxford University Press, 2008).

151. Paul Lubeck, "Nigeria: Mapping the Shari'a Restorationist Movement" (working paper, Center for Global, International and Regional Studies, University of California, Santa Cruz, 2010); see also Abimbola Adesoji, "The Boko Haram Uprising and Islamic Revivalism in Nigeria," *Africa Spectrum* 45, no. 2 (2010): 95–108.

152. See the interesting blog http://www.isvg.org/follow/blog/2011/11/07/nigerian-nightmare-visualizing-terror-in-africas-most-populous-nation; see also Jason Burke, "Boko Haram," *The Guardian*, January 17, 2012, http://www.guardian.co.uk/world/2012/jan/27/boko-haram-nigerian-sunni-militant. See Paul Lubeck, Michael Watts, and Ronnie Lipschutz, *Convergent Interests: US Energy Security and the "Securing" of Nigerian Democracy*, International Policy Report (Washington, D.C.: Center for International Policy, 2007).

153. The head of the US military's Africa Command claimed in August 2011 that Boko Haram was collaborating with the Algeria-based Al-Qaeda in the Islamic Maghreb, while a report published by the US House of Representatives Subcommittee on Counterterrorism and Intelligence in November 2011 pointed to links with Somalia's Al-Shabab. Yet no evidence has been presented to the public. In a video released on January 15, 2012, a Boko Haram leader, Abubakar Shekau, made it clear that the group's primary motivation remained redress for the government crackdown. Negotiations with Islamist groups in the north suggest that the Islamists demand troop withdrawal, mosque reconstruction, and compensation for loss of life. It is not at all clear that this is language of jihad. The danger of defining Boko Haram as terrorist and resorting to a heavy-handed military response is that it will further energize the insurgents and alienate a vast swath of the Muslim poor who are already estranged from northern ruling elites who have failed them. The consequences will be disastrous.

154. Tijjani Muhammad Naniya, "History of the Shari'a in Some States of Northern Nigeria to Circa 2000," *Journal of Islamic Studies* 13, no. 1 (2002): 31.

155. Paul Lubeck, "Nigeria," 44.

Aerial view of Katsina town looking north, February 1930. The National Archives, Kew, United Kingdom. Reference CO 1069-62-31, 1930.

The emir of Katsina, royal slaves, and district headmen, Katsina, 1911. The National Archives, Kew, United Kingdom. Reference 1069-59-3, 1911.

The Katsina agricultural show outside the city walls, Katsina town, 1911. The National Archives, Kew, United Kingdom. Reference CO 1069-59-5, 1911.

Livestock on display at the Katsina agricultural show, Katsina town, 1911. The National Archives, Kew, United Kingdom. Reference CO 1069-59-8, 1911.

Constructing a granary, northern Nigeria, circa 1920–29. The National Archives, Kew,
United Kingdom. Reference CO 1069-66-11, ca. 1920–1929.

A shaduf watering fadama plots, northern Nigeria, circa 1920–29. The National Archives, Kew, United Kingdom. Reference CO 1069-66-03, ca. 1920–1929.

A portrait of a Fulani farmer, northern Nigeria, circa 1920–29. The National Archives, Kew, United Kingdom. Reference CO 1069-66-31, ca. 1920–1929.

A portrait of a rural Hausa woman, Kano, circa 1920–29. The National Archives, Kew, United Kingdom. Reference CO 1069-66-28, ca. 1920–1929.

Touring district officers, northern Nigeria, 1922–23. The National Archives, Kew, United Kingdom. Reference 1069-84-04, 1922–1923.

Touring colonial official gathering tax and related information, Bauchi Province, circa 1920–29. The National Archives, Kew, United Kingdom.

Laborers working on the Baro–Kano railway, Gwari, May 1908. The National Archives, Kew, United Kingdom. Reference CO 1069-59-14, 1908.

REPORT

ON

Famine Relief

IN THE

Northern Provinces

IN

1927.

Printed by the Government Printer, at the Government Printing Office, Lagos.
To be Purchased from the C.M.S. Bookshop Lagos, and from
The Crown Agents for the Colonies, 4 Millbank, Westminster, London, S.W.1.
Price 6d.

Cover, report on the 1927 famine, Government Printer, Lagos, 1927.

K. 2151/3
K a d u n a.

THE HONOURABLE, THE CHIEF SECRETARY,   July, 1926.
L A G O S.

Principal Famines in Hausaland - Record of.

I am directed by the Lieutenant-Governor to forward
for the Governor's information the following notes on the
principal Famines recorded during the last century in
Hausaland from information collected by Sir William Gowers:-

    Famine called Dawara   1847.

    "Banga-Banga   1853

    "For 30 days at a time no gero, dawa, wheat or rice
"were to be had at Kano. People ate vultures.
"Attributed to defective rainfall

)   1863
)   1864
"Slight famines recorded in)   1873
)   1884
)   1889.

    "Fairly severe famine   1890.

    "Wide spread scarcity   1907-1908.

    "Severe Famine   1913-1914

    "Probably more severe than any
"since Banga-Banga.
"Mortality very great.

    "Frequent famines are recorded in Bornu during the
"second half of the 18th Century."

                          (Sgd) H. Hale Middleton.
                          Acting Secretary,
                          Northern Provinces.

ELF.

A copy of a memorandum written by the acting secretary of the Northern Provinces, Kaduna, July 1926 to the chief secretary, Lagos, on the principal famines of Hausaland over the previous century.

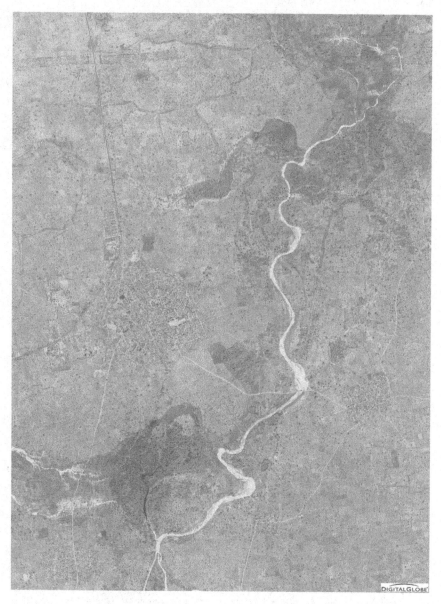

Aerial View of Kaita village and surrounding farmlands 2011. Digital Globe, Walnut Creek, California.

Satellite imagery of Kaita Village showing new road to the east of the village and *fadama* (wetlands) to the west, 2011. TerraServer, Raleigh, North Carolina.

Dirt road from Katsina leading into Kaita village, rainy season, 1977. Michael Watts.

The weekly Kaita market prior to the 1977 harvest. Michael Watts.

Farmer and donkey passing through mature millet and sorghum, Kaita village, 1977.
Michael Watts.

Tall millet prior to harvest, Kaita village, 1977. Michael Watts.

Fadama (wetlands) agriculture and irrigated plots, dry season, 1978. Michael Watts.

Indigenous shaduf in the floodplain area to the west of Kaita village, 1978. Michael Watts.

Junior and senior wife of a prosperous farming family, Kaita village, 1978. Michael Watts.

Junior son in a land-poor household, Kaita village, 1977. Michael Watts.

Head of household of a poor farming family, with his two young sons, Kaita Village, 1978.
Michael Watts.

My two assistants sitting outside of the district offices, Kaita village, 1977. Michael Watts.

Fulbe (Fulani) pastoralists purchasing grain in Kaita market, 1977. Michael Watts.

Emir of Katsina and his entourage, Sallah (Eid-el-Kabir) celebrations marking the end of Ramadan, Katsina town, 1977. Michael Watts.

SILENT VIOLENCE

[The peasant] is driven to increasing dependence on the market which he finds even more moody and incalculable than the weather.

—Karl Kautsky

For too long the ruling classes have attributed to "Nature" . . . the inequalities for which the organisation of society are responsible.

—Sebastiano Timpanaro

1

INTRODUCTION: THE POLITICAL ECONOMY OF FOOD AND FAMINE

Just as the progress of a disease shows a doctor the secret life of a body, so to the historian the progress of a great calamity yields valuable information about the nature of the society so stricken.

—*Marc Bloch*

Famines do not occur, they are organised by the grains trade.

—*Bertolt Brecht*

Food was very much at the forefront of development thinking in the 1970s. Following the large grain glut in the immediate postwar world food economy, a massive shortage of staple foodstuffs emerged, seen most dramatically perhaps in the crisis and famine of 1972. This resulted in a reduction of world food stocks by 42 million metric tons. Starvation of a frightening order now threatens many low-income countries who have not only ceased to be self-sufficient food producers but are faced with spiraling debt repayments and an inflated oil import bill; and not least, they are confronted by an increasing dependence on food imports purchased in a highly volatile world market. As Harriet Friedmann (1979) convincingly demonstrated, this global crisis is part of the decomposition of the old global food system and the recomposition of a new food order based on the separation of aid from trade, the increasing commoditization of grain transfers, the decline of U.S. concessional food sales, and a new form of American domination of the world cereals trade associated with the use of food for geopolitical purposes. Furthermore there is every indication that such trends will continue and deepen in the 1980s. When shortfalls occur the global market channels grain to the highest bidder; bilateral grain agreements often protect a considerable share of limited supplies for more affluent countries, increasing the price instability of the remaining market volume during poor years. As one recent report puts it (Barr 1981, p. 1095), the basic realities of the global economy "are not conducive to an automatic stabilizing process for the world's hungry." By 1990 in fact the developed world will

1

account for 24 percent of global population, 85 percent of all economic activity, and roughly 50 percent of the world's grain production and consumption.

There has been a great temptation, of course, to pose the food crisis as simply another variant of the Malthusian problematic; we are entering, to use the current parlance, an "era of permanent scarcity" inexorably propelled by untrammeled demographic growth. From 1950 to 1980, for example, world food production doubled with the increase in the developing countries actually exceeding that of the developed countries (table 1.1), but population in the former grew at more than twice the rate of the latter. Per capita food production in the developed world has increased by almost 50 percent since the end of the Second World War; in the Third World, conversely, while total production between 1950 and 1980 increased by 120 percent population almost doubled. Yet this purported shift to a new era of sustained dearth is a highly dubious proposition on at least two counts: first, famine and food shortage have been an integral part of social evolution generally, and of the evolution of capitalism in particular; and second, contemporary scarcity cannot simply reflect natural, demographic, or technical limits. Even after the increases in cropped acreage of the 1960s and 1970s, almost half of all available fertile land is *not* used for any type of food production (Johnson 1973) while cereal productivity in the periphery remains abysmally low. More critically, it is clear that the chain of causality runs from poverty to overpopulation rather than the other way around.

Neo-Malthusianism, in all of its various guises, certainly does not exhaust the myriad explanations of the food crisis however it is defined. There are individuals who clearly cling to a form of technological determinism in spite of the inability of such theorizing to account for the uneven occurrence and success of the Green Revolution. There are those who conversely point to systematic market distortions and unfavorable terms of trade between sectors—conventionally attributed to neglect, ignorance or mistakes by state apparatuses—or to structural stagnation, the latter usually being synonymous with inequitable land tenure that blocks the development of a fully capitalist agriculture. In this book, I adopt a somewhat different stance which draws upon three related theoretical threads. The first is the work of Keith Hart (1982) whose own political economy starts from the notion of the increasing commoditization of West African agriculture. He asks the question, What have been the consequences of an increased dependence on agricultural commodity production in rural areas that were previously restricted to a high degree of food self-sufficiency? In approaching this question, Hart analyzes the critical role of the state in rural development and yet observes "a growing discrepancy between the apparatus of the modern state and a dominant,

TABLE 1.1
POPULATION AND FOOD PRODUCTION

	1951–1953 to 1978–1980		Compound annual rates of increase (%)			
Item and region	Total increase (%)	Compound annual rate (%)	1951–53 to 1959–61	1959–61 to 1969–71	1969–71 to 1978–80	1973–75 to 1978–80
Food production						
World	102.0	2.6	3.3	2.5	2.1	2.1
Developed countries	95.0	2.5	3.3	2.4	2.0	1.8
Developing countries	117.0	2.9	3.0	2.9	2.8	3.1
Population						
World	64.0	1.8	1.8	1.9	1.9	1.8
Developed countries	33.0	1.1	1.3	1.1	0.9	0.8
Developing countries	88.0	2.4	2.1	2.5	2.4	2.4
Per capita food production						
World	24.0	0.8	1.6	0.6	0.3	0.4
Developed countries	47.0	1.4	2.0	1.3	1.1	0.9
Developing countries	15.0	0.5	0.8	0.5	0.2	0.4
Total agricultural trade						
World	397.0	5.3	5.3	3.7	5.0	5.0
Developed countries	N.A.	N.A.	N.A.	4.0	3.0	2.8
Developing countries	N.A.	N.A.	N.A.	3.6	8.0	9.1

SOURCE: Barr (1981, p. 1088).

NOTE: N.A. = not available.

decentralised agricultural sector operating at low levels of productivity" (1982, p. 14). The second theme is provided by Robert Bates's (1981) analysis of food policy in African states, which in spite of its somewhat Ricardian proposals, recognizes that the state has a dual yet contradictory function in the countryside that embraces both the desire for cheap wage goods and the development of a political constituency, that is to say a class alliance. Bates moves us beyond a simple pluralistic view of the state to one in which the state is firmly situated in the process of capitalist development, specifically the *demands* made upon the rural sector and the *concessions* granted to certain of its members.

And the third thread is provided by the brilliant work of Alain de Janvry (1981). He sees the food issue as part of a larger "agrarian question," and specifically the variety of forms or roads which capitalist development in the peasant sector may actually assume. De Janvry begins with what he refers to as peripheral disarticulated economies in which there is a powerful logic to sustain capitalist development on the basis of cheap labor and cheap food. This frequently occurs within the context of a peasant agrarian sector that is transitional, that is to say one in which land and labor are unevenly commodified. De Janvry identifies a type of transitional and contradictory "functional dualism" between the peasant sector and the import-substitution industrial economy, and attempts to relate the transformation of Latin American agrarian structure to the specific class alliances and state forms associated with it. While there are evident problems in transposing an ostensibly Latin American analysis to the African continent, de Janvry's work nonetheless is significant insofar as it addresses the varieties of paths that capitalism follows in agriculture, and also emphasizes the limits to which absolute surplus extraction from peasants can proceed in providing cheap wage foods and/or export commodities. Indeed, I argue that in the case of Nigeria the rapid oil-funded industrialization of the early 1970s has forced the state to confront the persistence of a large but low-productivity smallholder economy. By weaving these threads together, then, I hope to show how capitalist relations have developed among northern Nigeria peasant producers over the past century, and how these complex and contradictory changes in household production contribute toward an understanding of the series of food crises and famines that litter the contemporary era.

In any discussion of the present food crisis we should recognize of course that hunger is not a new phenomenon and famine is not the invention of the contemporary period; millions confronted hunger and absolute poverty not only in the era of grain surpluses in the 1950s and 1960s but throughout human history. Famine and subsistence crises in the past were the expression of vulnerable precapitalist modes of production, in which undeveloped forces of production had to often unsuccessfully adjust to (rather than control) environmental forces. However, such crises have been an integral part of capitalist development—though obviously not unique to it—and much of this book is an attempt to document the changing form and character of food crises as capitalist relations developed historically in northern Nigeria. The food issue must, then, be situated historically with respect to the particular phases of capital accumulation in the world economy and its uneven impact upon peripheral economies. There is not simply one form of subsistence crisis but many historically specific variants.

DIMENSIONS OF THE CURRENT FOOD CRISIS

Although the food crisis of the 1970s was not new, in a sense its scope and magnitude was unparalleled. The 1972–73 famine, which struck much of the semiarid tropics, was the apical point of almost two decades of chronically poor agricultural performance in the Third World. Nowhere is this structural malaise more evident than in sub-Saharan Africa, which in spite of the overwhelmingly rural character of its labor force—in the order of 65 percent—imports massive quantities of staple foods.[1] Africa is in fact the only region in the world where per capita food production has actually declined over the past twenty years.[2] Most African countries (see table 1.2) exhibit severe to moderate production declines, and by 1978 per capita food production in Angola, Benin, Ethiopia, Ghana, Nigeria, Zimbabwe, Senegal, Sierra Leone, Uganda, and Upper Volta was less than 90 percent of the 1961–65 average. Declining food production moreover translates into inadequate nutrition, and in most sub-Saharan countries caloric intake fell below minimal nutritional standards (table 1.3.)[3]

The current dilemma in the African food economy is, as the influential Berg Report (1981) makes patently clear, part of a more general malaise in agricultural development that is captured by five major trends since 1960. First, by the 1970s the growth rate of agricultural production lagged markedly behind population growth. In the 1960s agricultural growth (by volume) was 2.3 percent per year, but during the following decade production dropped to 1.3 percent per year, less than half the rate of population growth. In the low-income and oil-exporting countries, agricultural growth was especially sluggish—roughly 1 percent annually—while middle-income countries achieved a growth rate compatible with the rate of demographic increase. All groups of countries, however, registered declining per capita production, and only eight of thirty-nine countries showed rising agricultural production per capita. Second, agricultural exports stagnated and the African share of world trade declined for many commodities.[4] Third, food production per capita was at best stagnant over the 1960–1980 period. Where output increased it was due

TABLE 1.2
INDEXES OF PER CAPITA FOOD PRODUCTION
(1961–65 = 100)

Region and country	1970	1971	1972	1973	1974	1975	1976	1977	1978	1979
Sahel
Mali	84	86	65	67	86	88	97	82	105	75
Niger	104	109	105	66	91	76	103	92	106	85
Senegal	64	87	56	68	90	100	87	59	88	68
Upper Volta	76	70	66	58	72	76	74	67	69	67
West Africa
Benin	92	89	88	93	89	84	85	88	89	82
Cameroon	97	102	97	93	97	96	97	96	97	97
Ghana	99	93	81	87	88	75	74	71	68	70
Guinea	107	110	109	108	98	94	101	93	102	101
Ivory Coast	107	113	105	109	120	142	129	125	128	132
Liberia	81	84	84	91	100	94	96	98	96	97
Nigeria	95	93	95	87	90	89	88	86	84	84
Sierra Leone	93	98	96	95	92	96	92	95	87	82
Togo	108	103	102	96	98	96	97	93	97	96

Region / Country										
Central Africa										
Angola	104	95	88	95	92	72	65	58	53	51
Zaire	119	109	106	112	107	105	106	103	97	97
East Africa										
Burundi	117	119	119	117	98	113	110	109	108	109
Ethiopia	99	99	91	87	84	67	63	58	52	54
Kenya	96	91	99	97	96	102	113	117	111	110
Rwanda	123	122	115	118	112	121	119	121	119	119
Sudan	110	115	107	101	114	125	122	123	129	123
Tanzania	102	104	100	101	114	117	99	98	100	105
Uganda	95	92	87	82	79	81	77	73	76	68
Southern Africa										
Madagascar	108	107	107	98	102	105	105	107	108	99
Malawi	96	108	118	109	110	97	101	95	96	90
Zambia	95	117	132	110	135	139	153	142	128	104
Zimbabwe	79	93	103	78	102	92	88	86	83	69

SOURCE: USAID (1980, p. 3).

TABLE 1.3
Calories Per Capita, 1977

Region and country	Percentage of nutritional requirements
	Percent
Sahel	
Chad	74
Gambia	–
Mali	90
Mauritania	86
Niger	91
Senegal	95
Upper Volta	79
West Africa	
Benin	98
Cameroon	89
Ghana	86
Guinea	84
Guinea-Bissau	–
Ivory Coast	105
Liberia	104
Nigeria	83
Sierra Leone	93
Togo	90
Central Africa	
Angola	–
Central African Republic	99
Congo	103
Equatorial Guinea	–
Gabon	–
Zaire	–
East Africa	
Burundi	97
Ethiopia	75
Kenya	88
Rwanda	98
Somalia	88
Sudan	–
Tanzania	93
Uganda	91
Southern Africa	
Botswana	–
Lesotho	99
Madagascar	115
Malawi	90
Mozambique	81
Zambia	87
Zimbabwe	108

SOURCE: World Bank, *World Development Report* (1980).

principally to an expansion of cultivated area; productivity per unit of land and labor was wholly stagnant. Ironically, these declines were coincident with an era of expanded international concern with food production; between 1973 and 1980 $5 billion in aid flowed into agriculture, almost half from the World Bank. Fourth, commercial imports of food grains grew more than 300 percent over two decades (see figure 1.1); cereal imports leaped by 9 percent per year after 1960 and commercial food imports stood at 5 million tons in 1979.[5] And fifth, there was a significant change in consumptive tastes as wheat and rice came to account for 82 percent of gross cereal imports. Between 1970 and 1979, moreover, the real price of wheat rose by 153 percent (USAID 1980, p. 8).

Virtually all attempts to project Africa's food situation conclude that major changes in domestic trends are required to avert a further deepening of the crisis in the 1980s. The International Food Policy Research Institute (IFPRI) estimates that historical rates of growth in domestic food production in Africa, coupled with a constant 1975 level of per capita income, would produce a 1990 cereal import of 17 million tons—roughly three times the 1979 level. Estimates by the Food and Agriculture Organization (FAO) and the United States Agency for International Development (USAID), based on a more optimistic trend analysis, suggest a food deficit of roughly 12 million tons by 1990. The projected food import bill still leaves a significant calorie gap, namely, the difference between food demand and the quantity necessary to meet minimal caloric intake requirements. The IFPRI for example estimates this calorie gap will be equivalent to 13 million tons by 1990.

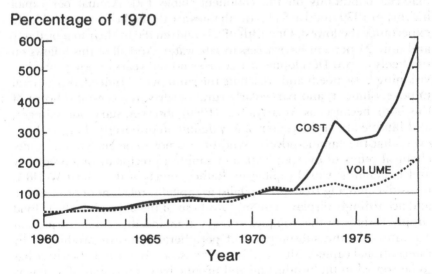

Figure 1.1. Sub-Saharan Africa: Indexes of grain imports. From FAO Trade Yearbook.

The poor performance of the agrarian sector has naturally generated a good deal of debate on which, at least according to the World Bank's *Accelerated Development in Sub-Saharan Africa* report (1981), there is a widespread consensus. This collective wisdom embraces civil strife, poor rainfall, population growth, government neglect, misallocation of funds, misdirected marketing and price policies, and organizational weaknesses in the public sector.[6] The World Bank's free-market emphasis, what it refers to as internal "structural" constraints derived in large measure from excessive state intervention and an unfavorable physical environment, neglects however the more general socioeconomic crisis on the continent in relation to the international division of labor. Between 1960 and 1979 per capita income in nineteen countries grew by less than 1 percent per year, while in the 1970s fifteen nations recorded a negative rate of growth of income per capita. Output per person rose more slowly in sub-Saharan Africa than in any other part of the world. Even the robust states like Kenya, Senegal, and Ivory Coast took a severe economic battering. Current account deficits rose from $1.5 billion to $8 billion between 1970 and 1980; external debt climbed from $6 to $32 billion over the same period, and debt service rose from 6 to 12 percent of export earnings. The World Development Report (1981) of the World Bank, using an "optimistic" set of assumptions about the world economy, forecasts no growth in per capita income for the continent as a whole during the 1980s; with less sanguine conditions, a negative rate of growth seems almost inevitable for the poorest states.

The human tragedy of the 1980s crisis is embodied in the appalling material conditions on the continent (table 1.4). Annual per capita income in 1979 stood at $411; death rates are the highest in the world, life expectancy the lowest. One-fifth of all children die by their first birthday and only 25 percent have access to safe water. And all of this follows on the heels of two Development Decades and ten years of ostensibly provisioning basic needs and "reaching the rural poor." Indeed, this general impoverishment, and particularly rural poverty, is a central concern of this book because, as Amartya Sen (1980) observes, starvation, hunger, and famine are at the center of any definition of poverty. I argue, however, that the famine-poverty syndrome is not to be analyzed as a mechanical reflex of overpopulation or simply a precipitate of a predatory and hegemonic world capitalism. Rather, much of the Third World is transitive, moving from precapitalist to capitalist relations of production, and accordingly displays a unique synthesis of the old and the new; food supply resides in this complex conservation and dissolution of peasant economy—in the subsumption of peripheral forms of production by international capital. The current food crisis in Africa and elsewhere has to be rooted in the production and productivity constraints of an emer-

TABLE 1.4
Sub-Saharan Africa and the World: Basic Data

Countries	Population (millions) Mid-1979	GNP per capita average annual growth rate (%)		Per capita growth 1970–79 (%)		Adult literacy rate (%) 1976	Life expectancy at birth (years) 1979	Child death rate per thousand (ages 1–4) 1979
		1960–70	1970–79	Agriculture	Volume of exports			
Sub-Saharan Africa	343.9	1.3	0.8	−0.9	−3.5	28	47	25
Low-income countries	187.1	1.6	−0.3	−1.1	−4.5	26	46	27
Nigeria	82.6	0.1	4.2	−2.8	−2.8	–	49	22
Other middle-income countries	74.2	1.9	−0.5	−0.4	−3.5	34	50	22
South Asia[a]	890.5	1.5	1.5	0.0	0.6	36	52	15
All developing countries	3,245.2	3.5	2.7[b]	0.1	−1.5	57	58	11
Low-income countries	2,260.2	1.8	1.6[b]	0.1	−3.1	50	57	11
Middle-income countries	985.0	3.9	2.8[b]	0.6	1.9	72	61	10
All industrialized countries	671.2	4.1	2.5[b]	0.2	5.2	99	74	1

Source: World Bank, *Accelerated Development in Sub-Saharan Africa* (1981).

[a] Bhutan, Bangladesh, Nepal, Burma, India, Sri Lanka, Pakistan.
[b] 1970–80.

gent and changing peasant commodity production system (Bryceson 1981). In northern Nigeria, I suggest that food supply is to be situated in the differential involvement of peasants in commodity production. This was an uneven process because the expansion of cash crop production by peasant producers was not always at the expense of food production or security; equally, population growth might be accommodated at the land frontier. But productive techniques stagnated, the colonial state often ignored food security issues, and the expansion of commodity relations exposed producers to new risks, undercut many indigenous food security mechanisms, and deposited peasants in new relations of exploitation which left them vulnerable to crises of subsistence. In an area subject to recurrent drought, the market proved to be, as Kautsky noted, as incalculable as the weather; peasants under capitalism were doubly vulnerable. In the process, the genesis, character, and dynamics of famine and food supply changed quite dramatically as new social relations of production emerged.

FOOD SYSTEMS, RISK, AND FAMINE

> The peasant had to survive the permanent handicap of having a "surplus" taken from him; he had to survive, in the subsistence half of his economy, all the hazards of agriculture—bad seasons, storms, droughts, floods, pests, accidents, impoverished soil, animal and plant diseases, crop failures; and furthermore, at the base frontier, with the minimum of protection, he had to survive social, political and natural catastrophes.
>
> —John Berger

Far from being a novel source of fear, famine is an ancient and persistent human experience. Most human societies have suffered food calamities grave enough to undermine health and well being, and to cause migration, political upheaval, and occasionally human mortality on an enormous scale. Each society has its own characteristic cognitive style which frames these food crises. Where it is recursive—and this is especially true of the Sahel—a specialized famine vocabulary may arise to express different degrees of severity, causation, and effect. The study of famine moreover is not new. Cornelius Waldford made a historic attempt in 1878 to make an inventory of food crises, the League of Nations addressed itself to "a scientific study of calamities" in the early 1920s, and the Brazilian geographer, Josué de Castro, conducted a systematic analysis of world hunger for almost half a century prior to his recent death. Yet in view of the fact that Europe suffered a major food crisis in one region or another every two or three years from the beginning of the Christian era until the late nineteenth century, the literature dealing with chronic food shortage is surprisingly fragmentary, particularly in comparison to other social disasters. Much Euro-American disaster research dates to the Cold War era and accordingly reflected a morbid preoccupation with the spectre of nuclear warfare. Famine studies have, until quite recently, exhibited an obsession with the biology of starvation in spite of the heteroclite nature of its subject matter.[7]

Famine is simultaneously a biological and a social experience. Its etiology may be as profoundly economic as environmental and its effects as much political as physiological.[8] For the purposes of this study, I use famine to refer to a societal crisis induced by the dissolution of the accustomed availability of, and access to, staple foods on a scale sufficient to cause starvation among a significant number of individuals. As a United Nations Research Institute on Social Development (UNRISD) report suggests, a systematic study of recurrent famines rests on the idea that their episodic career has a certain logical, sequential structure:

> [A food crisis] has three distinct phases: an initial period of gestation in which a number of factors converge in attenuating food supplies; a period in which accessibility of food reaches critical dimensions in terms of human survival . . . and a period of recovery . . . or dissolution of settlements and migration of groups. [UNRISD 1977, p. 3]

These phases are catenary events involving agronomic changes, rising prices, loans, borrowing, asset sales, and migration to catalog but a few of the characteristic constituents of the crisis itself.[9] I attempt to illustrate how these heterogeneous events constitute premeditated patterns of action made by households and individuals who modify their behavior in accordance with their perception of the food situation. Families adopt characteristic modes of famine behavior following the dictates of tradition, personal interest, local understanding, and (more critically) their relative position in the circuits of production, exchange, and consumption.

Any understanding of famine presupposes a grasp of the form and functioning of the food system[10] in question, including the manner in which the pattern of food supply is affected by environmental perturbations, such as drought. This is notably the case among rural producers in transition but for whom the forces of production remain relatively undeveloped. Of course, the relation of social reproduction to the physical environment strikes to the core of a good deal of contemporary social theory, of which two domains are especially apposite. The first embraces natural hazards research and human ecology, addressing questions of adaptive structure in social systems.[11] The second concerns the role of risks and risk aversion in peasant behavior. Underlying these approaches is a belief in the desirability of focusing on environmental events that constitute threats to individuals experiencing them. These environmental perturbations carry the risk of mortality, of losing the existential game in which success consists of staying in the game. As Vayda and McCay put it:

> Any event or property of the environment which poses a threat to the health and ultimately the survival of organisms, including people, may be regarded as a hazard for them and that responding adaptively to such hazards involves in our view . . . not only deploying resources to cope with the immediate problem but also leaving reserves for future contingencies. [Vayda and McCay 1977, p. 411]

The focus on hazards and environmental risk is especially pressing in northern Nigeria, and indeed the Sahel generally, which is subject to intense variability in rainfall. Drought constitutes *the* major hazard for peasant producers in Hausaland, and accordingly assumes considerable practical and cultural significance. Such semiarid environments, which are characterized by enormous spatial and temporal variability in precipitation and where "normal rainfall" is something of a statistical fiction, afford an opportunity to examine the complex relationships between environmental crises and the essential strengths and weaknesses of social and economic systems. But in the process of examining the changing character of food production and environmental risk in northern Nigeria, however, I emphasize that both hazards research and human ecology have suffered from a neurotic obsession with individual rationality, a profound ahistoricism and not least a neglect of political economic structure. Waddell (1977) and Torry (1979) among others have identified these shortcomings in the geographic study of environmental risks, but they are as pernicious in human ecology where change is often treated as "disturbance." In this respect it is parallel to ecology in its preoccupation, until very recently, with stasis and equilibria. It is as though the environment itself determines the rules of behavior so that once a production system is adopted the problem simply becomes one of Pavlovian response to environmental signals. But we clearly live not only in an environment constituted by natural processes but also in one of our own making, socially constituted by human practice and subject to ongoing change and historical transformation.

Some recent attempts have been made to overcome these limitations in an examination of the processes by which low risk, autarkic communities are subsumed into international economic systems. Clarke in particular examined what he calls "the changing structure of permanence," that is, the rupture of local systems as they become part of coherent and highly integrated global networks.

> As society and economy are enlarged in the course of development, as communities trade autarky for access to a wider range of goods and services, new

and coarser patterns of resource evaluation and selection replace old, finer patterns. Specialisation replaces diversity; economic risk is added to natural risk. [Clarke 1977, p. 374]

Grossman's (1979) recent work on coffee and cattle in the Papua New Guinea Highlands is one of the first attempts to examine empirically this changing structure of permanence. He explores the impact of cash-earning activities on the natural environment, the subsistence system and the structure of social relationships through an uneasy marriage of human ecology and economic development theory. While this genre of work is akin to what I call political economy, it often fails to specify the structure of the entire productive system. This is true both of the self-sufficient, internally regulated subsistence systems on the one hand, and the external market systems on the other, which are characterized by the use of such loose terms as "subsistence system" and "cash economy." Put somewhat differently, there has been a concern with *exchange* and its role in the linkage of two apparently contradictory but unspecified production systems; cash figures prominently in these discussions although money per se conveys nothing of the laws of motion of the economic system itself. To the extent that production is considered, a priority has been lent to the operational attributes of productive systems measured as inputs (energy, caloric expenditure) and outputs (production expressed in monetary or caloric units), rather than access to and control of productive assets. Of course this type of work has yielded some excellent and valuable information on the implications of economic change on local regulatory autonomy and processes of ecological degradation. But what is lacking is an analysis of the qualitative aspects of the entire system of production, most especially the social relations of production.

The second theoretical corpus, largely the domain of agricultural economists, concerns the role of risk and risk aversion in peasant behavior.[12] The axiom here is that operating environments are intrinsically unstable, and planning is uncertain. Decision makers, drawing on reservoirs of cultural and personal knowledge, attempt to survive in poor seasons and exploit the favorable years. Farmers are posed as risk averters though there is little consensus either on "average" risk aversion among farming communities or the proportion of individual attitudes that differ significantly from mean risk preferences. Ironically in spite of the acceptance of risk as a critical element in peasant reproduction, a recent colloquium organized by the Agricultural Development Council found little consensus on the definition and measurement of risk or risk aversion, or its purported effects on peasant strategies.[13] Nevertheless, much of the work of the International Center for Research in the Semiarid Tropics (ICRISAT) in India on the effect of risk on smallholders has not slid into a semantic quagmire and is of great value for any study of famine.[14] Working in an area subject to enormous variability in rainfall, ICRISAT has examined the relationship between riskiness—measured as variability in yield and prices—and risk aversion, and in particular systems of self-insurance and risk diffusion. The former included measures taken before damage (i.e., drought) may occur that include crop diversification, adjustment of sowing times, and water management techniques. The latter were designed to deal with the consequences of losses and embraced storage, accumulation of assets, reduction of financial commitment in drought years, borrowing, and so on (Jodha et al. 1979). Effective risk reduction and loss management would permit a farmer to assume substantial levels of risk without exposure to a reduction in customary consumption or loss of assets, even in drought years.

The centrality of risk and subsistence security in peasant life has been employed by James Scott (1976) to construct a more general model of precapitalist communities. According to Scott, the technical arrangements of the "safety first" principle correspond to a "subsistence ethic" within peasant social structure and constitutes what he (following Edward Thompson) calls a moral economy. The peasantry were, he says, up to their necks in water so that even a ripple might drown them; producers were quite naturally preoccupied with subsistence and the omnipresent fear of shortage that translated into a premium for long-term sustainable income rather than short-term maximization. There was little room for bourgeois calculus in peasant life; as risk-averse individuals, their goal was the achievement of low fluctuations in consumption streams through time, regardless of fluctuations in income and production. The moral economy, then, was all about survival and simple reproduction.

There is a great danger, however, that risk aversion however defined emerges as a sufficient condition for understanding a massively heterogeneous peasant economy. Risk-averse behavior becomes, in other words, a universal trait of rural smallholders in the same way that, according to critics of the moral economy approach, all peasants are "rational utility maximisers" (Popkin 1978).[15] Equally, by concentrating on the purportedly risk-averse qualities of individual peasant decision making, farmers are seen as isolated atoms, whereas the opportunities and the constraints to which individuals respond at any point in time arise out of interactions among individuals and social groups (Berry 1980). Nonetheless, although risk is a protean term, it is clear that farmers consider variability of outcomes when making agricultural decisions, and this accordingly bears directly upon food availability. In this study, I take risk to be the probability distribution of an event that threatens normal consumption (see Cain 1981). Among most peasants it is not unreasonable to assume that household heads wish to safely ensure adequate consumption streams, that is, simple reproduction. I am especially concerned with events that pose threats to reproduction, and how they are dealt with and accommodated within the food system. In northern Nigeria high risks are posed by weather variability, especially rainfall, but other sources of risk are socially determined. In any case, risk must be fundamentally grounded in the form and quality of social relations in which peasants necessarily participate. Some people's productive choices constitute other people's productive constraints, and this strikes to the core of what I call political economy.

And all this is of great pertinence to this book. For in the first place it suggests that there is no predetermined relationship between high-risk environments and food availability. Drought does not necessarily "cause" famine, as much of the discourse surrounding the Sahelian famine of the 1970s implied.[16] To make such an assumption is to make a major methodological error since it poses drought as a natural cause; natural both in the sense of being of nature, but also of being logical (i.e., arising naturally). Yet had thousands of people died in Great Britain during the 1976 drought, it would be inconceivable that such a human disaster would have been labeled "natural" insofar as it was climatically induced. In this sense much of what passes as natural hazards are not really natural at all; drought may be a catalyst or trigger mechanism in a sequence of events that lead to famine conditions, but the subsistence crisis itself is more a reflection of the structural ability of the socioeconomic system to cope with the unusual harshness of ecological conditions and their effects.[17] To neglect this tendency is to resort to an ideology that sees natural disasters as "acts of God," placing responsibility upon a malevolent nature. Second, from the political-economic perspective adopted here, an analysis of risk not only probes the darkest corners of environmental relations, but throws into sharp relief the organization and structure of social systems generally. The impact of a drought on human communities for example presents the social scientist with a particular optic through which to view the functioning of the social formation. And third, to appreciate the fact that risk is mediated by and embedded in the socioeconomic structures of the societies affected is simultaneously to recognize that "modernization" or "development" has not necessarily solved the age-old problems of subsistence crises or vulnerability to environmental threats, and in some cases has actually aggravated them. To conclude, as Popkin (1978) does for Indochina, that colonialism was ugly but the quality of the minimum subsistence floor improved requires much circumspection, at least for northern Nigeria.

This discussion of social forms dovetails nicely with a theoretical projection of famine because if environmental or social risks do not necessarily reduce food availability or result in starvation, then starvation and famine may arise *without* a decrease in food availability. In this regard, recall that a famine is a food shortage leading to widespread death from starvation. Characteristically it is, to use Currey's (1978) terminology, a syndrome; that is, a decline in food-grain intake per capita leading to characteristic behaviors or responses such as migration, sale of assets, breakdown in social bonds, widespread mortality, and ultimately a series of postfamine adjustments. But as Sen (1980) observes, starvation has nothing directly to do with food supply or what he calls food availability decline (FAD) in the Malthusian sense. It is a matter of command over and access to food, or entitlements. Put differently, in a society in which food is heavily commoditized and a private market economy prevails, command over food may concern asset endowment, real income, and purchasing power; that is, how the individual can translate his/her initial endowment of labor power into food goods. In a precapitalist system, command over food may be bound up with patterns of social obligation reciprocity, patronage, gift exchange, and the like; in short, Scott's moral economy. Famines may develop, then, when prevailing patterns of exchange entitlement collapse on a massive scale.

   In light of these observations, there are three famine motifs to which I return throughout this book. First, the evolution of famine must be traced through a configuration of changing food availability, exchange entitlements, and the historically specific political-economic context in which they operate. As Alamgir (1980, p. 384) puts it, famine must be grounded in good availability and command over food (i.e., real income), *both* "superimposed over a set of social relations that are inherently exploitative." Second, because social relations and exchange entitlements are historically determined, it follows that famines can and should be sharply distinguished in terms of their etiology and effects. Sen (1980) for instance talks of boom and slump famines; the former refers to inflated food prices fed by the expansion of monetary demand (e.g., Bengal 1943); the latter refers to falls in food output that reduced purchasing power and caused derived destitution among the suppliers of goods and services (e.g., Wollo 1973). Alamgir (1980, p. 14) refers to a class famine, the burden of which falls on one social group that stands in a vulnerable position in relation to real income and the social relations of production.[18] Nonmarket famines or precapitalist crises may have a different character altogether. Famines that occur in societies in the process of transition to capitalism may not fall neatly into any typology. And third, the responses to and effects of famine can only be fully comprehended if they are seen as part of a wider political economy. Variation in famine response among peasant households, for example, reflects the transition from precapitalist to commodity production; famine relief by the colonial state was an attempt to secure the reproduction of a transitional peasant class that had been partially destabilized. Famine might in some circumstances strengthen semifeudal relations in agriculture, and in others hasten the penetration of capitalism.

Seeing famines this way, the history of subsistence crises is of some political interest. In particular we can begin to approach the paradox of a phaoroic sequences of famines in northern Nigeria since 1900 in an almost wholly peasant society during which period the men and women who worked the land were those who perished for want of food. Those who experienced the silent violence of famine were those who produced, a fact which is of some political significance.

> The crisis created by a famine reveals the workings of the economic and social system and affords an insight into that structural violence which has the effect of denying the poorest . . . the right to feed themselves. . . . The fact that . . . town dwellers can still get something to eat while the country people starve . . . is a sign of the power relation between urban and rural populations. [Spitz 1977, p. 3]

Analyzing famine, then, ultimately demands a careful deconstruction of the social, political, and economic structure of the society so afflicted, and of its historically specific systems of production. Such a project implies that this work might, with some justification, carry the subtitle 'the social production of famine.'

PEASANTS AND THE DEVELOPMENT OF CAPITALISM

> Between the time when the bulk of the peasantry, i.e., the bulk of the pre-industrial population, exists largely outside the capitalist market, and the time when the bulk of the surviving agricultural population can be regarded as "capitalist," there is a long period when we can claim no more than that the peasantry adapts itself to the dominance of a capitalist economy, as it might, under other circumstances, adapt itself to the dominance of a noncapitalist economy. For the "peasant economy" is not hegemonic but subaltern; at most it is independent, namely where the economic and socio-political mechanisms for extracting its surplus are too weak to establish effective domination through the market or otherwise.
>
> —Eric Hobsbawm

In Africa smallholder production still predominates. Peasantries were the bedrock of the colonial state, and what Marx called "the pygmy property of the many" has persisted in the face of "the giant property of the few." Goran Hyden (1980) recently argued that this peasant resiliency makes for the peculiarity of the African situation; specifically, he argues that African peasants were "made" in the colonial era in the sense that smallholders using family labor were inserted into a wider social economy. And that the survival of household production into the present represents an active and independent precapitalist "peasant mode of production," characterized by what he refers to as an economy of affection. Hyden is correct in his assertion that the survival of peasants must be theorized in relation to the Marxist proclivity to assume instant eradication; equally, he is right to point to the problems of labor control or "capture" by the state where no capitalist labor process exists, what he calls the peasant exit option. But there are two important respects in which this study departs from Hyden. First, in northern Nigeria peasants existed as part of the precolonial Sokoto Caliphate; strictly speaking, peasantry is here understood as a historical category in which commoditization is or has been resisted by the reproduction of institutional and social relations limiting the mobility of land and labor (Friedmann 1979*b*).[19] Colonialism progressively, but in highly heterogeneous ways, transformed peasant households into petty commodity producers, the central characteristic of which is the circulation of commodities in both directions. This transition marks the partial displacement of personal or institutional mechanisms for the mobilization of land, credit, labor, and the means of production by market-determined prices. And second, the process of commoditization has profound implications for the complex forms of household differentiation, accumulation, and proletarianization, phenomena which Hyden neglects by virtue of his concern with an idealized affective economy.

These theoretical debates surrounding the agrarian question in Africa are of direct relevance to the food crisis. For those like Wallerstein (1976) who defined as "capitalist" any agriculture functioning within an economic system whose global structure is market oriented, the immiserization of the peasantry—the "underdevelopment" of smallholders—followed quite naturally. Paradoxically, also from an avowedly Marxist perspective, Bill Warren (1981, p. 130) sees underdevelopment as an "illusion" and dependency as "nationalist mythology" and argues that colonial rule actually contributed to the disappearance of famines among peasants after the 1920s. For others,[20] peasants are at various times and places posed as nascent accumulators—kulaks behind every cotton plant or every rubber tree—while for Fred Cooper (1981) they are above all remarkably ornery, producing the wrong quantity of the wrong commodity at the wrong time, and causing much hair pulling among frustrated colonial bureaucrats. What is at stake, of course, in the proliferation of peasant studies is certainly not new since it is what European Marxists tried to confront in their debates on the agrarian question between the late 1890s and the outbreak of the First World War.[21] These volatile confrontations arose from a recognition that it was critical to specify the manner in which capitalism affected the internal structure of agricultural production, not to assert a priori its dominance. As Hobsbawm (1980, p. 22) observes,

> while these debates demonstrated clearly enough that peasant farming was being eroded and transformed by capitalism, they also demonstrated that politically socialists did not quite know what to do about the large body of

peasants in developed countries who could be classified neither as rural bourgeois nor as rural proletarians or quasi-proletarians except in those cases where
a traditional, and almost by definition non-capitalist, peasantry could be regarded more or less as a collective revolutionary mass, and appealed to
accordingly.

The present "mode of production" approach is a continuation of the
turn of the century dialogue but addresses the general characteristics
behind the variety of appearances of the relations of production and
surplus extraction from peasants (Boesen 1979). What emerges, rather
than the classical Leninist-Kautskyian search for the capitalist farmer,[22]
are two lines of thinking. The first poses the peasant as a semiproletarian
as capital destroys precapitalist relations of productions though their
forms might be preserved.[23] The second is the "articulation" perspective
in which capital subordinates peasants by a dialectical process of preserva-
tion-dissolution or destructuration-restructuration.[24] In this work, I draw
heavily on the latter in accounting for the effects of the uneven pattern of
incorporation of northern Nigeria into a capitalist international division
of labor. The forms of production that survived in northern Nigeria were
not doomed to rapid erosion; the vital point is that "noncapitalist forms of
production were articulated into capitalist forms of commodity circulation without themselves necessarily being—or becoming—strictly capitalist enterprises" (Murray 1981, p. 492). In actual fact, the syncretism
resulted in the emergence of hybrid forms of production, a heterogeneity
of forms of household reproduction, and an uneven transition toward
capitalism. More critically for this study, however, is that the essential
change that articulation involved was, as Lenin noted, that "the small
farmer becomes a commodity producer, whether he likes it or not" (cited
in Hobsbawm 1980, p. 22).

My theoretical starting point is the category of natural economy, a
huge abstraction that implies a social formation characterized largely by
production of use-values. Lenin and Luxemburg described a natural
economy largely in terms of relatively homogeneous household units,
self-sufficient and self-contained; it stood opposed to commodity production and exchange generally and to the expanded reproduction of capital
in particular. In nineteenth-century northern Nigeria, natural economy
should be used with great caution since it was constituted by a specific
form of appropriation of surplus labor, an equally specific structure
governing the relations of production, and an overarching prebendal
state mediated through a hegemonic Muslim ideology. The primary
focus here is the denouement of the precolonial natural economy
through the insertion of capital under the aegis of the colonial state. In
northern Nigeria the transformation of natural economy did not necessitate widespread appropriation of land, massive forced labor, or a
transformation of the forces of peasant production. Indeed, the colonial

state rather ironically was seen to act in support of "local custom," against private property, and hence indirectly to retard the process of proletarianization. Colonial integration did nonetheless initiate the process of primitive accumulation, which projected Nigeria into a global division of labor in which it was integrated into the world capitalist economy as a supplier of industrial raw materials. And I will illustrate how such changes, achieved without expropriation of producers, were of tremendous significance both for food production and for the genesis of famine in a drought-prone environment.

The colonial annexations of the late nineteenth century reshaped the global division of labor, but in Africa, as elsewhere, it did not (to paraphrase Lenin) demolish the natural economy at a single stroke. Rather specific forms of international capital took labor as it found it; only later did identifiably different social relations appear. Godelier for instance notes that

> as Marx and Engels have endlessly repeated, it is impossible to analyse and understand the forms and routes taken by the transition from one mode of production and social life to another without taking fully into consideration the "premises" from which this transition develops. Far from their disappearing from the scene of history at a stroke, it is these earlier relations of production and the other social relations which transform themselves, and we must start from them in order to understand the *forms* which the effects of the new conditions of material life will take and *places* where they will manifest themselves within the previous social structures. [Godelier 1978, p. 107]

The process of subsumption, then, must address the historic form of international capital in relation to the noncapitalist formation that it confronts. This means that we cannot assume a priori that capital singlemindedly shapes and forges labor to maximize profits or that the state bears a singular stamp; equally, there is no reason to suppose a homogeneous spread of commodity production. In northern Nigeria, the process of primitive accumulation remained only differentially completed in the face of foreign dominance by metropolitan capital. As Murray (1981, p. 7) notes, this halting and uneven process was less a function of peasant psychology than "the internal class structure of the noncapitalist modes of production [and the] historical time, location and impulse for outward metropolitan expansion."

As I have already suggested, the hybrid forms of production were the result of the historically specific syncretism of capitalist and noncapitalistic production processes, a tendency noted long ago by Kautsky in his account of capitalist transition in agriculture in Europe and Russia. Lenin also echoed Kautsky's sentiments that agrarian capitalism could apparently cohabit with precapitalist relations of production.

It should be added that our literature frequently contains too stereotyped an understanding of the territorial proposition that capitalism requires the free landless worker. This proposition is quite correct in indicating the major trend, but capitalism penetrates into agriculture particularly slowly and in extremely varied forms. [Lenin 1964, p. 178]

In both prefamine Ireland and Scotland, for instance, capitalist development did not conform to a simple model; many factors contributed to the resilience of the smallholder, particularly domestic industry, seasonal migration, and (not least) the ability of the peasant to reduce his living costs to the lowest denominator (see Hobsbawm 1980; Carter 1979; Hazelkorn 1981). Much of the recent work on agrarian change in Africa has borne out Lenin's claim of the unmanageable heterogeneity of a transitional commodity economy. In Kenya for example, Cowen (1980, 1976) proposes that in Central Province there has been a historic *expansion* of middle peasant production and a reduction in income inequality measured through gini coefficients of milk and tea production;[25] Kitching (1980) has also illustrated the extreme diversity of labor situations in Kenya, which do not rest easily with watertight definitions of "peasant" or "proletarian." This points to the absolute necessity of recognizing the variety of paths of agrarian development and the great difficulty of theorizing peripheral societies as a singular mode of production.[26]

In colonial Nigeria, European and local merchant capital and an indigenous ruling class played a central role in the drama of commodity production.[27] At a theoretical level merchant's capital is contradictory insofar as it does not necessarily establish control over production but is nevertheless socially corrosive. In Marx's words,

the development of commerce and merchant's capital gives rise everywhere to the tendency towards production of exchange values, increases its volume, multiplies it, makes it cosmopolitan, and develops money into world-money. Commerce, therefore, has a more or less dissolving influence everywhere on the producing organization, which it finds at hand and whose different forms are mainly carried on with a view to use-value. *To what extent it brings about a dissolution of the old mode of production depends upon its solidity and internal structure.* And whither this process will lead, in other words, what new mode of production will replace the old, does not depend upon commerce, but on the character of the old mode of production itself. In the ancient world the effect of commerce and the development of merchant's capital always resulted in a slave economy; depending on the point of departure, only in the transformation of a patriarchal slave system devoted to the production of immediate means of subsistence into one devoted to the production of surplus value. However, in the modern world, it results in the capitalist mode of production. It follows therefrom that there results spring in themselves from the circumstances other than the development of merchant's capital. [Marx 1967, III, 332]

Kay (1975), then, is right to emphasize that independent merchant capital was the form of existence of industrial capital in much of Africa, but one needs to ask how such capital irregularly controlled production and yet constituted a barrier to further agrarian development. The overall result in northern Nigeria was that capital maintained only a partial control over the labor process; peasants lost their autonomy but not their means of production. The union of merchant capital and the colonial state established a commercial hierarchy of Hausa traders, commission agents, brokers, and farmers presided over by European traders and held together by complex lines of credit and patronage. I attempt to trace the specific linkages between merchant capital and social differentiation and, more critically, their implications for subsistence security and famine. In tracing the organic connection between the changing form of subsistence crises and the progressive development of capitalism in northern Nigeria I have chosen to emphasize the changing social bases of household production[28] and the growth of commodity production,[29] which ruptured the cycle of peasant reproduction.

In summary, this view of historic change in Nigeria recognizes that individual capitals were part of accumulative processes that developed in contradictory directions and spawned a variety of other forms. In Nigeria the accumulative process was a two-phased development. In the period up to the Great Depression, metropolitan capital and its agent the colonial state attempted to secure its commercial hegemony, and to this extent conservation prevailed over dissolution. After 1930, with the expansion of commercial activities and the fiscal security of the colonial state, rural producers were increasingly incorporated into the market economy and the commoditization of labor, and the means of production proceeded apace. In this sense, the extended reproduction of capital was marked by what Murray (1981, p. 123) in referring to Indochina calls "advanced dissolution." Moreover, patterns of uneven development in Nigeria suggest that we be sensitive to the fact that capital accumulation during the colonial epoch, far from banishing smallholders to the history books, might sustain household production while partially transforming them into commodity producers. However, Brenner (1977) has rightly pointed out that the peasant economy is not simply a precipitate of uneven development; rather, the situation of colonial producers in Nigeria was a reflection of forms of exploitation that emerged as a result of the prior constellations of class relations and their engagement with a market economy supervised by the colonial state. The point is, of course, that capitalism is not an entelechy, and in its colonial expression experienced both conflicting interests within itself and highly resistant class structures in the periphery. Colonialism was as much about failure as success. All this makes for complicated if not convoluted dialectical developments, not simple unilinear change.

THE STUDY AREA

The broad geographical region chosen for this study is Hausaland (figure 1.2), an area of roughly 120,000 square miles spanning northern Nigeria and southern Niger, inhabited largely by Hausa-speaking people. The 15 million Hausa-speakers are settled principally between 10° and 14° north and 4° and 10° east, throughout the Sokoto Basin and the Hausa plains to the east. Hausa is in fact a linguistic not an ethnic term; it refers to those who speak the language at birth, and hence includes many Kanuri, Fulani, and Kebbi people who have little in common ethnically. The Muslim Hausa are, however, sometimes differentiated from pagan Hausa (*Maguzawa*). In spite of the ethnic diversity, the Hausa region does possess an underlying uniformity, as Daryll Forde noted long ago. For several hundred years, Hausaland has comprised a number of discrete emirates, each presided over by a titular ruler, the emir, who owed allegiance to the Caliph at Sokoto. During the nineteenth century these emirates were welded together into a single political entity; this state structure, referred to as the Sokoto Caliphate, was subsequently dismembered following colonial conquest in 1903, though the emirates formed the basic building blocks for the colonial administrative system. The Caliphate was the largest, most populous, and probably the most complex state in precolonial West Africa which, through its conquest of non-Muslim communities and slave raiding, absorbed and socialized populations into a highly differentiated Muslim society. Although it was a cultural periphery of the North African Islamic diaspora, the ecological limits of the Sahara and its geographic isolation from the coast permitted the Caliphate to develop distinct institutional and cultural patterns prior to the colonial presence.

While Hausaland provides the broad cultural frame of reference, my geographic focus is almost wholly Nigerian Hausaland, and in particular the core emirates—Kano, Katsina, Sokoto—of the old Northern Region. This is an area of Sudan and Guinea savanna, which in the extreme north of the country becomes increasingly Sahelian in character. These two ecological zones are quite distinct in spite of the fact that the undulating landforms of the Hausa plains, broken occasionally by mesas, lateritic ridges and outcrops, and irregular watercourses, are often seen as relatively uniform and undifferentiated. In the Guinea ecological zone, which occupies much of southern Hausaland and the Middle Belt, the granitic basement complex tends to produce leached ferruginous soil, while in the

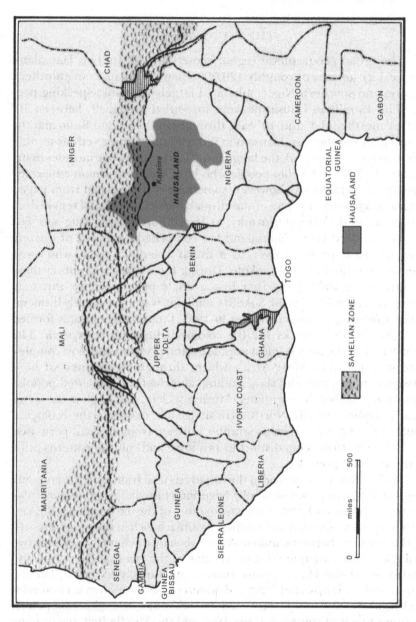

Figure 1.2. Hausaland and its West African context.

northern Sudan savannas sedimentary structures result in fragile sandy soils, low in silt and clay. In the seasonal river valleys and flood plains (*fadama*) that dissect the uplands, heavier and poorly drained hydromorphic clay soils predominate, which can be exploited for dry season agriculture. While both zones are vegetatively distinct, a high population and long-term continuous cultivation has invariably reduced the ecological landscape to a farmed parkland appearance.

Rainfall is, of course, the critical limiting factor in peasant rainfed agriculture. The whole area has a distinctive rainy season with a pronounced unimodal peak in August and a seasonal length of four to six months. However moving northward from the Guinea savannas, rainfall decreases markedly (table 1.5); precipitation of 900 to 1,400 mm is characteristic of southern Hausaland, while 500 to 900 mm is representative for the Sudan zone. The length of the rainy season and growing period progressively diminish toward the north. Of particular significance for this book is the considerable annual (and spatial) variation in the amount and distribution of rainfall, most especially the enormous irregularity of precipitation at the onset and termination of the rainy season. Indeed, in a real sense drought is almost a normal part of the agricultural routine.

Throughout the north of Nigeria local farming systems are still characterized by simple hand-tool technology with only limited use of modern inputs. Since peasant rather than settler or estate production was the material bedrock of the colonial state in Nigeria, household production remains critical in an economy that is still, at least in terms of employment, overwhelmingly agricultural. As in the past, the household economy is sustained and dominated by the production of sorghum and millet, with groundnuts and cotton as the most upland export commodities. In spite of quite rapid population growth, the increasingly high population densities especially in the close settled zones (Kano, Zaria, Katsina, Sokoto), and the limited availability of virgin bush land, landlessness remains (as it was throughout the colonial period) quite undeveloped.

Northern Nigeria provides an intriguing forum for the examination of the changing form of food production and famine, quite apart from its size and political importance. First, in the nineteenth century Hausaland was firmly embedded in the affairs of the central Sudan, a huge desert-edge mosaic in which drought, famine, and the grain trade were integral elements of its culture and historical development. Second, from the fall of the Sokoto Caliphate until Independence in 1960, the colonial state constantly wrestled, often unsuccessfully, with problems of food supply, and peasant producers faced at least four major subsistence crises over a fifty-year period. And third, northern Nigeria, and indeed the entire West African Sahel, was deeply affected by the massive famine of the

TABLE 1.5
CLIMATIC VARIABILITY IN NORTHERN NIGERIA

Area	Location	Ecological zone	Mean monthly temperature Min.	Mean monthly temperature Max.	Total rain in in. (cv)[a]	cv[a] in monthly rainfall	Length of rainy period (days)	Growing season Length (days)	Growing season Start	Growing season End	Months when water is surplus
Sokoto	13°01'N 5°15'E	Sudan	15.0	40.0	29.6	137	120	150	June 1–10	Oct. 21–30	July–Sept.
Zaria	11°11'N 7°38'E	Guinea	13.9	35.0	43.9 (14.9)	115	160	190	May 11–20	Nov. 1–10	June–Sept.
Bauchi	10°17'N 9°49'E	Guinea	12.8	36.7	43.4 (19.0)	127	150	180	May 21–30	Nov. 1–10	June–Sept.

SOURCE: Kowal and Knabe (1972).

NOTE: The start of the rains and the start of the growing season is defined as the first ten-day period in which the amount of the rainfall is equal to or more than 25.4 mm followed by a subsequent ten-day period in which the amount of rainfall is at least equal to one-half the evapotranspiration demand. The end of the rains is assumed to occur when the water storage in the top four inches of soil is used up. Water-surplus months are defined as those in which rain exceeds evapotranspiration and soil water storage.

[a]cv = the coefficient of variation.

early 1970s, an event that came to be seen as a watershed in a new era of global food shortages.

In conclusion, it is perhaps appropriate if not especially uplifting to note that Nigeria's agricultural sector is entirely representative of the depressing continental trends noted earlier in this chapter (Wallace 1981). In many respects, of course, Nigeria as an OPEC member with a huge domestic market (in the order of 85 million) and a nascent, if energetic, manufacturing economy, is quite atypical. The huge increase in oil revenues after the 1973 crude petroleum price hike permitted a massive expansion in public capital expenditures (see Kirk-Greene and Rimmer 1981). The last decade has accordingly seen a considerable growth in state centralization, a proliferation in the number of states (figure 1.3), a rapid if uneven growth of manufacturing, the creation of new national institutions, and a tardy commitment to development planning expressed through universal primary education, parastatal organizations and infrastructural development (*African Business*, December 1981). Yet, as the recent International Labor Office report concludes (ILO 1981, p. 5), while the advance on these fronts has been considerable "it has not been matched by comparable social programs or even economic development." While the gross domestic product (GDP) per capita in 1980 stood at $670, there is every indication that since 1973 real private consumption per head has been falling, and "there has been a worsening of income distribution" (ILO 1981, p. 220).

Like Gabon, another OPEC member, Nigeria had a relatively robust agricultural economy in 1960; in 1964 Nigeria was in fact self-sufficient in staple foods and a leading exporter of palm oil, cocoa, and groundnuts. Gabon then produced double its food requirements. Yet between 1957 and 1980 nonoil exports fell by 60 percent in real terms in Nigeria and 72 percent in Gabon; agriculture as a percentage of GDP shrank by almost 50 percent in both countries over the same period, and official estimates suggest that agricultural production per head fell by 47 percent in Gabon and 31 percent in Nigeria between 1970 and 1980 (*The Economist*, December 5, 1981). In Nigeria alone, U.S. rice imports, which were nonexistent in 1970, stood at $92 million in 1980; total staple food imports have spiraled over the last decade (table 1.6) and amounted to a colossal 2.5 million tons in 1980. The index of per capita food production fell from 100 in 1969 to 85 in 1980. The staple food import bill in 1980 stood at $3.1 billion, more than 15 percent of gross calorie supply. This would require an 11 percent per annum growth rate in food production to close the food gap by 1985. The ILO mission concluded that the Nigerian food balance sheet calculations revealed (a) a huge national food deficit, (b) inadequate calorie and protein supply, and (c) a widening gap between production and national food requirements. I hope to provide a historical context for

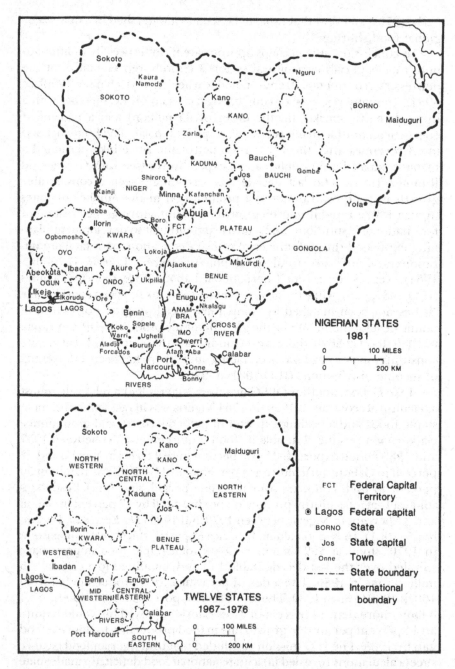

Figure 1.3. State structure in Nigeria. Adapted from Rimmer and Kirk-Greene (1981).

TABLE 1.6
IMPORTS OF MAJOR GRAINS
(1000 tons)

Year	Wheat	Rice	Maize
1970	266.4[1]	1.7	8.8
1971	406.7	0.2	3.8
1972	292.0	5.8	2.3
1973	494.1	1.1	1.8
1974	318.3	4.8	2.4
1975	407.3	6.6	2.2
1976	733.1	45.3	9.8
1977	746.0[2]	413.3	36.8
1978	1683.3[3]	770.0	116.3
1979	1350.0	700.0	71.1
1980	1400.0[4]	350.0[4]	140.0[4]

SOURCES: World Bank Nigerian Agricultural Sector Assessment Report, 1979, p. 36; *Economist Quarterly Review of Nigeria*, 1st Quarter 1981.

[1] Includes wheat flour converted to wheat equivalent.

[2] Comprising 719,700 tons of wheat and wheat equivalent of 23,700 tons of flour (at 90% milling rate)

[3] Comprising 1,300,000 tons of wheat and wheat equivalent of 345,000 tons of flour (at 90% milling rate)

[4] Provisional: *Economist Quarterly Review* – 1st Quarter 1981.

this crisis in terms of changing patterns of food availability in the colonial era, and more recently in relation to the oil boom and state intervention.

FACT, FICTION, AND METHOD

Colonial rule is particularly subject to the distortions of bureaucratic structures which mistake the report for the bullet, the plan for the action and what one clerk says to another as history.

—Eric Stokes

The object of historical knowledge is "real" history where evidence must necessarily be incomplete and imperfect. . . . Historical practice is . . . [a] dialogue; with an argument between received, inadequate and ideologically informed concepts or hypotheses on the one hand and of fresh or inconvenient evidence on the other.

—E. P. Thompson

Particularly since the publication of Edward Thompson's epochal *Poverty of Theory* and more generally since the theoretical debates conducted in the pages of *History Workshop* in the 1970s, epistemological concerns have become central to much historical writing. Thompson, of course, raised the thorny problem of evidence in all historical inquiry and the appropriate concepts for understanding historical process, but these are questions that naturally underpin much social scientific discourse (Anderson 1980). I wish to raise these issues here not because Africanist historiography is insensitive to the absences and silences of the historical record (see Bernstein and Depelchin 1978), but because I have been personally troubled by the difficulties they represent for this study. Moreover, these murky epistemological waters often flow uninterrupted under the bridge of contemporary political economy which quite frequently relies on one overrepresented source of information. Even a powerful and informed work such as *The Roots of Rural Poverty*, for instance, contains an overwhelming dependence on archival materials that, as Terence Ranger observes, necessarily distorts the process of peasantization that it seeks to explain (1978, p. 107). I have quite deliberately employed an eclectic array of sources including oral evidences and a local-level field-work (village) study of some duration, which in themselves raise other unique problems of evidence and interpretation.

With regard to the primary and secondary historical materials, the latter requires little comment save to say that Nigerian Hausaland is no longer *the* understudied region that Polly Hill believed it to be in the early 1970s. The primary sources, which I take to be oral and written documents that have information about the past but whose sources cannot be checked and verified, are quite diverse. The oral evidence presented here largely pertains to historical information on nineteenth- and twentieth-century famines and famine chronologies, and descriptive material on nineteenth-century household production and productive changes in the colonial period. The majority of this information was derived from extensive discussions with elders (*dattawa*)[30] in northern Katsina and Daura. Of course, it is widely accepted that these oral sources need to be examined in light of the world outlook of the informant and an understanding of the cultural context and personal biases—of class, lineage or status—inherent in individual perception. If much of the discussion conducted in Katsina did not pertain directly to overly sensitive political or ideological content, it quickly became clear that individuals who were themselves famine refugees were reticent to speak directly to their own experience. The interviews, about fifty in all, are supplemented by an assemblage of oral verse and poetic recitation (*kirari*) collected principally from the Sarkin Tabshin Katsina. In some cases, praise songs and the like were devoted entirely to the elucidation and characterization of famine conditions; they appear in the Appendix.

Two other primary data sources were of special significance. First, I utilized journals, diaries and travelogues written by a handful of nineteenth-century explorers who in varying degrees resided in *Kasar* Hausa. Bovil, Clapperton, and Barth all passed through Katsina—indeed Barth spent a considerable period of time in and around the town—leaving exquisitely wrought and evocative descriptions of the Hausa landscape. Usman (1977), however, quite correctly suggested that such sources require the same textual analysis as is demanded of oral sources since they were products of a racially obsessed culture. The penetration of the historical density of these sources is critical for they represent a definite and historically specific conception of nature and society.

The second source consists of a wealth of colonial archival materials located in Nigeria and Great Britain.[31] Chapters 5 and 6 make extensive use of assessment reports, touring documents, private papers and diaries, and provincial administrative papers in the reconstruction of socioeconomic changes in the Hausa countryside. They have been supplemented wherever possible by secondary sources and a plethora of governmental papers, which are still littered throughout northern Nigeria buried in local government store rooms and in district center offices, partially consumed by local wildlife. These colonial "oral traditions" naturally have their shortcomings. Many administrators did not understand Hausa and the possibility of profound misapprehension was correspondingly high. Obviously, the collection of rural information was a highly political act; the spectre of taxation made the systematic collection of accurate rural data, if not impossible, terribly difficult. Few colonial administrators were trained in historical recovery and even the colonial ledger itself appears in hindsight to be inconsistent, confused, and contradictory; much of what passes as imperial administration resembles deliberate obfuscation and self-congratulation. Take for instance the following two descriptions of 1942–43—a famine year—abstracted from official colonial memoranda:

> It is probable that the requisitioning of grain from the harvests of 1942 and 1943 has stimulated the farmers to increase their farms. There are, indeed, evident signs that in the latter half of the year people in the North had more to eat than they had had for some years [cited in Kuczynski 1948, p. 458].
>
> In the Northern Provinces, the late rains caused a food shortage which affected the health of the population. In Katsina province this was regarded as the responsible factor for an increase in the death rate and a decline in the birth rate. Meat has been very scarce and expensive in most areas, and the cost of essential foodstuffs has increased [cited in Kuczynski 1948, p. 458].

At the same time, northern Nigeria was the training ground for some extraordinarily gifted colonial political officers whose observations seem as insightful and acute as much of what passes as social science. A good assessment report can compare favorably with a good contemporary farm management survey.[32] All this may make for epistemological messiness but it is inevitable unless one adopts the crude idealism of some recent work that denies the validity of history altogether. In this respect I can do no better than quote a scholar who seems particularly sensitive to the dialogue between theory and fact and the failings of commonsense empiricism.

> Thus, historical records have never been seen here as sources of "facts" but as class products, and at that almost always products of the capitalist and intermediate classes. Peasants and workers did not write despatches, departmental reports or Colonial Office minutes . . . therefore, they have to be subjected to a process in which theory is used to constitute data from them by a critical examination, a paring away of their ideological elements, and a re-assembly of what is left. Given the nature of records as class products, the ability to learn much of the class struggles of the workers and peasants is thus greatly circumscribed; the reactions of their enemies is almost always more clear, and we write history, therefore, as if from a reversed image in a distorting mirror.
>
> For now, and painfully so in the case of the present study, we have to be aware of the profound limitations on what we can do. What I have tried to do here, then, is to be very conscious of theory and to place it literally in the forefront, and then to use it to constitute the data which I have chosen to present, more especially . . . to assign priorities and levels of importance to them. [Post 1978, pp. 466–67]

The distorted optic provided by a wholesale dependence on archival sources can, and I would argue must, be complemented by oral fieldwork.[33] The value of such work is manifold in a work such as this, but I fully endorse Ranger's belief that "fieldwork is perhaps the only way of making systematic sense of the African side of the multiple 'intermediate' positions between peasant and proletarian" (1978, p. 117). The vast majority of chapter 7, which addresses famine in the current era, is based on a fourteen-month village study in Kaita village, located north of Katsina town (Kaduna State) in a sandy and rather infertile district adjacent to the international border. There were several reasons for selecting northern Katsina, and Kaita village in particular, as a research locale. First, it is an extreme northern district, fringing the Sahel, with a recorded history of food shortage and drought. Second, Katsina emirate is fortunate in having an enviable pedigree of historical and economic work, which provides an unparalleled wealth of contextual materials. Third, the national and local archival materials are especially rich and well documented for the reconstruction of socioeconomic changes throughout the Katsina countryside during the colonial period. And fourth, the selection of Kaita village as a community for study fulfilled several important requirements concerning size, access, the presence of a market garden sector, and a periodic rural market. As is often the case with such choices they appear on reflection to be almost embarrassingly arbitrary.

In Kaita I knew the district head, it was an attractive community, and I felt comfortable there.

During the village study in 1977—78 I collected field data using a variety of what I refer to with some trepidation as methodological techniques; sometimes they involved large-scale survey methods and on other occasions small, nonrandom samples of householders and farmers. Initially, I determined a sampling frame through a village-wide population census and socioeconomic survey; this could be compared directly with both Kaita village tax records and a 1978 election census. From subjective estimates obtained from a carefully selected group of five village elders (*dattawa*), I was then able to stratify the population of householders (*masu gidaje*) according to indigenous categories of economic status: namely, the traditional elite (*masu sarauta*), wealthy and successful farmers (*manyan noma* or *masu arziki*), farmers who are neither rich nor poor, and finally the poor and destitute (*matalauta*). These two data sets—the village census and the householders stratified into economic groups—constituted the two frames from which smaller samples were taken to conduct intensive interviews on agronomy, drought, trade, and general economic activities. In all the series of interviews, I generated either 10 or 20 percent random samples of informants; in the event of nonresponse, another informant was randomly selected.

Exceptions to this procedure concerned historical data, detailed agronomic exegesis, and socially or politically sensitive issues, notably credit, grain sales, and migration. In these cases, individuals were interviewed who were recognized locally as skilled cultivators or oral historians. With respect to indebtedness and food sales, it quickly became clear that survey methods using sampling techniques were wholly inappropriate. Reliable data could be obtained only from a small number of individuals—householders whom the author knew well—painfully compiled over a long period. Accordingly, what emerges is a small, patchy and perhaps unrepresentative picture; yet to resort to large-scale sampling on such sensitive subject matters would, in my opinion, magnify the error factor to a wholly intolerable degree.

All this is not an apology but to suggest that I am somewhat disillusioned by the empirical products of some aspects of field research. I confess that I am even more astonished by the fact that so few skeptical individuals apparently acknowledge these limitations in their own work since the difficulties that emerged in my own endeavors are presumably not unique to Kaita village but are intrinsic to much research. I have attempted to make my own misgivings as explicit as possible, and to indicate, to the extent that I am able, areas where the data seem unreliable or perhaps specious. For some survey work, of course, such as farm measurement, agronomic practice, and the demographic censuses, I have much more confidence in the quality of the data collected.

During the actual process of data collection and interviewing I was always present and participated in the discussions, though I may have worked with an assistant and initially with an interpreter. By the end of my stay in Kaita, I conducted interviews without an assistant, which was necessary in discussions with acquaintances on debt, credit, and personal family matters. I conducted farm measurement during the dry season of 1977 at considerable expense to my mental well-being and health. My one field assistant provided help throughout the research period; he was excessively laconic toward my endeavors, which my explications did nothing to improve, but an extraordinary source of information on the intricacies of smuggling and, more important, a good comrade.

Field research thus combined orthodox participant observation with farm management methods. Both have their limits but this is not a variable that can be readily committed to a footnote or disguised as an acceptable error factor, for these difficulties sustain systematic, and not so systematic, biases which effectively remove large realms of village life from serious enquiry.

This process of obfuscation is not only related to taboo areas of enquiry, which are to be found in all cultures, but to the frequent equation of expatriate researchers with the traditional hierarchy and external political authority, in particular with local village heads. Hausa farmers are rightly suspicious of outsiders and of their rulers, for the village head is, as often as not, perceived as the local representative of a predatory government and hence is both feared and resented. The researcher has to do much more than simply obtain the sanction of the local leader to allay the fears and antipathy of the farmer. In this light, Hausa farmers plan their responses to the intrusion of the field researcher and display a good natured resignation if not loquaciousness. But few individuals put much effort into their responses and are especially uncooperative on matters pertaining to economic status. Accordingly, splendid examples of exaggerating poverty, affluence, or influence, abound.

There are naturally many sensitive subjects about which accurate data is extraordinarily difficult to obtain: numbers of young girls are regularly underestimated as are adopted children; grain sales tend to be very sensitive; numbers of large livestock and manure sales are invariably fictive; and various forms of land tenure, especially pledging, rental, and sales, are difficult to document either through obfuscatory use of language or through verbal agreement. Credit, moneylending, and loans are all fundamentally off limits. In Muslim Hausa society much behavior is filtered through a complex ideological screen, which presents a somewhat distorted picture of human praxis; some sensitive aspects of interpersonal relationships are institutionally disguised by formal or informal arrangements. The web of relationships that bind Hausa communities together do not, moreover, miraculously materialize with time or linguistic proficiency. The best one can do is to be methodologically careful and consistent, cross-check frequently, and be patient. In my opinion, it certainly helps to be anal compulsive. Much of my early information collected with and without assistants, with and without questionnaires, was quite useless. Indeed, it was worse than useless, for I constructed wonderfully elaborate edifices on foundations of nonsense.

And finally to complete this tale of Hausa hazards, it bears reiteration that my perspective is ashamedly, but not naively, sexist. In a society where the incidence of rural wife seclusion has risen dramatically since 1900, access to married women and their economy was largely secondhand. I was, of course, able to speak to the elder women who were exempt from seclusion and who ironically were often the most forthcoming informants. I could also supplement this information with data gleaned from other sources, but clearly the majority of my time was necessarily spent with male farmers.

In conclusion, any discussion of facts and statistics would be woefully incomplete without at least a passing reference to Nigerian government and official sources. It is, of course, commonplace to bemoan the absence of meaningful or accurate survey data throughout much of Africa and little more needs to be said on that score. In the case of Nigeria, however, these absences have reached a new zenith. None other than the *Economist* (January 23, 1982) published a recent survey of Nigeria in which it lamented that "this is the first survey published by the *Economist* in which every single number is probably wrong" (p. 4). At an aggregate level, nobody really knows within an acceptable margin of error how many people live in Nigeria, what their material standard of living is like and how much they produce. The Annual Report of the Central Bank of Nigeria in 1981 was not able to publish any data on federal government revenue, expenditure, or trade! By early 1982, the Central Bank, the state bureaucracies, and indeed the electorate generally, are none the wiser. The situation for the state governments is doubtless much worse. This state of affairs led the *Economist* reporter to conclude that an oil-rich Nigeria was all too Hobbesian in character; Nigerians were, in his words, "chucking it away." I return to these questions of apparent anarchy and decay in relation to the current food crisis in the last chapter.

In this work, I attempt to weave together the archival and field data into a sort of historical tapestry that sheds some light on the changing character of food production and famine in Nigerian Hausaland. The blending of source materials and the synthesis of field and archival information is, I suspect, a particular strength of the geographic approach. In the following chapter, largely using published secondary material and to a lesser degree oral and archival sources, I briefly outline the salient characteristics of the social structure of the complex Islamic state structure that prevailed in nineteenth-century Hausaland, the Sokoto Caliphate. In doing so, I hope to provide a context for the following discussion concerning the nature of food production and hunger in the precolonial period, and the changes associated with colonial overrule. In chapter 3 I examine the nineteenth-century patterns of famine and food security in relation to environmental risk and household production. Chapters 4, 5, and 6 deal with the impact of the colonial state and European merchant capital on the precolonial cycle of household reproduction. Patterns of commoditization, trade, and rural differentiation are traced with respect to new patterns of food production and subsistence insecurity. Chapter 6 specifically addresses the sequence and changing character of famines and subsistence crises between 1900 and 1960 in relation to the partial and distorted patterns of transformation among the Caliphal peasantries. In chapter 7, using materials collected from a 1977–78 village study, I examine the major famine of the early 1970s especially with respect to the commodification and differentiation trends initiated in the colonial era. The conclusion deals with the current crisis in the Nigerian food economy following the oil boom of the early 1970s. In doing so I try to show not only that the contemporary crisis is organically connected to the long and complex historical pattern of food shortage but also that the 1980s mark a new phase of capital accumulation in Nigeria that threatens the persistence of the small-scale commodity producer.

2

HAUSALAND AND THE SOKOTO CALIPHATE IN THE NINETEENTH CENTURY

[There is little] to compare with the political and cultural sophistication of these ancient Hausa states, with their walled red cities, crowded mosques, literate mullahs, large markets, numerous crafts . . . far ranging traders and skilled production of a wide variety of crops.

—*Margery Perham*

The military slave-guards . . . frequently formed the capstone of Islamic political systems [and] wore a praetorian guise. Religion saturated the whole ideological universe of the Muslim social system. . . . Islamic towns were tangled, aleatory labyrinths and [the Islamic world] typically exhibited juridical monopoly of land.

—*Perry Anderson*

Almost half a century after the foundation of the Sokoto Caliphate, the German geographer Heinrich Barth arrived in northern Hausaland after an eleven-month trek from the shores of the Mediterranean. There are obvious difficulties of historical recovery in Barth's political and social writings, but the power of his glowing and eloquent testimony to material life and welfare in the Hausa states remains. The manicured parkland of the Hausa plains, intensively cultivated riverine margins, bustling rural markets along the desert edge, international textile commerce and the brilliance of ancient cities like Kano and Katsina, which constituted the cells of a vibrant political community are the very substance of Barth's encyclopaedic journals. When Barth entered Kasar Hausa, the Sokoto Caliphate and Borno were effectively a single, if heterogeneous, region in which the Caliphate was the dominant partner. The holy war (*jihad*) of 1806 forged some thirty territorial units into the largest and most populous state in nineteenth-century West Africa. The hegemony of a Hausa-Fulani emirate system marked the economic and political ascendancy of the Caliphate over the entire central Sudan, a complex and variegated ecological and economic

mosaic embracing both northerly Sahelian biomes along the desert edge
and the moist Sudanic savannas of the lower latitudes. Viewed through
the lens of social and material change the jihad "assumes the character of
just one event in a large process in which Islamization, economic growth
and increasing centralization of state structures were interrelated" (Baier
1980, p. 24). By the time of Barth's emergence from the desert in 1851,
the Caliphate powers had already quelled the political disquiet and military insecurity of the immediate jihad aftermath and embarked upon a
policy of economic expansion that included settlement of bush land, the
establishment of new communities, continuing immigration of servile and
free labor, huge investment in agricultural infrastructure, a general
broadening of commodity production, and a further deepening of the
Hausa trade diaspora; this implied an extension of the cowry currency,
burgeoning textile exports, and popular consumption of European imports. The prosperous eastern emirates, particularly Zaria, Katsina, and
Kano, were principal agents in the genesis and sustenance of this new
economic trajectory.

The history of the central Sudan, like so much of West Africa, is an
attestation to Coquery-Vidrovitch's (1969) claim that African societies
have never lived in isolation because their genealogy and ancestry have
always been indissolubly linked with movement, trade, and migration.
But by the same token commerce has become the talismanic slogan for
precapitalist Africa and this analytical concern with exchange alone has
assuredly lent a specious dynamic to indigenous social systems. The study
of Hausaland has been especially subjected to this, and other related
biases. First, in spite of the explosion of historical research on the emirates,[1] the obsession with trade has characteristically been at the expense
of material production, and more critically of the role of labor (Shea 1975,
1981). Second, individual scholarship of a "representative emirate,"
encourages generalization across the Caliphate on the basis of limited
historical experience, impoverishing the political and economic diversity
that has become a hallmark of the Hausa states. And third, the proclivity
for empiricist political or dynastic histories has muddied our understanding of the essential timbre of the Caliphate itself, namely, the political
economy and economic structure of an agrarian formation. These weaknesses are, I suspect, embedded within African historiography as a
whole,[2] which Crummey and Stewart (1981, p. 21) stridently claim to be
idealist, empiricist, and theoretically barren. The new wave of materialist
social history[3] is an attempt to return precolonial African history to its
rightful place.

In his denunciation of the scope, method, and content of African
historiography Clarence-Smith (1977) has invoked Braudel and the *Ecoles
des Annales* as a model for future intellectual development, an agenda

which I find especially amenable not only because of its explicit treatment of history and geography as a necessary unity but, more appositely, because some of the most epochal work on climate, famine, and society has emerged precisely from the Annales school itself (Ladurie 1971). In this chapter I cannot claim to present such a new social history, but I attempt a simple theorization of the Caliphate at the end of the nineteenth century. I emphasize the economic structure of society in a manner that lends priority to production and its social context.[4] My intent is to grasp the dynamic of the Caliphate so as to understand how it reproduced itself as a totality—as a system of social reproduction. This should not seem far removed from my ostensible interests of food and famine, for if history is indeed the discipline of context, then this structure is central to an understanding of agrarian economy. Indeed, it is only in terms of the relations between the household and the wider social formation that the moral economy of the peasantry can be understood.

HAUSALAND, THE CENTRAL SUDAN, AND THE SARAUTA SYSTEM

The cultural history of Hausaland (Kasar Hausa) is inextricably associated with the affairs of the central Sudan, an area encompassed by a rough parallelogram extending from the Tibesti Massif to the Kebbi Lowlands, and from Azben to the Gongola basin (see fig. 2.1). It is an enormous area of Sahel, desert, and savanna, almost half a million square miles in extent and now occupied by the Republics of Niger, Nigeria, Chad, and Cameroun. Though relatively free of tectonic activity, historically the central Sudan has been subject to substantial climatic change presumably associated with long-term secular changes in pressure conditions. The palaeoclimatic record is woefully incomplete and the implications of climatic variability for the human ecology of Sudanic West Africa are murky (Nicholson 1979). Smith (1971) and Grove and Warren (1969) suggest that the entire region was bisected along an axis running southwest from Kawar to the northeast edge of the Jos Plateau.

> The zone east of this line 20,000 years ago was almost entirely occupied by a large lake, the Mega-Chad . . . the western zone of our region . . . was a swell of land traversed by rivers . . . support[ing] a parkland flora. [H.F.C. Smith 1971, p. 166]

Nicholson (1976), recognizing at least four climatic episodes since the late Pleistocene and Holocene, believes that the dessication of the Mega-Chad began roughly 8000 B.P., stabilizing at present levels approximately 4,000 years ago. In spite of several moister oscillations, the dessication prior to 4000 B.P. left Lake Chad a shallow body of water and hastened the retreat of the humid tropical biomes farther southward, leaving in their wake a

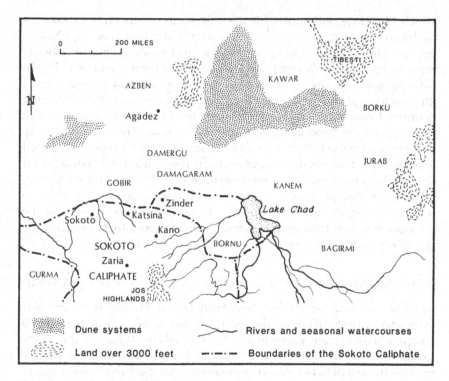

Figure 2.1. The Central Sudan. Adapted from H.F.C. Smith (1971, p. 160).

xerophytic, Guinea savanna woodland. It seems probable that both edaphic and hydraulic systems of agriculture emerged in the Sudan during this period in a broad millet-sorghum zone. Harris (1973) and Harlan (1971) both reason on the basis of exiguous evidence, that pearl millets were initially cultivated in the island delta of the Niger and in the Air, perhaps by simple hydraulic methods such as flood retreat or lakeside cultivation. In contrast to the vegecultural systems of the humid south, seed systems are, for edaphic, nutritional, and ecosystemic reasons, intrinsically expansive and spatially unstable. It seems likely that long fallow swidden systems diffused outward from these early centers.

Prior to A.D. 1000, the archaeological record is extremely thin. Shaw (1971), nonetheless, suggests that the period of dessication produced a new physical configuration throughout the central Sudan, which isolated, culturally, the east from the west. The rift, reflected in the emergence and persistence of two different language groups, was paralleled up to the fifteenth century by two semiautonomous political systems; the Hausa states to the west, and the Kanuri empire to the east. Though the origins remain obscure, it has been assumed that the southward migration of

Hausa-speaking populations in the period after 4000 B.P. provided the cultural foundation stones for a Kasar Hausa, a land of the Hausa speakers, bounded roughly by Asben, the Jos Plateau, the Chad basin and the river Niger. The area possessed a cultural integrity that has remained largely intact down to the present in spite of spirited infringements upon its territorial limits after A.D. 1500.

In a compelling thesis, Sutton (1979) has inverted the conventional reasoning of the northern origins of Hausa culture. Rather than a southward migration from Air pushed by a combination of long-term desiccation and Touareg hostility, Sutton's analysis of linguistic and cultural evidences posits a recent east-west expansion across the Hausa plains. In its embryonic stage, perhaps one millennium ago, the Hausa diaspora arose from a series of small settlements probably centered on granitic inselbergs in the eastern plains (Mortimore 1971). During this formative period, there were no territorial states or massive city walls. Commodity production and external commercial or intellectual linkages were circumscribed, and Islam notably absent. Society was small-scale and corporate: a relative equality endured among corporate descent and occupational groups in which the patriarchal heads of these lineages and craft associations assumed significant political functions.

The geographic expansion from the eastern heartland was multivalent; it not only forged a Hausa ethnic identity and an identifiably Hausa way of life in the northern savannas but also simultaneously "domesticated" the bush savanna and woodland into something like farmed parkland, which supported grain cultivation and vastly higher population densities. Sutton's collective reference to these developments as Hausaization obscures the fact that the creation of open savanna by Hausa cultivators was quite literally coevolutionary in the sense that the reduction of tsetse-infested bush expanded the frontiers for Fulani pastoralism and concurrently opened up a natural environment that hitherto had not been particularly conducive to human mobility, trade, and interchange. It was, above all else, a cultural ecological motion in which human practice left its indelible imprint on the ecological landscape and necessarily fabricated a distinctive mode of material life in the process. The simultaneous elaboration of an identifiable Hausa culture with an expanding agricultural frontier constituted the basis for the prismatic process of state formation in the central Sudan.[5]

Until more elaborate and detailed work is undertaken along the lines of that pursued by Y.B. Usman (1973), our grasp of the early politics and evolution of the Hausa states will necessarily be partial. Most analyses see the period between 400 B.C. and A.D. 1000 as the temporal crucible from which Sudanic civilizations emerged, for it was during this epoch that exchanges with North Africa were regularized, iron technology was in-

troduced and adapted, and camels and horses became fundamental vehicles of travel and warfare. Yet the historic detail of state formation
remains opaque except for a simple recognition that it is deeply implicated in the creation of "Hausaness" itself. We can be fairly sure that the
earliest agricultural communities in Kasar Hausa were independent
patrilineal family groups (sing., *gida*; pl., *gidaje*) organized into small,
relatively corporate communities (*kayuka*). Perhaps in some primordial
state the autonomous world of the gidaje was subject to no other higher
authority than the household head, but Horton (1971, pp. 78, 79) has
convincingly argued that ecological and demographic conditions were
especially conducive for the emergence of simple lineage forms, and even
institutional differentiation. Abdullahi Smith suggests that the contours
of these communities were provided by

> nucleated hamlets organised for crop production and consisting of family
> groups whose farmland (*gona, gandu*) was contiguous and separated from that
> of other kayuka by waste (*daji*). [H.F.C. Smith 1971, p. 162]

Sustained largely through the extensive long-fallow swidden cultivation
of millets and sorghums, the communities were constituted by a crude
social asymmetry along sexual and occupational lines. The rudimentary
division of labor provided an avenue for social stratification since the few
positions of authority beyond the household were characteristically associated with lineage totems and ancestor worship (Nicolas 1965). How-
(*sarkin noma*) and the patron of hunters (*uban farauta*) were certainly of
great antiquity and their activities probably involved ritual practice associated with lineage totems and ancestor worship (Nicholas 1965). However, the authority that such titular positions conferred was tightly circumscribed; they were in no sense governing offices and , in spite of the
emergence of the lineage idiom, the territorial criterion of group identity
was undeveloped.

Usman's study of political transformation in Katsina has shown that at
some unspecified time well before the fifteenth century, the parochial
forms of a rural life were superceded by the genesis of large settlements
composed of constellations of lineages. These towns (sing., *gari*; pl.,
garuruwa), though able to develop a more sophisticated division of labor
than the villages including full-time craft specialists, remained in many
essential respects agrarian. The protourban forms were nonetheless presided over by a town head (*mai gari*), usually the ostensible representative
of a senior lineage, who exercised direct control over individual households. In Katsina, Usman identified the authority of such rulers as based
on their control of (and identification with) the ancestor cults centered on
the tombs (*Kusheyi*) of Durbi-ta-Kusheyi. The executive authority of these
corporate settlements supervised the distribution of land, the provision of

security, and probably some forms of worship. The growth of the towns, fueled by migration and the efflorescence of trade, witnessed a parallel increase in the authority of the mai gari. Slowly, mature urban forms emerged, which subsumed the older towns and villages and proved to be embryonic forms of the territorial kingdoms. By the middle of the fifteenth century the walled town (*birni*) had displaced the town as the crucible of economic and social change, and the authority of rulers of the tombs had been undercut with the emergence of a political system centered on the institution of Sarkin Katsina. The cities were centers of exchange and migration, and acted as poles to attract migrants in search of farmland, security, trade opportunities, or a potent spirit cult (*iskoki*).

The appearance of cities (*birane*) as centers of political authority provided the basic building blocks for the territorial kingdom, the *sarauta* system, which arose in Katsina by the mid-fifteenth century and in Kano somewhat earlier.[6] Several commentators have observed the close correlation between early Hausa centers and granite inselbergs (*duwatsu*), which had a religious connotation for the pre-Islamic iskoki pantheon. In Katsina, it seems that one of the factors that encouraged the institution of kingship was the florescence of a religious center in direct opposition to the traditional ancestor cults. For example, the Earth Mother (*Inna*), a central figure in the iskoki pantheon, overrode the particularistic traditions of the past largely in response to the increasing occupational diversity and ethnic heterogeneity coterminous with large-scale immigration. New forms of worship, which transcended the parochiality of lineage idioms, were therefore capable of providing the ideological unity for the heterogeneous forces that Sutton calls Hausaization.[7]

The patterns of authority associated with the somewhat fluid urban hierarchy marked a qualitative separation from the past. The urban officeholder was not simply a titular head of the birni but was *sarkin kassa*, the ruler of the territory; he presided over both town and country. The birane were, in other words, not only diverse and cosmopolitan centers but were the loci of new forms of power. Government evolved into a complex hierarchy of specialized offices presided over by an urban-based king (*sarki*) who held jurisdiction over satellite villages and towns. While essentially dynastic in form, government was not a simple hereditary autocracy.[8] Some of the subordinate state officials (*sarakuna*) exhibited a measure of autonomy, but they were all in the shadow of the sarki's refulgence. Usman's study shows clearly how, from the powers of the Sarki Katsina, the central government derived its hegemony over territory and inhabitants alike.

Concurrent with the rise of urbanism, then, came an elaboration of the state apparatus, which gave form to the fledgling territorial kingdom. As senior lineages were invested with hereditary state offices (*sarautu*), this hierarchy of *masu sarauta* came to regulate major forms of economic activity, orchestrate palace practice, and control the army. Much compressed, this was the social form of the early Hausa states, of the famous Hausa *bakwai*.

ISLAMIZATION AND THE CALIPHAL STATE

By the end of the fifteenth century Hausaland had become "fully integrated into the commercial and ideological nexus which linked the Western Sudan societies together [and into] . . . the wide Islamic world" (Adeleye 1971, p. 492). The three centuries of development preceding the overthrow of the sarauta system involved two integrative processes. First, the network of towns, villages, and hamlets encompassing immigrant communities of heterogeneous origin was welded into a political community under a class of sarakuna. And second, expanded commodity production, migration, and long-distance trade integrated the kingdoms, in varying degrees, into the *bilad-al-Sudan*. Both tendencies were predicated on considerable descent and occupational diversity and on elaboration of central governmental functions, an important consequence of which was the expanded position that Islam came to occupy in social life. The Islamization of Hausa society seems to have been coterminous with the rise of the birni, beginning in the fourteenth century when Islam entered Kasar Hausa initially through the efforts of a community of Malian traders and clerics. By the sixteenth and seventeenth centuries, Islam had been adopted by a significant proportion of the urban commoners (*talakawa*) and throughout those densely settled and ethnically diverse rural areas fueled by immigration. In providing a matrix for social cohesion and a code for personal conduct, Islam was especially relevant for those embedded in an emerging commodity nexus since it provided an appropriate juridical framework for the proliferation of exchange, trade, and craft production. Usman (1973) is very much to the point in his observation that while the old iskoki pantheon addressed the definition and control of the individual's relation with nature, Islam concerned the regulation of social discourse and man's interaction with his fellow men.

In its historic mission Islam gradually penetrated the sarauta system, and produced a Muslim intelligentsia capable of providing leadership among rural and urban commoners distinct from the sarakuna. There were instances of Muslim sarakuna—Mohammed Rumfa (1463–1499), for instance, was the first Muslim king in Kano and in fact adopted Al-Mahili's treatise on Islamic government—who lent political support to both Islam and the clerics (*ulema*), but the latter as a class were unequivocally distanced from the loci of authority. The eighteenth century efflorescence of state power and the birth of something like an

Islamic theocracy was ultimately built on a rickety foundation. For while the populace was largely Muslim in terms of values, conduct, and identity, the nominally Islamized rulers sustained their authority from a dynastic context wedded to the iskoki pantheon. An increasingly influential Muslim intelligentsia had no institutional function in government, which was overseen by a cadre of slaves and eunuchs.

By the close of the eighteenth century the contradictions between the ideals of Islamic piety and the reality of dynastic practice and sacerdotal kingship on the one hand, and an urban elite and a rural peasantry on the other, sharpened considerably. The tension between social cohesion and political authority was expressed in a fundamental split between the *cikin gida*, the palace clique, and the *cikin fada*, the influential Islamized commoner class. The eighteenth century had, in any case, seen massive political disruption with the collapse of the Kebbi cities and the leveling of the Zamfara Kingdom. In this ethos of great political insecurity, the escalation of interbirni conflict was critical, for it necessitated increased taxation and the growth of military conscription, and doubtless much agrocommercial dislocation. It was amidst this emnity and discord that the preachings of the *malamai*, and especially of the reformist intelligentsia centered on Usman dan Fodio, offered an appropriate avenue for the expression of political disquiet.

Over a relatively short period beginning in 1796, and more formally with the defeat of Sarkin Gobir in 1804, Fodio forged a militant community (*jama'a*) that posed a direct challenge to the hegemony of the sarauta system. The ideology of the jihad supported religious reform in anticipation of a Mahdi, subverting political loyalty to the sarakuna by appealing to a nascent caliph, the *amir-al-mu'minin* (*sarkin Musulmi*). The jihad movement was governed by several distinct military contingents, led by jihadist intelligentsia (*mujahidun*) whose legitimacy was grounded in piety, learning, participation in the holy war, and association with the Shehu. It is not my purpose to review the etiology or the chronology of the jama'a period (1796–1816), which remains subject to intense debate.[9] Though many have seen the revolutionary disintegration of the sarauta government as principally an ethnic conflict in which the Fulani were pitted against the Habe ruling class, Usman (1973) has drawn attention to the limitations of sharply drawn ethnic categories that have little explanatory value in themselves other than as means of social identification. And while the revolution was necessarily bathed in a religious illumination, the territorial and occupational units that constituted the political constituency from which the jama'a was drawn indicate that the jihad was principally concerned with authority. From this perspective the following to whom Fodio appealed was, strictly speaking, transethnic; they were principally the downtrodden, disenfranchised commoners, who were for the most part heavily taxed, misguided by the officeholders, and inequitably judged.

The social blueprint held by the Muslim intelligentsia was, of course, quite unlike the model of society envisioned by the former Hausa kings. Fodio, above all else, aspired to establish a community of believers under the aegis of the Muslim state nourished by the security of *Shari'a* rule. The jihad projected a new social order; the king was to be replaced by an emir, a first among equals, whose legitimacy rested on personal piety toward Allah, in whom all authority was ultimately vested. Political process was relatively unbureaucratic, designed to limit the excesses of palace-centered sarauta rule and to redress the hypocrisy of a nominally Muslim kingship sustained in some measure by local religious belief. The architecture of the new emirate system was explicitly detailed in Fodio's exegesis on the Kano constitution, the *Diya'al-hukkam*, which was modified, adapted, and reformed by the Shehu's Caliphal successors. As Last (1978, p. 3) observed, in a sense the political and intellectual history of the nineteenth century was an extended exercise in the implementation and reform of the original blueprint. The practical political consequences of this grandiose social design was the birth of a huge Muslim community, the Sokoto Caliphate (see fig. 2.2), covering some 150,000 square miles,

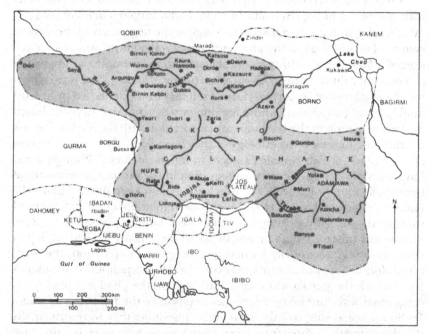

Figure 2.2. The Sokoto Caliphate. From P. Lovejoy (1978. p. 52).

which welded together the thirty emirates. This emirate system survived for one century from the accession of Usman dan Fodio as amir-al-mu'minin at Gudu in 1804, to the death of Caliph Ahmadu at the hands of the British colonial forces at Burmi in 1903. The Sokoto Caliphate was to become the largest, most heavily populated, most complexly organized, and wealthiest state system in nineteenth-century West Africa, if not sub-Saharan Africa as a whole. By 1838, the Caliphate stretched from the Touareg-controlled Air in the north to the Yoruba emirate of Ilorin 600 miles to the south, a territory that took some two months to traverse.

CALIPHAL ADMINISTRATION AND JIHADI IDEOLOGY

The presence of Shari'ah, waglis and Sufi orders thus made possible the a'yan-amir system as a viable universal pattern. . . . But [this] system in turn (with its rural foundation in a free peasantry) allowed the Shari'ah in particular to rise to the top . . . and so to maintain the universality of the whole society. . . . The only explicit unity was the Dar al-Islam itself; and that was actually effective.

—Marshall Hodgson, *The Venture of Islam*, vol. 2

The central institution of the new emirate system was the Sultan (amir-al-mu'minin), resident at Sokoto, whose authority derived from his investiture by the entire Muslim community as supreme ruler. The Caliph was bound to rule according to the Shari'a and the Sunnah, mediated through a complex process of advice and consent from the Islamic intelligentsia. Within the political community of the Caliphate, the constituent units, or cells, were the emirates. Unlike their sarauta predecessors, they were not sovereign but were subject to the discretionary powers of the Sultan who devolved power to his representatives, the emirs, who had direct jurisdiction over their territorial domains. The emir was an official of the Caliph vested with specific powers (most notably the performance of religious duties, tax collection, and material improvement) whose appointment or dismissal was the sole prerogative of the amir-al-mu'minin. The execution of emirate functions was undertaken by elected administrators who were merely functionaries of the emirate government. The territory was thus held in a quasi-vassal status with respect to Sokoto authority; the latter was in fact physically represented in the provinces by a Caliphate sarauta, usually the vizier (Last 1967). In contrast to the sarauta system, which was administered through a bureaucracy of slaves, eunuchs, and freemen, the emirate was characterized by a discrete and clear-cut aristocratic component. In practice, the aristocracy consisted of families or lineages, frequenty with genealogical connections to the Sultan, who drew their wealth from periurban estates given as territorial grants by the Caliph.

The success of the jihad, however, was followed by a period of profound political fluidity and economic deprivation in which Fodio and the jihadist leaders wrestled with the loose confederation of emirates. The gains of the jihadists were continually threatened by the guerrilla forces of the conquered Habe dynasties. The defense of the birni necessitated a far more regularized military force than the guerrilla forces of the earlier period. Furthermore the jihadists had inherited a centralized state apparatus of tax and tribute collection, which although reformed still demanded a significant bureaucratic structure. More ominously, rivalries and competition within the jihadist community soon surfaced and the struggle for state control commenced even before the initial military phase of the jihad was brought to a close.

After the death of Fodio in 1817, the new Caliph Bello retained control of the wealthy eastern emirates, which were materially critical to the economic survival of Sokoto, while the western emirates were the domain of the vizier. The central Caliphal administration deployed a plethora of personnel for the maintenance of emirate revenue, on which the Caliphate depended heavily. Household retainers, the mujahidun, the Caliph's immediate kin, leaders of local Fulani clans, and Muslim intelligentsia were all incorporated into a weighty administrative superstructure in the capital.[10] These cadres were especially active in the appointment or sanction of the emirs, in the resolution of disputes and succession, and also in the receipt and collection of taxes and tribute from the constituent emirates. Payments were made at least twice each year in addition to the revenue generated from death duties and accession tribute. Last (1978, p. 8) believes that Caliphal fiscal demands increased as the century wore on, not least because a growing international reputation could not be materially sustained by the Sokoto hinterland, which was resource poor and lacked dense agglomerations of agriculturalists.

That the Caliphate survived the serious political and economic challenges to its survival in the first part of the nineteenth century was partly due to its ideological manifesto. The exegetical nature of the early jihadi treatises on government and religious practice were intended to upgrade and purify the quality of Hausa-Fulani culture within the matrix provided by a theocratic state. In this sense, the jihadi ideology consolidated the hegemony of Islam in the Hausa states to the extent that it determined the canons of social conduct and personal behavior. The Muslim state, as von Grunebaum (1961) elaborates it, had a moral teleology and foundation, which it revealed in the enforcement of Shari'a as the supreme object of all government. The role of the state in sustaining the community of believers (*Umma*) thus became ideologically central.[11] Yet the Caliphal hagiography was distinctly sub-Saharan in timbre and Sokoto was, in a double sense, textually and geographically peripheral to the Muslim world system.

[The Caliphate] was not integrated into a single division of labor nor organized as a political- administrative dependency of North Africa. Instead, contact with the center of the Muslim world was informal. Linkages were made through the trans-saharan trade, the obligatory *Hajj*, and wandering Muslim scholars and mystics as well as the more formal organization of the Islamic brotherhoods. *Jihadi* ideology, therefore, became a theory of state building, wherein the Muslim community could expand, prosper, and disseminate Islamic learning. Moreover, by becoming a self-conscious cultural frontier of Islamic civilization, they believed themselves to be participants in a *universalistic* Muslim community. [Lubeck 1977, p. 15]

The progress of a theocratic state went hand in hand with the encouragement of literacy and the creation of a patrimonial bureaucracy, the success of which was partially dependent on Islamic scholarship and knowledge of Muslim jurisprudence.

Insofar as Caliphal rule initiated an attempt to reproduce the classical Islamic models of the early caliphs, jihadi ideology not only affected material life directly but also sustained a particular ideal of social justice.[12] Koranic precepts sought a state directed in accordance with principles revealed by Allah, the equal treatment of all believers before Divine Law and the practice of a form of mutual assistance between rich and poor. Nonetheless, an ideology of equality still left what Rodinson (1974, p. 28) calls "an irreducible residue of inequality" between slave and freeman, between merchant and farmer, which was seen as a wholly natural condition. By the same token, the jihadi mentality encouraged incorporation of nonbelievers into the Islamic diaspora through military conquest. This geographic imperative enslaved pagan populations or placed nonbelievers under direct protection (*dhimma*). Thus the fulfillment of jihadist dictates simultaneously extended political jurisdiction and absorbed and gradually reintegrated productive labor. As Anderson (1975, p. 505) observed, these ideological tendencies lent Islamic civilizations a warrior cast.[13] The state machinery of the Caliphate was not overwhelmed by a consortium of professional soldiers, but its political tone is nicely captured by Sourdel in his notation of classical Islamic society.

> The world is before all else a verdant garden whose enclosure is the State, the State is a government whose head is the prince, the prince is a shepherd who is assisted by the army, the army is a body of guards which is maintained by money and money is the indispensable resource which is provided by subjects. [1968, p. 327]

The resonance of these qualities produced a type of military predation, what Smaldone (1977) calls the war complex; it also nourished a state paternalism and slight contempt for agrarian production which is perhaps classically embodied in Fodio's poem that claims "peasants should be protected because they are orphans" (cited in Paden 1973, p. 15). Both dispositions gave rise to a powerful praetorian slave guard that capped the state apparatus. In any case, the clique of palace slave functionaries (*bayan sarki*) was structurally significant in dynastic politics, and Fika's (1978) belief that slaves had come to dominate Kano politics by 1893 is probably of some general relevance to the emirates.[14]

The point I wish to emphasize here is the centrality of the state apparatus in the Sokoto Caliphate. If Shari'a law permitted commodity production and a flourishing merchant class, neither became autonomous from the political and ideological muscle of a centralized, Muslim state. Under precapitalist conditions, superstructures necessarily are constitutive of the prevailing modes of production which "cannot be defined *except* via their political, legal and ideological superstructure since these are what determine the type of extra-economic coercion that specifies them" (Anderson 1975, p. 404).[15] I argue strongly that in the Caliphate the apparatus of exploitation was embedded in the superstructures themselves, and this is especially critical in understanding the property system—of "social relations in their totality" as Marx put it—through which the ruling class appropriated its surpluses.[16]

And yet in spite of the analytic priority I have lent to extraeconomic sanctions expressed in jihadi ideology it is perhaps appropriate to conclude with a caveat concerning the social adoption of Islam rather than with its intervention in state functions. Salamone (1978, p. 44), for instance, suggests that only 5 percent of the population in Hausaland at the turn of the century was Muslim. The persistence of prejihad iskoki cults among non-Muslim Hausa (*maguzawa*; sing., *bamugaje*) was, according to this view, considerable, perhaps because pagan communities were able to exercise a measure of self-determination predicated upon a tax payment (*jizia*) for Caliphal protection. Unlike their Muslim counterparts for whom state centralism led to the attenuation, and finally the disappearance, of unilineal descent groups—except among the Fulani aristocracy—the maguzawa social organization was based on the patrilineal sib. Down to the present, the maguzawa of Niger have maintained agnatic exogamous clans and their religion, unlike monotheistic Islam, was a clan affair associated with particular spirits (iskoki).

It is almost impossible to estimate the number of maguzawa residents in the Caliphate at the end of the nineteenth century. But the scanty evidence suggests that the proportion of non-Muslim Hausa may have been surprisingly high, lending some support to Trimingham's speculation (cited in Salamone 1978, p. 44) that nineteenth-century Islam in Hausaland was aristocratic, and ironically it was colonial rule that favored wholesale Muslim conversion. According to a 1905 resident assessment,[17] 85 percent of the Katsina emirate was "pagan," and M. G. Smith (1978, p. 33) estimates that maguzawa still constituted at least 10 percent of the Hausa emirate population in 1958. H. R. Palmer, early in his Katsina residency, observed the following at the time of conquest:

except in towns where Fulani chiefs eg: Headmen reside, eg: Ingawa, Mani, Karofi, I have never seen a "massalachi" ["mosque"]. . . . I was under the impression originally that nearly all Fulanis were Mohammedans. . . . I have frequently made inquiries on tour, and came to the conclusion that except where Fulanis have settled down side by side with Habes, they are nearly all pagans. [NAK Katprof 1 ACC 162 1905]

Much of the confusion arises, I suspect, from the persistence of prejihad institutions, which were putatively "pagan," and the strongly syncretic character of rural Islamic behavior. As Last and Al-Hajj (1971, pp. 231–240) convincingly demonstrated, the boundaries of Islamdom are fluid, and nowhere is this clearer than in the contemporary juxtaposition of a monotheistic Islam and the pantheon of individuated spirits among the residual maguzawa communities (see Barkow 1973; Nicolas 1975).[18] The patina of Muslim conversion does not alter the substance of my argument on the relations between state and Islam, but the existence of maguzawa communities and their institutional or behavioral correlates in an ostensibly Islamic countryside is of some consequence. In particular, the non-Muslim realm—if that term can be rather loosely employed—possessed a unique complex of political offices and social practices, many of which were actively maintained and widespread among their Muslim brethren, that were of great functional significance in subsistence security.

THE EMIRATES: POLITICAL AND SOCIAL STRUCTURE

Over the past thirty years almost all of the Hausa emirates have been the subject of important historical studies, the majority of which have concerned questions of political structure and dynastic development. Yet despite the growth of Nigerian historiography, essential research into the conditions of material life and the dominant forms of economic activity are still lacking. A political economy of the Caliphate remains to be written. What has emerged from the proliferation of Hausa studies, nonetheless, is a recognition of the substantial political diversity within and between the emirates. In most cases emirs were appointed on principles of heredity and seniority within a single aristocratic lineage, although in some cases appointments alternated between lineage segments and sometimes, as in the unique instance of Zaria, rotated between distinct lineages. Government in the emirates proceeded through a system of titled offices each of which was in theory an indissoluble legal corporation with rights, powers, duties, and special farms, land, and slaves. The offices constituted a hierarchical edifice built upon relations of clientage, each level of the pyramid cemented by myriad messengers (*jekadu*). The precise function and distribution of offices within the emir's domain did not, however, conform to one model. Last (1978, pp. 14–16) believes there were two broad categories. First, the lineage-based emirates in which government functions and territories were distributed among large, cohesive groups. This category can be graduated along a centralization-decentralization axis. In Zaria and Kano officeholders resided in the capital and constituted a ruling council, while in Sokoto and Katsina masu sarauta resided in the countryside. As a consequence, authority tended to be politically diffuse and orchestrated through an arabesque multitude of intermediaries and agents. And second, a minority of emirates without officeholding dynasties relied on heterogeneous aggregations of individuals, both free and slave, and were clients of the emir. In spite of the plurality of offices and its taxonomic complexity, it seems probable that the nineteenth century witnessed an increasing centralization of power, whatever the intentions of the Shehu (Paden 1973, p. 162). This contamination of the jihadi mission was a reflection of growing security, the stabilization of the *ribats* in the periphery, and economic growth.[19] But as many central offices usurped the authority of their territorially based counterparts, ruling lineages sought to remove the encumbrance of central opposition—and hence the threat of seizure of the emirship itself—by an expansion of royal slave appointments (*cucanawa*).[20] The growth of central bureaucracies simultaneously provided the opportunity for expanded state intervention in production itself.

Figure 2.3 illustrates the ideal-typical tripartite structure of government in Katsina emirate during the 1870s. First, the slaves of the emir (bayan sarki), as the primary executive arm of the government, were responsible for the conduct of official palace business. The most senior slave, the *magayaki*, supervised the collection of the principal tax, *kudin kassa*, and stood at the apex of a diverse yet corporate clique; and whose authority extended to the regulation of economic activity, militarism, law and order, protocol, fiscal matters, and commerce. Second, the lineage-based free *sarakunan sarki* as senior advisors to the emir presided over the middle-level administrators, the *hakimai*, who themselves held jurisdiction over frequently noncontiguous territorial "fiefs." And, third the *'yayan sarki*, the city-based royal kin who, though politically potent, were administratively weak; they were often given towns which they absentee managed via a complement of "representatives" (*jekadu*). Hill (1977, pp. 1–3) describes the major responsibility of the organs of central government as the regulation and supervision of the "fiefholders," the *sarakunan kassa* or hakimai, all of whom were attached to definite lineages and who operated through their own agents in the lower echelons of the settlement hierarchy. As Weber's description of patrimonial bureaucracy suggests, the affairs of the state were inextricably grounded in the consummate authority of the emir; consequently dynastic change necessitated a dramatic turnover in the emirate personnel who occupied client

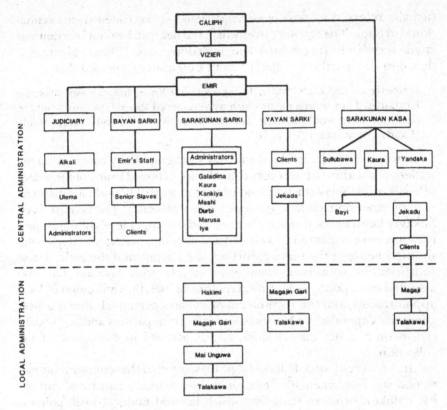

Figure 2.3. Pattern of government and administration, Katsina emirate about 1880.

niches within the bureaucratic edifice. In sum, then, high-level emirate government was composed of offices each vested with unique rank, prestige, tradition, rights, and authority (*iko*); territorial administration was effected through prebendal allocations[21] from which taxes, labor, and military forces were levied; and each emirate capital, irrespective of the extent of bureaucratic decentralization, contained a palace (or court), a treasury, a prison, markets, mosques, a prayer ground and state compounds.

The grass roots levels of the administrative hierarchy were probably more uniform than central superstructures since, like much of West Africa, the fundamental social unit was the household aggregated into larger entities specified by territorial or kin affiliation. Within the local territory of each *hakimi*, settlements were presided over by village or town heads (*masu garurnwa*); the towns, as in the prejihadic period, constituted the basic administrative unit. Town representatives, like the hakimai, appointed their own officials for hamlet (kayuka) or ward administration (usually referred to as *masu unguwa*), generally recruited from occupational groups. The territory over which the hakimai held jurisdiction was characteristically fragmented and noncontiguous. Palmer, giving evidence to the Northern Nigeria Land's Committee, reported that

> formerly the big chiefs lived in the big towns like Kano, and they were absentee landlords. They owned towns which were scattered about. One town would be east, one town would be west, another would be north, and another south. [Lands Committee 1910, p. 78]

Even where an individual hakimi held a geographically coherent estate, settlements within that territory could be apportioned to any of the palace officials, while small tracts of land or even groups of households might be held by other nonresident patrons or palace officials.[22] The decentralized linkages between local representatives and the upper levels of the administration were cemented by a class of agents (sing., *jekada*; pl., *jekadu*) who shuttled between the masu garuruwa, the hakimi, and the emir. These functionaries concerned themselves largely with taxation but also assumed basic police and juridical responsibilities, the ratification of local appointments, and the recruitment of military personnel. Junior offices generally depended on benefices and gifts from patrons and an "unofficial income" from the talakawa, largely accrued in the course of tax collection.

In her recent work Hill (1977, p. 16) suggested that emirate administration was fundamentally flawed in its hierarchical structure of authority. Unlike European feudalism which labored under a weak political summit, the Hausa state had an apex with no substructure, a distortion that stemmed in part from a settlement hierarchy dominated by a primate city. She believes that Kano people were "people lacking hierarchical systems of chieftancy and village administration" (p. 22) and is accordingly puzzled by the question "How was the socio-political structure [of Kano] maintained in the absence of both a . . . institutionalized hierarchy of authority and of segmentary lineage systems" (p. 16). This is a confusing issue since Usman, whom she quotes, argues quite convincingly that the emirates were, to a very large extent, politically integrated entities. Under the massive load of rural autonomy, which Hill imposes, the state apparatus and its reproductive demands almost disappear altogether. But the state necessarily intervened *directly* in the internal nexus of surplus extraction, and it is the imbrication of economic exploitation with extraeconomic institutions that gives the Caliphate its unique political form. Moreover, even if we capitulate and assume that the formal properties of authority were attenuated, the administrative structure top heavy, and the fiscal demands of the state slight, this should not obscure how other political networks fostered integration between town and country. Two of these subsystems are crucial: first, the cleric (ulema) and merchant networks and the Islamic brotherhoods described by Tahir (1975), which I discuss in some detail later in this chapter; and second, the so-called *chaffa* or *chappa* system.[23] The latter, referred to by Glenny[24] as a "confusing system of administration," has superficial parallels with the *uban daki* functionaries described by Low (1972) in Hadejia whose nominal power overran that of local village heads. Local administrators were the nonresident chappa heads who had fief over *families*, not land. These ties were not necessarily by location, occupation, or some other classification but were "partly based on historical connection and custom and for the rest on inclination" (NAK Sokprof 85/1906). Chappa patrons accentuated the confusion by employing separate collectors for each tax.

> The confusion is rather accentuated by the . . . custom of employing a separate collector—not for each unit—but for each tax . . . i.e. a unit consisting of 25 compounds may own 5 separate ubandakis who employ 3 separate collectors each, the total of all taxes shown under that particular unity having therefore been contributed to by 15 different collectors [NAK SNP 7 6166/1909, p. 30].

The chappa system amounted to ramifying sets of patron-client relationships, extending far beyond the geographical proximity of the border emirates in the eastern plains, where it was undoubtedly widespread. An early Katsina Resident noted, for example, that

> the people who did not recognize the local head had chaffa with some other important chief. Though they resided in the town, they only recognized the local maigari insofar as they paid him land rents if they farmed there. . . . I found exactly the same state of affairs in the large towns of [Kano] . . . quite one-fifth of the inhabitants of Isa (?) and Dawaki districts had chaffa with some important personage in Kano, so that in many cases the maigari where they lived dare not collect . . . rents from them [NAK SNP 10/6 3835/1909].

M.G. Smith (1978) describes a parallel system of territorial administration in nineteenth-century Daura referred to as *tarayya* or *tarewa*.[25] These words had two overlapping connotations; one subsuming informal clientage and the other pertaining to the jurisdiction exercised by two or more officials over individuals who were scattered in local communities.

> the specifically political form of *tarayya* was based on relations of personal allegiance between a commoner and some official other than the fiefholder and was normally established by the commoner, who sought out the *ubandaki* and declared his *cafka* (loyalty, allegiance) in return for the official's protection and aid. Normally commoners only took such action to secure political assistance in the face of repeated threats or oppression from agents of their lord [Smith 1978, p. 72].

Through these sorts of bifurcating chains of allegiance and clientage, through Hill's "mysterious tax collectors and 'political officers' " (1977, p. 17), rural communities were linked to centers of power.[26] To obsess over administrative "deformities" as Hill does is to misconstrue the nature of the state and its material basis. Indeed, I argue that it is these sorts of connectivities, whether of quasi clientage or of formal state intervention, that constituted critical threads of the moral economy of the peasantry.

Caliphal society in the nineteenth century was stratified along two principal axes; first, between officeholders (including their kin, clients, and slaves) and those engaged in farming, trade, and craft production; and second, between free and slave populations. The former included aristocratic lineages, the palace client community, the ulema and the commoners (talakawa) and the latter "luxury slaves" (Fisher and Fisher 1970), the praetorian guard who were part of the emir's palace entourage, and domestic or predial farm slaves. The boundaries between classes so defined are necessarily pervious; scholars and slaves, for instance, are not easily situated in such a social matrix. But as Last (1978, p. 21) suggests, distinctive features of the office-oriented were both their relative immobility and a concern for genealogical descent, dynastic alliance, and the rules of patrilineal inheritance. Conversely, the talakawa maintained (with the exception of the non-Muslim Hausa) a territorial or ethnic identity rather than a precise genealogical notation. M.G. Smith (1978) and Tahir (1974) both suggested that Hausa society was also stratified through a number of relatively fixed occupational classes recruited through agnatic descent.[27] This ranking included both dynastic officeholders, whether hereditary or achieved, and Koranic scholarship.

Ranking below the masu sarauta and the Islamic intelligentsia were the wealthy merchants (*attajirai*), long-distance traders, tailors, blacksmiths, commission agents, builders, weavers, dyers, tanners, barbers, butchers, eulogists, drummers, and finally field slaves. These status differences were both informed and reinforced through ramifying networks of clientage, a form of social relation not found to the same extent among maguzawa or nomadic Fulani. In its institutional expression, clientage embraced menial domestic clientage (*baranci*), relations among craftsmen (*mutumci*), and political affiliation (*barantaka*). Finally, the role of women in these systems of occupational stratification and clientage was decidedly secondary insofar as Hausa custom and Islamic law defined them as political and legal minors. Women nevertheless maintained clientage relations among themselves, were active in the household economy, and contributed valuable labor time to craft and agricultural production.[28] In the nineteenth century, only the wives of men of high rank were in purdah (*auren kulle*).

From the sixteenth century onward, slavery was a critical element of emirate social structure. In spite of the proliferation of historical research concerning both palace and farm slavery, estimates of the proportion of slaves to free men—which range from ten to sixty percent—are still the subject of considerable debate.[29] It seems probable that slavery grew significantly throughout the nineteenth century since captives were a solution to a chronic manpower shortage and, through ribats and slave settlements (*rumada*), a means of securing political stability along the margins of Caliphate territory. We are, however, currently in a much better position to evaluate the "relation of slavery" in the Caliphate, namely, how servility was represented legally, culturally, and ideologically. For the most part, Caliphal slavery has been viewed through the lens of kinship (see Miers and Kopytoff 1977) in which slaves were incorporated or absorbed as quasi kinsmen. Slaves were allowed to own property (including slaves), to devote labor time to their own ends, and to redeem themselves.[30] Slaves begotten on their master's estate and reared as Muslim Hausa were, by custom, inalienable and were socially incorporated through kin solidarities (M.G. Smith 1978, p. 44). Of course, royal slaves with political or administrative functions enjoyed wide political immunities and privileges compared to first or second generation farm slaves.[31] But both were nonetheless slaves in the sense that they were equally subject to "an individualized condition of powerlessness, natal alienation and dishonor" (Patterson 1979, p. 40).[32]

Work by Smaldone (1977) and Tambo (1976) has explained how the acquisition and concentration of slaves progressed, particularly in the aftermath of the abolition of the slave trade. The critical role of emirate warfare and close ties with indigenous merchant's capital enabled the ruling class to partially produce their means of production and build a "plantation system" through labor control. Hill (1977) quite correctly emphasized that slaves also worked alongside sons in gandu on small-scale farms. Hogendorn (1977) and Lovejoy (1978) clarified the labor process under slave conditions, particularly supervision, discipline, punishment, and work routinization, all of which suggest that the purported integrative mechanisms, especially on large slave estates (*gandaye* or *rinji*), may have operated tardily at best. Suffice to say here that slavery was a significant, not an epiphenomenal, social relation in the Sokoto Caliphate. The extent to which slavery was a major structural force, and in some sense was determinative in the social order, is explored in a more explicit theoretical fashion in the following section.

THE ECONOMIC STRUCTURE OF SOCIETY

In all forms of society it is a determinate production and its relations which assign every other production and its relation their rank and influence. It is a general illumination in which all other colors are plunged and which modifies their specific tonalities. It is a special ether which defines the specific gravity of everything found within it.

—Marx, *Grundrisse*

Production, simply put, means making things. But humans do not just make textiles or chop wood; nor do they produce as an abstraction. Rather, they fabricate and fashion things in specific ways that necessitate particular social relations with others engaged in production. All human beings, then, "enter into definite connections and relations with one another and only within these connections and relations does their action on nature, does production, take place" (Marx 1849, p. 80). Production, as Marx observed, is a twofold relation, being both natural and social. He also established, however, that these determinate, productive relations and ideas about production are produced and reproduced along with the products themselves (see Corrigan 1980, pp. 1–3). Social life while predicated on material production, also requires the renewal, on a continual basis, of the means and forces of production.

> Whatever the form of the process of production in a society, it must be a continuous process, must continue to go periodically through the same phases. A society can no more cease to produce than it can cease to consume. When viewed, therefore, as a connected whole, and as flowing on with incessant renewal, every social process of production is, at the same time, a process of reproduction. [Marx 1967, I, 531]

It is an understanding of the Sokoto Caliphate as a system of social reproduction that I seek to schematize here. My exegetical remarks start with the economic structure of society,[33] which, following Cohen (1980, p. 63), I take to mean the whole set of its productive relations. These relations are "relations of effective power over persons and productive forces, not relations of legal ownership"; the productive relations that form the economic structure Marx referred to as the *social relations of production*.[34] Productive forces, conversely, are understood as the means of production (instruments of production, raw materials, or space) and labor power (the productive faculties of producing agents). Marx posed these forces as "elementary moments" of the *labor process*.[35]

THE LABOR PROCESS AND MATERIAL LIFE

The Sokoto Caliphate was overwhelmingly agrarian in character. If Hill's (1977, p. 18) demographic speculation of ten million at the turn of the century is at all plausible, then at least 80 percent of this total resided in the countryside engaged very largely in agricultural pursuits. In the savannas of the central Sudan wealth lay in "the production of an agricultural surplus and proximity to the desert, with its strong demand for grain, other foodstuffs and manufactured articles" (Baier 1980, p. 21). This was not an urban society as conventionally understood, regardless of the flattering European descriptions of Hausa assiduity or cosmopolitan trade termini like Kano and Katsina;[36] it was a rural economy, an agrarian society based on a complex admixture of long-term swidden (shifting), short-term fallow, and permanent systems of agriculture diversified by the raising of cattle and small livestock and dry season irrigation. This "Sudanic complex," to use Murdock's epithet, was a seed culture—principally sorghums and pennisetum millets—thriving on the light, sandy upland soils (*jigawa*) of the Hausa plains. In his turn-of-the-century description of Hausa agronomy, Imam Imoru actually inventories over twenty major cereal, root, and legume domesticates including peppers, indigo, groundnuts, and cotton, the latter confined largely to the heavier *laka* soils and higher rainfall zones in southern Katsina, Zaria, Kano, and parts of the Sokoto-Rima valley. The particular constellation of cultigens grown varied latitudinally, sorghums predominating in the wetter southern plains while the northern limit of rainfed (roughly 300 mm per year) millet agriculture lay in the Sahel proper, bisecting Adar and Damerghou.

The upland millet-sorghum complex, which provided the bulk of the means of subsistence for rural households, was complemented by three other agricultural endeavors. First was irrigation of low-lying riverine (*fadama*) gardens devoted largely to "luxury crops" like manioc, sugar cane, onions, tomatoes, rice, tobacco, cotton, henna, and a variety of herbs.[37] These labor-intensive horticultural systems achieved higher technical levels, and thrived where edaphic and market conditions permitted, notably in the penumbra of Hausa cities for which many of the market garden commodities were ultimately destined.[38] Richardson (1853, p. 275) and Barth (1859, vol. 3, p. 57) both described in detail the emir of Damagaram's magnificent gardens near Zinder and Mirria.[39] The second endeavor was game hunting and the gathering of sylvan produce, including the fruits of a large number of semicultigens used as supplementary foodstuffs and as the raw material for local craft and petty commodity production (see Echard et. al. 1972; Dalziel 1937).[40] And the third was livestock production, which formed a mixed economy in association with upland cultivation. Virtually all households possessed a number of small ruminants, especially sheep and goats, which functioned both as organic (and relatively liquid) capital and sources of manure for farms. Cattle, which were not equitably distributed among households, were entrusted to Fulani shepherds in districts of high population densities and land scarcity where the risks of crop trampling and fodder shortage were accordingly magnified.

By the early eighteenth century precolonial agricultural systems were able to support very high population densities—in some areas in the order of 300 per square mile. These close settled zones (CSZ) in Kano, Katsina, and perhaps the Sokoto-Rima valley, were sustained on permanently cultivated holdings by considerable inputs of organic fertilizer and crop rotation. Certainly in Kano emirate, and very probably in the vicinity of *birnin* Katsina also, districts were actually deficit in grain production, a condition no doubt related to the proliferation of full-time craft specialists. This underproduction was made good by large-scale food imports from regional breadbaskets like Zamfara, southern Katsina, Damagaram, and Gobir. But as a general rule, there is no reason to assume that the extension of cleared land by settled pastoralists, immigrant households, and imported captive labor significantly reduced uncultivated bush which remained in surfeit in the peripheral emirates.

Given the configuration of a short growing season and potential redundancy of household labor during the long dry season (*rani*), the majority of adult males devoted considerable labor time to at least one craft or trade (*sana'a*). Artisanal and petty commodity production were generalized household functions that far surpassed the sufficiency of immediate needs. Blacksmiths forged agricultural tools, axes, and housewares while potters, dyers and weavers, calabash makers, mat weavers, roofers, granary builders, cobblers, and tanners all plied their trades in a vital artisanal exchange economy. Craft production nonetheless was located within the household rather than in formal guild or lineage structures. Labor originated and was predominantly controlled from within the gandu unit; production, usually undertaken on a part-time basis, resonated with the small-scale qualities of a peasant economy.[41] Shea (1975) demonstrated, nonetheless, that for the rurally based Kano textile industry, the development of a huge export-oriented dyed cloth industry was predicated on full-time specialists and an influential merchant class who engaged in a limited form of petty commodity production secured through the employment of client, slave, and wage labor. But even artisans who were engaged in year-round commodity production still secured familial subsistence through slave-labor farming (M. G. Smith 1954, p. 19).

In some cases the manufacturing industries were significant economic enterprises; Barth's (1857, vol. 1, p. 511) conservative estimate of the annual turnover of Kano cloth sales alone was over 300 million cowries during the 1850s. The character and organization of textile production also highlights the fact that the geographic loci of these trades was unequivocally in the Hausa countryside not in the birane. Data presented in table 2.1, abstracted from a turn-of-the-century colonial assessment report in Katsina emirate, highlights the variety and volume of rurally based crafts, confirming Shea's supposition of nonagricultural commodity production beyond the urban arena. This complex artisanal division of labor was characteristically based on convergent productive

TABLE 2.1
RURAL CRAFTS, YANDAKA DISTRICT, KATSINA ABOUT 1909

Craft	Number
Builders	33
Shoemakers	9
Barbers	32
Tailors	305
Tanners	65
Butchers	148
Beekeepers	163
Brokers	52
Blacksmiths	94
Salters	39
Weavers	1,282
Dyers	769
Total:	2,991

SOURCE: National Archives Kaduna (NAK) SNP 20 266p/1909 Yandaka District Assessment Report.

NOTE: Total population, 27,827; total compounds, 6,826; compounds with no craft-trade activity, 317.

interests; occupational strata were catenary systems linked through customary preferential marriage (for instance weavers and dyers) or clientship (leatherworkers to tanners).

A good deal of craft production in the countryside was clearly intended only for local consumption, that is, for barter and exchange rather than strictly for exchange value.[42] Conversely, Kano produced textiles that entered the international circuits of trade centered on the northern Saharan termini, while other rurally produced commodities, particularly cotton cloth, leather goods, small livestock, and minerals such as natron, iron, and tin, were also projected into wider regional trade systems. Using the significant work of Shea, Polly Hill (1977, pp. 14–16) has resolved that the division of labor between town and country was tightly segregated. Much transport and production, in Kano at least, was certainly rurally based. But she has pressed much farther and asserted that (i) there were very few linkages between the birane and the countryside,[43] and (ii) *most* artisanal production was located in rural environs. With respect to the latter, the cities evidently engaged in specialist craft production, particularly some forms of metal working, the production of military hardware, and perhaps tanning (see Collion 1981). Furthermore, the hypothesis of rural autarky completely ignores the form and function of urban-based merchant capital, which had secured a prominent site in the political and economic architecture of the Caliphate, particularly as agricultural investment and commodity production grew in the course of the century. Tahir's (1975) work on early merchant-ulema networks reconstructed what he rather spuriously calls "primitive corporations," which seem reminiscent of pre-Restoration Japanese patrimonial firms; they were enormous commercial edifices resting on complex patterns of kinship, clientage, slave labor, and religious affiliation. These wealthy merchants stood at the apex of patrimonial commercial organizations that integrated the production of crafts and food—especially cloth and grain—with credit services, patronage, protection, and commercial support. In the Sokoto Caliphate, as in many other African societies, the merchant and the scholar tended to be closely linked, if not one and the same person.[44] Tahir's (1975, p. 275) recovery of Tulu Baba's mercantile empire during the 1830s is instructive for it consisted of fifteen slave estates in four emirates, one factor agent in Gwanja, and three cloth "corporations" in Kano. One leather merchant, Sharuf-na Tsakuwa, produced annually in excess of 22 million cowries worth of leather goods and supported 150 slaves, 20 commercial clients and 50 wage laborers in eleven Kano villages, which en masse constituted the primary production center. In addition, Tsakuwa controlled rural clients, suppliers, and manufacturers in nine northerly emirates. The conflation of merchant capital and the Muslim clerics produced vast, ramifying networks that were not residual elements in a predominantly peasant economy. On the contrary, merchant-ulema complexes were predicated on extensive geographic ties of primary clientage and trust (*amana*), and the mai gida stood as the fountainhead of a huge commodity producing edifice, that locked town and country together in a mutually supportive embrace.

The expanded function of what Rodinson (1974, p. 6) terms precapitalist merchant capital is also in evidence in the mine economy. Though basic historical research remains to be undertaken on the subject, it is probably safe to assume that strategic raw materials such as iron and tin fell within a regional trade system in which merchant capital appropriated, through unequal exchange, a large surplus, but was (as Shea observed in the Kano textile industry) increasingly exerting its hegemony at the point of production itself. The principal iron ore deposits seem to have been located along the southern edge of the Hausa plains between Mandara and Yauri (Jaggar 1973, p. 24; Usman 1973, p. 11); conversely, tin was geographically confined to southern Kano and the plateau (Freund 1981). In both cases, mineral deposits attracted migrant labor; iron workers (*yan tama*) from Daura and northern Katsina for example traveled south in the dry season to Kankara, Birnin, Gwari, and Koriga. Mining and smelting were labor-intensive, employing large numbers of wage and slave workers; but it seems to have been the smelter owners and the merchants who controlled regional distribution to the urban centers and to specialized artisans.

A full understanding of the Caliphate formation, however, must be grounded in the wider matrix of the central Sudanese regional economy, a human ecological mosaic in which the sedentary agricultural system was fully imbricated in the affairs of the pastoral sector (Baier 1980, pp. 12–21). Although the northern Sahelian desert edge was climatically marginal for the cultivation of rainfed millets, a vibrant livestock economy sustained large numbers of nomadic pastoralists and the complex confederacies of the Air massif. The extreme spatial and temporal variability of Sahelian precipitaton, which supported the traditional rangelands, necessitated considerable herd mobility. These dry-season circuits of transhumant activity, particularly the seasonal southward retraction into the moister savannas, provided the ecological basis for a sort of pastoral-sedentary mutualism, a mechanism that actually surpassed a simple dry season visitation by Touareg or Fulani herds.

The pastoral sector consisted of two ethnically discrete communities: the northern Berber-speaking Touareg centered on the fertile valleys of the Air massif, and the cattle Fulani of the northern savannas. The former, while subsisting in large measure on cattle products, also required grain to supplement their diet, particularly during the dry season as livestock lactation rates fell off markedly. In part the grain demands were met from Touareg sedentary estates staffed by individuals of servile ancestry, frequently located within Hausaland in the savannas.[45] The bulk of the grain requirements were met, however, through the *asalay* trade[46] in which Hausa-produced millet (principally from Damerghou and Damagaram) was exchanged for goats, sheep, cattle, and salt. The Ful'be were savanna pastoralists properly speaking, with a long record of interaction with sedentary agriculture throughout the western and central Sudan. The patterns of movement and the detail of the Fulani transhumant circuits in the nineteenth century suggests a fluidity modulated in relation to military activity and the ongoing process of sedentarization. Immediately prior to the arrival of the colonial forces in Nigeria, there were at least three major pastoral circuits in northern Katsina, for example, principally associated with a series of active market towns along the northern periphery of the Caliphate. Ful'be nomads traded with sedentary Hausa farmers exchanging animals and milk products for grain, cloth, leather, iron tools, and weapons.[47] Pastoral households made arrangements with farmers to graze their animals on postharvest crop residues in return for the provision of manure or specialist herding services like cattle entrustment.[48] But above all, the division of labor between pastoral and agricultural economies was dynamic and changing. Throughout the nineteenth century sedentarization was encouraged by the emirate administrations; and the continuum of mobility was inextricably bound to the changing economic and climatic fortunes along the desert edge.

The Caliphate was firmly situated in a regional economy in which a dazzling array of social adaptations to the savanna environment—involving ethnic, occupational, political, and religious associations—were woven together into a human ecological tapestry. Specialized commodity production fitted into a wider nexus of West Africa trade. At the end of the nineteenth century, the Kel Ewey and Kel Gress Touareg confederations dominated the trade corridor between Air and the emirate birane while the Hausa trade diaspora controlled the agricultural, craft, and mineral exchanges to the south and southwest. Both circuits supported diaspora communities in the savannas, providing brokerage, security, and other service functions. Wealthy Hausa merchants, Ful'be noblemen and Touareg aristocrats all invested in agricultural production and artisanal manufacture, simultaneously fulfilling crucial merchant and finance capital services.

The complicated social and technical division of labor[49] that I have sketched was constituted by a variety of definite labor processes, which were structured by a set of social relations of production. The transformation of nature requires that production be divided into discrete functions requiring specific forms of labor cooperation and use. In the Caliphal economy, the fundamental unit of production and reproduction was the household (gida),[50] a corporate body for economic and social functions, which defined the dominant labor process, the abode as it were of production itself. In its most protracted guise, the gida embraced sons, clients, and slaves in a cooperative gandu structure:

> In the nineteenth century . . . the *gandu*, which was the primary type of organization for farming, included slaves and their descendants. They were assimilated in some degree as kinfolk of the *gandu*-head. . . . Sometimes the slaves' huts were situated within the same walled or fenced enclosures as those of the owners' family, though in a different section, . . . [It] functioned as a single unit for production and consumption of food, the payment of tax, the provision of farm tools, and seeds, the common exploitation of land . . . and other resources and the provision of brides for members of the group. [M. G. Smith 1954, p. 27]

The expectations, reciprocity, and obligations within the gandu structure have been well documented.[51] What concerns me here is less the institutional expression than the cooperative forms of the labor process. The collective basis of household production was often expanded into larger work groups (*gayya*) essentially cooperative in nature and called by individual farmers to overcome labor bottlenecks in the agricultural cycle.[52] Of course, few societies are monotypic, and most span a variety of labor processes that are unevenly subsumed by the dominant relations of production. In the case of the Caliphate farm slavery was prominent, if regionally variable, but it was not in a statistical sense dominant. Many farm slaves were woven into household fabrics as quasi kin or clients. Equally, the political economy also included corvée labor service generally recruited by officeholders for purposes of estate production, military recruitment, or civic reconstruction and, if we are to believe Rowling (1949) and Last (1967, p. 104), there was a nascent sharecropping system. And in spite of Hill's obdurate claim to the contrary (1977, p. 129), the commoditization of production had also extended to the labor relation itself.[53] Wage labor (*kwadago*) existed for dry-season rice cultivation in the Kebbi valley, among migrant cotton workers in southern Katsina, and fadama market gardening in Damagaram, not to mention the appearance of the wage relation in other spheres of commodity production like house construction, leather manufacture, iron working, and the dyed cloth industry. Yet in all cases these systems of labor mobilization in agricultural production were subservient to the household.[54] This applies equally, I believe, to craft production and the mine economy. In characterizing a highly commoditized tin sector, Freund correctly observes that:

> [I]t seems likely that wage labor, slave labor and other forms of labor control were present at the various stages of the production process. However none functioned definitively outside of the context of the *gida* . . . tin production may have distended *gidaje* relationships but it did not apparently break them. [Freund 1981, p. 28]

In one important respect, however, artisanal production did differ from agriculture insofar as the forces of production in the agrarian sector, irrespective of the labor process, were relatively undeveloped. Based on an ancient farm technology, the technical division of labor was simple, at least in upland cultivation.[55] Shea's work (1975, p. 157) on technical innovation in the dyeing industry (from clay pots to *laso* lined pits) and Freund's proleptic discussion of tin smelting (1981) both suggest a vastly more sophisticated precolonial technical division of labor.

THE SOCIAL RELATIONS OF PRODUCTION

[I]n all forms in which the direct laborer remains the "possessor" of the means of production of his own means of subsistence, the property relationship must simultaneously appear as a direct relationship of lordship and servitude, so that the direct produce is not free; a lack of freedom which may be reduced from serfdom to a mere tributary relationship.

—Marx, *Capital*, III, 771

The period following 1855, the Caliphate experienced a boom in trade and production, based in large measure on a prodigious investment in agricultural infrastructure. The settlement of new areas made possible by imported captive labor proceeded apace; land was cleared and gradually improved through fertilization, drainage, and crop rotation.[56] Cattle routes were protected, wells dug, and ribats staked out for a hitherto unprecedented security. Increased agricultural output, according to Last (1978, p. 27), permitted an increase in acreage devoted to cotton, onions, and groundnuts, which plausibly fostered a proliferation in trade and craft production. Urbanization and commoditization flourished in a manner that suggests that the Caliphate economy was no less dynamic than its politics. As Shenton (1982, p. 8) noted, the possibilities presented by the social relations of production were continuing to unfold on all levels.

While the minimal productive unit throughout the nineteenth century was incontrovertably the household, this is an otiose conclusion because the domestic unit is therefore deposited as a "digit in a series," to use Edward Thompson's (1975, p. 487) felicitous phrase. Rather, a proportion of household labor was expropriated by a ruling class (masu sarauta) as a socially defined surplus. And my remarks here address the social relations of production that permitted this siphoning of surplus labor from the commoner economy. That is to say, those relations of effective power over persons and productive forces that can be conveniently represented as relations of ownership (Cohen 1980, p. 63).[57] I argue that control over labor and land in the Caliphate, upon which surplus extraction ultimately rested, must be understood in relation to political intervention and in the ideological basis of state power.

The largely self-sufficient world of the gidaje was integrated into a state structure through the expropriation of surpluses by taxation. The aristocratic hakimai had tenure over territory, either as contiguous tracts or as widely dispersed settlements drawn together by ties of clientage. Irrespective of the geography of residence or lineage affiliation of the officeholder, the territory was granted as a gift by the emir. As Shenton and Freund (1978) suggest, these fiefs functioned as tax farms. Virtually all officeholders and notables among the ulema-merchant community, in addition to administrative territory, also possessed private estates (gandaye) worked by kin, slaves (bayi), clients (barori), and wage laborers (yan kwadago). In these precapitalist circumstances in which an overwhelmingly agrarian economy did not, as a dominant relation, presuppose the separation of the laborers from the means of production, appropriation of surplus labor can be understood as a form of precapitalist rent (Hindess and Hirst 1975, p. 189).[58] The direct producers—that is, the vast majority of Hausa-Fulani hoe farmers—had possession of the means of production of their own labor power. Precisely because this condition held, precapitalist rents presupposed a mechanism by which surpluses could be appropriated since there was no economic compulsion to do so. In short,

> pre-capitalist rent presupposes the political/ideological subordination of the direct producers to the exploiting nonlaborers. The surplus product is extracted in the form of rents (payment for the right of the use of the land) and by a noneconomic mechanism . . . [by] a form of state in which direct producers are subject to the exploiters. [Hindess and Hirst 1975, p. 190]

Ideological and political intervention in the Caliphal social relations of production did not, however, follow a classically feudal model of the European ilk (Nzimiro 1978). Rather, the state itself, sustained by Muslim ideological apparatuses, directly extracted peasant surpluses. This configuration is what Hindess and Hirst (1975, p. 192) refer to as a tax-rent couple, a form also evoked by Marx.

> Should the direct producers not be confronted by a private landowner but rather . . . under the direct subordination of the state . . . then rents and taxes coincide. . . . The state is the supreme lord. [N]o private ownership of land exists although there is both private and common possession and use of land. [Marx 1967, III, 771–72]

This theoretical derivation poses land as state property, cultivated by subjects who have effective possession of the means of production. Surplus assumes the form of taxation for the right of possession, and use, and it is this fiscal system that sustains the state apparatus. I now turn to the totality of these social relations, beginning with the Caliphate tax-revenue system.

The major source of emirate income was derived from an arabesque assortment of taxes levied on agriculture, manufacture, trade, and personal properties and collected through legions of subordinate officials. A number of taxes were designated generally as *kharaj* or kudin kassa (literally "land money"), the latter being a legacy of the prejihad period co-opted after 1804 as a legitimate Islamic impost. For the most part, however, revenue systems varied enormously between and within emirates and accordingly have been a source of much intellectual debate and confusion, perhaps most painfully evinced in the proceedings of the Lands Committee in 1910. There was, for instance, no kharaj in Sokoto and Gwandu since all land was declared territorial *wakf*; that is, it was not conquered territory but Dar-al Islam. Land taxes were sometimes graduated with distance from the birni,[59] sometimes levied per head as a poll tax, occasionally on the household, or per plot and, in the unique case of Zaria, on the hoe. What is certain amidst this prodigious diversity, nevertheless, is that taxation was ideologically legitimate. As Palmer (in Paden

1968, p. 1305) observed, kudin kassa was "customary and legal" while all the levies lay within the rubric of Islamdom.[60]

> All taxes on Mohammedans which we found in existence, (except the Kurdin Kasa) were based upon the Zakat. Even though the imposts on certain crops, trades and individuals had the appearance of capitation rates arbitrarily fixed, they were in origin an attempt, and apart from abuses in collection, to some extent, a sensible and practical attempt to arrive at the prescribed fraction of the annual income of the taxpayer. [Gowers 1921, p. 51]

Doubtless corruption in the collection system and the excesses of levies on accession to office (*kudin sarauta*) or *gaisuwa* (gifts) tainted the purity implied by Gowers, but what concerns me is less the circumvention of Shari'a norms than the fact that it underwrote state appropriation.[61]

The surpluses appropriated by the state assumed three fundamental forms: (1) labor rent, largely drawn as corvée for public works and on demand (*girma da arziki*) on the farms and estates of the officeholders (*gandun sarauta*); (2) rent in kind, most particularly the grain tithes; and (3) monetary rents levied on some special crops and craft goods.[62] The principal tax-rent triumvirate of the late nineteenth century consisted of, first, *zakkat*, a 10 percent canonical grain levy obligatory for all adult Muslims, which being paid in kind supplied the sarakuna with their means of subsistence through extra-market channels.[63] Zakkat also embraced the cattle tax (*jangali*) raised on nomadic pastoralists and levies on nongrain commodities, particularly *kudin shuka* (on groundnuts, cassava, cotton, and gourds) and *kudin rafi* (on irrigated crops like wheat, tobacco, sugar cane, and onions).[64] Second, the kudin kassa or kharaj, an impost on all householders, which was, according to Palmer, "an ancient family tribute for the right of cultivating certain hereditary property" (cited in Lubeck 1968, p. 11).[65] And, third, the taxes on crafts (*kudin sana'a*), collected by elected occupational officeholders, but which varied enormously in their incidence between trades and emirates. Shea (1975) showed how levies on textile production, for instance, were held deliberately low in the Kano close settled zone to encourage the dyeing and weaving industry,[66] and were abandoned altogether in Sokoto and Gwandu. A brief inventory of the major tax-rents in Katsina and Damagaram at the turn of the century appears in table 2.2.

It is probably safe to assume that rents fluctuated throughout the nineteenth century both in terms of their individual magnitude and relative importance. Usman suggested that the *kudin tausa* (kharaj) in Katsina oscillated between one and three thousand cowries, finally settling down to approximately 1,200 by the arrival of the colonial forces.[67] In a similar fashion, the division of revenue and the collection of taxes was highly variable; Fika (1973, p. 267) cites, as a general principle in Kano, a

TABLE 2.2
Tax Systems About 1900

Tax	Katsina	Damagaram (Zinder)	Kano
Kudin kassa (tausa, karo)	1200 c. per farm (gona)	5500 c. per adult male	4000 c. per farm
Jangali	5000 c. per householder	1 calf per herd	10,000 c. per herd (?)
Zakkat	one-tenth of grain harvest	110 zacca**	one-tenth of harvest
Kudin shuka			
Potatoes (dankali)	1200 c. per plot (garka)	1200 c. per plot	3000 c. per plot
Groundnuts (gyada)	1200 c. per plot	1200 c. per plot	3000 c. per plot
Cassava (rogo)	1200 c. per plot	1200 c. per plot	3000 c. per plot
Kudin rafi			
Onions (albassa)	3000 c. per farm	2200 c. per plot	3000 c. per plot
Tobacco (taba)	3000 c. per farm	(no data)	(no data)
Henna (lalle)	3000 c. per farm	(no data)	(no data)
Wheat (alkama)	3000 c. per farm	2000 c. per plot (?)	1200 c. per plot
Al'adu (Kudin sana'a)			
Weaver (masuka)	2400 c. per person	1200 c. per person	none
Dyer (marina)	3000 c. per dye pit	1200 c. per person	700 c. per dye pit
Tanner (majema)	2400 c. per person	1200 c. per person	none
Butcher (mahauta)	2500 c. per person	10,000 c. per person	(no data)
Salt cutters (masu gishiri)	2400 c. per person	5,000 c. per person	(no data)
Blacksmith (makera)	10,000 c. per person	10,000 c. per person	(no data)
Brokers (dillalai)	5000 c. per sale	3,000 c. per sale	(no data)
Bori* (masu bori)	1200 c. per person	(no data)	(no data)

SOURCES: National Archives, Kaduna (NAK) SNP 17/8 History of Katsina; Palmer papers, Jos Museum; Collion (1981); Salifou (1971); Gowers (1921).

NOTE: c = cowries

*Spirit cult practitioners

**Zacca = 0.875 kg.

holy trinity that divided the rural surpluses: one-third to the *dagatai* and jekadu, one-third to the hakimai and one-third to the emir. In Katsina it is less clear whether, and how, a formal distribution such as this eventuated, and certainly Palmer paints a picture of a much more erratic system.

> The point is that you have a clique, viz., the governing class. In Kano it is specially large. There are thousands of men who formerly were the minions of the Emir, and who collected the taxes. A very large proportion of the population of Kano are of this tax-gatherer class—the upper classes. In fact, I know one little town which has a hundred tax-gatherers—Dan Zabua. [Lands Committee 1910, p. 75]

Palmer modified this entropic view of taxation a few years later when he pointed out that prior to 1905 the jekadu collected all taxes excepting in those districts that conspicuously controlled their own revenue systems. The craft taxes were certainly collected by individuals assigned to specific occupational groups, and who paid a fixed sum to the emir. What is less opaque, however, is that in spite of the organizational diversity, and apparently labyrinthine and fragmented character of the fiscal system, the state consciously participated in the buoyancy of the regional economy.

The legal basis for precapitalist rents rested upon the intricate ideological and political relationships between the state and prevailing categories of property. In his important discussion of the classical Muslim empires Perry Anderson establishes that state monopoly of conquered land became a traditional legal canon of Islamic political systems. And yet the limited authority of existing political machinery, and the fact that the juridical existence of a land monopoly mitigated against precise concepts of property, produced "endemic vacillation and chaos" with respect to Muslim landed property (Anderson 1975, pp. 497–99).[68] This extreme juridical indetermination in the agrarian sphere "beyond the ultimate claim of the rule of the totality of the soil" (Anderson 1975, p. 498) was classically represented in the Caliphate, and was doubtless one source of the astonishing confusion expressed by early political officers in northern Nigeria in coming to terms with the tremendous local variation in peasant land and occupancy rights.[69] The indeterminacy arose from the threefold derivation of land tenure: (1) Shari'a law; (2) local custom, often involving prejihadic elements of great antiquity; and (3) *iyasa*, or the discretionary power of the ruler (Meek 1957, p. 63; Frischman 1977, p. 70). Under malikite interpretation all land belonged to the Muslim community vested in the amir-al-mu'minin who held it in trust for the faithful.[70] As Withers Gill (NAK SNP 76565/1908), an early political officer succinctly put it, land was on loan (*abin aro*) from the emir through his representatives, the village heads. The emir was in practice the trustee or agent (*wakil*), for all land belonged, in an ideological sense, to the Mohammedan state. According to Koranic law, all land was vested in the community, and hence juridically private property could not exist; rather a secure right to possession was based on tax payment mediated by and subject to the ambiguities of local custom.[71]

> "Thus it is seen that though the peasant has not a fee-simple in his land"—that is to say, not the absolute property in his land—"he has in theory, even now, a right of possession subject to the payment of taxes of a farm that he has bought." [Palmer, Lands Committee 1910, p. 70]

In spite of the purportedly "communal" character of land, property relations were a unique synthesis of maliki law and native custom. This should come as no surprise since "in each historical epoch, property has developed differently and under a set of entirely different social relations" (Marx cited in Corrigan 1980, p. 4).[72]

For the upper classes, land over which they had power (*malaka*) was of two kinds: first, the district, territory, or settlement they supervised; and second, land occupied either as a private estate or as a gandu attached to political office. As regards the first, the masu sarauta were the agents of the state, though possessed, in theory, a certain veto power over who could and could not cultivate. While they could not sell or rent this land, by custom many of the hakimai, for example, did sell the right of possession to commoners. Emirate rulers could and did grant land to influential and well-connected merchants (Tahir 1975, p. 299). Furthermore, many of these ruling class properties were tax exempt as *hurum, haraji,* or chaffa holdings.[73] As regards ordinary farms, the peasantry cultivated land that was transmitted to their heirs, and was obtained either by occupation of bush (daji) with, in theory, the consent of an agent of the state, or by a grant of an already existing farm. Subject to the payment of rental on a year-by-year basis, the average peasant had exercised considerable security of tenure within the bounds of local custom albeit bounded by the juridical capacity of the emir to dispossess. Throughout the emirates, hire (*ladan gona*), pledge (*jingina*), loan (*aro*), gift (*kyauta*), and inheritance (*gado*) were all permitted with respect to land transactions.[74] In practice, then, to use Palmer's words,

> in letting or transferring his right [of possession] an occupier is dealing with a right which is his own, for the consent of the Malikin Kassa is neither sought nor required. [NAK SNP 7 6565/1908, p. 4]

As Palmer's observation suggests, because of the autonomy of local tenurial systems, the plasticity of Shari'a law and the pressures imposed by population growth, land scarcity, and increasing commoditization, the much vaunted "communal" principle of nonalienation of land was seriously under siege by the late nineteenth century.[75] Palmer also noted that irrigated plots (*rafi*) and houses stood in a unique class since they were rented, leased, and (more critically) bought and sold as private property (*dukia*). It is clear, however, that in areas of high population density in which village and field boundaries had been well established for hundreds of years, the distinction between possession and freehold was increasingly chimerical.[76] Forde and Scott's observations on farm purchase are worth citing at length in this regard.

> After the Fulani conquest, the office, which offered opportunities for lucrative tax farming, was often bestowed on followers or sold by the new rulers. While the district head was always in theory only a functionary with no property rights as such in the district he supervised, he was often able, where the demand exceeded the resources, to exact large presents for assigning farmland to new claimants and for recognizing succession by descendants. Thus a practice of disguised purchase has grown up in some heavily farmed areas and regular transfer values for land have become established. [Forde and Scott 1946, p. 121]

In practice, the private estates of the masu sarauta and the farms of many peasants were de facto private property in the strict sense of paying no tax, having security of tenure, little possibility of dispossession and being highly commoditized. In this sense, Hiskett (1968) and Anderson (1970) seem quite correct in their assumption that freehold in its most complete form was at least known in precolonial Hausaland varying in degree from place to place.

MODES OF PRODUCTION AND THE MATERIAL BASIS OF THE CALIPHATE

> The specific economic form in which unpaid surplus labor is pumped out of the direct producers, determines the relations of rulers and ruled, as it grows directly out of production itself and in turn reacts upon it. Upon this, however, is founded the entire formation of the economic community which grows up out of the production relations themselves, thereby simultaneously its specific political form.
>
> —Marx, *Capital*, Vol. III

It has not been my purpose to present a general political economy of the Caliphate but instead to sketch the contours of its economic structure and specifically the matrix of powers in which production occurred. It presents, however, a somewhat flat, lifeless view of human practice and requires both a genealogical depth and internal dynamic to render a historic perspective and depth of field. The recent modes of production debate is an attempt to revivify African historiography by identifying the dominant forms of extraction of surplus labor and the practices that occupy the determinant place in the social formation.[77] Much of this discourse has degenerated into an abstract and sterile taxonomy of lineage, pastoral, slave, or Asiatic modes or of "overlapping modes of production." Rather than enter directly into this debate, I believe there is good reason to decompose these highly abstract theoretical precepts into a number of lower-order concepts (see Kitching 1980, p. 5). For this reason, my reference to a mode of production is embarrassingly specific, which, following Cohen (1980, pp. 79–84), refers to three constitutive concepts: the purpose of production, the form of the producer's surplus labor, and the mode of exploitation.[78] The question is, then, how the dominant mode of surplus extraction provides (to use Marx's marvelous phrase) the general illumination that colors other productive activities and modifies the specific tonalities of social and cultural life. To do so is to grasp the Caliphate as a "societal field of force" (Thompson 1978, p. 151), of antagonisms, contradiction, struggles, and reconciliations, which, I argue, provides the basis for both an understanding of the moral economy of the peasantry and of the impact of the colonial state.

In light of the earlier discussion of the labor processes and the social relations of production it is now clear that the surplus labor that sustained the state apparatus and its ruling cadre did not enjoy a single origin. Taxation of rural producers, slavery (either as exchange capital or through their labor time on elite estates), and long-distance trade (especially in luxury commodities) have all been elevated to the status of structural determinants in a characteristically African mode of production. Amin (1972) and Coquery-Vidrovitch (1976)[79] in particular have emphasized "the combination of a patriarchal agrarian economy . . . and the exclusive ascendancy of one group over long-distance trade" (Coquery-Vidrovitch 1976, p. 106). Shackled by the low level of development of the forces of production and a marginal physical environment, precapitalist rents were meager; they were symbolic gestures that "maintained" a social structure rather than providing a material substance for society at large.[80] In such a case,

> long distance trade makes possible, through its characteristic monopoly profit, the transfer (not, of course, the generation) of a fraction of the surplus from one society to another. For the receiving society, this transfer may be of vital importance, and may serve as the principal basis of the wealth and power of the ruling classes. [Amin 1972, p. 508]

Of course it is well known that exchange was intrinsic to the Caliphal political economy whether it was the honeycomb markets of local households, the peripatetic short-distance traders centered on rotating or periodic marketplaces, or the acclaimed trans-Saharan trade systems (Hopkins 1973). However a close examination of regional exchange suggests that the social reproduction of the Caliphate can hardly be accounted for, either theoretically or empirically, through the realm of circulation.[81] First, internal long-distance trade, which involved relatively few commodities, was often rurally based and, as Richmond Palmer noted, "the bulk of the trade does not come to [towns] at all." Caravan tolls certainly generated revenue but a heavy incidence threatened the vitality of trade itself and risked merchant antagonism. However, the international systems—to Asben and Hoggar, to Borno-Kawor-Tibesty, to the northern Saharan cities like Tuat and Ghadames, and to Gwanja[82]—did not lay in the hands of the sarauta class, who in any event did not participate *directly* in trade (Tahir 1975, p. 232). Rather Touareg, North African, and Hausa merchants' capital organized and controlled the operation of the caravans. Clearly an alliance existed between the sarauta and the merchants since the realization of surplus depended upon the consumption of elite goods by the state functionaries.[83] But the state apparatus was comprehensively dominated by the officeholding class and (while the merchants reaped the benefits of unequal exchange and the deepening of commodity relations) sumptuary laws, maliki inheritance, and the land tenure system all mitigated against long-term capital accumulation by merchants as a class. The sarauta, conversely, desired revenue from trade, and acquired luxury goods through which their ideological hegemony over the talakawa was measured and maintained and, particularly in the first half of the century, benefited materially from the slave trade since captive labor was both an export commodity and productive capital on sarauta estates. Trade may indeed have had more than a cameo role in the genesis of the state, but its structural significance at the end of the nineteenth century was less a measure of its own ability to appropriate surpluses for social reproduction than the increasing commoditization and dynamism of a society in which state, merchant capital and Muslim intelligentsia were historically conducive to trade expansion.[84]

Slavery conversely is of some consequence because captive labor was directly involved in the productive process—on large estates, alongside familial recruits on household farms, and in local manufacture—and because Hausaland is conventionally seen as a "high density" slave formation (Klein and Lovejoy 1979, p. 208). The Sudanic pattern of slave recruitment and use actually entered a new phase in the late eighteenth century, which the postjihad warrior state further deepened through a military-commercial alliance. First, while state militarism became the principal instrument of slave production, the Islamic warriors depended on merchant capital for the realization of the value of captive labor. And second, the demise of the Atlantic slave trade coupled with the dictates of

Caliph Bello's (1817–37) mandatory settlement policy, "internalized" the role of slavery as captives were settled productively on rinji, in ribats, and incorporated into the household farm system (Last 1978; Lovejoy 1978). Lovejoy has traced the genesis of a distinctive plantation sector to this internalization; plantations apparently "dominated" agricultural production by 1850, most especially of grain, cotton, and indigo. They were controlled by merchants and officeholding aristocrats and worked by large-scale, supervised gang labor. Indeed, according to Lovejoy and Klein slavery assumed a determinative quality and a distinct "mode of production";[85]

> it was self perpetuating, for it was based on enslavement as an institutionalized process. It was therefore related to a different mode of production, a slave-producing mode. The functioning of the slave-producing state was based on the export of slaves either within Africa or outside. In this system of production, control was confined to a relatively small class of people who directed the military and headed the states that negotiated exports. Before the nineteenth century, the slave "producers" were often not slave exploiters. They absorbed slaves largely as warriors and not as farm labor, and sold the majority to traders. It was within the commercial sector that nineteenth century slave-exploiting states emerged . . . slaves were essential to the reproduction of society. [Klein and Lovejoy, 1979, p. 209]

The theoretical question of the existence of a slave mode of production is not my principal concern here but I believe Meillassoux to be correct in his surmise that "slavery always appears in association with other relations of production . . . and the ruling class cannot be defined strictly only in relationship to it" (1975, pp. 20–21).[86] Rather, I wish to understand the dynamics of the relation between slavery and society. This mode of articulation presupposes three social aspects: (i) the dependence on slavery, (ii) the nature of that dependence, and (iii) the direction of dependency in systemic terms (Patterson 1979, p. 60). It is uncontestable that captive labor was politically and ideologically significant in the Caliphate; military slavery was an intrinsic part of the jihadi mentality, political and administrative structures were inconceivable without this institution, and individual slaves exerted a profound influence in politics, public administration, and warfare. If slaves were agents of state power they were also the means of accumulation in the agrarian sector. Masu sarauta employed farm slaves on estates attached to political office largely for grain production to support their huge kin- and client-based households. Hill (1977, p. 129) is certainly right to point out the lucrative opportunities for large-scale slave-based production in an expanding and highly commoditized economy. But Lovejoy (1978) has implausibly inflated the degree of dependence on the institution. In some of the northern and peripheral emirates, perhaps less than 10 percent of the populace was servile,[87] and while Kano and Sokoto may have been high-density systems, we are after all referring to a society constituted by perhaps 8 to 10 million "free" peasants. Further, one obvious test of internal dependency is to examine the process of abolition, which was effected in northern Nigeria quite painlessly.[88]

To understand the political economy of the Caliphate is necessarily to grasp the complex interdigitation of warfare, jihadi ideology, and the "production of slaves" by the sarauta class. To this extent slavery enters into the equation of social reproduction. But the systemic articulation of slavery in society was a reflection not simply of labor shortage per se but of the costs of slave acquisition,[89] labor control,[90] and slave reproduction. The latter, for second generation captives, was not inconsiderable, particularly in an agrarian system in which labor was potentially idle throughout the dry season with the result that patterns of slave rights emerged to defer these reproductive costs. The rights of ownership and production that farm slaves possessed converged with the slaveholders' ideology of the Islamic patriarch, assimilation, and the possibility of manumission. In short, the political, economic, and ideological tendencies in the Caliphate were toward the *production of peasants* who, if not entirely free, could at least be taxed or retained in a quasi-client status.[91] This process of peasantization was entirely congruent with the growth of the Caliphal economy after 1850 and embodied in the increasing trend toward wage labor, especially in high-value commodity production like fadama cultivation, textiles, and mining. In sum, then, one finds a dynamic sectoralization of a dual economy, a slave sector and a peasant sector of free or semifree labor.

My own position is that the material basis of the Caliphal economy was provided by the political and ideological control of land through a state dominated by an officeholding class. Following Suret-Canale (1969, p. 120), I believe that "the fundamental exploited class [was] the working peasantry."[92] In a society in which the vast majority of direct producers maintained possession of land and experienced a low level of economic subsumption, surpluses were accrued through rents, that is "a politically based exaction for the right to cultivate . . . [whose] level will depend upon the coercive means available through the State" (Hindess and Hirst 1975, p. 258). This resulted in what Marx called the "overlapping" or "mixedness" of the state and economy.[93] The state, then, becomes central in the Sokoto Caliphate because

> State-forms are related to the social relations and conditions of specific modes of production in their historical development: State-forms are not related

contingently and accidentally, nor are they related externally . . . as a coercive set of relations, but rather *internally*. [Corrigan 1980, p. 5, emphasis mine]

After the jihad, Islam naturally fulfilled a legitimizing function providing the ideological basis and justification for state extraction and coercion and, as the century wore on, for increasing political centralization and state involvement in production.[94] The Caliphal state operated in a wider "field of force" in which merchant capital and the institution of slavery were of signal importance. But the fundamental polarity was between subject and state; the state apparatus and the sarauta class were coterminous in their hegemony over the talakawa. The presence of slaves, merchants, craftsmen, laborers, and malamai complicated this class division but did not transform it.[95] Nonetheless, as I explain in chapter 3, these were real limits to state predation in the countryside. Hegemony was expressed in complex patterns of strength and weakness, imposition and deference, choice and constraint.

SUMMARY

I have sought to show how the Sokoto Caliphate was a complex agrarian formation in which merchant capital, petty commodity production, slave estate agriculture, and wage labor all flourished in varying degrees. In the social reproduction of this system, however, the relation between state and peasantry dominated the political economy. The state-form under Islamic hegemony was overwhelmingly the domain of a prebendal officeholding class. To the extent that the masu sarauta held the reins of the state apparatus they were sustained individually by slaveholding and estate production and by the class of Muslim clerics and intelligentsia from whom they, in part, derived and nourished their ideological legitimacy. The extraction of surplus labor through precapitalist rents and the state's involvement in the Caliphal economy were both given expression through an admittedly indeterminate jurisdiction over land and territory. Since the state was able to participate directly in the regional economy, and also benefited from expanded commodity production of cotton, wheat, tin, and iron through direct taxation, it is to be expected that the sarauta developed symbiotically with merchant capital. The alliance between the sarauta and merchant capitalist classes was in fact sealed through the canons of deference (girma da arziki), and what Tahir (1975, p. 223) refers to as "grace, favors or protection (*alforma*)."

Commoditization proceeded apace, reducing the autarky of rural communities and providing new opportunities in trade as the circulation of commodities intensified. A greater proportion of the social surplus was canalized to the merchant capitalists, who increasingly interposed themselves in the actual process of craft and agricultural production.[96] By the mid-nineteenth century, merchants had coevolved with ulema ties in the countryside and laid the foundations for the emergence of huge commercial but nonetheless patrimonial enterprises subsuming estate grain production, wage, client- and slave-based manufacture, and highly integrated regional distribution networks.[97] It seems probable that inheritance and sumptuary laws mitigated against long-term accumulation among merchants, although our understanding of the changing political tension between merchants and officeholders is usually lost amidst the detail of dynastic histories.

In some respects, this exegesis resembles Taylor's (1979, pp. 182–84) description of the Asiatic mode of production in which the state extracts surplus labor (as tribute) and is ideologically legitimized in this function. The state also acts as an organizer of the means of production through massive agricultural investment, communal land redistribution, and the organization of crop rotations. The Hausa states certainly participated in the reproduction of the prerequisites for production—largely via fiscal measures, grain storage, and the production of captive labor—but in no way did it organize the means of production. In a sense the Caliphal state was partly parasitic, in some respects suspended over and loosely anchored in society. For this reason, while the role of ideology was critical in the reproduction of society as a whole, it did not impose massive restrictions on capital accumulation or private ownership of land, as Taylor suggests for the Asiatic mode. Accordingly the brief history of the Caliphate was far from "unchanging" or "stagnant," as Marx described the Orient. The emergence of wage labor, land transactions, and merchant corporations pays eloquent testimony to this dynamism. Indeed I suggest that it is the peculiar role of merchant capital that simultaneously exerted a corrosive influence on socioeconomic structures (Marx 1967, III, 323–27) yet reinforced the power of the existing ruling elite that lends Caliphal society its progressive and contradictory qualities.

In summary, the configuration of state-form and the complex alliances between merchants, ulema, and officeholders made for a dynamic political economy. And yet without labor and land as fully commoditized the Caliphate could not be characterized by commodity production in the full sense of the term (Brenner 1977, p. 51). In Marx's words,

> money and circulation can mediate between spheres of production of widely different pre-capitalist organization whose internal structure is still chiefly adjusted to the output of use values. [Marx 1967, I, 328]

Brenner's (1977, p. 36) observations on precapitalist structures (systems of surplus extraction and property), which tend to fetter the application of the means of production in relation to the development of cooperative production, are entirely relevant to the Caliphate.[98] The prevalence of individualized household production, the predominance of politically based surplus extraction and the peculiar property relations encouraged by the amalgam of Shari'a and local custom, tended to mitigate against massive investment in land or industry, but fostered expanded participation in trade (see Hodgson 1974, p. 136 ff.). Yet the very significance of mercantilism provided its own contradictory dynamic, nourished by the ulema and sarauta alliance.[99]

Class consciousness was not, however, a simple reflection of these material stimuli. While the basic issues around which class conflict centered were largely those of land tenure and taxation, the ideological framework of the Caliphate mediated overt conflict. From the time of the jihad, grievances were given expression through support or opposition to the Caliphal structure, reflected through the prism of dynastic politics, through the commitment to a particular Islamic brotherhood, or via a commitment to the Mahdist tradition. Tyranny, as Shenton and Freund (1978, p. 12) put it, was primarily understood in terms of a deviation from or violation of Islamic norms, and rebellion was usually directed toward a particular ruler rather than at the ruling class qua class. So fashioned, political or class consciousness did not pose a direct threat to the hegemony of the Caliphal state system.

* * * * * *

These skeletal remarks on the Caliphate economic structure provide a critical context for the following discussion of security, risk, and food production in which I focus largely on the rural sector and, more specifically, on the minimal unit of production, the peasant household. One can quite legitimately refer to peasants in the Caliphate insofar as household reproduction was primarily based on vertical and horizontal reciprocal ties for the renewal of the means of production and subsistence (Friedmann 1980, p. 163). Though direct producers were part of the commodity circuit, access to land, labor, and credit, was still mediated through institutionally stable nonmarket ties. I argue that food and famine can be understood only in terms of these nonmarket ties, in terms of a moral economy. Yet to grasp this moral economy among peasants (their cycle of reproduction) one must necessarily return to Thompson's wider field of force that embraced both the state-form and the constellation of productive relations that I have schematically portrayed.

3

FOOD, FAMINE, AND CLIMATE IN THE NINETEENTH CENTURY

*L'accident climatique n'est, comme il arrive souvent, qu'un
élément provocateur; et il fait jouer des causes profondes,
humaines, plus durable que lui.*

—*Le Roy E. Ladurie*

During the early 1970s, much of Sahelian and
Sudanic West Africa lay in the clutches of a crushing famine that devastated the pastoral and agricultural sectors along the desert edge. Its basis lay in a run of consecutive drought years beginning roughly in 1968–69. Since that time, the Sahel has gained a sort of textbook notoriety, including an appearance on the cover of *Time* magazine under the somewhat dubious notation of "creeping deserts." Depending upon one's ideological spectacles, the desert edge calamity is viewed as an archetypical example of poor land use, desertification, local or global climatic change, "bad ecology," Malthusian population pressure, or massive economic dependency. A substantial literature on the consequences of famine for the social fabric of Sudano-Sahelian societies, most especially the impact on pastoral communities, has specifically addressed the deterioration and demise of indigenous institutional and cultural practices. There is a strong implication in much of this work that the drought eroded the institutional basis of these historic societies, and that the *malaise paysanne* was, in part, an environmental problem; it was the legacy of long-term occupation of what is a rather poor piece of agricultural real estate. Much of the early work implicitly assumed, quite wrongly I believe, that drought and famine were phenomena for which the savanna dwellers were conceptually and practically unprepared. I am not intimating of course that the impact of climatic variability was not real or potentially disruptive; but if scholarship addresses only questions of harm done, then "climatic history must remain wedded to the study of short-term crises" (de Vries 1980, p. 630). Le Roy Ladurie raises, however, another problem entirely in his simple observation that climate is a function of time, "it varies; it is subject to fluctuation; it has a history" (1971, p. 7).[1] Because climate is

historical—because the long term is important—we cannot naively assume that Sahelian farmers were (or are) wholly ill-equipped for meteorological anamolies like drought. In fact, in the semiarid tropics in particular "normal" rainfall is something of a fiction; for those whose survival is secured largely or wholly through rainfed agriculture, variability is *the* existential norm. In the long run, in other words, societies adjust and adapt.[2]

An appreciation of the long term, of the environmental context of social evolution, is exciting because it throws the individual climatic event into a new light and reaffirms the central role of human agency. All historians of climate run the grave risk of a naive anthropocentrism that converts the contextual significance of climatic variation into the climatic interpretation of human history. Geographers have been particularly sensitive to this legacy of determinism bequeathed by Elsworth Huntingdon. But it has perhaps been the Annales school that has pushed farthest in the historiography of climate, armed with a healthy respect for climatic context yet with a skepticism, if not distrust, of simple meteorological determinism (Le Roy Ladurie 1959; de Vries 1977; Piuz 1974). It was Fernand Braudel, for example, who pronounced in his *Capitalism and Material Life* that there was

> the possibility of a certain physical and biological history common to all mankind [which] would give the globe its first unity well before . . . the industrial revolution. [Braudel 1973, p. 19]

The dimensions of the debate on climate and society extend, of course, well beyond the Annales work, and a wide-ranging exchange has endured between members of a series of frontier disciplines.[3] What has emerged, I think, are two broad thematic areas of discourse. The first is *climatic reconstruction*, the documentation of short- and long-term chronologies of climatic change, a task shared by meteorologists, geographers, palynologists, dendrochronologists, and historians. And the second is the impact of climate on history, whether fluctuations of climate react on social life—what Le Roy Ladurie (1971, p. 22) calls "ecological history," and what I term *conjunctural*. The latter embraces the empirical consequences of annual climatic perturbations on prices, harvest quality, disease, demography,[4] the communication of cyclical variations in weather to economic life,[5] and long-term, human adaptation to climatic variability.[6]

I touch upon both climatic and conjunctural themes but my principal concern is adaptation in the broadest sense: on the one hand, the relation between long-term climatic variability and social life; and on the other, how long-term structural adaptations operate in relation to short-term climatic change, particularly drought. These foci raise two important

methodological questions. First is the question of climatic chronologies
and meteorological data in an African context. Over the past twenty years
our historical understanding of tropical climates has advanced immea-
surably, particularly for the African Pleistocene. Yet a chronic paucity of
lake-level, dendrochronological, and palynological research still hampers
the reconstruction of past environments and of the climatic conditions
that produced these geographies (Nicholson 1976). Although only the
broad contours of late Pleistocene and early Holocene paleoclimates are
available to us, the patterns of climatic anomaly in the recent past are no
less opaque. In her exciting work on climatic oscillations in the Sahel over
the past half-millennium, Nicholson (1979) mined a huge, if somewhat
patchy, deposit of geological, historical, geographical, and meteorological
data.[7] Yet, of her own admission, there are extraordinary limitations
imposed by the absence of written climatic records prior to 1900, not to
mention the historiographic pitfalls of an overdependence on travel
journals, oral accounts, and inconclusive palynological studies. Sadly,
there is no equivalent in northern Nigeria to Titow's (1960) extraordinary
discovery of thirteenth-century manorial archives in Winchester, which
extensively document local meteorological change. In comparison with
the surfeit of quantitative data in Le Roy Ladurie's work on the history of
European climate since the year 1000, the poverty of African climatic
sources is overwhelming.[8]

The second question relates to a caveat concerning my preoccupation
with rainfall. Quite clearly, the environmental context to which Hausa
farmers have historically adapted was not simply climatic. Other environmental perturbations that constituted threats to savanna dwellers included not only variability in rainfall but also disease, pest and weed
infestation, and erosion. However in an agrarian society almost wholly
dependent upon subsistence provided by rainfed upland agriculture,
precipitation becomes *the* critical parameter.[9] Since temperatures in
Hausaland rarely fall below 42°F. (the critical threshold for plant growth)
the growing season is contingent upon the quantity and distribution of
annual rainfall. Further, the predominantly aeolian and highly perme-
able soils characteristic of the Caliphate carry a large soil-water deficit at
the onset of the rains, and cereals are largely dependent on the distribution and quantity of precipitation. The historically changing character of
the relationship between drought and subsistence provides the frame of
reference for this study.

NATURE AND SOCIETY

From the specific form of material production arises a specific relation of men
to nature.

—Karl Marx

Any study that purports to address the relationship between climate and subsistence security is, in the widest sense, attempting to illuminate the complex and historically changing form of the dialogue between nature and society. An understanding of this relation lies at the root of much geographical enquiry, and it is entirely appropriate that geographer Clarence Glacken (1967) in his epochal intellectual history of the idea of nature should insist that any knowledge of the natural world is intrinsically historical. Glacken was at pains to establish the antiquity and embeddedness of particular views of nature and culture—the organic analogy for instance—and the historic watershed in the eighteenth century after which ideas of nature were

> [of] an entirely different order, influenced by the theory of evolution, speciali-
> sation in the attainment of knowledge and an acceleration of the transforma-
> tion of Nature. [Glacken 1967, p. 705]

The emergence of Darwinism, and later of ecology (the study of evolving living systems as integrated complexes), and the adoption of the ecosystem concept marked a new phase in the interactive approach to society and nature. This powerful ecological framework spawned a host of new intellectual devices, such as cultural ecology and natural hazards, and relied heavily on concepts derived from general systems theory to provide "a holistic view of Nature" (Anderson 1973, p. 180). I believe nonetheless that all such ecosystemic approaches are confined by an often subtle dependence on one or more varieties of the organic analogy; they reflect, therefore, a specific view of society as a living system and of man as an ecological dominant. This is perhaps most explicit in the influential work by Vayda and Rappaport (1967) in which human society is conceptually treated like any other biological population in a web of ecosystemic relations. The character of "man-environment interactions" is then seen through the particular biological lens of adaptation. Rappaport (1979) voices this opinion in its most sophisticated form when he talks of human society as one form of living system; in all living systems, processes of adaptation—or adaptive structure—inhere within them. In his words,

> I take the term adaptation to refer to the processes by which living systems
> maintain homeostasis in the face of both short term environmental fluctuations,
> and by transforming their own structures, through long term nonreversing
> changes in the composition and structure of their environments as well [Rap-
> paport 1979, p. 145].

It is at this point that the intellectual conduit which links biology to systems theory becomes clearest. Ecological anthropology in particular, eager to throw off the earlier criticisms of adaptation as a protean term that was seemingly tautological, has adopted a cybernetic view of adaptive process in social life. Specifically, societies are seen as *general purpose systems* whose goal is nothing more than survival; that is, they can be conceived of as a class of "existential games" in which "there is no way of using winnings ('payoff') for any purpose other than continuing the game for as long as possible" (Pask 1968, p. 7). Society and nature are engaged in the specific forms of interaction that follow the general model of Slobodkin and Rapoport (1974) on orderly adaptive structure. In this view,

> successful evolution requires the maintenance of flexibility in the response to environmental perturbation and that this flexibility must be maintained in the most parsimonious way. The parsimony argument is that organisms must not make an excessive or unnecessary commitment in responding to perturbation, but at the same time the deeper responses must be ready to take over to the degree that the superficial responses are ineffective. [Slobodkin and Rapoport 1974, p. 198]

At the instant of environmental change a series of responses is triggered within complex systems that can be ordered in terms of activation time and commitment of resources. The graduation of responses with respect to time also orders them in terms of depth of commitment. As a theoretical focus, then, adaptation becomes cybernetic, organized, and hierarchical, since "all biological and evolving systems . . . consist of complex cybernetic networks" (Bateson 1972, p. 13). Building upon this parsimony model of human adaptation, Vayda and McCay (1975) advocated an approach that begins with environmental perturbations like drought to highlight both the Darwinian character of social life, and the capability of human systems to reproduce themselves in variable, and often threatening, environments.

This recognition of adaptive capability even in technologically undeveloped cultures has been of some interest in African historiography, particularly with regard to the vitality of precolonial economy. Feierman (1973) for instance, working on the history of the Shabaa, devoted much attention to the "complexity of adaptation . . . to their environment." Patterns of local exchange, a skilled understanding of local ecology, and a variety of socially constructed coping mechanisms, permitted the Shabaa to "defeat famine, to cheat death." Kjekshus (1976), also writing on East African precolonial economic history, pressed still further. Reacting against the view that precapitalist social life was largely indolent and slothful, he stresses their "dynamic and integrated character," the buoyancy of local productive systems, and the variety of agricultural adaptations.

> The precolonial economies developed with an ecological control situation—a relationship between man and his environment which had grown out of centuries of civilizing work of clearing the ground, introducing managed vegetations, and controlling the fauna. The relationship resulted in an agro-horticultural prophylaxis. [Kjekshus 1977, p. 8]

Kjekshus goes so far as to suggest that famines were actually "less preva-
lent in the pre-colonial period"; that periodic catastrophes due to structural imbalances and maladaptations of colonialism replaced the random
disasters that characterized the nineteenth century.

I have raised the whole question of adaptation in relation to my
concerns because at one level I wish to distance myself from it, most
especially from any theoretical axiom that poses society as a type of
self-regulating, self-organizing living system isomorphic with nature itself. This is not the place to engage in a critique of human ecology, but its
essential weakness is captured in Bateson's favorite illustration of man-
nature interaction.

> Consider a man felling a tree with an axe. Each stroke of the axe is modified or
> corrected, according to the shape of the cut face of the tree left by the previous
> stroke. The self-corrective (i.e. mental) process is brought about by a total
> system, tree-eyes-brain-muscles-axe-stroke-tree; and it is this total system that
> has the characteristics of immanent mind. [Bateson 1972, p. 317]

I argue that such relations, including the complexities of drought and
subsistence, are never a priori cybernetic. To return to the Batesonian
motif, humans never simply chop wood. Rather humans enter into a
specific relation with the wood in terms of a meaningful project whose
finality governs the terms of the reciprocal interaction between man and
tree (Sahlins 1976, p. 91). For Sahlins this is a cultural project, a symbolic
order of intersubjective meanings in which nature is harnessed in the
service of culture. But it is above all *social*, and presupposes a wider system
of material *production*; as Marx put it, animals collect but only humans
produce "through the appropriation of nature by the individual within
and through the mediation of a definite form of society" (cited in Schmidt
1972, p. 68). This production is not simply survival, for societies survive in
a *specific, historically determinate way*; they reproduce themselves, albeit as
systems, but also as certain kinds of men, women, classes and groups, not
as organisms or aggregates thereof.

In this chapter, I assume—in keeping with the human ecological
work—that social systems are conceptually prepared (and able) to reproduce themselves in the face of recursive stress, such as drought.[10] But I
believe that the specific form of this reproduction in the Sokoto Caliphate
cannot be understood by posing Hausa farmers or the Hausa state as
cybernetic entities.[11] Rather I adopt a political economic perspective in
which nature somewhat separate from society has no meaning. This is not
simply to suggest that nature is mediated through, and related to, social
activity but rather that, in both historical and practical senses, nature
resides at the locus of all human practice. People rely on nature for the
fulfillment of basic needs; the first premise of all human history is the
production of material life, which always involves a relation between

producers and nature, or what Marx calls the labor process. There is, then, an irreducible unity between society and nature that is differentiated from within. The socially active producer

[c]onfronts the material of nature as one of her own forces. He sets in motion arms and legs, heads and hands, the natural forces of his [sic] body, in order to appropriate the material of nature in a form suitable for his own needs. By thus acting through this motion on the nature which is outside him and changing it, he at the same time changes his own nature. [Marx 1965, p. 177]

With this "metabolic" view of man and nature (Schmidt 1971, pp. 76–77) Marx introduced a new understanding of the relation between what had been conventionally seen as a static polarity. The content of this metabolism is that "nature is humanized while men are naturalized" (Schmidt 1971, p. 78) in historically determined forms. Nature, then, is historically unified through the labor process.

In the abstract, labor is the active and effective relation between society and nature; labor is transformative and social. Labor as the relation between people and nature is historical in two senses. First, we must ask what kind of labor, or laborer, or labor process? There is no historical inevitability about why interaction with nature is mediated through slave or serf or wage relations. But in any given period, the metabolism of humans and nature is locked into a historically determinate structure of social relations (Sayer 1979). And second, this metabolism is historical in the sense that it is not voluntarist, for "men make their own history, but they do not make it just as they please . . . but under circumstances directly encountered, given and transmitted from the past" (Marx 1972, p. 10). In laying stress on human agency, history, the nonteleological quality of social systems, and structured social relations, a materialist perspective clearly does not simply translate into the geographical notion of "man as an ecological dominate," which is a strong thread in the weft of contemporary human ecology.

In sum, then, a focus on labor as the embodiment of the society-nature relation affirms the critical importance of social context. In particular circumstances labor is refracted through the prism of *specific* social relations of production, that is, the social relations that determine the "rationality" of the economy, the differential control, the means of production, the distribution of social labor time, and the total social product.

The manner of appropriation of Nature, i.e. the form of our metabolism with Nature, is determined by the social relations, chiefly to do with ownership and control, and these forms of appropriation have the effect of reproducing those social relations. The separation of workers from the means of production means that their appropriation of Nature is governed by the interests of capitalists, and in turn this serves to reproduce the workers as wage-labourers because it does not give them the control of the means of production to enable them to become anything else, and it reproduces the capitalists as the owners and controllers of production. Therefore there is a necessary relation between the form of appropriation of Nature and the social relations of production [Sayer 1979, p. 29].

This is a very different picture of "adaptation" and has much in common with Godelier's (1974, p. 124) supposition that "[adaptation] désigne avant tout la logique interne de l'exploitation des resources et les conditions de reproduction de ce mode d'exploitation." This definition implies that adaptive processes are (i) not uniquely constrained by nature but also by the social relations of production, and (ii) often have a contradictory character, which emerges from the labor process itself.[12] Robson (1978, p. 326) is correct when she argues that if adaptation is to designate a compatibility between society and nature, these mechanisms must have specific social forms and be elaborated in terms of the conditions of social reproduction of society. Thus, if environmental relations are instances of the labor process, climatic extremity can, as I argue in the following section, be seen as moments or crises in the system of social reproduction.

I have entered upon this theoretical ellipse because this chapter is built around the notion of a precapitalist moral economy, that is, the social provision of minimum income in the face of high risk. While the institutional or sociological and technical expressions of the moral economy may be posed as "adaptive strategies," they are ultimately predicated on a radically different view of social relations and human ecology. The moral economy does not arise from a presumed Darwinian or cybernetic tendency; neither is it, as some critiques of the moral economy have alleged, principally a question of morality or ethics (Adas 1980). The moral economy arises from the class structure of society itself; it is embedded in the social relations of production, in the historically specific form of the relation between nature and society of the Sokoto Caliphate. To pose it in this manner is to see subsistence and survival as moments in a total system of social reproduction.

THE ENVIRONMENTAL CONTEXT OF HAUSALAND

The country through which we passed formed one of the finest landscapes I ever saw in my life. The ground was pleasantly undulating, covered with a profusion of herbage not yet entirely dried up by the sun's power; the trees, belonging to a great variety of species, were not thrown together into an impenetrable thicket of forest, but formed into beautiful groups, exhibiting all the advantages of light and shade.

—Heinrich Barth, 1851

Throughout the nineteenth century, Hausaland consisted, as it does today, of open, rolling savanna plains some 1,500 feet above sea level, broken occasionally by granitic outcrops and thickly wooded watercourses. Even at the turn of the century following fifty years of expanded settlement and population growth, there were large tracts of uncultivated bush dominated by perennial mesophytic grasses and fire-resistant woody components. Much of the Hausa plains, however, had felt the touch of human practice and approximated a fire proclimax, the result of centuries of burning, grazing, and farming, which prevented the restoration of a closed woodland "natural" climax. Vegetatively, the ecology of the Caliphate had almost certainly degenerated under these influences into several scrub communities:[13] *anogeissus* (savanna woodland), acacia thickets (especially on moist sites), *guiera* shrub savanna in areas of poor soil and long fallow, and *Combretum micranthum* or open shrub savanna. In areas like the close settled zones, which had been subject to high population densities and permanent cultivation for several centuries, the acacia thickets and shrub savannas had disappeared altogether, replaced by a highly manicured and selectively wooded parkland[14] (Pullan 1974). The phytogeography of these farmed parklands was dominated largely by baobab, winter thorn, dum palm, silk cotton, locust bean, and a variety of shrubs and forbs, all of which had some local use-value (see table 3.1). Toward the northern margins of Hausaland, the savanna complexes merged with the increasingly xerophytic biomes and the relic dune systems characteristic of the Sahel. The narrows limbs of diverse riparian vegetation, known locally as fadama,[15] were much less widespread but had also been subject to considerable modification largely through dry-season grazing by Ful'be pastoralists, firewood collection and repeated gathering by Hausa peasants, and increasingly during the second half of the nineteenth century by dry-season irrigated agriculture.

It is often supposed that savanna soils in West Africa are generally thin, being "particularly low in organic matter and may have poor structures, poor nutrient reserves and poor moisture storage properties" (Ahn 1970, p. 237). Of course, this type of generalization is of little practical utility at the local level and, in any case, in spite of the low esteem in which tropical soils are held, the Hausa plains were quite fertile and readily worked,

> lying between the deserts to the north and the forest to the south, [the Nigerian plains] are analogous to the loess belt of Europe. Both have long been zones of easy movement, both are unusually productive and owe their fertility . . . in part to soils derived from wind and water land deposits that accumulated under climates differing markedly . . . from the present. [Grove 1961, p. 108]

The drift deposits varied in depth and texture but the light, aeolian soils of the northern reaches were well suited to cereals, and the sandy loams of

TABLE 3.1
FARMED PARKLAND: COMMON TREES, SHRUBS AND GRASSES

Hausa name	Botanical name	English name	Use
TREES			
Gawo	Acacia albida	Winterthorn	Fodder, tanin
Dorowa	Parkia clappertoniana	Locust bean	Fodder, dye, mortars
Tsamiya	Tamarindus indica	Tamarind	Shade, fruit
Kadanya	Butyrospermum parkii	Shea butter	Oil, wood, utensils
Kuka	Adansonia digitata	Baobab	Food, rope
Goriba (kaba)	Hyphaene thebaica	Dum palm	Fruits, mats
Giginya	Borassus abyssinica	Borassus palm	Fruit, weaving, wood
Kirya	Prosopis africana		Hardwood
Faru	Odina barteri	Neem	Shade, medicine
Kurna	Ziziphus spina-cristi	Christ's thorn	Food, fodder
Aduwa	Balanites aegyptiaca	Desert date	Fruit, fodder
SHRUBS			
Sabara	Guiera senegalensis		Food, medicine
Geza	Combretum micranthum		
Kalgo	Piliostigma reticulatum		Cordage
Runhu	Cassia singueana		Medicine
Dilo (zayi)	Boscia senegalensis		Food
Gwandar daji	Anona senegalensis	Custard apple	Fruit
GRASSES			
Gamba	Andropogon gayanus	Elephant grass	Matting
Gatsaura	Aristida longiflora		Thatch
Katsemu	Aristida stipoides		Thatch
Garaji	Brachiaria spp.		Fodder
Kiri-Kiri	Cynodon dactylon	Bermuda grass	Fodder
Harkiya	Digitaria debilis	Finder grass	Fodder
Datanya	Thelepogon		Horse medicine
Komayya	Eragrostis spp.		Famine food

Kano were, in particular, "highly amenable to intensive cultivation" (Mortimore 1967, p. 118). The laka soils of southern Hausaland—notably southern Katsina and Zaria—were of a finer drift material, somewhat heavier to till, and with a pronounced clay horizon. Subject to inundation and waterlogging, the laka soils were especially suitable for intensive cultivation of sorghum and cotton (Buchanan and Pugh 1955, p. 39). Riverine environments and depressions were distinguished by the extreme diversity of their hydromorphic soils, typically with pronounced clay or silt fractions and inferior drainage (Turner 1977). In spite of the agronomic constraints imposed by alluvial or colluvial deposits, the fadama niches were nonetheless the sites of intensive commodity production, notably cotton, wheat, indigo, cassava, and rice.

The Hausa agricultural calendar was markedly bimodal, polarized between a long dry season (rani) culminating in a ferocious hot spell (*bazara*) in April, and a short, intense wet season (*damana*) commencing in May or June in northern Hausaland, during which time the landscape, as Morel (1911, p. 116) aptly put it, was transformed into "a carpet of green . . . white [with corn] until harvest." The pattern of precipitation depended largely on the movements of two major air masses: the Tropical Maritime (mT) and the Tropical Continental (cT).[16] The latter, the dry northeast trades, centered on the Saharan massif, whereas the southwest monsoon was characteristically moisture laden and the harbinger of the rainy season. Precipitation reflected the conjunction of these two air masses, that is, the movement of the intertropical convergence zone (ITCZ).

> the surface location of the [ITCZ] is often identified by the surface wind direction and humidity as indicated by the dewpoint. In the moist equatorial air mass the wind has a southerly component. . . . The drier (cT) . . . has a northerly or easterly component and a dewpoint of 14 C. The depth of the moisture layer is of the order of 1500–3000 meters during the rainy season . . . and under 1500 meters in the dry season. [Oguntoyinbo and Richards 1977, p. 116]

The advance and retreat of the ITCZ had a profound influence on the onset and termination of the rains (figure 3.1). At its northern apex, the location of the ITCZ was approximately latitude 20°N, which it usually attained in August; the southern limit, in January or February, was approximately latitude 7°N.[17] Using contemporary data from 146 stations in northern Nigeria, Kowal and Adeoye (1974) have shown how mean annual rainfall, the start and termination of the monsoon and the length of the rainy season are closely correlated with latitude.[18] The "normal" patterns that these authors document in their statistical analysis are subject to the important caveat that the ITCZ has never acted like a front in temperate regions, for there is no direct correspondence between the

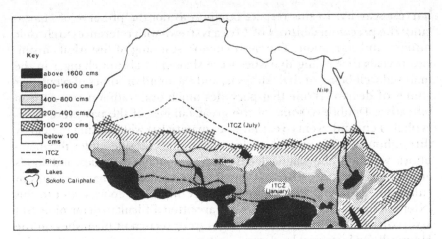

Figure 3.1. West African precipitation patterns in relation to the intertropical convergence. From Nicholson (1977).

surface front of the ITCZ and rainfall.[19] Furthermore, today as in the past, the advance of the ITCZ is not regular but comes in a series of surges, halts, and retreats. Much of the precipitation is actually derived from disturbances, line squalls that move from east to west but are generally south of (and parallel to) the surface front of the ITCZ. So in practical terms the regular round of the seasonal precipitation was cloaked in enormous variability and discontinuity. In these circumstances mean statistics, in practical terms, mean very little;[20] risk, as Oram (1977, p. 18) observes, is the name of the game in rainfed agriculture.

The climatic precariousness and pronounced seasonality of the Sudanic savannas had two obvious implications. First, the temporal rhythm of the agricultural cycle imposed constraints on food availability, which was naturally contingent upon the quality of the upland millet and sorghum harvests. For this reason, foodstuff consumption was frequently scheduled throughout the dry season to ensure that grain was available to sustain adult males during the critical cultivation period. Nevertheless, as the nineteenth-century chronicler Imam Imoru made explicit, the *bazara* (wet season) was characteristically the *lokacin yunwa*, the time of hunger. In his early tenure in Katsina, H. R. Palmer similarly noted that grain was invariably scarce six weeks prior to the early millet harvest, a deficit that was often made good by cereals imported from Damagaram and Damerghou (NAK Katprof 1928/1908).

The second implication of rainfall irregularity was that a harvest shortfall presented the real possibility of intense hunger, and perhaps the prospect of a fully fledged subsistence crisis rather than normal preharvest scarcity. In this respect famine was not the preserve of Hausa-land; the precolonial history of Africa is strewn with references to chronic hunger and starvation. The most cursory scanning of historical chronicles reveals that ruling dynasties were shaken by abrupt changes in the material well-being of their subjects, and the motif of "times of plenty" or "times of dearth" is one that pervades much oral tradition and African narrative. Doubtless, some of the great famines of the past were apocryphal. Ten- and twenty-year famines materialize with striking regularity throughout the Bornu Chronicles, entire cities subside under the metaphoric weight of the plague, locusts consume ruling dynasties, and floods erode entire polities. Environmental crises become dramatic symbols of ruling lineages and metaphors for entire historical epochs, and to this extent their exact empirical referents are often difficult to determine. But assuredly, famine and food shortages were recurrent blemishes on the Hausaphone historical landscape, and in some cases tarnished the entire desert edge from the Hausa heartland in the east to the Wolof-speaking regions in the west. At the other end of the subsistence spectrum, the long wave of serious, regional famines has superimposed upon it an epicycle of more regular local shortage. Limited in spatial extent and in the social hardship they generated, these crises in food availability occurred regularly, as the early colonial administrators readily discerned. In view of the endemic vascillations in food supply and the variability of rainfall, famine and the spectre of starvation were in no sense epiphenomenal in nineteenth-century Hausaland. They were, on the contrary, very much a part of the social fabric, and the threat of starvation was incorporated into some of the fundamental goals of peasant behavior. The famine-subsistence dialectic was, in short, one primordial axis about which peasant consciousness and practice revolved.

DROUGHT AND FAMINE IN THE CENTRAL SUDAN

> I thank Allah
> Who gave me sight and hearing,
> And the multifarious gifts of thought.
> O Blessed one, I crave they help;
> Give me good fortune in the rains.
>
> — Na'ibi S. Wali, *Song of the Rains*

Rainfall comes and goes. This is prosaically true whether the time reference is seasonal, millennial or geologic. In the central Sudan and the Saharan margins generally, there is an emerging body of knowledge on climatic variability and absolute trends of variation since the Pleistocene (Mauny 1971; Nicholson 1976). Three Quaternary episodes since about

20,000 B.P. emerge with some clarity. The Wisconsin, or Wuerm, glacial (20,000–15,000 B.P.) was characterized by a southward shift of climatic and vegetative zones and increased aridity throughout the southern Sahelian and Sudanic margins of the Sahara.[21] An interglacial period, about 10,000 B.P., indicated a sharp volte-face, notably a marked increase in precipitation throughout the semiarid tropics,[22] followed by a moist altithermal episode about 5000 B.P.; this period was interrupted by an arid millennium about 7000 B.P., quite similar to the preceding epoch with vegetation and climatic thresholds being situated northward of their present position. By 4000 B.P. climatic conditions approximated those of the present throughout the central and western Sudan. This stabilization was achieved by a marked trend toward increased aridity between 5000 and 4000 B.P., followed in most areas by extreme aridity until about 3500 B.P., and then a humid phase toward 2000 B.P. and another about 800–1200 A.D. (Nicholson 1976, pp. 96, 97).[23]

At least since the last major humid phase (ca. 1500 A.D.), a finer grain of historical data is available, which enables us to analyze shorter-term climatic periodicities and rainfall anomalies. The burden of historical reconstruction is lightened by the close association between severe drought (*fari*) and famine (*yunwa*) throughout Sudano-Sahelian Africa and the cultural significance of drought and hunger in the collective mentality of desert-edge societies. Plague, natural disasters, and famine frequently served as the backdrop for millennial expectations; they were connotative, dramatic symbols of moral decay or turpitude in keeping with the political prophecies of "times of trouble."[24] The centrality of subsistence crises was further reinforced by the fact that influential Hausa elders (*tsofuwa*) invariably directly experienced periods of severe hunger; they were and are repositories of famine lore. Virtually all of the elders in the village in which I worked could vividly recall personal anecdotes pertaining to the turn of the century famines. Through these narratives and anecdotes the *Babban Yunwa* (the great hunger) was given a real world presence. Further, there is a complex lexicon of terms (see table 3.2) that denote subtle distinctions in rainfall quality and quantity, harvest attributes, and in access to staple foodstuffs. These same themes are incorporated in the most significant cultural and artistic forms; the Hausa, like other African societies, tend to date periods and epochs in the past by reference to natural events. The "year of the locust" or "year of the famine" continue to serve as historical markers as most Nigerian historiographers and census officials will testify. Famines may become temporal beacons sprinkled over the historical landscape but may also come to signify periods of political leadership or kingly rule. Hausa praise epithets (*kirari*) and verse reveal that famines often are assigned distinctively human attributes.

TABLE 3.2
A DROUGHT-FAMINE LEXICON

Famine-Hunger: Yunwa	Drought: Fari
Babban yunwa: great hunger, famine	Fari: a major drought
Dan mudu, kunci, matsi, askare: small famine	Bushi, budi, dan iska: small drought
'Yar madegu: slight hunger	Yayyafa: a slight rain that does not penetrate the soil
Kadigiri, kwambo: destitute	Firwata: a dry spell during the rains
Talauci: poverty	Soki: serious pest or drought
Rafta, rafto: famine refugees from the north	Cafandare: to use water sparingly during a drought
Majanga: having to travel a long distance to obtain corn during a famine	Kauje: shortage of water
	Lagadam, ajawal: wilting of corn due to drought
Dan mudu, hir ka zaka: a small corn measure used during famine	Kiri, kwazar: early rains
Buda rumbu: forcible confiscation of grain during famine	Rubali, cin ruwa: ruining of crops due to water surfeit
Tsefe: unripe corn roasted during famine	Bursune: sowing prior to rains due to a lack thereof
Sha dunku: name of a child born during a famine	Busau, shira: drying up of corn prior to maturity
	Kwafe, kwafi: resowing after failure of first rains
	Zirnaniya: shower provoked by a small storm
	Dadada noma: late showers

Epithets: Kirarai

Yunwa, ba kau da hali: famine, thou makest an honest man dishonest.

Tashim marah hatsi ba shi da wujia: migration during famine is no hardship for the destitute.

SOURCE: G. Bargery (1934); R. Abraham (1946); Donaint (1975); and field data.

In keeping with the centrality of subsistence crises, the naming of famines—often with reference to detail·of their local impact—is commonplace throughout the Sahelian and Sudanic zones. In Nigerian Hausaland, for example, some of the late nineteenth-century famines were referred to as *"Ci Kworiya"* (eat calabash), *"Kumumuwa"* (suffering) and *"El Commanda"* (the commander). Moreover, oral traditions embellished and exploited the existential dilemmas perpetrated by extreme food shortage. Hausa folktales (*tsatsunyoyi*), fables (*almara*), poetry, and anecdote (*labarunda*) all pay lucid testimony to the social consequences of extreme deprivation. As Johnston (1966, p. 92) put it,

> the famine . . . provides the overture for many Hausa stories [and] in earlier times it must have been a regularly occurring phenomenon.

This is nicely illustrated in Schon's *Magana Hausa* (1885, pp. 168–72) in a tsatsunyoyi entitled "How to Keep Up Appearance," which describes the great Hausa famine in the middle of the nineteenth century, called *Banga-Banga*, and reflects the premium placed on the proper personal conduct even in situations of extreme adversity. The power of a subsistence crisis to threaten or to invert the customary social order and to transgress the conventional canons of authority, was a simple reflection of the fact that possession of (or access to) scarce foodstuffs became the new criterion accorded to social status and rank. Famines were, therefore, preeminently social crises as the following piece of famine verse, collected in Katsina, reveals.

> Where are you, princes? My kinsmen
> You inhabitants of the palace you had better reduce
>   your swaggering
> You cannot show off on an empty stomach
> Something pitiful is there in the country
> Yandaki, Gafiya, Abdallawa,
> Going from one dum-palm to another knocking down the nuts
> Elderly men are fighting at Haben Birni
> The children went to get relief but there was none
> The elders were thinking that it was due to the children's
>   lack of strength
> But the whole issue is not concerned with strength
> Even if strength is your boast, (you become) soft
> Borau, husband of Tayimba, who has lion's strength
> We went to get relief but could not get any
> We thank the Chief of the Warlords
> Cassava flour is the Kaura.[25]

In a society in which social order and status were so starkly delineated, and in which there was an absolute hierarchic segmentation between rulers and ruled, the radically disruptive capability of famines must have cast it in a strong moral light.

These broadly specified cultural attributes of famine and hunger hopefully illustrate that food shortage was neither socially nor symbolically peripheral, or indeed a statistical rarity. I suggest in fact that the memory of subsistence crises and the threat of recurrence were very much at the forefront of peasant consciousness. Rather appropriately, tradition has it that a partial famine resulted in the original concentration of peoples in the birnin Kano and necessitated both the election of a sarki and the construction of the first city walls.[26]

Over the past several centuries Hausaland and the central Sudan more generally have been affected by a series of severe droughts. While much empirical information has been collated from the Sudanese chronicles, European travelogues, and the somewhat thin palynological and dendrochronological records, any fine-grained chronology of rainfall anomalies must remain elusive. Nicholson (1976, 1979), assembled six long-term chronologies for Sudano-Sahelian West Africa covering the period from 1500 to the present. Using exiguous evidence she argues that the first two centuries of this episode experienced considerably moister conditions than the later centuries.[27] Cissoko (1968) for example reviewing sixteenth-century Arab *tarikhs* of the Niger Bend concluded that the century was one of unrivaled prosperity in which famine "could not break out." The Bornu Chronicles also paint a prosperous picture of the sixteenth and seventeenth centuries. Nicholson (1979) believes that following the moist conditions of the early historic past, there were three periods of intense drought—about 1681–87, 1738–56 and 1828–39—all of which embraced much of, if not the entire, Sudano-Sahelian region. In actual fact, a more complex drought chronology emerges (see table 3.3) in which even the regional correspondence during periods of purportedly severe droughts is often not at all clear. It is probably safe to assume that the droughts of the late seventeenth and mid-eighteenth centuries were "international" in scope, although it is difficult to determine whether Hausaland or Bornu were as seriously affected as Nicholson implies.[28] A major perturbation in the eighteenth century was the massive drought of mid-century which quite literally subsumed much of western Africa and was not matched in intensity until 1969–74.[29]

Another climatic anomaly occurred in Hausaland in the 1790s according to the Tedzkiret en-Nisian though of lesser significance than the Great Drought forty years earlier. Baier (1980, pp. 30, 31) believes the nineteenth century was "remarkable for the absence of prolonged drought"; Lovejoy (1978, p. 350) also posits that after 1817 there were no

TABLE 3.3
DROUGHT CHRONOLOGIES: CENTRAL AND WESTERN SUDAN

Niger Bend[1]	Bornu–Chad[2]	Lake Chad[3] (low levels)	Hausaland[4]
1617	1540s	1565–95	1590s (?)
1639–43	1560	1750	1750s
1669–71	1657 (?)	1828–29	1793–95
1695	1681–87	1873	1790s
1704	1738–51 (?)	1895	1840
1711–16	1751–53		1855
1721–22	1790s		1863
1738–43	1810		1864
1756	1831–36		1873
1770–71	1834–37		1884
1772–75	1896–98		1889–90
1853–54			
1864			
1865–66			

SOURCES:

[1]Cissoko (1968); Nicholson (1976); Curtin (1975); Monteil (1939); Schove (1977).
[2]Palmer (1928); Palmer (1936); Urvoy (1949); Plote (1974); Nicholson (1976).
[3]Nicholson (1976); Schove (1973); Schove (1977).
[4]Watts (1979); Lovejoy and Baier (1975); Oral data, northern Nigeria 1976–78.

major climatic catastrophies in Hausaland.[30] This is, however, a dubious supposition, not simply because there was in fact a recurrent drought in the Chad basin between 1810 and 1840,[31] but because the first quarter of the century witnessed the massive social dislocation of the jihad, which almost certainly colored the nature of entries into the local chronicles. In any case the period 1840–95 was actually one of successive rainfall failures of regional significance (see table 3.3).[32] Throughout the tropical and temperate margins of the Sahara, from 1875 to 1895 precipitation was continuously above normal (Nicholson 1976); lake-level data and the meteorological evidences of the first synoptic stations established by the early colonial states all point to moister conditions, though the only data specifically relevant to Hausa territory indicate recurrent, if localized, drought (Watts 1979).[33] The hiatus of the early 1890s was followed by a pronounced arid episode over much of the central Sudan, peaking with the devastating drought years about 1910–20.

To summarize then, the mesoscale pattern of Sudanese climate appears to have been relatively stable over the last millennium. Superimposed upon it were epicycles of greater or lesser dryness; the sixteenth and seventeenth centuries for example seem to have been subject to pluvial conditions throughout the desert margins. The eighteenth century was a period of "rapid fluctuations," to use Nicholson's (1976, p. 176) term, and increased drought incidence. By 1800 conditions in the central Sudan were probably identical to those of the twentieth century. Within the past four centuries, however, one can identify four synoptic rainfall anomalies; the Great Drought of the mid-eighteenth century, and three lesser aridities in the 1680s, the 1790s and the last quarter of the nine-teenth century.[34] Hausaland was unequivocally subject to these capri-cious conditions, but also to the annual effects of the intense local variabil-ity in rainfall characteristic of the semiarid tropics.

A HAUSA FAMINE CHRONOLOGY, 1800–1900

Oh Almighty God! Protect us against evils: Poverty and sickness, famine and indigence!

—Imam Imoru, *Wakar talauci da wadata*

Recent work on famine chronologies for sub-Saharan Africa reveals that the record remains embarrassingly incomplete and often highly ambiguous,[35] Perhaps the most widely cited study of precolonial drought and famine in the Sudanic belt, the excellent work of Cissoko (1968) on the Niger Bend, in spite of its strengths, illuminates the pitfalls of such historical reconstruction. His evidence is quite straightforward, consist-ing mainly of the explicit references to drought, famine, and pestilence in three chronicles. In the sixteenth century, there were recurrent pesti-lences in 1536, 1548, and 1551 and again in 1582–83, but on balance this was a period of stability during which there are records of plague but rarely famine; it terminated abruptly with the consolidation of power by an administrator class, an attendant decline in economic well-being,[36] and the conquest of Songhai by the Moroccan army in 1591. Throughout the seventeenth and eighteenth centuries the Niger Bend was the site of intense political competition and internecine strife. According to Swift,

Throughout the seventeenth and eighteenth centuries the area was fought over by competing groups. The least shortage of food or a natural disaster such as drought, floods, or locusts was liable to turn into a famine. Great famines were recorded every 7 to 10 years during the seventeenth century, every 5 years during the eighteenth century. In 1738 nearly half of the population of Tim-buktu, and probably of the whole region, dies. [Swift 1977, p. 471]

Cissoko discovered that famines were described vividly and explicitly, dwelling particularly on the numbers dead, the uncontrolled price infla-tion of foodstuffs, and an occasional hint of cannibalism.

In historical recovery of this genre, the dependence on a limited number of tarikhs, and an even more limited collection of veiled and ambiguous literary or journalistic references to starvation, is methodologically problematic. Not only is the cause and effect sequence hard to trace but it is doubly difficult to gauge the actual extent and magnitude of the disasters. There is at least the suspicion that a certain standard phraseology has crept into the chronicles. In any case, prior to 1800 the record is scanty, leaning heavily upon a very few written sources.[37] Palmer (NAK Katprof 1389/1916) refers to decade-long famines in Bornu and Kano during the seventeenth century, and Lovejoy (1978) supposes that the food crisis of the 1750s, spanning almost two decades, effectively leveled the desert edge. While the capacity of subsistence crises to provide the mechanism for the sort of social change Lovejoy envisages—the mass evacuation of the Sahel, the dissolution of slave estates, and an enormous recession in the Sahel-savanna economy—is certainly not in question, the evidence on which he bases his conclusions is necessarily skimpy and partial.[38]

A very crude attempt at a famine chronology for the central Sudan and Nigerian Hausaland is presented in table 3.4. Most of the empirical detail on the Caliphate was derived from informants in northern Kaduna and Kano states[39] and refers to the period up to the formal conquest by colonial armed forces. M.G. Smith (1978, p. 147) and Last (1970, p. 346) both refer to early famines in Daura and Sokoto between 1804 and 1808 that were almost certainly perpetrated by the military maneuvers of the jihad, compounded perhaps by the poor harvests of the 1790s. Oral testimony from Katsina suggests that the entire Jama'a period (1796–1816) was one of variable food supply and of sporadic hunger. A famine struck Katsina town in 1807 following the jihadi siege of the same year. During this time lizards sold for 50 cowries and vultures in excess of 500 cowries. The first half of the nineteenth century, nevertheless, appears relatively free from the classic *babban yunwa* of the preceding century, and Lovejoy for one sees this as a period of consolidation, expansion, and prosperity in the aftermath of the devastation of the 1750s. Lavers (cited in Fisher 1974) however documented a famine called *Dala Dema* following a severe drought during the last year of the reign of Mohammed al Amin al Kanemi about 1835, which ravaged Bornu and eastern Hausaland. For the second half of the nineteenth century we are fortunate in having a famine chronology for Kano collected by Resident W. Gowers (NAK SNP17 K2151). The famines of 1847 and 1855, referred to as *Dawara* and *Banga-Banga* respectively, were, as table 3.4 indicates, not simply confined to Kano emirate. Yunwar Banga-Banga, attributed to defective rainfall, was particularly severe and in the birni:

> For thirty days at a time no gero, no dawa, wheat or rice were to be had in Kano.
> People ate vultures. [Gowers NAK SNP17 K2151]

TABLE 3.4
A FAMINE CHRONOLOGY

Date	Central Sudan
1543–61:	Bornu, a "great famine" called "*Bu Ihagbana*" during the reign of Dunama Muhammed.
1561–68:	Bornu, a seven-year famine called "*Sima Azadu*" during the reign of Abdulla Muhammed.
1582–1618:	Kano, an eleven-year famine during the reign of Mohammed Zaki.
1644–80:	Borno, a famine called "*Dala Dama.*"
1680–92:	Funj, famine and smallpox.
1681–1717:	Darfur, a seven-year drought.
1696:	Agades, "the war of famine."
1699–1717:	Borno, a great famine of seven years during the reign of Sultan Dunama bn Ali.
1734–49:	Borno, a two-year famine called "*Ali Shuwa.*"
1738–56:	Niger Bend, Hausaland, a twenty-year period of famine and epidemics.
1747–50:	Borno, a famine during the reign of Sultan Dunama Gana.
1781–1807:	Kano, a famine during the reign of Sarkin Mohammed.
1780–90:	Hausaland, out-migration from Air.
1793–95:	Northwestern Hausaland, severe food shortage.

HAUSALAND

Daura	Name	Kano	Name	Katsina	Name
1805–07		1807–10		1807	
1858 (?)		1830s		1855	
1868		1847	Darwara	1888	Yar Mani
1872		1855	Banga-Banga	1890	Ci Kworiya
1879	Malali	1863		1893	
1898	El Commanda	1873		1899	Tashi Namaka
		1884			
		1889			
		1890			

SOURCE: S. Nicolson (1976); P. Lovejoy and S. Baier (1975); Gowers (NAK SNP 17 K2151), and oral data from Katsina and Daura.

This was presumably the great hunger that Imam Imoru (Mischlich 1942, p. 166) refers to in his *Travels in Hausaland*, which he recalled from his early childhood. The slight famines that Gowers notes for 1863, 1864, 1873, 1884, and 1889 are difficult to appraise; they were almost certainly geographically contained within one or more districts in Kano emirate. In such cases, as was clear from my own field discussions, a famine that occurred in Daura during the 1870s and may have caused considerable hardship there might be wholly unknown to the inhabitants of birnin Katsina, forty miles distant.

In examining the actual historic record of famine in Hausaland, hunger should not be posed simply as the mechanical reflex of a capricious rainfall.[40] Many cities were brought to the point of collapse by epidemics, locusts wrought havoc in Bauchi at the end of the nineteenth century, and cattle epizootics decimated Fulani herds, perhaps most notably through the rinderpest epidemic called *Sannu* in 1893.[41] There is a strong suggestion that the jihad had seriously disrupted agricultural operations. To the north of birnin Katsina considerable disruption and depopulation was precipitated by the continued conflict between Dan Baskore and his Maradi-based supporters and the Katsinawa centered on the birni.[42] An intriguing example of this sort of military famine is provided by the yunwa el Commanda, in Damagaram Sultanate during the late 1890s.[43] The name in fact denotes the assassination of one Captain Garbriel Cazemajou of the Mission de Haut Volta during 1898 by supporters of Sarkin Zinder Ahmadu. The killing of Cazemajou prompted a particularly violent response from the Mission Afrique Centrale (MAC). The march of the MAC across Niger left massive devastation in its wake; whole villages were sacked and burned. Their inhabitants, including women and children, were taken prisoner or summarily executed. As Salifou (1971) describes it, the mission, under Lieutenant Joalland, reached Zinder, leaving a swath of carnage in its wake across northern Hausaland, only to find the town deserted. The disruption that accompanied the MAC campaign that was conducted during the wet season of 1898 provided the catalyst for the abandonment of entire farming communities, and the rupture of normal agricultural activities. Since the death of the French captain also coincided with the eruption of conflict between Zinder and Kano, one can safely assume that the food production cycle over a significant proportion of southern Damagaram was never fully completed and the harvests were correspondingly poor. The refugees (*yan yunwa*), torn from their village areas, drifted southward to birnin Daura into an area barely self-sufficient in grains at the best of times.

Nevertheless, drought seems to have had the closest kinship with famine throughout the central Sudan during the eighteenth and nineteenth centuries. This is perfectly congruent with Hausa sentiment, in which the great hungers of the past were almost the inevitable outcome of excessively poor rainfall (fari), either because seasonal totals were grossly inadequate or the rains terminated abruptly prior to maturity (*kumshi*) of the upland grain crops. Clearly the babban yunwa were the exception rather than the rule; but we should not lose sight of the lesser crises, for periods of shortage in Hausaland had typically been of a much smaller scale. Echoing Scott's (1976, p. 2) findings in Southeast Asia, the threat of starvation might fall upon an isolated community or be confined to a single household whose land might have suffered localized drought, or whose working head fell ill at harvest time or whose children were too many for its small patch of land. These localized food shortages, called *dan mudu*, *kunci*, or *matsi* in Hausaland, were much more regular occurrences. At the district level at least one village area—or part of it—would be subject to irregular food availability of this order of magnitude perhaps every four or five years. Hardship that extended over larger territorial domains, perhaps embracing large tracts of entire emirates, was less frequent and perhaps more congruent with Hill's (1972, p. 21) suggested periodicity of seven to ten years.[44]

In summary, the drought-famine chronologies for Hausaland are, perhaps inevitably, woefully inadequate. In an ecological realm as large and diverse as Hausaland with so variable a climatic regime, a comprehensive chronology must remain elusive. Nonetheless, it appears that the 150-year period from the 1750s to 1913 was free of a massive subsistence calamity that embraced the entire savannas and desert-edge community. Regional crises occurred with much more frequency—especially during the second half of the nineteenth century—superimposed upon by an irregular pattern of local shortages. Although drought was a regular if unpredictable environmental attribute, and raised the specter of starvation, famine was not an *inevitable* outcome. It is worth recalling that drought is a *climatic* phenomenon, and famine a *social* crisis. To the extent that a relationship of causality existed between drought and famine in the Caliphate, or indeed any society, it is mediated through the political and economic architecture of the social system. Grounding environmental events in a natural order points toward "harm done" and individual passivity rather than to learning, long-term adjustment, and human agency.

MORAL VERSUS POLITICAL ECONOMY?

We must see [the moral economy] as it was, sui generis, with its own objectives, operating within the complex and delicate polarity of forces of its own context. And I find the critical clue to this structural equilibrium . . . in the gentry's jealousy of the State, the weaknesses of the organs of the State and the particular inheritance of Law. . . . . This is the central structural context of the reciprocity of relations between rulers and ruled. It was not a price which was gladly paid.

—E. P. Thompson

In light of the recursive quality of rainfall variability and harvest shortfalls, it is to be expected that rural communities were in some sense cognitively aware of environmental risk; they possessed, in other words, a long-term adjustment capability with respect to drought and the threat of starvation. James Scott (1976) suggested that this adaptive flexibility, the capacity to cope in a risky environment, was characteristic of peasant communities dependent upon their own labor for the provision of the means of subsistence. Precapitalist societies were, to a large degree, organized around the dual foci of risk and subsistence security. Scott was concerned with the wider issues of the impact of the colonial state, the expansion of markets, and more particularly with peasant rebellion, but his materialist touchstone led him to begin with the existential conditions of the rural producers. The high costs of agricultural failure—the omnipresent reality of living close to the margin of biological survival—projected subsistence security onto the screen of peasant rationality. Using the Chayanovian model of peasant households as units of consumption, production, and reproduction, each farming family was, according to Scott, faced with an irreducible domestic demand to secure short-term survival. These minimal needs translated into a behavioral conservatism such that safety and reliability took precedence over long-run profit.[45] Individual agronomic decision making was, to use the current parlance, risk-averse. In this sense, much of the peasant universe was an investment against instability. In practice, peasant households preferred to minimize the probability of having a disaster rather than maximize a particular output. Narrowly defined, the "safety-first principle" presupposes welltried, adaptable, and flexible agronomic strategies[46] unlike the rigid minimax program that Allan (1965) sees as characteristic of African husbandry.

The safety-first maxim extended beyond the realm of technical or agronomic practice for it was given social expression at the level of the community and the descent group. There developed, to use Joel Migdal's (1974, p. 72) words, "community mechanisms to maximise security for the household." Welfare and insurance was, then, writ large in the social superstructure of the corporate peasant village. Scott argued that these social forms constituted a "subsistence ethic," which found expression in the "patterns of social control and reciprocity that structure[d] daily conduct" (1976, p. 40). The right to subsistence subsumed both horizontal and vertical ties as primary normative concerns. Webs of kinship reciprocities maintained a collective resiliency among households dependent upon pooling and sharing of the domestic product.[47] The logic of gift giving was most intense among close kin, within descent groupings, and between bond friends, but variants of reciprocity were evidenced in more formalized associations, often between individuals of different social status. Vertical relations between patron and client,[48] for instance, reflected special cases of a mutuality in which reciprocal obligations, rights, and norms were closely defined and morally enforceable. In a similar vein, elite responsibilities appeared grounded in the moral attributes to the peasant's right to subsistence. A characteristic of the peasant milieu was, in fact, that economic inequities had specific redistributive parallels.

Because these suprahousehold institutions were in some sense seen normatively they embodied standards of justice and fairness; Scott suggested that they constituted a "moral economy of the peasantry." Scott borrowed the concept of "moral economy" from E. P. Thompson (1963, 1971) who focused specifically on British food riots and popular protest during a period of profound socioeconomic transition. Thompson argues that these highly complex forms of political expression were approved by popular sanction and constituted efforts by the laboring poor to uphold the ethical precepts—the moral economy—of an ostensibly nonmarket grain economy. These precapitalist norms inhered in the politics of plebian and patrician culture, in royal policy making, and in the popular consciousness; food riots by the plebs were attempts to gain what was legitimately theirs through custom, common law, and paternalistic market patterns. For Scott, a moral political economy was one in which elite demands—either of the patron or the state—took account of peasant subsistence needs and exigencies. In sum,

> this precapitalist normative order was based on the guarantee of minimal social rights in the absence of political or civil rights. Peasants expected of elites the generosity and assistance that they imposed within the village on their better-off neighbors; social rights were, in this sense, village morals writ large. [Scott 1976, p. 184]

In a sense, the normative (and morally enforceable) quality of the subsistence ethic ramified throughout the entire peasant universe in ever widening orbits of responsibility from the household, to extended kin, to village patrons, and ultimately to the state itself.[49]

In spite of the wide acceptance of the moral economy interpretation, Scott's work has been subject to recent criticism.[50] Perhaps the most sustained critique has been leveled by Popkin (1979), who from his self-proclaimed "political economy" perspective,[51] deductively derived and rejected the core assumptions of the moral economy approach.[52] Popkin's work on individual peasant politics is intriguing but it is flawed insofar as he ignores the moral economy notion itself in its most expanded Thompsonian form, and misrepresents the moral economy "school," which he believes characterizes peasant society as "moral, efficient and stable" (1980, p. 431).[53] Furthermore, he levels criticisms that Scott himself addresses[54] and does not provide a theoretically coherent alternative. Popkin apparently sees the peasant world as not composed of so-called conservative, risk-averse minimizers, but of gamblers, free riders, and investors. It is difficult to know whether these propensities to gamble and invest in children, goats, or durables is a universal peasant trait or something that emerges through capitalist subsumption.[55] Popkin, steeped in the tradition of public choice theory of Olson and Arrow, accordingly derives the explanatory power of his work from an assumption of rational goal seeking; that is, "individuals evaluate the possible outcomes associated with their choices in accordance with preferences and values" (Popkin 1980, pp. 31, 32). I am at a loss to know how this assists our understanding of precapitalist society.[56] A large part of this failure derives from his attempt to universalize peasant behavior; rural producers are (or were) either risk-averse Whigs or Schumpeterian gamblers. Of course, as Bates (1978, p. 140) claims, rural producers most certainly gamble; reproduction is clearly a risky business, and the most risk-averse intercropping strategy cannot guarantee good rains. But I fail to see why investing in children or livestock is at all inconsistent with the view that most precapitalist peasantries preferred alternatives that offered the lowest probability of driving them below an irreducible domestic income level. These questions of individual propensity can only be understood in the historical context of the political-economic specificities provided by the wider ensemble of social relations of production that tie classes together.[57] There is not one peasantry, only peasantries.

While I draw heavily on the moral economy concept in the following discussion of food security in the Sokoto Caliphate, Scott's work is deficient in some areas that impinge upon my argument. Popkin (1979, pp. 72–79) is right to draw attention to the overly corporate quality of precapitalist village drawn by Scott; this corporateness is necessarily undermined where commodity production and merchant capital is well developed. Because the corporate community was, in many cases, much more attenuated, the intravillage leveling mechanisms also appear somewhat exaggerated. A common criticism leveled against the moral economy is that its proponents idealize the very sort of community denounced by Marx as "undignified," "barbarian," "vegetative," and the "solid foundation of Oriental Despotism" (see Adas 1980, p. 541; Genovese 1973, p. 161). Scott, in fact, comes very close to a Weberian ideal type in his discussion of Burma and Vietnam; he relies heavily on historical materials drawn from outside Southeast Asia, and not infrequently is forced to employ evidences that relate to nonpeasant agrarian groups to support his typology. Popkin's broader view of patron-client relations also reiterates that intravillage welfare cannot be assumed a priori but is the outcome of changing political struggles. In this sense, to assume that peasantries who adopt risk-averse technical arrangements ipso facto develop social institutions for minimizing risk would be highly specious.[58]

A more serious empirical weakness in Scott's work is that he has surprisingly little to say about the state, and specifically about the elites. In part, this reflects his admittedly magisterial marshalling of an enormous range of evidences from many areas to the neglect of the textual detail and richness of a single case study. Adas, in his Balinese research in particular, showed how the moral and ethical dimensions of state-peasant relations were

> far less important determinants of the peasant's welfare than the administrative and technological deficiencies of pre-colonial states and the defense mechanisms which these weaknesses allowed the peasantry to develop to buffer elites. [Adas 1980, p. 530]

The competitive nature of dynastic politics (what Adas calls the "contest state"), the undeveloped communicational technology, a measure of autonomy of the periphery from the center, and the low level of military development in most precolonial states, all meant that the peasantry were practically buttressed against oppressive demands, in addition to the moral and ethical mediations of a patrimonial system.

In the final analysis, however, these caveats are not inconsistent with the moral economy concept; rather, I adopt a broader rubric entirely in keeping with Thompson's original formulation in which the tensions, constraints, and controls of the moral economy emerged from the political, economic, and ethical-legal systems as a whole, from the very structure of the precolonial economy. I begin with the assumption that Hausa peasant households reproduced themselves through nonmarket systems of reciprocal vertical and horizontal ties.[59] Within this system of social reproduction, the moral economy refers to ideologically legitimate and enforceable social and technical arrangements, spanning all levels from the household to the state. It resulted from the persistence of an economy of use-value production in which work and consumption were united in the family. But the sociocultural reproduction of rural producers also had a wider social meaning which "grew out of the special working and living conditions of . . . producers and their location in a specific class structure" (Medick 1981, p. 67). That some social or productive relations were seen to possess moral or ethical qualities was a reflection of the centrality of political-ideological instances in precapitalist societies. The ostensible morality of precapitalist economy should not, then, obscure the fact that the moral economy arose from the peculiar social field of force, within the Caliphate itself. While the fundamental class contradiction with the Hausa emirates resided in the state-peasantry relation, exploitative conduits between classes were ultimately defined by the dependence of the sarauta on the revenue derived from the talakawa.[60] In sum, the moral economy was, as E.P. Thompson observed in his discussion of eighteenth-century England, a reflection of the contradictory strengths and limits of state power.

> But it is necessary also to say what this hegemony does *not* entail. It does not entail any acceptance by the poor of the gentry's paternalism upon the gentry's own terms or in their approved self-image. The poor might be willing to award their deference to the gentry, but only for a price. The price was substantial. And the deference was often without the least illusion: it could be seen from below as being one part necessary self-preservation, one part the calculated extraction of whatever could be extracted. Seen in this way, the poor imposed upon the rich some of the duties and functions of paternalism just as much as deference was in turn imposed upon them. Both parties to the equation were constrained within a common field-of-force. [Thompson 1977, p. 163]

In this way, the moral economy need not be saddled with the usual criticism of precapitalist idealism, of Hopkins's "myth of merrie Africa";[61] it is not necessary to be trapped between the Scylla of precolonial affluence and the Charybdis of primary misery. The moral economy was not especially moral and the Caliphate was certainly no Rousseauian universe of peasant welfare and benevolent patrons. Rather, the moral economy was necessary to the survival of ruler and ruled, and the price was paid by prevailing power blocs for the maintenance and reproduction of the social relations of production replete with its exploitative relations and class struggles. There is, then, no need to project a Hobbesian view of village life or to pose peasants as amoral rationalists, as Popkin implies. Rather the moral economy emerges as an outgrowth of class struggles over subsistence minimum and surplus appropriation, not as an attribute of a specific, isolated group. For didactic purposes, I have detailed the technical and social arrangements of the moral economy as a simple matrix (table 3.5) consisting of ever widening orbits of human practice, from the individual farmer through household, descent group, and village, to the state and regional economy.

HAUSA AGRONOMY, RISK, AND DROUGHT

There are three obvious attributes of arid and semiarid ecosystems; first, precipitation is so low that water is the dominant controlling factor

TABLE 3.5

SUBSISTENCE SECURITY AND RESPONSE STRUCTURES IN NINETEENTH-CENTURY HAUSALAND

Response level	Response Structure		
	Safety-first	Norm of reciprocity	Moral economy
Agronomic or Domestic Level	Agronomic risk-aversion Intercropping (crop mixtures) Crop rotation (moisture preservation) Crop experimentation (short-maturing millets, etc.) Exploitation of local environment (famine foods) Secondary resources (dry season crafts) Domestic self help and support		

Community Level

Interfamily insurance (risk sharing)
Extended kin groups (*gandu*)
Reciprocity (gift exchange, mutual support)
Elite redistribution to the poor
Storage, ritual sanctions
Antifamine institutions (*Sarkin Noma*)
Patron-Clientage (*barantaka*)
Communal work groups (gayya)

Regional or State Level

Regional and ecological interdependence between desert edge and savannas
Local and regional trade in foodstuffs from surfeit to deficit regions (*yan kwarami*)
Role of the State:
1. Central granaries based on grain tithe (zakkat)
2. State relief and tax modification

for biological processes; second, precipitation is highly variable through the year and occurs in discrete, discontinuous packages or "pulses"; and third, spatiotemporal variation in precipitation has a large random (unpredictable) component. From an anthropocentric perspective the water-controlled nature of arid ecosystems, principally due to the tight coupling of energy inflow with water inflow (Noy-Meir 1973) translates into agropastoral systems that are highly vulnerable to drought[62] and rainfall uncertainty. In marginal areas climate is bimodal, or as Ruttenberg (1981, p. 28) put it: "some rain, little rain." Precipitation is almost never "normal" over the short or long term; it is almost always considerably above or below any mean statistic.

In light of the extreme variation in rainfall, the site of subsistence security among nineteenth-century Hausa farmers resided in the lexical ordering of domestic goals to avoid starvation and ensure the capacity for agriculture, upon which the means of subsistence depended. These were practical priorities and can be derived from Chayanov's heuristic analysis of the peasant household in which the central feature was that its economic logic was not governed by the objective of either a monetary surplus or a net profit even though a proportion of peasant production was appropriated by the state. Since, to use his words, "the family could not maximize what it could not measure," the objective of productive labor was an equilibrium between producers and consumers.[63] The family attempted to maximize *gross* rather than *net* profit (Medick 1976, p. 298). The household entered into exchange relations as a producer of use-values, even where products necessarily became commodities. Chayanov also pointed out that at certain points in the trajectory of the household demographic cycle, families facing dependent labor-consumer ratios would be especially vulnerable to subsistence crises. But because this was the case, demographic natural histories reaffirmed the overriding importance of meeting domestic subsistence demands safely.

The identification of subsistence security[64] within the Caliphate requires, at the outset, a reaffirmation of the preeminently scientific quality of Hausa dryland agriculture. Ferguson (1973, p. 51), paraphrasing Imam Imoru, suggests that the strength of Hausa economy was centered on this agronomic affluence, on regular weeding, mixed cropping, fallowing crop rotations, and manuring, of a system marked by a relative poverty of the forces of production. The astute commentator E.D. Morel (1911, p. 115), touring the northern states at the turn of the century, went so far as to suggest that "there is little we can teach the Kano farmer." In moving beyond the spurious view of chaotic and maladaptive swidden systems toward one that emphasizes a measure of agricultural prosperity, one certainly need not resort to a wholly Panglossian vision. The acuity and industriousness of Hausa farmers were consistently lauded in the prose of the early European travelers, while geographic work on palaeo-technical swidden systems has established beyond question that, far from being destructive and unproductive, their labor returns per unit input were high, and uninterrupted polycultural systems bred a type of systemic stability. While a variant of long-term fallowing may have been the norm for large tracts of the lightly populated savannas, it is certain that permanent agriculture had replaced swiddening over large parts of the Caliphate territory, especially in the vicinity of Kano, Katsina, and Sokoto. In spite of high child mortality,[65] the continual importation of captive labor and constant in-migration throughout the nineteenth century suggest that the Caliphate experienced a consistent, if relatively low, demographic growth. These permanently cultivated and intensively manured areas were capable of supporting extraordinarily high population densities, largely through the increased application of organic fertilizers and expanded labor inputs, an intensification structurally akin to Geertz's (1963, pp. 32–37) notion of "agricultural involution." At the turn of the century, a visitor to Kano, described the system as follows:

> That they have acquired the necessary precise knowledge as to the time to prepare the land for sowing; when and how to sow; how long to let the land be fallow; what soils suit certain crops; what varieties of the same crop will succeed in some localities and what varieties in others . . . how to ensure rotation; when to arrange with the Fulani herdsmen to pasture their cattle upon the land. [Morel 1911, p. 234]

Soil fertility was maintained by the intercropping of nitrogen-fixing legumes, subtle use of crop mixtures, and intensive manuring from the dry season visits of Fulani cattle, domestic livestock droppings, ash, and *balbela* (egret manure).[66] The humus layer was naturally enriched through these manuring practices, which simultaneously raised the moisture-holding capacity of the soil. Techniques such as ridging and bunding served to preserve moisture and to minimize the possibility of seed erosion during intense storms.

Within the matrix of normal agricultural practice, Hausa farmers possessed an adaptive flexibility to accommodate the climatic risks intrinsic to tight water-controlled ecosystems. I refer to this precolonial knowledge and capability under the general rubric of risk aversion,[67] referring specifically to (i) crop mixes, (ii) cropping strategies, (iii) storage, and (iv) household diversification.[68] The assumption of a universal rationality such as risk aversion in communities marked by socioeconomic stratification and short-term intrageneration economic mobility is naturally open to criticism. But in a society in which for most households the object of production was the reproduction of the conditions necessary for family consumption, a risk-averse utility surface at low income levels is a useful and valid heuristic device.[69]

Crop Mixes: Intercropping and Polycultural Systems. Nicolas (1968) most aptly referred to the ancient indigenous crop mixtures of Hausa upland agriculture—namely, the polycultural production of sorghum, millet and beans—as an ecological "marriage" adapted to the unpredictability of Sudanic climates.

> The "marriage" [of] millet and sorghum . . . is a sort of insurance for the cultivator: millet adapts fairly well to a rather dry agricultural season; in contrast, a very humid agricultural season is better suited to sorghum. Thus the totality of the millet-sorghum harvest should be fairly consistent from one year to the next. [Nicolas et al. 1968, XXII]

Crop diversity spread risk, reduced the possibility of total crop devastation by insect or disease infestation, evened out agricultural labor inputs, and bred a sort of ecological stability. Only recently has research on crop mixtures and intercropping illustrated the adaptive value of indigenous planting practices for the semiarid tropics (Abalu 1976). Norman, for example, working near Zaria observed that

> there is a greater probability of obtaining higher returns per unit of input from growing crops in mixtures rather than in sole stands. Therefore under indigenous technological conditions growing crops in mixtures is consistent with the goal of security. [Norman 1974, p. 14]

These practices did not, however, constitute fixed agronomic programs that were automatically run every year (see MAB 1978). There was no one best cropping pattern or spacing system but rather a great deal of on-line flexibility. Nowhere was flexibility more necessary than under conditions of erratic rainfall, either when the initial planting rains failed and replanting was necessary, or when the onset of the planting rains fell beyond the bounds of normal expectation. Typically, the farmer adjusted his planting, cultivating, and harvesting schedule within the confines of water availability. Furthermore, he probably had a series of fall-back positions that depended upon alternative crop strategies as well as scheduling flexibility.[70] Hausa cultivators exploited short-maturing cereals, spacing variations, and variations in local soil moisture conditions. In addition, the Hausa-Arab star calendar provided a model from which deviations of the rainfall pattern from a hypothetical norm might be gauged. The following poem, which describes the relationships between the star calendar and the agricultural cycle, is a common piece of oral verse widespread throughout rural Hausaland and is of some antiquity:

When Surayya appears, O friend
Be sure that the time of planting is near.
When Dabaram comes, truly seeds must be sought,
Some even sow (their seed) early.
When Haka'a appears seed is sown; some are (already) tilling,
And the farmers must dig the ground.
When Hana'a is six days old, the drought comes in.
With Zira'a the corn (begins to shoot) everywhere in
the fields.
When Nasara comes the rainy season really sets in
With Darfa the period of constant rains begins.
With Jabha the rains become constant day and night.
Plump with the rains ripe millet heads (appear) on the farm.
When Harsan comes, pumpkins are plentiful,
And the rains are heavy and constant without doubt.
With Sarfa the harvesting of millet comes in,
And bundles of millet heads and threshed grain are everywhere
measured out.
With Iwwa destroyer of walls, the rain has settled in.
When Simaku comes there are fish in hand.
With Gufru the rains then say "Farewell,"
And the bean blossoms are abundant on the farms

[Hiskett 1967, p. 172]

Although the star calendar is subject to minor regional variations in detail, it provided a sort of agrometeorological template, against which the specific variations in the local pattern could be evaluated. In this way, each wet season demanded a slightly different agronomic plan grounded in the detail of local rainfall characteristics. Each wet season was unique from the cultivator's perspective, demanding a complex sequential decision-making process in which plant varieties, spacing, weeding, manuring, and other agricultural practices were manipulated and orchestrated.

Cropping Strategies. While the agricultural system was dominated by the production of cereals on an essentially upland (jigawa) environment, Hausa farmers also exploited two other ecological niches: the broad, flat alluvial river valleys; and the intermediary scarps, the margins between upland and lowland. These geographically restricted fadama environments, frequently subject to periodic inundation and high water tables year round, were used for the cultivation of rice and sorghum in the event of an upland harvest failure. Where edaphic and pedological conditions were appropriate, these bottomlands and alluvial flood plains were exploited for flood retreat cultivation or dry season irrigation (*lambu*). Barth described some of this fadama agriculture near Katsina during the 1850s.

Cotton and karasia fields interrupted the parklike scenery, and near Kamri, a small place surrounded with a low clay wall, we were delighted with the view of a green patch of low ground laid out into beds, and, with the help of a number of drawbeams, "khattatir" or "lambuna," producing wheat and onions. This ground is only worked with the gelma and the fertana or small hoe. [Barth 1851, III, 483]

The cultivation of cassava (*rogo*) along fadama margins was of particular significance during drought years.[71] Unlike other tubers, cassava can adapt to low rainfall conditions, being planted immediately after the sorghums and millets and harvested eight to ten months later when domestic foodstuffs are at their lowest ebb. Contrary to M.G. Smith's (1978, p. 36) belief, cassava was an important crop throughout Hausaland during the nineteenth century, and was particularly popular in northern Sokoto when Barth passed through in the 1850s. Imam Imoru for example was quite cognizant of the role of cassava and its utility as a famine (if somewhat low status) food.[72] Historical work in southern Kano near Kura (Palmer-Jones, personal communication) has suggested that large tracts of land were sometimes reserved specifically for hunger periods during which time the village head arranged for the cultivation of cassava and other foodstuffs to compensate for the possibility of general scarcity.

Storage. Storage of grain and seed was, of course, the usual mechanism that helped to mitigate the effects of a poor harvest. A relatively efficient storage system and a preeminently suitable commodity in the form of millets and sorghums permitted the long-term storage of grains. According to early colonial reports, indigenous granaries (usually mud vessels, subterranean pits, or woven bins) could preserve cereals for between five and seven years with minimal losses.[73] The following description from Clapperton written during the 1820s confirms the ubiquitous and sophisticated storage technology throughout Hausaland:

Their granaries are made in the form of a large urn or pitcher, raised from the ground about three feet by stones. They are made of clay and chopped straw, and are raised to a height of eleven or twelve feet. When the grain is put in, a conical cap of thatch is put over to keep out birds, insects, wet and moisture. The *doura* (dawa) and millet will keep well in these jars for two or three years, after that period it perishes and is destroyed by worms and insects. The jar itself will last seven or eight years, if taken care of by matting around the lower part with straw during the rainy seasons; if not, two or three years is the period it will stand unimpaired. [Clapperton, in Cardew 1960, p. 222]

Among the maguzawa storage was ritually sanctioned. The agricultural cycle was characterized by a ritual symmetry between, on the one hand, the "closure of the granary" (*kulle rumbu*) after the harvest in which seed required for planting and wet season consumption was stored, and on the other, the "opening of the granary" (*bude rumbu*) immediately prior to the rains, which was concurrent with an elaborate ceremony "releasing" the millet and sorghum seed.[74] The principal agricultural spirits, *uwar gona* and *kure*, were thus propitiated by the closure ceremony; granaries could not be opened prior to the rains without throwing into spiritual jeopardy the entire rainy period. Raynault (1975) refers to a similar precolonial system in Gobir where seed and sufficient foodstuffs for the preharvest hunger were placed into a clan or clan-segment granary protected for the period by the appropriate representatives of the maguzawa pantheon.[75] This period of granary closure often corresponded to the departed adult males on dry season migration (*cin rani*), long-distance trading (*fatauci*), or as corvée labor.

Household Diversification and Stability. Most Hausa families, extended or nuclear, must have had little slack to take up during periods of hunger. To the extent that domestic resiliency flourished it was in part with the assistance of food substitutes that were used to alleviate hunger and to safeguard the consumption of grains. In many instances, the foods that came to assume particular significance, such as *kuka* (baobab leaves), were usually part of the Hausa diet but simply came to occupy an expanded role in local consumption. The self-help philosophy also extended to the social relationships within the gandu unit. In a period when it constituted the fundamental productive unit, the gandu conferred a degree of collective security for its constituent members.

> Peasants find many advantages in the gandu as a productive unit. It combines joint insurance against individual distress due to illness, pests, or crop-failure, with economies due to the better management which large resources of land and labour permit, and to the spreading of ceremonial expenditures at marriage, childbirth naming, or Sallah ('Id el-Fitr and 'Id el-Kabir). [M. G. Smith 1965, p. 214]

Its intergenerational character also permitted an averaging-out of the consumer-producer ratios of component nuclear families, which in turn reduced the level of vulnerability of these component units to a crisis of simple reproduction.

Several other characteristics suggest why the extended household was a resilient and adaptive unit under conditions of dearth, in addition to advantages conferred by size. First, women exhibited a large measure of economic autonomy as Hill (1969) illustrated in her discussion of "hidden trade" and the "honeycomb market"; female petty trading added economic diversity to the gandu and, in an era when the incidence of rural wife seclusion was slight, female labor power and the agricultural production from wives' farms contributed significantly to the domestic unit. Male-female roles were *complementary* and *cooperative*, which added fiscal security to the household. Not only did women provide credit, grain, and income but—and this is still the case today—the sale of small livestock, invariably owned by women, provided the liquidity to buy cereals during the crucial preharvest period. Adult males and youths could diversify the economic foundation of the gandu through dry season trading and crafts (particularly hand weaving during the nineteenth century) while migration (cin rani) might relieve pressure on domestic granaries.[76] Table 3.6 is a rendering of the contribution of craft, sylvan, and livestock in the household economy taken from a colonial assessment report in Sokoto, but early enough to be representative of the vitality of off-farm production.

Though my principal concern has been with the sedentary economy, it bears reiteration that risk-aversion and security was very much embedded in nomadic practice. All aspects of nomadic livelihood were in some sense subordinate to the reality of drought.[77] Operating in biomes marginal at best for sustained yield agriculture, Ful'be and Touareg households were especially sensitive to the variability in rainfall; indeed their survival depended upon it. To run the risk of poor pasture was to risk the loss of accumulated domestic capital and a massive decapitalization of livestock that was not readily reconstituted. Caldwell's (1975, p. 57) observation that "mitigating the effect of downswings in economic misfortune [rather] than on getting most out of the upswings" captures the stockholder's concern for security in the face of constant threats against daily sustenance and access to the primary means of production. The cognizance of risk among pastoralists is seen in the emphasis on recuperative power, the capacity of a household to continue as an independent unit with sufficient stock after a loss (Dahl and Hjort 1979, p. 18). Absolute family size was doubtless of some significance for Sudano-Sahelian pastoralists in their desire to buffer themselves against drought, but other strategies included the construction of social ties and links of lineage solidarity.

The risk-averse qualities of the Ful'be and Touareg production systems were reflected in five pastoral strategies: mobility, herd diversification, herd dispersal, herd maximization, social relations, and investment. Mobile adaptation, whether the daily patterns of trekking or the seasonal transhumant circuits in search of quality pasture, constituted the basis of pastoral reproduction, but the intensity, frequency, and distance of herd mobility increased noticeably under conditions of diminished pasture availability (van Raay 1975; de Leeuw and van Raay 1974). Pastoral households able to maintain a diversity of species, as was typical among Ful'be and Touareg who held goats, sheep, cattle, and camels, also benefited from a more complete utilization of forage and graze, a more even access to food, and a reduced risk of total herd loss.[78] The spatial separa-

tion of livestock units—loan animals via kin networks—served to minimize the impact of local calamity, while access to a large number of
animals was in itself a precaution conferring a greater margin of security.[79] Stock associateship and clientage used social ties as a hedge
mechanism, for household participation in extensive kin networks with
other stock allies magnified their recuperative power. Reciprocity claims
could be activated following, or in anticipation of, a major stock loss. And
finally, both Ful'be and Touareg lineages invested quite heavily in agrarian and commercial infrastructure in the savannas, which involved servile communities of grain producers (as in the case of *buzu* farm estates,
which provided annual cereal tribute, broker services, and refuges during
the cycle of drought recovery) or semisedentary stock breeders. In any
case, these commercial investments were emblematic of the gradations of
mobility and sedentarism along the desert edge between which livestock
herders necessarily oscillated in response to the demands of climatic
perturbations and animal loss.

THE POLITICAL ECONOMY OF SUBSISTENCE

> The minimal formulation was that elites must not invade the subsistence
> reserve of poor people; its maximal formulation was that elites had a positive
> moral obligation to provide for the maintenance of their subjects in time of
> dearth.
>
> —James Scott

In an intriguing exegesis on the *jamani* system of South Asia, Epstein
(1967) suggested that the inherited and fixed exchange relationships
between village specialists actually maximizes the distribution of grain
during bad harvests. The lower-caste households were willing to accept a
fixed, minimal payment in grain regardless of services provided on the
grounds that it granted them security even during a bad harvest. The
system thus reflected a logic that focused on the long-term minimum
product rather than the short-term marginal product. This general concern with long-term stability and insuring minimum subsistence requirements in poor years, appears to be a general characteristic of precapitalist
societies. For many households whose livelihood and local environment
leave them close to the survival level, many social arrangements make
sense as disguised if limited forms of social welfare. The anticipation of
food shortage gives rise to practices and behaviors that attempt to preserve a margin of economic security and the demands for subsistence
security emerges from the concrete conditions of peasant life.

The transgression of the disaster threshold, however, does not mean
that peasant families automatically starve. Indeed, Polly Hill (1972) noted

TABLE 3.6
OFF-FARM PRODUCTION MARIKI DISTRICT, SOKOTO, ABOUT 1906

Trade	No.	Annual profit			Sylvan	No.	Annual value	
		£	s	d			s	d
Dyers	591	2	9	8	Kuka	1,066	5	
Weavers	923	2	5	0	Kaiwa	974	3	
Salt sellers	40	2	5	0	Tsamiya	358	3	
Butchers	186	5	0	0	Dinya	366	5	
Builders	25	1	1	6	Dorowa	1,258	5	
Potters	28	2	5	0	Kiria	52	2	6
Saddle makers	4	2	5	0	Aduwa	586	1	
Snuffmakers	9	3	10	0	Magoria	1,215	2	
Leather workers	25	2	5	0	Bagorua	478	3	

	No.	Value		
		£	s	d
Kurag	50			9
Livestock				
Horses	74	3	3	0
Mares	220	3	10	0
Donkeys	942	1	7	0
Sheep	4,543		3	0
Goats	12,221		2	6
Cattle	5,484	No data		

	No.	£	s	d
Barbers	34	1	19	0
Mat makers	89		13	0
Smiths	152	3	0	0
Tanners	82	2	5	0
Tailors	510		13	0
Brokers	72	1	19	0
Total Trades	3,881			
Average trade per adult male = 0.75				

SOURCE: NAK SNP 10 472p (Mariki District Assessment Report, Sokoto Province).

NOTE: Area, 90 square miles; population, 21,825; density, 246 per square mile; total males, 5,147.

in her study of contemporary Batagarawa, near Katsina, that while individual poverty was commonplace, few actually starved. An early political officer in Kano captured the essence of this individual resiliency in Hausaland and the social arrangements that underscored it, when he referred to

> the fact that a man can always get a handful of grain here and there is probably due to the simple charity inherent among peasant folk; but it may perhaps be also due to an instinctive feeling . . . that bad times may place them, too, in a position dependent on other humanity. [NAK SNP 9 5785/1912]

I refer to the character of this peasant charity as the "logic of the gift" used in a loose sense to refer to the social character of exchange, gift giving, and redistribution, which can act as insurance and as welfare mechanisms. In doing so, I argue that this norm or logic of reciprocity inheres in several social levels from the household to the state. In his discussion of the Sokoto Caliphate, Murray Last's (1967, p. 186) observation that "the household, like the village, was a microcosom of the state" captures the isomorphism between these different social levels. In the following discussion, I simply pose the question, "how did the peasantry survive during periods of food shortage?"

Village Sociology. In contrast to Popkin's (1979, pp. 131, 132) portrayal of corporate village identities in precolonial Vietnam, communities "with clear boundaries between insiders and outsiders . . . a well developed public sector and village citizenship," it would be spurious, I believe, to claim the closed corporate community as a model for Hausaland. The Northern Nigeria Lands Committee (1910) was correct to point out the antiquity of traditional village boundaries, but in many ways, as H. R. Palmer noted, the corporateness of Hausa communities required careful qualification. First, the hegemony of the village head (mai gari) over a contiguous community was partly undermined by the existence of chaffa ties, household heads who owed no allegiance to the mai gari or the village as such, save for the payment of kudin kassa. Residence was, then, no measure of community corporateness, and Palmer in his commentary on Katsina villages—which he typified as a nucleus of 300 walled compounds—noted that it was not unusual for 20 percent of the residents to have chaffa status with other patrons.[80] Second, many farmers held individual holdings in communities other than the one in which they resided; absentee farming (*noma jidi*) obviously transgressed the conventional limits of village autonomy.[81] And third, the level of development of merchant capital (and hence commoditization) and the existence, especially in the close settled zones, of dispersed homesteads and hamlets, runs counter to the archetypical autonomous, nucleated village.[82] Also, villages were not egalitarian or necessarily harmonious. In any economy in which the market was not instrumental in household reproduction, we can assume that some of this "innate inegalitarianism," as Hill (1977, p. 130) calls it, can be accounted for by the Chayanovian model of family natural history.[83]

Yet in spite of these caveats with respect to corporate village identity, and of the limited extent of village-wide institutional forms in Hausaland, there is no need to view rural life as wholly Hobbesian.[84] In his work on peasant rebellion, Barrington Moore (1966) captured the minimal social norms and reciprocities that can emerge from peasant communities in which the production of use-values and the sharing of risks predominates.

> The essence of these standards is a crude notion of equality, stressing the justice and necessity of a minimum of land [resource] for the performance of essential social tasks. These standards usually have some sort of religious sanction. [Barrington Moore 1966, p. 49]

This model had two dimensions in Hausa society; first, horizontal reciprocity among equals, most particularly gift exchange between individuals or households; and second, vertical redistribution among unequals, notably between patrons and clients, and officeholders and commoners. The latter, while often distinguished from reciprocity was, as Sahlins (1972) has shown, a variant of it.

These reciprocal norms imposed certain standards of performance on its better-off members; Raynault describing nineteenth-century Maradi points out that these obligatory roles were most pronounced when households were incapable of meeting basic biological requirements from their own resources.

> When, during periods of dearth, family reserves were unable to last the year and to cover the period of peak hunger, chiefs and dignitaries from various offices in the political hierarchy, were expected to open their granaries—filled in large measure by the labor power or rents collected from the peasantry—and to provide assistance to the local inhabitants. [Raynault 1975, p. 12]

Beyond the purely familial, then, various networks, institutions, and exchanges acted as shock absorbers for the peasantry. In particular, it seems safe to assume that Hausa communities in the nineteenth century were characterized by a rapid circulation of wealth through complex patterns of exchange and gift giving, in much the same way that Nicolas (1965) described this "circulation de richèsse" in the 1950s in Nigerian Hausaland. The system of gift and countergift provided the very fabric of village, and indeed intervillage cohesion.

The Hausa language contains a varied vocabulary that denotes the complex typological gradations in gifts, from those that are socially nonspecific to others with quite definite attributes, gifts with a clear-cut social personality given in tightly regulated ritual or ceremonial contexts. There were, for example, gifts of homage, thanks, or salutation (*gaisuwa, kudin godiya*), gifts of piety especially associated with Muslim festivals (*sadaka*), gifts of alliance and friendship (*gudumuwa*) frequently related to important life cycle occasions such as birth and naming, and finally "le don ostentatoire" (Nicolas 1967, p. 136), which embellished complicated political and redistributive networks. The formality and obligatoriness of gift giving varied enormously according to social context; those associated with bond friendship or ceremonies of great collective significance were rigidly adhered to. In spite of their institutional or contextual differences, however, their general function in Hausaland was quite clear. It was a language with implications of social support (Nicolas 1967, p. 71).

I attempt to demonstrate that while gifts were multiplex in character[85] they all possessed a strong instrumental quality; simply put, these gifts and exchanges provided the social context of famine occurrence and constituted the admittedly brittle strands of an indigenous relief program.

Obligatory gifts and countergifts between equals penetrated almost every nook and cranny of Hausa life; personal friendships (*babban abokinci*), spirit possession, circumcision, investiture, political election, and the great Islamic festivals of Id-el-Kabir and Id-el-Fitr, were all accompanied by social exchanges of some form. Some were highly structured and subject to rather strict ceremonial protocol. Gifts associated with formal ceremonies were usually referred to as *biki*;[86] that is, any gift or contribution to a friend celebrating a special occasion that would necessarily be recompensed later. Biki commonly between male and female friends, co-wives, and close kin were motivated by love and trust (*amana*). In addition to the biki and gudumuwa circuits, bond friendships, adashi relations, complimentary exchanges (*kori*), maguzawa rituals, and *bori* initiations all had this reciprocal thread running through them. Gift exchanges associated with the important life cycle developments—child naming, marriage, and death—were doubly significant. These ceremonies not only cemented new social bonds—as in the case of marriage and naming—but in a strategic sense acted as enormous local investment networks. Nicolas (1967) estimated ceremonial expenditures at the end of the nineteenth century in Nigerian Hausaland, which highlight the magnitude of gift exchanges at marriages, funerals, and naming ceremonies (table 3.7). The magnitude of these ceremonial funds varied according to the economic status of the household—and in this respect the richer households were able to generate larger social networks—but the structures of performance were similar. In addition to the great number of social linkages involved, another aspect of ceremonial exchanges was the inclusion, in a rather perfunctory manner, of

TABLE 3.7
Ceremonial Gift Exchange in Hausaland at the End of the Nineteenth Century

Funeral		Naming ceremony		Wedding	
Category of gift	Amount (cowries)	Category of gift	Amount (cowries)	Category of gift	Amount (cowries)
Burial ritual		Sheep	4,600	Gifts to wife's parents*	
Shroud	4,000	Kola	?	Shinin ba iko	10,000
Gifts to the marabouts	10,500	Food	millet	Sa arme	10,000
Gifts to the infirm	50	Gifts to mother	1,000	Sa lalle	200
Gifts to the grave diggers	200	Gifts to paternal aunt	meat	Dauren arme	?
Total cost:	14,750	Gifts to maternal parents	meat	Sadaki	12,000
Seventh-day alms (sadaka)		Gifts to paternal parents	meat	Trousseau	24,200
One sheep	10,000	Gift to the matron	50	Gifts	10,000
Gifts to the marabouts	10,000	Marabout	5,000	Alwali	1,200
Gifts to the infirm	500	Butcher	60	Marabout	200
		Griot	450	Kola	?
		Village head	?	Total cost:	67,800
Total cost:	20,500	Blind	100	Cost of kola	12,500
Grand Total:	35,250	Total Cost:	11,260	Countergifts to spouse's parents	40,000
					1 horse

Source: Nicolas (1967).

*Consists of a series of formal gift exchanges, which are listed here using their Hausa names.

the village elite. In most of the cases documented in table 3.7, gifts were usually granted to the village head. This was not only an acknowledgment of parochial authority but also an affirmation of elite obligations and peasant rights. In this fashion, the fundamental ceremonials that cemented interfamilial linkages at one level symbolically reproduced village-wide patterns of authority and local obligation at another. This ambiguity is, of course, intrinsic to the notion of hegemony itself.

The prosaic point I wish to make with respect to all Hausa ceremonies and their gift-giving attributes is the pan-family linkages they represented. Family groups were joined and strengthened, individuals and groups were incorporated into the community, and solidarity was affirmed. A powerful form of collective security was guaranteed because village bonds were coterminous with complex networks of social indebtedness. This takes us, moreover, far beyond the anarchy of individual self-interest and peasant distrust. Participation in these circuits did not level inequalities in one mighty redistributive act but, more crucially, confirmed that in times of hardship certain social relationships—biki partners, bond friends, and so on—were measurably reliable sources of support. In some instances these links extended beyond the village boundaries, a tendency that was encouraged by the Hausa cultural preference for village exogamy in marriage. Gift exchange in Hausa communities was a symbolic token of future claims against the insecurities of an unpredictable future.

Transcending the parochial resources of the gandu unit or nuclear family (iyali) was very much part of the peasant world where shared values, obligations, and norms seemed to reinforce mutual assistance. Among the maguzawa, the clan segment (*GIDA*),[87] which was the locus of much gift giving and reciprocal support, served this welfare function in times of hunger.

> [The GIDA] has but one function: when the grain stores of one household are exhausted, its head may borrow grain from another GIDA household and repay that grain at harvest without interest. [Faulkingham 1971, p. 123]

Of course, a man could not count with as much certainty on assistance from a nonrelative or distant kinsman as he might from household members, and this tended to be especially the case among bilateral kindred, where reciprocal help diminished markedly with kin distance. But because of this graduation toward the periphery, reciprocity was ensured and, wherever possible, intensified.

While it is easy to idealize village reciprocity and the sort of welfarism that emerged from it, most commentators on peasant society have not failed to note the extent to which it operated (Scott 1976). Not only did this involve horizontal reciprocities between households of roughly equal status but also vertical divisions between elite and commoners, mirrored by a standard package of morally laden redistributive rights. The general end to which these rights were directed was, in a minimal sense, simple reproduction, and more generously to permit peasants to discharge ceremonial and social duties, to feed themselves, and to continue to cultivate. To the extent that peasant households fell below this level, the village heads, merchants, patrons, and ultimately the sarki had specific responsibilities. Indeed, they were in part legitimized by these duties and ideologically bound to them by the Shari'a. I now turn to these chains of interdependence and redistribution among unequals in nineteenth-century Hausaland. In doing so, I concentrate on three related Hausa institutions: the communal work group (gayya); patron-client relationships (barantaka), and other elite responsibilities, most particularly the institution of sarkin noma (king of farming).

Communal Work Groups. Although of little practical importance today, the gayya—which Bargery (1934, p. 264) defines as the collecting together of a number of people to assist one another in a piece of work—was formerly commonplace among free farmers, and frequently levied compulsorily by officeholders. There were at least four varieties of gayya: (1) for brideservice when a work party was sponsored by a daughter's fiancé, (2) by a client for his patron, (3) by contract to wealthier men (*masu arziki*) and (4) compulsory gayya for officeholder, when youths worked on the large estates (gandun sarauta) of the village elite or as corvée labor for state-sponsored construction. Irrespective of its precise form and function, adult men and youths were to perform gayya usually to overcome labor bottlenecks, most notably hoeing and weeding. In return for labor services, the gayya group would receive kola, food, cash, and perhaps presents. A gayya was generally called by a wealthier mai gida, the poorer households providing labor, while food, gifts, and such were given in return. Gayya also released foodstuffs during the critical preharvest period. As Raulin (1964, p. 71) put it "[gayya] appears as a redistributive and equilibrating mechanism in [Hausa] society since [it operates] in this sense at the moment when food resources begin to diminish and when scarcity makes itself felt."

Patron-Client Relationships. Though kinship provided the fundamental setting for the most important social relationships in Hausaland, a great number of individuals participated in client networks. M. G. Smith in describing nineteenth-century Zaria suggested that ties of political patronage and clientage constituted the very fabric of Hausa society.

Clientage (barantaka)[88] in Hausaland was a highly variegated social relation and assumed four basic associational forms: (1) *political*, pertaining to a patron's aspirations to (and support for) political office,

(2) *domestic*, as a type of substitute kinship in which a person assumed ties of consanguinity or affinity, (3) *commercial*, between merchants or traders and their associates, and (4) *female* clientage. All forms of barantaka, however, demanded similar standards of performance.

> [Client-patronage] had the premise of a voluntary, dissoluble consociation entered upon to the mutual benefit of the contracting parties, and certain enjoined obligations encumbent on each for the period of this connection. [Low 1972, p. 19]

In practice, the ties of loyalty (*cafka*) intrinsic to dynastic politics and patrimonial state systems (particularly between the Sultan and emirs, between emir and courtiers, or between a village chief and his superiors) were, strictly speaking, all forms of clientage. Local clientage within, and occasionally between, Hausa villages often constituted the lower end of vast catenary tarayya systems, or merchant networks, which frequently terminated in the cities at the seats of urban patrons.

The attenuated village patronage systems were more commonly tied to the local elite, the village head (mai gari or mai unguwa), the wealthy traders, the merchants (attajirai) and the officeholders. For clients, these relations afforded protection, reductions in the tax burden, and in some cases the provision of food, clothes, and marriage expenses. Unlike Asia, clientage did not interface with landlord-tenant relationships, which to the best of our knowledge existed nowhere in Hausaland. Nonetheless, effectively controlled clients (barori) were instrumental in large-scale agricultural production and political support. In reality, barantaka was far more complex than simple dyadic unions and intertwined large sections of the community in huge social networks.[89] In a society in which officeholding was an object of intense political competition between persons eligible by birth for appointment, clients were attracted in proportion to the local estimate of their prospects (M. G. Smith 1960, p. 12). The merchant-ulema networks were also matrices of primary clientage centered on the patriarchal, all-encompassing mai gida, who acted as patron for his slaves, wage laborers,[90] and *yara* (boys). In contradistinction to Popkin's (1979, p. 75) assertion that in spite of the patriarchal self-image of the patron "he himself lacked the managerial competence to perform such a role," Tahir (1975) has shown how these massive, extended patrimonial merchant households in nineteenth-century Kano were reproduced precisely through centralized, managerial functions.

Of course, we cannot assume that the terms of exchange, or the maintenance of dependency and resource distribution among patron-client dyads was exogenously given. Competition among clients (and especially between clients and kin) was intense and the patterns of reciprocity that emerged reflected relative bargaining power as much as the binding power of local ethical standards. But in Hausa society in which clientage was a critical means for soliciting political support, and in which labor power was in short supply, the institution of patronage ultimately depended upon how well it fulfilled local claims. Clientage provided a vehicle for subsistence security, but it also assisted in the reproduction of agrarian inequality. Yet because it provided an opportunity to demonstrate trust, integrity, and courage it was a relation of moral equality. In Hausa society where notions of honor and shame (*kunya*) had—and continue to have—enormous normative significance, clientage could stubbornly demand, and fulfill, a security function by virtue of its moral force. From the peasant's view, barantaka opened up new claims on his labor power but also was a channel to larger resources. That these resources sometimes lay beyond the community was indeed an asset, particularly in an environment where rainfall variability was localized.

Correlatively, the Koranic school and Islamic networks in nineteenth-century Hausaland had much in common with the extant systems of patronage. The ulema were, of course, directly supported by the emirs, officeholders, state functionaries, and wealthy merchants, but many talakawa and common folk were incorporated into these webs of Islamic learning. This participation was in fact part of a peripatetic tradition taking the form of seasonal migration (cin rani) of youths to study with respected malamai. The dry-season departure of aspiring scholars relieved pressures on household granaries. The tradition of the peripatetic mallam offered a positive economic inducement, not simply in an ideological sense of deepening the practice of Islam or achieving upward mobility as a scribe in the patrimonial bureaucracy but it assisted household reproduction and lowered the risk of famine. Koranic students resided in town and country alike and often engaged in casual wage labor.[91] The ethics and status norms of Caliphal society demanded that Koranic students receive alms, which was in fact "a form of redistribution of wealth from the more affluent urban dwellers to the sons of rural dwellers under the norms of Islamic charity" (Lubeck 1980, p. 5).

Elite Responsibilities, the Sarkin Noma (King of Farming). In his observations on precolonial Maradi, Claude Raynault declared that in the Hausa-Fulani social system "the possibility of accumulation [found] an institutional counterpart in the obligation to redistribute ... the wealth produced" (1976, p. 88). Social relations functioned, in other words, as mechanisms of collective security. The institution of kingship was part of such an embracing normative order that imposed canons of proper social conduct. By mandate, the sarki, literally the sarkin kassa (the master of the territory), was directly responsible for emirate welfare; indeed, the geographic locus of his power, the birni, was not simply a citadel and a palace but was also a granary (Nicolas 1969, p. 137).[92] Among Muslim communities redistribution was sustained by a religious ideology in which the image of the Islamic patriarch was all powerful.[93] This open-handedness constituted one important part of the Hausa concept of *mutum kirkii*, the good and righteous person, and among many communities, but particularly the maguzawa, found institutional expression through some individuals invested with clearly defined redistributive powers attached to their political office, perhaps the most important being that of sarkin noma.

The office of sarkin noma is an ancient one long predating the jihad, and survives, in a purely honorific way, among many Muslim communities.[94] The institution embraced on the one hand, the ceremony by which the sarkin noma was elected, the *dubu* or *ruga*, and on the other, the discrete functions of the office within the village and local economy. The rather complex procedure by which the sarki was proposed and ultimately elected need not concern us here. Suffice to say that any individual who proposed to (and eventually did) harvest 1,000 bundles of grain (*demin dubu*) could appeal to become a member of the prestigious regional community of *sarakunan noma*. In nineteenth-century Kazaure and Daura for example a village might possess two or more sarakuna, both of whom held prominent clan positions and who effected, through their allegiance to the sarakunan noma, alliances with other maguzawa clans.[95] At the apex of the community of farming kings was the *sarkin lafiya* (king of well-being) surrounded by *shugaba* (guides) and high-ranking dignitaries (*ajiya, sarkin hatsi, kaura noma*) all of whom were instrumental in the accession of a new sarki. The preparatory rituals and ceremonies were closely interconnected with the spirit (*iskoki*) pantheon, especially those whose domain concerned farming, fertility, and rainfall. But it is the culmination of the proceedings, the dubu,[96] that directly concerns me.

> The term "dubu" means 1000. It evokes the fundamental prerequisite of the clan or lineage candidate, who proposes to accede the title [of Sarkin Noma]: to have accumulated a large number of bundles of millet. . . . The dubu is in effect a ritual ceremony, a rite of passage . . . in which the new Sarkin Noma must distribute his wealth. [Nicolas 1960, pp. 160, 161]

The dubu actually rested on two community principles: first, reciprocal exchanges characteristic of most domestic occasions; and second, interclan competition enacted through enormous redistributive feasts. In this sense the dubu was a type of potlatch in which the production, consumption, and distribution of wealth of the ritual was partially geared to the accumulation of symbolic capital. The presence of the sarkin lafiya and other regional sarakunan noma ensured that the sarki elect lived up to, in a stylized, competitive way, his clan's claims of generosity, wealth, and largesse. Nicolas has argued on the basis of his ethnographic studies in southern Niger that the principal beneficiaries were artisans, griots, clan allies, religious dignitaries, the village chief, and local or regional sarakunan noma. These exchanges hardly conform to the simple model of rich to poor assistance, but the sarakuna had precise public functions within their own communities and hence the passage of wealth between officeholders ultimately served the same redistributive end. In this particular case intervillage grain allocation of some magnitude went some way toward balancing local deficits and surfeits of food.[97]

The second relevant institutional attribute of the sarkin noma pertains to the prescribed functions of elected officials. In addition to a legitimate claim of 100 bundles tribute and a ram's leg from any other individual who harvested in excess of 1,000 bundles of grain, the sarki was also responsible for the organization and payment of communal work groups. The centerpiece of the office, however, was the obligation that the sarkin noma annually present the village chief 200 headloads of grains and also act as a famine reserve.[98]

> [Sarkin Noma] generally posesses a larger piece of land than the other *masugida* and as a result controls a considerable harvest surplus. If the grain runs out in a *gida* before the new harvest, the *maigida* takes himself to the *Sarkin Noma* and asks for help. Either grain would be sold to him or loaned until the next harvest. Interest would not be paid on its return. [Reuke 1969, p. 25]

It is interesting to note in regard to these subsistence concerns that rain rituals, rites, and prayers—many of which are now moribund—were commonplace among Muslim and maguzawa communities alike. Among Islamic communities, a preferred rite was a "water chase" (*farautal ruwa*), exclusively effected by married women and seen as an act of ritual purification in which the drought was clearly endowed with a moral etiology.

> In the towns and cities, all the married women, without exception, must participate in the ceremony. Unmarried women must find husbands and prostitutes are chased out. This action appears as a positive rite designed to produce rain . . . , and is based on the perceived tie between women and rainfall. . . . The exclusion of prostitutes corresponds . . . to an act of purification. [Nicolas 1975, p. 394]

In the event of a sustained drought, the masu sarauta and the clerics— usually in the larger towns and birane—organized a prayer for rain (*rokon ruwa*), sometimes actually led by a senior wife (*uwar gida*).[99] In extreme circumstances, spirit (bori) adepts were called upon who appealed to the pagan authorities to perform their hereditary rain rites. The maguzawa rain rites, conversely, necessitated the propitiation of agricultural spirits or influential representatives in the cosmic hierarchy, through the use of sacrificial offerings effected through clan leaders and distinguished officeholders such as the sarkin noma or sarkin lafiya.[100]

The detail of both sets of ritual practices is of less pertinence than their structural and functional similarities, which bear directly upon the discussion of famine and subsistence crises. First, the *publicity* of the rituals was at once a public denotation of an environmental problem and simultaneously a signal—not least to the elite—of the possibility of a crisis. That such an eventuality was grounded in ritual, religion, or cosmology did not detract from its importance, for it reaffirmed the central functions of the state, the elites, and the oligarchy in times of dearth. And second, like all rituals, the rain rites emphasized social bonds—and in this sense were in keeping with (and supportive of) the norms of reciprocity and collective sentiment—and the moral order of which the ritual was a part. Insofar as the rituals demanded the participation of those upon whom the peasantry might ultimately depend in times of dearth, they also preemptively affirmed the obligations encumbent upon those powers.[101] Among the maguzawa for instance, the sarkin noma frequently conducted the rain rites since it was he who had guaranteed a bountiful harvest in the ceremony of the "opening of the bush" (*budin daji*) prior to the wet season. Poor precipitation was not only a reflection on the purported agronomic prowess of the sarkin noma—or the morality of the community in the case of the Muslim Hausa—but it also generated a response that was an affirmation of the social order and the roles the elite were expected to perform. Far from being obfuscatory, therefore, of the real "scientific" causes of drought, these rites were functionally adequate in relation to subsistence security. It may well be that the rites conform to Rappaport's (1971) model of ritual regulation in the sense that they are responses to environmental signals that convey information about the response system and its normal functioning; at the same time they send messages to the "higher-order regulators," which ultimately play an important part in the indigenous system of famine relief.[102]

Village, State and Region. As a preface to the discussion of state performance and the struggles revolving around the disposition of the surplus product, I briefly recapitulate some of the regional mechanisms of food security. These regional issues pertain especially to the human ecology of the desert edge, and in particular to the activities of specialist grain traders who evacuated foodstuffs from areas of surfeit like the Zamfara, Bornu, and Gobir granaries, and traded them to the central close settled zones like Kano and Katsina, which were almost certainly net grain importers. In times of dearth, the grains trade provided a limited bulwark against starvation.

In their seminal work on the precolonial savanna-desert edge economy, Baier and Lovejoy (1975) showed how the Sudanic savannas and the

Sahel were closely intertwined. These symbiotic relations were thrown into sharp relief when the desert-side system suffered severe drought.

> During hard times, nobles, their families, and retinues depended on the hospitality of dependents on estates in the savanna, including many Agalawa villages as well as servile villages and farms close to Tuareg grazing camps. Nobles remained at the southern end of their network until the weather improved and the herds began to grow again, so that these southern communities in effect acted as a safety valve in times of scarcity. [1977, p. 404]

Patterns of social structure, most particularly the gradations of servility among Touareg lineages, contributed to the general pattern of cultural plasticity and symbiosis among adjacent ecological niches. This view, however, of Touareg and buzu diaspora communities and associated patterns of trade and movement actually depicts a sort of parasitism, for the southerly emirates provided the haven to which the Sahelian populations retreated during periods of hardship. A simple retreat-expansion model calibrated with the drought cycle actually oversimplifies a rather complex two-way interdependency. Under closer scrutiny, the northern emirates in particular were to a large extent dependent upon grain production in the southern Sahelian regions of Adar, Damagaram, and Damerghou.[103] H. R. Palmer, for example, while the Resident of Katsina, noted that at the turn of the century much of Hausaland proper was not a huge granary as the colonial administration hypothesized.

> But in this connection when I was touring in the northern part of the Province I met a great number of caravans going to fetch or returning with guinea corn from French territory. I learn that they have to resort to outside sources for their supply of guinea corn at this time of year. I mention this matter as it is the impression that Katsina Province is the granary of the Protectorate. [NAK Katprof 1789/1904]

Thus while the horizon of the Touareg communities was toward the southern refuges in the savannas, Hausa farmers as often as not looked north (*arewa*) to meet grain deficits.

It has long been appreciated that internal migration, in part stimulated by famine or food shortage, has been central to the evolution of Hausa emirates. These movements left an indelible stamp on the social and political constitution of Hausa communities. In Katsina and Kano, migratory patterns favored the rapid growth of social and trading networks that constituted part of the infrastructure of the early territorially defined communities. Much of this movement was closely related to, and often coterminous with, the local and regional grains trade, which grew up in response to the subsistence crises characteristic of the northern savannas. These exchange circuits were the domain of a particular class of traders, *yan kwarami*, frequently drawn from specific ethnic communities especially buzu (servile Touareg) and maguzawa. In 1907 the Kano Resident was embarrassed to report that "administrators have never realized how much corn is imported from the north. I had always looked upon Kano as self-supporting . . . but I find this is not the case" (NAK SNP 7 3095/1907). A Sokoto District Assessment included a comment upon the continual "igidi" trade to Gobir in the north, farmers returning "loaded with grain" (NAK SNP 10 379/1913, p. 10). Where the trade was localized and small-scale, single donkey-based *dan kwarami* purchased grain directly from the household producers. In other cases there was a permanent need to import food grains over much greater distances. The buoyancy of the grain market was reflected in the tendency among merchants to devote slave-based gandu production to millet cultivation (Tahir 1975).[104] In nineteenth-century Zamfara, the attajirai were invariably those who had a close connection with either grain production or distribution. Kaura Namoda emerged as an important locus of the regional cereals trade, and local grain merchants (*yan sakai*) built a reputation for their enormous wealth, none more so than the Touareg from the north (Na Dama 1976).

Although the precise character and organization of nineteenth-century trading remains murky, it characteristically carried a strong ethnic tone. Buzu traders certainly dominated the foodstuffs network in the Sokoto area, bringing millets from the Adar and returning with cotton; thus,

> many of the Bugaje are merely traders and transport-men who perform every year a valuable service by fetching grains from districts where it is plentiful and selling where there is a demand. [NAK SNP 10 102p/1915]

Kebbi yan kwarami from Argungu and birnin Kebbi took rice to the more arid northern reaches of Sokoto, and the famous long-distance trade in cereals from Zamfara and southern Katsina was associated with maguzawa, who had a reputation for farming excellence. The general impression, at any rate, is that grain was not a marginal commodity in these Caliphate distributive circuits; the usual academic emphasis on elite goods, slaves, and kola, and the northerly movement of foodstuffs purchased by seasonal immigrants from Air, has actually disguised the ubiquity and magnitude of the long-distance trade in staples. In view of the erratic nature of rainfall and the fear of poor harvests, the precolonial grains trade had great practical virtue. It was one element in the response system, a bulwark that attempted, as far as technical conditions permitted, to level regional imbalances. Not only was this network of special significance in relation to the drought recovery cycle but, with due respect to

Lovejoy and Baier, it reflected the dependence of the savannas on the Sahelian surplus-producing regions to the north. The axis of dependence, in other words, tilted the other way.

The role of the food network is thrown into a greater illumination when it is recalled that a good deal of historical evidence establishes that large areas within Hausaland—especially the close settled zones—were permanently grain-deficit by the nineteenth century, if not before. In the Kano region, the vulnerability to food deficits was doubtless related to high population densities, land shortage, and the emergence of a large commercial textile sector that absorbed many full- and part-time specialists. I raise this issue because it highlights that Hausaland was not a homogenous surface of self-sufficient, corporate villages, and also because it bathes the dependence on northern grains in a new light.

Clearly, the efficacy of the grains trade was tightly constrained by the nature of precolonial transportation. Its antediluvian character prevented the rapid transmission of large quantities of staple foodstuffs. The Caliphate was shackled by distance; a round-trip grain expedition from Katsina to Zamfara or Damagaram was a three to four week undertaking with no guarantee of immediate purchase or of local purchasing power being sufficient to match famine prices.[105] In light of the limits imposed by the technological forces, and by volatile prices and low purchasing power, the role of state apparatus and emirate elites assumed a signal importance.

The struggle over the appropriation of surplus labor is, as Scott (1977, p. 288) observes, the central class conflict in all precapitalist states. Yet in spite of the centrality of the state apparatus and of the ideological hegemony that legitimated the role of the sarauta class as appropriators of peasant surpluses, in a sense (as Lukacs noted of most precapitalist states) the state was insecurely anchored in the real life of society. The independence of much of rural life from the fate of birni politics was complex and contradictory. On the one hand, the legitimacy of Hausa state authority (iko) was inseparable from religiously defined social tasks, for which it was held responsible. These obligations, moreover, had practical consequences for the fate of individual kingly rule, and dynastic competition was tightly bound to harvest quality, the onset of the rains, and peasant welfare; kings lost the mandate of heaven when famine stalked the land (Nicolas 1969). Yet, in part the peasantry developed separately from the state; the talakawa developed a culture of resistance that embodied both a symbolic and geographic isolation from the apex of power (Scott 1977a; 1977b; 1977c). From these tensions and struggles emerged the peculiarities of village-state relations during the Caliphate, a moral economy in which the hegemony of the masu sarauta was vacuous if "vital [subsistence] needs were ignored or violated by elites, for these needs [were] an integral part of peasant consciousness" (Scott 1977a, p. 280). But, to say as Scott does that the important question in village-state relations was "what is left and not so much what is taken," actually leaves much unsaid; this is true because of the *nature* of struggles within the Caliphate, and because of the limits upon elite exploitation imposed by moral and ideological norms, by technological undevelopment, and by the relative bargaining power of the "talakawa." Subsistence security in relation to state power did not arise from central benevolence but from the politicoeconomic and technological constitution of class relations.

What, then, were the limits on state exploitation and on the bulwarks that peasants developed? Relatively poor communications, the limited level of military control (Last 1978), and the partial autonomy of local-level administration meant that massive forceable appropriation was impractical. If force was at all significant it operated through the catenary systems of clientage typical of patrimonial systems. But in emirates where population density was low and bush available in quantity, labor control could only be maintained through patron-client reciprocity. Furthermore, under conditions of labor shortage changing patrons or fleeing into other districts was a highly significant political act. The centralized form of dynastic politics—what Adas (1980, p. 537) calls the "contest state"— posed limits on direct administrative control in the countryside,[106] fostered by the parochial traditions and the village-centered culture of peasant life, which marked itself off from the practice of urban elites. Migration, then, was a legitimate form of dissent that placed limits on central predation (Last 1970). Equally, the oppressed peasant had final resort to banditry as a possible means of resistance to exorbitant demands, or to the influential rurally based ulema to whom the sarauta looked for ideological legitimation.[107] No emirate administration, no matter how despotic, could afford to eliminate or even excessively tax those upon whom it ultimately depended for its revenue; I have suggested that with this limit the nature of class relations within the Caliphal state was such that there were objective limits to exploitation.[108] The Sokoto Caliphate, to use Last's (1978, p. 26) phraseology, was imbued with a low degree of exploitation and control.

How, then, were these limits translated into the customary practice of a moral economy? Much balanced on the fulcrum of rents, their magnitude, timing, and rigidity. In his evidence to the Lands Committee in 1910, H. R. Palmer emphasized the fiscal latitude in emirate revenue systems.[109] Hull (1968) refers to tax "rebates" in late nineteenth-century Katsina while the following categories of tax exemption[110] conferred some security for those likely to be most vulnerable:

1. *Rongomi:* the "compounding" or "bargaining" between the tax collector and the payer due to the alleged poverty of the latter.

2. *Bakonchi:* a reduction in tax payment due to the recent arrival of the taxpayer in the village area.

3. Payment of the kudin kassa at half the usual rate for the first two years of occupancy if the resident is an immigrant or a new mai gida.

4. Exemption of civic duties (*aikin kaya*) on the grounds of poverty.

While there is still much historiographic work to be undertaken on the revenue and tax collecting systems in the Hausa states, it seems that the agents, collectors (jekadu), and masu garuruwa took account of harvest quality in their annual revenue assessment. This is the picture that H. R. Palmer painted for the Northern Nigeria Lands Committee:

> The Jakadas had wonderfully good memories, and when you went to them they would tell you the taxes of many hundred towns down to the smallest details. They carried all these in their heads. They would tell you in a wonderful way what each village produced. When it came to the actual collection, if there was a short harvest or anything special they would strike off a certain amount of taxes. The Emirs did not mind very much because they got quite as much as they wanted. [Palmer, Lands Committee 1910, p. 69]

The strength of this system, of course, was that the tax adjustments and state intervention were both predicated on the knowledge and perception of persons who had, by virtue of residence or work, first-hand knowledge of the local situation. Patron-client ties, chappa connections, and links to merchant networks could also serve to modify the tax burden; indeed, oral testimony collected in Katsina and Daura indicates that a complete suspension of taxes was not uncommon in the event of severe hunger. There was, in short, fiscal flexibility in what was nominally a fixed-rate system.[111] According to Dunbar, Damagaram State actually imposed extra taxes to cover the seed requirements of the poor.

> Occasionally during hard times an additional tax upon millet was levied. Called bude rumbu it consisted of half the millet remaining to a family after the seeding time, in order that the by now extremely scarce millet could be distributed to people who did not have fields or who had to depend upon the charity of the Sarki or the community at large [Dunbar 1970, p. 158].

Claims upon peasant subsistence were necessarily carefully graduated because the dividing line between legitimate expropriation and exploitation was, from the peasant's viewpoint, a thin one. Exploitation, in fact, had political-economic limits and the revenue system reflected this in its flexibility.

On balance, there is good reason to accept Orr's (1911, p. 157) judgment that nineteenth-century taxation systems were "never really onerous." The zakka grain tithe was certainly difficult to transport, collected sporadically and haphazardly, and according to Hill (1977, p. 51) "much of the grain held back as zakka was sold or eaten."[112] In his early touring of

northern Katsina, Palmer reported that all towns knew exactly what they
had to pay as traditional levies and "I have had no complaints" (NAK
Katprof 1769/1903).[113] Furthermore, it seems probable that the rate of
increase in kudin kassa did not keep pace with the rate of inflation of the
cowry; using Barth's tax estimate of 2,500 cowries in the 1850s and
Cargill's figure of 4,000 in 1900, the kudin kassa increased by 70 percent,
while the value of the cowry correspondingly fell by roughly 100 percent
over the same period.[114] While some emirates, such as Kano, may have
suffered a decrease in real tax revenue, revenue from the *shuka*, rafi and
industrials expanded considerably.[115] This is in concert with the deepening commoditization of the Caliphal economy and the growth of cash crop
production to which Last (1978) refers. Moreover, insofar as the cultivation of noncereal crops was a lucrative commodity sector and was often
assessed on actual yield, the burden of these levies fell more equitably
than kudin kassa, which was nominally regressive. Therefore, the level of
taxes on free men was acceptably low and sensitive to the exigencies of
peasant livelihood.[116] In view of the comparatively high population densities, the ratio of officeholders to tax payers was sufficiently low that a
relatively small tax burden levied on a large talakawa was sufficient to
sustain a state machinery and finance the elite consumption patterns that
were the mark of social class.

The second dimension of state responsibility was direct famine relief
through regional- or urban-based granaries, public works employment,
and grain relief. Throughout the Caliphate these sorts of central responsibilities were firmly embodied in notions of adequate government. Indeed Usman dan Fodio's treatise on government lay considerable emphasis on the particular administrative functions of material improvement,
charity, and relief.[117] The zakkat grain tithe, as irregular and variable as it
may have been, at least ensured the possibility of grain accumulation
during the bountiful years. In precolonial Gobir, for example,

> a part of the agricultural surplus of producers was appropriated by the local
> aristocracy who only sold and consumed part of it. The enormous quantities of
> grain thus accumulated were stored in mud granaries inside the birni . . . when
> a drought came, it was encumbent upon the Sarki to open the granaries . . . and
> to redistribute their contents to his subjects. A Prince who strove to avoid this
> obligation lost his throne [for] the local populace had the capacity to intervene
> in the political life of the court. If the granaries were empty . . . the sovereign
> mounted an expedition into the interior . . . to bring back grain bought in
> exchange for his treasures. [Nicolas 1977, p. 163]

The accumulation of foodstuffs was not simply an instance of state
benevolence, or an overwhelming concern for peasant welfare. The
urbanites clearly benefited from the security that large granaries conferred, especially in an epoch when military siege was not infrequent.

Equally, the zakkat sustained the enormous palace household of the emir, the dry season state projects, and corvée labor employed on public works. In Katsina emirate, some of the zakkat was deliberately held in the district capitals and the larger villages under the jurisdiction of palace clients, hakimai, and village heads.[118] Rural storage minimized the technological constraints on large-scale grain movement and the burden of long-distance migration by refugees searching for urban welfare. For the talakawa, the central granaries, generally under the jurisdiction of the sarkin hatsi, constituted the last desperate gasp in the hierarchy of famine assistance.[119] If all else failed, as peasant wisdom had it, "the Emir never ran short of food."[120]

FAMINE GENESIS AND DYNAMICS

The "general crisis" was a crisis of actual scarcity, typical of pre-capitalist modes of production and reflecting their inability to develop their productive forces. It was not a crisis indicative of the dominance of capitalism, exemplified by "poverty amidst plenty."

—Robert Brenner

I have tried to show that drought and famine were integral parts of the economic ebb and flow of the desert edge of the central Sudan during the nineteenth century. For agriculturalist and herder alike, capricious rainfall and the threat of starvation were both real and experienced. That the history of this area has been colored by long- and short-term cycles of growth, famine, and recovery provides the context for an understanding of what de Vries (1980) called the capacity for adaptation. At least since the time of Joseph's biblical promise of seven years of prosperity and dearth, societies have found social and technical mechanisms to grapple with fluctuations in climate and food supply.

In the short term, famines did occur in Hausaland and unquestionably caused a great deal of socioeconomic dislocation. Like subsistence crises elsewhere, these famines had an episodic career of three distinct phases: first, an initial gestation period in which a number of factors converged to attenuate food supplies; second, a period of crisis, and of characteristically "disaster" behavior that deviated markedly from customary routines; and third, a period of recovery and reconstitution. These episodes must, however, be situated in the seasonal round of rural activities in the Caliphate in which, even during a normal year, the critical months prior to harvest were generally of some hardship. Accordingly, a poor upland harvest due to drought might make itself felt by the following dry season (bazara), although the precise onset of actual shortage would depend on the quality of harvest during the preceding years.[121]

When the cereal crop failed completely the hunger threshold was considerably advanced.[122] Equally, the ability to refurbish granaries following a subsistence crisis was in large measure dependent upon a succession of good harvests.[123]

From this simple temporal pattern, two practical consequences can be derived: first, a food crisis was to a degree predictable both in the long term (insofar as it was expected) and in the short term (from the moment of irrevocable damage to the millet crop). And second, the famine itself had a certain logical sequence as a chain of interacting events, which were in a sense predictable. In Hausaland this sequence of disaster signals involved diverse elements such as changes in crop mixes or grazing patterns, the use of famine foods, household decapitalization, and out-migration. These activities were an expression of the "normal" operation of local adaptive flexibility, which I have colloquially referred to as an indigenous relief system. In spite of the Western image of Islamic fatalism, Hausa farmers did not sit and starve, or respond randomly when harvests failed; they adopted characteristic modes of famine behavior graduated with respect to time.[124] In the parlance of moral economy, the households had a clear vision of where they might turn for direct assistance and, as Scott (1976) puts it, a "social map" of expectations. A typical temporal sequence of strategies involved the following (see Jodha 1975):

1. Domestic mutual support; intensification of "fall back" activities by household members, including the collection of famine foods.[125]
2. Minimization of current commitments through suspension or cancellation of resource allocation, including tax relief and grain loans.
3. Disposal of inventories of home-produced goods, village charitable relief, grain purchase, and patron support.
4. Sale or mortgage of assets, especially small livestock.
5. Short- or long-term migration.
6. Famine relief from state or patron assistance.
7. Possible return, recovery, replanting, and reconstitution of reserves.

The gradation of famine behavior[126] corresponded to the resources contained within different social orbits. Self-help contained the most reliable output but it yielded only what a household could mobilize; wider social realms—the descent group, the patron, the village—controlled a greater resource pool but carried higher risk, or (more accurately) less certainty of return. At any rate, these social and temporal gradations marked off famine behavior from contextual relations of normal conditions (figure 3.2).

A precise historical reconstruction of actual precolonial famines, save for the sordid anecdotes of child sale, consumption of carrion, and the

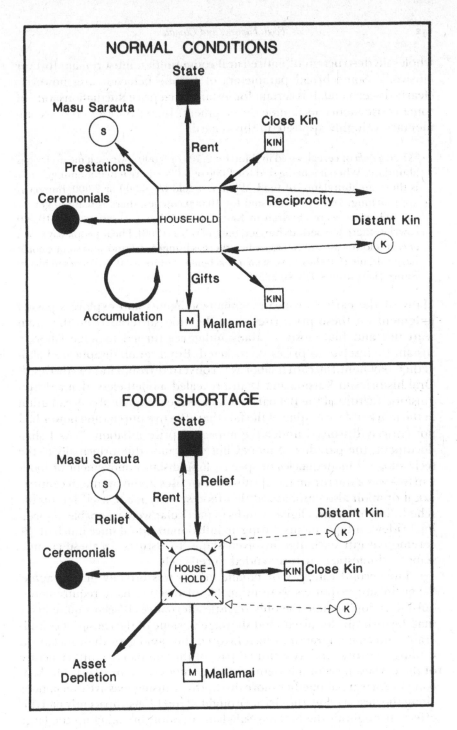

Figure 3.2. Nineteenth century drought-famine dynamics

wholesale destruction of entire rural communities, must remain forever elusive.[127] Some broad parameters of famine behavior are, however, clearly discernable. It is certain for instance that price fluctuations were of some consequence in famine development. Imam Imoru's cryptic commentary is highly apposite in this regard.

> When a *taiki* of cereal is sold in Kano for 2,500 or 3,000 cowries, it means food is abundant. When it is being sold for 4,000 or 5,000, there is neither hunger, nor is there an abundance of food. When it is sold for 6,000 or 7,000, hunger is approaching, and when it is sold for 10,000 cowries, there is real hunger.
>
> When we were children in Kano [ca. 1840] and it was sold for 10,000 cowries, there was serious hunger, but today [ca. 1900], I hear people say that a *taiki* is sold for 30,000 cowries when there is hunger in Kano, and some people have told me that they have seen a *taiki* being sold for 40,000 cowries in birnin Kano. [Ferguson 1973, p. 325]

Many of the early European commercial agents and explorers passed judgment on these price rises since they too suffered from the grain scarcities and high costs.[128] Many indigenes turned to wage labor to sustain themselves as prices skyrocketed. But as grain disappeared altogether payment for casual labor was converted from kind to cowries.[129] Oral histories in Katsina and Daura revealed, nonetheless, that a distinguishing feature of the Babban Yunwa was the complete absence of grain in the marketplace in spite of the fact that effective purchasing power had not entirely dissolved under the impact of price inflation.[130] As I shall document, the paradox of money but no grain—due principally to the technological inadequacies of speedy, long-distance movement of foodstuffs—was a mirror image of subsistence crises in the twentieth century. Local opinion also emphasized that food scarcity made itself felt on the scheduling of births; eligible youths in particular were incapable of meeting bridewealth payments during an inflationary spiral since much of the ceremonial gift exchange involved staple foodstuffs. In these circumstances, domestic structure tended to retrench.

The second category of famine effects was broadly demographic. When in situ responses were incapable of meeting basic requirements, out-migration became the only realistic alternative. It seems quite likely that, historically, localized food shortage was one of the causes of considerable internal migration, which favored the rapid growth of social and trading networks that constituted part of the commercial infrastructure of the earliest territorially defined communities (Usman 1974). The babban yunwa were altogether more disruptive, causing massive evacuations along the desert edge; the Great Drought of the 1750s apparently had this effect throughout the Sudano-Sahelian corridor, breaking up the large gandaye, leveling whole communities, and forcing the abandonment of large estates. Some of the first signs of impending hardship in the northern emirates came with the appearance of farmers and pastoralists fleeing from the Sahelian heartland, especially Adar, Gobir, and Damerghou. The traces of this north-south axis remain, with the diaspora communities dotted throughout the Hausa plains as emblems of past hardship. Adarawa communities in the Kebbi floodplains, buzu villages southwest of birnin Katsina, Agalawa, and beriberi estates in Kano all testify to the presence of famine refugees. Many of the famine victims (*yan cin yunwa*) drifted into the emirate capitals in the hope of locating short-term causal employment, a benevolent patron, or the doubtless erratic alms provided from state granaries. The Hausa migrants were, of course, readily assimilated into their new urban abodes, but northern refugees, referred to locally as *rafto*, are still to be found in relic communities and wards in the northern cities. The Asben ward in birnin Katsina, presided over by a titular head (the Sarkin Asben), traces its historic origins to famine displacements in the eighteenth century.

Other demographic consequences pertaining to mortality must remain largely unknown. Oral histories tend to confirm what is common sense, namely that infants, aged, and infirm suffered highest mortality.[131] Famine had a direct impact on slave-holding though it is unclear whether, as Lovejoy (1978) suggests, slaves were actually freed or escaped. Aliyu's (1974, pp. 711, 712) historical work in Bauchi suggests rather that slaves circulated with great rapidity, a surmise lent some credence by the Kano Resident who reported that the "inevitable result" of the 1907–08 famine "was that a certain number of slaves are transferred . . . the owner being unable to support them and the slaves are hungry . . . desiring to be transferred" (NAK SNP7/10 2035/1909 par. 166). This type of decapitalization involving the disposal of assets and inventories was part of a famine cycle in which gradual replenishment occurred during the good years between droughts. Naturally, the drought-famine recovery cycle was neither inevitable nor as predictable as this might imply. Recoupment of famine losses for the vast majority of the rural poor was never a certainty.

The famine recovery cycle among pastoral households bore remarkable similarities to, and indeed was closely bound up with, the sedentary economy. The threat of periodic droughts imposed a need for geographic and social flexibility among Touareg and Ful'be herders. Baier and Lovejoy (1977) have shown how the Touareg social system provided a clearly delineated blueprint of hierarchical access to resources during periods of scarcity, which linked the aristocratic lineages of the north to the servile farm estates in the savannas. Nobles claimed the hospitality of their dependents in the savannas, both in the Agalawa villages and the servile communities close to the grazing camps. They remained there until the end of the drought, using the southern communities as safety valves.

As herds recovered . . . they enlisted more dependents. Surplus animals were
distributed from their herds . . . new slaves acquired by purchase . . . and
farmers from the south joined the Touareg in a dependent capacity of their
own free will . . . when climatic conditions were favourable. [Baier and Lovejoy
1977, pp. 405–406]

While this complex process of retraction, sedentarization, and recovery
was probably unique to Hausa-Touareg relations, the principle of graduated responses to drought was nonetheless intrinsic to the pastoral livelihood (see table 3.8). Unlike the sedentary economy, however, pastoralists
were subject to other recovery pressures, which emanated from the peculiar capital constitution and terms of trade characteristic of all livestock
systems. In the first case, Touareg and Ful'be were dependent, in varying
degrees, on purchased grain, and it is clear that as the terms of trade (i.e.,
millet prices) moved against them, herding households were faced with
the possibility of immediate decapitalization (i.e., animal sale) to cover
essential grain purchases. Poor harvests, drought, and inflated grain
prices among the savanna communities reverberated throughout the
desert edge with much practical consequence for the nomadic economy;
in the most extreme scenario, pastoral households might face the possibility of compulsory sale of prize fertile cows, on which herd recuperation
depended.

Second, the impact of severe drought on pastoral herd losses posed
unique and debilitating constraints on recuperative capability. Dahl and
Hjort (1976, 1979) simulated the impact of severe two- and three-year
droughts—associated with 70 to 90 percent loss rates—on herd dynamics

TABLE 3.8
SCENARIO OF NOMADIC RESPONSE TO LARGE-SCALE REGIONAL DROUGHT

Stage	Response
1 (Deepening drought)	Restricted movement around permanent water sources; overgrazing near wells; death of weakest animals; raiding; some animal sales if near a market.
2 (Intense drought)	Crucial move-stay decisions; massive herd die-offs, especially of water-demanding species; depletion of animal and material capital reserves; livestock sales wherever possible, but poor price since stock condition is poor.
3 (Total, prolonged drought)	Drought of several years duration; most of animals consumed, dead, or sold; capital reserves expended; involuntary sedentarization.
4 (Drought recovery)	Use of remaining capital reserves, surviving stock, and labor sales to rebuild the herds.

SOURCE: Johnson (1975, p. 80).

and restitution. Their demographic model projects severe age and sex distortions in herd composition, and hence in the subsequent rate of reproductive regeneration.[132] The consequences of a drought that disequilibrated the pastoral economy was felt for an extended period after the return of the rains. Herders continued to struggle with scarcity for at least one generation, having too little milk and too few animals to sell. Furthermore, normal seasonal fluctuations were felt with much more vigor than during periods when herd size and constitution were optimal.

The practical consequences of drought, herd dynamics, and pastoral terms of trade were thrown into sharp relief during the large regional famines, which perturbed sedentary and nomadic economies alike. Obscenely inflated grain prices turned the terms of trade sharply against pastoral products;[133] Ful'be and Touareg herders relied heavily on servile- or kin-based grain production but invariably faced massive capitalization as they were projected onto the distorted cereals 'market'. A common response to drought among pastoralists was to try to sell animals in anticipation of their eventual demise. Herd losses due to reduced pasture further decimated their herds with the result that nomads abandoned livestock altogether and took up cultivation. During the famine itself the terms of trade were highly adverse for herders but in its immediate aftermath, as grain prices fell and livestock was in short supply, they turned sharply in favor of the pastoral sector. Of course, from the perspective of the herder who had suffered a 90 percent animal loss, the cost of recapitalization was excessively high. The delay in calving during the drought created a shortage of male calves in the immediate recovery period, while, as a rule, older male stock or old cows had been sold or slaughtered during the emergency. Rapid recuperation of goats and sheep (which were prolific producers) involved a major element of risk since small ruminants were highly susceptible to high epizootic mortality. This, combined with the age and sex distortions, made for tardy recovery even with the assistance of stock alliances, clientage, and servile-run refuges. In a long-term recuperative sense, then, the pastoral economy was especially vulnerable to the drought-famine cycle, a vulnerability reflected in the constancy with which nomadic families commuted in and out of the sedentary economy. If their recovery trajectories differed, it was nonetheless the case that the fortunes of both pastoral and sedentary economies moved in an uncomfortable harmony with the climatic uncertainties of the desert edge.

* * * * *

In this sort of analysis there is a great danger embodied in Kjekshus's (1977) claim that the precolonial rural economy in Tanganyika possessed a cultural adaptation that "developed to defeat famine; to cheat death."

There is no need in a political economic analysis to glorify what is long gone. Equally there is no need to saddle the moral economy with the legacy of Durkheim, Rousseau, and Ruskin. The Sokoto Caliphate was not, as I have implied, a universe of satisfied peasants, benevolent patrons, and welfare-minded sarauta. Seasonal hunger and famine occurred in the nineteenth century with some regularity; subsistence crises wrought much harm and, perhaps because they did, were embedded in the social and cognitive fabric of Caliphal life. Furthermore, to evoke the moral economy is not to conjure up a perfectly calibrated social machinery that guaranteed survival. In light of its limited productive forces, production was ultimately constrained; village or suprafamilial assistance worked unevenly and social sanctions were not unfailingly effective; patrons and chiefs were not always reliable and the rhetoric of state responsibilities could not live up to the rigors of political practice. The moral economy was, in short, not always especially moral.[134] State relief was a restricted form of aid, which at best could only amount to the value of a region's annual levy and in any case could not be readily mobilized and transferred to the deficit districts. And not least, we can quite plausibly anticipate the class character of famine itself. Imam Imoru's ostensibly populist poetry appropriately confides that it was after all the wealthy who ate *fura*, *tuwo*, milk, and honey during the great hungers, while the talakawa scrambled for wild roots.[135] Many of the offices and institutions that I have described must have had a distinctly ambivalent function in peasant life for they simultaneously made claims on individual resources, fulfilled insurance functions, and assisted in the reproduction of inequality.

I have emphasized that a famine reveals the inner workings of the economic and social systems affected; it affords an insight, to quote Spitz (1978, p. 868), "into the structural violence of [society]." A major environmental crisis, like drought, provides a searchlight that probes the shadowy corners of the relations between society and nature, bathing the essential strengths and weaknesses of the social systems in a new illumination. Marx saw crises not as aberrant but as integral and embedded in economic systems; they exposed the contradictions, productive and technological, inherent in social life. In a precapitalist context, Marx identified crises with an underproduction of use-values; material reproduction was, in other words, in jeopardy. This was precisely the character of famine in the Sokoto Caliphate. Subsistence crises were precapitalist in the specific sense that food availability declined.[136] Social reproduction was vulnerable to the vicissitudes of nature as a consequence of the low level of development of the productive forces. The systematic barriers imposed by small-scale precapitalist property forms, by individuated peasant production, and the fetters of Caliphal class structure all mitigated against the emergence of large-scale specialized or cooperative labor, which were crucial conditions for technological development (Brenner 1977). Famines in the Sokoto Caliphate were what Sen (1980*b*, p. 617) calls direct entitlement failures[137]; that is to say, these subsistence crises contained a peculiar relation between persons and commodities in which there was an *absolute* shortage of the foodstuffs.

Correlatively, the predominance of household production in Hausaland placed an existential priority on the reproduction of the producing unit; the equation of self-consumption with the necessary product. This was reflected in the constellation of technical and social arrangements that constituted the moral economy. There may have been a weakness inherent in Caliphal technology but there was a strength in the social relations of production. This strength and resilience arose, specterlike, from the ashes of class relations. The critical, if prosaic, qualities of subsistence rights, food scarcity, and moral demands for survival were ultimately grounded in political economy. They arose, to use Edward Thompson's phrase, in a particular political and economic context in which "each fact can be given meaning only with the ensemble of other meanings" (1972, p. 45). The moral economy of the peasantry arose as much from the subaltern power of rural producers and from the limits of state power as from the hegemony of a state dominated by a Muslim sarauta class.

Food, then, was an essential part of material reproduction and (at low levels of development of the productive forces) became a critical if not volatile element. Although the Caliphate society was singularly ill-prepared for the babban yunwa, it did provide some household social insurance against the normal risks of agriculture. In the following three chapters I examine how the context of security and food shortage was transformed under the aegis of colonial domination. The period after 1900 witnessed changes in the conditions of reproduction of the Hausa peasantry, the making of another state apparatus, and the gradual and necessary erosion of a moral economy as new struggles and class relations took shape. The very form and etiology of famine changed.

4

CAPITAL, STATE, AND PEASANTRY IN COLONIAL NORTHERN NIGERIA

When I was a maiden the European first arrived. Ever since we
were quite small the mallams had been saying that the Europeans
would come with a thing called a train. . . . They would stop wars,
they would repair the world, they would stop oppression and
lawlessness.

—*Baba of Karo*

In the early 1800s when Hausaland was em-
broiled in the political turmoil of Usman dan Fodio's jihad, novel patterns
of world commodity trade had transformed the Niger delta from its
original dependence on slaves to a new emphasis on the production of
palm oil. This transition to so-called legitimate commerce, which principally reflected changing European demands for vegetable oils, did not
alter the extant system of coastal trade.[1] The informal trade empire of the
first half of the nineteenth century synthesized the merchant interests of
Victorian capitalism with the spiritual and philanthropic demands of
evangelism. The expansion of agricultural production for a capitalist
market, particularly after 1850, was dominated by intense competition
among European merchants, capital which had penetrated the local circuits of production and consumption in coastal communities. The ascent
of mercantile activity did not, however, transform the social relations of
production. Since the European merchant class was formally subsumed
by industrial and financial capital, commercial capital throughout its West
African trade diaspora helped realize the surplus value of European
workers.[2]

The efflorescence of trade in agricultural and manufactured products and the deepening of merchant capitalist penetration witnessed the
emergence of an African petite bourgeoisie which, in the absence of
political control over the means of production (especially land), attempted through the juridical form of slavery to directly control labor
itself. By the 1880s, however, this commercial symbiosis along the coast
had been plunged into an acute economic crisis.[3]

The demand for West African vegetable oils slumped. Developments in transport and finance increased opportunities for competition in West Africa. The invention of the Gatling and Maxim guns made coercion cheaper and easier. European powers eventually resolved the crisis by bringing all African territories under formal colonial rule. [Williams 1976, p. 15]

For Great Britain, the depression marked the terminal point in its spectacular domination of world production and trade. As prices, profits, and trade fell drastically, unemployment rates grew markedly, and Britain faced effective competition and protectionist legislation from newer, more sturdy European states. Not unexpectedly, the response of British capital was an aggressive search for untapped markets in tandem with a drive to procure steady, cheap, and abundant supplies of industrial raw materials. For essentially similar reasons, several other European powers sought to preserve and extend their own commercial interests by carving spheres of geopolitical influence, largely through treaties of protection, which were the forerunners of formal colonial rule.[4] Such renewed competition and the reduced level of merchant profits not only provoked a confrontation between European and indigenous African merchant capital—which ultimately resulted in its subsumption by European firms—but also reaffirmed the necessity of explicit political control of peasant production. Further commercialization was contingent upon the establishment of formal colonial rule, capable of extending cheap bulk transport and consolidating a profitable trading network. The realization of Chamberlain's "national estate" demanded imperial occupation, for as Lugard wrote in 1901,

> trade cannot be established on a satisfactory basis until the northern Hausa states are included in the provinces of the protectorate rendered safe for all small traders. [Lugard cited in Okediji 1972, p. 52]

To the extent that the colonial conquest actually represented a competitive annexation by an essentially free-trade imperialism, the British takeover of Nigeria was a type of "defensive colonialism."[5]

And so it was that in the aftermath of the chaotic territorial scramble for Africa in the 1890s, the proclamation of the Protectorate of Northern Nigeria was finally made in January 1901. Yet as the Union Jack was hoisted over Lokoja, British knowledge of the north was imprecise and fuzzy, and the exact form and extent of colonial responsibility was obscure, if not contradictory. But in spite of the severe limitations on manpower and finance, the British imposed their rule in northern Nigeria with singular comprehensiveness and dedication. The Colonial Office developed a system of indirect rule, a peculiar synthesis of indigenous Islamic authority, nineteenth-century emirate administration, and direct intervention by a Bonapartist colonial state. In the process, the cowry was replaced by a rational currency; emirate taxation was simplified, systematized, and incorporated into an embracing system of revenue and assessment; slavery was tardily abolished; and the colonial state organized both voluntary and forced recruitment of labor, largely for construction and porterage. The colonial courts quickly extended their jurisdiction, embracing the activities of mercantile companies and agents, which facilitated the extension of commerce into the interior proper. European firms were free to combine at will, while the conservative fiscal and currency policy of the banks served the firms whose merchant monopoly mitigated against new activities. Surplus money capital was repatriated to Great Britain with the profits of the firms and large portions of government salaries.[6] In other respects, the colonial state actively inhibited the development of the forces of production, particularly in agriculture, by using state sanctions to increase the extraction of absolute surplus value. Plantations, for instance, were subservient to domestic or household systems of production, and not given the opportunity to develop at the expense of peasant economy which, as Governor Clifford put it in 1922, was a "natural growth," self-supporting and cheap.

Although the constituent unity of the Sokoto Caliphate was shattered by colonial conquest, indirect rule resurrected a mock feudal structure that cemented a class alliance between traditional emirate officeholders and the European bureaucracy. The colonial edifice was decidedly patrimonial, but it enlisted the dominant status groups and preserved a class of rural producers insulated from white settlers or from "the African land grabber and usurer" as H. R. Palmer put it. This measure of political, ideological, and economic continuity, which indirect rule constituted, goes some way toward explaining the widely held belief that the colonialism in northern Nigeria was not a radical hiatus; there was continuity rather than disjuncture. Perhaps, the most dramatic economic expression of this can be traced to Myint's (1967, 1971) vent for surplus theory—recently resuscitated by Hogendorn (1978, p. 2)—according to which, economic growth measured by the massive expansion in the volume of exports was achieved without (1) a proportional increase in population, (2) a corresponding decline in either land or time devoted to "traditional" commodity production, or (3) a radical transformation in the forces of production.[7] As Myint observed (1971, pp. 141, 142),

> the surplus productive capacity provided these countries with a virtually "costless" means of acquiring imports which did not require a withdrawal of resources from domestic production but merely a fuller employment for their semi-idle labour. Of course, one may point to the real cost incurred by the indigenous peoples in the form of extra effort and sacrifice of the traditional leisurely life and also to the various social costs not normally considered in the comparative-costs theory, such as being sometimes subject to the pressure of

taxation and even compulsory labour. . . . But for the most part it is still true to say that the indigenous peoples of the underdeveloped countries took to export production on a voluntary basis and enjoyed a clear gain by being able to satisfy their developing wants for the new imported commodities.

Growth was thus directly attributable to surplus factors in underutilized areas; the international market exposed a vent and hence a costless mechanism for increasing exports while preserving domestic self-sufficiency.

According to Hogendorn (1978, pp. 2, 3), all of the major predictions of the Myint model are confirmed in the case of northern Nigerian groundnut exports[8] with the notable exclusion of indigenous entrepreneurship. While not wishing to underestimate the laudable and pioneering entrepreneurial talents of the average Hausa peasant so effusively praised by Hogendorn, the vent for surplus model itself is highly problematic. To suggest that the expansion of export commodity production in Hausaland was achieved without a technological revolution or additional risks to the peasant producers, and that export production was self-financing, is to simultaneously argue that the cycle of simple reproduction at the household level remained almost anesthetized. If indeed the Myint thesis were valid—and assuming no long-term secular change in rainfall patterns—the food shortage problem after 1900 would be structurally identical to the precolonial era save for the fact that expanded investment in transportation might actually have smoothed out the uneven surface of regional grain surfeits and deficits.

However, I endeavor to show that this was categorically not the case; as both Berry (1970, pp. 17–19) and Smith (1979, p. 54) have hinted, Myint's myopic vent was not entirely costless. This is in part due to his conception of precolonial economy and society, his adherence to "voluntaristic" notions that ignore important reallocations of land and labor, and a strange conception of capitalism as a sort of global vacuum cleaner. Export growth demanded, in fact, considerable population movement while petty commodity trades and crafts were unevenly disqualified; in some locations—most notably the northern close settled zones, which were neither land surplus economies nor self-sufficient in grains—the export revolution deflected domestic productive activity away from cereal production. Thus, with due regard to Myint, greater output was often achieved through new forms of agronomic and productive organization. Even though the Hausa entered, and emerged from, colonialism armed with little more than the hoe, technological stasis should not obscure the disruptiveness of a colonial epoch that transformed class relations and political institutions and the conditions of peasant reproduction. Colonial rule did not create "modernity" from "backwardness" by simply harnessing a traditional state of low-level equilibrium; neither was a dismembered Sokoto Caliphate somehow historically frozen and then reconstituted intact under imperial domination. As Shenton and Freund (1978, p. 8) noted, colonialism wrought productive, political, and social change, and at the same time preserved some dimensions of precapitalist society in order to supply cheap commodities including labor power. This "changelessness," which Bettelheim (in Emmanuel 1972, p. 297) referred to as the law of conservation-dissolution, transformed the context of hunger in northern Nigeria.

Colonial changes, then, provided a new context for ecological variability that had implications for the genesis of, and vulnerability to, food shortage. Not only were segments of peasant communities made increasingly vulnerable to environmental perturbations and incapable of responding adequately to variability in food supply, they were subject to the novel stresses imposed through their subsumption into an expanded commodity economy mediated through the price system. In fact, I argue that the process of colonialism was coincident with the social production of famine; moreover, the dynamics of famine were less a reflection of an environmental disaster than of the moodiness of the market and the social relations of production among rural producers. Any understanding of hunger in the colonial period must be grounded in a recognition of the gradual and selective transformation of peasants into small commodity producers and semiproletarians, and the logic of a retarded capitalism which did not revolutionize the productive forces.

In this chapter I lay the groundwork for an analysis of food crises in colonial northern Nigeria along two lines. First, by specifying the nature of the colonial social formation as a totality, and the manner in which human practice was determined within it. And second, by examining the specific economic and political practice—that is, the production and reproduction of the material conditions of human existence and class power—among Hausa peasantry in relation to the colonial state. In the first section I discuss the structure of colonial capitalism in northern Nigeria as a totality, arguing that it should be conceptualized as an outcome of the syncretic interplay between preexisting social relations of production and the reproductive requirements of metropolitan capital. The structure of northern Nigeria was constituted by—to use Rey's (1973, p. 15) terminology—a complex economic and political articulation. The first phase of articulation was given expression by the dominance of European merchant capital acting as the agent of a hegemonic industrial capital. One can legitimately refer to this process as *mercantile subsumption*, for the reproduction of merchant capital requires some form of monopoly. Economic practice accordingly developed along two related fronts and constituted the movement from natural economy[9] to increasingly generalized commodity production. Initially, the product of labor was transformed into the commodity form; that is, use-values were super-

ceded by exchange-values, which gave rise to differentiated petty producers enmeshed in a web of commodity relations. And concurrent with
this expansion of exchange values—but nonetheless, proliferating as the
commodity form became more generalized—the commoditization of
labor power itself. In Lenin's words, one witnessed the beginnings of
production of commodities by means of commodities.

FOUNDATIONS OF COLONIAL CAPITALISM

The independent and predominant development of capital as merchant's
capital is tantamount to the non-subjection of production to capital and hence
to capital developing on the basis of an alien social mode of production which is
also independent of it.

—Marx 1967, III, 327, 328

In some situations it is more beneficial to capital to dominate agriculture by
controlling the conditions of reproduction of the small farmer rather than by
expropriating him. This means that capital is spared certain costs it would have
to bear were it to directly organize agriculture production.

—Bernstein 1976, p. 58

The British conquest of the Sokoto Caliphate was a shattering experience, a fact often overlooked by the rhetoric surrounding Lugard's theory
of indirect rule. And yet the government of northern Nigeria, which
supplanted the commercial hegemony of the Royal Niger Company,
consolidated its military overrule with relative ease. Following the defeat
of Adamawa in 1901, until the fall of Sokoto and Kano in 1903, most
northern resistance was comprehensively quashed.[10] Indeed, with the
exception of the bloody uprising and butchery at Satiru in 1906 and the
longer-term guerrilla resistance of the hill peoples of Jos and southern
Zaria, the imperial armies were never seriously threatened.[11]

In light of the clinical efficiency with which conquest was effected, the
agency of the colonial state in northern Nigeria, which played a critical
role in the restructuring of African production, was far more complex.
The centrality of the colonial state apparatus in the political economy of
the colony is, however, often seen either as a reflection of the needs of the
metropolitan bourgeoisie or as "overdeveloped" in relation to the needs
of European capital. Whether one is a convert to the "structural" or
"instrumental" schools, the case of northern Nigeria shows clearly how
the colonial state was not constituted simply as a metropolitan reflex.[12] To
the extent that one can conceptualize the state as determined by structural
needs of the center expressed through the necessary continuity of primary commodity production, such an analysis,

> cannot in itself account for why particular crops were introduced in particular
> colonies or, more importantly, explain the variant forms of colonial production

that develop in different areas, e.g. peasant commodity production, corporate plantation production, settler estate agriculture. Nor is it sufficient to explain the variant forms and differing trajectories of development of colonial state apparatuses in particular colonies. [Berman and Lonsdale 1980, p. 57]

In Nigerian Hausaland, the state needs to be situated with the contradictory historical circumstances and class forces that emerged from the articulation of metropolitan capital with indigenous forms of production. I have suggested that articulation was an ongoing process by which the precapitalist formation of the Caliphate was subjected to preservation, dissolution, and transformation by specific forms of European capital. Contained within this historically specific process in northern Nigeria— largely dominated by merchant capital at the service of industrial capital—the colonial state provided the institutional apparatus for capital accumulation and was the ultimate agent for political practice, namely the control and legitimation of class domination. Such an approach[13] to the state recognizes that the demands of capitalist accumulation and reproduction on the one hand and of state control and legitimacy on the other may be mutually contradictory.[14] Insofar as the colonial state in Nigeria straddled two levels—between metropole and colony and between capitalist and indigenous modes of production—it condensed within it these conflicting interests. Over northern Nigeria, the "condensate of struggling classes," to use Holloway and Picciotto's (1978, p. 24) felicitous phrase, were fractions of European merchant and industrial capital, the bureaucrats of the Colonial Office (including the Treasury) in London and Nigeria, the newly emerging Hausa-Fulani salaried administrators, officeholders, and commercial elites and the peasantry. Given the priority of metropolitan demands,

> the state takes on the central role of managing and representing the myriad encounters and struggles between classes and agents of different modes. The state provides economic, social and political services for capitalist penetration, orchestrates the de- and re-structuring of elements of the precapitalist mode . . . and "copes" so to speak, at the level of cohesion of the whole social formation, with the dislocative consequences of the expansion of the capitalist mode. [Lamb 1975, pp. 131, 132]

SLAVES, LANDLORDS, AND PEASANTS

It is the task of civilisation to put an end to slavery.

—Lord Lugard, 1922

Generally speaking the intervention and policy of Government is not to interfere with the relation of master and slave [in northern Nigeria].

—Lord Lugard, 1919

The British assessment of the Sokoto Caliphate at the turn of the century was unquestionably tainted by the prevailing European views on race, slavery, and social development.[15] Strong antislavery sentiment naturally situated some of the centralized, highly stratified African states (such as the Caliphate) in the broad phalanx of barbarous and savage societies that occupied, as Social Darwinism dictated, the bottom rung of the social evolutionary ladder. The ideology of racism was embodied in the two canons of the dual mandate itself, in which there were economic advantages for the civilized world and moral benefits conferred upon backward Africans. Lord Lugard, one of the most respected "experts" on African affairs, revealed a strong commitment to social evolutionary theory both in terms of race and social progress. He quite clearly believed that private ownership, for instance, represented the pinnacle of a long process of economic change.

> Conceptions as to the tenure of land are subject to steady evolution, side by side with the evolution of social progress from the most primitive stages to the organization of the modern state. In the earliest stage, the land and its produce is shared by the community as a whole; later the produce is the property of the family or individuals by whose toil it is won, and the control of the land becomes vested in the head of the family. Later still . . . the conception of proprietary rights in it emerges, and sale, mortgage, and lease of the land, apart from its user, is recognised. . . . These processes of natural evolution, leading up to individual ownership may, I believe, be traced in every civilization known to history. [Lugard 1922, p. 280]

On balance, then, the paternalistic view of the Sokoto Caliphate held by the British contained elements of unashamed Social Darwinism—"they are positively antediluvian" as Sir Percy Girouard (1908, p. 335) referred to the Hausa—with a begrudging recognition of the "light skinned" Fulani artistocracy who had conquered and enslaved a backward black people.[16] The century of Caliphal rule was accordingly characterized by a sort of cultural degeneracy: miscegenation, slavery and warfare.

The gains to the industrial classes that Nigerian colonialism would confer were closely intertwined with the growth of a British capitalism heavily dependent on the production of textiles for the internal market and for export. However, the periodic irregularities in the U.S. supply of raw cotton had plunged the British cotton textile industry into successive economic crises. Further, adverse shifts in the terms of trade between Britain and the U.S. at the turn of the century amplified the strains on an already ailing British economy. In this light, Lugard's demand for conquest of the Caliphate found favor among the influential industrial capitalists of the Lancashire cotton lobby. The famous Kano textile industry represented not only enormous cotton lint producing capability but also, as Birdwhistle (NAK SNP 7/8 1765/1907) noted in his Commercial Intel-

ligence Report of 1907, "the possibility of creating new wants." It was
amidst this euphoria for Nigeria's economic future—a view held by
R. Churchill, E. D. Morel, and Alfred Jones in spite of their contradictory
opinions concerning the precise *mode* of development—that the Lancashire cotton interests sponsored a joint state-merchant firm, the British
Cotton Grower's Association (BCGA).[17] In a statement emblematic of the
historic mission of capitalism in northern Nigeria, the BCGA waxed
lyrical that "Kano, the Mecca of the Lancashire spinning trade, will be
brought into economical touch with the rest of the world" (BCGA 1907,
p. 26).

The progressive sphere of British capitalism may have seen investment as an immediate necessity to capture the resource potential of the
Hausa plains, but this was equivocally not the case at the British Treasury,
which provided funds for both the conquest and subsequent administration. In short, a highly dubious colonial venture could be justified only
through self-finance and general parsimony. Shackled by the poverty of a
minuscule grant-in-aid sufficient to support only a diminutive cadre of
political officers,[18] the colonial state was straitjacketed in terms of the
manner in which development might be undertaken. In practice, this
meant few European bureaucrats, no significant standing army, and
economic change under the auspices of private entrepreneurial initiative
bound to indigenous resources. To satisfy the demands of political stability and fiscal self-reliance, indirect rule emerged not as a sophisticated
or mystical creation but as a pragmatic necessity. A class alliance was
forged with cooperative members of the ruling emirate aristocracies,
guarantees were given to the sanctity of Islam, Christian missionaries
were tightly controlled, and priority was lent to merchant monopolies
who, in the pursuit of commodity production and exchange, provided the
fiscal basis for colonial taxation systems. Colonial imperatives bore a
striking similarity to the groundwork laid by Goldie in the late nineteenth
century in establishing the Royal Niger Company's commercial domination over northern Nigeria.

Clearly, then, the British needed the ruling class to rule, and in
abstaining from any interference with Islamic religious principles they
"allowed the ruling class to define virtually all the prerogatives of their
class" (Lubeck 1979, p. 199). In the case of domestic and farm slavery in
Hausaland, the juxtaposition of imperial ideology with the practicalities
of indirect rule presented glaring contradictions on an issue that had
purportedly been a major moral justification of the conquest itself. The
1901 Proclamation on Slavery prohibited slave raiding, abolished the
legal status of slavery, and declared that all individuals subsequently born
of slave parents would be free. Yet Lugard in his 1906 *Political Memoranda*
made no attempt to disguise his solicitude for the slave-owning class,

which "it was the object of the government to preserve and strengthen" (Lugard 1970, p. 221). As part of the alliance with the emirate aristocracy, Lugard had hoped to prevent fugitive slaves from occupying land (1906, p. 142) in an attempt to temporarily preserve the relation of master and slave. His own position is made strikingly clear in the 1906 Memoranda.

> If, after inquiry, the Resident comes to the conclusion that the slave has no good case, that there has been no cruelty and that the person is simply a bad character or loafer . . . he would discourage the assertion of freedom. [Lugard 1906, p. 140, para. 13]

Imperial survival was closely bound to the welfare of the Sultan, the emirs, and traditional *masu sarauta*. And to the extent that the institution of slavery shored up the authority of the indigenous ruling class, the abolition of human servitude constituted a political threat to the agents of imperial control. As a northern Resident put it to Lugard in 1908:

> I am very much afraid that if slavery disappears and with it the wealthy class we will find in some ten to twenty years time that the Fulani administrative machinery has disappeared and that we have nothing to replace it with. The only solution I can think of . . . is that domestic slavery in some modified form be legalised, it would be a temporary measure and help to bridge the next twenty years at the end of which one hopes that the revenue of the country will have increased so much that it will be possible to provide adequate remuneration for native administrators. [Howard, Rhodes House, Mss. Brit. Emp. 263]

Since Lugard recognized, however, that slavery would eventually—and in practice did—die a slow death, the legitimacy of the Hausa-Fulani was to be maintained by its transformation into a landlord class organically linked to an ex-slave, farm-laboring class. The Lugardian project to (at a single stroke) produce a landlord mode of agriculture—a strange dose of eighteenth-century England in the northern provinces—stands in stark contrast to the later theology of gradualism and indirect rule encapsulated in the *Dual Mandate*. In holding that slavery was pervasive if not predominant in the Caliphate formation, Lugard wrote that

> Government, by the very act of introducing security for life and property, and by throwing open fertile land to cultivation, adds to the difficulty of the problem it has to solve, namely, the creation of a labouring class to till the lands of the ruling classes. [Lugard 1906, para. 8]

The genesis of a wage-laboring class, Lugard believed, could be lent the weight of the British courts, which would ensure that the nascent landlord class obtained "free labor" by contract and hence was enforceable by law. The fulcrum on which the new system balanced was to be the recognition of the *right of private property in land*.

The majority of cases of assertion of freedom take place among the agricultural population, and the most effective way of preventing a too sudden and pre-mature tendency to desertion, is, as I have said . . . by enforcing proprietary rights in land. In other words, by not permitting fugitive farm slaves to occupy land to which they had no title, nor to build new villages at will, and by upholding the landlord's right to charge rent to his tenants. [Lugard 1906, para. 14]

The Lugardian vision was complete: a bureaucratized Islamic theocracy presided over by a traditional Caliphate aristocracy assuming newfound legitimacy as wage-paying landlords. And all this dressed up in the rhetoric of indirect rule. By 1910, however, with the appearance of what is arguably the single most important piece of legislation in the history of colonial northern Nigeria, the Lands Committee had comprehensively undermined Lugard's model of colonial political economy.

REVENUE, HENRY GEORGE, AND THE LAND QUESTION

Capitalism can never immediately and radically eliminate the preceding modes of production, nor above all the relations of exploitation that characterize these modes of production.

—Pierre Philippe-Rey

In contrast to the conservative trends in British imperial affairs—of which Lugard was exemplary—there emerged in the post-1914 period, a group of reformers who, in using the collectivist language of radicals such as Hobson and Lenin, felt strongly that European impact in Africa had been disastrous.[19] The doctrinaire works of Leonard Woolfe, E. D. Morel, and Norman Leys argued strongly against the dual mandate theory, demanding a limit to the operations of private capital and a preference for peasant proprietorship. These liberal reformers had a forerunner in the guise of Charles Temple, a northern Nigeria Resident from 1901 to 1910, who was subsequently promoted to Lieutenant Governor in 1914. Temple, who was a close friend of Charles Strachey, was a devotee of the North; he spoke Hausa, admired the aristocracy, despised individualism, and regarded industrial capitalism as preeminently decadent.[20] His fanat-ical support for indirect rule was the cornerstone of a policy to protect the virtues of an aristocratic and bucolic culture from the vulgar barbarism of a crudely expansionary British capitalism.

Following the departure of Lugard to Hong Kong in 1906 and the appointment of Sir Percy Girouard, Temple and Strachey were pre-sented with an opportunity to undercut the Lugardian schema. The new cadre of northern political officers found the perfect foil for their inten-tions in the form of Henry George, an American economist who believed in a fundamental contradiction between capitalist and worker qua class on the one hand, and the landlord on the other. His fixation with the unearned income that accrued to the landlord class led him to promote state control of land, and accordingly to tax all rents that would ordinarily have lined the pockets of private landowners. George's influential views provided a perfect justification for the Temple-Girouard formula, namely the nationalization of land in the Protectorate and the transformation of emirate elites into a salaried bureaucracy which, as Gowers (cited in Tomlinson and Lethem 1927, p. 9) put it, "creates a body of chiefs whose interests are closely bound up with the Government."

As a transport engineer and representative of merchant interests, Girouard welcomed the coming of the Baro railway to the North, yet feared a large influx of white settlers demanding land. Indeed Lugard's twofold distinction between private Crown lands (acquired from the Royal Niger Company) and public lands vested in the government (acquired by right of conquest) simply formalized colonial control over the protectorate in a manner that seemed to open the floodgates to the landgrabber.[21] How could this be otherwise when Lugard sought to inculcate the notion of freehold

> so that the Native Rulers and Alkalis who devote their time to executive and . . . administrative work, may be provided with a private income to supplement their official salaries, and replace the wealth which formerly consisted in ownership of slaves. [Lugard 1906, p. 131]

Girouard (NAK SNP 6 C 162/1907) on the contrary, found such views "cumbersome" and "indefinite," yet sought to consolidate his nationalization stance not by a direct confrontation with Lugard but through the necessary complement to any resolution of the land tenure question, namely land revenue.

Both Lugard and Girouard were in general agreement on the necessity of direct taxation in the protectorate. A landlocked location, the parsimony of the Treasury, and the strong sentiment against indirect levies such as customs duties—since the levies fell heavily on European merchants with the possibility of stifling trade on the North—all necessitated that a good deal of state revenue be generated through direct taxation.[22] Lugard recognized, of course, that taxation was an established tradition in the "Koranic model" as he called it, but the entire project had, he believed, fallen into gross abuse, rife with extortion and corruption. Nonetheless, the retention of ancient forms of taxation, sanctioned by tradition, was vindication of the existing machinery while simplifying the mode of collection. The jekadas were to be abolished, the hakimi despatched to district capitals, and the Hausa-Fulani bureaucrats (while initially to receive a share of the receipts) were to be ultimately transformed into salaried officials, assigned private officeholding estates, and fully incorporated into the colonial state. Through Lugardian spectacles taxation provided the pivot about which all else revolved.

> As a stimulus to production, as a source of revenue for the support of the colonial administration—"it marks the recognition by the community of the protecting Power"—and finally as the basis for the development of his system of indirect rule which meant the modernisation of traditional institutions through their own agency. Without income from taxation they could not provide for development, let alone the payment of officials on a regular basis. Without a tax there can be no treasury, and without a treasury no eventual measure of self-rule. [Lugard 1922, p. 218]

Though Lugard cherished the thought of a rationalized indigenous taxation system lubricated by the native treasury, the immediate post-conquest period resembled a Kafkaesque nightmare; a strange conflation of extortion, plunder, and administrative chaos. In the first instance, the Residents preserved much of the Caliphal fiscal structure—with the notable exception of the jekada collectors—simply consolidating the myriad nineteenth-century petty taxes and levies. Accordingly, political officers demanded from the emirs a large proportion of emirate income; yet this plunder, particularly in Katsina, prompted more extortion from the jekadas to compensate for the decline in the emir's income. Tax-gathering parties resembled punitive expeditions, and the "raiding" quality they projected once again raised the spectre of peasant revolt (Fika 1978, p. 113). In fact in the pagan areas, which had invariably been peripheral to central revenue collection, peasant resistance was met with brutal retaliation. Villages were torched, granaries destroyed, and looting widespread across much of southern Zaria and the plateau region. All this was a far cry from Lugard's model of an individual income tax based on political office assessment levied on private property owners.

And so from 1905 onward, the British attempted to systematize and monetize all taxes, appropriating a portion of the surplus (initially 50 percent) that had formerly been appropriated by the masu sarauta. Monetization acted as a spur to export production but was at the expense of the long-standing grain tithe (zakkat) which, in the eyes of the administration, was too flexible, too bulky and, of course, relatively unnegotiable. In Katsina, Palmer merged the kudin kassa and zakkat into a single farm tax calculated as three shillings per "median household." Zakkat as a charitable yet voluntary gift was restored as a fixed rate placed on plantation or garden crops that oscillated between one and three shillings per plot. Of course, all this possessed a certain contingency, for in the early years a large degree of discretionary power was necessarily devolved to the Residents in the northern provinces, who adapted the revenue system to local and historical circumstances. A complex—and often contradictory—balancing act emerged to procure a stable income: simplifying the battery of precolonial levies yet instituting a new compound tax; abolishing taxes on nonirrigated gardens and dye pits yet resurrecting a compulsory zakkat; dissolving the standard three shilling farm tax yet replacing it by a levy on grain farmers of one shilling per acre.[23] Practice and theory, then, were light-years apart and the tax issue assumed an arabesque quality as a Niger Company representative noted to Lord Scarborough.

> Taxation is really getting too funny. One Resident writes, "I have taken so much Plantation Tax" Sir F [Lugard]: "Plantation Tax! What is this! However don't stop until I can go into the matter" Another — "I have instituted something like a poll tax." Sir F: "Oh you have have you, you know that that is directly against my ideas! How dare you! However, leave matters until I can get around to see for myself." [Rhodes House, Mss. Afr. RNC, vol. 12]

After a decade of ostensibly Lugardian practice, then, the revenue issue was quite simply a mess; spatially inconsistent, regressive, and frequently arbitrary, the lion's share of the tax burden fell on peasant grain producers. In Katsina, for instance:

> By 1910, taxpayers in Katsina Division were paying nearly twice as much as the Kano Division in proportion to its population; and the burden was falling almost entirely upon the corn farmers [Hull 1968, p. 262].

Such was the prevailing state of affairs when the Northern Nigeria Lands Committee met in London in 1908–09 and launched a frontal assault on tax assessment and Lugard's early scheme. In his preparatory documents circulated to all northern Residents, Girouard strove to show first that Caliphal assessment had degenerated into a poll tax, and second, by invoking the case of Lower Burma, that a precedent existed for the codification of Henry George's ideas. Shenton (1982) in particular documented Girouard's careful manipulation of Baden-Powell's exegesis of the Burma Land Act of 1876 to provide a justification for a full revenue assessment in Nigeria along the lines of the India experience. The Lands Committee was in fact a fait accompli for Girouard's loosely collectivist economic rent model;[24] the principal witness in the hearings was Temple, who had earlier written to Lugard that "land belongs to the community not to the individual," and was ably supported by the Resident of Zaria, Charles Orr, and by the legal talents of H. R. Palmer, Acting Resident in Katsina.[25] All three waved the flag of land "nationalization," clinging desperately to the entirely fallacious idea that a "fee simple" or freehold tenure did not (and had never) existed in the emirates (Temple 1918, pp. 138, 139). As a consequence, the Committee testimony is a mass of contradictions, half-truths, and a large measure of outright speculation

presented with a certain Anglo-empirical smugness. Palmer set the tenor
for much subsequent discussion by suggesting that the peasant had no fee
simple but "a right of possession, subject to the payment of taxes, of a farm
that he has bought" (Lands Committee 1910, p. 70). Yet in Kano, "owing
to the influence of the Arabs," land and residential property was bought
and sold without reference to the emir. Palmer's vacillation on the tenure
issue and his muddied thoughts on freehold versus possession were both
highlighted by Temple, the purported land expert. Chairman Digby and
Mr. Wedgwood in particular elicited from Temple the inconsistencies
between the apparent absence of freehold and the existence of precolonial taxes levied on the *value* of land.

> 676. Is not the annual tax that the chief extracts from the inhabitants in the
> village that you have mentioned to all intents and purposes the annual value of
> the land which the chief gives to his followers to cultivate?—I did not quite catch
> that.
> 677. What I mean is this. Is it not a fact that land has a certain value, which
> value is paid by the native to his headman every year in the form of taxes?—I
> cannot answer that straight off.
> 678. Although you say that the land has no value it has a value which is
> represented by what the native is prepared to pay every year in taxation rather
> than go elsewhere outside the village?—I do not feel that I can answer that
> straight off. I am very sorry. It is deep water rather.
> 679. (*Chairman.*) Directly you begin to talk about rent of land, survey of
> land, and so on, and at the same time say that your leading principle is that there
> is no such thing as private property at all, and that the State is to have the
> control, you must beware that you do not get into inconsistencies?—Yes.
> [Temple, Lands Committee 1910, p. 88]

So amidst a good deal of confusion and contradiction, the "socialistic"
principles of the Lands Committee, Girouard's "economic theory of land
tenure," had won out. Having established that neither leases in perpetuity
nor a landlord class existed in the North, Girouard's coda saw no need to
introduce a system of tenure in which modern nations were spending
"untold millions," trying to serve the "full rental value of the land" (NAK
SNP 6 C. 162/1907, p. 68). Since the Muslim community owned land prior
to conquest, the whole of the North—occupied or unoccupied—became
subject to government control.

> [The indigenous occupier] has no legal right to security of possession; he
> cannot sell or mortgage the land . . . nor does he transmit indefeasible title to his
> heirs. [Lands Committee 1910, p. 31]

The colonial state naturally held the right to dispossession—principally for nonpayment of tax or voluntary sale without consent—and
hence at a single stroke the Lands Committee undermined Lugard's
projected landlord class.

466. You do not see any danger of the Emirs and district headmen and so on becoming intermediate landowners?—Not unless they acquire some power of dealing with the property as owners, which at present they have not got.
467. That resolves itself into a question of tenure?—Yes.
468. (*Mr. Wedgwood.*) It would also be obviated, would it not, by giving them a fixed salary instead of a percentage?—Yes. [Palmer, Lands Committee 1910 p. 79]

The irony of the Temple-Girouard triumph was, of course, that it was grounded in a fundamental misunderstanding of precolonial political economy. The Lands Committee thought only in terms of private property as an absolute right to use and abuse as defined in Roman law.[26] Temple was, therefore, only prepared to recognize community property mediated by customary rights in the Muslim state, which obviated any notions of private occupation and land sale. Accordingly, land was valueless.[27] However, as Clarke has shown (1980, p. 180), communal possession—and here I include Caliphal society qua community—refers to the conditions under which members of a community gain access to land, and is perfectly compatible with purchase and legal title. This was particularly the case in the land-scarce close settled zones and among the rich fadama lands, as for instance in Kura south of birnin Kano, both of which were highly commoditized.[28] As Arnett, Resident of Kano, observed,

> But in the Hausa states and in this Emirate [Kano] especially, land is so fully occupied that it has for years past acquired such a value and private ownership of land is therefore coming into being and must if the present course of events continues be eventually recognized as part of the customary law of the land. [cited in Shenton 1982, p. 91]

If there was a communal possession in the sense articulated by Temple, it was perhaps among the peripheral non-Muslim Hausa communities (maguzawa) in which access to land was contingent upon membership in patrilineal or patrilocal households subsumed in landholding segmentary lineages (Greenberg 1946; Starns 1974). But the maguzawa certainly constituted a statistical minority in 1900. And in any case, a wealth of empirical evidence indicates the customary nature of land sale and farm commoditization in some Caliphate locations. The district officer of Raba District in Sokoto Province observed in 1914 for instance that preconquest farm prices to strangers ranged from £1 to £5; in the same year, Mr. Liddard reported twenty-five cases of farm sale in Jega District, Sokoto Province during a three-month period totaling £105.10.0. District officer Liddard noted that not only was farm purchase a long-standing phenomenon but also that even after a total prohibition of such sales by the colonial government in 1910, "for every one case reported . . . 20 are not reported" (SNP 10 274p/1915). Resident Arnett, who interestingly was not called to testify for the Lands Committee, was closer to the mark when

he observed the absence of any sharp distinction between private possession subject to customary community rights characteristic of the Caliphate
peasant proprietor and the notion of private ownership or freehold of the
European genre. The duplicity of the Lands Committee was perfectly
captured by Watts of the Niger Company.

> Two facts strike me very forcibly in connection with the evidence taken before
> the committee, firstly the evidence of the parties principally interested i.e. the
> natives of Northern Nigeria was not sought, and secondly benefit was not taken
> of Sir William Wallace . . . in the country prior to British occupation. . . . the
> socialistic principles of the Lands Committee will prove to be utopian and
> unworkable in practice. . . . I cannot agree with Mr. Temple's conclusion that
> under no possible conditions could a private estate exist in Northern Ni-
> geria. . . . I am well aware that in the Emirate of Bida under emir Maliki, circa
> 1885 – 1895 private individuals were fully allowed to dispose of their interests in
> such property and this is confirmed by Dr. Cargill's assertion that in Kano the
> right of the user of a plot of land could be purchased and such right was
> inheritable. This official had experience in the country prior to British occu-
> pation and to my mind his conception of land ownership under Fulani rule is (a)
> much more accurate one than Mr. Temple's. [Watts, Rhodes House, Mss. Afr.
> RNC, vol. 15, 1910]

I have dwelled on the land-revenue issue at some length because the
Lands Committee marked a watershed in the political economy of northern Nigeria and set the tenor for subsequent social and economic development. Indeed, the implications of the Lands Committee were tremendous: first, the white settler route was effectively undermined in spite of
Temple's murmurings to that effect. Second, the denial of private property obviated the possibility of a feudal landlord class that usurped rental
payments that would otherwise accrue to the capitalist class via the state;
in its place stood the traditional officeholders converted into a salaried
bureaucracy financed by direct taxes levied on peasant incomes. Third,
the maintenance of peasant smallholders in Nigeria sealed the predominance of merchant capital which, according to Temple and Girouard
were "the primary European interests" in Nigeria. And fourth, the new
mode of revenue assessment, was finally consolidated.

> 686. (*Mr. Morison.*) You contemplate, then, that the Emir will fall into the
> position of an official of the Government?—Yes. With regard to taxation
> settlement, the political staff is enjoined in the memorandum on taxation to
> avoid giving the natives to understand that any settlement has been made. It is
> out of the question, I think, at present, to make any settlement without in-
> curring the risk of doing great injustice either to the Government or the native.
> It is stated on page 148 of Baden-Powell's "Land Revenue in British India" that
> *the general requirements for a settlement are a survey, a detailed valuation of land, a
> record of rights, statistical information. We have none of these at present.* The amount

that can be paid as "general tax" depends entirely on the crops. There is little accumulated wealth in the country. A yearly revision by the political staff, with the assistance of the native administration, based on the "Resident's assessment," is, I think, absolutely necessary. There is one precedent in the Punjab and Burmah. [Temple, Lands Committee 1910, p. 88, emphasis added]

In 1909–10 a new revenue assessment was introduced clearly based on the Indian paradigm. Prior to this date, following the Native Revenue Proclamation of 1906, districts were both resident- and native-assessed for the kudin kassa tax (land money), which amounted to a standard, and hence regressive, poll tax. The new *taki* system,[29] however (which attempted to replace the customary kudin kassa in many of the northern provinces), was a fixed annual rent of sixpence per acre, each peasant holding being measured by an appointed official, the taki mallam. By 1911 the five home districts in Katsina Division had been taki-assessed (NAK Katprof 1897, p. 31) and by the following year almost 3,000 square miles in the northern provinces had fallen under the preliminary survey system. In some districts the old kudin kassa persisted, perhaps until the postwar period, but generally taki gained widespread institution. The only attempt to transform the rudimentary pace-measurement method into a full cadastral survey was undertaken in Kano Division. The Kano revenue survey never really extended beyond the home districts but by 1924 all land transactions were in theory recorded, and income assessment graduated with respect to soil type. By 1934, though 1,253 square miles of the emirate were embraced by the full cadastral system, it was estimated that a comprehensive survey of the twenty-one Kano districts at the then prevailing rate of progress would have taken roughly seventy-six years to complete (NAK Kanoprof 5/1 1708, vol. 1).

Irrespective of its specific form, the introduction of the new taki assessment prompted a dramatic increase in revenue, in excess of 150 percent in fact in Katsina Division between 1908 and 1913 (NAK SNP 10.6 134p/1913). Gross revenue aside, however, taki was highly problematic, not least with regard to its strikingly regressive incidence. Not only was taki highly inequitable with respect to farmers who cultivated large holdings in infertile districts, but in addition the taki mallams usurped the authority of an already unstable local administrative class. District heads found themselves drawn to corruption and embezzlement, while the local-level clout wielded by taki mallams further contributed to a centralized and increasingly alien system of bureaucratic control (Hull 1968, p. 268). These shortcomings carried debilitating consequences for subsistence security among peasant proprietors.

In spite of mounting criticism, the taki system persisted in some districts into the 1920s but was increasingly replaced after the war by a new revenue policy referred to variously as "kudin arziki," "haraji," or "lump sum assessment." The general aim of haraji was to subsume the multitude of regionally variable taxes (kudin kassa, compound tax, zakka, kudin shuka, kudin rafi) into one consolidated levy. In contrast to the per-unit area tax of the taki system, haraji involved community-wide assessment (NAK Katprof 1 1835/1926); in other words, gross revenue derived from agriculture, crafts, and livestock at estimated yields per acre or income per craft year. The lump-sum assessment of the village unit was then levied at a rate of approximately 10 percent of total annual income, which would be apportioned by the village or hamlet head congruent with the household's assessed income. According to the haraji system village or district assessment was established empirically, usually by a British political officer, and the individual tax by the village head on the grounds that he was necessarily competent and sufficiently knowledgeable to compute a household's income and its capacity to pay. The emergence of lump-sum assessment marked the apical point in the British preoccupation with tax and revenue in northern Nigeria. The base of taxation could be steadily broadened and, as the recruitment of British staff progressed, reassessment became more regular and closely supervised. By the Great Depression the foundations of colonial revenue policy had been established and consolidated.

ADMINISTRATION, BUREAUCRACY, AND ISLAM

Northern Nigeria is not, and probably never will be, wealthy enough to bear the weight of direct European administrations. It is, therefore, necessary that the Government rule the individual through native administration. For the efficient working of such administrations in these circumstances two conditions are necessary: (1) that they be effective, that is; that their authority be recognised by the individual; (2) that their acts should be readily controlled by the Government and not regarded as irreversible by the individual. It is sufficiently hard to fulfil these two conditions. The granting of the freehold of land to individuals would render both impossible of fulfilment. [C. Temple, Northern Nigeria Lands Committee, 1910]

Prior to 1918, the system of colonial administration was still experimental to the point of being haphazard. But the eventual product of overrule was an essentially theocratic pattern of traditional authority that had been secularized and bureaucratized in some fundamental ways. British support of indigenous religious structures, and of tradition generally, should not obscure this point. As is well known, the interpretation of precisely what indirect rule meant in practice was a highly contentious issue. For Lugard, indirect rule was synonymous with the preservation of, and administration through, indigenous Caliphal institutions, continually prompted and monitored by a British political officer. The entire edifice was, in the first instance, supported by a small and reluctantly given imperial grant-in-aid sufficient for a minuscule cadre of officers, and subsequently by various direct and indirect tax revenues. In effect, Britain designed a system, grafted onto the existing Muslim social structure, to integrate native institutions into a colonial totality which was at once racist and paternalistic. In Lugard's words,

> The policy of the Government was that these Chiefs should govern their people, not as independent, but as dependent rulers. The orders of the Government are not conveyed to the people through them, but emanate from them in accordance, where necessary, with instructions received through the Resident. While they themselves are controlled by Government in policy and matters of importance, their people are controlled in accordance with that policy by themselves. [Lugard cited in Crowder 1968, p. 217]

The Resident was to be a nonobtrusive, "sympathetic advisor" to the emirate hierarchy such that real authority was seen to emanate from the native authorities (NAs). Lugard's interpretation of the advisory capacity was largely "interventionist" while his successors, particularly Bell and Girouard, withdrew much more. The directness of colonial rule was therefore subject to enormous personal and provincial variation, an inevitable consequence of devolving power and authority to the Residents. Lugard's Political Memorandum—the "Book of Genesis," as Heussler (1968, p. 59) calls it—was in practice a redundant and unconsulted text.

The broad distinction between degrees of colonial intervention should not obscure the fact that in some spheres administrative rule was, of necessity, direct and blunt. H. R. Palmer was chided by Cargill for excessive and heavy-handed meddling in Katsina in removing an uncooperative emir and imposing an alternate who was clearly peripheral to the royal line. Indeed it was Palmer, accused by Temple of an obsessive hatred of Fulani rulers, who reestablished the Habe dynasty in Daura (NAK SNP 16/3 CC 0109). Likewise, political officers tended to use tax as an instrument to remove lower-level officeholders, usually on the grounds of embezzlement, yet might grant political immunity to favorites who apparently embodied the proper colonial aspirations and attitudes.[30] A paradigm of the directness of colonial rule is provided by a Bornu resident who candidly admitted that "it is good for the people that one District Head should bite the dust each year" (cited in Heussler 1968, p. 75).

The use of existing emirate machinery coupled with the poverty of imperial support led Polly Hill (1977, p. 21) to argue that indirect rule in the period up to the First World War was in actuality "rural non-rule." This is only true in a limited sense. First, for reasons of fiscal restraint, colonial personnel were thin on the ground. In 1903 a protectorate of 20 million people was administered by fifty-two European officers, and Palmer apparently ran Katsina Province alone save for two clerks. And second, district administration initially misjudged the extent to which it could provide strong village and district authority. Many of the nominated hakimai were nonlocal Fulani aristocracy, strangers in their own right, whose horizon was the capital rather than the community, and who were clearly clients, if not creations, of colonial authority. In Katsina emirate in 1916, for instance, forty-eight salaried village heads were not natives of the towns over which they presided (NAK Katprof Acc. 1280). Their legitimacy was grounded in clientage to what Gavin Williams (1976, p. 15) calls the "Great White Patron," a fact confirmed to the peasantry themselves by the large turnover in district- and village-level administrators and officeholders, apparently at the whim of distant colonial officers. The district heads were the middle-level transmitters of colonial dicta not, as Hill (1977, p. 23) observes, "the facilitators of upward rural demands." In short, indirect rule was very much a one-way street. At the same time, it would be mistaken to assume that rural nonrule is synomymous with a sort of colonial anarchy in the countryside. On the contrary, to the extent that the efficacy of the colonial state was in large part measured by its tax receipts, rural rule was tangible, concrete, and felt by everyone. In a sense not implied by Hill's "nonrule" view, colonialism in the North was an incorporative process with profound ramifications for peasant welfare and subsistence security. Administration was one thing, revenue and taxation quite another.

The model for the conversion of Caliphal institutions into Lugardian native authorities was provided by Katsina emirate.[31] Largely under the skillful direction of H. R. Palmer, a formal administrative hierarchy had been established within several years of conquest (figure 4.1). The legitimacy of the emir was preserved while judicial, executive, and legislative functions were constituted in a manner that affirmed the centrality of the provincial Resident (Paden 1973). In addition, Palmer recognized the need, in view of the demands for self-finance through direct tax, to consolidate the scattered and amorphous fiefs into nineteen contiguous administrative districts (see figure 4.2) and place each under a district head or hakimi directly responsible to the emir.[32] This new political alignment of power also involved the creation of subdistricts, either through the amalgamation of hamlet and village areas or the reconstitution of small fiefs. The lower echelon in the administrative hierarchy was the village unit presided over by a resident village head. District reorganization was in fact part of a larger scheme designed specifically for the reform of Caliphate taxation systems. In the 1906 Land Revenue Proclamation, Lugard—who was relatively uninterested in rural functions with no direct bearing on revenue—was quite candid about the function of territorial reorganization.

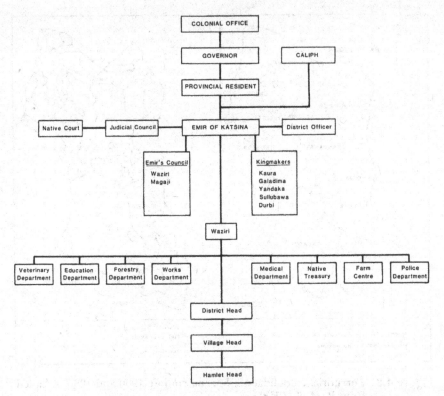

Figure 4.1. Pattern of government and administration, Katsina emirate about 1920. From R. Hull (1968), Y. Usman (1974) and field data, Katsina 1977–78.

A Resident may from time to time appoint chiefs or other suitable persons to be district headmen and village headmen *for the purpose* of supervising and of assisting in the collection of tributes and taxes under this Proclamation. [Lugard cited in Hill 1977, p. 35]

Territorial reform, then, was at once fiscal reform. Nowhere is this more in evidence than in the move to push all precolonial hakimai into their districts, ostensibly to undermine what the British saw as "absentee landlordism," and to abolish in one deft movement the insidious jekada system of tax collection. Unlike Kano, many of the Katsina sarauta and territorial magnates had been resident outside the birni during the pre-conquest era for at least part of the year, but by 1910 all the Katsina district heads were living in their district centers. While Palmer must have been cognizant of the historical significance of the Caliphate territorial units, the new administrative boundaries were quite artificial, with little concern for the political contours of the Sokoto Caliphate. District re-composition from the British perspective fulfilled the needs of admini-

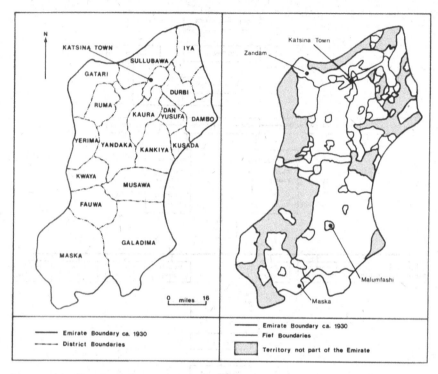

Figure 4.2. Territorial consolidation, Katsina emirate 1900 and 1930. Adapted
from R. Hull (1968).

strative convenience although the precolonial chain of authority was
inverted in the process. The institution of jekadanci was dealt a fatal blow,
while the hakimai became the true administrators whose legitimacy rested
largely on the hegemonic shoulders of the British. The erosion of traditional jekada authority in conjunction with the abolition of slavery—
through five antislavery proclamations between 1900 and 1907—marked
the watershed in the gradual bureaucratization of the old officeholding
class. Palmer's resurrection of the Caliphal treasury (beit-el-Mal) was a
critical element in this process. It provided for the departmentalization of
the NA, and hence filled the vacuum created by the dissolution of the
palace cliques. Its inauguration also systematized all financial transactions, intensified revenue collection, and prepared for the transition of a
masu sarauta class into a salaried stratum in the form of what Shenton and
Freund (1978, p. 14) call a "mock-feudal structure." As Fika (1978, p.
160) observed in his social history of Kano, taxation and the Treasury
"decisively pushed [the emirates] . . . toward bureaucratization."
    In some respects, of course, the territoriality issue was never ade-
quately resolved since the absence of a well-articulated hierarchical

structure linking birni to *kauye*, particularly in Kano, presented insurmountable problems with regard to authority and legitimacy in the countryside. In Katsina Division, further district reorganization in 1916 created large and unwieldy units, which grossly overextended the capabilities of administrative staff and undermined the salaries of the officials themselves. Subsequently, as the native administrations expanded and became increasingly bureaucratic, there was in fact a gradual regression to the earlier territorial framework. Village areas were reduced in size on the grounds of efficiency of tax collection, but generally at the expense of district coordination. The 1938 Provincial Report noted:

> We do not for one moment suppose that the Village Head is able to carry out all his duties on the official remuneration made to him. Yet his position and responsibilities must demand a high standard of morality. At the same time it is almost essential that he must augment his income by various devices, which if come to light bring down official reprimand, dismissal, or imprisonment. [NAK SNP 17/4 30876]

By 1940 Katsina emirate, encompassing roughly 9,466 square miles, consisted of 548 village units, some of whose tax revenue was incapable of supporting the local administrative official. Whether this constituted an efficient rural system is a moot point but it did (as Polly Hill observed) create inoffensive village territories "which would cause no trouble" (1977, p. 49).

In conclusion, it bears reiteration that the vast literature on indirect rule shows clearly how the British conquest and subsequent policy actually deepened the control of Islam. As Lubeck's work indicates (1979, p. 199), the Islamic nationalist reaction to conquest by Christian infidels consolidated Muslim hegemony in the emirates. Equally, the cultivation of precolonial administration supported Islamic institutions, particularly in the absence of a white settler community and a significant missionary vanguard. Indeed bureaucratization favored the position of emirs, and through them elements of the traditional aristocracy who were presented with new offices to bestow on clients (Abdullahi 1977). In the Weberian sense, the rationalization of the bureaucracy involved no leveling, for the prerogatives of the Muslim ruling class were preserved intact. The rise of a compradore Islamic elite was thus expressive of the removal of the traditional constraints on centralized emirate power. The emirs, supported by the military and communications apparatus of the colonial state and mediated by a hegemonic Islamic ideology, could retain and even extend their domination over the talakawa. As Abdullahi (1977, p. 79) put it, the colonial epoch in the North was above all a reflection of the seemingly endless capacity of the elites to accommodate and contain the British political officers without loosing its hold on the peasantry.

Merchant's Capital, Rural Development, and Colonial Political Economy

Merchants are the messengers of this world and God's faithful trustees on Earth.

—Prophet Mohammed

I am so anxious . . . to provide for . . . the contingency of the exclusion of a section of natives from the land causing the primary interests of the Europeans which are trade, to be subservient to the secondary interests [of] planting and production.

—Sir Charles Temple

The role of the colonial state as an agent for the expansion of European trade interests set the stage for all subsequent development in northern Nigeria. I have suggested that the genesis of a salaried mock feudal bureaucracy, the de facto nationalization of land, and the gradual emancipation of a large slave population did not contribute to the genesis of a wage-laboring class, but rather blocked the development of a plantation sector (or a landlord class) financed by European capital. As a consequence, merchant's capital was guaranteed a hegemonic role in the northern Nigeria economy. The function of commerce houses is complex and is explored in depth in the following chapter. Suffice to say here that European merchant's capital acting on behalf of industrial capital battened itself onto preexisting indigenous Hausa-Fulani and Tripolitanian merchant networks that long predated the colonial presence. This unholy alliance was supervised by the colonial state. Merchant's capital, the practice of buying cheap and selling dear, is what Marx referred to as an ancient or "antediluvian" capital and one spanning a variety of social formations, particularly within the Muslim diaspora. Nowhere is the correspondence between Islam and trade better highlighted than in the central Sudan in the nineteenth century, a phenomenon labeled the "merchant-ulema" complex by Tahir (1975). The traffic in commodities showed clearly that the preconditions for the expanded role of European trade—namely money and commodities—were present in the Sokoto Caliphate. The British did introduce a more generalized specie—which Palmer believed was in widespread circulation by 1908—to replace the increasingly impractical cowry currency, but the prevalence of the commodity form, a buoyant craft sector, and the regularity of exchange behavior obviously struck a positive note among the early commercial intelligence officials. In particular, the cotton textile sector stirred the hearts and minds of the European trade community. Yet in spite of the early enthusiasm of Churchill, Hesketh Bell, and the BCGA, the active promotion of cotton cultivation by the government, and the extension of the railway in 1907, the projected cotton boom (sponsored by foreign capital) was never to materialize (Hogendorn 1978, pp. 16–35).

To break into the existing commodity production system, the BCGA was forced to offer competitive lint prices in a vigorous rural textile industry that produced for domestic consumption and for export throughout the desert edge. The BCGA, intent on high profitability through commercial exclusion, was granted monopoly buying rights in 1905 by the colonial office, and set to work using other merchant companies, including Levantine firms, as buying agents on a fixed-price commission basis (NAK SNP 7 1521/1905). The project to curtail speculation, competitive buying, and price fluctuations ultimately failed to transform the Hausa plains into a new American South.[33] A major reason for the failure is unquestionably reflected in Governor Bell's lament that local market prices for cotton lint were at least 20 percent higher than the fixed price offered by the commercial firms.[34] The price that rural producers could demand from Hausa spinners and weavers in a highly integrated regional textile trade peripheral to the global commodity market, was thus well above the prevailing world price.

And so with the arrival of the railway in Kano in 1912—and with it the first flush of expatriate trading companies, which totaled eighteen by December 1913—cotton prospects were bleak. Ironically, as the Niger Company, John Holt, and the like erected buildings in the township, the railhead was deluged, not with cotton lint but with groundnuts. What began as an experiment was rapidly seized upon by rural producers as a means to procure tax payment. The "groundnut revolution" proceeded apace, recovering quickly from the temporary setback of the 1913 drought and further boosted by the new British oil demand after 1916.[35] Like the abortive cotton trade, groundnut purchasing assumed an oligopolistic quality particularly in the decade of struggles and mergers up to 1929, which culminated in that year with the formation of the United Africa Company. In the course of the emergence of the trading combines, the structure of middleman operations changed as the European firms made use of the influx of Levantine and Arab capital after 1917.[36] To be sure, large numbers of Hausa merchants were employed by European agents particularly among the remote buying stations far from either railhead or motorable roads. But, as Hogendorn (1978, p. 141) observed, the big influence of the Hausa middleman of the early period was gradually usurped by Levantine traders like Saul Raccah.

The ascendancy of the groundnut did not sound the death knell for cotton. Rather the BCGA changed its strategy from one of competition with to destruction of the local market. The local textile industry proved remarkably resilient nonetheless for it was estimated that 50,000 people dyed traditional cloth in the 1930s, and 50 million square yards of cloth were produced on local hand looms. But under the 1916 prohibition of local seed and the massive impact of cheap European cloth, which was frequently advanced on credit by buyers to peasants in the dry season to secure harvest sales, cotton production gained significant inroads (see table 4.1).[37] From 1915, purchase figures climbed steadily and by 1934 the BCGA felt confident enough to relinquish its purchase monopoly, thereby reducing its commission costs while preserving the supply of lint to Lancashire.

By the end of the First World War the dominant role of merchant's capital in northern Nigeria was consolidated. The European firms came to regulate and control the conditions of export crop commodity produc-

TABLE 4.1
COTTON PRODUCTION IN THE NORTHERN PROVINCES, 1915–1940

	Export of cotton	Price of seed cotton
Year	Bales (400 lb. net)	(pence per lb)
1915–16	121	1.75
1916–17	433	1.75
1917–18	855	2.5
1918–19	2,248	2.75
1919–20	3,568	3.75
1920–21	5,403	4.5
1921–22	9,883	2.0
1922–23	11,224	2.5
1923–24	15,683	3.0–4.0
1924–25	27,966	3.0
1925–26	37,556	2.5
1926–27	16,659	1.2–1.75
1927–28	16,316	2.4–2.2
1928–29	24,686	2.1–2.2
1929–30	34,389	1.6–1.2
1930–31	13,849	0.8–0.5
1931–32	4,811	0.6–0.8
1932–33	22,228	0.8–0.9
1933–34	23,013	0.9–1.2
1934–35	50,022	1.1–1.5
1935–36	49,795	1.1–1.6 falling 1.1
1936–37	49,196	0.9–1.3
1937–38	23,174	0.6–0.8
1938–39	19,588	0.7–0.6
1939–40	50,000 (approx.)	1.4–1.2

SOURCE: Compiled from NAK SNP 17 10199 Vol. I, "Agriculture Dept. Reports on Cotton Growing Industry in Nigeria 1923–29. Report on the Cotton Export Industry for the Half-Year Ending March 31, 1927," and NAK MINAGRIC 20121 "Crop Marketing and Cotton Export Tax."

tion and exchange without transforming the nature of actual production. Their trade operations were conveniently complementary; income acquired through advances or crop sale furthered what Birdwhistle called "the creation of new wants" (NAK SNP 7/8 1765/1907), consumer goods that gradually undermined indigenous craft production as they became items of necessary consumption. The evacuation of agricultural commodities was paralleled by the simultaneous influx of "incentive goods": European cotton goods, soap, kerosene, high grade salt, cigarettes, metalware, and bicycles. The entire import-export trade, including the financial superstructure that supported it, was a vast corporate oligopoly. In fact, throughout British West Africa one company alone controlled four-tenths of the external commerce, while a few banking operations— dominated by Elder Demster's Bank of British West Africa—established themselves as suppliers of specie and financiers for the firm's advance system.[38] By 1945 a cartel of six major firms, known collectively as the Association of West African Merchants, had come to dominate Nigeria's produce trade (see table 4.2). This oligopoly, which handled 80 percent of the foreign trade, was presided over by the United Africa Company (UAC), a subsidiary of the Unilever combine. Prior to 1939 the firm, in collusion with the colonial state, attempted to set prices and market commodities through involuntary compliance and sanctions. Internal policy was inevitably troublesome and cut-throat competition in the countryside (especially between Syrians and UAC) frequently led to litigation and physical violence.

Interposed between the corporate interests on the one hand and the peasant producers on the other, there developed myriad intermediary agents, brokers, traders, and middlemen. The evolution of this enormous commercial edifice provided salaried district and village heads, bureaucrats, and local merchant capital generally, with an opportunity to spread a lucrative but highly usurious credit system. Well before the harvest, commercial agents were advanced considerable sums by European firms, which in turn were lent directly to the producer who pledged his crop to an agent in return for borrowed cash to cover tax or other

TABLE 4.2
SHARE OF PRODUCE TRADE IN NORTHERN NIGERIA, ABOUT 1945

Firms	Groundnuts %	Cotton %
3 largest firms	58	79
5 largest firms	76	96
1937 "syndicate"	90	100

SOURCE: Bauer (1953, pp. 312–13).

social obligations. Baldwin's (1956, p. 26) *Groundnut Marketing Survey* in the mid-1950s estimated that there were 950 such middlemen directly accredited to the firms, 2,000–2,500 agents delivering the middlemen, and 3,500–4,500 buyer's boys. In a nutshell, the most successful traders stood at the apex of a vast hierarchy of credit and clientage, which rested firmly on the shoulders of low-level rural agents and middlemen. The merchant class, whose development was truncated by the dominant position of European capital, lived in the interstices of a colonial economy constituted by peasant households increasingly committed to export commodity production.

The centrality of merchant capital and its ability to penetrate deep into the Hausa countryside not only furthered peasant commodity production but provided the building blocks for the enormous increase in administrative revenue following the establishment of the native treasury system.[39] Governor Bell laid down preliminary regulations in 1910 for NA expenditure, which was to be divided equally between payment to district and village heads involved in actual tax collection, and the Beit-al-mal. The latter was to fund the salary of the emirs and officeholders, a fiscal reserve, and public works within the jurisdiction of the NA. My concern here lies less with fiscal policy than with expenditure in the rural sphere in light of the preservation of peasant proprietorship. Gervis (1963) and McPhee (1926) extolled British achievements in this respect, leaving, as Gervis put it, "a land with new industries, with agriculture and mining developed" (1963, p. xv). The enclave mine sector on the plateau did benefit from productive investment but there is a wealth of colonial financial information that documents how general imperial parsimony and a conservative monetary policy tightly constrained material improvement. Indeed, the pattern of government expenditure for agriculture and rural development was already inculcated by 1910. Tables 4.3 and 4.4 highlight the complete neglect of indigenous agriculture and capital

TABLE 4.3
GOVERNMENT EXPENDITURES IN NORTHERN NIGERIA, 1910–1911

Head	Amount	Percentage
Political	£ 76,515	43
Posts and Telegraphs	17,455	9
Medical	32,715	17
Agriculture and Forestry	2,654	1.5
Education	923	0.5
Public Works	30,188	16
Railways	24,443	13
TOTAL	£184,893	100%

SOURCE: *Annual Reports on Northern Nigeria, 1900–1911.*

TABLE 4.4
Distribution of Funds, 1910–1911

Item	SOKOTO £	SOKOTO App. %	KANO £	KANO App. %	KATSINA £	KATSINA App. %	BORNU £	BORNU App. %
Administration and Treasury	25,303	85	41,946	74	4,408	55	9,100	71
Judicial	552	2	2,760	5	1,220	15	1,248	10
Police and Prisons	2,688	9	3,207	6	636	8	647	5.1
Public Works	600	2.2	4,836	8	1,178	14	342	2.7
Education	250	0.8	1,240	2	200	2.4	300	2.2
Hospital and Sanitation	–		1,024	1.9	–		1,080	8.8
Special Grants for Economic Development	–		500	0.9	300	3.7	–	
Miscellaneous	300	1	1,500	2.2	144	1.9	25	0.2
TOTAL	£29,693	100%	£57,013	100%	£8,086	100%	£12,742	100%

SOURCE: *Annual Reports on Northern Nigeria, 1900–1911.*

investment in the rural sector. With the exception of an abortive (and elitist) mixed farming program that started in the 1920s, and an unsuccessful flirtation with irrigation, the organic composition of capital in agriculture remained low, if not antediluvian; Rodney's dictum (1972, p. 60) that "the peasant went into colonialism with a hoe and came out of it with a hoe" certainly testifies to the continued undeveloped forces of production among the Nigerian peasantry.

A consequence of agricultural neglect and the increasing efficacy with which direct taxes were collected was the accumulation of unutilized balances, or the reserve fund. At the end of 1915, the reserves of all NAs totaled £121,449.1.2; of this princely sum, £56,445.10.11 was invested in low-interest bonds abroad and £65,003.10.3 remained on deposit with the Nigeria government at 4½ percent. This reserve continued to grow and stood at £1,418,699 during the depression (see table 4.5). Indeed the increasing surpluses during periods of declining revenue—as obviously accrued in the 1930s—was at the expense of development. Hence Kano Province had a cumulative reserve of £320,769 in 1928 yet steadfastly refused to undertake any "special expenditures" for economic development or welfare. What emerges, then, is not only relatively wealthy NAs but increasing investment abroad despite the 1930s recession, the locust invasions, and the constant threat of famine. These investments were relatively fixed in Europe and generally used for the support of British business. The NAs received low interest on their vast surpluses while the peasantry, who were after all the fiscal grist for the NA mill, received considerably less. In what is a perfect condensation of colonial attitudes to rural and agricultural improvement, an administrator concluding the Land Utilization Conference in the 1930s suggested in an intriguing meteorological metaphor that rural development in the northern Provinces "could only be a gradual drip-drip process not a sudden deluge" (NAK Kadminagric. 1/1 2401).

So at the opening of the twentieth century northern Nigeria was confronted with colonial merchant's capital, relatively autonomous in the form and extent of its operation but formally subsumed by European industrial capital. As Kay (1975, p. 95) alluded, in order to sustain its primacy as an autonomous moment in the circuit of industrial capital merchant capital sought the appropriation of surplus value through the market, competing with other capitals and preventing direct access to the circuit of peasant production and consumption.[40] This historically specific form of capital, supervised and abetted by the colonial state, did not, as Tahir (1975) would have us believe, herald a bourgeois revolution, rather it blocked, distorted, and truncated capitalist development. What, then, were the precise forms and effects of this truncation?

First, the legislative decision of the Lands Committee to nationalize land crushed Lugard's projected creation of a landlord class. Instead, the

TABLE 4.5
FINANCIAL RESERVES, 1933–34

Province	Cash on current, or savings account			Fixed deposits			Invested abroad			Total surplus		
	£	s	d	£	s	d	£	s	d	£	s	d
Bauchi	33,644	12	6	67,050	0	0	66,237	16	1	166,932	8	7
Bornu	23,235	14	11	33,150	0	0	54,044	19	9	110,430	14	8
Kano	72,541	1	6	173,073	0	0	118,435	13	5	364,049	14	11
Plateau	25,864	10	3	17,000	0	0	20,133	4	1	62,997	14	4
Sokoto	54,404	5	8	53,649	0	0	104,182	5	1	212,235	10	9
Zaria	45,624	4	10	17,400	0	0	139,364	18	4	202,389	3	2
Totals	£303,643	5	8	£472,839	4	7	£642,217	4	1	£1,418,699	14	4

SOURCE: Jacob (Rhodes House, Mss. Afr. +16, 1934, appendix).

colonial authorities worked through the traditional officeholding class converting them into a salaried bureaucracy supported by surpluses appropriated from rural producers in the form of rents.[41] The aristocracy lost a source of surplus appropriation with the abolition of slavery—the freed slaves becoming peasant producers, not a wage-laboring agricultural proletariat—but retained their control over the peasantry, not only as revenue collectors for the state but in many instances as agents for the European firms. Accordingly, the accumulation of capital via the direct control of the means of production was never realized. Second, and as a corollary of the first point, Leverhulme's 1906 scheme for plantation agriculture—or a white settler variant of it—was averted in view of a legal framework that did not sanction either the expropriation of landed property or the coercion of a wage-labor class. Leverhulme, however, called for a revision of the land tenure laws in 1918 because

> [the] African native will be happier, produce the best and live under the larger conditions of prosperity when his labour is directed and organised by his white brother. [cited in Buell 1965, p. 769]

Yet the Chief Secretary to the Colonies responded that Leverhulme's ideas were "diametrically opposed to the government of Nigeria." The preference for peasant commodity production was rationalized in its most complete form by Governor Clifford in his address to the Nigeria Legislative Council.

> As further agricultural industries in tropical countries which are mainly, or exclusively in the hands of the native peasantry (a) Have a firmer root than similar enterprises when owned and managed by Europeans, because they are natural growths, not artificial creations, and are self-supporting, as regards labour, while European plantations can only be maintained by some system of organized immigration or by some form of compulsory labour; (b) Are incomparably the cheapest instruments for the production of agricultural produce on a large scale that have yet been devised; and (c) Are capable of a rapidity of expansion and a progressive increase of output that beggar every record of the past. . . . For these reasons I am very strongly opposed to any encouragement being given . . . to projects for creation of European owned and managed plantations to replace or even supplement, agricultural industries which are already in existence, or which are capable of being developed by peasant. [cited in Buell 1965, p. 772]

In practice the ecological and economic risks of export crop cultivation were born entirely by the direct producer, though merchant's capital could (and did) present itself as the savior of peasant culture. Moreover the propensity of merchant's capital to intensify the preexisting unity between direct producers and their means of production provided no immediate incentive for the colonial administration to develop an agricultural policy. In fact, with the exception of cotton, the soporific Department of Agriculture was content to dabble with cash crop seed development and multiplication on experimental stations, to provide a flimsy marketing infrastructure, and to effect a simple but often ineffective produce inspection system.[42]

A third effect was the fragile imbrication of interests between merchant's capital, the state bureaucracy, and the traditional elite, sealed through the tax-money-trade nexus. The objectives of colonial tax nicely interdigitated as Lugard noted.

> To avoid the trouble of transporting bulky produce, the native quickly appreciates the advantage of securing sufficient cash to pay his tax, this promoting the adoption of currency, which facilitates trade. [Lugard 1968, p. 251]

The spread of commodity relations and the contagion of monetary relationships were therefore the instruments of a successful alliance between the trading firms, the colonial state, and the local ruling class. Direct taxation, however, upon which indirect rule and the export-import trade ultimately rested, was also a critical factor in the genesis of a wage labor force. The precedent for the commodization of labor had been set by the use of "compulsory nature labor" for road construction beginning in 1903. The extension of the Baro and Bauchi light railway lines, however, marked a new era of what came to be euphemistically known as "political labor." In Nupe Province for instance between 1907 and 1912, over 250,000 laborers had been recruited (Mason 1978, p. 71); by 1912 at least 10,000 seasonal, semiproletarianized laborers were employed in the plateau mine fields. Yet in spite of tax demands, the prevailing low wage rates—9d per day in the 1920s—amplified the need for political labor. As late as 1925, 3,000 men were forcibly recruited for railway and public works construction (Crowder 1968, p. 208). The cash incentive still provided a major impetus for seasonal migrant wage labor, especially in remote districts where agricultural or artisanal commodity production were not viable economic options.

In conclusion, it is worth noting that the apparent unity of interest between merchant and bureaucrat was itself contradictory. On the one hand, customs duties—while easy to collect and impose—conflicted with European trade interests, being value-added taxes for the prospective Nigerian consumer. On the other hand, direct taxes, while capable of generating income, were difficult to impose, frequently aroused African opposition, and (more critically) could discourage peasant consumption of imported wares. Every penny appropriated through tax was a penny denied to the trader's coffers. On balance, there was a move from custom duties, which formed 51.2 percent of Nigerian revenue in 1913, to direct taxation, which constituted 73.7 percent in 1918. Nevertheless, the tensions among administrative self-finance through direct taxation, the necessity for export commodity production, and the need for local purchasing power to sustain the European import trade, are critical to an understanding of the peasant predicament in the colonial period.

CONCLUSION

To study the agrarian question according to Marx's method we should not confine ourselves to the question of the future of small scale farming. . . . We should ask: is capital, and in what ways is capital, taking hold of agriculture, revolutionising it, smashing old forms of production and of poverty.

—Karl Kautsky

In this chapter I have argued that the colonial social formation in northern Nigeria needs to be seen as a complex and contradictory articulation of a capitalist system with persisting noncapitalist forms of production. Articulation here implies syncretism rather than a mechanical linkage; it invokes the practice of one social formation within the practice of another, each wrestling to transform the other to meet its own reproductive requirements.

This articulation of one practice within another is governed both by the reproductive requirements of the capitalist mode and by the restrictions on [it] either by the limits within which the penetrated instance can operate as set by the non-capitalistic mode of production, or by the continuing reproduction of elements of the non-capitalist mode. [Taylor 1979, p. 227]

To construct a universal model then for the penetration of what is erroneously seen as a monolithic metropolitan capital into Third World formations is wholly wrongheaded. The historical development of the relation of capital to agriculture—which is the principal thread running through this book—expresses such a diversity. The conjunction of metropolitan capital and noncapitalist social relations in northern Nigeria produced a truncated capitalism characterized by complex, varied, and hybrid forms of economic activity. European capital did not unashamedly call the shots, and what emerged was, to use Murray's (1981, p. 9) description of colonial Indochina, a transitional society, a syncretic combination of the old and the new. This was necessarily the case because "people do not create society for it always pre-exists" (Bhaskar 1979, p. 46). The dynamics of agricultural production in colonial Nigeria, then, can be understood in terms of this dialectic, that is, in terms of the needs and tendencies of specific capitals and their agents, and the characteristics of specific agrarian systems of production.

In northern Nigeria, at least until 1945, merchant capital acting on behalf of industrial capital under the aegis of the colonial state constituted the principal mode of capitalist penetration. Because merchant's capital does not have to organize production on a capitalist basis to extract value from the productive process, it is dependent on the noncapitalistic class that organizes the exploitation of labor, even as it tends at the same time to undermine the economic and social basis of the noncapitalist ruling class. This contradictory nature of capitalist penetration in the form of merchant's capital is echoed in Rey's (1976) first two stages of articulation: in the first stage capitalism reinforces the precapitalist mode, and allies itself with its ruling class. In the second phase, where capitalism has taken "root" it begins to corrode the social organization of production itself, although still depending on the noncapitalist mode to supply labor and raw materials. Since a major characteristic of merchant's capital is its dependence on, and even reinforcement of, extant forms of production and exploitation in the noncapitalist mode, the structures reinforced or created by merchant's capital can serve as a barrier to the eventual reorganization of production on a capitalist basis. That is to say, industrial or productive capital must necessarily struggle against merchant or circulation capital to bring the latter under its dominance. In Nigeria these conflicts were in evidence over the land question, and in particular Leverhulme's attempt to overthrow the dicta of the Lands Committee.

In addition, however, the restructuring of the Caliphal relations of production proceeded through merchant and interest-bearing capital.[43] Historically, of course, as Marx recognized, the two forms are inseparable.

> Interest-bearing capital, or, as we may call it in its antiquated form, usurer's capital, belongs together with its twin brother, merchant's capital, to the antediluvian forms of capital, which long precede the capitalist mode of production and are to be found in most diverse economic formations of society. [Marx 1967, I, 593]

Capital thus asserted itself in the North through two basic economic mechanisms: trade and credit. Both involved the interaction of forms of capital already existing in the Caliphate precapitalist formation with corresponding forms originating in the metropole. As I document in detail in the following chapter, merchant capital was able to reorganize the conditions of production and reproduction in the peasant household without intervening directly in the process of production or necessitating primitive accumulation properly defined. While the peasantry gradually lost autonomy, they were not separated from the means of production. As Banaji (1977, p. 34) maintains, "the capitalists' control over the labor process [necessarily] retains a partial and sporadic character." The outcome was simply that value created in the noncapitalist realm was transferred to the capitalist domain through unequal exchange and usury; merchant and interest-bearing capital increasingly controlled the product if not the production process as a whole. The protectorate provided raw materials in the first instance and increasingly came to serve as a market for European exports. The circuit of commodity exchange within the precapitalist mode was gradually inserted into the international circuits produced by European capitalism.

Why, then, did a truncated capitalist penetration assume this specific form? First, the presence of long-distance trade, of merchant's capital, and of limited commodity production at the time of conquest provided a firm basis for further commodity production. Subsequently, the expansion of the home market, the export of agricultural production, and the imports of manufactures all provided for a considerable increase in commodity circulation, and for a strengthening of the merchant class. And second, at the political level, the colonial state was strapped by the constraints of Treasury parsimony, the need for self-finance and by the trade interests of a manufacturing lobby. Further, in light of the violence of conquest in the Caliphate the necessity for law, order, and security became paramount. All this translated into a need to work through the Caliphal ruling class and forge a political alliance embodied in the rhetoric of indirect rule. In this regard, Lugard's vision of such an alliance in the form of a landlord class based on private property was radical and ultimately problematic since it opened the way for the landgrabber and usurer, widespread proletarianization through mortgage and debt, and conceivably the presence of a white settler class that might threaten the authority of the aristocracy. In addition Leverhulme's plan for large-scale capitalist agriculture was seen to be constrained by biological and seasonal characteristics of Hausa agronomy, which posed significant obstacles to the development of a fully industrial agriculture.[44] However, the preservation of independent family farms producing export commodities appeared highly advantageous: the risks of production were borne by the households, it was cheap and efficient; the costs of reproduction of seasonal wage laborers to the mine or the urban sectors were incurred by the peasant family, which accordingly permitted lowered wage levels; and the import-export trade could be conveniently controlled by direct tax on all adult males in the countryside.[45] In short,

> the industrial interests, the trading companies, and the state combined to attempt to regulate what was grown, how it was grown, the quality of the produce, as well as to establish monopolistic pricing and marketing arrangements. . . . While the immediate organization of the production process remained in the hands of the peasant, their production and reproduction was determined by the development of commodity relations, including the eco-

nomic and political measures such as cultivation bye laws, compulsory land improvements schemes, and credit and extension services, which tied the producers more closely to particular kinds of production. [Bernstein 1978, p. 64]

All this suggests the rather obvious point that colonialism in northern Nigeria did not bring a capitalist revolution in agriculture, if by that we mean a primitive accumulation process in which direct producers are separated from their means of production.[46] On the contrary, the peasantry—Marx's sack of potatoes—showed remarkable resiliency. Moreover, the colonial state was not simply an "agent of capital" but actually intervened in support of custom and against private property for essentially political and fiscal reasons. In this sense agriculture was derivative of the state which in actual fact attempted—albeit unsuccessfully because of the corrosive effect of the market—to resuscitate some attributes of mutual economy. In Nigeria, a dominant impulse was provided by precapitalist labor anchored in the family. The household economy made it possible for merchants to profit through it, "from a special relation of capital in which the family economy bore the risks . . . without any benefit" (Medick 1981, p. 53). In both instances, however, Lenin and Kautsky point to heterogeneity of agricultural production under conditions of capitalist incorporation. In Nigeria, I argue that such heterogeneity appears as a series of unresolved tendencies: the uneven appearance of the wage form, the increasing generalization of commodity relations, new forms of peasant differentiation, and the dissolution of precapitalist social relations. The ambivalency and complexity of these developments are perfectly captured by Bettelheim in what he calls conservation-dissolution.

> Inside social formations in which the capitalist mode of production is predominant, this domination mainly tends to expanded reproduction of the capitalist mode of production, that is to dissolution of the other modes of production and subsumption of their agents to capitalist production relations. The qualification "mainly" indicates that this is the *predominant tendency* of the capitalist mode of production within the social formations under considerations. However, this predominant tendency is combined with another *secondary* tendency, that of "conservation-dissolution." This means that within a capitalist social formation, the non-capitalist forms of production, before they disappear are "restructured" (partly dissolved) and thus *subordinated* to the predominant capitalist relations (and so *conserved*). [Bettelheim, in Emmanuel 1972, p. 297]

Among Hausa-Fulani peasant households during the colonial epoch, the conservation tendencies are synonymous with what Marx called a formal subsumption of labor by capital, that is to say a subordination on the basis of existing technical conditions, division of labor, and control of the means of production. At the same time new social forms arose, not least the sale of labor power, whether as seasonal migrants to the mines and cities or as rural farm laborers. For the peasant farmers in the Caliphal period, the relations of exploitation determining the appropriation of surplus were *extra-economic*, requiring direct political intervention through taxes, labor service, and so on. In contrast, the colonial period saw the emergence of surplus extraction in the *economic* realm, namely, through the necessary consumption of imported goods, through unequal exchange and usury, and through the wage form. In the following chapter I detail the nature of these changes and the concomitant transformation in political, social, cultural, and ideological levels among an increasingly differentiated Nigerian peasantry. In doing so, my aim is to detail how the penetration of capitalist relations into the agricultural sector impinged upon food supply and subsistence security. In what follows, I draw heavily on empirical data drawn from three provinces: Katsina, Zaria and Kano. I argue that as the development of capitalism progresses in agriculture, initially through expanded commodity production, the noncapitalist relations of production decompose in a manner that presents new threats to subsistence security. Colonial capitalism broke the cycle of household reproduction such that peasants could not "overcome simple reproduction due to surplus extraction that cancel[led] accumulation" (de Janvry and Deere 1979, p. 610). Periodic food crises in Hausaland not only accelerated the processes of social decomposition but were also expressive of limited accumulation within the peasantry and of the chronic vulnerability of some rural producers to both environmental and economic perturbations.

5

HUNGER, RISK, AND HOUSEHOLD
SECURITY

*The moral of history, also to be deduced from other observations
concerning agriculture, is that a rational agriculture is
incompatible with the capitalist system (although the latter
promotes technical improvement in agriculture), and needs either
the hand of the small farmer living by his own labour or the control
of associated producers.*

—*Karl Marx*

*Without revolutionizing the mode of production [merchant
capital] . . . only worsens the condition of the direct producers . . .
under conditions worse than those under the immediate control of
capital.*

—*Karl Marx*

Among household producers the domestic
group possesses the means of production, provides labor, and disposes of
at least part of its collective product. In view of the variety of historical
circumstances under which household agricultural production occurs,
the internal composition and division of labor within households and the
character of their constituent members are largely conditioned by the
household's relation to the larger economy (Friedmann 1979*b*). During
the Caliphal period, households produced surpluses over and above
consumption requirements to support the nonproducing *masu sarauta.*
But surplus generation could remain static without jeopardizing the cycle
of simple reproduction. During the colonial period, however, there was a
type of extended reproduction and an increasing scale of surplus appropriation. In spite of the fact that in northern Nigeria surpluses were also
appropriated by peasant elites and by merchant capital, the relation of
rural households to the market and the state generally appears markedly
different under colonialism. Following conquest the effect of the law of
value was reflected in the development and intensification of commodity
production, and later in the uneven emergence of wage labor. Several

authors have written on this process of commoditization among African peasantries[1] and much of the literature is pertinent to the Nigerian experience. In particular, two concepts are of special theoretical significance in grasping the nature of agrarian change in Hausaland. First, *reproduction*; that is, the annual renewal of the forces and relations of production. As Friedmann (1978a) puts it, if reproduction is to occur the renewal of the means of production and the distribution of the social product must be affected such that production may recommence in its previous form. And second, *transformation*; that is, the dissolution of the cycle of reproduction and a recombination or reconstitution of some of the old elements into new productive relations. I have argued that the colonial experience in northern Nigeria needs to be understood as a breaking of the cycle of peasant reproduction, that is, as a gradual transformation of the conditions of peasant production. Bernstein says

> we are trying to pose relations between capital and peasants as simple commodity producers "deposited" historically by the destruction of natural economy (manifested in various pre-capitalist modes of production). By this we mean that the destruction of the reproduction cycle of natural economy gives way to a different process of social reproduction in which the reproduction of households takes place increasingly on an *individual* basis through the relations of commodity production and exchange. The relations between individual households, whether at the village level or at the level of the regional, national, or international division of labour, are increasingly mediated through the place *each* household occupies in the total nexus of relations of commodity production and exchange. [Bernstein 1979, pp. 426–27]

In chapter 2 I showed how household producers in the Sokoto Caliphate reproduced themselves as *peasants*; that is to say, the cycle of reproduction was secured by a partial resistance to commoditization. This is not to suggest that there was no commodity production per se; rather it suggests (1) that use-value production predominated, and (2) that household reproduction was based on horizontal and vertical reciprocal ties for the renewal of the means of production and subsistence (Friedmann 1978a). Access to land, labor, and credit was mediated by nonmonetary ties and by stable institutional mechanisms that linked households to other productive units and classes. This entire "culture of reproduction" corresponds closely to Scott's (1976) moral economy of peasantry. Colonialism promoted the deepening of commodity relations within the cycle of reproduction; in fact the individualization of production was synonymous with the severing of households from precapitalist reciprocal ties. Market relations, in other words, came to mobilize land, labor, credit, and the means of production.

The progress of simple commodity production may potentially involve two developmental paths: first, the increasing specialization of commodity producers, which reflects an advanced division of labor in a developing capitalist economy; and second, as a logical extension of commodity proliferation, the complete separation of the household from all ties save those of the market. Northern Nigeria did not witness the genesis of simple commodity production in this latter sense; rather there was an intensification of commoditization. That is, the proportion of household necessary consumption purchased at market-determined prices substantially increased; the mobility of land, labor, and credit assumed market forms;[2] and the survival of the household itself became contingent upon the production of exchange-values, and in some instances, upon quite specialized commodity production.

In the following discussion I am less concerned with a general political economy of commodity production in northern Nigeria than with the relations between commoditization and household security. Accordingly, my emphasis on the rupture of peasant reproduction has as a corollary the decomposition of a complex of local-level institutions and the disqualification of an entire culture of production. Of course, this process, which was a reflection of the struggle between direct producers and capital over the conditions of labor in the spheres of production, distribution, and realization of value, involved a measure of resistance. Particularly under conditions of peasant proprietorship, rural producers could sabotage or refuse new agrarian technologies, call rural "strikes" against depressed producer prices, avoid or ignore administrative dicta, and on occasion participate in acts of outright violence, whether individual or collective, against the agents of the state. However, the partial transformation of the peasantry had important ramifications for food supply, hunger, and household security. Indeed, in terms of subsistence security, colonialism was a two-edged sword. The transport revolution removed some of the geographical constraints on food trade and famine relief characteristic of a precapitalist technology; yet those very same improvements in mobility provided a vent to evacuate rural surpluses out of the countryside in the form of taxes, rents, food, and export commodities. Colonialism pioneered the expansion of the agricultural frontier in Hausaland and the state was instrumental in encouraging the cultivation of export crops; but in both instances these developments subjected peasant producers to the unfettered clutches of the firms, middlemen, advance system and, of course, to the instabilities of the global commodity markets. In this light, I endeavor to show the following:

1. Colonialism changed the context of environmental variability to the extent that the response systems described for the Caliphate (social and agronomic mechanisms that served to guarantee a margin of subsistence security) were gradually eroded.

2. The process of colonial integration in transforming the culture of production also changed the character and genesis of hunger and famine, for the incorporation of northern Nigeria into a global system imposed new stresses on peasant households and changed the very organization of agricultural production.

3. The continued low level of development of peasant forces of production rendered subsistence a highly discontinuous process in the face of physical variability and climatic seasonality. In spite of the dependence of the colonial state on an essentially "backward" rural sector, the continuity of a simple farm technology after 1900 ensured the persistence of peasant vulnerability to natural calamities such as drought, disease, or insect infestation.

Clearly, the connection between famine and environmental variability such as drought, is mediated by the prevailing social and economic relations of the stricken social formation. Not only can some forms of societal arrangements either accommodate or amplify the effects of environmental variability or harvest shortfall, but chronic hunger may become a structural feature of society itself. Necker described this sort of condition in fourteenth-century France,[3] identifying virtually all civil institutions as self-serving for large landowners in a manner that denied the poor the fundamental right to food. As Lavoisier, the French chemist, commented in 1777, subsistence crises were less the result of a malignant Nature than a consequence of the social institutions which Nature confronts. It is, then, the form and mechanisms of inequality which explain that:

> subsistence crises were unavoidable in France because the forms of surplus extraction in an absolutist state which was based on the small peasant proprietor excluded any possibility of increased production. The old mode of production was simply "sucked dry"; it was in no sense altered. [Lis and Soly 1979, p. 100]

Food crises, in other words, appeared as social products.

HAUSA AGRONOMY AND HOUSEHOLD PRODUCTION

And all the time the country's riches lay at our very feet, in the blessed groundnut.

—African Mail, 1914

In spite of the frequent criticisms of agricultural incompetency leveled against the Hausa farmer by British administrators, colonial officials made almost no attempt to transform indigenous farm technology. Indeed, even in the 1970s the organic composition of capital among Hausa hoefarmers was little different from that of their nineteenth-century ancestors. The colonial government did, however, enthusiastically encourage the expansion of what were to become the twin supports of the northern Nigerian export economy, namely cotton and ground-nuts.[4] Neither crop was, of course, a colonial introduction: both Barth and Staudinger had commented upon the profusion of groundnuts through-out the northern Hausa plains during the 1850s and the famous Kano textile industry was entirely supplied by locally grown cotton lint.[5] After the early economic intelligence reports by Birdwhistle and his colleagues, however, the production of both groundnuts and cotton was deliberately encouraged by the Department of Agriculture and the BCGA. There were, of course, various interests involved in the propagation of cash crops in the colonial economies. These included the metropolitan indus-tries that consumed the export commodities as elements of constant capital; the large commercial firms and trading companies who orches-trated the collection, marketing and export of the crops to the metropole; and the colonial state itself which was interested not simply in the genesis of income to finance infrastructural development and the costs of admin-istration but also, at an ideological level, in the creation of "economic men" as part of the "mission civilatrice."

In the course of changing the condition of household reproduction by coercive means (i.e., taxation, forced cultivation, the use of market mechanisms), the protectorate experienced a sharp increase in the culti-vated area, due in part to the emancipation of several million slaves, and in the volume of export commodities. From a gross production of 9,000 tons of groundnuts and 1,500 tons of cotton in 1915, the trade grew by 2,000 and 700 percent, respectively, over the following twenty-year period (Helleiner 1966).

In a spatial sense, groundnuts and cotton were complementary.[6] The latter flourished in the more humid climes, particularly on the rich laka soils of the southern Hausa plains; groundnuts, conversely, thrived in the more arid jigawa regions of the northern provinces, most especially Sokoto, Katsina, Daura, Kano, and Borno. In the intermediate zones, the central regions edaphically suited to both, the production of groundnuts and cotton vacillated annually in accordance with the prevailing or antici-pated export prices offered by the buying agents and the firms.

A common position on the relation of colonial export crops to hunger, as reflected in the work of O'Keefe and Wisner (1975) and some of the French Marxists (Comité Information Sahel 1974; Derriennic 1977) is that cotton and groundnuts displaced traditional foodstuffs in a linear fashion. De Castro (1976) was one of the first to argue along these lines, situating peasant production within colonial underdevelopment rather than in the Malthusian problematic of uncontrolled biological reproduction. The rupture of the balance between use- and exchange-value is seen in this view to have occurred through the increased labor time and land devoted to export commodities, which undermined food-stuff production; in addition, the market and price systems that accompany commoditization "do not adequately provide substitute purchased use values" (Bryceson 1980, p. 282). In its most perverse form, self-sufficiency in foodstuffs was quickly eroded, occasionally to the point of full-blown cash crop specialization, which (as in the Senegalese case) required large-scale food importation. Crowder and Suret-Canale exemplify the displacement view.

> Progress in export production was also brought about—mainly in Senegal—at the expense of traditional food production, of which the shortfall was not made good by consumption of imported rice. . . . The pre-colonial crop system, within the traditional social setting, provided a complete and permanent equilibrium between man and nature. Compelled thereafter, with means which were unchanged, to provide for his own subsistence and to furnish a surplus of export products as well, the peasant succeeded only in reducing this subsistence to a minimum, or even below: reserves kept back for traditional feasts or bad years disappeared. Every year there was famine. Malnutrition became a permanent feature. [Suret-Canale 1977, p. 128]

> The colonial administration did nothing to prevent situations such as that in Gambia where rice that could have been grown by the peasant more cheaply was imported and to pay for it he devoted more of his energies in the cultivation of groundnuts. Indeed it favoured the colonial economic system, for French rice exports in Indo-China could find a market in Senegal. [Crowder 1968, p. 348]

In northern Nigeria the colonial experience is much more refractory and less clear-cut. First, at no time did export crops *completely* replace cereal production. In this sense full petty commodity production—in which subsistence production succumbs entirely to the mediation of the marketplace—is not characteristic of agrarian formations in much of the Third World. And indeed there were very good reasons for the preservation of "mixed production." The colonial state required foodstuffs for the supply of military, minefield, and administrative personnel, while household food production subsidized the costs of labor; in any case food production made much practical sense in an area of considerable ecological variability.

> The input-output balance of the reproduction cycle remains within a system of circulation which is amenable to control and planning. This prevents famines due to economic causes for example. The peasant with an intact subsistence production allocates his factors of production to meet the needs of his household in such a way that even in the event of a bad harvest, there would be sufficient food. [Elwert and Wong 1980, p. 504]

Virtually all hoe farmers attempted to cultivate at least a portion of their food requirements, although the ratio of foodstuffs to cash crops oscillated from year to year in accordance with the nature of household demands for cash and liquidity.

And second, some scholars have argued that in any case groundnuts were incorporated into intercropping patterns and crop mixtures *without* either significant additional demands being made on land or labor time or a reduction in the volume of cereal production. This view suggests that groundnuts were successfully integrated into cropping regimes without seriously affecting the number of grain stands planted or their resultant yields. In other words, in comparing farms that were sole cropped with guinea corn with those that were intercropped with guinea corn and groundnuts, no significant differences were found in plant densities of the former or the yield per stand. Furthermore, it has been suggested that groundnuts do not impose additional fertility constraints on savanna soils since, as a leguminous crop, they are nitrogen-fixing.[7] On balance, then, these positive attributes unique to the groundnut, in addition to its local use-value for oil production and as a source of food in periods of extreme hardship, have led some to argue that the "region continued to be self-sufficient in food" (Lubeck 1979, p. 201).

While it is unquestionably true that groundnuts stand in sharp contrast to cotton on all these counts, the case in praise of "the blessed groundnut" is far more desultory. Raynault's figures from Maradi (1976, p. 292) in Niger, and Norman et al.'s data (1976, p. 192) collected in Sokoto indicate that for the aeolian jigawa areas, at least, cereal yields fall off markedly when intercropped with groundnuts (table 5.1). Irrespective of the density of stands per acre, yields of most crops tend to be depressed when grown in mixtures rather than as sole stands, principally because of lower plant populations and interspecies competition for space, light, and moisture. This is especially the case on low-fertility, lightly manured farms. This means first that the poorer households, strapped by small peripheral farm locations and inadequate livestock for manure inputs, stood to suffer disproportionately from yield reductions through groundnut intercropping. Second, in a region in which household labor shortage was a major productive constraint, groundnuts necessarily absorbed labor time in planting, extra weeding, and harvesting. Third, while the groundnuts were edible—and indeed contained critical sources of vegetable protein, fatty acids, minerals, and vitamins—they could not be consumed as a staple for they provide insufficient nutrition and caloric intake over extended periods (Altman and Dittmer 1968; Roberts 1980). And fourth, the relative vulnerability of cash crops, even groundnuts, to the vicissitudes of the Sahelian climate increased the threat of underproduction as ever larger proportions of farm holdings were devoted to export commodities.

Of course, groundnuts grown as part of local crop mixtures may be perfectly compatible with the goal of security. But this should not detract

TABLE 5.1
CROP YIELDS

	Yields in sole stands*			Yields by intercropping*						
Location	Millet	Sorghum	G. nuts	Millet and sorghum		Millet, sorghum and g. nuts			Millet and g. nuts	
Maradi	423	404	500	313	142	281	56	153	307	261
Sokoto	657	582	383	796	166	499	63	79	581	282

SOURCE: C. Raynault (1976, p. 292); D. Norman et al. (1976, p. 192).

*Maradi statistics refer to kilos per hectare. Sokoto statistics refer to pounds per acre.

from the practical need among all families for a type of commodity production to cover tax demands and to purchase items of necessary consumption and which resulted in correspondingly reduced cereal yields. In the case of cotton, which in any event makes high demands of soil nutrients, the displacement view is far more apposite. The BCGA actively encouraged monocultural cotton production in the northern provinces, fearing that the new improved American Allen seed was susceptible to pest infestation and reduced productivity when cultivated in crop mixtures (NAK SNP7 267/1905). Land in the major cotton lint areas—notably southern Katsina and Zaria—was probably not at a premium, but without hiring labor power, the extension of domestic production could only be achieved through a reduction in the area devoted to cereals. Furthermore, the labor demands of cotton production—especially planting and weeding—conflicted with domestic grain production demands during crucial labor bottleneck periods (Tosh 1978; Kassam 1976).

The precise conditions of export commodity expansion in relation to food supply during the colonial period can only be pieced together from wholly inadequate archival materials. But even with a paucity of empirical evidence it appears that cash cropping made profound inroads into the northern Nigerian food economy. The case of groundnuts is particularly instructive since the early expansion in cultivation occurred largely in the land-scarce and densely populated zone in Kano Province. During the 1920s in Tudun Wada District (Kano Province) the average peasant holding was approximately 3.5 acres of which almost one-third was devoted to cotton or groundnuts. According to Forde (1946, p. 125),

> the household will require at existing levels of grain consumption the harvest from 1 – 1½ acres of grain per adult unit for its own needs. *A small household of 1 man, 1 wife and 2 children would thus require from 3 – 4 acres of grain for its own needs, while a large unit of 2 men, 2 wives, 2 aged people and 4 children (= 8 adult units) would require from 10 – 15 acres of cornland.* The assumption that children [who in northern Nigeria appear to be taken as girls of under 14 or 15, and boys under 15 or 16] and aged persons normally consume half the quantity of grain required by adults appears to be made generally by agricultural officers and others. [Emphasis added]

Backhouse's (1932) reassessment of Dan Zomo District, a largely land surplus region in Gumel emirate, established an average holding of roughly five acres of which four were devoted to cereals interplanted with cowpeas and the remainder sown to groundnuts. Yet, the potential problems posed by overproduction were exacerbated by the critical function of groundnuts as a source of necessary cash in relation to price fluctuations. The Resident of Kano noted in 1933 that:

> Economically, groundnuts provide the lifestream for this Province. A falling price last year stimulated the extension of cultivation. There is a large crop,

possibly larger by 25%, but the drop in price to 50/- a ton is too great to prove less than disappointing—roughly this year it takes the peasant twice as much in groundnuts to meet his tax and there has been little over for expenditures.

Not only was the acreage under this crop greatly increased by the farmers already acquainted with its value as a ready money crop but in the Northern Division resident Fulani and peasants in distant buying centres planted nuts in hope of obtaining money to pay taxes. . . . In consequence the acreage planted showed an increase of probably 20% over last year.

It is improbable that the low prices this year will adversely affect production in the immediate future. For the bulk of the Province it is the easiest money crop and whatever the price it does represent a certain sum of hard cash. [NAK SNP 17 21326/1933]

Even in isolated areas such as Tarke hamlet, Sokoto Province, and in Bomo village near Zaria, where average holdings were 9 and 7.4 acres respectively, a large proportion of households were "net purchasers of grain" during the 1930s (Corby 1941, pp. 106–109). The grain harvest in many areas of the north had been reduced to the level of household self-consumption needs and "even to somewhat below this" (Forde 1946, p. 125).

The temporal and spatial pattern of export commodity penetration was, however, far from even. During the first quarter of a century, both groundnuts and cotton revolutions were largely confined to the Hausa heartlands, most especially Kano, Katsina, and Zaria. The combination of suitable ecological conditions and accessibility were the hallmarks of this expansionism. Gradually, throughout the depression, the export crop frontier was pushed outward subsuming Sokoto, Bornu, and the Middle Belt. Yet even within these provinces cash cropping was far from generalized. In some peripheral districts the relegation of export commodities to a secondary position was compensated by other cash-earning activities, notably artisanal production, the export of wage labor, or the commercial production of staple foodstuffs, whether grains or lowland fadama crops. This conversion of use- to exchange-values was neither fully generalized (i.e., did not necessitate the development of a specialized or "mature" simple commodity system) nor geographically homogenous over space. These uneven qualities are of some relevance to the subsistence scarcity issue in colonial Nigeria.

THE INTENSIVE EXPORT ZONES

The periurban districts surrounding birnin Kano have been closely settled since at least the nineteenth century. Mortimore and Wilson (1965) and Hill (1977) have both shown that, prior to 1903, peasant holdings in several such areas adjacent to Kano, Katsina, and Sokoto were small, intensively manured, and permanently cultivated. Archival work has also established that these districts, most particularly near Kano, were very probably net importers of grains. As early as 1905, H. R. Palmer observed the enormous regional grain trade between northern Katsina and the emirates of Gobir and Damagaram, former breadbaskets in what is now south central Niger (Raynault 1977a). Two years later the Resident of Kano was struck by the same phenomenon.

> I do not think that people have ever realised how much corn is imported from the north. I had always looked upon Kano as self-supporting in this respect but I find such is not the case . . . we [receive] corn from the north . . . [and] from the Gwari country west of Zaria. [NAK SNP7 3095/1907]

In an assessment report of Dan Iya District by Mr. Webster in 1912, the "inability of the district to feed itself even in a good year" was attributed to the profusion of profitable subsidiary trades (sana'a), especially textiles, which permitted the purchase of grain and the deterioration of local soils that had been intensively cultivated for several centuries at least.[8] The absence of fallow, the purported deterioration of yields, and the prevailing regional food deficits cast the export crop revolution in a new light. In these close settled zones, where considerable inroads had been made into the use-value and exchange-value balance prior to the arrival of the Europeans, the new colonial demands on household surplus labor amplified the precariousness of an already fragile food system.

The extent to which groundnuts in particular were embedded in the rural economy of the close settled zones is reflected in their centrality in household tax payments, which had steadily risen since 1903. In Garki District (Kano Division) in 1934, the sources of income to pay taxes during the preceding year were as follows: groundnuts 85 percent, sale of grain 4.2 percent, sale of livestock 3.5 percent, other income sources 7.3 percent (NAK Kanoprof 3027). The pressures for expanded groundnut production in Kano are seen clearly in assessment data from Kura District, roughly thirty miles southwest of the city. In 1929 the total acreage devoted to cotton and groundnuts was between 16 and 20 percent (NAK Kanoprof 9117); by 1943, 40 percent of the district was devoted to groundnuts (Jackson 1980, p. 25). The agronomic situation in the central districts adjacent to the city walls was worse still, as shown in MacBride's classic assessment of Dawaki-ta-Kudu District in the 1930s (NAK SNP17 30361). MacBride determined that 85 percent of the total surface area was registered farmland at an average population density of 348 per square mile. Average holdings were just under four acres, and 31 percent of the cultivated land area was devoted to groundnut production alone. MacBride's data revealed that for a household concentrating on cereals and groundnuts, the value of production for direct consumption was nearly twice that of sales, while production for export constituted roughly one-third of total output. Under conditions of variability in commodity prices or harvest shortfall, the insecurity of household finances and domestic income is quite striking. This vulnerability is highlighted in Forde's comment (1946, p. 153) that

> the high local prices of both grain and ground-nuts as compared with those in more remote areas, such as Kazaure and Misau, must be borne in mind when considering this budget. *In this instance, where subsistence production accounted for little more than a third of the total of the £ 18 6s. 3d. of recorded income, the household was far from self-sufficient in food supplies including those for the stock.* Household purchases of grain were estimated at £3 18s. [Emphasis added]

Of all productive activity, then, almost two-thirds was fully commoditized, in this instance largely through craft production and groundnuts.

The household budgetary data from Dawaki-ta-Kudu indicate much more than the growth of exchange-values in local circuits of production and reproduction. MacBride indicated that approximately 40 percent of the total value of net adult male production was derived from off-farm income, almost half of which was earned from "craft, trading and wage labor" (see table 5.2). However, these multifarious and fluctuating "supplementary" incomes from sylvan produce, livestock, donkey transport, and trades (including dry-season irrigation) were not widely accessible. First, the fadama lands were productive (£9 per acre compared to roughly £1 per acre on jigawa upland), but only 3 percent (the "prosperous specialists") actually benefited from local irrigation. Second, the trades and crafts while more generalized in incidence (one in three reported some craft output) revealed a great variability in annual incomes, from £18 among grain traders to £1.2.0 for the "industrious weaver," probably the most widespread of trades in rural Kano before the depression. And third, donkey transport though lucrative, especially in the suburban ring of Kano, was, in view of the socioeconomic distribution of donkeys, accessible to approximately one of three or four households. This reflection on the extent of off-farm production among households in the close settled zones and the growth of price-mediated relationships also highlights the differentiation among rural producers in conditions of vulnerable, if not declining, food supply.

Toward the periphery of the close settled zones, holdings were certainly larger and probably under short fallows but intensified export production placed additional pressure for permanent cultivation and accordingly increased manure application to maintain productivity.[9] This type of involution was already apparent in Kazaure emirate, 60 miles north of Kano, in the 1930s (Leslie 1934). The household budgets fluctuated enormously in tandem with prevailing export prices, which to a large degree determined both the extent of food or craft sales and the buoyancy of the local economy. Table 5.3 indicates, nonetheless, that unlike the

TABLE 5.2

ESTIMATES OF TOTAL PRODUCTION; DAWAKI TA KUDU DISTRICT, KANO, 1937

Production	Total for district to nearest £100		Per adult male					
	Gross	Net	Gross			Net		
	£	£	£	s	d	£	s	d
Dry farm produce[1]	168,500	148,500	5	4	8	4	12	2
Irrigated plot produce[2]	5,900	5,600		3	8		3	6
Total farm produce	174,400	154,100	5	8	4	4	15	8
Sylvan produce	16,100	16,100		10	0		10	0
Stock sales	9,600	8,000		6	0		5	0
Donkey transport	8,000	6,500		5	0		4	0
Craft, trading, and wage labor	64,400	58,000	2	0	0	1	16	0
Household maintenance	8,045	8,045		5	0		5	0
Total output[3]	£280,545	£250,745	£8	14	4	£7	15	8

SOURCE: Adapted from Forde (1946, p. 149).

NOTE: Information concerning many items of output was not available (e.g., especially self-produced domestic and farm equipment and repairs). The total refers, therefore, only to the sum of items reported on. However, the omitted items would not make a significant difference to the value of the true total.

[1] From a total of about 150,000 acres.
[2] From 626 acres.
[3] Apart from other unrecorded items, no allowance is made for self-supplied domestic services, which might be reasonably valued at 10s. per one-man household.

TABLE 5.3
Budget Estimate for Farming Households, Kazaure Emirate, Kano, 1934

Item	Gross value[1]			Deducted costs[2]			Total			Net value								
---	---	---	---	---	---	---	---	---	---	Subsistence			Sales locally			Export		
	£	s	d	£	s	d	£	s	d	£	s	d	£	s	d	£	s	d
A. Crops and By-products																		
1. Grain, ca. 2,500 lb.[3]	3	5	0		5	0	3	0	0	2	17	0		3	0		—	
2. Corn stalks at 10% of (1)		6	0		—			6	0		6	0		—			—	
3. Beans		7	3			3		7	0		7	0		—			—	
4. Cassava		5	3			3		5	0		3	0		2	0		—	
5. Sweet potatoes[4]		7	3			3		7	0		2	0		5	0		—	
6. Minor crops		2	3			3		2	0		2	0		—			—	
Cash Crops																		
7. Groundnuts		17	0		1	0		10	0		1	0		—			15	0
B. Livestock																		
8. Goats or sheep		12	6		2	6		10	0		—			5	0		5	0
9. Donkey		7	6		1	6		6	0		—			3	0		3	0
C. Sylvan Produce																		
10. Firewood		5	0		—			5	0		5	0		—			—	
11. Fruit and leaves		5	0		—			5	0		5	0		—			—	
12. Honey		1	6		—			1	6			6		1	0		—	

	Gross value	Deducted costs	Total	Subsistence	Local exchange
D. Marketing and Transport (values included in output values of crops, stock, etc.)					
E. Crafts					
13. Rope, basketry, and matting from own materials	6 0	—	6 0	6 0	—
14. Spinning, cooked food, etc., by women	1 0	—	1 0	1 0	—
F. Household Maintenance					
15. Maintenance and repair of house, well, and household equipment with own materials (20 days at 3d.)	5 0	—	5 0	5 0	—
Totals for household	£7 18 6	£0 12 0	£7 6 6	£4 14 6	£2 12 0
Total per adult male	£3 19 3	£0 6 0	£3 13 3	£2 7 3	£1 6 0
Total per adult unit	£1 6 5	£0 2 0	£1 4 5	£0 15 9	£0 8 8

SOURCE: Adapted from Forde (1946, p. 140).

[1] Assuming no net depletion or enhancement of soil fertility and other resources.

[2] Estimated to include seed, materials, repairs and replacement of tools, granary, etc.

[3] No exact records are available; the quantities are based on local estimates of typical production. Values are at local harvest prices.

[4] The value of tops, etc., is assumed to be included in the return on livestock below.

central districts, the value of production for direct consumption was nearly twice that of sales, and export production constituted less than a third of total output. In addition, small food "surpluses" were sold in 1934 when groundnut prices were depressed (roughly £2.10.0 per ton). Of total exchange values, however, groundnuts remained the largest single item, roughly 30 percent of net sales value. These figures are not significantly different from the rather limited information (from Misau near Bauchi, and from Soba near Zaria) pertaining to cotton-producing zones, which indicates that just less than 50 percent of farm produce was sold.

On balance, then, what emerges from an admittedly scanty survey of the Kano close settled zone, which was earmarked by colonial authorities as a high-potential export producer, is the following: a relative scarcity of uncultivated bush, family farm holdings of less than four acres of permanently cultivated land in the central districts, and a regional food deficit inherited from the precolonial period. Pressures exerted by population growth, Muslim inheritance practices, and increased export commodity production placed additional strains on already overburdened farm holdings; ever increasing proportions of total household output were mediated by the price system as use-values were converted to exchangeable commodities. While groundnuts constituted (in value terms) a large part of the exchanged product, it is worth noting that in Kano Division,

> this sum was less than the general tax assessment of the division as a whole, not including the *jangali* on cattle, viz. £41,000. *Further production of marketable products was therefore, needed to meet the rest of the tax and for other payments including those for purchased consumption goods.* [Forde 1946, p. 144, emphasis added]

In a region in which mean statistics and averages mask considerable economic inequality, these figures give some indication of both the importance of off-farm income for household reproduction and the chronic underproduction of foodstuffs for large segments of the rural poor.

THE REMOTE AND PERIPHERAL REGIONS

In the more remote districts of perhaps lower fertility, longer fallows, lighter population densities, and more uncultivated bush, the penetration of export commodity production was, even as late as the depression, surprisingly slight. In the hamlet of Tarke, adjacent to the Nigerian border in northern Sokoto Province, an assessment conducted in 1939 indicated that market exchange was confined to homespun cotton, small livestock, and millet surpluses. In regions less isolated from railheads or from the middlemen operations, surplus land could easily accommodate the introduction of groundnut or cotton production. However, the constraints of domestic labor supply, of labor conflicts and bottlenecks over

different crop regimes, and the limited opportunities for income generation to cover hired labor, all mitigated against an easy accommodation of
expanded export crop production. Indeed, the general character of these
peripheral districts was one of balancing money income (secured through
temporary dry-season migration) against cash outlays. The 1939 assessment of Gwadabawa District estimated that almost half the adult able-
bodied men were seasonally absent.

The Tarke situation is exemplary of the crisis in simple reproduction
even in land surplus districts, albeit of low fertility. Estimates of local grain
production were about 3,000 pounds per holding, of which half to two-
thirds were required to meet the normal food requirement for "a small
household" (two adults only). In a good year, a surplus product of perhaps 1,000 pounds of grain would, at midseason prices, total about £1. Yet
at harvest time, when tax and other monetary obligations were due, grain
prices were low (about 2d per bundle), perhaps only one-third of the
prevailing price during the wet season.

> Direct enquiry showed that few households had in fact sufficient reserves of
> currency or carry-over of grain to be able to wait for the highest price and sold
> almost all their surplus at the low harvest price. Household grain stocks were
> usually so short towards the end of the growing season that about a quarter of
> the crop was generally eaten as, or even before, it became ripe, and the lack of
> reserves compelled the immediate sale of a good part of the harvest at low prices
> to meet the tax-payment. [Forde 1946, p. 154]

In short, given the mid-1930s tax levy computed at midseason prices plus
a tithe to the hamlet head, *extra income was a necessity*. Assuming relatively
stable yields and price levels, the sale of labor power—usually outside of
the district—in order to cover fixed monetary charges, was required to
balance household budgets (see table 5.4). In similar conditions in Dan

TABLE 5.4
ANNUAL HOUSEHOLD PRODUCTION: TARKE, SOKOTO PROVINCE, 1939

	Production for					
	Subsistence			Sale		
Item	£	s	d	£	s	d
Farm produce	1	13	6	0	17	0
Homestead maintenance		5	0			
Sale of goat					3	0
Spinning					5	0
Seasonal wage labor				1	5	0
	£1	18	6	£2	10	0

SOURCE: NAK SNP 17/23006 and Forde (1946, p. 155).

Zano District (Gumel emirate) Backhouse (R.H. MSS Afr. S 601) reported a decline in food production over a fifteen-year period (1917–32) while Corby's (1941) study in Zaria estimated that in spite of large average holdings in excess of seven acres, there were no food surpluses. In such isolated, low-fertility districts where food self-sufficiency was marginal and cash cropping unlikely, the seasonal export of labor fulfilled the new monetary demands for tax and grain purchase.

Farther south in Bida emirate, Nadel's (1942) study of rural household budgets (in an area where neither groundnuts nor cotton were adopted to any great extent) highlights the commoditization of foodstuffs. Nadel's studies revealed that, strapped by extraordinarily high tax demands in the 1930s, roughly 50 percent of the total household product was realized on the market. Further, of total family income among rural households, at least 50 percent (and usually much nearer 75 percent) was realized through the sale of foodstuffs, notably sorghum, cassava, yams, and rice (see table 5.5). These middle-belt provinces, and to a certain extent Zamfara, Kebbi, and Bornu, became the principal breadbaskets for the colonial administration in fulfilling the new governmental, institutional, military, and minefield food requirements. The provincial Residents also repeatedly turned to these same surfeit areas when faced with the presence of mass starvation in the North.

The general impression that emerges from the 1930s, then, is of a northern region whose residents produced at best a small food surplus above and beyond domestic requirements. The archival and secondary data seem to support the claim that the development of the colonial export trade had the effect of undermining subsistence production, particularly in the intensive export-producing regions. Forde's somewhat conservative estimate of the impact of these export trends by the 1930s is worth quoting at length.

> Except in the immediate vicinity of Kano and perhaps of a few other large centres of population and market activity such as Zaria, the levels of consumption in recent years have been very low. The data on production and the returns on crops, craft activity and labour suggest that the incomes available to the ordinary rural household have been barely sufficient in a year of reasonably good crops to support the native norms of consumption, which are themselves very modest and, so far as food is concerned, are probably physiologically inadequate.
>
> The need to secure a sufficient cash income to meet tax-payments and allow for customary native expenditure frequently leads to immediate sales of produce at the lowest prices and even to failure to maintain a sufficient reserve of grain for food supplies from one harvest to the next. The high rate of interest on borrowed corn reduces the amount which can safely be borrowed when reserves are exhausted and, at the same time, makes serious inroads on future income. All this reacts unfavourably on the level of food consumption.

. . . the outstanding conclusion from these investigations is that the ordinary farming household in northern Nigeria is at present unable to count on obtaining an adequate supply of the essential items of the traditional native diet. Even in a good farming year, resources are often insufficient for the purchase of other needs including clothing, small luxuries and personal services. [Forde 1946, p. 163]

Subsistence insecurity and the threat of severe hunger was underscored by McCullogh's work (1929–30) on the diet of rural and urban Hausa Fulani in northern Nigeria. Patterns of consumption varied enormously across economic strata, but McCullogh determined that, for the vast majority of the rural poor, grain consumption per adult per day was less than two pounds. Regular consumption of high-quality protein, outside of the aristocracy and the merchant class, was negligible and the incidence of vitamin-mineral salt deficiencies was noticeably high. Data collected by Meyer Fortes on the urban laboring poor in Jos during 1941 were equally depressing.[10]

TABLE 5.5
HOUSEHOLD BUDGET: BIDA 1935

Crops and trees	Total yield	Kept for household consumption	Sold	Additional income
Bulr. millet	Bad crop	No yield	–	Sold 2 young goats for 3s each to obtain rest of the tax
Late millet	10 loads	–	9 loads for 9s	
Sorghum	5 loads	1 load	3 loads for 3s	
Beans	7 loads	–	all, for 5½d	
Locust beans	9 loads	–	all, for 3s	

	s	d
Income from farm produce	15	5½
Total income	21	5½
Money expenditure: Tax	21	0

SOURCE: Nadel (1942, p. 341).

NOTE: *Tunga* near Bida. Labor unit: father (old) and married son (invalid); family of five.

FULANI PASTORAL ECONOMY, TERMS OF TRADE, AND AGRICULTURAL PRODUCTIVITY

A little-studied facet of Caliphate political economy is the changing relationships between sedentary Hausa-Fulani agriculturalists and nomadic cattle Fulani, particularly the Wo'daa'be and Bororo. Usman (1974) briefly referred to the complex circuits of transhumance and seasonal migration among the Wo'daa'be of northern Katsina emirate at the turn of the century, especially the continuing process of sedentarization that had commenced after the jihad. The Wo'daa'be maintained a strong cultural and economic identity, reproducing themselves exclusively by livestock herding and trade. Doubtless the local patterns of household mobility have changed historically but the fundamental axis, a north–south oscillation graduated to the onset and termination of the rains, is a pattern of some antiquity (de St. Croix 1944; Dupire 1952). During the dry season the Wo'daa'be withdrew from the northern Sahel zone near Aderbissinat and Tahoua in search of crop residues and lowland (fadama) forbs and grasses, particularly to the Kebbi, Rima, and Challawa floodplains (see Hopen 1958; Stenning 1959).

The Wo'daa'be economy, like other contemporary nomadic systems, was never fully self-sufficient. Dahl and Hjort (1976) for instance, estimate that for a nomadic family of six to subsist *entirely* off their animal produce—assuming a herd of usual age and sex composition—would require a dry-season population of 593 animals with a lactation rate of 4 percent. Recent studies in Niger (Sutter 1980) and surveys conducted in the 1930s in Sokoto (Sharwood-Smith in Jacob 1934) indicate that the mean herd size was between 18 and 25 animals. In short, the Wo'daa'be depended on trade and in particular in exchange for cereals [Hopen 1958, p. 152]. Cattle were unquestionably sold for other purposes, characteristically for ceremonial expenses and precolonial taxes (jangali) or under conditions of extreme adversity when the terms of trade turned sharply against pastoral products; but the principal means for the genesis of revenue was sale or barter of milk (and milk products) for cereals and occasional trade items.

This dependence upon purchased foodstuffs goes some way toward explaining the purportedly symbiotic relationships between agriculturalists and nomads along the desert edge. In the absence of detailed historical work, much discussion of Hausa–Fulani interaction has a myopic quality. Doubtless, the forms of communication between the two communities have varied enormously historically but one might venture to suggest that a model of sorts is provided by the following description abstracted from an early colonial report:

As to manuring, the practice followed in [Raba] District seems to be thus: in the dry season a Fulani with cows and sheep is asked to let his flocks wander over the farm. One about 3300 sq yards would be thus manured by 200 sheep and 100 cows in a week for which payment of 2 bundles of gero and 2 of dawa would be made. [NAK SNP 10 609p/1914]

Hopen (1958, p. 154) described a similar system in Gwandu, and Hill (1972, p. 287) refers to an infrequent yet "highly competitive" manuring by Fulani in Batagarawa near Katsina town. Sharwood-Smith estimated that in the 1930s a herd of twenty cattle grazing in Sokoto farms between December and April produced a rate of return of one shilling per week (i.e., 30 lbs of millet). From what little is known of precolonial Hausa-Wo'daa'be interaction, it is evident that colonialism transformed the conditions under which products and services were exchanged. In a simple descriptive sense, there has been a geographical displacement; in northern Katsina, for instance, in Kaita and Dan Kama districts the seasonal visitations of the *filanin gawo* are long gone. In most instances, the Katsinawa lineages of the Bororo were pushed northward into Niger, principally toward Dakoro, Tahoua, and Tanout. De St. Croix (1944) documents similar displacements from Sokoto and Bauchi during the early period of colonial rule. The changes in pastoral economy were, however, not only locational; more fundamentally they concerned an increasing integration into a fully commercialized livestock network, which magnified its susceptibility to the vagaries of volatile and changeable terms of trade. The context of these changes in Wo'daa'be production and exchange is formidably complex but is seemingly related to the following developments:

1. The intent of both British and French colonial administrations to incorporate and commercialize the pastoral sector in a manner that would generate revenue through jangali taxes levied on each animal, provide the rapidly growing coastal urban communities with meat, and stimulate hides and skins production.[11]

2. The loss of dry-season pastures along wet bottomlands as the fadama areas were increasingly employed for agricultural purposes to supply urban food markets.[12]

3. The increasing incidence of crop destruction and land or track conflicts in highly populated close settled zones.[13]

4. Changing terms of trade as Fulani faced unstable grain markets and fluctuating livestock prices. The former needs to be seen in light of the growing cereal underproduction along the desert edge concurrent with the inroads made by cotton and groundnuts. The latter gains additional significance as new or expanded items of necessary consumption in

Wo'daa'be budgets (sugar, tea, cloth) demanded the sale of livestock rather than milk (Sutter 1980).[14]

The practical significance of these changes was reflected in the crisis of the pastoral economy during the 1930s. The Wo'daa'be economy had been dislocated by the rinderpest epidemic of 1885 but had recovered sufficiently by the turn of the century not least because, as Baier (1974, p. 123) shows in his study of Damagaram, cattle-grain price ratios were apparently favorable to herders. Conditions were obviously subject to regular market failures, particularly in famine periods when grain was scarce and livestock flooded rural markets, or during periods of general economic recession. The temporal variability in terms of trade is indicated in a proleptic fashion in table 5.6. The squeeze imposed by price fluctuations and a deepening market involvement is reflected starkly in the Wo'daa'be budgets determined by Sharwood-Smith (1933) in 1930 in Sokoto Province (table 5.7). The family income is high in light of typical farming budgets in northern Nigeria but cash outlays for food procurement were considerable. The gradual demise of grazing on crop residues in return for grain, however, projected Wo'daa'be households further into the price-commodity nexus. In the 1930s Forde (1946, p. 208) estimated annual grain purchases at £1.15.0; however, from contemporary estimates of average cereal consumption (Sutter 1980) of 4,380 pounds per year for five adults plus children, I have determined that the millet bill would have been between £6.12.0 and £9.2.6. Even Forde's conservative calculations recognize that cattle tax on twenty head of cattle would certainly have exceeded household income.

> From the balance of £2 17s there has to be paid not only the cattle tax (*jangali*), which at the reduced rate of 1s 6d introduced in some areas in the early 'thirties would amount to £1 10s., but also the general head tax payable by all farming Fulani which would probably amount to another 5s or 10s according to the number of taxable males in the household. Thus, a margin of only £1 or less would remain for all "non-essential" expenditure and emergencies, while at the earlier *jangali* rate of 2s per beast practically no margin would exist. [Forde 1946, p. 208]

The conflation of poor terms of trade and a heavy tax burden bore heavily on pastoral households, as is evidenced by the proportion of profits absorbed by the colonial administration. Sharwood-Smith and Jacob (1934) both estimated that jangali incidence was in excess of 15 percent of net household income. As a consequence, livestock sales to cover tax was at least equivalent to and often somewhat higher than natural herd increase. A run of poor years was catastrophic for herd composition, in other words, as the proportion of cull cows—which normally represent a high proportion of revenues—diminished in num-

TABLE 5.6
FULANI TERMS OF TRADE: MILLET-CATTLE RATIOS

Year	Location	Millet price per lb. (pence)	Cattle price (export bull) £	s	d	Millet equivalent (lbs.)	Millet equivalent Niger Republic[5] (lbs.)
1903	Katsina[1]	0.1	2	10	0 to	6,000–7,200	1,936
			3	0	0		
1914*	Kano[2]	3	5	1	0	4	4–6
1928**	Sokoto[3]	7	5	7	0	1,814	1,571
1939	Sokoto[3]	5	1	8	0	672	506***
1949	Katsina[4]	2	9	0	0	1,080	586

SOURCE: [1]NAK Katprof 1769; [2]NAK SNP 10/6 170p/1915; [3]Sharwood-Smith (1933) cited in Werhahn et. al. (1964, p. 66); [4]NAK Katprof 1743; [5]Baier (1980), data refers to Zinder, Niger Republic.

*Famine year
**Year following 1927 famine
***Estimate

TABLE 5.7
Estimates of Output, Fulani Households, About 1930

	Home consumed			Marketed income			Purchases			
	£	s	d	£	s	d	£	s	d	
Stock				2	12	0	1	15	0	(Grain)
Dairy produce	3	5	0	3	5	0		10	0	(Meat)
Manure (included in crop value)					10	0		5	0	(Salt)
Farm crop	1	0	0					10	0	(Natron)
Spinning					5	0		15	0	(Cloth)
	£4	5	0	£6	12	0	£3	15	0	
				Tax	£2	0	0			

Source: Adapted from Forde (1946, pp. 206–08), Jacob (R. H. Mss. Afr. +16, 1934), and Werhahn et. al. (1964).

Note: Composition of household: about 5 adults plus children, twenty cattle.

ber, young males were increasingly presented for sale. In this regard, it is significant that the number of animals shipped by rail from Kano and the export of cattle hides from the North both increased markedly in the late 1930s after several years of deteriorating terms of trade. Between 1933 and 1939 the weight of hides exported increased by almost 30 percent, and over the same period railed cattle grew by over 80 percent.

I have dwelt at some length on the pastoral economy and its interface with the agricultural sector because it indicates the essential complexity of colonial impact along the savanna-desert edge. Implicit in this analysis is the assumption that in the nineteenth century the northern savannas and the Sahelian biome constituted a human ecological unity in which the affairs of Hausa agriculturalists and semisedentary Fulani were closely integrated with pastoral Wo'daa'be, Touareg and other nomadic groups to the north. These spatial linkages were embodied in the strong currents of exchange bridging the two regions—the desert cultures providing salt, natron, dates, and livestock; and the savanna providing cloth, foodstuffs, and craft products—which conferred a measure of security in the face of recurrent climatic variation. The colonial impress, however, marked a major reorientation of trade; the imposition of the frontier constituted a somewhat pervious barrier to geographical mobility and trade as customs tolls were systematically levied from 1903 onward. More critically, however, Baier (1977) showed how the arrival of the French and the demise of the trans-Saharan trade, due to the decreasing cost of shipment on alternate routes into the interior, eroded the hegemonic rule of the Touareg confederacies in the Nigerian Sahel. The secular decline in the desertside economy was sealed by the volte-face in the export trade; in particular the Touareg economy, devastated by the 1914 famine and subsequently smashed by French military action in 1916, was almost laid to rest; many nomads, bereft of animals, actually retreated to the savannas to take up farming. Grain producers in Damagaram and Damerghou, who previously supplied the nomadic communities of the Air massif with millet, increasingly turned their attention to lucrative markets in northern Nigeria.[15]

In northern Nigeria a counterpart to these changes occurred in the transformation of the Wo'daa'be economy, which is conventionally seen as a peripheral society. The rigorous imposition and collection of cattle tax[16] (which in Sokoto Province amounted to 26 percent (£300,000) of NA revenue in 1933), the general deterioration in the food economy, and the propensity of the terms of trade to turn sharply against cattle herders pushed the Wo'daa'be firmly into a commercialized livestock network (Okediji 1973). Between 1900 and 1920 (doubtless prompted by the 1914 famine which necessitated extensive cattle sale) Hausa merchants moved to a greater degree than before into the livestock trade, profiting from rapidly rising southern incomes fueled by the cocoa and palm oil trade that permitted increased consumption of luxury foods. At the same time, pressure on dry-season grazing, increasing land scarcity, a high incidence of jangali, and periodic deterioration of the terms of trade placed new strains on household reproduction. In some instances the crisis was contained through semisedentarization; Fulani herders produced millet for local consumption until such time as herd reconstitution permitted a return to a fully nomadic lifestyle. This temporary sedentarization frequently became permanent, as was the case in much of northern Katsina during the first three or four decades of colonial rule. In 1956 the Resident of Katsina Province indicated that:

> Of the 497,769 population of the 14 northern districts of this Province, 245,499 claim to be Fulani. The ancestors of nearly all of these were at one time nomads though the 161,067 cattle in these districts almost all belong to farmers now. [NAK Katprof 1/1 File 1329 1956, p. 33]

Worsening economic conditions, especially in the 1920s and 1930s, also displaced Wo'daa'be herders northward into Niger, toward Dakoro, Tessaoua, Tahoua, and Tanout where French well construction, lower tax levies, and available grazing represented a more favorable residence. New and expanded livestock markets emerged along the Niger-Nigeria border—Jibiya, Dankama, Mai'aduwa—frequented by Hausa cattle merchants and agents who provided commercial outlets for the livestock which now resided further north.

From the perspective of Hausa farmers in northern Nigeria, the migration of Wo'daa'be constituted a loss of organic manure in an area where the application of animal wastes is a critical element in farm productivity and land value. Of course, it is impossible to estimate in any empirical sense the loss of organic inputs over time for some statistically average Hausa farm plot. Scott, however, observed in northern Katsina during the 1960s that

> the accepted notion of a symbiotic relationship between nomadic Fulani and sedentary Hausa farmers . . . is not as strong as it apparently was in the past. In fact, I never observed Fulani cattle grazing on hoe farmers land. [Scott c. 1976, p. 11]

Scott ventured to suggest that the realignment of the pastoral economy necessitated a reduction in quantity and quality of manures applied by Hausa farmers in comparison with the early colonial period. Small livestock, particularly goats and donkeys, continued to provide a major source of organic fertilizer of course, but it is significant that these manures had become trade items, especially in the densely settled, permanently cultivated zones. Further, it is not insignificant that in interviews conducted with farmers in the Katsina-Daura area, many farmers lamented the historic decline in yields on upland farms.[17] The colonial archives, moreover, are replete with references to deteriorating productivity in the northern districts. This deterioration provided a partial justification for the introduction of a mixed farming program in 1924 designed explicitly to improve crop productivity by simultaneously harnessing the draft power of cattle with the provision of manure. The deterioration of yields in the close settled zones very probably emerged during the late nineteenth century, compounded by the loss of dry-season cattle. In Dan Iya District, Kano Province, these developments had already caught the attention of the district officer by 1912.

> The deterioration in yield/acre is apparently . . . at least 50% in the last 20 years. It is due in part to closer cultivation and at the same time deprivation of the manure formerly applied, but which now cannot be obtained as practically all cattle have to be sent south before the crops are cut, instead of being as formerly kraaled on the farms, partly due to the excess of darawa which tho' a most valuable asset in times of shortage is apt to . . . [be] a . . . notorious exhauster of land. [NAK SNP7 4055/1912, p. 9]

The purported decline in cattle wastes assumes further significance with the genesis of what is usually referred to as the entrustment system,[18] in which cattle owned by farmers are loaned to pastoral or semisedentary Fulani. This form of symbiosis, in which the Fulani gain milk *gratis* in return for grazing the animals, is closely related to two developments: first, cattle had become lucrative capital investments for rich peasantry; and second, the absence of pasture, the potential for crop damage, and labor scheduling conflicts had rendered intravillage possession or fattening of cattle increasingly difficult. In Kaita village, where I conducted research in 1977–78, the vast majority of local cattle had been entrusted to semisedentarized remote Fulani households who grazed animals farther south, usually in the vicinity of Runka. Where Fulani cattle were observed grazing on postharvest stubble and crop residues

> they were on large farmers land who were able to pay higher prices than hoe farmers . . . the inescapable fact is that Fulani . . . [are] demanding higher prices both in cash and kind for their services . . . [and] the result is an increasing concentration of organic fertilizer on a few large farms. [E. Scott 1976, p. 12]

The reorganization of the pastoral economy, then, in conjunction with the elitist mixed farming scheme deflected domestic utilization of organic manures; in some cases the manure was evacuated entirely from the district and in others onto the fields of the wealthy.

THE SOCIOLOGY OF THE HOUSEHOLD AND THE "CULTURE" OF REPRODUCTION

> Little by little, market relations founded on the mediatory role of money . . . displaced the relations of solidarity and reciprocity which constituted the living tissue of village communities and families.
>
> —Claude Raynault

During the Sokoto Caliphate the dominant unit of residence (the gandu), encompassing several generations of kin, clients, and slaves, was coterminous with the unit of production. Ideally the gandu was a conjugation of male agnates plus their families with maternal and paternal kin. In the past, very high prestige was accorded these large and cooperative farming units. Since 1900, however, social structure has undergone substantial modification and change, and the model gandu has lost its former preeminence, both ideologically and in practice. Buntjer, for example, presented evidence of the decomposition of such complex farming entities in Zaria and concluded that

> in comparison with the past, *gandaye* are less frequent, and that where a gandu arrangement is held, this only involves a limited number of persons. [Buntjer 1970, p. 162]

Both Hill (1972) and Goddard (1973) documented the demise of three generational households in both Katsina and Sokoto.[19] Changes in family sociology can be identified with variations in the classic constitution of the gandu as outlined by M. G. Smith (1955), which indicates a decentralization of familial authority and a gradual retraction of the extended family structure itself.[20] In a historic sense the trend has been toward domestic, if not residential, fission: from the extended to the nuclear family (iyali). In the words of Raynault,

> it is the case that the gida has been more and more reduced to a simple monogamous or polygamous family: a man, his wife and their children. . . . The cohabitation of [father and married sons] in the same compound enclosure is quite frequent but in the majority of cases work is not communal. . . . In this new context . . . the notions of family fields and collective work have lost their [traditional] meaning. [Raynault 1976, p. 289]

Nadel (1942, pp. 246–47) observed similar trends among the Nupe in the 1930s. He noted that the cooperative labor unit (efako), like the Hausa gandu, ensured against the normal risks of agriculture. A large cooperative group was capable of utilizing fully the highly diversified, polycultural agricultural system—both in terms of spatial extent and crop diversity—so as to minimize the possibility of a total harvest failure. Mobilization of efako labor power could also compensate for the temporary, but commonplace, elimination of a worker through illness; aged or invalid workers could be given lighter tasks and the pooling of off-farm income provided a type of familial welfare. Yet by the Great Depression, scarcely a quarter of a century after conquest, the zenith of the efako system had already passed. Only three of Nadel's fifty-one households had working units composed of more than four adults. Naturally, there are no reliable statistics for earlier periods; moreover, any calculation of either gandaye or efako as a percentage of all farming units does not relate actual to potential incidence, nor does it reveal the changes in family authority, most notably of the household head. But aside from these computational problems, the changing form of classical gandu or efako authority is clear nonetheless; M. G. Smith's (1955, p. 17) Zaria study found only 25 percent of households in gandu form, while Goddard (1969, p. 43), working in three Sokoto villages, found 23.7, 14.5 and 9.3 percent of all adult males in complex farm units.

In light of the superior efficiency and security conferred by large working units, the gradual demise of the gandu is a process that highlights not only the effect of commoditization but shows clearly how colonialism ushered in changes in the ideological and social environment, and in individual attitudes toward what one might call family politics and domestic social relations. An appropriate starting place for the analysis of this social fragmentation is the contemporary form and function of the gandu; the classical model of labor mobilization and economic obligations within paternal gandaye has changed radically, while the incidence of fraternal gandaye, always structurally unstable, remains low. Goddard (1973, p. 214) found that in Sokoto 80 percent of the sons in gandu were expected to provide their own tax; Buntjer (1970, p. 11) discovered that extended families frequently consist of only one son subordinate to paternal authority, usually the youngest who is morally obliged to assist the father after elder agnates have left. In many gandaye, the decentralized authority of the household head (mai gida) has resulted in relatively autonomous domestic units within the putatively extended household; each male gandu member provides food and tax from his own *gamana* field, though communal farm operations are still organized by the mai gida. A study of five elderly householders by Goddard documented the decomposition of gandaye over a period of two to three generations, nourished by intergeneration conflicts over paternal hegemony and the demands for economic independence. These structural contradictions within the domestic unit further contributed to the instability of familial unity as the *masu gidaje* grant more gamana farmland and reduce labor time obligations in lieu of the demands to develop viable off-farm employment.

> For the *gandu* head to meet both the food requirements and the social obligations of a large family, it is necessary to derive a substantial income from the communal activities of *gandu* members on the common farm. The tendency to substitute income from off-farm employment to meet these social obligations in areas with land shortages weakens the central authority of the *gandu* by substituting the earnings of individuals for communal earnings under his direction, and at the same time diminishes the benefits accruing to subordinate members of the *gandu*. [Goddard 1973, p. 235]

Hausa family cooperation was failing on two counts: first, an increase in the needs and demands of individuals that the gandu could not readily accommodate; and second, a deterioration in the ability of the large farming family to fulfill acceptable standards of maintenance and social obligation. In this sense Nadel (1942, p. 247) was correct in surmising that the failure of efako (or indeed of the gandu) in Nupeland was not simply culture change externally generated but was a much wider phenomenon, namely, "the readjustment between productive organisation and needs existing in the society." The atomization of extended households was a precipitate of the solution of a domestic economy into the fluid circuits of a global system. The basis of domestic fission, then, resided in the crisis of simple reproduction whose complex etiology I hinted at in chapter 4. Faced with chronic subsistence difficulties, the mai gida was incapable of fulfilling gandu demands; empty granaries and wet season indebtedness undercut his ability, for instance, to provide sons in gandu with basic food requirements. The structural tension between father and son was magnified as culturally conditioned norms of domestic cooperation were eroded. In particular the demands on the mai gida for the son's tax payment—which rose steadily throughout the colonial period—and the traditional expenditures on bride-price bore heavily on family finances. These monetary pressures could only be fulfilled by sons in gandu generating off-farm revenue to cover part of their own reproductive needs, by the mai gida delegating larger gamana farms to ensure that sons could meet their own tax demands by cash crop production, and finally, by a reduction in the authority of the household head. As M. G. Smith (1966, p. 265) observed, the new economic opportunities available to gandu sons as wage laborers, seasonal mine workers, or petty traders pushed the weakened gandu structure inexorably toward dissolution. These changes were fueled by an ideology of separatism; namely, the preference of newly married sons to reject the yoke of paternal authority. In practice this meant a larger measure of freedom and leisure, discretion in planning farm work, and what Nadel (1942, p. 246) calls "spiritual freedom" from family dictates. Without the benefits to be gleaned from a substantial gandu income to provide for the social obligations of the entire domestic group, there were few attractions for the father but especially for his sons to remain together. Changes in land availability—due to demographic growth, massive immigration from the French territories, and the freeing of several million farm slaves—only served to hasten the demise of gandu in closely settled districts. Gandu holdings were divided upon the death of the mai gida, often into parcels barely adequate for subsistence needs let alone to fulfill the demands of extended kin groups. This is not to imply that the gandu farm is entirely a thing of the past; in Kaita village in 1978 28 percent of all farm units were gandaye while 51 percent of all married men were in gandu units. But significantly, the incidence was much higher among richer households. Fifty percent of all wealthy households (n = 56) were in paternal gandaye in contrast to 3 percent of the poorest farming families (n = 93) [see table 5.8]. These statistics suggest that historically the poor producers have been unable to maintain the economic basis of the gandu, and have accordingly lost the cooperative benefits that complex farm units can confer. Even among middle peasants, where the gandu is far from moribund, the actual practice of familial cooperation may deviate markedly from the *modus classicus*, which severely limits some of the security provided by functioning complex farm units (Wallace 1979).

An intriguing exception to this dissipative trend was described by Hill (1977) in the "big houses" of the Kano close settled zone, which she saw as a "direct consequence of the persistent and intensifying pressure on land" (p. 180). Working in an extraordinarily densely populated and land-

TABLE 5.8
INCIDENCE OF *GANDU*: KAITA VILLAGE

Unit	Class I	% of I	Class II	% of II	Class III	% of III	Total	% of Total
No. of farm units	56		226		93		375	100
No. of paternal gandaye	28	50	54	24	3	3	85	22.7
Average size of paternal gandu	12.2		8.87		5.6			
No. of fraternal gandaye	2	2	19	8			21	5.6
Average size fraternal gandu	10		9.9					
No. of iyalai (nuclear family)	26	48	153	68	90	97	269	71.7
Average size iyali	6.9		5.1		3.7			

KEY: I = Poor households
        II = Neither rich nor poor households
        III = Rich households
(For a discussion of this classification see chap. 6)

scarce district outside the birni walls, Hill documented a high incidence of extended residential and production units;[21] large gandu-like structures under the jurisdiction of one male and frequently incorporating twenty or more married males. Under the prevailing conditions of extreme poverty, minimal off-farm income and obscenely inflated land prices, there may be enormous pressures to preserve gandu-type households. The precariousness of economic activity and the permanence of chronic hunger for some segments of society has resurrected the large household, rendering it again adaptive and viable in the face of extreme insecurity. Yet Hill notes that even in these cases there is no necessary congruence between theory and practice since "it seems unlikely that economically insecure men benefit from living in big houses" (Hill 1977, p. 189). Appearances are deceptive particularly when there are ideological reasons for denying the loss of the old ways. In Hausaland, only the patina of the traditional gandu remains. Social relations among rural producers have been altered in a manner that makes households more isolated, economically weaker, and dependent upon the world conjuncture for survival. One need not glorify the past, invoking traditional structures with mythological welfare functions, to appreciate the strength of co-operative household relations of production. Nadel was certainly near the mark when he wrote that

> we cannot claim to be able to describe exactly how the labour-unit was working under traditional conditions, and to state categorically that the scheme of insurance entailed in it operated without difficulty or friction. But on the evidence which we possess it is reasonable to assume that under certain conditions, with a small taxation and protected from severe, incalculable, market fluctuations, the large co-operative group represented—or would represent—an eminently stable and successful labour-unit. [Nadel 1942, p. 374]

It was clearly a sign of the growing instability of these complex farm units and the demise of domestic insurance against agricultural risks that Nadel commented on the emergence of borrowing and credit as regular items in household budgets. All this pays eloquent testimony to Bernstein's (1979) remark that commodity production individualized peasant society.

As a corollary to the atrophy of extended kindred units—and indeed related to it—two other social structural changes impinged upon household security. Both are anchored in the ideological realm of Hausa society and are part of what I have referred to as the culture of reproduction. First, is the remarkable growth since 1900 in the incidence of full or partial wife seclusion (auren kulle), by which married women are geographically confined to the compound (gida) in daylight hours, and generally prevented from engaging in direct agricultural labor. The current incidence of wife seclusion varies considerably within Hausaland; Raynault (1976) and Sutter (1980) working in south central Niger where the presence of married women in the agricultural sector is pronounced found that women's gamana fields were a major source of cereal production, accounting for between 25 and 37 percent of total village production (Raynault 1976, 1977). Across the border, however, the unusually severe enforcement of purdah is widespread; Hill's work in Dorayi, Kano (1977, p. 84), and Batagarawa, Katsina (1972, p. 22) and my own in Kaita confirm the uniquely high proportion of women between the ages of fifteen and sixty years in strict seclusion. The ideological underpinnings of what is now an almost universal restriction of female freedom in rural areas is perhaps related to the desire to demonstrate a cultural equality between urban centers and the countryside. Whatever its origins, the practical ramifications on household economy are of some interest since the poverty of some families is obviously exacerbated by the withdrawal of female labor from farm work. Hill (1977, p. 84) alludes that the generality of secluded marriages is a postwar development, but archival materials indicate that district officers were fully cognizant of a proliferation in rural purdah by the 1930s. While women remain important economic agents in seclusion through the "honeycomb market" of hidden trade, the withdrawal of married female labor from the agricultural economy of Muslim Hausa households had profound implications, especially in a region where a major economic constraint had been that of labor.

A second change that impinged upon household security concerns kinship ceremonies and rites of passage—naming and burial ceremonies, and particularly marriage exchanges—provided from what Wolf (1966, pp. 5–9) calls the "ceremonial fund." It is well known that the festivities and highly stylized ritual gift giving that seals Hausa marriages are critical elements in the cementing of interfamily alliances, and hence become principal strategies in the consolidation of domestic security and welfare. Marriages in this sense have obvious social and economic as well as biological reproductive functions. To be a fully paid-up member of Hausa society—to avoid shameful behavior in fulfilling the demands of proper conduct—is necessarily to participate in these ceremonies, and by extension in the complex circuits of gift exchange. In the context of household security these cultural behaviors have a direct bearing on production most clearly expressed in marriage. The wedding expenses borne primarily by family heads, which consist of a formal and protracted exchange of gifts between prospective partners and their parents, changed both in form and quantity. That is to say, the ceremonial fund came to absorb in real terms an ever greater proportion of household reproduction costs, and the necessity of fulfilling these necessary and obligatory ceremonial demands thrust rural households further into the commodity nexus. Nadel (1942, p. 350) noted that in Bida emirate, bride-price increased from £3 prior to 1900 to £20 by 1930; similarly in Zaria, average marriage expenditures incurred by the groom's family for a first wife increased from £1 at the end of the nineteenth century to £9.10.0 about 1949 (M. G. Smith 1955, pp. 56–57). A principal component in the marriage inflation was the position that imported wares came to occupy in the ceremonial exchanges. Not least in this regard were European cloth and decorated enamel bowls and plates (*kwano*). Smith (1955, p. 54) noted that by the 1940s the bridegroom was obliged to give his bride at least three imported cloths (*mayafi*, *kalabi* and *fatalla*) which cost £2.10.5 in rural Zaria. The penetration of such wares into fundamental Hausa exchanges was part of the general process by which export commodity production was promoted through the firm's policy of advancing, among other things, European cloth to ensure harvest sales. The firms maintained a series of stores or canteens dotted throughout the countryside selling and advancing imported goods through an arabesque legion of clerks, agents, and middlemen. By the 1930s, these same commodities were regularly hawked by peripatetic bicycle creditors who sold cloth and advanced various "ceremonial" items on short-term high-interest credit. The complicity of the firms, the middlemen, and the colonial state provided the context for substantive changes in marriage expenditures, which then became a vehicle for the canalization of imported manufacturers into the locus of the household economy.

In view of the crisis of simple reproduction that emerged from the new relations between capital and household, the function of crafts (sana'a) and what was previously referred to as fallback or secondary resources assumed a new significance. Small-scale dry-season commodity production was relatively elastic, bringing welcome relief in times of hardship and helping to absorb the debilitating effects of local harvest failure or personal calamity. Crafts were an established part of local activity and their intensification did not disturb the web of village life. Families remained in situ, which gave craft activity a "retreatist quality," as Scott (1976) called it. The impact of household incorporation into a world economy did not, as is sometimes supposed, simply destroy at one stroke the Hausa industrial sector. Some of the more esoteric skills—civet cat farming, perfume production—disappeared quite quickly, but in the Tureta District in Sokoto Province, for example, of the 380 trades in 1914, at least 60 percent were gradually undermined by the flood of cheap European wares. Equally, community-wide "free resources" became imprisoned in a maze of native ordinances and laws or were simply overwhelmed by demographic growth. Native authorities regulated, for example, such traditional activities as collecting firewood, establishing forest reserves that were tightly controlled, and limited access to community dry-season pastures.

Naturally, colonialism did not wholly displace indigenous petty commodity production; some crafts such as pottery, blacksmithing, butchery, grains trade, and house construction and repair were as much a part of the rural economy in 1980 as they were a hundred years earlier. Other skills were stubbornly resistant to European competition; the rural textile industry in Hausaland is a case in point since in 1910 European cloth had captured only 10 percent of the local market. Furthermore the commercial disruption of the 1914–18 war and the inflated textile prices in its aftermath provided some protection to the Hausa cloth trade. But, as Nigerian cotton lint export proceeded apace local costs of production increased and, through the advance system, cheap European baft supplanted the products of Hausa weavers. Colonialism also created new economic opportunities at the same time the traditional pursuits were disappearing; fadama production blossomed, petty trading niches appeared in the interstices of the colonial economy, and a battery of administrative and bureaucratic positions emerged with the extension of rural administration.

These new crafts were instrumental in the reproduction of the household. M. G. Smith (1955, p. 147) estimated that in Zaria emirate in 1949, concentration on the production of services and commodities for local exchange had actually displaced food production. The crucial point, however, is that dry-season off-farm income—which was clearly a necessity for all poor households—could assume two broad forms. Adult males could migrate to sell their labor at wage rates that were incapable of covering reproductive costs. Political labor (paid 9d per day in the 1920s) was barely adequate to cover food expenditures (Mason 1978, p. 74), and forced labor continued into the depression because hired labor could not be attracted at prevailing wage rates. According to Fortes's calculations (in Forde 1946, p. 157) conditions were much the same throughout the plateau minefield.[22] The second alternative was to participate in local craft production or to exploit the plethora of merchant opportunities that opened up in the circuits of the colonial economy. As M. G. Smith's (1955, p. 224) data show, many of the trades were extraordinarily lucrative, but it is equally important to recognize that access to new commercial activities was frequently limited to those capable of extensive capital outlay or with the requisite political influence. Traditional crafts, conversely, while integral to the rural economy, accessible, and relatively secure from international competition, only offered small profit margins. The implication, then, was that while a wholesale eradication of off-farm employment never occurred, and indeed new opportunities arose, the benefits were not borne equally. For many of the poor and middle households, the reproductive needs for craft production, trade, or wage labor either projected adult males into a highly exploitative wage sector in which reproductive costs of labor were partly met by the household itself, or thrust them into a competitive exchange economy whose buoyancy was contingent upon the state of the export market.

Thus, the demand for gowns, for dyers' cloth, sugar-cane, porterage and for trading services, will fluctuate in sympathy with the size of the cash incomes received by the great majority of the farming households from the sales of their ground-nuts. [Forde 1946, p. 158]

It would, of course, be mistaken to imply that the process of colonial integration somehow undid the entire sociological fabric of Hausa society. The preservation of close bonds of kinship is to be expected in some measure. Rather, at a domestic level, peasants were swept up into the commodity boom; the colonial experience as a consequence was contradictory, vacillating between processes of decay and continuity on the one hand, and new economic horizons and opportunities on the other. On balance, subsistence options were narrowed, adaptive flexibility undermined, and households increasingly subject to price fluctuations outside of their control. There was a profound sense in which rural life was distinctively atomized. For some, not only was life on the margin relatively insecure but the margin itself was narrowed.

GRAINS TRADE, DOMESTIC STORAGE, AND THE MINESFIELD

While historians have laid some stress upon the growth in cash crops [for export], the increased commercialization of food crop production even more directly affected the foundations of peasant household production. The tin mines played a major role here.

—Bill Freund

Long-distance and local trade in grains predated the British conquest. Large-scale production of grains on merchant gandaye, short-distance movement of millets by yan kwaramai and, in spite of a high volume-to-weight ratio, caravan trade in cereals, were all commonplace in the nineteenth century. Baier (1977, p. 53), for example, estimated that millet imports into lightly populated Air from the northern savannas was in excess of 3,000 metric tons per year, while regional grain surfeits in densely settled emirates like Kano necessitated much larger food imports, not infrequently from non-Muslim (maguzawa) territory. After 1900, however, demands for staple foods increased sharply in the protectorate due in large measure to the proliferation of nonproducers—colonial armies, seasonal or permanent mine workers, forced laborers for railway and public works construction, and the expanding cadre of colonial and NA bureaucrats—all of whom had to be sustained by local food grains, notably millet and sorghum.

A measure of this expanded market for cereals is contained in the rapid growth of political labor and the Jos mine community. In the case of the former, in April 1909 in excess of 15,000 men were at work on the railway earthworks, which stretched from the Niger to Kano; in 1911 another 5,000 were added with the construction of the Bauchi Light Railway. Between 1907 and 1912 a quarter of a million laborers were recruited in Niger Province alone. This figure does not include, moreover, the demands made by the West African Fighting Force (WAFF), the garrisons, and the standing army which, though not large, was sufficient to cause a major food shortage in 1905 in Zaria and Bauchi due to "the large demand for corn for the horses and the men of the mounted infantry" (PRO Cd. 2684 1905, p. 44). The mining communities exerted still greater demands on food supply. By 1911, when the mines alone employed 41,000 laborers (Ndama-Egba 1974, p. 56), the ability of local plateau districts to supply cereals was clearly overwhelmed:

During the past summer, it was realised that the mining district could not supply nearly sufficient food for the largely increased population with the result that a famine was narrowly averted. . . . This is a new additional reason for [the Bauchi Light] railway. [CO 446 109 ref 37400 1912, pp. 282, 283]

By the outbreak of war in 1914, 70 separate companies worked claims covering a total area of 3,816 square miles (Calvert 1912; Morrison 1977) and the labor rose steadily to 46,000 in 1927, falling to 15,000 in 1933 at the height of the depression, and rising again to over 80,000 during the peak demand of the Second World War. Before 1945 the vast majority of migrants hailed from Hausaland, southern Bornu, and Chad; the local pagan communities, or the plateau, proved obdurately uninterested in wage labor preferring to pay the colonial tax burden in grain. After the First World War, the terms of trade moved sharply against plateau peasants, however, since the tax burden (which was raised significantly on the plateau in 1919) grew much more quickly than cereal prices. Muller's (1980, p. 83) work among the Rubuka estimates that this differential inflation over a couple of decades forced direct producers to increase their grain sales tenfold to cover tax demands. The mine economy had simultaneously threatened the stability of the local agro-ecosystem, as a subcommittee on land rehabilitation made clear.

At the time of the arrival of Europeans, the Plateau was savannah woodland. The pagan villages farmed pockets of arable soil and terraced the rocky hillsides. At this time there were few cattle, few immigrants, and a small indigenous population. Under these conditions there was ample grass cover, rainfall was conserved, rapid run off and soil wash were relatively slight, streams were perennial and springs common. The only serious source of damage was the annual burning of the bush. . . . With the coming of the European followed closely by the Fulani, Hausa and other immigrants, the position rapidly deteriorated. The pagan, no longer fearful of attack, abandoned his thrifty but laborious system of intensive farming and adopted shifting cultivation; wholesale clearance of woodland and trees took place also to provide fuel for the mining companies and their labourers and of thatching grass for labour camps; the cattle population increased to such an extent that the area soon became grossly overgrazed; and the loss of woodland led to the use by the pagans of straw, grass and manure as fuel. The combined result has been an accelerating impoverishment of the soil. Soil wash and erosion has taken place on a vast scale and the surface soil, built up in the course of thousands of years, has within a generation or two been largely washed away. [Land Rehabilitation, n.d.]

A combination of ecological deterioration and a hefty tax burden pushed pagan peoples inexorably into the wage economy and further deepened the minesfield's dependence on imported foodstuffs from other provinces.

Until 1918 grains were still forcibly requisitioned in many provinces to meet NA requirements (NAK SNP 148p/1917), a policy that was reinstituted during the Second World War in order that high-priority wartime targets such as the mine enclaves could operate at maximum output. Prior to 1914, the plateau appropriation of grain was part of a violent attempt to subjugate local communities and expropriate lineage lands for the mine companies. In the process over 1,000 individuals were killed. In Sokoto Province, Resident Arnett used district heads to acquire millet, but the entire exercise suffered from considerable extortion (NAK SNP 9 1218 p/1917, p. 15). In 1919 Arnett again failed to make provision for the purchase of military grain needs and was forced to travel 120 miles to procure corn because of locally high prices.

> Without some pressure from the NA on the farmers, the quantity would not have been obtained except at an extravagant price. When prices are forced up . . . a good deal of hardship is caused to poorer towns people. [NAK SNP 9 289 p/1919, p. 63]

Gradually, however, the provision of foodstuffs to the colonial administration fell into the hands of Hausa merchants and middlemen. The grains trade, dominated by urban-based indigenous merchant's capital, drew sustenance from the ever increasing NA food demands, and also from the structural crisis in the northern food economy which meant that, given the vagaries of Hausa climate, virtually every dry season saw the threat of food shortage in at least one of the emirates.

The provincial Residents accordingly came to depend upon Hausa merchants like the Dantata family in Kano, many of whom were involved in the groundnut buying network. Though the European firms, especially UAC, were actually contracted by the NA to provide millet and sorghum, virtually all of the local buying was undertaken by Hausa merchants. The large urban grain buyers stood at the apex of enormous pyramidal commercial structures constituted by client middlemen and buyers who operated at the local level; they purchased from remote grain surplus regions like southern Katsina, Zamfara, Bornu, Nassarawa, and increasingly into French territory, notably Damagaram and Damerghou. The grains trade frequently circumvented the marketplace altogether as a district officer in Yandaka District, Katsina emirate noted:

> The export trade in corn is rarely done through . . . markets. There is an influx of traders from the Kano region at the time of the harvests who deal directly with the farmers. [NAK SNP 7 K.C. Series K8833 1929, p. 9]

This new expanded yan kwarami trade, making extensive use of the improved transport network provided for the evacuation of cotton and groundnuts, assumed overt political significance. First, the merchants themselves had placed the colonial administration over a barrel; it was impossible for the NAs or the companies to buy in bulk directly in the marketplace fearing huge price distortions were inevitable. But Hausa middlemen could not only make use of their oligopolistic position in rural markets, cornering the grain market, but also charge inflated prices to NAs who were desperate for staples. The provincial administrations could of course import corn, but past experience had shown this to be both excessively costly and much too tardy. The Katsina Resident was not alone when he lamented the high price of foodstuffs in 1949 due to "an attempt to corner the market by lending traders from Kano, Katsina, and Sokoto" (NAK SNP 17/5 47603 1949, p. 3). Some years earlier, the grains situation approached high irony with the representatives of the mines pleading to the Northern Provinces Advisory Council that hoarding grain merchants were accruing what they called "excessive profit" at the expense of the mine companies.

The trade in foodstuffs was political in another sense. Provinces with grain surpluses, particularly in periods of local harvest failure, were loathe to see them appropriated by merchants from other provinces, and regions. A suspected shortfall in Katsina or Kano could bring profiteering grain merchants to Bornu, Yauri, or Nassarawa syphoning off local surpluses that might otherwise have fulfilled in-house NA needs. The tension between provinces—and occasionally between NAs—over food movements deepened as the crisis within the peasant economy deteriorated. Since each NA could control, by native ordinance, the movement of food within its jurisdiction, the cereal supply issue became politically charged. Indeed the Sokoto NAs (Gwandu, Yauri, Argurgu, and Sokoto) considered a system of permit accession to regulate provincial exports of grain (NAK Sokprof 87 Vol. II, p. 13), an extraordinarily bureaucratic task necessitating the issue of licenses to every owner of a pack animal! The Resident, commenting on the proposed Native Authority Law, concluded that such legislation was inappropriate because "Rule 4 [prohibiting the movement of food on pack animals] . . . would bring agricultural life to a standstill."

The structural crisis in the northern Nigeria food economy was in many respects highlighted by the deepening commoditization of staple foodstuffs. The rapid growth of nonproducers, whether proletarianized mine workers, military personnel, or NA employees, placed excessive demands on a food system already subject to the inroads made by export crop production, and in some areas already suffering from long standing grain deficits. The low level of development of the forces of production among household producers ensured that productivity not only remained low but also that grain production as a whole remained vulnerable to adverse physical conditions. Low household productivity, and the drive to expand nonfood export commodities all served to shatter the self-sustaining character of the peasant economy. The colonial state was accordingly faced with the contradiction of expanding cash crop production to balance NA budgets and to fulfill metropolitan demand, yet depending on local food surpluses to ensure that households had the means to survive and a regular and cheap wage food was available for all salaried personnel and workers. The colonial government presumed that traditional breadbaskets such as Zamfara, Bornu, and the middle belt provinces would continue to supply foodstuffs, since grain production represented a lucrative income source for households faced with monetary pressures for tax. In spite of French murmurings to the contrary, the northern government made no attempt to regulate grain imports from French territory; traders were attracted to the Hausa cities by favorable price differentials.

On balance, a colonial food supply system emerged that embodied the contradictory intentions of the state itself: continued grain requisition to procure NA foodstuffs in spite of the recurrent spectre of famine; simultaneous appeals to "grow more food" and maximize export production while making no efforts to modernize agriculture or reduce direct taxation; and competition between and within provinces and NAs to procure their own wage foods. All these tendencies within the food system created conditions conducive to high merchant profits. Middlemen exploited commercially the annual fluctuations in harvest quality, the spectre of widespread starvation throughout the northern provinces, and the demands of the colonial government to acquire enormous quantities of food—almost at any price—to ensure the continuity of basic state functions.

Some provinces became deficit food producers during the colonial period; Katsina was reputedly importing 20,000 tons by the late 1950s. Zaria Province, increasingly devoted to cotton production in spite of the demands of the adjacent mine communities, was probably a net importer of grain when M. G. Smith conducted his study in 1949. At the household level accumulation or storage of foodstuffs sufficient to act as a famine reserve were increasingly chimerical. Raynault (1975) for example, believes that the Islamization of maguzawa communities during the colonial epoch selectively displaced the iskoki pantheon upon which the ritually sanctioned storage system was predicated. Among the Muslim Hausa, colonial officials lamented, with justified alacrity, the trend away from both long- and short-term storage, quite wrongly attributing its causation to native deviancy, agronomic backwardness, and a fickle peasant personality. But by the 1930s it was the penetration of exchange relationships, the extortion of the colonial state, and the general shakiness of the domestic economy that was largely antithetical to cereal accumulation.

The limited information available suggests that, save in a few areas where definite links with an urban or other corn importing market have been established, the rural household in the north produces at best only a small surplus of food crops beyond its own needs for the ensuing year. Even when surpluses are produced, they, like the cash crops, are sold without delay in order to secure money and are not held as an insurance against crop failure in the following agricultural year. [Forde 1946, p. 158]

Underproduction of foodstuffs is thrown into sharp relief by the budgetary data collected by M. G. Smith (1955) in postwar southern Zaria. In district P to the south of Zaria city and in communities E, F, and G the percentage of the total volume of grain consumed which was acquired through the market was respectively 14.6, 25.8, 20.6 and 26 percent; that is to say, between two- and three-months' grain supply was purchased. In terms of value, however, a somewhat different picture emerges; recomputing data pertaining just to village G (see table 5.9) shows that purchased foodstuffs constituted an average of 18 percent of net cash income and 41 percent of the value of domestically produced grains. This suggests that millets and sorghums were procured during the preharvest period after a considerable seasonal price rise.

CLASS RELATIONS AND RURAL DIFFERENTIATION

A change toward a material productive end, the shift from production for self sustenance . . . to production for an external market must necessarily bring on radical transformation if not the social destruction of the communities.

—Claude Meillassoux

There are now the beginnings of a wealthy class of agriculturalists in the North.
—H. R. Palmer

The Land and Native Rights Proclamation of 1910 was an attempt to shield northern Nigerian society against the corrosive effects of non-Muslim agents, whether they were white settlers, Ibo middlemen, or Yoruba agents. While Clifford deliberately undermined this policy of sheltering in the North in the postwar period, the colonial administration nonetheless strove to preserve at all costs the authority of emirate aristocracies upon which colonial rule ultimately depended (Okonjo 1974, p. 52). The necessity of forging a class alliance with the *masu sarauta* did not mean that the Caliphal elites were maintained intact. On the contrary, the British meddled constantly in emirate and dynastic politics, deposing and instating high-ranking palace officials with great regularity. Yet in spite of the directness of colonial intervention, dispatching emirs to Ilorin, reestablishing the Habe line in Daura, dismantling palace cliques, and pushing the *hakimai* into the countryside, the *sarauta* as a class was

TABLE 5.9
GRAIN SELF-SUFFICIENCY: SOUTHERN ZARIA, 1949

Total acreage	Food millet or sorghum (acres)	Cotton (acres)	Total cash income £ s d	Trade income £ s d	Craft income £ s d	Labor income £ s d	Staple food purchases £ s d	Staple food purchases as % of cash income	Staple food purchases as % of staples grown* (by value)
0.65	0.65	—	29 14 0	—	19 10 0	10 4 0	5 6 6	16.3	62.5
2.60	2.60	—	22 13 10	—	20 11 4	—	1 0 6	4.4	8.7
3.78	2.32	1.25	26 7 8	9 12 0	—	— 15 —	5 8 6	20.4	42.2
3.11	2.84	—	27 6 11	—	27 6 0	—	7 5 7	27.0	77.5
6.41	5.27	—	37 10 6	4 16 0	14 8 0	—	— 5 0	0.6	0.9
5.34	4.91	0.3	24 15 6	—	14 0 0	—	4 7 0	17.5	21.6
1.93	1.64	—	16 1 2	3 0 0	14 0 0	—	2 0 0	12.5	16.9
2.15	2.15	—	22 10 11	3 0 0	19 0 0	—	3 13 10	16.6	26.5
0.55	0.55	—	32 10 5	32 10 5	—	—	19 18 0	62.5	100.0
1.07	1.07	—	19 19 0	— 14 0	—	7 6 0	1 17 8	9.1	25.0
0.76	0.76	—	30 10 0	—	29 14 0	—	7 18 4	25.6	109.0
1.36	0.90	0.40	21 4 6	15 4 0	—	—	3 6 3	15.6	55.2
3.65	2.61	1.07	28 13 0	—	12 12 0	—	3 1 0	10.9	11.5
1.85	1.85	—	29 9 8	20 8 8	—	—	— 17 0	3.0	5.2
2.18	2.18	—	22 1 6	—	19 10 0	—	2 7 8	10.9	23.8
Average:									
2.5	2.1	0.20	£26 1 0	£6 15 0	£11 8 0	£1 4 0	£4 5 0	18.1%	41.8%

SOURCE: M. G. Smith (1955, pp. 180, 186, 189, 201, 210, 228).

NOTE: These data refer to market town on a road and old trade route.

*Domestically produced foodstuffs are valued at harvest prices and include the local sale price of stalks.

maintained. From the British perspective this was both inevitable and necessary; indirect rule was the grand coalition between the Fulani and the British, sealed by the Satiru uprising and the Native Courts Proclamation, both of which were strategic statements of mutual support. In rallying the Fulani around the cause of peace, order, and stability, the Fulani were simultaneously bound to the British and given a stake in colonial stability (Okonjo 1974, p. 36). As a consequence the traditional basis of society and its ideological platform was retained by the British.

The military supremacy of the colonial state, starkly highlighted in the fall of Kano and Sokoto in 1902, actually changed the nature of aristocratic legitimacy; the tacit support of the state apparatus placed the new rural administrators in a sturdy political position with respect to the talakawa (Abdullahi 1977). In cases where rural officeholders had no legitimate claim to office, and in view of the regularity of deposition, the district and village heads were clearly the clients, if not the puppets, of colonial rule. Equally, these neophyte elites, often from Fulani aristocratic lineages, quite naturally gazed outward to the Resident via the emir rather than inward to the community for political legitimacy. The increasing bureaucratization of the NAs and the creation of a salaried class of rural bureaucrats reinforced the sense of detachment between resident sarauta and the village community as a whole. It was Resident Festing of Kano who complained that district heads had "no sympathy for the talakawa," but many others bemoaned the inability of the colonial government to inculcate a local commitment among salaried rural officials beyond the desire to maximize tax receipts. The newfound authority of the village-level administrators found expression in their renewed attempts to deepen their exploitative control over the peasantry. The obvious avenue for this exploitation was taxation but other opportunities presented themselves, not least as commercial agents; village and hamlet heads quickly became local-level representatives in the groundnut and cotton buying networks. By the 1920s, for example, the Galadima of Zaria was a successful trader.

> His buyers bought hundreds of tons of produce by . . . using his authority to compel sale at a profitable price and to get transportation for nothing. . . . The Emir, many District Heads and even Village Heads had used such labour . . . to increase the acreage of their farms [and] for mercantile profit. [Arnett, R. H. Mss. Afr. 952.6/2, pp. 81-82]

The fact that administrative salaries remained low in relation to expected ruling class social obligations (the village head salary was a measly £2.0.0 in 1917 but was actually reduced in the 1930s) naturally pushed local sarauta toward illicit trade, extortion and embezzlement. What often emerged, then, were district and village areas which, as a touring officer noted of Dankama, were "run like private estates" (NAK Katprof 1 #4 1926, p. 79).

The new structural conditions in which the traditional aristocracy found themselves allowed for a deepening of their control over rural producers. An inventory of the manner in which officeholders extracted surpluses is hardly necessary in view of the considerable literature on political corruption and administrative malpractice. Since all colonial dicta including taxation passed through the rural administrators, excessive grain requisition, underpayment for NA grain levies, illegal forced labor, and illicit tithes were regular ammunition in the sarauta arsenal. M. G. Smith (1964a, p. 188) estimated in Zaria that an underpayment of grain in one season produced roughly £800 for one district head. The preservation of precolonial officeholding estates, which Lugard saw as a necessary corollary for buttressing Fulani privilege, also went hand in hand with obligatory unpaid village labor on sarauta farms (NAK Sokprof 368/1911). Tax extortion was of course commonplace, appearing amidst much moral proselytizing in almost every annual report as one might anticipate in view of Lugard's preoccupation with revenue. District heads often collected taxes in advance (*kudin falle*) to provide the capital for their market speculations, especially buying grain in bulk to be resold during the following wet season. In 1912, Webster estimated that the village heads were levying 30 percent more on zakkat and kudin kassa taxes, since receipts were rarely given to each individual taxpayer. The lump-sum assessment system actually compounded the likelihood of tax embezzlement since computation per household lay directly in the hands of the sarauta. Palmer depressingly concluded that speculation and a measure of exploitation was probably an inevitable externality of the administration's devolution of central authority.

> It is extremely difficult to inculcate the idea that Government is interested in method as opposed to the result of [tax] collection, and the Native mind considers that Government has no right to complain of a chief who renders to Caesar as much as Caesar can find out to be due, even though he incidentally makes a good deal for himself. [Palmer NAK SNP 170 p/1916, p. 25]

This is not to imply that the administration did not intervene in tax embezzlement issues. Indeed the first two decades of colonial rule are flooded with cases of deposed hakimi and village heads who overstepped the license that British political officers had granted. In a two-month period in 1910, twenty-eight officials were deposed in Katsina Province (NAK Katprof 1/1 1865/1910); in 1931 in Zaria, forty-one village heads "proved unequal to the responsibilities of tax collection" (NAK Zariaprof 7/1 125/1931). These depositions did not lessen the political clout that the rural oligarchy wielded; rather they were catalytic in two senses. First the elites developed systematic devices to shield themselves from complaints or investigation.

The *hakimi* tries to prevent complaints being made against him by use of a system of agents, ('*yan labari*), who endeavour on his behalf to prevent complainants gaining access to the Administration. This practice is concisely expressed in the Hausa idiom "*An yi mashi gobe, jibi*" (They did him to-morrow and the next day"). The *hakimi* seeks to frustrate such complaints, partly because of his uncertainty concerning the Administrative reaction and the processes of English Law, partly to avoid any exposure which may threaten his security of office or chances of promotion, and partly from the desire to avoid situations involving him in heavy expenditure on gifts. [M. G. Smith 1955, p. 90]

And second, the mass depositions provided ample opportunity for the emirs to consolidate their political hegemony in the countryside. Emir Dikko of Katsina carefully used the tax issue to place his clients at strategic points in the villages. In 1917, forty-eight of the salaried village heads were nonnatives of their towns, being relations or servants of the emir, relations of the district heads (who were inevitably closely tied to the ruling lineage), or former jekadas. Ola's (1974) suggestion that indirect rule proved to be a centralized "ruled coercion" is not too far from the mark.

In part, this gigantic edifice of gaisuwa and aristocratic privilege was both encouraged and consolidated by indirect rule. C. Temple said that the political officer must

shut [his] eyes . . . to a great many practices which though not absolutely repugnant to humanity are nevertheless reprehensible to our ideas . . . you have to make up your mind that men are not all equal before the law. [Temple, in Kirk-Greene 1963, p. 49]

It is, then, difficult to see why Sharwood-Smith should conclude that it was "the rarest of events" for a Resident or D.O. to close his eyes and ears to abuses (1969, p. 142). Rather, deceit or neglect was a *sensible* reaction to the rigid procedural rules of a hierarchical and competitive civil service system (Okonjo 1974, p. 284). British officers who exposed the corruption of the system were especially vulnerable to abuse as Edwardes discovered in Sokoto in the 1920s. His fall from grace came about not only due to his deserved denunciation of the Sultan's despotism but also because he was "notoriously a friend of the peasants" (Heussler 1968, p. 124). The system selected for sycophancy in a manner that allowed the emirs unrestrained autocracy. Ironically, Sharwood-Smith (1969, p. 68) charged that a submissive Sokoto peasantry in the 1930s permitted much evil to go undetected unless staff did otherwise. Indeed, it is perhaps apposite to conclude with Smith's desultory comments on Zaria emirate twenty years later.

This village provided instances of as many administrative malpractices as could be wished. I found cases in which the Village Head and native departmental officials together exacted (unauthorised) fines (*tara*) or bribes (*toshi*) from individuals alleged to have certain diseases, themselves or in their households; or to permit certain transactions, such as sale of cotton, hides or skins; together with both forms of levy (*agama* and *tausa*) on the local market. N.A. funds sent to pay men who had worked on the sleeping sickness clearance had not been disbursed. The Village Head maintained a personal staff of 19 agents, *jekadu* and other youths. The District concerned, like others, was also administered through *jekadu*.

In another District an eyewitness recorded the irregular receipts of his District Head, intermittently over eight months . . . this District Head received gifts from all Village Heads under him to repair their meeting-house, when he had a motor accident, when the Village Heads brought in tax, when the District Head went to the capital on official business, and when a British Officer visited the District. An informal collection from the pastoral Fulani in lieu to tax was also rewarding, and so were gifts received by the District Head when he appointed a prison warder, a wardhead, a Chief Praise-singer, and when he considered appointments to a Village Headship. . . . A village Head who had committed some offence, and a villager seen talking alone with a visiting British Officer both produced their gifts. When the District Head formally installed a new Village Head, the villagers collected an amount to express their loyalty, an act shortly afterwards repeated when their new Village Chief had a son. This District Head also had access to loans from the Native Authority for cattle fattening and similar schemes, and continued to use unpaid labour on his farm, which adjoined my quarters. At the harvest he considerably overpurchasd grain for the N.A., but paid the official price, and sold some at a profit to merchants in a nearby Emirate. The District Court totalled £54. It will be seen that almost every practice prohibited by Shehu was to be found in Zaria during 1949–50, together with many innovations by which modern administrative duties and opportunities were reinterpreted to fit traditional patterns. [Smith 1964, pp. 189–90]

From the British perspective, as long as the colonial state relied on noncapitalist relations of production in the countryside, these surpluses retained by the elites were necessary costs to be incurred.

Another issue concerns rural differentiation within the talakawa as a class. This is a highly contentious subject and Polly Hill (1972) adamantly adheres to the classlessness of rural Hausaland in light of her estimation of the strength of leveling mechanisms, principally intergenerational dissipation of wealth upon death. Further, she sees the moral economy as decidedly intact.

Village responsibilities for providing social security are much wider [than those of "rich merchants in cities"] and inhibit capital growth. [Hill 1972, p. 198]

Hill's work falls within the phalanx of Chayanovian theory or "cyclical kulakism," which gives analytic priority to innate abilities, chance, personal enthusiasm, and inheritance. Chayanov identified a peasant economy regulated by its own developmental laws, particularly the demographic cycle of the household, which determines the producer-to-consumer ratio. In the absence of the market, the causes of peasant poverty pertain directly to lack of domestic labor, natural disasters, or personal attributes (Williams 1976).

To view the household economy in colonial Nigeria as simply subject to internal, ahistoric developmental tendencies is, however, an essentialist explanation that fails to recognize how the reproduction of the farm unit was dramatically altered by the role of merchant's capital. This is not to deny the role of household demography since the majority of rural producers still own their means of production. But the Chayanovian model operates *within* the confines of incipient class formation, of the distillation of commodity producers into different strata. Within the differentiated peasantry, the "natural cycle" of demographic growth and fission may be of greater or lesser significance. Hill alludes to this distinction since she observed in Batagarawa that "the system [of economic mobility] is sticky," and more recently in Dorayi near Kano that the hamlet "is incipiently, if not actually, economically stratified." Colonialism did not merely change rural inequalities in some quantitative sense but changed the nature of productive relations and surplus extraction.

> What is new in the societies of the Sudantic belt, traditionally organised on a strong hierarchical basis, is not the existence of inequalities, but the emergence of disparities which are no longer based on the social structure and stable values, but which arise and spread from the manipulation . . . of goods and money. [Raynault 1977, p. 28]

For Hill, however, northern Nigeria is, and was, rural capitalism through and through. Colonialism skimmed cash crops off a stagnant agrarian base; there was not so much differentiation in the countryside as lateral adjustment and internal circulation of elites, compounded perhaps by persistent population pressure.

For others, colonialism had its economic cake and ate it too by producing capitalist goods with precapitalist workers on precapitalist land. This seems to be Williams's view (1976) in which peasants persist by producing cheap commodities, often through "self-exploitation, by clinging to a system of production which sees wage labor as slavery." I suggest, however, that the agricultural mode of production in northern Nigeria changed from predominantly peasant production—household simple reproduction through use-values—to simple commodity production; that is to say the household production is "expanded" to include exchange-values, the production of which became internalized in the cycle of reproduction. This is perhaps best viewed as an intensification of commodity production at the household level; as Kautsky observed, the rural producer comes to depend more and more on the market and credit.

Peasantries were thus dissolved and reconstituted; they were, in short, transformed. An understanding of this transformation must recognize how capital penetrated the countryside generating new inequalities, and how surpluses were extracted through these new class relations. As Paine puts it,

> differentiation between the various agricultural classes is based on the hiring out of land, hiring in labor, practising usury and accumulating profits by commodity transactions. [Paine 1977, p. 366]

The process of differentiation and its implications for food scarcity are dealt with in detail in the following section. Here I simply want to draw attention to the increasing land transactions and the quantitative aspects of household differentiation in the colonial period that highlight the transition toward commodity production. In the first instance, the sale of farms increased significantly in spite of the Lands Proclamation (Frishman 1977). Rowling's study in 1946 showed that of eighteen case histories at Dawaki near Kano, eleven involved outright sale. In addition, Rowling (1949, pp. 49–50) documented the rapid proliferation of other land transactions, notably pledging (jingina), lease (aro, Kudin goro), and sharecropping (kashi mu raba) as follows:

(i) *Pledging.* An entire field or farm is taken over in exchange for a money loan. Rowling felt that in Kano the sum paid bore no necessary relation to land value, no term was stated and the creditor farmed until the debt was paid. Tenure was invariably precarious and hence productivity or investment (in manure) tended to be low. Local opinion varied on whether redemption or ultimate sale was more frequent but the transaction was widespread and in a case study at Gama one-third of the farmers had experience with jingina transactions (Rowling 1949, p. 50).

(ii) *Lease.* The terminology for lease in the Hausa language is *aro* which also means loan, but this is deceptive for leases should be recognized for what they are. The transaction runs for one season and quite frequently a second-year renter will be given a different farm "to avoid any risk of his establishing a claim to title" (Rowling 1949, p. 50). The Kano information indicated that rates varied according to size, fertility, and type of farm; for upland fields the range was 21 shillings to 10 shillings; for irrigated patches, which, by virtue of their scarcity and productivity had been regularly leased since 1900, the rates were often in excess of £1 per season.

(iii) *Sharecropping*. Rowling also identified a type of *metaye* system in Kano, although other references to sharecropping are notably absent. In some districts the practice is still unknown since lease is a preferable transaction. Rowling (p. 51) claimed to have found sharecropping in Rano where land was not scarce. In this case, there may be a connection between domestic clientage and ex-slaves. The system continues to be found largely on irrigated farms—in the 1940s Rowling discovered that twenty-eight farmers at Wudil sharecropped fadama lands—in which the title-holder supplies the land, his share being between a quarter and a third, depending on the richness of the silt.

In many instances, of course, the hiring out or in of land in whatever form was rarely reported to village heads since Islamic dictates on interest pose obvious practical limitations on such transactions. Language acts to obfuscate these land dealings since aro, for instance, may mean loan although the nature of the exchange can be one of formalized direct rental. The undeniable fact, however, is the emergence of farmland as a rentable commodity, and of a class of agriculturalists who derived income (whether in cash or labor power) from such dealings. The commoditization of land is indicative of the extent to which new relations of production had emerged, although quantitative measures of differences between households in the colonial period are difficult to gauge, in spite of survey assessments at the village level. The most accessible statistics pertain to landholding; in 1937 two communities studied for revenue purposes in the Kano close settled zone showed that 35 percent of all holdings were less than four acres, while 33 percent were in excess of seven acres per farm household. A much clearer picture emerges from a study by Morrison (NAK Kanoprof 5/1 6551/s.1) of the Dawaki-ta-Kuda District in 1947 (table 5.10). Dawaki village had a mean household holding-size of roughly six acres; 25.9 percent of all households held less than three acres each, while 27 percent of households owned just over 50 percent of all farmland (NAK Kanoprof 5/1 655 / s/1). Seventeen percent of all households held less than one acre, and 13.1 percent were landless, presumably renting or borrowing land. In light of the critical role of household labor, it is perhaps worth noting that 50 percent of all households consisted of five or less individuals, while 27 percent consisted of ten or more. Morrison also estimated that between 1937 and 1947, the percentage of holdings in the less than three-acre category had increased in the three communities studied by 1.7 percent; the proportion in the over six-acre group, conversely, had fallen by 2 percent.

TABLE 5.10
LANDHOLDING DISTRIBUTION IN KANO ABOUT 1947

Size of household	Total	Holding size in acres									
		0	<1	1–2	2–3	3–4	4–5	5–6	6–7	7–10	>10
1	135	30	5	10	11	11	16	16	14	18	4
2	98	21	4	7	8	6	6	6	13	15	12
3	82	10	2	3	2	7	4	4	4	21	25
4	49	3	2	3		6	3	3	3	10	16
5	34	1		1		1	2	4	3	4	18
6	25						3		5	7	10
7	10		1	1	1					2	5
8	12				1	1				3	7
9	13						1	1		3	8
10	7				1		2			1	5
10+	30								1	2	25
Totals	495	65	14	25	24	32	37	34	43	86	135

SOURCE: NAK Kanoprof 5/1 6551/S.1 1947.

The differentiation issue is given further clarity in Smith's (1955) budgetary data collected in 1949 in Zaria emirate (table 5.11). The smallness of the sample size severely prevents a detailed examination of household stratification, but a recomputation of Smith's household tabulations reveals a striking economic polarity. The households were ranked by gross income per adult male; the differences in mean incomes and farm acreages between rich and poor households varied by a factor of almost four. The rich peasants owned roughly three to four times as much farmland and generated four times as much gross income per adult male than the poor families. While the community as a whole was grain deficient, poor farmers clearly purchased more as a percentage of domestic foodstuffs grown on family farms, than their wealthy brethren. Cotton and groundnuts were both significant income sources, though the rich households produced almost four times more by value; 18 percent of the cultivated area was devoted to export commodities among the wealthy peasantry as opposed to 30 percent of the farm area among the poor. Perhaps most significant, however, was the extent of commoditization in the nonagricultural sphere—principally crafts and trade—and the contributions these activities made to household reproduction. Among both rich and poor the value of off-farm income was seven to ten times greater than that of agricultural export commodities. Differentiation found expression in this sector, however, since well-to-do households monopolized the lucrative merchant and trade occupations; the poor families conversely were saddled with high-turnover, low-return crafts such as mat weaving and the provision of community services (praise singing, barbers). The wealthy peasant was in fact in this regard a "kulak," that is as an all-round agent of commodity relations, functioning as moneylender, transporter, credit facilitator, and renter of land and machinery.

The craft economy provided an alternative to the sale of labor power, in spite of the fact that 25 percent of all household heads did not practice a craft. The relatively low incidence of wage labor in areas subject to intense merchant activity was not necessarily universal, but it is interesting that even by 1947 in Dawaki-ta-Kudu District (Kano), Morrison estimated that only 10 percent of households regularly hired in labor. The undeveloped nature of wage laboring was not unrelated to the attractiveness of mercantile operations, given the backwardness of the circuits of commodity circulation. As Bernstein observed, the higher rate of return in trade versus reinvestment in production

can help account for the limited formation of agrarian capital and the limited differentiation of units of production simultaneously with the extension (and intensification) of commodity relations. [Bernstein 1979, p. 432]

TABLE 5.11
HOUSEHOLD INEQUALITY AND DIFFERENTIATION: SOUTHERN ZARIA, 1949

House-hold	Income[1] per adult male			% cash income	Acreage	Cotton/ groundnut production			Trade profit			Craft profit		
	£	s	d			£	s	d	£	s	d	£	s	d
Rich	114	15	2	70.6	6.3	10	10	0	–			–		
	78	10	0	70.4	7.8	5	9	0	102	10	0	–		
	69	2	0	25.9	3.8	5	3	0	–			10	11	0
	66	1	0	40.7	8.7	4	14	0	48	9	0	–		
Av.	81	15	0	51.9	6.6	6	10	0	37	15	0	2	15	0
Poor	15	6	0	22.8	3.0	–			6	4	0	0	16	6
	27	4	0	47.2	2.1	3	18	0	15	7	0	3	10	0
	21	17	0	52.8	1.2	1	0	6	–			9	7	0
	17	2	0	67.4	1.2	–			–			19	17	0
Av.	£20	5	0	47.0	1.87	£1	5	0	£5	7	0	£8	5	0

SOURCE: M. G. Smith (1955).

NOTE: These data refer to an old market town on a trade route and road.

In some respects any estimates of the extent of wage laboring is bedeviled by the shame that surrounds the act of working another man's farms.[23] Furthermore, the high incidence of indebtedness almost certainly indicates that repayments were not infrequently made in labor power. Hence Morrison's survey in 1947, which noted the widespread use of gayya (collective farm labor) may be rather deceptive. Neither should this obscure the extent of dry-season migration (cin rani) for the purpose of wage employment. Prothero's (1958) survey, for instance, estimated a quarter of a million migrants passing through Sokoto Province alone.

By using the village as a type of social laboratory for an analysis of the impact of colonialism in northern Nigeria, I have argued that the penetration of capital unraveled the social and cultural fabric of rural Hausa society. I do not mean to suggest that colonial rule destroyed peasant "culture," or led to a sort of community anarchy leaving villages somehow bereft of their history. In some respects, indirect rule did just the reverse, not least with regard to the untrammeled authority of Islam. M. G. Smith's (1955) budgetary information in the late 1940s shows clearly that, even among food-deficit households, a large proportion of grain still entered the traditional circuits of gift exchange. At the same time, the

TABLE 5.11 continued

Gifts in			Gifts out			Tax			Women's profit			Staple food purchased			Purchased staples as % of staples grown
£	s	d	£	s	d	£	s	d	£	s	d	£	s	d	grown
8	9	0	4	11	0		14	8	35	8	0	13	4	0	50
3	19	0	–			1	10	0	32	8	0	8	15	0	25
5	12	1	–			1	1	0	12	10	0	3	11	0	10
5	0	8	–			2	13	6	18	7	0	7	14	0	16
5	15	0	1	3	0	1	8	0	24	17	0	8	5	0	25.25
–			–				11	5	21	0	0	5	10	0	33
–			–				7	0	9	3	0	2	19	0	20
–			–				7	0	7	12	0	2	2	0	30
10	8		–			–			10	6	0	8	3	0	250
4	2						6	5	£12	0	0	£4	15	0	83

[1]Gross annual income per adult male; the other craft, trade income, and so on refer to household incomes.

world of the gidaje was progressively weakened. Complex farm units were less attenuated, cooperative labor groups (gayya) were of "declining importance" by the 1930s (Forde 1946, p. 158), and among the magu-zawa, the acceleration of Islamic conversion and the extension of the market signaled the disappearance of the iskoki pantheon, and most especially of redistributive authority like the sarkin noma (Nicolas 1977). The form and function of patronage changed as externally supported village elites could afford to ignore local opinion, and as a shift occurred from domestic to individualistic and cash-credit clientage. On balance, the precolonial tension between what Nicolas calls "*le don*" and "*le marche*" moved inexorably in favor of the latter.[24] All this is faintly reminiscent of Scott's (1978) "post-peasant society": of increasing tendencies toward agricultural involution or labor export, of the erosion of local kindred and social ties, and of a peasant culture that resembles a provincial variant of national culture. The contours of such a postpeasant society are such that the village "may come to represent little more than geographical proxim-ity of resident households" (Scott 1978, p. 151). This is a convenient encapsulation of the petty commodity form of production that emerged in northern Nigeria.

MERCHANT'S CAPITAL AND SIMPLE REPRODUCTION

The English trader can have all his own way in Northern Nigeria.

—Sir Hesketh Bell

The mere death of his cow may render the small peasant incapable of renewing his reproduction on its former scale. He then falls into the clutches of the usurer, and once in the merchant's power, he can never extricate himself.

—Karl Marx, *Capital*, Vol. III

The various interests involved in the production and supply of cash crops, most notably metropolitan capital, trading firms, local merchant capital, and the colonial state, could not simply depend on the apparently erratic and agriculturally backward Hausa peasantry for the supply of export commodities. The state was compelled to intervene directly through taxation and the support of monopolistic pricing and marketing arrangements. Merchant capital, however, which organizes the circulation of commodities, generally acquires profit through the market mechanisms, and particularly through a process of unequal exchange. Yet the necessity to regulate what was cultivated and in what quantity, demanded intervention by the firms at the level of the conditions of production. While the organization of production remained in peasant hands, commodity relations exercised increasing control at the point of production. The regulation of production was fashioned in two ways. First were the colonial bylaws, extension schemes, fertilizer programs and quality control legislation, which tied rural producers to specific forms of agricultural production. And second, was a variant of what Walter Rodney called policing the countryside, namely, the advance crop mort-gaging system, which binds producer to buyer through webs of credit and indebtedness. The intervention of antediluvian forms of capital under conditions of limited development of the forces of production and of periodic deterioration in the terms of trade, constituted a serious threat to simple reproduction of households. In the following discussion I examine two aspects of the pressure on peasant reproduction, what Bernstein (1979, p. 427) calls the "simple reproduction squeeze"; the efflorescence in rural indebtedness, and the market insecurities associated with price variability and changing terms of trade.

RURAL INDEBTEDNESS AND THE ADVANCE SYSTEM

It is clear from the work of Hogendorn (1978) that the foundations of the trading firm—buying agent edifice—were already consolidated by the first decade of colonial rule, initially through the skin trade, and more significantly after 1912, by the groundnut revolution. The early European firms and commercial representatives were not in touch with potential export commodity growers and had little choice but to work through the indigenous merchant (ulema) networks and their agents in the countryside, and the influential local-level bureaucrats, particularly the district, hamlet, and village heads. By state compulsion, advancing salt and cloth, and doubtless by a measure of political persuasion on the part of the masu sarauta, groundnut production spread rapidly. The subsequent development of the produce trade created multiple commercial opportunities for intermediaries, agents, and middlemen who were active in the sale and purchase of export commodities. A complex hierarchical structure of traders emerged welded together through ties of credit and clientage.

The fortunes of the commercial sector naturally vacillated in response to prevailing global economic conditions, but by the early 1920s the colonial pattern of trade in cotton and groundnuts was firmly in place. There were the European firms—UAC, CFAO, the London and Kano, and the like—who alternated between intense competition between themselves in an effort to capture a large share of the produce market and restrictive pricing or purchase agreements to divide the spoils. The firms generally plied their import-export trade through canteens, which functioned as buying and assemblage points in the provinces, run in most cases by Ibo and Yoruba commercial clients (*angulum kanti*). The canteen system flourished during the interwar years and provided expanded buying opportunities for Hausa merchants who could establish trade domains in the more remote, isolated districts. The Levantine and Arab merchants constituted a second, but not entirely independent, buying network. After 1917–18, the Lebanese in particular gained favor with the European firms and acted as middlemen in the groundnut commerce, using Hausa agents for local-level purchases. As licensed buying agents, the Levantine merchants came to dominate the groundnut trade until the 1950s; their robustness not only displaced Hausa middlemen, pushing them into the lower orders of the buying networks, but also spawned large Lebanese trading companies like Saul Raccah, which competed directly with the European firms. And finally, there were the Hausa merchants themselves who acted sometimes as independent middlemen, sometimes as agents for the Yoruba, Ibo, Lebanese, and Syrian clerks, and occasionally as autonomous mercantile houses, of which the Dantata empire is perhaps the model. The Hausa merchants expanded their role in the produce trade after the Second World War, and by the 1950s Sanusi Dantata alone is reputed to have financed 60 percent of all licensed buying agents (LBAs) through free cash credit. The development of an influential indigenous merchant capital was built upon and developed through the precolonial merchant-ulema networks, which Tahir discusses in nineteenth-century Kano. After 1900, however, these networks further diversified, perhaps in part as a response to discrimination in the export produce trade, and pursued other commercial lines in imports (cloth, salt), kola, transportation, grains, property development, and building contracts.

Though Hausa merchants did not initially occupy apical positions in the produce-buying pyramid, they were nonetheless predominant and influential at the local level. It is important to appreciate that the Hausa agents and middlemen, while subsumed into the European or Levantine systems, also constituted important commercial diasporas in themselves. A typical groundnut merchant operation in Kano during the interwar period consisted of at least four levels. First, were the relatively autonomous merchants who operated their own networks yet were business associates (abokin ciniki) of an urban patron who frequently advanced cash, goods, and imported wares to them. Second, smaller and less autonomous primary clients who operated within the merchant network. Third, the agents who acted as middle-level wholesalers. And fourth, a network of lower-level traders, the rural speculators (madugai), balance men (yan balas), and rural agents (attajirai) who took quite small cash and cloth advances from the merchant patron and distributed credit, as a corollary to buying activities, through village- and hamlet-level networks. A hierarchy of this sort including various categories of business patronage and client behavior might have a vast geographical range, covering virtually every growing area and buying center in the emirate. The complicity—and in many cases the direct intervention—of the village and district heads in merchant functions ensured the profitability and success of local-level buying operations. By the 1920s, the Zaria Resident observed that the Sokoto and Katsina cotton trade was, in this de facto sense, in the hands of the emir (NAK SNP 386/1918).

Like many other parts of the Muslim world, the extension of merchant capital in colonial Nigeria went hand in hand with usury or interest-bearing capital; through this form, merchant influence extends beyond the realm of circulation into production proper. In many instances, credit is employed to support what Marx dramatically referred to as a "system of robbery" to enhance the conditions under which produce can be bought cheaply and sold dear.[25] The antiquity of credit-based crop purchase in northern Nigeria dates back to the beginning of the groundnut trade in Kano, where salt and cloth were advanced to rural producers by buying agents to secure harvest sale (Hogendorn 1978, pp. 77–89). The rationale for this crop mortgage system was well articulated by early Kano district officers.

> The export merchant to arrange properly for freight, storage and sale abroad must try to get delivery of assumed supplies at fixed points and within fixed

periods. He arranges to advance money to the smaller traders on guarantees that they will deliver the produce at periodically fixed prices and at fixed points. The small traders . . . then have the same problem. . . . If they waited till harvest they would have to join in a hectic scramble for produce. . . . They adopt the same solution—advances to the grower. [NAK SNP 17 1864]

The advance system not only provided a means to regulate household production but was also a lucrative method for surplus extraction in the form of interest. The form of antediluvian relations in the countryside in Hausaland is, nonetheless, a dauntingly complex issue. Clearly usury predated the advent of colonial rule, for much of the long-distance trade was cemented through ties of merchant clientage and credit. The extent to which usurious activities were vehicles for merchant profits in the countryside is, however, a moot point; Palmer's statement to the Lands Committee in 1909 that all the peasantry were in debt is doubtless a reflection of the precariousness of an agricultural economy subject to the vagaries of climate, disease, and personal calamity. But equally, the nature of debt had a strong familial basis in which community standards of equity and justice could be brought to bear on loan activity. The colonial period witnessed a spatial expansion, as it were, of credit relations since producers were progressively subsumed into lineages of debt whose origins lay ultimately in the advances of the European firms. A second point concerns the manner in which advances and crop mortgages varied both spatially and temporally. Cash advances progressively succeeded the early cloth-salt system, though the latter was still prominent in Katsina in the 1940s; further, interest rates and forms of usurious activity showed some variability between provinces and between sectors, notably between cotton and groundnuts. And not least, advances per se need to be seen as part of a much broader credit nexus that developed in tandem with the deepening crisis within the peasantry as a whole. Where producers enter into commodity production through merchant middlemen who advance to secure crop sale, it is inevitable that households should turn to these same agents for productive or consumptive loans. The loans—either in cash or kind—can be paid either by presale of corn or export crops at predetermined but usually undervalued prices, or at usurious interest rates in cash or commodity form, the value of the latter determined at the time of delivery.

The sheer magnitude of advances by the trading firms in view of the frailty of legally binding credit enforcement was quite extraordinary. In the early 1930s, an average firm engaged in groundnut purchases advanced in the order of £30,000 per season, of which as much as £8,000 might be made available to the larger Syrian merchants; this capital was then used for local-level Hausa *dan baranda* middlemen, village and district heads, and wealthy villagers who attempted to secure the crop as it was raised. The quantities of money advanced to local agents obviously varied considerably, but in the late 1930s A.D.O. Hall estimated that a large groundnut dan baranda might receive £800 per season. The Resident of Sokoto alleged several years before that district heads engaged in the cotton trade regularly received advances in excess of £1,000 (NAK Kadminagric 19735). The crop mortgage system had emerged and proliferated in the fertile laka cotton districts of southern Katsina in the early 1920s; each clerk (*fuloti*) of the firms, who received a commission of 12/6d per ton of cotton purchased, advanced loans to five to ten of his *yan baranda*, who were also paid on a commission basis. The filoti offices opened prior to the official buying season (usually December 1st), perhaps in October when food and tax requirements needed to be met. The dan baranda made use of the preharvest cash-hunger by making loans to secure the cotton crop in the face of competition from other agents. If the crop failed, the dan baranda and the clerk had the security of interest on the cash loan. The dan baranda had a monopoly until the loan was paid off and the middlemen took advantage of this dependency, since "the farmer sells 15/- or £1's worth of cotton before he is told that he has repaid [the] 10/- debt" (NAK Katprof 234). In Katsina emirate, the emir had ruled that by Mohammedan law loans could not be made on the security of standing crops, but the provincial resident reported in the 1940s that

> lenders now make loans without mention of security [in order] to bring action for recovery.... However they seldom resort to the Courts... in fact the majority of them... prefer that a portion [of the loan] is outstanding so as to retain hold over the borrowed. [NAK SNP 17 1864]

Advances continued unabated. In 1949, 80 percent of UAC purchases were financed by capital loaned to middlemen (Hogendorn 1978, p. 143); in 1956 Baldwin's survey of firms estimated that 94 percent of export crop purchases were procured by advances through 950 middlemen, 2,500 agents, and 4,500 buyer boys. By December of the purchasing season, £1 million was outstanding.

Producers could, of course, circumvent the yan baranda altogether by marketing direct to the fuloti, assuming there was no demand for short-term loans. In fact the situation was far more complicated since, as the emir of Katsina noted, the middlemen were active year-round using their own capital, and exploiting the scarcity of cash for ceremonial occasions and other reproductive needs. By the depression, there were at least three credit avenues. First, were crop "future" purchases against cash loans during the wet season. As Giles described it in 1937,

> a merchant says he will lend [the peasant] so much and hands him a sack or bowl; the loan is to be repaid by so many measures at a certain price... it is of course assumed that the grower will fill the sack... but if his crops fail he will not be let off the bargain. [Giles, R. H. MSS Afr. S. 887, p. 44]

Second, foodstuffs were purchased prior to maturity as the crop began to ripen (*farkon gyartuwa*). Premature crop purchase usually necessitated losses of 30 to 50 percent over anticipated harvest price levels. And third, was the advance system in its classical mode. The pervasiveness of rural indebtedness was brought home in Giles's study in the late 1930s, commissioned by the colonial administration for a major cotton growing area in Zaria emirate (table 5.12). His study revealed an incidence of indebtedness between 30 and 42 percent of all households; at least one-third of all families faced a recurrent reproduction crisis that was resolved through borrowing. This is hardly surprising in view of Forde's interwar assessment of northeast Zaria.

> No close estimate of the extent of corn borrowing in north-eastern Zaria was made. But it was sufficiently general to indicate that, with abundant land and reasonable fertility, a very considerable proportion of farming households fail to produce crops sufficient to build up reserves of the food staple to meet their regular subsistence needs. [Forde 1946, p. 162]

Table 5.12 indicates that food, tax, and marriage expenses constituted the principal motives for borrowing,[26] that the majority of loans were taken in cash form, and that local hamlet or village heads were instrumental in securing creditors, working on a commission basis for the canteen clerks. Loans were generally secured in two important ways. First by mortgaging invested crops to farmer-traders in return for grain, principally during the wet season when labor demands prevented local sale of labor power. Grain, up to five or ten bundles, was borrowed and repaid in cash or kind several months later at harvest time. According to Forde (1946, p. 167) the usual rate of interest on these grain transactions (generally referred to as *kudin falle*) was "one bundle for two to be repaid at harvest." And second, by advances from produce buyers or clerks against unharvested crops. In this case, the interest was compounded in several ways; either the debtor faced short-weighting or uncompetitive pricing,[27] or, since buyers rarely advanced full cash loans, the farmer was forced to accept overpriced credit in kind, particularly cloth, which was then sold on the market at a loss. Usurious lending[28] under conditions of considerable insecurity, low agricultural productivity, and limited capital quickly devolved into chronic cyclical indebtedness.

> To repay at this rate of interest (100%) often means that the farmer will be short of corn again next year . . . [but] the farmer *must* have corn and may be paid to take 5 bundles for 10, but he recognises it as an injurious transaction. Hence some men prefer to get by working on other men's farms . . . [but] it is only employed when you have been unable to borrow corn. [NAK Zariaprof 1486A/1937]

The rapid proliferation of rural indebtedness quickly reached crisis proportions. During the 1940s public outcry surfaced on the pages of the

TABLE 5.12

LOANS AND CREDIT: ZARIA PROVINCE, ABOUT 1935

Statements of typical canteen clerks operating in cotton-buying areas

Loan details	Local opinion	A	B	C	D
Why taken	Food, tax, clothes, marriage	Hamlet head takes £5–£30 from clerk for tax payment. Farmers borrow from hamlet head at usurious rates.	Hamlet head takes up to £20 from the clerk; repaid in kind after the cotton harvest.	Hamlet head takes £7–£15 for his area. He directs farmers to sell their cotton to the clerk who lent him the money.	Lends to hamlet head or merchants who will in turn lend to farmers. The hamlet heads direct the farmers to the clerk after the cotton harvest.
How taken	25% in kind 75% in cash	60% in cash, 40% in kind. Loans in kind resold at less than par often to the money-lenders.	75% in cash, 25% in kind. Goods borrowed in the local market, especially salt.	Cash and salt. The latter sold at prices 10–15% below their cost price. Mallam C loaned £300 to 600 farmers in 1935–36.	Cash. £5–£11 to the hamlet head, £5 to farmers and up to £10 to middlemen.
Repayment	25% not recovered by fixed date, 5% never recovered.	30% not recovered after a good season, 40% after a bad one. More trouble from the hamlet heads than from farmers.	10% not recovered in normal year, 5% never recovered.	20% not recovered from farmers in a good year. 20% not recovered from middlemen. But much of this is regained from them in the following year after court proceedings.	10% of loans to farmers not recovered in a good year but it is usually regained the next year; 15–20% default by middlemen, most of which is finally recovered.

SOURCE: L. Giles (1937, p. 42).

leading northern Nigerian daily newspaper, *Gaskiya ta fi kwabo*, which referred to "general profligacy," "falling social standards," and the "evils of debt." Much of the discord that surrounded the public interchange on debt centered on the emergence of a salaried administrative class in the northern provinces and the burgeoning southern populations in the Sabon Gari townships. The NA officials quickly built up a reputation as "sons of debt" (*yan albashi*) for their tendency to consume in advance and incur heavy short-term *hiyal*-type debts. A further study in the late 1940s by a provincial agricultural office confirmed the excessively high interest rates among Syrian, Hausa, and southern clerks (NAK Argungu NA 1284). The Governor of the North was somewhat distraught by the debt furor and not unexpectedly haunted by the specter of the Indian experience.

> The conditions described in the All India Credit Survey are in general very similar to those that exist in the northern Region of Nigeria. It is common knowledge that a very large proportion of agricultural communities make a habit of mortgaging crops . . . and such high rates of interest are charged that it becomes extremely difficult for the victim ever to escape the clutches of this creditor. [NAK SNP MSNC 1358 1955, p. 36]

It is in this light that one can readily comprehend the colonial government's enthusiasm in the 1930s to Strickland's proposal for West African cooperatives, which was designed in some measure to remedy the ills of usury (Adeyeye 1978). However, the northern Nigerian cooperative movement failed in its efforts both to alleviate the impasse of rural credit and to improve agricultural productivity in the face of the contradiction between increasing commodity production and attempted self-sufficiency in foodstuffs. Instead, the Agricultural Permanent Secretary observed in 1955 that

> until steps are taken to break the moneylenders domination, little progress can be expected from the co-operatives. [NAK MSWC 1358 1955, p. 29]

It was, nevertheless, the tepid reception and ineffectual implementation of the cooperatives plus the rising tide of discontent concerning debt that prompted a further rural credit survey. Finally, in the late 1950s, Vigo collected data from 37 different villages and questioned 2,400 individuals (NAK MSWC 1358/s.1, vol. 1). Vigo's painstaking study, abstracted in table 5.13, simply confirmed most of the worst fears and suspicions held during the 1920s and 1930s.[29] The survey findings, although confined to Katsina, Sokoto, Bauchi, and Bornu, captured perfectly the general conditions of subsistence in security and food under production for the rural poor as they had emerged during the interwar years. Vigo's principal findings were as follows:

1. The period of maximum indebtedness occurred during the pre-harvest months, especially May–August.

TABLE 5.13
RURAL INDEBTEDNESS IN NORTHERN NIGERIA, 1956

Village Debt Data	Katsina	Sokoto	Bauchi	Bornu	All Areas
No. of villages	8	10	9	10	37
No. of informants	600	650	550	600	2,400
No. in debt	281	502	456	389	1,628
% in debt	47	77	83	65	68
Sources (%)					
Traders	39.9	56.7	53.5	42.2	48.9
Canteens	10.9	2.2	–	.5	4.2
Produce buyers	1.4	3.9	.1	.7	1.3
Cooperatives	6.9	1.3	–	.1	2.0
Relations	12.3	19.3	24.8	20.5	19.9
Friends	9.8	16.5	21.7	35.5	19.0
Village heads	10.1	.1	–	.1	2.5
Unspecified	8.7	–	–	.4	2.2
Purposes (%)					
Food	22.2	43.6	53.2	67.4	47.2
Clothing	6.4	5.8	9.2	12.1	8.5
Fines or taxes	.7	.5	.6	.5	.6
Manure	.5	.1	.1	.2	.2
Labor	15.7	12.6	18.3	7.1	13.7
Farm expenses	4.2	6.3	3.7	1.9	4.0
Ceremonies	15.3	19.2	12.9	4.7	12.8
Unspecified	35.0	11.9	2.0	6.1	13.0
Rates of Interest (%)					
Nil	1.0	.3	–	–	.1
50–55	–	–	–	–	–
55–60	–	–	–	–	–
60–70	7.7	–	–	–	.3
70–80	–	4.2	–	22.0	10.1
80–90	39.6	18.4	11.7	20.0	18.1
90–100	27.1	77.1	64.5	–	39.0
Over 100	24.6	–	23.8	58.0	32.4
Total	100.0%	100.0%	100.0%	100.0%	100.0%

SOURCE: A. Vigo (1958, pp. 23–46).

2. Sources of credit were principally traders and merchants (48.9 percent).

3. Interest rates were without exception high, and indebtedness as a proportion of village adults quite frequently in excess of 70 percent.

4. Farmers were often "compelled to dispose of foodstuffs to clear debt."

5. Crop pledging was "common everywhere," and "too much emphasis is placed on the cultivation of cash crops. Shortage of grain was one of the primary reasons for indebtedness."

6. Grain production had fallen and continued to fall due to lack of fixed prices.

Vigo's study stands in sharp contradistinction to Giles's credit survey in the 1930s. While food (46 percent) and ceremonies (13 percent) remained important items for initiating loans, the extent of indebtedness had grown considerably, reaching 83 and 77 percent respectively of all informants interviewed in Sokoto and Bauchi provinces. In addition, the 1957 data revealed new trends in both sources and uses of credit; with respect to the farmer, produce buyers and canteens had declined significantly, compensated by village traders who had grown to absorb a greater proportion of credit activity (48 percent of all loans). Coterminous with the transformation of loans sources was the demise of export commodities as loan security; the mortgaging of cotton and groundnuts had in fact fallen to 13 percent by the time Vigo conducted his study. Equally, only 5.3 percent of all loans were repaid in agricultural export commodities, while cash repayments had climbed dramatically to 48 percent. Perhaps most striking of all was the usurious nature of interest rates—almost three quarters (71 percent) of which were in excess of 90 percent—and the emergence of rural wage labor; 13.7 percent of all loans in fact were made ostensibly for the purpose of employing farm laborers. A study conducted in 1956 in Dambarta District, Kano Province by the Registrar of Cooperatives confirmed Vigo's findings; in Ajumawa village, the Registrar identified six prominent moneylenders and concluded that

the average peasant farmer was indebted to one of the few wealthy farmers of his village. There are peculiar things about money lending in the rural areas . . . [they] are not professional moneylenders . . . but big farmers who have become rich. These people also practice unpatriotic food hoarding. [NAK Kano Sec 2711/s.2]

The shift in credit relations can be accounted for by the postwar changes in produce marketing. The wartime creation of state monopolies (groundnut and cotton marketing boards) had the effect of displacing European firms and their clerks from their comfortable position in the countryside. Competition between buyers accordingly fell[30] and the state produce boards were not compelled to provide LBAs with advances to procure commodities prior to harvest. While the crop mortgaging system had seen its heyday, Hausa middlemen came to dominate the produce trade as licensed buying agencies interposed between state and rural producers, and rapidly displaced Lebanese and Syrian competitors. The LBAs could compensate for the loss of the traditional advance system by utilizing their local merchant function as a vehicle to fulfill the general demand for credit among the rural producers. The structural conditions that encouraged widespread borrowing were spelled out in a sixteen-village study of Bornu and Bauchi provinces, which indicated 38 and 19 percent respectively of farmers interviewed had exhausted domestic grain reserves prior to the commencement of the farming season (NAK MSWC 1358). By July these figures had leaped to 90 and 94 percent. Under such circumstances, households turned to local farmer-traders as sources of loans to cover domestic needs. Those who, by virtue of their poverty and low credit worthiness, could not raise loans would "seek work on the farms of better off farmers to earn money to buy food, leaving their own fields [untended]" (NAK MSWC 1358/S.5A). Vigo's work pointed strongly to a new commercial hegemony by Hausa buying agents and rich farmer-trader agents, using local capital rather than acting as fronts for the advances by the European firms.

> Moneylenders have agents in villages or districts in which they operate. Usually they have a confederate working with them. Agents living in villages operate through a number of leading farmers called "madugus." They are kept informed of the movements of moneylenders to whom they are attached. . . . Money lenders agents often reside in the same village or area as their clients . . . and therefore know about the state of their crops and their ability to pay at harvest. These agents with the help of harvest heads as well as [madugus] are responsible for repayment of loans. For this service they may have their own loans interest free. [NAK MSWCD 1358/S.5 vol. 1, pp. 35, 36]

In addition, there were "hundreds of itinerant traders [moneylenders]," especially Ibos, who traded year-round in the rich agricultural regions like Kebbi and southern Katsina. Dealing mostly with women, these peripatetic usurers sold goods (cloth, beads, head ties) on short-term credit (8–12 weeks) and collected repayments on a fortnightly basis.

In view of the low proportion (17 percent) of "productive loans," Vigo's report highlighted the extent to which households faced simple reproduction crises on a regular (if not annual) basis. Debts still outstanding in the harvest period were generally extended to the following year rather than negotiated through the native courts, which may cause the moneylender to be faced with the possibility of both losing a client and exposure to public abuse for extortionate interest. The shame (*kunya*) that surrounds all moneylender transactions, for creditor and debtor alike, ensured a marked silence in public discourse; default on debt payment was not in this regard legally enforceable, but large outstanding debts were necessarily carried at the expense of long-term credit worthiness. In conditions of economic insecurity, the inability to command loans in the future should the need arise constituted a fundamental social impediment in the cycle of household reproduction. The creditor (though shackled by Mohammedan law) was satisfied with part repayment since outstanding small debts tied the debtor to him in a quasi-client status. As Vigo observed, "the farmer, like a wound, is best bound."

Vigo's recommendations, which grew naturally out of what he perceived to be the contradictions in the northern Nigerian household economy, were: moneylenders should be controlled by compulsory registration;[31] expanded cooperatives should be established to free the smallholder from "the crushing system of credit"; grain prices should be regulated to prevent the debilitating season price rises, which fell heavily on the poor; and not least, a reorientation should be made away from the priority of export production. Not surprisingly the governmental and ministerial responses to Vigo's survey were uniformly negative. The Ministry of Agriculture defended its position with much passion, rejecting any disinterest in food supplies and arguing rather that the northern region was in food surplus but shackled by the poverty of transport infrastructure (NAK MSWC 1358/S.6, p. 111). The Economic Planning Division, conversely, derived inner strength from other sources; the incidence and structure of debt was after all "no different from any Western country," land pledging was "interesting," cash crop specialization a necessary response to overpopulation, and a purported reduction in export commodity production wholly "contrary to sound economics." All governmental agencies found great solace in the fact that 1957 was a "poor year"—abnormal and untypical as the Agriculture Ministry called it—which demanded that all Vigo's uncomfortable conclusions be treated with considerable reserve. In actual fact, rainfall had been deficient only in Bornu, Bauchi, and Azare, and certainly went some way toward explaining the high incidence of grain shortages in those areas. But more accurately, the 1957 drought threw into sharp relief the structural vulnerability of the entire agrarian sector. On the eve of independence, the colonial government shelved Vigo's potentially subversive report, preferring to adopt a position articulated by Polly Hill twenty years later that "most credit . . . is internally generated . . . [and] universal indebtedness is nothing new" (1972, p. 330).

MARKET INSECURITY AND PRICE VULNERABILITY

The anomaly of the agrarian markets forced the marginal subsistence producers into an unequal exchange relationship through the market. They did not benefit from the market under these circumstances; they were devoured by it. . . . Especially in bad years . . . petty producers were compelled to buy additional grain and go worse into debt. Then in good years and low prices they found it difficult to extricate themselves from . . . accumulated debts.

—Hans Medick

As household production became mediated through a formal price system, and as portions of the harvest were valued at prevailing market-prices, so did security become subject to the irregularities of that system, and absolute value was of less practical importance than real market value. In northern Nigeria where export crops were largely sold to clerks, fuloti, and buying agents, there was no assurance in advance of an adequate return to labor, irrespective of harvest quality.[32] First, insofar as the global commodity market determined the price ceiling for the Hausa peasant's crop he was vulnerable to the insecurity of the market failure. In any case, notwithstanding this variability, rural producers in northern Nigeria received only 26 percent of the total f.o.b. price for export commodities in the early 1930s (Jacob, R. H. MSS Afr. T16, p. 76). And second, blatant exploitation in the actual marketing and sale of export produce further expropriated peasant surpluses, even (and perhaps more so) during recessionary periods. A combination of shortweighing at the scales and underpricing through crop mortgaging conspired to reduce the real value of marketed produce. In 1927, the secretary to the northern provinces estimated that "at least a quarter of the price of the cotton does not reach the producer" (NAK SNP 386/1918, p. 2). As Zaria cotton farmers commented to M.G. Smith in the late 1940's on the cotton scale system: "ba dama: ya wuce sata" ("there's no choice: it's worse than theft").

The relation between local village price and harvest was ruptured, and income frequently varied more or less independently of village production. The amplitude of price variation—not simply for export commodities on a year-to-year basis but also the interseason oscillation of foodstuffs—ensured that peasant income varied within much wider limits on average than in the precolonial period. The entrapment of peasants into a wider global net also rendered households subject to various forms of external perturbations and political insecurity over which they had neither control nor understanding. The case of variability in export prices is perhaps the most dramatic (see figure 5.1). The price of cotton and groundnuts between 1902 and 1921 fell from £220 and £24 per ton respectively to £64 and £21. Ten years later during the depression

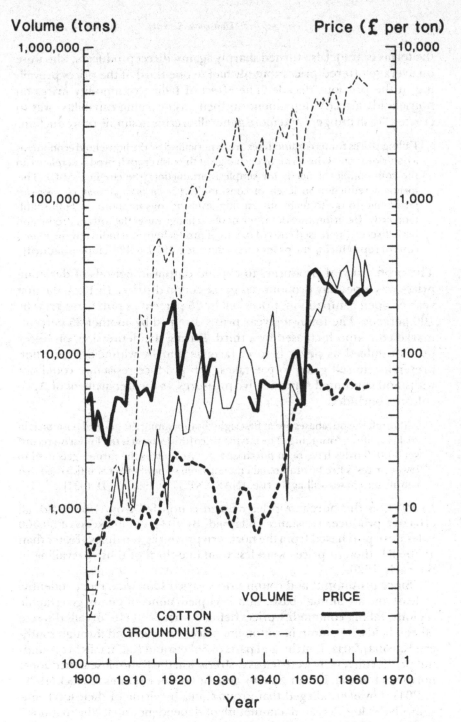

Figure 5.1. Export prices in Nigeria 1900–65. Adapted from Helleiner (1967).

the terms of trade also turned sharply against direct producers, who were on average offered prices roughly half to one-third of the prices prevailing in the previous decade. The effect of falling commodity prices on households already dependent on their cash-earning capability, was to create a "cash hunger" and more generally a crisis in simple reproduction.

> Falling prices for its commodities are experienced by the household economy as a deterioration of the terms of exchange of the cash crops it produces relative to the commodities it needs for simple reproduction (the circuit C-M-C). This means a reduction in levels of consumption *or an intensification of commodity production* (to try to maintain existing levels of consumption), or both simultaneously. Deterioration of the terms of exchange raises the costs of production both directly (increased costs of means of production) and indirectly (increased costs of reproducing the producers). [Bernstein 1979, p. 428, emphasis added]

The propensity of producers to expand output in periods of declining prices was especially pronounced in the cotton districts. In 1924, the first year of open competition, prices fell by 25 percent as purchases grew by 100 percent. The following year prices dropped by another 25 percent; marketed cotton increased by a third. During the depression, producer prices tumbled as never before; farmers initially withheld production preferring to sell grain to pay taxes. But produce resistance could not withstand continued reproductive pressures, as the Department of Agriculture concluded.

> Although the purchases are at first sight disappointing the general position is in reality quite encouraging. The buying price [this] season is the lowest on record yet 14,000 bales have been purchased. . . . As soon as the farmer gets used to lower prices, since he must obtain money from somewhere, it is anticipated that cotton purchases will again rise. [NAK SNP 17 10199 Vol. II 1931]

In 1931, as the purchase price of seed cotton fell from 1/6d to 8d, all effective producer resistance collapsed. By 1934–35 in excess of 50,000 bales were purchased from the northern provinces, ten times greater than 1920–21, though prices were less than one-third of those prevailing in the early 1920s.

Since groundnut and cotton prices varied somewhat independently, at least on an annual basis, and occupied noncontiguous geographic regions, falling commodity prices defined what Scott (1976) calls discrete "shock fields." A slump in cotton lint prices reverberated through southern Katsina, Zaria, Bauchi, and parts of Sokoto and Kano; falls in groundnut prices conversely were felt as cash crises in the Kano close settled zone, northern Katsina, Bornu, Sokoto, and the border emirates. Lubeck (1979, p. 201), however, alleged that groundnuts, by virtue of their local consumptive value, "created a minimum of dependency on its fluctuations." But by the 1930s, Kano producers depended *completely* on groundnuts for tax payment (NAK SNP 17 14686 Vol. I); consumption of groundnuts may have prevented short-term starvation but did not, as Lubeck (1979) suggests, "reinforce the stability of the system." Rather its incorporation as a commodity into the cycle of household reproduction amplified the likelihood of instability in the form of Bernstein's "reproduction squeeze." In times of favorable prices, producers stood to benefit, meeting ceremonial, tax, grain, and household expenditures and perhaps even accumulating a small cash reserve. In times of falling producer prices, groundnut producers could even benefit from the illicit international trade, smuggling their produce into Niger where prices might be marginally higher, as appeared to be the case irregularly between 1939 and 1951 (Collins 1974, 1976). To talk of a minimum dependency, nonetheless, is highly spurious.

STATE CRISES AND STATE DEMANDS

All this means . . . that the relative autonomy of the . . . State stems precisely from the contradictory relations of class power between the different social classes.

—Nicos Poulantzas

Northern Provinces' exported produce prices fell from an index of 100 in 1926 to 37 in 1933 . . . The direct taxes proposed for the Provinces for 1933/34 was £1.337 millions, or nearly 35% over [the 10% maximum].

—S. M. Jacob

The Nigerian colonial state internalized the contradictions embodied in Lugard's *Dual Mandate*. On one hand, it acted as an agent of metropolitan capital, and on the other, as a supervisor of tensions internal to the colony itself. In acting as the guarantor of social order the colonial state had to contend with conflicts generated within Nigeria as a function of its support for European trade expansion. In this regard the state expressed a measure of autonomy with regard to the prevailing mercantile class domination. Of course it intervened directly and extensively in the economic life of the colony to further trade, but as Lonsdale and Berman (1979, p. 490) observed, the state cannot be the obedient servant of capital, "only the protector of capitalist social relations." The imperial demand for self-sufficiency gave the Nigerian government a primordial interest in direct taxation to finance NA expenditures and salaries for political officers. The state actively assisted merchant capital (the European firms in particular) and could partially fulfill its own demands for revenue in doing so. The state's self-interest with revenue, so clearly spelled out by Lugard, was not entirely compatible, however, with the European firms' bias toward the genesis of a domestic market for cheap imports because a heavy tax burden necessarily reduced local purchasing power. Nonetheless, the imperial preoccupation with self-finance and law and order—its own demands for survival and reproduction—provides the context for understanding the latent tensions between the firms and the bureaucracy and the steady growth of the direct tax burden. While direct taxes constituted only 15 percent of Nigerian government revenue, the tax bill—which amounted to more than £2 millions by 1930—amounted to a significant proportion of household income. Table 5.14, using tax data from Daura emirate covering the period 1911 to 1961, depicts the relationship between taxation and the terms of trade with millet and groundnuts. The onerousness of taxes, which grew in a quantitative sense throughout the colonial period, vacillated in real terms in relation to prevailing crop and consumer prices. In the depression, the terms of exchange turned sharply against the taxpayer; the postwar years seem by comparison relatively prosperous. Whether rural producers suffered material impoverishment through fiscal demands was to a large extent dependent upon the degree of unequal exchange by merchant capital. As Bryceson observed,

> peasants could receive a fair return based on average socially necessary labor time in exchange of their commodities if the struggle between capital and the peasantry had reached a point where it was advantageous for the state to safeguard peasant commodity production against excessive merchant profits. [Bryceson 1980, p. 283]

In Nigerian Hausaland, the colonial state actively intervened in support of peasant commodity production by attempting to regulate the pernicious advance system, refusing to grant the BCGA their demand of tax payment in cotton lint, experimenting with mixed farming (during the interwar years), supporting cooperatives and small-scale resettlement, and finally, establishing state marketing boards in the postwar period. I pursue these themes in more detail in the following chapter, arguing that these interventions and regulations need to be seen in relation to the structural weakness of rural producers. But the reproductive requirements of the state apparatus generated a single-minded preoccupation with tax revenue, even to the extent that huge NA reserves accumulated during the 1930s. It is the effect of this neurotic fiscal obsession that concerns me here; this is not to argue that the realization of subsistence was not jeopardized by the irregularities of the market, the unequal exchange perpetrated by merchant transactions, or the vagaries of Sudanic climate. Rather, the centrality of taxation for households and provincial administrations alike warrants separate treatment in regard to the residuum of the moral economy. I emphasize three specific attributes of revenue and the claims of the state, which suggest that the *quantitative* burden of taxation may be eclipsed in importance by its form, timing, and rigidity.

TABLE 5.14
TAX AND GROUNDNUT-MILLET TERMS OF TRADE: DAURA EMIRATE

Year	Tax per adult male s	Tax per adult male d	Millet price per lb in pence	Groundnut price per lb in pence	lbs of millet to cover tax	lbs of groundnut to cover tax
1911/12	3	6	0.1	0.44	420	93
1923/24	7	4	0.33	1.3	270	67
1934/35	9	1	0.66	0.3	165	363
1950/51	11	7	1.6	2.3	86	60
1951/52	12	8	1.7	3.9	89	40
1960/61	25	10	2.2	3.7	136	81

SOURCE: M. G. Smith (1978); NAK KAT. Div. KAT-FOO 2 1964; NAK Kadminagric. 1/1 9101 Vol. I, 1937; NAK SNP 9/10 3267/1923; NAK SNP 7/10 1872/1911.

MONETIZATION AND THE DISSOLUTION OF ZAKKAT

The Koranic grain tithe (zakka or zakkat) levied on all households to the tune of one-tenth of all guinea corn and millet production continued to be collected after 1903. Hewby (NAK SNP 111/1908) felt, however, that zakka had never been honestly paid or uniformly collected; doubtless the problem of transportation made for limited transit, substandard quality of grain, and ample opportunity for extortion. Palmer (NAK Katprof 1289) complained bitterly that zakka could only be collected after the guinea corn harvest, and dragged on into the dry season when many men were absent on cin rani. Taxes in kind were, moreover, hardly compatible with colonial needs for monetization, which had to proceed hand in hand with commodity production if the much vaunted "trade economy" was to be established on a firm footing. Within the first decade zakka was accordingly commuted to a cash payment and absorbed into the new farm tax; in the Kano districts this commutation was initiated in 1909, and a year earlier in Katsina. The gradual proliferation of specie was at the expense of a ready-made cereal supply, and indeed undermined the precolonial birane granaries. In light of the growing NA food demands, the bad press which zakka received is all the more paradoxical; Palmer, in fact, subsequently lamented the passing of the traditional grain levies.

> It would be a boon to have a great reserve of grain store, to be sold off gradually throughout the year, thus ensuring a constant supply of grain in the wet season when, as is known, there is often a serious shortage in Kano. [NAK SNP 10 951/1911]

In some peripheral districts, zakka was still collected in spite of logistical problems following the First World War (NAK SNP 9 179p/1918), and much of what came to be institutional grain requisitioning was in actual fact justified by the NAs as zakka under another name. But the clear preference for negotiable tax payments undermined the famine-relief grain reserve; indeed, it is remarkable in view of the shortage of cereals that plagued most provincial administrations, and the occasional desultory discussion of grain storage systems, that the resurrection of taxes in kind was never seriously considered.

THE MAGNITUDE AND RIGIDITY OF THE TAX BURDEN

In sharp contrast to the precolonial Caliphal revenue system, colonial taxes were regular, predictable, and above all rigid. This fiscal inflexibility (largely in response to the high proportion of administrative fixed costs, particularly European salaries) took no account of the vagaries of Hausa life, such as late rains, locusts, price variability, disease, and personal calamity. The unyielding character of colonial tax policy stood in contradistinction to the precolonial jekada system which, as Palmer (Lands Committee 1910, p. 69) acknowledged, "could strike off a certain amount of taxes in the event of a harvest shortfall." Though surely not innocent of extortion, the jekadas graduated taxes with respect to local circumstances, a capacity predicated on an acute understanding of village life, and firmly grounded in a knowledge of village administration and the value of other sources of government revenue—notably slavery and trade.

Colonial taxes, however, were cast in view of the procedures and method by which they were computed and collected. The state was in many respects a bureaucratic sloth and functioned through an unwieldy web of ordinances, rules, and laws. It was centrally administered by a cadre of political officers who of necessity, given the enormity of their task and limited financial resources, were horrendously overworked and wholly incapable of coming to terms with the problems of several districts, let alone entire emirates. The implications of these administrative pathologies were most pronounced in the realm of revenue assessment, upon which taxable capability was ultimately based. During the first decade, prior to the adoption of an Indian model of revenue assessment by the Lands Committee, the protectorate taxation system was an arabesque mosaic of confusion. Taxes were amalgamated, dropped, and resurrected with great abandon; a compound tax introduced in 1909 by Temple in Kano to solve the nonresident taxpayer issue and to strengthen the dagaci in the face of widespread cheppa (patronage) ties, fizzled in 1917. Kudin shuka and kudin rafi taxes on nongrain crops and irrigated plots both experienced checkered histories, sometimes levied per unit area, occasionally on furrow length (NAK SNP 10 2607/1909), and ultimately abolished due to embezzlement and the need to encourage fadama cultivation. Even the kudin kassa seemed remarkably unstandardized (Hill 1977, p. 50). With the area-based taki (farm measurement) system, and later the lump-sum assessment, the entire tax process though relatively formalized in theory was in practice somewhat arbitrary. Witness, for instance, the following candid anecdote from Lethem, one of the most able of political officers, concerning his assessment of Fika:

> His Honour's comments on my Fika report were very funny . . . he . . . said it was the best assessment report he had seen from Bornu . . . which—remembering my eyewash and tongue in cheek method—will tickle you as much as it does me. [cited in Heussler 1968, p. 59]

The practical implication was that the establishment of a reasonable tax estimate with due regard to net income was simply shooting in the dark. Temple for example remarked in a 1909 Annual Report for Kano (NAK SNP 6/5 44/1909) that the peasantry were paying tax "without demur" yet the massive rural exodus from the province into the border emirates in that year was due to the excessively high tax incidence. Migration in fact proved to be the litmus for the revenue experiment; short of rural rebellion, household mobility in the early years was a sensitive barometer for the prevailing tax burden.

Another point that amplifies the dubious character of assessment pertains to the procedure by which fragmented "fiefs" were transformed into contiguous districts. For revenue purposes these districts were treated as relatively homogenous regions, which meant quite simply that crucial microvariations in ecological conditions (soil, cropping patterns, and so on) were glossed over in order to create a uniform classification conducive to manageable administration. Once again, in practical terms this boiled down to a "representative village problem"; assessment was conducted at the district level from which a small sample of representative rural communities were selected. From household computations of agricultural and industrial income, each village was granted a lump-sum assessment to be allocated by the village or hamlet head in relation to his estimation of household income. Yet as Edwardes wrote in 1917,

> The variety of methods employed to arrive at the taxable capacity of the village is remarkable. . . . In only two cases have the officers compared their estimate of total yield with the total consumption of the inhabitants, in no case has an officer suggested that the corn produced in the district was insufficient for the feeding of the people though in nine cases production works out at less than consumption. [R. H. MSS Afr. 769, p. 123]

The arbitrariness and the inequity of local tax distribution was replicated at the provincial level. Not unnaturally, Residents were granted a large measure of autonomy in order to adapt procedures to cultural or historical variability within and between different emirates. But this necessary devolution of power, in conjunction with the confusion and ignorance surrounding the tax questions, made for extraordinary regional varia-

tion. In 1910, Palmer noted that the tax burden upon the Katsina peasantry was more than double that levied on their "wealthy and prudent"
Kano brethren! The abolition of the jekadas and their replacement by an
"alien" if resident hakimi, was also of some consequence for peasant
security. While the Caliphate administrators found it prudent to adjust
their claims as local circumstances demanded, the new agents imposed by
the colonialists had less interest in maintaining local support. They rose
or fell according to their efficacy in pleasing their bureaucratic superiors.
The survival of the district heads was contingent upon the pacification of
the provincial Resident through efficient bookkeeping and the maximization of tax receipts. Emirate revenue increased steadily as the means of
collection was tightened and as individual tax burdens were regularly
raised through district reassessment. Yet the distinctiveness of colonial
taxation rested not so much on the magnitude per se but in the form of
those taxes and the rigor with which they were instituted.

The likelihood of overassessment and the accuracy of tax computation was not altogether ignored by the Colonial Office since it simultaneously posed the threat of rural rebellion in an area without a standing
army, and presented a contradiction with the alleged support of merchant capital. The Lands Committee members, especially Wedgwood and
Digges La Touche, rigorously interrogated Temple on this point,
inquiring whether an individual farmer who considered himself overassessed might have a right of appeal (Lands Committee 1910, p. 86).
Temple naively believed that such an appeal lay in the lands of the
hakimi. The Chairman was, however, skeptical.

> 615. (*Chairman*) Do you think that you can rely on the right of appeal? Has
> the village headmen any power or any means of making it so disagreeable for
> the appellant as to deter him from exercising the right of appeal? You see what I
> mean?—Yes.
>
> 616. Would the people as a matter of fact freely exercise the right of
> appeal?—Yes. *They do appeal very readily against the village headman, but not so
> willingly against the Emir, or district headman.* My point is that we have to trust to
> the village headman in any case.
>
> 617. You have to trust the village headman, but your real check on the village
> headman, as I understand, is the accessibility of a Court of Appeal?—Yes.
> [Lands Committee, 1910, p. 86, emphasis added].

Temple's convictions naturally sound hollow in light of the control exercised by the emirs over the election of village and district heads and the
pervasiveness of what political officers referred to as "peasant passivity."
M. G. Smith (1955) noted for instance the tactics by which rural bureaucrats could prevent the public expression of local discontent. In the face of
the dominant position of rural masu sarauta and their complicity with the

palace cliques, Temple's expectation that overassessed masu gidaje
would, of their own volition, approach emir, Resident, or district officer
was wholly unrealistic. Mr. Morison recognized as much (Lands Committee 1910, p. 86) when he suggested in any case that a peasant's right of
appeal was contingent upon an understanding of the principles upon
which taxation was imposed and assessed. Temple responded that it
would be impossible to "educate the natives on [the tax] principles" (1910,
p. 86), in large measure because the principles were in large measure
unknown to the colonial officers themselves!

For the majority of the northern provinces, then, the colonial land
taxes were strikingly regressive, consisting of fixed annual levies bearing
little relation to taxable capacity or subsistence security. Kudin kassa and
amalgamated *kudin arziki* taxes, though hardly as incidious as the poll tax
system of the French territories, were nevertheless based on assessed
acreage subject to average yields. Taxes, in other words, constituted a
fixed proportion of production independent of variability in wealth, since
taxes were collected on the basis of agricultural wealth, "it is not so much
in the nature of the rich man paying more, as of the man who has . . .
more land paying more" (Lands Committee 1910, p. 78). The tax burden
thus fell particularly heavily on those with large farms in the low-fertility
districts. Palmer was even more sanguine, confiding to the Lands Committee (1910, p. 78) that the institution of a graduated income tax was
"quite impossible." It is all the more significant that assessment was
enacted without reference to variable harvest quality; tax revenues in fact
exhibited quite remarkable stability in relation to crop yields. Table 5.15
shows clearly how tax revenue in Katsina emirate, irrespective of harvest
quality or commodity prices, grew consistently between 1910 and 1924. In
this respect Mary Bull is quite correct in her surmise that in northern
Nigeria

> revenue figures were commonly taken as the yardstick by which to measure the
> success of the [colonial] administration, both because they indicated progress
> towards financial self-sufficiency, and because of the general belief that only by
> paying taxes did the African acknowledge himself to be under the control of
> government [Bull 1963, p. 79].

Kudin kassa represented a substantial proportion of total household
income since district officers generally determined tax at 10 to 15 percent
of gross annual family income, which frequently amounted to 20 percent
or more of net returns. In 1908, a year of poor rainfall and harvest
shortfall, Festing estimated, for example, that taxation amounted to 50
percent of gross household income (NAK SNP 7 5490/1908). By the
1930s, Jacob (R. H. MSS Afr. 5769, p. 105) estimated in his report on
taxation for the Colonial Office that rural producers paid a minimum of

TABLE 5.15
KATSINA DIVISION: ANNUAL TAX RETURNS

Source	1910–11	1913	1915	1917	1919	1921–22	1923–24	% increase 1910–1924
Direct tax (£)	18,741	23,189	28,874	37,762	50,605	53,147	44,910	140%
Adult males	149,612	158,083	216,180	201,580	208,904	211,017	193,211	40%
Total population	386,841	441,422	516,587	570,974	no data	792,165	716,455	88%

SOURCE: Katsina Museum, File 1629, Tax Returns.

30 percent of their net income to the state; in several cases the direct taxes amounted to almost double that figure.

The administration's concern with fiscal rigor and detail extended to the actual process of tax collection, enforcement and administration. The *beit-el-mal* was the embodiment of this concern, its establishment marking the rapid and continued growth in revenue that was the hallmark of overrule. As Fika (1978, p. 130) observed, no amount was considered too small or insignificant, "even small returns of revenue were considered good per se." The degree of slippage was reduced as the colonial apparatus plundered the North, as much through the reams of NA paperwork as through military hardware. To document the consolidation of the colonial state is to follow the inexorable progress of surveys, settlement reports, and a growing body of regulations. The bureaucratic state reached its zenith with the Kano land revenue survey, which unlike its *taki* predecessor, strove to record the size, status, and productivity of each farm holding. Generally, however, the extent to which assessment actually pursued the modalities of household income is a model of compulsiveness. A district assessment by Mr. Harris in Marusu District, Katsina in 1920 is exemplary in this respect; dry-season irrigation (*lambu*) incomes, which were subsumed by the industrial tax (*kudin masu sana'a*), was based on average onion production of 20,026 per acre, and of 23 tobacco leaves per plant! Annual sylvan productivity, mind-boggling calculations of goat fecundity, the annual number of haircuts per barber, and the seasonal yields of fish were all entered into a vast budgeting exercise. In the interest of moral turpitude, Mr. Harris even instituted a tax of 3/- per person on "*banzan gori*," that is, people who "sponge on friends" (NAK Kat. Loc. Auth. HIS/40 1920).

As I detail in the following chapter, the oppressive character of colonial revenue systems was not received without a measure of peasant resistance (Fika 1978, p. 140), albeit in terms that could hardly be labeled rural rebellion. The important point is that colonial commitment to stable income for its own reproductive demands placed additional burdens on household security. This commitment, often in the face of merchant opposition, explains the warped reasoning of increasing tax levies during and after subsistence crises in order to compensate for loss of administrative revenue.

THE TIMING OF TAX COLLECTION

In simplifying Caliphal taxes, provincial governments also sought to regularize the collection periods, ostensibly to be congruent with the budgeting procedures of the fiscal year. The British in northern Nigeria imposed tax collection dates, however, with scant regard for household needs in relation to the agricultural cycle. Tax payment dates, like everything else, actually varied considerably between provinces, usually falling somewhere between August and February. A memorandum on the timing of tax collection, circulated to agricultural departments in 1937 (NAK Kadminagric. 3503, vol. 1) illuminated the difficulties that arose from overly eager revenue officials in the southern Katsina and Zaria cotton belts, where tax collectors moved into the countryside during November, at least two months prior to the sale of the cotton lint.

> The influence of tax collection on agricultural practice is that many farmers are attacked when they are least prepared to pay tax i.e. when their cash crops are not ready for the market. In such cases they are compelled to dispose for cash whatever they can sell. . . . Guineacorn . . . is frequently sold by a farmer against his will . . . [which] is a staple crop which if sold has to be bought again at all costs . . . [groundnuts] are sold either when they are not fully matured . . . or properly dried, thereby depressing their commercial value. [NAK Kadminagric. 3503 vol. 1]

The timing problem was certainly not new. Resident Orr urged in 1906 that collection be pushed back from October–November to January–February, after harvests were completed (NAK SNP 7 4867/1907). By the 1930s early tax collection either prompted early crop sale or—as was frequently the case in the cotton districts—pushed rural producers headlong into the eager hands of the buying agents who advanced money or paid taxes in return for crop sale. The Katsina administration refrained from any action on the grounds that the period of budgeting was relatively fixed, and because "the system [of advances] . . . only results in short-term indebtedness" (NAK Kadminagric. 2503, vol. 1). In the 1940s it was paradoxically the Association of West African Merchants who intervened, also arguing that early tax collection in Katsina provoked indebtedness. Not unnaturally, their interest lay entirely in irrecoverable capital, which the firms themselves had fronted (NAK Kanoprof 211/1944).

The consistent rejection of a later tax collection date by Crown Counsel and provincial Residents alike, placed a special temporal constraint on household reproduction. The quantitative aspects of direct taxation were, in this sense, of less significance than the biological cycle of agricultural production. Seasonality meant that the smallholder had little choice but to sell grains when prices were lowest—only to be repurchased at inflated "hunger season" prices—or alternatively to submit to the usurious practice of crop mortgaging and moneylending against future crops. The groundnut zone was, to a degree, less vulnerable to the fiscal machinations of the colonial state since the harvest followed closely on the heels of the millets and sorghums. Yet here too the pattern was far from uniform; Sokoto Province, for instance, progressively advanced the collection date during the first twenty-five years of colonial rule until, during the 1930s, taxes were gathered during August and September, prior to the harvests of both cotton and groundnuts (NAK Kadminagric. 3503 vol. 1, 1937).

CONCLUSION

To the already considerable risks of drought, flood, pests, and plant disease the colonial economy added price fluctuations and credit crises. Returning to the felicitous metaphor of Tawney, it is as if the colonial government had found a peasant smallholder up to his neck in water and had first proceeded, by its tax policy, to raise the water level to just beneath his nose and then, by integrating him into a cash economy, to increase the wave action enough to drown him.

—James Scott

The emergence of commodity production in northern Nigeria cannot be simply identified with colonialism per se since peasants in the Sokoto Caliphate were, to some degree, producing exchange-values. Nonetheless, in the rural sphere the production of use-values was dominant. Colonialism, then, is perhaps empirically captured not so much by the destruction of natural economy as by the *intensification of commodity production*, and more specifically by a change in the conditions of peasant reproduction. I have argued that the colonial state working through class alliances played a crucial role in reorganizing the conditions of exploitation of the Nigerian rural producer and establishing the basis for capital accumulation. As Lenin and Kautsky both pointed out, there is not one model that explains the conditions under which capital confronts and transforms precapitalist agriculture. In northern Nigeria, the hegemony of European merchant capital in conjunction with a coercive colonial state established the historical conditions under which commodity production was intensified. These new conditions involved the withdrawal of labor from use-value production, and the monetization of some—if not most—of the elements of household reproduction, which projected rural producers further into production for exchange. The generality of commoditization in the northern provinces progressed rapidly; the household budgetary data provided by Forde (1946) indicate that cash earnings constituted at least 50 percent of total household income by the 1930s. But within peasant households, food production remained a short-term possibility.

In this chapter, however, I have been less concerned with the nature of capital and peasantry in northern Nigerian than with the general impact of capital on peasant security, and in particular the risks of hunger and starvation vis-a-vis physical vagaries. The insular world of the gidaje and the kyauta was disrupted; commodity production acted to individualize households as units of production and reproduction. Moreover, the continued dependence of rural producers on a precapitalist agricultural technology perpetuated their vulnerability to natural calamities. To this was added the irregularities of the market, the vicissitudes of the price system, the unequal exchange and usurious behavior of merchant capital, and the persistent pressure of demographic growth and land fragmentation. The realization of subsistence was, then, in considerable jeopardy. Indeed, I have suggested that for large sections of the Hausa peasantry, the margin of subsistence security was progressively undermined by a retarded capitalism; the bases of the moral economy were eroded in a significant way. To return to the earlier motif, colonialism transformed the adaptive structure of the Sokoto Caliphate; in complicated and often contradictory ways, colonialism dissolved many of the response systems that served to buffer households from the vagaries of a harsh and variable semiarid environment. In addition to the risks of ecological variability and limited technological development, the colonial economy simultaneously weakened social relations and imposed new burdens associated with export price oscillations, indebtedness, and rigid tax levies. Peasant income in the colonial era fluctuated within much wider limits than in the Caliphate era, a tendency exacerbated during periods of global depression. Colonial fiscal policy ate into the already marginal family budgets of some rural producers. The fixed charges imposed upon householders during periods of intense economic recession caused severe reproductive crises, and in some cases outright ruin. The patterns of change that I have documented not only altered the extent of hunger in a statistical sense but changed its very etiology. The genesis of famine, which I pursue in the following chapter, came to reflect the changing process of incorporation of Hausa producers into a global division of labor. Northern Nigeria moved from its peripheral position in a vast Muslim diaspora during the nineteenth century to its new niche as a peripheral capitalist formation in a twentieth-century world system.

The crisis in simple household reproduction, which compounded the vulnerability of producers to environmental variability in the face of the low-level development of the forces of production, is highlighted in table 5.16. Both figures (i) and (ii) suggest that necessary consumption was barely matched by household production; in both cases the possibility of household accumulation was low, and under these circumstances the tax burden appears especially onerous. This was notably the case in Bida, where foodstuffs constituted the principal cash-earning commodities. The budgetary data on a model northern household refers to an average groundnut and subsistence mixed production unit characteristic of the Kano close settled zone; here the surplus of production over necessary consumption was marginal to say the least. Forde's far from sanguine conclusion captures the plight of peasant immiseration.

The data on production and the returns on crops, craft activity and labour suggest that the incomes available to the ordinary rural household have been barely sufficient in a year of reasonably good crops to support the native norms of consumption, which are themselves very modest and, so far as food is concerned, are probably physiologically inadequate. [Forde 1946, p. 263]

The need to secure cash assumes significance not only in relation to necessary consumption and the demands of the state but particularly with regard to the temporal qualities of cash and liquidity requirements. The magnitude of the tax burden certainly necessitated the production of a monetized surplus, which reduced the fund of necessary consumption; the exchange-values produced to pay taxes detracted from food production, and the sale of labor power reduced labor availability for households during critical periods of the agricultural cycle. However, the need for postrains liquidity frequently led to either indebtedness—which had in any case proliferated through the activities of the European firms—or to postharvest sales at seasonally depressed prices. A failure to accumulate sufficient grain reserves to cover the period from one harvest to the next found expression in patterns of cyclical indebtedness, often involving high-interest corn credits that made profound inroads into future income.

At the same time that the Hausa peasantry showed clear signs of a long-run subsistence crisis throughout the colonial period, Popkin (1979, p. 79) inferred correctly that the commercialization of agriculture need not necessarily be wholly deleterious to all commodity producers. Periods of buoyant commodity prices—as was generally the case during the first twenty years of overrule—and a transitory cash surplus might enable even the rural poor to expand their purchase of luxury items, such as cloth. Equally, the degree of exploitation effected through unequal exchange and merchant capital "was contingent upon the exigencies of capital at any particular historical moment" (Bryceson 1980, p. 283). Furthermore, the fact that the confrontation of capital and the peasantry promoted social differentiation implies that some producers benefited enormously from the new commercial opportunities presented by the colonial apparatus. All this simply affirms the absurdity of an argument that posits that colonialism witnessed the gradual immiseration of *all* rural producers. Like any historical development that involves the articulation of radically different productive systems, rural economy in the northern provinces contained contradictions inherent in the nature of the accumulation process itself. A fundamental contradiction that directly concerns this study has been eloquently expressed by Bryceson.

Merchant capital was most instrumental in developing commodity production, and the exchange component of peasants' simple reproduction may well have

TABLE 5.16

ESTIMATED VALUES OF ANNUAL CONSUMPTION AND PRODUCTION AMONG RURAL HOUSEHOLDS

(i) *Average Household, Northern Provinces**

Item	Production for subsistence			Net value of sales			Item	Costs		
	£	s	d	£	s	d		£	s	d
Food crops	3	17	0		10	0	Foods	1	3	0
Groundnuts		1	0		15	0	Tobacco		3	0
Livestock		–			16	0	Kola		5	0
Sylvan produce		10	6		1	0	Clothes		12	0
Crafts		1	0		10	0	Clothes		5	0
Household maintenance		5	0		–		Services		5	0
Additional crops		–			10	0	Tax		7	0
Household Total	£4	14	6	£3	2	0		£3	0	0

SOURCE: Forde (1946, pp. 141, 164).

*Composition of household: 1 man, 1 wife, 2 children

(ii) Household Budget, Bida Emirate**

Crops and trees	Total yield	Household consumption	Sold	Additional income
Early millet	5 loads	All	—	Mat weaving, for 9d each
Late millet	3 loads	All	—	Total earnings 5s
Sorghum	8 loads	5 loads	3 loads, for 2s	
Beans	v. little	All	—	
Sw. potatoes	?	—	All, for 3s	
Cassava	?	All	—	
Locust beans	5 loads	—	All, for 1s, 3d	

	s	d
Income from farm produce	6	3
Total income	11	3
Money expenditure: Tax	9	6

SOURCE: Nadel (1942, p. 340).

**Composition of household: 1 man, family of four

been enhanced through the introduction of commodities such as cloth that saved their labour time allowing them to specialize in commodity production. On the other hand, merchant capital placed great pressure on peasants' subsistence food production without being able to introduce innovations or structure peasant production to generate the surplus food production demanded. As a result, merchant capital was very deeply constrained by the lack of surplus food production of the peasantry. [Bryceson 1980, p. 289]

The intensification of commodity production under the aegis of merchant's capital to fulfill metropolitan resource demands simultaneously presented the colonial state in Nigeria with the dilemma of underproduction of foods and massive economic insecurity. Not only were administrative food demands in jeopardy but the likelihood of starvation threatened the continuity of the entire colonial project. Either way, the colonial state was saddled with the additional expenditures of famine relief to bolster a vulnerable peasantry, or the improvement of agricultural productivity through a transformation of extant precapitalist technology. However, the advantage of the maintenance of functional dualism lay in its ability to produce cheap commodities, partly through the subsidization of labor costs via self-sufficiency—what Bernstein calls the devalorization of peasant labor—and partly through the ability to ensure commodity production even under conditions of depressed or falling prices. The canalization of labor power out of the rural sector to the mines and urban areas further compounded the likelihood of food underproduction. The state found itself, then, in a tenuous position mediating between its own economic and political survival, the demands for the maximization of cheap commodity production, an unfettered commercial environment for the European firms, and the need to keep peasants alive.

Although the relationships between colonialism and household security in northern Nigeria were often ambiguous, it would nonetheless be wrongheaded in my opinion to conclude, as Popkin (1979, p. 33) does, based on his Asian experience, that "the expansion of markets is of particular benefit to poorer peasants"; or indeed that "peasants clearly benefit from the growth of law and order . . . and wider systems of trade, credit and communications . . . [which] helped keep [them] alive during local famines" (p. 81). Colonialism was not only oppressive but seriously threatened the quality of the minimum subsistence floor. In the next chapter, I examine how this long-term structural subsistence crisis—the corrosion of the moral economy—and the inability of households to maintain short-run security or to accumulate capital, was reflected in periodic crises of simple reproduction; that is to say, the complete breakdown of the food system. In this sense, Popkin's suggestion that, in contradistinction to the views of the moral economists, peasants will make risky investments or gambles has a hollow ring; for the bulk of the poor and some middle peasants in the North, *every year was an enormous gamble.* Moreover, the stakes, as the pharaoic sequence of famines testifies, were frighteningly high.

6

FAMINE OVER HAUSALAND, 1900–1960

*The climate in particular influenced the fluctuations between
normal, good and bad harvests which led to crises of the 'old type.'
Yet the effects of such natural factors were also socially
determined. . . . Crises [developed] because the productive forces
in agriculture were little developed which must in turn be seen in
connection with the relations of production which failed to
stimulate their development or even prevented it.*

—*Jürgen Schlumbohm*

In spite of the silences that are intrinsic to any
colonial reconstruction based in large measure on archival sources, the
drone of continual food shortage resonates throughout the sixty-year
period of colonial overrule in northern Nigeria. The most cursory gloss
on colonial administrative practice invariably reveals the omnipresence of
famine and the threat posed by huge grain deficits in the face of increasing urban, military, and administrative demands.[1] It is entirely appropriate—and emblematic of the entire imperial era in Hausaland—that one
of the earliest cables by Lugard to Lyttleton at the Colonial Office in
August 1904 was a request for famine relief. Nowhere is the spectre of
food security thrown more into stark relief than in the voluminous annual
and semiannual reports from the provinces; each wet season brought
renewed fears of crop failure, of inflated urban food prices, of additional
NA expenditures incurred for relief or market rigging, and even the
possibility of a major calamity of Indian proportions. The monotonous
regularity of subsistence crises and the sequence of famines after 1900
was matched only by the frequency with which provincial administrations,
shackled by fiscal parsimony and a dire shortage of political officers, were
incapable (and often unwilling) to either monitor the extent of food
shortage or effectively respond to it. I argue that one of the principal
contradictions embodied in the colonial state was simply that while peasant production constituted the bedrock of imperial accumulation, the
drive toward expanded commodity production, the needs of an ever
growing nonproducing sector, and the changed conditions of peasant
reproduction generally—what I refer to as the partial erosion of the

moral economy—all seriously jeopardized the simple reproduction of rural producers. That is to say, at the same time that the state extracted surpluses for its own imperial mission it threatened those upon whom it ultimately depended. Crudely put, to starve to death the rural producers who were the material foundation of the colonial state was not an especially astute long-term exploitative strategy. Throughout its existence, the colonial state confronted this contradiction and never really resolved it. The four major famines—to say nothing of the litany of more localized crises—that occurred in the half-century following Lugard's conquest provide useful instruments for an analysis not simply of the conditions of rural poverty but of the evolution and penetration of capitalist relations under the aegis of the imperial state.

In the previous two chapters I tried to chart the changing relations of production among Hausa farmers after 1902. There was in the first place a quantitative expansion in the utilization of peasant labor, which included the newly established holdings of immigrant families from the French colonies and thousands of freed slaves who took up cultivation largely by clearing virgin bush land. For the vast majority, then, output increases came overwhelmingly from expansion of cultivated area and from rising output per unit of land due to increased labor time. Unlike Kenya, this was achieved without the incorporation of female labor in spite of the pressures on long-term seasonal migration by adult males and the growth of rural wage laboring. Hausa peasants increasingly entered into commodity production of cotton, groundnuts, and in some areas staple foodstuffs. A rising proportion of socially necessary labor time among households was, therefore, expended in the production of commodities rather than directly consumed use-values. The cycle of peasant reproduction was broken and marginally commoditized. The creation of new wants, the introduction of new use-values and tax liabilities all projected households into the money nexus, with the result that the estimation of monetary returns, as much as use-value returns, became a part of the household calculus. The rise of wage laboring and the intensification of commodity production was a reflection of this calculus. Of course, these developments possessed a markedly uneven character in time and space and emerged in tandem with subtle and complex forms of household differentiation. The latter is best conceptualized not as a pyramid of wide-layered strata but, in Kitching's words (1980, p. 154), "as a finely graded spectrum from richest to poorest with the closely intertwined and interdependent criteria of size of off-farm income and size of landholding as the twin axes around which differentiation revolved." But peasant commodity production was still secured through the realization of peasant subsistence based, for the most part, on undeveloped productive forces. I wish to show how the procurement of subsistence for many of the rural poor became increasingly problematic. This was not simply a technological issue or, as many of the political officers believed, a function of peasant indolence or sloth, which incidentally provided the state with an ideological justification for taxation. Rather it was an outcome of the historic confrontation between various forms of capital and a precapitalist Caliphal economy. In this chapter I show how the changing nature of this confrontation, and of the conditions of peasant reproduction in particular, was captured in the occurrence of several massive famines.

The analytic priority lent to the changed conditions of peasant reproduction does not alter the capriciousness or the signal importance of rainfall. An analysis of rainfall trends between 1900 and 1970 shows at least four short-term anomalies in 1912–15, 1926–28, 1941–43 and 1948–51 (figure 6.1), which correspond closely with the incidence of the principal colonial famines. The low level of development of the productive forces, at least until the first attempts at irrigated agriculture and mixed farming, naturally rendered peasant production vulnerable to adverse physical conditions. But the specific conjunction of environmental uncertainty and rural political economy determined the character of famine itself. The impact of the colonial state and merchant capital exposed vulnerable Hausa peasants to additional stresses, which actually amplified their susceptibility to drought under conditions of technological stasis. One manifestation of this dilemma was that famines, far from being classically precapitalist crises, came to be increasingly characterized by failures in exchange entitlements, that is by market distortions and constraints imposed by the commoditization of social and economic life.

1900–1918: CONQUEST, INCORPORATION, AND TRANSITION

[The Nigerian peasant] is earning so much . . . money he does not know what to do with it.

—E.D. Morel, *The African Mail, 1914*

From August 1913, the subsequent 12 months brought intense famine, war and . . . an informal [commercial] arrangement . . . to reduce the prices paid [to the peasant] for groundnuts.

—Jan Hogendorn

The first two decades of the twentieth century in Hausaland must have been quite extraordinary. This was the period of the commercial frenzy of the groundnut revolution, the brutal repression of Islamic resistance to imperial conquest, the butchery at Satiru, and the sporadic emergence of self-proclaimed Mahdis saturated with millennial visions and predicting the end of the world. And with good reason. What began

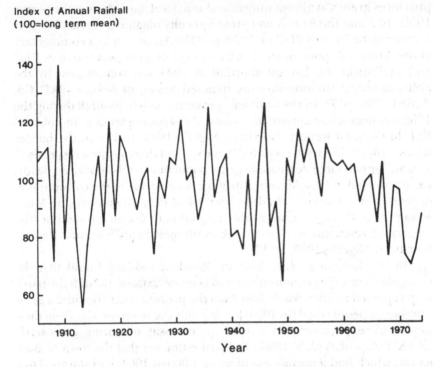

Figure 6.1 Annual rainfall indexes, Northern Nigerian Stations, 1900–70. From climatic data, Institute of Agricultural Research, Zaria.

with the fall of Kano successively witnessed the dispatch of a posse of emirs to Ilorin, massive dislocations in territorial boundaries and political jurisdictions, the abolition of the slave trade (if not slavery), the outbreak of the First World War, large-scale forced labor for the minesfield and railroad construction, a postwar commodity boom, and a stunning economic crash in 1920. District heads, pushed from their comfortable seats in emirate birane, were propelled into their new districts; they rose and fell with comic rapidity, accused of abetting peasant rebellion, embezzlement, slave dealing, and general administrative incompetence. British officers grappled with complexities of tax, court politics, and the threat of popular rebellion which, in view of their numbers and a motley West African Fighting Force (WAFF), was quite futile. But this was also the period of the 1913–14 famine, perhaps the worst food crisis in over a century.

From the very outset, Lugard inherited a series of poor harvests and a general downturn in rainfall, spanning the twenty-year period up to the outbreak of the First World War (Nicholson 1976). In the middle belt provinces grain was almost unprocurable in local markets over the period 1902–08,[2] and the British had great difficulty obtaining cereals for their military detachments (Tukur 1979, p. 903). According to a commentary in the Annual Report for the Northern Region, grain was scarce in 1902 and in Bauchi the harvest shortfall in 1903 was complicated by the political unrest surrounding the deposed Sultan of Sokoto (PRO Cd. #2684 1905, p. 7). In the southerly provinces, patchy rainfall during the 1903 wet season had apparently caused a "distressing famine" in Yola and Bauchi (Annual Report, Northern Nigeria 1904, p. 12); in the border states, Low (1972, p. 49) recorded "a measure of demographic dispersion" and an "appreciable decrease in gross population." One hundred deaths were reported in Bauchi township alone, largely due to the consumption of poisonous roots and "children [were] sold in large numbers" in Muri, Katagum, and Nupe. A large-scale migration to Bornu ensued but "the emaciated remnants were too weak to till their fields" (Annual Report, Northern Nigeria 1905, p. 13).[3]

In the following year, Assistant Resident Liddard found that the Gongola river valley communities had been devastated, though the hardship reported in 1906 was lighter than the previous year "because a great number of people died [in 1905] leaving only the stronger who from their deplorable experience had learned the necessity of storing grass seed" (NAK Yolaprof. Vol. V 1906). Liddard estimated that the town of Banjeram, which had a population of some 4,000 in 1904, had slumped to a paltry forty-three souls in 1906. Lugard wrote to Lyttleton at the Colonial Office in April 1905 that the effects of the previous year's famine had "carried over" especially in the Benue districts where food was scarce (PRO CO 446 19358, p. 81). In fact, it was the military conquest that interrupted the normal agricultural activities in 1902 and 1903, compounded by the food demands of a considerable armed force at Zungeru. The political factor, in this instance the deposition of the emir, was also critical in Katsina, when a localized famine occurred in the wet season of 1905, referred to locally as "*ci abinki ta rimin gora*."[4] Farther south, the new colonial townships and their military attachments made heavy claims on already scarce local grains.

> [In Zungeru] the famine . . . was accentuated by the large demand for corn for the horses and men of the mounted infantry. . . . Zaria is not a great grain producing province [anyway]. [Annual Report #476, Cd. 2684 1905, p. 7]

In spite of these pressures, the governor reported in 1905 that the tax burden was collected in full, and went on to suggest, in a remarkable piece of Victorian nonsense, that "the experience of hunger will stimulate the people to cultivate larger areas."

This early famine episode is of some consequence not only in its relation to imperial conquest but also in regard to the prototypical response illicited from the colonial administration; a response that set a precedent for the entire colonial era. Lugard actually wrote Lyttleton in August 1904 with the following request:

> What expenditure will you approve for famine relief. Great mortality due to last years' drought blight. [PRO CO 446 ref. 30658 1904, p. 283]

Lugard must surely have had his tongue firmly in his cheek, for even had funds been available—in practice a near impossibility—the administration would have been powerless to assist the countryside. Nevertheless, the reply from Lucas (at the Colonial Office) is singularly instructive. Lucas informed Lugard that all famine relief was to be met from some mysterious "savings" not from the grant-in-aid, and went on to suggest, in a master-stroke of British instrumentalism, that

> this is a very impractical communication . . . we have no information whatsoever that there is any existing or impending famine. *If there is a famine in the districts near Zungeru it ought to solve temporary difficulties which exist in obtaining labor for transport.* [PRO CO 446 ref. 30658 1904, p. 283, emphasis added]

Even with the best philanthropic will in the world, these early years were necessarily chaotic. Not only did five different men, for example, hold the post of Kano Resident during the three-year period after October 1906, but the entire rural population of some 6–7 million was administered through 1,000 man-days of work annually. In 1908 there was a severe preharvest famine in Kano—referred to in the northern divisions as *Yunwar Kanawa*[5]—which, having persisted for roughly six weeks prior to the millet harvest, provides the first glimpse into the changing form of colonial hunger. On that occasion, the governor did not appeal to the Colonial Office for the very good reason that he learned about the famine only in 1909 on reading the annual report! The acting Resident was unashamedly frank.

> Yes, the mortality was considerable but I hope not so great as the natives allege—we had no remedy at the time and therefore as little was said about it as possible. [NAK SNP 9 472/1909, p. 18]

The previous Resident, Mr. Festing, while no less shamefaced in his candor was at least better informed.

> The talakawa have suffered greatly . . . [due] to our not having realized how great was their want, and for the last few months the old people, the women and the children have literally been starving. [NAK SNP 7 5490/1908, p. 2]

The Kano cereal harvest had been one-third of normal, grain prices leaped eightfold to 4d per pound, and zakkat—still levied in kind at this point—made the taxes claimed by the NA "as much as half of what was grown."[6] The failure spanned a fifty-mile radius of birnin Kano[7] and was not simply attributable to drought, as Festing acknowledged, but to "the constant call for . . . labor and human transport" and to the predation of district heads making up tax arrears.[8] Festing was also astutely cognizant of what was to become commonplace during later years:

> The big men cornered the market (for food) in Kano and the big towns and called on the talakawa to bring in more . . . it is of course not possible to prevent this. [NAK Kadminagric. 14429/1908]

In what came to be standard colonial rhetoric the peasantry were accused of being innately "improvident," squandering what little they had and not making provision for what they might need. Alarming reports were spread about ensuing famine for the following year, prompting a widespread rash of looting but, as Festing confessed, it was "by our own people." In a somber conclusion Festing surmised that he had been, first, misled by a local populace of inveterate rural liars, and second, duped by their administrative agents who hoped for a remission of zakkat. Duplicity aside, he was not mistaken in his observation that "people have [never] realized how much corn has . . . come from the North nor that Kano Province . . . is hardly self-supporting as regards corn" (NAK Kadminagric, 14429/1908). Large numbers of famine refugees from Kano poured northward into Katsina Province in a desperate search of food, but ran straight into Katsina's own localized subsistence crisis, referred to as *Yunwar Dikko*.[9] Immigrant and resident farmers alike were largely dependent upon yan kwarami plying millets from the north (arewa), notably from Gobir and Damagaram. These desert-edge grain bins, which had been so critical in the precolonial period, were in fact in their twilight years; the French administration was, as Festing remarked in 1908, in the process of regulating the now international grain trade. In any case the huge capitation levies of the French rapidly accounted for any local household surpluses.

In one sense there is a legitimate case to be made for a series of mediocre rains immediately following the conquest, which confronted a neophyte administration wholly incapable of distinguishing its right hand from its left. Indifferent and poor harvests clearly took their toll on domestic grain reserves and peasant assets generally. Grain prices rose steadily, fed by the demands of a resident military force and a growing minesfield laboring class; by 1911 in Gumel emirate, for example, sorghum reached 1/6d per bundle, almost 150 percent higher than the prevailing price several years earlier.[10] As one district officer of the time noted, full granaries and decapitalized assets were not reconstituted overnight; ideally two or three good harvests would be required to minimally replenish domestic grain bins. On the eve of the First World War, quite apart from the exactions of a predatory colonial state, the security of the northern Nigerian peasantry was not all that it might have been.

To stop here, however, would be to neglect the most significant developments of the pre-1914 period, and in particular of the manner in which colonial demands exposed households to the vicissitudes of climate. From my conversations with elders, it is clear that weakness of the household economy resided in the systematic erosion of grain reserves attributable to the constancy of high tax levies extorted during several poor harvests.[11] In Katsina, for example, taxes were collected in kind until the generalization of specie in about 1910, during which time the admittedly chaotic and ad hoc imposts averaged roughly 12,000 cowries per household, almost double the precolonial level.[12] During 1908 Palmer (NAK SNP 15 Acc. 162/1908–09) lamented the fact that the northern division, and Katsina in particular, was "taxed up to the hilt" and in a telling minute confided that he did not understand "how the great majority of these people are going to live during the year" (NAK Katprof 1386). The heavy levies on special and irrigated crops (kudin rafi, and kudin shuka)—items that served as buffering mechanisms during periods of general shortage—had taken huge areas out of cultivation. Palmer noted again in Katsina, that "a slight increase in [special crop] tax will stop cultivation . . . altogether" (NAK SNP 10 3035/1909).

The compulsiveness of colonial officers with respect to taxation can only be understood in terms of the fiscal crisis of the colonial state. Between 1903 and 1906 the administration ran deficits of over £400,000 per annum (Kesner. 1981) on an expenditure of just over half a million pounds. Continued debt financing on this scale was impossible. Nigeria, and more specifically the rural producer, had to be made to pay for the reproduction of the state itself. This fiscal imperative underwrote Lugard's obsession with revenue, and explains the centrality of revenue demands. In this regard the early Resident assessments were executed entirely by trial and error. The limits of surplus appropriation were reached when the administration sensed or actually faced rural protest—witness the Cargill fiasco in Kano in 1908[13]—or as producers migrated out of the district altogether, voting with their feet in evasive dissent. Migration was a barometer that measured the odiousness of tax pressures; Daura peasants migrated *en masse* in 1911 in response to a huge increase in kudin kassa, while the Katsina districts experienced almost continual household mobility in the first decade of overrule. It is crucial not to underestimate the magnitude of these early tax experiments; an assessment on Azare District (Katagum) in 1912 prompted an increase of 120 percent over the previous native assessment (NAK SNP 10 6249/1912). In Fawa District the incidence of the land tax was raised in 1907 from 1/4d to 3/3d per adult male. In the adjoining district of Kotorkoshi the levy rose by 200 percent.[14] Direct taxes in the northern provinces totaled £300,000 by 1914.

The repercussions of the fiscal burden can be intuited from early cost-of-living estimates in Sokoto Province. The total subsistence costs for an "economical" family of three in Raba District were estimated at £2.14.1d; baseline taxes per adult male—excluding the levies on irrigated crops or industrials[15]—varied between a minimum of 3/- and a maximum 6/-, that is between 5 and 10 percent of reproductive costs (NAK SNP 10 609p/1914).[16] In Zaria emirate, the standard rate by 1909 was 5/8d per adult male, notwithstanding rafi rates of 5/- per plot (NAK SNP 7 4252/ 1909). Some emirates, like Yola, were even taxing Muslim women by 1910.[17] All this is a far cry from Perham's claim (1962, p. 105) that taxes represented no more than 2½ percent of net income and were "binding rather than dissolving force[s] upon the [village] community" (p. 53).

The Tolstoyan load of early taxation can only be effectively weighed in light of several other postconquest developments. First, the relative scarcity of British currency in which taxes were to be paid fostered a brisk seasonal trade in moneychanging. Birdwhistle made it clear however that in Sokoto merchants deliberately deflated the value of the cowry by roughly 100 percent, for which the talakawa, pressed for tax payments in cash, paid dearly (NAK SNP 7/8 1765/1907).[18] Second, prior to the adoption of the groundnut (beginning in 1912) as the principal vehicle for cash generation, rural households were largely dependent on the sale of cereals. Colonial assessors, however, based their early calculations on high-water market prices; obligatory sales at harvest times, when most peasants required immediate liquidity for the tax collector, cast those revenue assessments in a new and more somber light. In Dan Iya District, Kano Province, for example, the land tax was predicated on guinea corn sales of 1/6d per 60 lb bundle but the district officer commented when the value of domestically grown guinea corn was realized in September or October "[the value] is not more than 6d" (NAK SNP 10 4055/1912). By this estimate the farmer paid 40 percent of his gross farm produce in taxes. Third, the new wave of district heads, slighted with low salaries[19] but empowered with unregulated authority, took their own perquisites over and above the standard levies. A Zaria Resident estimated in 1910 that roughly 100% more taxes are being paid than are being returned to us.[20] And fourth was the unestimable impact of forced labor conscripted for the minesfield and the Baro—Kano Railway. Road and riverbed clearance and the construction of rest houses were all executed by compulsory labor, in spite of Lugard's stipulation to the contrary.[21] The railway accounted for huge numbers of rural laborers, especially in the preparation of earthworks. During the construction of the Bauchi Light Railway Extension, the Zaria administration complained bitterly that all their time was absorbed by efforts at large-scale labor mobilization (NAK SNP 10 107p/1914),[22] even during the rains; at the height of the rainy season in June 1914 almost 5,000 laborers were deployed on construction projects. During 1911 some 12,000 head porters were pressed into service on the plateau routes of the Niger Company (cited in Freund 1981, p. 63).

The plateau mine economy was a different case entirely. The corvée labor force was almost wholly transient and the government resisted the pressures from mine capital for the creation of a recruiting bureau of the Rhodesian genre. The problems of labor control in a "voluntary" system plagued mine labor supplies at least until market forces and taxation ensnared seasonal migrants in large numbers (Freund 1981). The sheer numbers involved in this partially proletarianized work force were, nonetheless, instructive. In 1912, at least 12,000 workers per month labored in the mines; while this figure fell by half during the rains as farmers returned to their villages, Freund (1981) estimates that this "floating population" was underestimated by half. Households had adjusted to allow for dry-season out-migration, but there were objective limits on how far this withdrawal of labor could develop. Among impoverished Hausa, Birom, or Kanuri families the very fact of casual work on the plateau was indicative of their economic marginality. Depressed wages, family misfortune, and dependent producer-consumer ratios all conspired to lend mine labor a last-gasp quality; in time, fewer migrants returned to their villages and peasant production slumped to new crisis levels. But even if farming households remained tenable by the evacuation of young men to the mines, the huge plateau labor force still had to be fed. In this regard, the plateau was ill-suited to sustain a massive influx; geographically isolated, it had never been a granary or a significant surplus producer of staples. Each year food demand escalated, and by 1911 the London and Kano Company was shipping large quantities of *dawa* from Bornu, Zaria, and southern Katsina. A conservative estimate of food imports suggests that about 1910 a minimum of 10,000 tons of corn was channeled into the plateau annually. Mining capital was pressed into furious competition with the fledgling NAs for the irregular grain surpluses; later they faced the additional incursions of groundnuts and cotton into domestic grain production.

The tax bill, then, and the burden of early economic change fell almost entirely on Hausa smallholders dependent upon the sale of grain and seasonal wage labor for the necessary specie to cover onerous tax payments. Perhaps inevitably, the downtrodden *talakawa* were at best indifferent toward the imperial presence, and frequently resisted tax payment altogether. Britain dealt with popular protest with military measures; in the early period the new overlords were compelled to repeat the same process almost every year (Fika 1973).[23] Tax collection usually necessitated sizable mounted patrols—what the Colonial Office called punitive expeditions—and in one notable incident, 2,000 recalcitrant peasants fled, at gunpoint, from a western district of Kano into Katsina. The threat of rural rebellion convinced the colonial government to actually disarm their rural subjects in response to what they termed "fanatical anti-European propaganda." In part because of the military reaction that peasant unrest solicited, the colonial state adopted a new farm-holding-based system of taxation in 1911 referred to as "taki".[24] Revenue accordingly expanded enormously, growing at rates of 20–30 percent per annum in Kano Province; in the face of these new surpluses Governor Bell suggested in 1912 that surplus funds be invested through the Crown agents. Ironically, it was also at this time that the first serious proposal to invest colonial reserves in famine relief was actually advanced. The proposal was shelved, as other similar proposals were shelved between 1913 and 1945, and in its place the administration accumulated huge quantities of surplus capital, for the most part invested in low-interest government bonds in Britain.

If the taki system ensured that colonial self-finance was finally realized, its success was a Pyrrhic victory. Taki was unpopular from its institution, especially in the low-density, low-fertility districts where tax burdens were at least comparable to those in the rich laka regions. Blackwell's 1912 assessment report of Azare District in Katagum determined that taki was approximately 40 percent of the average peasant household annual gross production (NAK SNP 10 6249/1912). Furthermore, taxpayers repeatedly complained that taki was rigid, making no allowance for harvest failure or local calamity; it came to be seen as a fixed rent charge irrespective of yield or prevailing market price.

> I think an inelastic tax like *taki* is bound to cause inequalities . . . it is in practice a flat rate per acre on all farms regardless . . . of production and soils . . . a farmer in the east may have good rains . . . and farmer B in the west late or poor rains and a partial failure . . . assuming each has four acres and is equally industrious Farmer A's income may be twice that of farmer B . . . yet both men pay the same tax. [NAK SNP 9 603/1924]

According to the Katsina Resident, taki was a "big mistake" for the very good reason that it resulted in land actually being taken out of cultivation in the northern districts,[25] especially Sullubawa, Iya, and Dankama (table 6.1). The appeal procedure for peasants wrongly assessed by taki was Kafkaesque, and by 1913 the backlog of claims was vast. As if to add insult

TABLE 6.1
THE EFFECTS OF TAKI TAX, KATSINA PROVINCE

District	Cultivated area in acres, 1913	Cultivated area in acres, 1917	% increase or decrease	Population increase or decrease
Durbi	64,710	63,585	− 1.5	+ 2.0
Sullubawa	56,779	45,109	−20.0	+25.0
Ingawa	101,771	97,329	− 4.0	no data
Magajin Gari	10,466	9,796	− 8.0	no data
Mallamawa	4,839	4,619	− 4.0	+20.0

SOURCE: National Archives Kaduna, (NAK) Katprof 1938, Taki Assessment Katsina Division.

to injury, a mere three years after the devastating 1914 famine taki rates were doubled by the Kano provincial administration.

The overall pattern that emerges from the immediate postconquest revenue data (table 6.2) is the remarkable growth of colonial receipts. The administration stuck doggedly to its collection policy in order that the central and local governmental administration could be self-supporting. This obsession with stable income perhaps goes some way toward explaining the strange reasoning of the Bornu Resident who, in 1915, raised the taxes for an already impoverished and hungry Kanuri peasantry on the ground that "[the raise] was intended to balance the losses due to disease and starvation [during the famine]" (cited in Mshelia 1975, p. 54). In the few instances where tax remission was considered or actually undertaken, the quantities involved were insultingly insignificant. At the zenith of the 1914 famine, Resident Malcolm of Sokoto in a magnanimous gesture reduced taxes by £517 "owing to human suffering" which, on a per capita basis, amounted to a 2 percent reduction in the annual levy (NAK SNP 10 476p/1914).

The other colonial development that relates directly to the 1913–14 famine was the overnight sensation of the groundnut trade. Purchases by the Niger Company vacillated around 1,000 tons between 1907 and 1911. The watershed in groundnut cultivation was in 1913, however; the completion of the Baro–Kano Railway, the competitive prices offered by the firms, and the talakawa's desperate need for specie all conspired to produce conditions conducive to an enormous expansion in the area devoted to groundnuts, especially in the Kano close settled zone. Bush and fallow farms were brought under cultivation, significant proportions of domestic labor were devoted to groundnuts, and there were even rumors that cattle Fulani participated in the frenzied planting activities. Not without good reason, Emir Abbas of Kano expressed deep concern for the city's food supply.

TABLE 6.2
Tax Revenue: Katsina Division

Year	Amount (£)
1909	20,000 (?)
1910	27,013
1911	37,664
1912	42,727
1913	50,914
1914	50,411
1915	54,801

Source: National Archives Kaduna, (NAK) Katprof Acc. 1289, Katsina Division, Annual Report, 1915.

The planting season of 1913 is remembered at Kano as an extraordinary year. Mohamman Ilori recalled a decline in planting of grain. . . . The condition was such that . . . Abbas became worried about food supply . . . but the appeal [to grow more food] was not effective and before the end of the year there was shortage and traders tried to buy grain from non-traditional areas . . . at high prices. [Okediji 1972, p. 194]

The production figures speak for themselves; there was a tenfold increase in marketed groundnut production in Kano Province between 1912 and 1913.[26] Not surprisingly, in view of the underproduction of foodstuffs and the succession of generally poor harvests, very little of the crop actually appeared on the Kano market for the very good reason that the peasantry faced starvation.

[In 1914] although there was supposed to be a good crop, the natives would not bring in the groundnuts because they said they were going to hold them for a better price. They stored them and fortunately they did. Owing to the groundnut planting, they did not provide their yams [sic] and their guinea corn, and were faced almost with starvation and so far as they could they ate the groundnut and held some over till the next season [Trigge in HMSO: Cd. F247 1916, p. 61].

Despite the use-value of groundnuts, the situation was not as sanguine as Trigge believed. The mounting pressures of tax obligations and the inflated groundnut prices offered by buying agents drew groundnuts onto the market even though the volatility of the grain market subsequently undermined any benefits that might have accrued from a favorable sale price. The hollowness of the high prices was brought home later in the year as an informal pooling among the European firms set a ceiling on the groundnut prices offered by the buying agents. The provincial administrations simply hiked taxes. In the Kano area, the real site of the groundnut revolution in these early years, the provincial government raised taki from 8d to 1/- per acre. In an act of sublime stupidity that is entirely emblematic of this period, in 1910 the Resident of Kano converted a famine reserve constructed by the emir of Katagum into a prison house (NAK SNP 7 951/1911).

THE FAMINE OF 1913–1914, YUNWAR GYALLARE

> Kakalaba, bakar yunwa
> Gyallare, mai sa maza kuka.

> Kakalaba, black famine
> Gyallare, making brave men cry.*

In the years immediately preceding the First World War, the climate of the entire Sudano–Sahelian zone was drier than it had been at any time during the last half of the ninteenth century.[27] In particular, 1913 was especially dry, the isohyets for that year lying 150 km or more south of their mean positions (figure 6.2). All three years covering the period 1912–14 were considerably below long-term means for the major north-

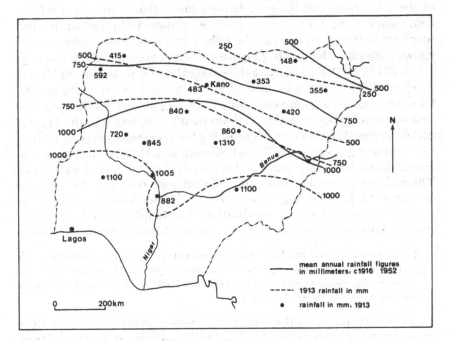

Figure 6.2. Rainfall in northern Nigeria, 1913. From Grove (1973).

*For other Hausa verse on the 1914 famine see the Appendix.

ern stations (table 6.3). During the drought period Lake Chad contracted and divided into two separate lake systems. The spatial ubiquity of poor rainfall in 1913 is revealed in one of its local Hausa names, *Malali*, meaning "great flood," and by the wealth of oral testimony across the northern region.[28] Resident Gowers in Kano (NAK SNP 10/2 134p/1913) commented that almost no community in the province was left untouched; even 300 miles to the south in Bida, Resident Dupigny wrote that "there has been no rain for twenty-eight days and . . . crops are worthless" (NAK SNP 10.2 221p/1914). To the north in French territory, drought was especially intense—indeed throughout the entire desert edge of the central Sudan; the Zinder station, with a mean annual precipitation of 19.0, recorded 11.6, 8.6, and 9.0 inches, respectively, in the years 1911–13. The poverty of monthly or daily climatic data prevents any confident statement on the distribution of precipitation, but most elderly farmers in Katsina felt that the critical juncture in 1913 appeared with the early termination of the rain at the point of crop maturity (*kumshi*).[29]

The first famine distress signals appeared, as always, with the influx of Nigerian peasants, Asbenawa pastoralists, and Fulani livestock herders into the northern emirates during early 1913. However, it was the failure of the 1913 rains and the poor harvest that followed that sounded the death knell. Crop failures were massive; Withers Gill reported that the sorghum suffered on most of the light fakko soils, while millets on the jigawa uplands yielded only 25 percent of normal crop (NAK Kanoprof. 1 717/1913). In Damagaram food shortages became serious in March and April of 1914, just six months after the harvest (Baier 1980, p. 98). Gowers reported a "complete failure" in Katagum; but Matthews in Katsina was much more sanguine, and was clearly nonplussed by the deputation of Yerima farmers who "were asking for a remission of taxation [due] to a failure of gero and dawa" (NAK Kanoprof. 1 95/1914). In Sokoto, the crucial Rima basin rice crop "failed entirely" (NAK SNP 9 837/1914). Through its particular optic, the colonial state only saw the "native's incapacity for generalizing," a reference to the apparent quiescence of the peasants in the face of harvest shortfall. The simple-mindedness of this sort of explanation did not, however, escape Resident Arnett in Sokoto.

> The reason for this reluctance [to admit to shortage] being a fear lest interested parties i.e. the grain dealers . . . will use a report of shortage to inflate prices. . . . The operation is described as "sun yi yunwa da baki" . . . they make famine with their mouths. [NAK SNP 9 837/1914]

As the secretary to the northern provinces observed in early 1914 "news from the north is very bad" and with grain almost unprocurable in Zinder "there was a slow but steady influx of families across the French border into Kano emirate" (NAK SNP 10/2 134p/1913). The shortfall in

SOURCE: Climatic records, Institute for Agricultural Research, Zaria.

TABLE 6.3
ANNUAL RAINFALL DATA, NORTHERN NIGERIA

Station	Latitude	Longitude	Mean (inches)	1912 (inches)	1913 (inches)	1914 (inches)
Kano	12°03′N	8°32′E	33.1	32.5	19.3	28.2
Sokoto	13°01′N	5°15′E	28.3	19.4	16.5	no data
Maiduguri	11°51′N	13°05′E	26.0	18.6	14.0	11.6

SOURCE: Climatic records, Institute for Agricultural Research, Zaria.

southern Niger, traditionally a breadbasket for some of the northerly emirates, only served to amplify the desperate purchasing of grain in the few districts with small surfeits. By May and June conditions were especially acute; according to Baier (1980, p. 99) stricken parents had left as many as 200 children in the Zinder market in the hope that benefactors would sustain them. The entire northern region, with a population of perhaps eight million, confronted the prospect of an influx of as many as 1–2 million destitute peasants. According to the Sokoto Residents, half a million were at risk in that province alone (NAK SNP 9 837/1914). While the details of actual conditions are difficult to assemble, the following brief descriptions by the Kano Resident, Mr. Hastings, and by a Frenchwoman in northern Nigeria during 1914, render a poignant picture of the human tragedy:

> This year the effect of shortage showed itself in all its ghastliness. The gaunt ghost of famine stalked abroad through Kano and every other part. The stricken people tore down the ant hills in the bush to get at the small grains and chaff within these storerooms. They wandered everywhere collecting the grass burrs of the kerangia to split the centre pod and get the tiny seed. They made use of every poor resource their ingenuity could think of, and ravenous in their hunger, seized on anything they could steal or plunder. Mothers could not feed their babies at their breasts and cows' milk lacked, for the pasture had dried up and cattle were just skin and bone. The great city of Kano drew the starving thousands from the country in the faint hope of scouring in the streets and markets to pick up what they might, or beg the charity of the townsfolk. Not only the Nigerians but thousands from French country drifted down across our borders, passing through villages en route all bare of food to offer them. They died like flies on every road. One came across them in the town markets, emaciated to skeletons, begging feebly for sustenance, or collapsed into unconsciousness where they sat, and one poor wretch died in the Residency garden where he had crept at night with his last strength [Hastings 1925, p. 111].
>
> Several [persons] fell exhausted on the road, unable to pick themselves up. Some mature men, horribly emaciated, leant on their walking sticks; girls with eyes like trapped gazelles; women clenching their children to their shrivelled breasts. The children sucking feebly . . . all in vain. . . . In Katsina people are falling ill, poisoned by the overconsumption of meat. In the fields one sees bands of children . . . eating herbs and the soil. [Vischer 1915, pp. 130–31]

The evolution of hunger during the early months of 1914 was mirrored by a highly volatile grain market. As domestic reserves were consumed or snapped up by grain merchants anxious to hoard for a price rise, millet and sorghum disappeared completely from the marketplace.[30] Price data (figure 6.3) for cereals in Kano market indicate that the 1912 postharvest price for millet (one tenth of a penny per pound) had risen to

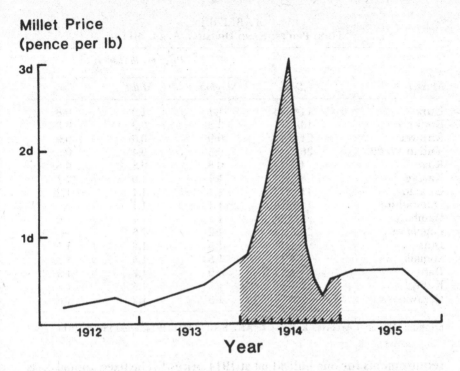

**Millet Price
(pence per lb)**

Figure 6.3. Millet prices, Kano Market 1912–15. From (NAK) SNP 10/6 93p/1920, Kano Province Annual Report 1920.

the obscene level of 3d per pound in July 1914.[31] Table 6.4 suggests that 1914 prices throughout the province were uniformly high; in a sample of twenty-two rural markets 85 percent experienced grain prices at least ten times above the 1911 level. Hogendorn (1978) believes that the relatively attractive prices offered by the firms earlier in the year induced the peasant to sell groundnuts,[32] but in reality they were almost unobtainable.

> Seven unshelled groundnuts cost one-tenth of a penny. . . . It is almost impossible to buy corn . . . and there is no longer any standard price. [NAK Katprof 1 3146/1913]

The anarchy that reigned in the marketplace—the fact that cereals could not be obtained "at any price" as the Katsina Resident put it— simply meant that the vast majority were entirely without food or the means for obtaining it (NAK Katprof. 1 1978/1914). The urban poor and fixed-income groups suffered terribly at the hands of food price inflation; the prevailing wage labor rate of 3d per day, which remained at that level into the 1920s, was clearly incapable of providing half the daily grain

TABLE 6.4
FOOD PRICES: KANO DIVISION, APRIL 1914

Market	Date	Price per *lb* (pence)		
		Sorghum	*Millet*	*Rice*
Kura	11/2/14	1.1	1.0	0.8
Bonkuri	13/2/14	0.8	0.9	0.8
Riruwei	21/2/14	0.9	0.6	0.9
Tudan Wada	26/2/14	0.5	0.4	0.5
Rogo	4/3/14	0.8	0.8	0.8
Karaye	8/3/14	1.1	1.0	1.1
Gwarzo	11/3/14	1.1	1.1	1.2
Dumbulum	13/3/14	1.1	1.1	−
Damberta	25/3/14	1.2	1.1	1.0
Fogolawa	28/3/14	1.2	1.3	−
Dutsi	9/4/14	1.5	1.8	1.5
Somaila	14/4/14	1.5	1.5	1.3
Dal	14/4/14	0.9	1.2	1.5
Kuniya	17/4/14	1.5	1.5	1.8
Gezawa	17/4/14	1.3	1.2	1.8

SOURCE: National Archives Kaduna, (NAK), SNP 7 231p/1914, Food Prices, 1914.

requirements for one individual at 1914 prices.[33] The fixed annual costs for a Katsina family of five during 1909 was roughly 11/-, which at the zenith of the price spiral would have covered grain costs for one and a half months only. The terms of trade moved sharply against the rural and urban poor, and in the ensuing instability theft and highway robbery proliferated.

The colonial relief effort in all its poverty failed entirely to provide immediate and large-scale assistance. The 1,000 tons of imported rice, ordered several months too late and arriving in Kano in October 1914 well after the apical point of the crisis, failed to fulfill any useful function;[34] as a British officer put it in a marvelous piece of understatement, the relief was "tardy." Generally, the quantities of foodstuffs were so small in relation to the huge demands for free relief and market rigging that colonial relief, chaotic in its organization right from the start, was doomed to fail miserably. The administration failed to appreciate that limited purchasing power in the countryside was inadequate, even to cover subsidized corn purchase. One month prior to the arrival of official relief, millet actually reached the preposterous level of 60/- per bundle, in excess of 1/- per pound, roughly equivalent to the prevailing sale price of one cow.[35] Hastings in Kano laconically concluded that, as a consequence of the tardy relief, "the number of deaths . . . were very heavy." The general situation in Kano Province—the hardest hit of the emirates—was as follows:[36]

1. Relief measures in Kano city lasted 74 days. About 160,000 free rations of grain were issued and 400,000 *mudus* of rice sold at subsidized prices between July and September.

2. Four hundred fifty tons of imported rice arrived two months late, by which time the native administration, already saddled with the costs of import, could only sell it at deflated prices, incurring an enormous loss in the process. Relief did not reach the northern districts of Kazaure until August, the second consignment having been attacked near Daura and sixteen bags stolen.[37]

The human toll of the 1914 famine cannot be adequately estimated, and the surrogate measures, particularly of mortality, are not easily interpreted.[38] In some districts, entire communities were abandoned and their inhabitants drifted southward, many turning toward the Zamfara valley where grain was reported in relative abundance. Thousands died in the course of fleeing starvation, perhaps as many as 80,000 from the French colonies alone (Baier 1980, p. 99). In Hadejia and Katagum, 40 percent of the total population apparently migrated; a figure not significantly different from the depopulation experienced in Bornu Province[39] (table 6.5). Flight unquestionably saved many destitute families, but few households were capable of returning to plant for the new rains, with the inevitable result that 1915 harvest prospects were bleak. For those who stubbornly clung to their rural abodes, the onset of the rains was far from a blessing because, as a Gumel district officer remarked, "much of the millet [is] spoiled . . . through the weakness consequent upon the lack of food" (NAK SNP 9 102p/1015). A contemporary in Kano further observed that some farmers remained in dire straits even in 1916 "having

TABLE 6.5
POPULATION, BORNU PROVINCE

Year	Population
1909	454,000
1910	674,000
1911	n.d.
1912	672,342
1913	513,388
1914	481,759
1915	626,500
1916	700,451

SOURCE: National Archives, Kaduna 89p/1918.

got into debt last year so that much [of the] good crop went to repay their creditors" (NAK SNP 10/6 518p/1916). In the popular consciousness 1915 is referred to as a famine year, usually by the name *Yar Kakalaba*, quite literally, "sister famine."[40]

Human mortality is perhaps even more indeterminate than migratory patterns. Hastings (NAK SNP 10/3 139/1915), in a flight of fancy, ventured the figure of 50,000 as the Kano Province death toll while the *African Mail*, in keeping with its sanguine outlook, opted for 30,000; Polly Hill (1972, p. 284) is less ambitious and suggests a figure of 4,000 for a much smaller area in northern Katsina. The Kano Province Annual Report estimated that deaths in Kano (including Kazaure), Katsina, Katagam, Daura, and Hadejia were 14,205, 5,000, 10,930, 6,747 and 7,769 respectively.[41] For the rest we have to be content with vague and uninterpretable colonial references to "very high death rates in Daura," "considerable mortality in Kazaure" and "heavy losses" in Gumel. A medical officer observed in 1914 that

> a remarkable feature of the mortality is that the deaths among the male section of the inhabitants have been much more numerous than among the females. There are numbers of small hamlets in the Daura [area] . . . which now cannot boast a single male inhabitant. I am assured that this is not due to flight. [NAK Katprof. 1 1978/1915]

Many deaths were apparently due to the premature consumption of unripe millet which caused intense dysentery known locally as *mai bashi*. In a pathetic irony, August 1914 (the peak hunger month) was designated the month of the fast of Ramadan.

Massive asset decapitalization during 1914 was not, of course, confined to the rural poor. Merchants with extended credit lines found them quickly terminated and the economic fortunes of men like Malam Yaro of Zinder, described by Baier (1980, p. 100), did not recover even by the Great Depression.[42] This was especially so for those whose income derived from the trans-Saharan trade, which was dealt a fatal blow by the 1914 famine. The plateau tin mines also felt the pinch of food shortage. In fact a famine was only narrowly averted in 1912 when the mine districts were incapable of providing grain surpluses for a rapidly growing labor force (PRO CO 446 109 ref. 37400 1912). Tera men from Bauchi, without access to commodity production, migrated to Jos as early as 1909 in search of tax monies, but the poor harvests of 1913 flooded the minefield with Hausa migrants desperate for casual work. Mining capital, eager to exploit this opportunity, renewed pressure for the reduction of daily wage rates from 9d to 6d.[43] In the crisis of 1913–14, the colonial state proved to be crucial in the resolution of the wage-food dilemma of the mine companies; they provided railway extension porters to the Niger

Company and subsidized the means of subsistence. Lugard, however, imposed taxes on mine labor to compensate for the decline in rural revenues, and actually closed the minefield in 1914. The chronic food deficits of that year threw into sharp relief the contradictory limits of simultaneously raising corvée mine labor, groundnut production, railway workers and maximizing government revenue. After 1913 mine companies began to stock grain on a regular basis, provide foodstuffs directly to the work force in addition to wages, and employ the European merchant houses, who moved increasingly further afield, as suppliers of wage foods. But the tensions between the minefield demands, labor, and export commodity production were never adequately resolved and resurfaced with particular intensity in the early 1940s.

1914 A PRECAPITALIST FAMINE?

In spite of its purported generality, the 1913–14 famine was uneven in its impact. Gombe suffered a poor sorghum harvest though millets flourished; rainfall in Kabba was well below average yet farther north in Zaria the wet season was moderately plentiful and harvests about normal. Kano, Sokoto, and Bornu provinces bore the brunt of hunger and high mortality. But I have suggested that the appalling rainfall of 1913 should not blind us to the new socioeconomic conditions presented by the first decade of imperial rule in the North. Coincident with the drought years of 1912 and 1913 was the excitement of the first groundnut planting, an experimental revenue system that significantly increased precolonial direct taxes and potential losses of male labor power to the mines and railways. In Bornu, grain reserves disappeared overnight in 1912, when 2,000 tons of cereals were evacuated to the plateau; taxes on adult men and women and the jangali rose by 200 percent between 1912 and 1914 (Mshelia 1977, p. 30) and large-scale grain requisition commenced with the outbreak of war. These developments, and additional demands placed by a resident fighting force along the German-held Cameroonian border, provided a particularly unfavorable setting for an admittedly severe harvest shortfall.

All this is to suggest that I am circumspect about the claims of the Hausa themselves that *Yunwar Malali* was entirely in the tradition of great Sudanese famines, with enormous physical and social dislocation, high mortality of humans and livestock, and grain almost wholly unprocurable. In these ways, 1913–14 was a precapitalist crisis; a period of absolute scarcity constrained by technological underdevelopment. The railway was completed in 1912 but was not employed for relief purposes; in any case, the movement of grain in the districts remained in the hands of yan kwarami using donkeys and camels. We are dealing with what Sen

(1980) calls a famine as a direct entitlement failure. But to denote 1914 as precapitalist also conceptually impoverishes it. The conquest had not smashed peasant relations of production at a stroke, but the capture of the circulation process by European capital brought a powerful, if uneven, drive to encapsulate, and ultimately erode these relations. The early 1900s brought the first flurry of development in this transformation of peasant life; in much of this the colonial state, preparing the way for merchant's capital, intervened to supervise and organize the conditions of exploitation of labor and land. It had not been entirely successful in its mission by 1913, and this was a period of sometimes chaotic transition. But these changes—the demise of zakkat granaries, the odious tax burden, the dislocation of agricultural routines—were all strategically significant in the peculiar character of Yunwar Malali. Indeed, there is a case to be made that if the famine itself was illuminated by the ambience of emergent commodity relations one of its effects was to intensify this luminescence. In short, 1914 was a watershed in the incorporative process. Its *genesis* was clearly inseparable from the decade of gradual impoverishment instigated by the colonial state; its *effect* was to further stimulate commodity production.

The pastoral sector in particular highlights the dialectical character of famine genesis and impact. Both Touareg and Ful'be herds suffered as a direct consequence of conquest; the French forces conscripted animals, particularly camels, and Lugard settled, by force, 2,000 to 3,000 Touareg in northern Sokoto (Thom 1972, p. 35). As early as 1901, the possibility of a highly commercialized cattle trade had been broached (Okediji 1973, p. 5) although the administration vacillated on whether livestock supply could be permanently enhanced without sedentarization. Through colonial spectacles, the nomad was the embodiment of economic irrationality, susceptible to no material or commercial inducement for animal sale. The cattle tax (jangali) provided a rather blunt but effective instrument for the commercialization of the livestock sector, but in the course of collection herd mobility was actively restricted, herds forcibly divided, and access to pasture reduced (Dunbar 1970). Many pastoral households fled to more remote pastures, Wo'daa'be lineages from Sokoto and Katsina migrating to Bauchi and Tanout (Sutter 1980; de St. Croix 1944). The Shuwa Arabs in Bornu were especially truculent in the face of the 3 percent jangali tax, but after five years of continual harassment, including massive fines by Resident Hewby, they were compelled to pay 20,000 head of cattle and 30,000 goats by 1911 (NAK SNP 19 1815/1905). In 1913, in a desperate attempt to exercise some measure of control, Hewby formed the famous Shuwa Patrol,[45] consisting of sixty *mallams* and a company of soldiers, to finally resolve the livestock census difficulties

(NAK SNP 15 CC0020/1913). Nine thousand animals were confiscated as most of the Shuwa families fled into the Cameroons.

The drought years of 1911–13 must have fallen particularly heavily on the pastoral economy since it was roughly coincident with the gradual demise of the trans-Saharan trade (Baier 1980). Furthermore, there was a major rinderpest epidemic in 1913 in which cattle losses were estimated to be roughly 100,000. The nature of decapitalization along the desert edge is difficult to gauge since small livestock were generally liquidated in periods of hardship. But the toll of the rinderpest outbreak assuredly meant that by the 1914 famine, pastoral households were compelled to sell immature and reproductive heifers and milch cattle. In the summer of 1914, Ambrosini Company in Kano purchased in excess of 60,000 calf skins. As the terms of trade moved sharply against herders, weak and poor-quality cattle glutted the livestock markets. At famine prices, a mature cow exchanged for three to six pounds of millet;[46] hides and skins abounded at ludicrously depressed prices (table 6.6). More than 100,000 cattle perished in the vicinity of Katsina town alone; according to Stenning (1959, p. 86), in 1913 "the [western] Wo'daa'be numbered 10,000 with 88,000 cattle; in 1914 they were estimated at 5,500 and 26,000 cattle."[47]

An unforeseen consequence of 1914 was the breaking of commercial resistance among herders. The influx of cattle and the proliferation of distress sales opened new avenues between urban merchants and the nomad sector and provided an incentive to break into the large urban consumer markets in the south of Nigeria. In 1908, roughly 20,000 animals trekked southward from Ilorin; by 1920 over 100,000 head crossed Jebba each year (Okediji 1973, p. 8). A jangali assessment in 1915 reported a major increase in the supply of cattle to Kano, and it is on record that the number of city butchers increased significantly during the First World War. The famous Wudil cattle market began about 1915 and from this period one can chart the meteoric growth of major rural cattle markets along the Niger-Nigeria border (see figure 6.4), which signaled the incorporation of nomadic households firmly into the market nexus.[48]

TABLE 6.6
LIVESTOCK PRODUCTS

Product	1913	1914
Hides	473,455	1,344,599
Skins	654,528	1,418,858

SOURCE: National Archives, Kaduna SNP 9/2 1915.

In sum, then, the 1914 famine effected a transition along the desert edge; the Sahel increasingly came to supply labor and cattle in highly commercialized networks held together through ties of merchant kinship and clientage. Nomad communities reduced their social and geographic flexibility, and the Touareg in particular gradually lost control over their grain-producing estates in the northern savannas.

> By the 1920's most nomadic Touareg retained only nominal ties with people who had once been under their control. Nomads occasionally visited farming villages but rarely stayed overnight, no longer recovered grain as tribute and were unable to stay . . . in case of drought. [Baier 1980, p. 138]

In this light it is hard to know why Baier should conclude that after 1914 the desert edge was "more isolated than it had been before the twentieth century" (p. 137); and more incongruously, that the 1913 drought "did not produce serious social and economic dislocation" (p. 139).

In Nigeria it would be absurd to deflate the significance of the 1914 famine, and equally specious to point to the spectacular recovery and growth of groundnut revenues. It was doubtless the groundnut revolution that led Palmer to pronounce that by 1916 "things were back to normal" (NAK Katprof 1 1242/1916). Ironically, it was probably the favorable groundnut prices of the postfamine period that made it possible

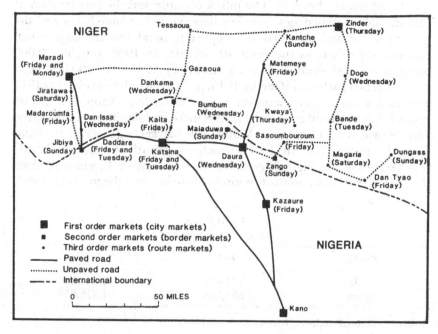

Figure 6.4. Principal border market centers, Katsina emirate.

for the rural poor to survive and accumulate reserves. But here, of course, lay the rub; Hausa smallholders, in the aftermath of such massive economic and social dislocation, had little choice but to plunge headlong into commodity production based on favorable prices. Debts incurred during 1914 and the doubling of tax in 1917 projected peasants inexorably into the complex circuits of colonial capital. The famine, then, served as a trigger for the rupturing of peasant reproduction. Still larger areas were devoted to the groundnut production, especially in the Kano divisions, and the dilemma of food provision became yet more critical. Groundnut production doubled every year in the postwar years, and famine actually seemed to have intensified and consolidated the very developments that were instrumental in its genesis.

The period 1905 to 1914 was a roller coaster pattern of boom and bust and set a precedent for the entire colonial era. Export commodity production grew as foodstuffs were neglected. A boom year such as 1913 saw quite serious food deficits, but this coincided with a catastrophic drought. With the outbreak of war and a trade depression in export crops, 1914 was an especially bad famine year. Yet this was followed immediately by a return to subsistence among rural producers that resulted in overproduction, the collapse of grain prices in the post-famine economy and a return to groundnuts. This trade cycle moved hand in hand with merchant rivalry and frequently market withdrawal, and with producers necessarily making planting decisions wholly based on the previous season's export prices in spite of the very real possibility of massive downswings in the international market. Not surprisingly, only six years after the famine came another boom and bust, although the worst was yet to come with the depression of the 1930s. Unfortunately, institutional learning by the colonial administration was minimal at best, and at worst, horribly misplaced; Resident Hastings, for instance, observed in 1915 after the Kano disaster that

> Nigerian farmers are not provident, they never take thought about the morrow, or keep a reserve in hand for times of scarcity . . . constitutionally they are lazy . . . and they trust to luck and allah. [Hastings 1925, pp. 111, 112]

By 1918 Resident Malcolm in Zaria was sounding the alarm over declining foodstuffs, rapid urbanization, and the extension of cotton production.[49] Yet amid the frenzy of expanded commercial opportunities, it was as though 1914 had never happened.

A Note on Irrigation

One offshoot of the food crisis during the First World War was the first serious suggestion of irrigation development in the North. The potential for water control in a highly seasonal regime subject to unreli-

able rains was quite evident, especially in view of the colonial project in
India. Indigenous flood retreat and hand irrigation of fadama areas had
expanded considerably in the nineteenth century, but it was the Resident
of Sokoto Province, Major Edwardes, who made the first systematic effort
at large-scale floodwater impoundment in the Sokoto and Rima valleys
(Mss. Afr. S. 769, Rhodes House). The first survey of irrigation potential
was undertaken by Colonel Collins, a military engineer with experience in
India, with the blessing of the Department of Agriculture. Yet in spite of
occasional bouts of enthusiasm in 1919 and again in 1937 (NAK Kadminagric. 26902, Vol. I) parsimony prevented any significant investment in
irrigation infrastructure, at least until the etablishment of the Irrigation
Division in 1949. The Sokoto schemes limped through the depression
years plagued by a host of technical and political difficulties. In 1922 the
structures for impounding the flood waters failed completely and were
destroyed by exceptional floods. But, in spite of reconstruction problems,
irrigation was sufficiently attractive to the Sokoto administrators to war-
rant a new effort along the Shalla floodplain. The Kwarre scheme, begun
in 1925, developed 600 acres for perennial irrigation (Swainson 1938).
The government actively pursued cash cropping but returns to wet-
season rice and dry-season irrigated vegetables were generally low and
variable; in many years flooding inflicted massive losses (Palmer-Jones
1977, 1981). These debilitating handicaps led to a low uptake of irrigation
farms, which, in the eyes of the colonial managers, was a stunning confir-
mation of peasant apathy, laziness, and "an incomprehensible lethargy"
(Swainson 1944). In 1927 the Marabawra bank broke and destroyed the
rice crop; and again in 1936 a burst bank cost the Sokoto NA in the order
of £1,000 in repairs.

Many of the early Kwarre problems centered on land tenure and
peasant compliance; it was not until the Sultan of Sokoto authorized
dispossession[50] that flood-protected areas were expropriated, consolidated, and allocated to "suitable farmers," all subject to eviction in the
event of poor agricultural performance.[51] The new clientele of mixed
farmers cultivated a minimum of four acres and were funded by a Sokoto
NA loans scheme, which displayed a pronounced bureaucratic and elite
bias.[52] The presence of the sarauta class could not, however, compensate
for continued technical problems, poor management, and the slow decline of the physical infrastructure. Palmer-Jones (1981) argues that land
expropriation, enforceable tenancies, and "economic" water rates were all
resisted in the 1930s, not least because they flouted indirect rule.
Demands for technical changes lapsed in the face of what the Chief
Secretary for Irrigation called "vested interests" and by the late 1930s the
entire system was a shambles (Carrow, Mss. Afr. S1443, Rhodes House).
Like so much that was to pass for postwar rural development, the early

irrigation efforts were grossly underfunded, shackled with inappropriate agricultural technology, overburdened by problems of farmer compliance and tenant conflicts, and ultimately confronted with the reality of elite usurpation. Perhaps appropriately, Kwarre was finally overwhelmed in 1940 by a flood.

1919–1939: CONSOLIDATION AND THE DEPRESSION ECONOMY

In most regions, the people are well nourished; they are well clad, and increasingly well clad; the professional beggar is as flourishing as he ever was, and knows nothing about any slump; and the appearance of the happy children simply inspires the observer with regret that there are not more of them; for any idea of adequate provision for them not being available, does not enter his mind. . . . Nigeria is one of those happy countries in which none need starve who is willing to work.

—Colonial Sanitary Director, 1933

[There has been] no cause for serious alarm [about famine] in the last 20 years . . . a famine policy is unwarranted.

—Lieutenant Governor Goldsmith, Governor of the Northern Provinces, 1919

The favorable economic trends of the first decade were firmly blocked by the First World War. The barter terms of trade declined because of the shortage and high price of imported goods; export expansion, conversely, was checked by the closure of European markets and the disappearance of shipping space. Faced with the prospect of depressed trade and great uncertainty in the world oilseed markets, the firms were determined to ensure low producer prices for groundnuts, especially after the soaring prices of 1913 fueled in part by merchant competition. A pool that had been formed to regulate the high prices prior to the war was resurrected in 1915, involving Holt's, MacInnes, London and Kano Company and the French Company. The following year, however, the pool broke down again and the local groundnut price reached £9.10.0 per ton; by February 1920 it was an unthinkable £36 per ton. The inflated postwar prices of both cotton and nuts turned the terms of trade in favor of peasant commodity producers. Prices of grains had settled down to a reasonable postfamine level of 0.5d per pound and as long as export commodity prices rose, which they did sharply after 1918, the tax burden and the debts incurred in 1914 were muted. This meant that credit remained available and a variety of employment opportunities were created in commerce and agriculture. Table 6.7 reveals that in spite of the

Famine over Hausaland

TABLE 6.7
Tax Levies and Cotton Prices: Maska District Katsina Emirate

Year	Population	Index of tax per adult male 1911 = 100	Cotton export price (£ per ton)
1911–12	9,814	100	67.1
1913	10,000	79	52.8
1914	10,000	123	56.0
1915	10,000	166	63.0
1916	14,454	133	46.5
1917	13,480	147	73.3
1918	13,502	225	99.3
1919	11,862	212	146.7
1920	11,130	222	161.1
1921	11,503	200	220.1
1922	11,518	212	64.0

Source: National Archives Kaduna NAK SNP 9 1044/1923, Katsina Division Maska District Assessment, 1923.

progressively heavier tax burden between 1914 and 1920 in a cotton district of southern Katsina, the favorable buying prices from the BCGA largely compensated for any deleterious effects of colonial assessment. However, buoyant commodity markets increasingly drew peasant producers into the export economy with the result that the shock field detonated by price recession embraced a much wider territory.

This first major boom terminated sharply in 1920 with an almost total collapse of the commercial sector. The upswing had in fact been the result of a sharp price rise fed by the accumulated commodity demand of the war period, which led to considerable stock and commodity speculation. Prices reached absurd heights, but as the surge was contained the real impact of wartime dislocation and low consumer demand was finally felt. The margarine industry was swept up into this boom-and-bust cycle (Shenton 1982); between 1919 and 1923 the price of margarine fell by 25 percent, a slump that was transmitted to the groundnut industry. In northern Nigeria, cut-throat competition between buying agents, middlemen, and the firms during 1919 had pumped export commodity prices to enormously inflated levels. The colonial howl of execration that ensued against the middlemen was crystallized in a combine of certain European firms with the object of regulating prices; yet no sooner had the cartel gelled than the crash came.

Home market prices fell almost hour by hour . . . home banks refused all further advances . . . local firms received orders to cease buying . . . and to dispose of their trade goods at below cost price. . . . With their purchased stocks unsaleable and the enforced sale of their local goods, the commerical gloom was intense. . . . The speculative competition benefited the few . . . the trader (who has enriched himself) the producer has not reaped the golden harvest. . . . It is to be hoped in the future that the cultivation of grain . . . will not be sacrificed to . . . the production of groundnuts. [NAK SNP 10 316p/1921]

The Kano Resident observed that the cessation in trade had, like a vast broom, "swept the Augean stable clean"; but not without cost. For a number of firms, the purchase of consumer goods and oilseeds at boom prices had been financed by bank credit. When the collapse came, the companies (particularly the Niger Company) found themselves shackled with overpriced stocks and much credit distributed in the countryside that could not be redeemed. The Niger Company, in the face of considerable debt, was bought out by Lever Brothers.

The crisis was also transmitted to the colonial state itself. It became painfully obvious that the official budget was subject to the variability so typical of open economies; revenue grew in the upswing of the trade cycle yet plunged downward as commodity prices and the level of commercial activity fell. Administrative expenditures were not readily cut in view of the fixed salaries, debt repayment, and constant costs. The net result was that the fiscal burden was stable as trade slumped. In Maska during 1921, cotton prices fell by 70 percent yet the personal direct tax burden was raised by 10 percent (NAK SNP 9 1044/1923). While the 1921–22 buying season saw cotton prices fall by 50 percent, in Zaria cotton sales— based on previous years prices—*increased* by 72 percent. The following year peasants returned to foodstuffs but with the Jos mines closed, causing grain prices to plummet, farmers returned to cotton production in spite of low producer prices.

The obvious glee expressed by European interests at the postwar export recovery was in actual fact something of a two-edged sword, for as Arnett, the Resident of Sokoto Province, commented in 1921 "the cultivation of grain . . . will be sacrificed to cash crops."[53] Although groundnut exports fell in 1922, by 1924 they had grown to 60,000 tons and more than doubled to 132,000 tons in 1924–25. Raw cotton grew from almost 3,000 tons in 1922 to 9,000 tons in 1926 (Helleiner 1966, p. 507).[54] Additionally, the amplified demands of the minefields, the deflection of household labor through voluntary labor, and the concurrent demands of grain requisition, only seemed to highlight Arnett's worst fears.[55] Immediately after the termination of World War I, the Zaria Resident nicely summarized the dilemma.

There is no doubt that corn supply in this Province is insufficient to meet the demand . . . unless cereals are imported. . . . The shortage is said to be due to two causes: the increased cultivation of cotton and groundnuts to the detriment of corn and the ever increasing nonfarm communities on the plateau [NAK SNP 9 2846/1918].

During the slump of 1920–21 a disastrous famine was narrowly averted in Sokoto where erratic rainfall in the western and northern districts had reduced the harvest by about 30 percent. Edwardes, a very much out-of-favor political officer in Sokoto, was correct to note that each year since the war, "the sowing and harvest months are times of enormous anxiety" (NAK SNP 10 26/1922).

From the postwar food crisis emerged the first serious discussion of famine relief.[56] Prompted initially in 1919 by a circular from the secretary for the northern provinces, the heated exchange between provincial Residents highlighted the astounding ignorance and misconception of food security and peasant economy in the North. And yet these groundless judgments actually come to constitute the touchstone for famine policy and food relief. In actual fact, for the remainder of the colonial period little progress was made beyond the 1920s debate.

In his original correspondence, the secretary had posed the likelihood of a major food crisis for which colonial resources were pathetically inadequate. Born in the aftermath of a severe famine in Uganda, due appropriately enough to the massive overproduction of cotton, the memorandum was especially apposite.

> Great as the danger is [of famine] owing to natural causes, the tendency in recent years has been to increase it. Owing to the inducements offered to the native to produce such products as groundnuts and cotton for export and also owing to the large demand for labor for other purposes than food production . . . in the case of a famine . . . the railway would be of little value. [Katsina Museum, #109/1920]

To the extent that the distributive aspect of relief was paramount, the secretary proposed a village-based granary system, a sort of "communal Provident club" as he called it, each adult male depositing a certain number of bundles of corn. A similar plan was offered by the Director of Agriculture, P. H. Lamb, who was also disturbed by "the increased risks of recent years," "grain scarcity," and "alarmingly high prices." Lamb's scheme obliged all masu gidaje to deposit grain with NA granaries for safekeeping, which after five or six years would constitute a reserve capable of provisioning the destitute for two successive seasons. Unfortunately, Lt. Governor Goldsmith, steeped in the tradition of laissez-faire, was deeply critical of both schemes, which he saw as neither practical nor "attractive to the natives." In an extraordinary display of stupidity he suggested that storage was wholly superfluous in view of the historic absence of any known subsistence shortage in over twenty years. Goldsmith went on to demolish a "local level" famine policy suggested by District Officer Browne and the emir of Katsina. Their proposal is nevertheless of signal interest if only for the weight it attaches to the sheer quantitative dimensions of regularizing the conditions of peasant production:

> The problem is how to secure food supply for 200,000 people. . . . It is proposed that the 1921 Haraji be taken in grain instead of money . . . from six districts . . . which represents 86,000 bundles. This will be done for three years. . . In 1924 when the grain is brought in by the farmers they will receive in exchange the same number of bundles in 1921 grain and they will pay their commuted zakka in currency. Similarly in 1925. . . . The granaries should be kept at each District Headquarters . . . they will be built from NA funds. [NAK Kadminagric. 12805/Vol. III, 1922]

The resurrection of what unknowingly was the precolonial zakkat granary system could, according to Browne, be complemented by food imports and purchases wherever necessary, subject to local estimates of a competent district officer who could reasonably judge, at harvest time, the future demand for relief. In impassioned responses, both Governor Clifford and Goldsmith objected that the reinstitution of zakkat was "retrograde," that it was burdensome on the peasantry, that exchange and resale was "complicated" and that the entire system was prone to "petty oppression." The criticisms were quite silly not least because the zakkat had in fact been successfully levied in the recent past, and much of the native authority structure was, by the same token, hopelessly complicated. The real issue was at once philosophical and practical; a general reticence to dabble with the invisible hand of the market as a matter of principle, and an obsessive economic parsimony as a matter of practice.

Ultimately, the fate of the famine scheme rested with the Residents, who seemed oblivious to the functioning of peasant economy and the nature of subsistence security, and apparently convinced that widespread famine was neither a potential nor actual problem. The site of the food dilemma, for higher echelon officers at least, resided with an improvident peasantry, a population of congenital reprobates who did not wish to store or put aside for the future. The possibility of some sections of the northern peasantry being simply too impoverished to store food or to accumulate in any fashion was, to my knowledge, never seriously considered. Even Resident Edwardes of Sokoto, in a complete condemnation of relief, and of his own intelligence, stated that the province had not suffered from food shortage since 1895, and that export crops presented no threat to grain production, which accordingly rendered a grain reserve completely superfluous.[57] Any such system Edwardes observed, was "too costly," "corrupt," and "wasteful." Edwardes was, at least, quite correct in his estimation of the potential costs of a major crisis; to support roughly 50 percent of Sokoto Province alone at a shockingly minimal nutritional level (one pound of millet per person per day) for two months would have cost approximately £250,000; that is to say about ten times the total annual tax revenue of Sokoto Province.

In spite of the prevailing antistorage sentiment, one lone, dissenting voice was that of Governor Clifford who quaintly observed that a temporal aspect of relief was characteristically underestimated, for "people have a nasty way of dying in platoons before relief can reach them" (Katsina Museum #109/1922). As the sole representative of some form of government intervention, Clifford considered selective NA granaries as the necessary wherewithal for the effective mitigation of inevitable future food shortages. The reserves issue was finally concluded by Lt. Governor Goldsmith in 1920 when he determined that granaries could not be maintained at public expense and were subject to "continual abuse." In lieu of relief, Goldsmith summoned up a hefty dose of Cartesian realism: the power of Reason and the merits of technology.

> To summarize my recommendations: moral pressure should be exercised by the Native Authorities to urge farmers to produce food . . . to continue to improve transportation . . . to increase water supply . . . and to encourage Prison farms to make each prisoner self supporting. [Katsina Museum #109/1922]

Quite how this spiritual and material development would forever lay the spectre of famine to rest was somewhat hazy.

In a manner somewhat reminiscent of early British famine policy in India, Goldsmith and the colonial administration had opted for laissez-faire. But while plans for action against famine were tightly bound and gagged in the early 1920s, the muffled cries of declining food production, grain scarcity and inflated prices were frequently heard throughout the interwar era. The prohibition of grain movement into Nigeria by the French colonial authorities placed provincial cereal production in serious jeopardy, especially in the heavily populated central regions. A famine was narrowly averted in northern Katsina in 1921, and a 1924 shortfall in Nassarawa Province required the import of 1,000 tons of rice after the Resident was incapable of procuring any food locally. All this renders Governor Clifford's 1919 statement all the more poignant.

> If you ever had at all a widespread famine in the northern provinces, your honor would find I fear, that even a good deal more than 10,000 of rice . . . would be but the proverbial pill to cure the earthquake. . . . I am not at all sure that we should be wise to content ourselves with assuring one another that we can sleep safely in our beds, which we all know is a habit to which Englishmen are addicted. . . . I see nothing improbable in the occurrence of a famine . . . on a really big scale; and if by that time supplies of locally grown food stuffs have declined [further] . . . large cash balances in NA treasuries will not avert a serious calamity. [Katsina Museum #109/1922]

Clifford did not have to wait long, for in 1927 much of the northern region was in the throes of another severe food crisis.

THE FAMINE OF 1927, YUNWAR KWANA

> Kwana bakar daga hana jere
> Auren da ta kashe ya yi zambar goma

> Kwana, evil charm, that prevents weddings,
> that dissolved marriages, to the tune
> of ten thousand.

As the *Report on Famine Relief in the Northern Provinces* explained, the 1926 harvest was "a partial failure." The very high prices of grains failed to come down to their normal postharvest level during late 1926, and by the early months of the 1927 dry season it became clear that a chronic food shortfall would strike several of the northern provinces. In Bauchi, Benue, and Bornu hunger was intense in isolated pockets while it was widespread throughout much of Kano, Sokoto, and Zaria. Two broad developments provide the context for the 1927 famine. First, the taki system of revenue collection was consolidated and enormously extended throughout the North after 1911. The levy itself raised governmental revenue overnight by leaps and bounds until its demise in the depression. Taki doubled in most of the northern provinces in 1917, and by the mid 1920s rates varied between 1/- and 1/8d per acre. In addition, the plethora of industrial taxes rarely averaged less than 2/- per craftsman. However, the taki tax was disproportionately heavy in the infertile and sparsely populated districts with the result that

> taki . . . curtailed cultivation; the peasant had hesitated to extend his hold [assuming] that his farms would be remeasured . . . and even reduced the size of those at hand. [NAK Zariaprof. 7/1 2575/1928]

Although domestic production sagged under the fiscal weight of taki, governmental revenue was remarkably stable, independent of ecological or market variability. During the famine year 1926–27, direct tax receipts for Kano Division actually rose by 15 percent (NAK Katprof. 1098/1927); similarly, jangali cattle tax collection revealed a notorious stability in the hard-hit northern divisions (table 6.8).

The second development was the deepening of cash crop production. By the late 1920s groundnut production had grown to 147,000 tons per annum, occupying in excess of one million acres of cultivable land; cotton production for export, though strapped by the resiliency of the indigenous textile industry, also showed a general upward trend. Both of these expansions were in the face of sharply declining commodity prices after the zenith of 1920. Groundnut prices fell almost continually between

TABLE 6.8
REVENUE STABILITY: JANGALI RECEIPTS, KANO PROVINCE

District	Amount 1926 (£)	Amount 1927 (£)	Increase or decrease (%)
Hadejia	4,506	4,509	+ 0.001%
Gumel	2,153	2,747	+29.0%
Daura	3,474	3,627	+ 6.0%
Kazaure	2,836	2,513	−10.0%

SOURCE: National Archives Kaduna, NAK SNP 17 K6892 Vol. II Jangali Receipts.

1921 and 1939 (Helleiner 1966, p. 110). This "perverse supply response" substantiates Fika's claim (1973, p. 397) that in Kano Province the average peasant household had come to rely totally on groundnut income to fulfill cash obligations, particularly tax. In Zaria Province a decline in cotton prices of almost 50 percent between 1923 and 1926 was matched by increased sales of 140 percent (Lennihan 1982).

The economic plight of the rural poor was increasingly bleak after 1920, contingent on the peculiar conjunction of taxes, commodity prices, cash demands, debt, and weather. An inflexible revenue system that limited cultivated areas conspired with the depressed condition of export prices to project households further into market exchange at the expense of foodstuff self-sufficiency. All this operated through a volatile price system and the exploitative crop-mortgaging network associated with LBAs and middlemen. In the cotton districts, however, open competition in 1924 combined with uncertainty in the British market to drastically reduce buying in the rural areas, and accordingly few advances were offered (Shenton and Lennihan 1981). Many farmers in 1926 were forced to sell grain to cover tax payments. Either way, the narrowed margin of security effectively blocked accumulation, either of assets or foodstuffs. Deficiencies in groundnut or cotton production was, the Resident observed in Kano in 1930, usually made good by food sales, which necessitated wet-season purchase at much higher prices (NAK SNP 17 14686 Vol. 1/1930).

The rainfall during 1926 was very erratic but generally below the computed means for the 1903–60 period (table 6.9). A more detailed monthly precipitation regime in 1926 for Katsina town indicates a low annual total (18.17 inches), an early termination of the wet season during September, and an especially poor showing in the month of July. Oral testimony hinted that planting was delayed until the first good rains at the end of May and the formation of mature millet heads was stalled by the very abrupt termination of the wet season.[58] Despite an inquiry into the

TABLE 6.9
ANNUAL RAINFALL NORTHERN NIGERIA

Station	Mean (inches)	1925 (inches)	1926 (inches)	1927 (inches)
Kano	33.2	34.6	28.0	30.7
Sokoto	28.6	27.0	22.3	30.6
Maiduguri	26.0	19.4	15.8	27.9

SOURCE: Rainfall statistics, Institute of Agricultural Research, Zaria.

food situation in December 1926 by the secretary to the northern provinces, an attempt at price control was shelved for reasons that are not entirely clear, and it was not until April 1927 that Residents were approached to make relief preparations, and efforts were made to acquire wage goods (NAK Kadminagric. 12805 Vol. 1/1927). The Katsina Resident noted that

the anticipated food shortage began to be apparent by the end of April and it was evident that without some assistance in the form of imported food much hardship and perhaps even death . . . will be the fate of a large proportion of the peasantry. [NAK Katprof. 1 2098/1927]

By the middle of the wet season some of the northern divisions, especially Gumel, Hadejia, and Katagum, were already severely depopulated; many Katsina farmers told me that 1927 actually brought more distress than 1914—a claim lent some support by the tenor of the district reports. Harvests throughout south and central Niger were fair, nonetheless, and the usual influx of peasants and pastoralists characteristic of 1914, did not materialize. Human mortality was probably much lower than in 1913–14 although no attempt was made by the colonial administration to estimate either human losses or social costs. Mortality statistics from Katsina emirate (table 6.10) indicate that death rates increased markedly, most particularly among infants. McCullogh claimed, nevertheless, that he saw no cases of "typical starvation" in Katsina town, only "malnutrition among the aged and the young."[59]

In the remote districts, extensive use was made of wild trees and shrubs notably *giginya, dinya, zure, cediya* and *ciciva*,[60] but most in situ coping mechanisms characteristically involved the liquidation of assets, especially small livestock owned by women. In Kano market, for instance, 60,218 sheep and goats were slaughtered in 1927 in contrast to 26,665 during the previous year. The number of cattle railed from Kano or slaughtered in the urban market remained relatively stable, suggesting that the northern pastoral Fulani economy may have escaped unscathed. Cereal prices, however, responded in a relatively predictable fashion

TABLE 6.10
MORTALITY STATISTICS

	Population		Birth rate (per '000)		Infant mortality (per '000)	
Location	1926	1927	1926	1927	1926	1927
Katsina town	14,682	15,000	17.8	28.13	229	261.7
Katsina emirate	598,940	644,940	20.3	44.0	277.6	438.3

SOURCE: National Archives Kaduna (NAK) Katprof 1/1 2098 Demographic Statistics.

(figure 6.5). Immediately following the trade boom of 1919–20 food prices soared to levels in excess of 1.5d per pound but by 1922 prices of both millet and sorghum had stabilized, subject to the usual seasonal variability of 30–50 percent, at roughly a half penny 5d per pound.[61] During June 1926, preharvest hunger prices of grains had risen sharply to 1.2d and remained at that high level even after the harvest of September 1926. At their zenith, the price of cereals was five to six times higher than the 1925 level, significantly less, however, than the amplitude of food-price variation during 1913–14. The comparison is instructive in view of the opinion reiterated by most farmers and artisans that foodstuffs were generally available in the marketplace in 1927, in contrast to 1914. If the 1927 market figures from Kano are at all representative, the prices of rice and meat were surprisingly stable (table 6.11). As a colonial report exclaimed, the problem was not *absolute dearth* but *relative accessibility*; less of total absence than of hoarded reserves and limited purchasing power. In Sokoto

> it soon became evident . . . that the 1926 harvest had failed to some extent . . . but there were supplies in the hands of a few hoarders. . . . When conditions became acute these hoards were put on the market at a price beyond . . . all but the richest. [Famine Relief Report 1927, p. 49]

The minuscule NA reserves and the small stocks of imported grain were patently inadequate for market rigging, not large enough to "break the corner" as the relief report put it. The Sokoto NA attempted to force the hand of the urban grain merchants by appealing to Muslim piety and respectable commercial conduct, but apparently with no success. As one Katsina elder put it, "in 1914 we had money but no grain, in 1927 we had grain but no money."

The colonial relief effort was, for the most part, another paltry and ad hoc affair. Six hundred forty-five tons of rice were imported into Kano

Province and distributed daily in the city market. During July and August, rice was sold at 2.8 pence per pound, barely below free market levels, with an upper limit of 5/- per individual. In the districts the sale prices were determined by the hakimai and the NA. Relief projects and public works, mostly road building, were conducted in Gumel and Katsina with payment made in cash. In spite of the colonial claims that the communications revolution during the first quarter of the twentieth cen-

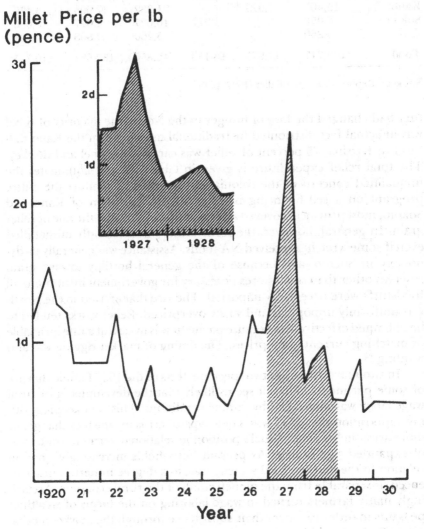

Figure 6.5. Millet prices, Kano Market 1920–30. From (NAK) Kanoprof 5/1 398/vol. 1 Famine Relief.

TABLE 6.12
FOOD EXPENDITURE, INCLUDING TRANSPORTATION

Province	United Kingdom (£)	Nigeria (£)	Local (£)	Total (£)	Receipts (£)	Loss (£)
Bauchi			306	306	21	285
Benue			1,975	1,975	1,975	
Bornu			3,900	3,900	3,900	
Kano	19,407	1,975		21,382	17,903	3,479
Sokoto	8,050		1,977	10,027	4,027	6,000
Zaria	5,260			5,260	4,808	451
Total	£32,717	£1,975	£8,158	£42,850	£32,634	£10,215

SOURCE: Report on Famine Relief (1927, p. 6).

tury had changed the face of hunger in the North, the majority of relief was in actual fact distributed by traditional means. From the Kano rail-head to Katsina, 75 percent of relief was carried by camel and donkey. The total relief expenditure is given in table 6.12 and illuminates the unqualified concern of the colonial government to conduct the entire program on a self-financing basis. With the exception of Kano and Sokoto, most provinces covered all expenditures through the sale of relief grain. In general, however, the relief effort was splendidly mishandled even if some wretches received NA foods. Assistance was generally tardy, notably in Sokoto, and because of the general hostility toward grain reserves other than small stores necessary for government institutions all foodstuffs were necessarily imported. The rice that arrived in the North was uniformly unpopular and vastly overpriced. Relief works tended to be of limited effectiveness because payment was in cash at a rate incapable of matching current grain prices. The timing of market rigging was also wanting.[62]

In summary, there are two specific effects of the 1927 famine that are of some pertinence. First, it seems likely that the development of rural wage labor was intensified by famine conditions. This is in keeping with my supposition that 1927 was a new type of crisis in which exchange, or more accurately an individual's position in relation to terms of trade, was of expanded significance. As peasant households increasingly stood in relation to the market, food scarcity was, to a degree hitherto unexperienced, inseparable from the monetization of the rural economy. Accordingly many farmers turned to wage laboring on the farms of wealthier peasants in order to secure their subsistence through the market mechanism. And second, the advance system, which had begun to take hold in the cotton districts in 1926, proliferated with renewed vigor in 1927.

Many farmers were naturally reluctant to plant cotton, and much of the seed distributed was in fact promptly consumed by a population desperately in need of sustenance. But the middlemen climbed on the back of the famine conditions, which they used to expand their credit policy and cash advances. According to Shenton and Lennihan (1980, p. 20, 21), the influx of cash benefited the prosperous peasants who promptly hired wage laborers from a labor pool swollen by the crisis. In a sense, then, the

TABLE 6.11
PRICES OF LOCAL FOODSTUFFS, KANO MARKET

			Price of foodstuff per lb (in pence)					
	Dawa	*Gero*	*Beans*	*Rice*	*Wheat*	*Cassava*	*Beef*	*Mutton*
1925								
March	0.8	0.9	1.0	1.5	2.0	0.48	3.0	4.0
June	0.6	0.7	0.8	1.32	3.0	0.3	3.0	4.0
September	0.56	0.51	0.8	0.75	0.3	0.24	3.0	4.0
December	0.66	0.71	0.69	1.09	–	–	–	–
1926								
March	0.8	0.9	0.87	1.0	3.0	–	3.0	1.0
June	1.20	1.26	1.45	–	3.0	–	4.0	4.75
September	1.1	1.1	1.0	1.3	1.7	0.5	3.4	3.0
December	1.1	0.89	0.96	1.24	2.4	0.5	3.0	3.0
1927								
March	1.5	1.7	1.7	2.0	3.0	0.6	3.0	4.0
June	2.7	2.7	2.8	3.0	3.0	0.8	3.0	4.0
September	1.57	1.0	1.5	1.0	4.0	0.48	3.0	3.0
December	0.7	0.9	0.6	0.9	2.5	0.5	2.4	3.0
1928								
March	0.8	1.0	0.7	1.0	2.0	0.4	3.0	3.5
June	1.0	0.8	0.8	1.0	4.0	0.4	4.0	4.0
September	0.6	0.7	0.7	0.8	2.0	0.3	3.0	4.0
December	0.6	0.6	0.6	0.7	4.5	0.4	2.4	3.0
1929								
March	0.6	0.7	0.6	0.9	2.0	0.6	3.0	4.0
June	0.9	1.2	0.7	1.8	2.4	0.4	4.0	6.0
September	0.5	1.0	0.6	0.7	4.0	0.2	3.0	2.0
December	0.6	0.7	0.7	1.0	2.0	3.0	3.0	4.0
1930								
March	0.6	0.7	0.6	1.0	2.0	0.8	3.0	4.0
June	0.6	0.7	0.9	1.2	3.0	0.21	2.0	2.5
September	0.6	0.7	0.9	1.2	3.0	0.2	2.0	2.5
December	0.5	0.6	0.4	0.8	1.5	0.3	2.4	3.0

SOURCE: NAK SNP 17 29652a, 1930.

1927 famine brought an end to peasant resistance to commoditization, and particularly to the wage relation that had historically been shrouded in shame and dishonor. As the new wave of buying agents burst into the cotton and groundnut districts after 1927, commoditization had irrevocably broken the cycle of peasant reproduction.

A NEW FAMINE POLICY

One concrete achievement that emerged from the 1927 food crisis was an attempt by the northern regional government to formulate a general scheme for famine relief in the northern provinces. The drought-prone northern provinces of Sokoto, Zaria, Kano, Bauchi, and Bornu were given primary attention since "the chief factor [causing] famine would be shortage of rainfall" (Famine Relief 1927, p. 3). Ironically, however, the first food crisis after 1927 occurred in the southern provinces, caused by locust infestation. At any rate, the scheme involved three stages. The first pertained to local shortage, for which NAs made their own arrangements. Second, a stage when famine conditions required government cooperation, the form of which was spelled out in the 1927 Food Control Ordinance.[63] And third, when the capability of NAs to cope was overwhelmed, executive functions passed direct to the central government. Rice was to be the principal relief item, distributed at subsidized prices at an allowance of one pound per person per day. The anticipated quantities required month by month were calculated on the basis of sustaining a stipulated proportion of the total population on minimal requirements (table 6.13). The absurdly high expenditure to support a relatively small proportion of the population in the northern provinces did not go unnoticed, and the relief report consoled itself with the firm belief that such eventualities could only materialize in the unlikely event of two consecutive harvest failures. The relief scheme threw into sharp relief the very real possibility of a regional famine that would grossly exceed the administration's capacity to finance or administer. Imported rice was estimated at £15 per ton at Kano, which meant in simple terms that the outlay for famine relief to cover a regional famine of some seriousness would comfortably exceed one million pounds sterling. The total annual direct revenue for Kano and Bornu NAs—two "wealthy" provinces—was £198,000. The self-help basis of the relief scheme assumed, of course, that imported rice would be sold to the needy but, as the 1927 experience revealed, the absence of requisite purchasing power among the rural poor necessitated free or at least massively subsidized grain distribution. NA losses, in other words, were inevitable.

Perhaps because of the contradictions embodied in the famine relief scheme it was rarely referred to after 1927 and responsibility for food distribution fell back on the NA arrangement referred to in the report.

In actual fact, there were no arrangements. This was not explicitly addressed until the early 1930s at the Proceedings of the Northern Provinces Advisory Council. Ironically, one of the prime movers in the resuscitation of NA grain reserves was European mining capital, which faced labor unrest and desertion as grain procurement on the plateau became ever more tenuous. The crux of the issue was that as export cropping ate into domestic food production, not only was the likelihood of regional scarcity and price instability magnified but the minesfield was held to ransom by Nigerian grain merchants who grew fat and happy on

TABLE 6.13
FAMINE RELIEF EXPENDITURES: 1927 SCHEME

Relief schedule

Month	% population to be fed
1st	4
2nd	8
3rd	12
4th	16
5th	20
6th	20
7th	24
8th	24
9th	28
10th	28
11th	32
12th	32

Food relief for Bornu, Bauchi, Kano, Sokoto, Zaria

Month	Tons
July	2,590
August	5,180
September	7,770
October	11,510
November	15,250
December	16,400
January	20,140
February	21,290
March	23,880
April	25,030
May	27,620
June	28,770
TOTAL	205,430 tons

SOURCE: Scheme for Famine Relief, pp. 6–17.

their speculative profits. Even the European trade houses like UAC, who generally supplied NA requirements, actually used Hausa merchants for grain purchase in the local markets. It was, then, high irony that a representative of European mine capital, Mr. Butler, should protest to the emirs that the Hausa grain mechant who bought at £5 a ton and sold at £12 was "making an excessive profit" (Northern Province Advisory Council 1931, p. 23).[64]

The issue of local granaries was the subject of much discussion at the Emirs' Conference in the early 1930s, if only because opinion was so divided (NAK Kadminagric. 9970/1930). The emir of Katsina, a vociferous proponent of centralized NA granaries sustained by voluntary zakkat contributions, confronted a muted emir of Gwandu who tabled a local, village-based scheme based on compulsory household contributions. Each blueprint raised questions concerning the location of reserves, NA purchase versus obligatory contributions, methods of disposal and renewal of stock and, not least, granary technology (cement versus local bins). In part because of the complexity of administration and the depth of divided opinion, the governor decided to advance on a small-scale experimental basis in 1931 though it is entirely unclear from the archival record who was to do what to whom. It should come as no surprise then that throughout the depression harvest shortfalls caught the NAs with their administrative pants firmly entangled around their ankles. In 1931 after the locust outbreak in the southern districts, the Resident of Zaria Province was found to be scrambling desperately for 1,000 tons of grain. Eight years later at the outbreak of the Second World War a memorandum from the Department of Agriculture in Ibadan requesting information on local storage was met with blank stares from the emirs and an embarrassing repeat of earlier debates by the Residents on "the realities of native habits of mind and custom" (NAK Kadminagric. 31657/S.#. Vol. II).

THE DEPRESSION YEARS, 1929–1939

The Europeans have brought many changes. There is nothing, our thought, our traditional way of life, which has not changed.

—Gaskiya Ta Fi Kwabo, 1935.

The idea of any form of economy by setting aside an odd six pence during months of prosperity is alien to their mentality and the consequence is that one receives an impression of poverty.

—Kaita District Officer, Katsina Province, 1933.

From its inception the groundnut trade depended upon a class of middlemen who acted as the lower-order buying agents for the European trading houses. In the early years the influential Hausa merchants gained access to the firms through the emirs and, using their own commercial networks and linkages, initiated a vital service by collecting produce in the outlying districts, buying direct from the producer, or using their agents, often village and district heads. By the 1920s a new group of intermediaries had emerged; they were of North African and Middle Eastern descent and came to dominate the middle rungs of the groundnut buying hierarchy. The "Syrians" as they were colloquially referred to, posed a competitive threat to the European companies, and in 1929 made an abortive attempt to bypass the firms altogether by exporting to Marseilles. In spite of the absence of any state support, particularly by regulating native produce markets, the firms responded with the formation of a buying pool, which the French agents joined two years later, leaving the Syrians completely in the cold. As in the past, the pool was not easily held together in the face of stiff competition from the likes of Saul Raccah. Indeed, the decade following the great crash was, above all, a frontal attack by the European firms on the Syrian and African middlemen in an attempt to preserve their commercial hegemony.

The strength of the Syrians' commerce lay in their control of the rural sector. But the extension of branch rail lines in the 1930s into Sokoto and Hadejia and the establishment of equalized freight charges reoriented the hinterland away from the powerful Kano-based Syrians. The stock market slump of 1929 greatly exacerbated the commercial strife. The price of groundnuts fell by 40 percent between March 1928 and March 1931, recovering slightly in 1932 only to plummet again in 1934. In a desperate attempt to stabilize their income, peasants expanded their output, exports rising from 135,000 tons in 1928–29 to almost 200,000 tons in 1932–33.[65] The cotton statistics show a similar trend. Yet in both cases direct tax revenue in relation to export price indexes remained quite stable (table 6.14). Expanded production occurred in the traditional export zones but the railway and buying agent competition had pushed the frontier of cultivation deep into the peripheral districts. In the annual report for 1933, the Resident of Kano observed that:

> Economically, groundnuts provide the lifestream for the Province. A falling price last year stimulated the extension of cultivation. . . . Roughly this year it takes the peasant twice as much in groundnuts to meet tax and there has been little left over for expenditure. [NAK SNP 7 21326 Vol. I/1933]

Pressures on producer incomes were such that in the northern divisions, pastoral Fulani were reported to have planted groundnuts to obtain tax monies.

The squeeze on producer income was felt by the firms as declining profits in their import trade. As more peasant surplus labor was appro-

TABLE 6.14
GOVERNMENT TAX REVENUE, EXPORT PRICES, AND COTTON PRODUCTION

Year	Index of total direct tax revenue Northern Provinces (1926 = 100)	Index of export commodity prices (1926 = 100)	Price of cotton per pound (pence)	Cotton exports** (Number of 400-lb bales)
1923–24	108	114	3–4	15,683
1924–25	99	109	3	27,996
1925–26	100	100	2.5	37,556
1926–27	105	116	1.2–1.75	16,659
1927–28	106	107	2.26–2.13	16.316
1928–29	78	83	2.25–2.13	24,686
1929–30	79	59	1.0–1.2	34,389
1930–31	77	47	0.8–0.5	13,849
1931–32	77	69	0.66–0.8	4,811
1932–33	77	37	0.8–0.9	22,228
1933–34	88	49*	0.9–1.2	23,013

SOURCES: Jacob (1934), Lennihan (1982), Northern Nigeria Agriculture Department Reports (1923–1929), NAK Kadminagric, 20121.

*Estimate
**Refers to purchased cotton in the Northern Provinces only.

priated for taxes by the colonial state, domestic demand for cotton baft and European wares necessarily diminished. Faced with declining rural income, renewed commercial competition and a demand for cash in the countryside, the companies and middlemen responded with a huge expansion of the advance-crop mortgaging system to at least secure a satisfactory portion of peasant production.[66] During the depression, the yan baranda system of cotton mortgaging flourished in southern Katsina and Zaria.[67] The system involved the establishment of buying clerks as "fuloti," who were advanced money by the firms for whom they purchased on a commission basis. The fuloti in turn advanced to his yan baranda employees, who negotiated with individual producers and received a percent of the fuloti's commission. During the early 1930s, grade B cotton was purchased at the farm gate at prices minimally 15 percent below the equivalent of the licensed buying stations. The farmers took loans from the yan baranda using the cotton crop as collateral. The practical implications of the mortgage were that

the dan baranda has . . . an absolute monopoly until the loan is paid off . . . the middleman takes advantage of this and the farmer sells one bundle of cotton before he is told that he has repaid the 10/- debt. Although the farmer could repay in cash, the lender will not take his money unless the crop has failed . . . [hence] the dan baranda makes money by manipulating the scales while the farmer is paying off his debt in cotton. [Katsina Museum, #234/1934]

As the tax burden absorbed an ever greater proportion of peasant income—estimated at 38 to 40 percent of total income by Jacob (MSS. Afr. T. 16 1934 Rhodes House) in 1934—cash advances took the form of the middleman paying the producer's tax and withholding the receipt until crop delivery. According to a conservative estimate in the 1930s, middlemen were estimated to absorb at least 20 percent of the total f.o.b. price for export commodities excluding usurious appropriations.

The proliferation of debt and the advance system hinged in many respects on the critical role of tax in the cycle of peasant reproduction.[68] The vicious pressures effected by the conjunction of high tax and low export prices is clearly illustrated in Parsons's assessment of groundnut cultivation in Roni and Yankwashi districts in Kazaure during the mid-1930s when export prices had fallen from an index of 100 in 1926 to 37 in 1933.

> The average farmer producing 10 baskets of groundnuts was just and only just able to pay his tax out of his groundnut [revenue] this season, for 10 buckets at 9d is 7/6d [and tax] is . . . 7/-. [NAK Kanoprof. 20007/1937]

Parsons observed that the price of groundnuts per bucket fluctuated from 5 d to 1/-, being generally higher near the railhead at Kano and Danbarta. The minimum price for groundnuts to cover tax was £2.13.0 per ton but every drop of 5/- a ton below this amount meant almost 2/- off the farmers income. Successive drops in relation to the tax can be represented as follows:

£2.10.0 = 95% tax
£2.0.0 = 71% tax
£1.15.0 = 60% tax

Not only were prices much lower in the more isolated districts—for example £1.10.0 per ton in northern Katsina—but as Parsons noted, needy farmers would sell crops in advance at depressed rates. By the late 1930s the prevailing Kazaure groundnut prices barely covered 75 percent of the tax levy. A district officer from Hadejia concluded from Parsons's study that

> the Kazaure farmer owning a donkey can just pay a 7/- tax with groundnuts at 55/- in Kano. . . . To achieve this the farmer must obtain a good crop and be prepared to sell it all and to devote the entire proceeds to tax. [NAK Kanoprof. 20007/1937]

Two points emerge from Parsons's study; first, the *relatively well-off farmer*—the smallholder with a donkey—could barely meet tax demands from groundnut production and was overwhelmingly dependent upon off-farm revenue to fulfill other cash demands. And second, in Kazaure where population pressure was relatively slight, the subsistence security of the average hoe farmer was surely greater than in the close settled zones where tax levies were on average higher, and where land was in short supply. Parsons concluded, like the Kano Resident a few years earlier, that the rural poor in Kazaure sold corn regularly "as the universal remedy for tax arrears."

A more general impression of the reproduction squeeze is presented in table 6.15 for three central Kano districts during 1933. Assuming that the Kano peasant depended upon groundnut revenue for tax payment, at 1933 prices the acreages required for groundnuts varied between 0.7 and 1.7 acres. Given the small size of an average peasant holding (roughly four acres in Kano in 1933) we have some measure of the proportion of holdings devoted to export production. The Resident assessment calculated that if prices remained stable, a below average harvest would mean "immediate hardship." Not surprisingly, the process of tax collection became exceedingly difficult.

> The very low prices prevailing during the present season has caused tax collection to be slower and the realization of the necessary amount . . . has entailed the expenditure of considerable time. [NAK SNP 17 14868 Vol. I/1930]

The rural tax collectors often compounded the fiscal crisis since their own salaries barely covered living expenditures and there was a positive inducement to embezzle, particularly by accepting and squandering tax payments in advance, a process known locally as kudin falle. It was, in fact, during this period that the idea of some form of sliding scale to graduate tax in accordance with price or harvest was first proposed. Sliding scales, tax remissions, and the like were never seriously considered, however, for the very good reason that a burgeoning state payroll demanded a large and stable revenue.

The outcome of the specific Nigerian conjuncture of a global market crisis and a predatory colonial state was the proliferation of rural indebtedness throughout the depression. A study of Zaria Province by Giles commissioned to estimate the extent of rural debt estimated that between 30 and 40 percent of all producers were seriously indebted (NAK Zariaprof 1486A/1937). Loans had become a necessary moment in the cycle of social reproduction. Significantly, Giles discovered that the three principal causes of debt were food shortage, tax, and marriage expenses. Haunted by the spectre of India, the colonial administration feared a further expansion of trade in standing crops; by 1932 almost 12 percent of civil cases in the northern provinces (roughly 20,000 in all) concerned debt, though quite clearly the vast majority of disputes did not reach the stage of formal litigation at all (Buell 1955, p. 692). The European firms attempted to use the credit issue to put more pressure on the middlemen,

TABLE 6.15
GROUNDNUT CULTIVATION AND TAXES: KANO DIVISION, 1933

| District | Tax per adult male | | Average yield of groundnuts per acre | Price per ton (shillings) | Acreage to pay tax | Estimated average holding (acres) |
	s	d				
Kumbotso	11	6	350 lbs	50	1.7	3.5
Bichi	8	–	420 lbs	50	0.85	4.5
Kura	8	–	460 lbs	50	0.77	4.5

SOURCE: National Archives Kaduna (NAK) Kanoprof 1 20007, Groundnut cultivation and taxation.

whom they accused of outright usury. But it was the firms who were necessarily slack with their advances in order to competitively secure the cotton and groundnut crop. In any case, the Northern Provinces Advisory Council concluded that it was impossible to legislate against the mortgaging system. Justice Butler-Lloyd decreed, in fact, that an employee of a company who advanced his employer's money, though he was forbidden contractually to do so, was not guilty of either larceny or conversion (NAK Kadminagric. 19735/1935).[69]

The vulnerability of the northern peasantry and of the food situation more generally was brought sharply into focus in 1930, not by poor rainfall but by the West African locust outbreak. The locust outbreak began at the end of 1928 when huge swarms of desert locust invaded Nigeria.[70] In December 1929 the migratory locust (*Locusta migratoria*) entered the southwest corner of Nigeria from Dahomey, and from April to July of the following year bred in Oyo and Abeokuta provinces and in much of the northern region. Most daughter swarms migrated to the northeast and a number oviposited near Lake Chad in August and September 1930. A return southwesterly migration of adults of the next generation occurred in October.[71] The northern provinces all suffered from flying swarms in the early 1930s, but it was Zaria, and especially Benue that felt the burden of the locust's appetite (table 6.16). Faced with widespread crop failure and little prospect of obtaining foodstuffs from other provinces, both Benue and Zaria regulated grain exports from their NAs, even though Benue markets in particular were frequented by middlemen and buying agents who provisioned the minefields and the northern cities. However, the control of the grain trade proved inadequate to the task; in the seventeen southern Zaria districts alone 5.3 million pounds of grain relief was required (NAK Kadminagric. 14429/1931). In 1931 sorghum reached 4d per mudu, roughly four times greater than the 1929 level (Okediji 1973, p. 163). Petty theft apparently proliferated during the months of shortage.

Food availability in 1930–31 was complicated by the renewed demands of the Nigerian Chamber of Mines for forced labor and grain requisitioning, which had been irregularly continued since the First World War. As a matter of principle, the state was generally loathe to interfere directly in food distribution and direct assistance for fear "the native would use his surplus corn for brewing beer or come to depend on the Government for assistance" (NAK Kadminagric. 14429/1931). In view of the shortages, however, the southern provinces resorted to the European firms for cereal provision and quickly discovered that virtually all Residents, in a vain bid to hold what grain they had, prohibited the export of grain across provincial boundaries. Fortunately, in spite of rising prices, the locust threat did not prove to be as serious as predicted,

TABLE 6.16
Locust Swarms, Zaria Province
(No. reported each month)

Year	Jan.	Feb.	Mar.	Apr.	May	June	July	Aug.	Sept.	Oct.	Nov.	Dec.
1930	0	0	0	16	9	12	11	6	57	6	6	2
1931	6	0	6	123	59	0	30	14	6	29	31	13
1932	1	2	20	13	32	4	12	0	0	0	3	15
1933	1	2	2	38	9	17	4	0	11	12	19	18
1934	0	0	0	47	42	43	70	18	8	54	51	17
1935	1	10	6	21	52	13	13	5	9	6	7	8
1936	1	6	12	52	12	4	11	0	5	30	7	24
1937	13	1	1	14	16	28	18	24	10	5	29	9
1938	7	4	4	32	47	19	35	14	4	1	5	9
Totals	30	25	51	356	278	137	204	81	110	143	158	115

Source: NAK Nat. Res. 10233B/1938.

due largely to the prompt and enthusiastic efforts of the NAs in their antilocust campaigns. Grain was nonetheless difficult to acquire and Zaria Province certainly could not obtain the 2,500 tons it required for relief in its southern districts. To make matters worse, most of the provincial administration had invested their capital in England during the 1920s and could not liquidate their assets for grain purchase because, as Resident Nash put it, "[the depression] would not appear to be a propitious moment for realizing investment" (NAK Kadminagric. 14429/1931). The secretariat to the northern provinces arranged for a meager 1,000 tons of maize to be imported through Lagos and distributed by UAC, the lion's share going to Zaria, Plateau, and Kano provinces. Ironically, producers were not able to benefit from the grain demand because the Jos mines were actually closed in 1931 with the result that prices slumped. Accordingly "the producer [had to] sell at Zaria . . . 480 lbs of threshed guinea corn to obtain [family tax]" (NAK SNP 17 16678 Vol. 1, p. 35). Not surprisingly, during the following year, in spite of dismal prices, cotton sales for Zaria Province increased by 519 percent.

In this light, Hopkins's (1973, p. 245) suggestion that the interwar period "improved crop storage facilities . . . and reduced seasonal variations in . . . availability of food" should be treated circumspectly. The advent of motorized transport, especially after 1937, certainly blurred the distinction between local- and long-distance transport, for it smoothed out the wrinkled surface of grain availability. Whether the peasantry could generally afford to buy what a newfound transportation system made available was another matter altogether.

MIXED FARMING AND THE COOPERATIVE MOVEMENT

The Great Depression was a watershed in northern Nigeria labor history. Wage labor could command something of a premium during the first quarter century of colonial rule, but by the 1930s prices of both commodities and wages fell drastically. On the plateau minefield, the African wage bill declined by one-third between 1928 and 1933 (Freund 1981, p. 82) yet labor, pressed by the needs of the tax collector, continued to be available for the ever dwindling number of jobs. A substantial reduction in production costs, then, enabled the likes of Anglo-Oriental to make a handsome profit even prior to the upturn in tin prices in 1933. Yet depression conditions also brought rebellion and starvation to the plateau. Indeed the very mechanisms that evacuated rural labor to the mines in search of cash simultaneously fueled the spectacular growth in export commodity production, achieved at the cost of domestic food sufficiency. But it was, of course, mine capital, as it transpired during the 1931 locust outbreak, that found itself at the mercy of a highly volatile foodstuffs market. In the 1930s the colonial state refused to actively intercede in the process of minefield grain acquisition, in part because of their own institutional, military, and relief needs. Many Residents attempted to tightly regulate grain movement, only too cognizant of both the constant tension between export and food production and the annual lottery of the millet harvest over which they had little control. By the late 1920s, then, there were murmurings of technological improvement for peasant producers to concurrently develop commodity production and a stable food production base.

The Nigerian approach to agriculture was nevertheless gradualist. Faulkner, the Director of Agriculture, held rigidly to a research-before-extension philosophy with the result that, in the face of limited NA allocations for agricultural development, most agricultural officers spent their limited time on isolated experimental stations (Forrest 1981). But low rural productivity combined with the regularity of food shortage, however, forced the hand of the colonial state. It approached the peasant economy on two fronts; first, in an attempt to raise rural productivity among what it took to be an essentially idle peasantry, the colonial government introduced a mixed farming extension service in the 1920s. And second, it experimented in the 1930s in a limited way with cooperative societies, principally credit and thrift societies in the northern provinces, to alleviate, among other things, the profusion of rural indebtedness, and to regulate the middleman trade.

In 1923 the Department of Agriculture first broached mixed farming, namely, the "simultaneous adoption of the practices of using cattle for ploughing and of deliberately making and storing farmyard manure" (Faulkner and Mackie 1933, p. 3). Experimental work at Samaru on soghum production had indicated that yields could be raised by between 50 and 120 percent through systematic and intensive manuring. A mixed farming colony was established at Bichi in Kano Province and later, on a more elaborate settlement scheme, at Daudawa near Katsina, for the specific purpose of harnessing draft power for intensive cotton production (Agricultural Report 1930, p. 4). As the mixed farming systems expanded the NAs came to provide working capital for the farmer with which the cattle and implements were purchased. In 1933, the cost of a complete outfit of bulls and technology amounted to £5, roughly equivalent in value to 5 acres of cotton. Loans were then paid back from the receipts of expanded commodity production. Corby's (1941) survey in Zaria revealed that the plough permitted a considerable increase in cultivated area; the acreage under cultivation by mixed farmers was 15.5 acres, more than double that of the hand farmers. Further, the adoption of the plough increased the proportion as well as the acreage of cash crops, reduced the amount of intercropping, and raised yields across the board by roughly 10 percent (Walker 1949, p. 28). The numbers of mixed farmers grew slowly prior to the outbreak of war, there being only 84 in the four most populous northern emirates in 1933 (NAK Daura NA 1/1 60/1945). Hill (1972, p. 307) estimates that by 1962 there were at least 20,000 mixed farmers on the books which, though a considerable improvement over prewar figures, remained singularly unimpressive in relation to the several million farming households in the North.

The purported benefits of mixed farming failed to materialize, and in any case was a technological package far beyond the means of the average hoe farmer. From its humble beginnings, the mixed farming program was elitist in practice and theory, "starting at the top and letting it trickle downwards" (NAK Kadminagric. 11019, Vol. 2), a system tailor-made for the private farms of the emirs and native authority officials in Kano and Zaria provinces.[72] In 1934, of a total of 121 mixed farmers in Katsina and Sokoto, 54 were NA executive officers, and 40 members of the sarauta class. An average plough farmer in northern Katsina in 1949 possessed fifteen acres and a gross farm revenue of £105 per annum (NAK Kat. Cent. Off. #898/1949), vastly in excess of the productive income of most rural Katsinawa. Even with the elite bias, the failure rate among adopters and the default on NA loans remained high; in 1939–40 no less than eighty-one village heads in Katsina emirate were written off the books because they had sold oxen to cover tax and debt repayment[73] (Agriculture Department 1940, p. 7). Furthermore, the technical legislation that the Department of Agriculture sought to impose—cattle pens, no sale of working oxen or hiring out of ploughs—was uniformly unpopular, requiring close supervision and doubtless contributing to the high failure rate. Tiffen's (1976) work in Gombe indicates how government policy actually impeded access to ploughs until it lost direct control over supply. In 1948 the West African Oilseeds Mission concluded that "it was impossible to conceive of any reasonable period within which [mixed farming] could have a marked effect on the volume of production in Northern Nigeria with a population of 11 millions" (Walker 1949, p. 30). Risks of disease, fear of loss, technical shortcomings, and the costs of initial capitalization all precluded the vast majority of the rural poor from the mixed farming program. In this respect, Nadel's (1942) fear that the policy promised the creation of a landed class of agrarian capitalists was hardly realistic. This is not to suggest that many rich peasants and rural bureaucrats did not benefit materially from the NA subsidies of plough-based commodity production, or that mixed farming did not encourage a further development of wage laboring.[74] But those who stood to benefit most invested in trade rather than agriculture, while the mass of the talakawa generally toiled with a simple hoe technology. In real terms, only a very few emerged from the colonial period with an agricultural technology significantly advanced beyond its nineteenth-century counterpart.

The cooperative movement was equally flawed although its foundations were laid by indigenous cooperative institutions.[75] As early as 1907 a cocoa farmers' organization was founded in Agege that provided credit, marketing arrangements, and construction assistance. By the late 1920s the Agriculture Department had converted these fledgling cooperatives into service organizations for the foreign firms in an attempt to both improve the quality of marketed cocoa and regulate conflicts in the produce trade. However, Strickland's report (NAK Kadminagric. 621/ 1934) in 1934 marked a turning point in cooperative history and provided the groundwork for the ordinance of the following year. In spite of the growth of societies in the southern provinces, progress in the North was tardy. Many of the emirates provided a lukewarm reception, Katsina rejecting thrift societies on the grounds that there was already an indigenous welfare state! Until 1951 the cooperative organization remained almost wholly a "stranger" movement; of the 128 societies in the region, 120 were thrift or consumer cooperatives. Virtually 100 percent of the membership was drawn from urban salaried workers, mostly of Yoruba and Ibo origin. The postwar credit societies experienced some success in southern Katsina, especially Maska, Danja, and Musawa, but it was not until the intervention of the government and the Northern Marketing Board in the mid-1950s that sufficient capital existed to transform the essentially local character of the movement. In 1956–57, £140,000 of preseason loans were granted, which according to Hill (1972, p. 218) was an attempt to keep farmers out of the clutches of moneylenders.

By the mid-1960s there were 139,000 members in the northern states, still a relatively unflattering statistic.[76] In any case, it was clear that credit societies constituted a direct threat to local merchants and money-lenders, who promptly monopolized the strategic positions in the cooperative hierarchy at the local level. This proved to be a relatively straightforward putsch on their part since the cooperatives had a formal association with the marketing boards and it was generally the case that the leading village creditors were also the local buying agents. The government relied heavily on existing village leadership to ensure the existence of the cooperative. As a result, membership was usually exclusive and the distribution of the benefits accordingly skewed. The cooperative procedures, such as democratic voting and regular meetings, were deliberately avoided, ostensibly because they fulfilled no economic function. Cooperative policy was not infrequently socially divisive rather than conducive to community development; from the villagers' perspective cooperative buyers were indistinguishable from private buying agents (King 1976). Those who could afford to make contributions and were well connected certainly benefited from the first flush of government loans. In Gombe in

1957—58 £68,000 was loaned; by 1964 the figure was in excess of £400,000 (Tiffen 1976, p. 112). But default on loans proved to be unacceptably high and by 1967—68 few societies received any loan capital. At any rate, by this time the cooperative movement had been completely politicized and, in a sense, made illegitimate. The largest loans ended up in the coffers of powerful Northern People's Congress (NPC) supporters, embezzlement flourished, and outstanding loans were never redeemed. When Arthur Vigo conducted his credit survey in the late 1950s, informal credit was clearly monopolized by local merchants and buying agents; the rise and fall of the cooperative movement had done little to fundamentally alter this state of affairs.

1939—1960: THE WARTIME ECONOMY AND ITS AFTERMATH

Plant a groundnut a day,
And keep Hitler at bay.

—Groundnut Propaganda, 1944

The outbreak of war imposed new economic constraints. The British government sought to maximize its dollar earnings to cover American wartime purchases, and strategic minerals such as tin came to occupy a prominent place in the consciousness of the colonial office. By the end of 1939 the United States had embarked upon a deliberate stockpiling of tin, and the British authorities pushed mining to the utmost (Freund 1981). With the fall of Southeast Asia, the Ministry of Supply placed yet more pressure on mine capital and, in the face of obvious wartime stringencies, reintroduced forced labor on a massive scale.

The prewar competition between the firms and the middlemen was also smartly terminated by the outbreak of war. Throughout the 1930s the companies had attempted to close out the Syrian and African buying agents, either through pooling and merchandise agreements or by the further extension of their canteens into the districts. As prices fell, however, competition became brisk and not infrequently erupted into violence. The famous Ghana cocoa hold-up in 1937 was a scenario that the Nigerian government found most troublesome and, in the aftermath of the Nowell Commission, the state toyed with the idea of cooperative marketing. The issue of state intervention was, however, prematurely resolved by the outbreak of the Second World War, which forced government to place cocoa, and later oilseeds, under the control of the West African Produce Control Board. The imposition of market share quotas and price structures not only spawned the postwar statutory marketing boards but provided a vehicle for the rapid expansion of export production generally, including the wartime groundnut campaign.

These institutional changes and the exigencies of war, placed extra demands on subsistence and the government rightly anticipated major problems of food availability.[77] The administrative dicta handed down to regional and local-level officers were specifically to monitor price trends and promote provincial self-sufficiency in cereals as a matter of wartime policy. The Department of Agriculture rightly predicted a dislocation in international shipping and accordingly promoted a grain reserve scheme in anticipation of emergencies. In practice, the colonial program during the war was a complex, and at times chaotic, amalgam of price control and grain requisition coupled with a vigorous forced commodity production policy. The axis about which much colonial policy revolved was, in fact, food. By 1942, at least, an allocative priority for grain purchased by or on behalf of the government had been agreed upon (NAK Gwandu NA 1253d/1942), which placed the military as the premier recipient, followed successively by the mines, government institutions, export, and famine reserve. But the good intent of wartime policy was ultimately jeopardized by its inherent contradictions. With one hand, the government exhorted the peasant producer to"grow more food" and to aspire to the lofty and laudable goal of surplus food production; and with the other placed unrealistic demands on direct producers for compulsory cash-crop pro-duction, conscripted military and mines labor, and obligatory grain requi-sitioning. As farm technology—and rural productivity—remained low, the forced labor syphoned from rural and urban areas alike to fulfill the seemingly infinite wartime demands of the plateau mines was of more than marginal significance. During the war the number of staple food-stuff consumers increased as the number of food producers declined, further fueling the inflationary spiral.The urban laboring poor were especially vulnerable to wartime consumer inflation since the cost of living allowance (COLA) emerged only toward the end of the war.

The Food Price Control Scheme, initiated in March 1941 under the direction of A. P. Pullen, had the specific intention of stipulating and enforcing ceiling prices for domestic foodstuffs. The translation of theory into practice was, however, fraught with problems because the government had no real means of enforcing its dictates, which would have necessitated another huge bureaucracy. In any case, many of the mer-chants and traders refused to cooperate; to have done so would have been against their own interests.

> It seems clear therefore that it was more rational for the dealer to go idle than to get ruined by selling at an impossible price. He did not in reality go idle. He just ignored the price regulation and sold at a price which guaranteed his own profits. And as long as ready buyers were available, the market performed smoothly, although illegally. (Oyemakinde 1973, p. 419)

Rather than resolving problems of regional food scarcity, price control introduced panic psychology into an already volatile situation. Several

northern provinces, keen to preserve whatever grain surpluses they possessed, made every attempt to limit the interregional movement of basic
foodstuffs. There was a proliferation of legislation designed explicitly to
forbid private sale of corn and to inhibit the movement of food commodities outside of NA frontiers. These restrictive measures, passed in Sokoto,
Katsina, Kano, and Bornu during 1942, reached absurd proportions
when Sokoto officers seriously proposed monitoring, controlling, and
even prohibiting each individual donkey in the interests of minimizing
the kwarami trade (NAK Sokprof. (C.87/1943). On balance, there is every
reason to believe that food price control actually compounded the wartime food crisis, and discouraged farmers from further production. It was
a naked attempt to milk farmers and dealers "to feed the more vocal clerks
and artisans in their arrogant municipal habitation" (Oyemakinde 1973,
p. 420).

   A necessary adjunct to price control was grain requisition. In 1939 the
Food Control Commission proposed large-scale grain reserves either
through requisition or a then unspecified village storage scheme.[78] Provincial Residents, like the emirs, were generally in agreement that NA
central granaries were "impractical" and conducive to peasant complacency (NAK Kadminagric. VI 31657/1940). The farming household was
to be the backbone of any reserve system in spite of the reticence of
dissenting voices like the Kano Resident:

> What we have to provide for is a crop failure. I doubt very much whether . . .
> household reserves [given current demands] would be sufficient to cope. . . . It
> might be possible to do so by increasing household reserves at the expense of
> cash crops but this is not desirable. [NAK Kanoprof. 5/1 3404/1940]

The Council of Chiefs actually passed a resolution in 1940 advising NAs
in cash crop regions to maintain reserves sufficient for government institutions. But requisition was the only realistic storage strategy given wartime imperatives.[79] Government agents or trading companies operating
in the open market would have contributed to an already inflation smitten
economy, while raising grain prices would have drawn peasant producers
completely out of cash crop production, which was a strategic part of the
war effort.

   During the early 1940s the colonial government began to requisition
grain on a small scale from peasant producers at fixed prices, principally
for military requirements and the plateau work force. From 1942 the
requisition program was stepped up in conjunction with the establishment of a Grain Bulk Purchasing Scheme (NAI CSO 26 36289/S.15
1942). By this time, the acute wartime strains were brought sharply into
focus as a crisis arose over grain supply to the Nigerian mines. During
1942 provincial requisition targets were agreed upon and, in an attempt

to minimize competition between minesfields and military purchasing, the West Africa War Council established a government supply authority for both.

1942−43, YUNWAR 'YAR BALANGE: BENGAL REVISITED?

> 'Yar Balange yunwar 'yan birni
> Mai dan Sanho ta bi da maza !Sarkin Barna!
>
> 'Yar Balange!Famine of the townspeople!
> Time of the little bag! Subduer of brave
> men! Supreme destroyer!

The intrawar famine of 1942−43, referred to generally as *'Yar Balange*, embraced much of Kano, Katsina, and Sokoto provinces.[80] The harvests throughout the northern region during the early war years were mediocre, although the rainfall data do not suggest a uniformly poor distribution. Indeed, in Katsina the picture was much more auspicious. Rather than a well-defined meteorological failure the 1943 famine was, in the broadest sense, precipitated by wartime economic pressures that placed excessive demands on domestic foodstuffs. The great hunger of 1942−43 was in some respects structurally akin to the great Bengal famine of the same year.[81] Indeed, most farmers in the Daura-Katsina region drew a sharp cognitive distinction between the *babban yunwa* in the classical sense and *'Yar Balange*, which is seen as largely *artificial* or, more appropriately, *aikin mutum* ("man-made"). The Katsinawa specifically attribute 1942−43 (known locally as *Yunwar 'Yar Dikko*) to wartime policy during which Emir Dikko of Katsina forcibly appropriated grain in large quantities.

The variable harvests of 1941 and 1942 are cast in a new, and more somber light by the desperate food situation on the plateau. In accordance with the International Labor Office (ILO) recommendations, a 1933 Ordinance banned forced labor in Nigeria but political pressure led by Harold Macmillan and the War Office resuscitated compulsory labor in 1942. The first year proved to be a disastrous failure—only 19,000 of an expected 30,000 recruits materialized—but the government stepped up the program in 1943 placing renewed pressure on local NAs. Between 1942 and 1944 at least 90,000 conscripts passed through the plateau (Freund 1981). At short notice, and with little feeling for the resiliency of the average northern smallholder, the colonial state also pressed for the prompt fulfillment of grain quotas for 1942. The computed 1942−43 quotas (table 6.17) were in fact preposterously high by any standard.[82] In some measure, the ambitiousness of grain requisition was grounded in wartime exigencies, but it also revealed a huge overestimation of the margin of peasant security, and a fundamental apprehension of regional

TABLE 6.17
MILLET AND SORGHUM REQUISITION: 1942–43
(in tons)

Commodity	Bauchi	Benue	Bornu	Katsina	Sokoto	Zaria	Total
Millet							
Amount due	1,000	250	2,500	4,000	3,000		10,750
Amount received	1,038	25	255	3,315	2,622		7,055
Sorghum							
Amount due	3,000	650	7,000	8,000	2,500	3,000	24,150
Amount received	2,464	445	6,848	5,873	2,415	2,882	20,937

SOURCE: National Archives Ibadan (NAI) CSO 26 36289/S.6 Grain Requisition.

self-sufficiency even during normal years. Northern Katsina is a particularly apposite case, for the food controller imposed excessive requisition demands on the arid, low-fertility districts adjacent to the Nigerian border, apparently unaware of Palmer's observation in 1906 that the entire emirate was barely self-supporting in a good year.

The "Grow More Food" program naturally had a tepid reception and was in any case largely offset by the wartime groundnut campaign, which was quite overtly directed at areas hitherto dominated by foodstuff production. War demands, then, imposed new burdens on an already attenuated peasant economy; the margin of security had been narrowed out of existence and only required the usual vagaries of peasant production—a below average harvest—to break the proverbial camel's back. While on tour in Katsina emirate during 1942, ostensibly gathering estimates for the director of supplies in Lagos, the Resident observed that the original quotas were quite ludicrous. Any grain appropriation would have been a threat, for the 1942 rainy season was extremely patchy requiring three or four sowings during May and June. Grain was in short supply and the 1941 tax hike, plus the disastrously low commodity prices of the entire war period (lower in fact than at any period during the depression), only served to highlight the Resident's worst fears.[83]

If the 1942 quotas were ignorantly optimistic, those of 1943 were quite simply ridiculous.[84] The chief supply officer in faraway Ibadan established requisition levels as follows:

Emirate	Millet	Sorghum	Total
Katsina	3,000 tons	7,000 tons	10,000 tons
Daura	1,000 tons	1,000 tons	2,000 tons

Although 12,000 tons was the stipulated requisition, the target figure was actually 17,000 tons. The Katsina emir argued convincingly to the provincial authorities that 6,000 tons *in toto* was the peak load that the emirate could be reasonably expected to bear. Though Dikko's request was summarily dismissed, by the end of January 1943 the agricultural officer had reduced the allocation to 6,150 tons "to avoid hardship." By March, the Katsina Resident reported a complete absence of grain to an unbelieving supply officer, concluding that

[there is] no corn in the markets at Katsina and the Northern Districts, continued export of corn or forced requisition is folly as it may be necessary to reimport [NAK Katprof 1/1 5277/1944].

Requisition reached 5,000 tons by the fourth month of 1943, approximately 75 percent of the original Katsina quota, but in Daura barely one-third of the initial demand was met. The Katsina Resident had, however, come to his senses.

At our meeting with the emir . . . in October 1942 he strongly opposed the target figure . . . on the grounds that the corn was not available. He then told an officer who was producing theoretical figures . . . that they should not trust such methods but see for himself in the farms compounds. . . . The emir's judgement has proved right. . . . Too much corn has been taken from the Province. . . . The idea that Katsina produces a considerable surplus . . . is greatly in excess of real conditions. Estimates of crop conditions and production are apt to be misleading [NAK Kadminagric. 1/1 3712/1944].

The final grain quotas are significant not so much for the total quantities they represent but because within three months corn and cassava were reimported into Katsina Province for relief purposes.

The outbreak of war touched off a rapid increase in the rate of domestic inflation. Imported goods, to the extent that they were available, rose sharply in price, while the internal foodstuffs market was seriously distorted by the Pullen price control legislation. The latter had actually contributed to illicit grain dealing, hoarding, and a general upward trend in wage foods. Following the harvest of 1942, corn prices in the north did not fall appreciably (figure 6.6), and the speculation mentality was nourished by the prospect of further requisitions. In spite of the Katsina

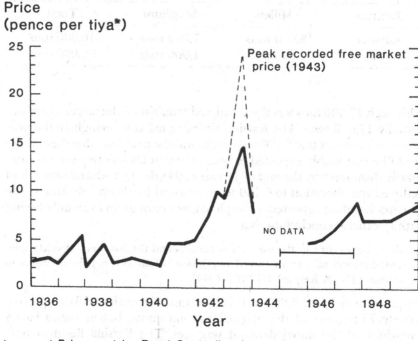

Figure 6.6. Millet prices, Kano Market 1936–43. From (NAK) SNP 17/4 38550
     Kano Province Annual Report 1944.

Resident's belligerent cry that few households were holding grain surpluses, the claims of the state were rigidly exacted. In some of the more
recalcitrant districts, armed collection parties forcibly opened household
granaries and confiscated the requisite quota. Shortly afterwards, the
hardest hit districts began to lose their adult men and in some cases entire
families moved southward in search of casual wage labor, or benevolent
patrons. In March 1943 the Resident of Kano commented upon the large
numbers of Katsinawa refugees passing through the division in search of
food.

> [Out-migration] was due to a corn quota; those who could not fulfill their
> allotment had what they did produce taken away and were told to go away and
> produce what they were originally told to bring in. [NAK Katprof. 1/1 5277/
> 1943]

In spite of the wealth of evidence to the contrary, a culpable Katsina administration denied all knowledge of hardship in the districts. A telegram from a Sokoto district officer in July reported "large numbers of destitutes, starving with no money" in the vicinity of Gusau, to which a Katsina counterpart, Mr. Nash, abruptly retorted that such "immigrants" were "all work shy and ne'er do wells who never farmed properly" (NAK Sokprof. 3/1 793/1943). As yet more refugees from Dutsen Ma, Rimi, and Batsari poured into the Gusau area—and as the irritation of the Sokoto administration visibly heightened with growing relief expenditures—the Katsina authorities finally denied that the famine refugees heralded from their province at all. By mid-August, with the first millet harvest at least two weeks away, Bindawa, Kankiya, Yandaka, Mallamawa, Durbi, and Tsagero districts were all in the midst of severe hunger. In Yar Gaga village area (Dutse District), 200 individuals died during the first two months of the wet season, and the vast majority of the wretched souls who lived subsisted on wild tubers and failed gero stalks. McCabe estimates that 40,000 persons—at least 5 percent of the total provincial population—emigrated from Katsina Province during late 1942 and the first half of 1943. A representative illustration of famine out-migration from six Katsina districts for the month of July alone is presented in table 6.18.

The relief program, such as it was, commenced in Katsina and Daura emirates during August. In the absence of any local or regional grain reserve, and in view of the evacuation of enormous quantities of grain to fulfill requisition quotas, the relief effort was, to use the district officer's euphemistic turn of phrase, "rather restricted in scope" (NAK Katprof. 1/1 403/1943). Cassava meal was somewhat sluggishly brought up from the southern provinces and small quantities of corn were distributed in several of the northern districts. One free meal per day was allocated to children in some of the periurban areas, while millet was retailed at one-third of market prices—2d per kwano—on the basis of half a kwano per person per day. The Katsina Resident accepted the limited efficacy of famine relief; in relation to the pious hopes of the 1927 Famine Relief Scheme, it was a pathetic mockery. Ironically, even though Katsina NA received only 120 tons of relief in 1927, the emir and his councillors rejected a storage plan for 250 tons of emergency relief in 1940 since it "created the impression among the peasantry that there is no need for traditional individual storage" (NAK Kat. NA VI 403/1940). As it was, the *highest* expectation in 1943, according to Resident Nash, was that the peasant could "set off to his farm with a full belly twice a week!" During August 140 tons of corn and 220 tons of cassava meal were distributed to the "distressed areas"; by that time a large proportion of able-bodied males had long departed in search of casual wage labor. As a consequence

TABLE 6.18
MIGRATION, JULY 1943

From Katsina Province			To Sokoto Province	
District	Village	Number of persons	District	Village
Dutsin Ma	Dutsin Ma	8	Chafe	Chafe
	Dutsin Ma	46		Yanwari
	Dutsin Ma	42		Yankuzo
	Dutsin Ma	15		Maraya
	Dutsin Ma	18	Gusau	Wonaka
	Dutsin Ma	7		Ruwan Bore
	Dutsin Ma	157		Mada
	Dutsin Ma	20		Baje
	Total	307	Gusau	Wonaka
Tsaskiya	Safana	22		Shemori
	Safana	12		Ruwan Bore
	Dan Musa	9	Chafe	Chafe
	Tsaskiya	9		Maraya
	Tsaskiya	25	Chafe	Chafe
	Total	77	Chafe	Yanwari
				Yankuzo
Musawa	Musawa	3		Yanwari
	Total	3		Yankuzo
			Gusau	Wonaka
Ruma	Wagini	40		
	Wagini	38	Chafe	Chafe
	Batsari	56		Yankuzo
	Batsari	57	Chafe	Chafe
	Ruma	12		Bilbis
	Total	203		Yanwari
			Gusau	Ruwan Bore
Kaura	Rimi	6	Chafe	Bilbis
	Kuraye	53		
	Total	59		
Kankiya	Kankiya	5		
	Kankiya	16		
	Kankiya	54		
	Kankiya	11		
	Dan Tsufa	24		
	Total	110		
	Grand Total	1,252		

SOURCE: National Archives Kaduna (NAK) Katsina Native Authority 1/1 403, Migration.

of farm abandonment, the potential for a swift return to normal conditions was rapidly extinguished.

> The majority of [refugee] farms were overgrown with weeds and contained no crops which returning refugees could harvest. . . . In the hardest hit districts, the average farmer will barely reap . . . sufficient for his own household needs. . . . The refugee will have no farm of his own to work, little prospect of . . . food and no means of providing himself with seed. . . . It is also . . . likely that the position [will be made worse] by a rise in the corn price. [NAK Katprof. 1/1 403/1944]

The hardship suffered by the northern peasantry as a consequence of requisition did little to alleviate conditions on the plateau. The period of the war in the minesfield is unquestionably one of the most hideous episodes in the history of colonial rule in Nigeria. The huge influx of conscripts overwhelmed the primitive camp conditions. Laborers from Katsina, fleeing the onset of famine, arrived in Jos dressed in rags only to be confronted by disease, declining real wages, and the barest of services provided by the mines. Between 1942 and 1944, Zaria (19 percent), Sokoto (16 percent) and Bauchi (15 percent) provided the lion's share of the recruits, but desertion ran at a constant 15 percent, being especially high among the recalcitrant Katsinawa.[85] Fortes's (cited in Forde 1946, p. 159) medical survey of Jos laborers in 1941 exposed the appalling health of most workers. Each laborer was granted eight lbs of grain per week but salt, meat, and foodstuffs generally were in short supply and, in any case, the 76 percent rise in the cost of living between 1939 and 1945 meant that real wages actually declined during the war (Oculi 1977). According to Freund (1981) 10 percent of the mines' workforce was, at any one time, too ill to work.[86]

The war effort, then, had taken its toll. Unfortunately, the administrative preoccupation with wartime stringencies, and the general reluctance to admit the extent of rural hardship during 1943, conspired to minimize the extent to which the social and economic costs of famine were either estimated or reported. Human mortality statistics are wholly lacking, migration data are entirely speculative, and physical dislocation barely assessable. The best that can be done is to cite Resident Hunter Shaw who lamely commented that

> the year 1943 will long live in the memory of the Katsinawa as a period of toil and tears. The poor harvest of 1942 was followed by widespread food shortage. Fodder was scarce and livestock mortality high. . . . Repeated sowings exhausted many households. The price of corn rose to abnormal heights and entire families left in search of food. [NAK Katprof 1/1 3333/1943]

But this was in many respects only shadowy and illusive pro forma reporting, since Resident Shaw had earlier concurred with his Kano counterpart that the 1943 famine had little to do with drought but principally with requisition and wartime inflation.[87] At a meeting of Katsina village and district heads during 1942, most local representatives coldly spoke out against brutal British demands; requisition was

> depriving [the talakawa] of their stocks of food for the coming months and threaten to leave them without adequate seed and food. [NAI CO 26 36289/1944]

A political officer from the northern division really said it all during the early 1940s in criticizing the cosmetic quality of annual reports on the condition of the peasantry; he observed that even in times of peace and stability "the *talakawa* lived in the shadow of famine."

RURAL DEVELOPMENT AFTER 1945

The ideology of colonial development that emerged from the Second World War contained an expanded role for the colonial state in all spheres and phases of the circuit of capital. In particular, the apparatus of the British state was mobilized in 1947 to expand colonial production by raising rural productivity (Cowen 1980).[88] The tenor of this new philosophy was distinctively Keynesian, building on wartime planning efforts. Plans, including the first Ten Year Development Plan for Nigeria, and national accounts became part of the state arsenal (Forrest 1981). Great weight was attracted to external assistance, which gave rise to a variety of schemes to transform peasant agriculture and introduce mechanized farming. Between 1924 and 1944 £18 million was expended on all farms of British colonial development, just *less* than the amount on development and welfare in the four-year period between 1945 and 1949. Many of these early prescriptions built upon and expanded early interwar efforts including farming, cooperative, seed improvements, and an inorganic fertilizer campaign. The native administrations were granted £3 million over a five-year period to pursue "community development," which amounted to the first systematic effort to improve rural health, education, veterinary service, town planning, and village reconstruction.

The postwar resettlement schemes were perhaps the most grandiose of the Fabian-inspired visions of a new Nigerian agriculture. Predicated on the assumption that mixed farming had been superceded by mechanized tillage, the prototypical efforts at Mokwa (the Niger Project) and Kontagora proved to be unmitigated disasters certainly the equal of the infamous Tanganyikan groundnut scheme (see Baldwin 1957). Settlers on the Niger Agricultural Project exercised minimal autonomy over their productive operations, lacking private incentives under the sharecropping arrangements. Each settler had a twenty-four-acre plot which, because of technological difficulties, had to be hand weeded, with the result that each farmer faced the impossible task of doing 408 days work in six weeks! When the Colonial Development Corporation withdrew its support in 1954, only eighty farmers had been settled, soil erosion was severe, a suitable cash crop had still to be adopted and, not least, a loss of £123,000 had been sustained (Baldwin 1957). Further north, mechanized rice and resettlement schemes were marginally more successful. A notable exception at Anchau in Zaria Province had housed 2,000 people in nine villages, cleared a tsetse-free corridor of some 700 square miles, and apparently benefited 50,000 persons (Nash 1948). Other experimental schemes attempted to regulate population movement from the Jos Plateau to the lowlands, which, if Shendam and the Wawa Bush projects are at all representative, proved to be high cost, low return, and limited in impact. One agricultural officer at Kafinsoli commenting on "planned farmed areas" and "resettlement" in Katsina stated that

> they are artificial and they only touch a very small section of the population. They strike me as window dressing to which eminent people are taken to see while the remaining 166,000 hand farmers are neglected. [NAK Katprof. 2960/1950]

This was doubtless congruent with the view of the Land Utilization Conference in 1950 which saw rural development as a "constant drip-drip rather than a deluge."

The establishment of the Groundnut and Cotton Marketing Boards in 1947 as statutory export monopolies also had its origins in the intrawar state intervention. The continuation of the West African Produce Control Board was supported on the grounds of price stabilization and reduced middleman extortion. As is well known, the boards were de facto revenue instruments, taxing the rural sector to finance "development" (Williams 1980).[89] The boards regularly purchased at well below the prevailing world price; groundnuts at the farm gate which brought £30 per ton fetched £220 per ton in Britain (Olatunbosun 1974). The huge surpluses financed party politics, state and private investments, education, industrial infrastructure, and the activities of the Regional Development Boards (Helleiner 1966). Bauer (1975), in his criticism of the state export monopolies, was essentially correct in surmising that the trading surpluses did little to promote general welfare. After 1954 when the boards were regionalized, the £81 million surplus held in British securities was gradually run down. Thereafter the peasant surpluses financed some regional development programs, a goodly amount of rather ugly regional and party politics, and a great deal of waste and corruption. The new boards, then, marked a new phase in the relation of the peasant to the colonial state.

The appropriation of surplus value was not brought more directly under the control of state machinery through its pricing, tax and credit policies. Public finances were used to support and subsidize the establishment of capitalist relations . . . and merchant capital lost its dominant role in the colony. [Forrest 1981, p. 231]

For the first time, the indigenous commercial capitalist class had come to occupy a strategic situation in the Nigerian social formation (Tahir 1975). The new licensed buying agent network was constituted by this very commercial bourgeoisie, a class that had historically established itself as a collective agent of the European firms. Ironically, however the much vaunted postwar increase in export crops was achieved, not through major advances in the organization of production but once again by expanded household commodity production.

The new marketing boards and the growth of domestic commodity production after 1945 did not significantly alter the mechanisms of crop purchase and peasant debt. The new LBAs advanced money, perhaps as much as £30,000 per year, to their agents, usually in September and October, which was used by village headmen and madugai to extend credit to direct producers. By the early 1950s, the Dantata groundnut empire in Kano funded at least 100 agents in a province-wide buying network. A slight change in the organization of crop purchase had occurred during the early 1940s when, owing partly to a shortage of animal transport and the need to protect the farmer who had not sold groundnuts or cotton by the new scale system, an instruction was issued prohibiting the purchase of decorticated nuts by scale except at gazetted buying points and at certain scale locations. In theory, the producer neither had to transport his produce to the buying stations nor employ middlemen with transport. This did not prevent buying in the villages, which was continued by "donkey middlemen," but it did cause the bulk of the crop to be brought to scale stations nearest to the farmer. In the postwar years, the buying activity continued at the village level because both middlemen and farmers found it to their mutual benefit.

The buying agents also benefited from the price differential between the rural scale stations and the railheads, and in some instances actually established illegal scale points of their own in order to reduce the distance to the nearest railhead. Direct producers were at liberty to transport their own produce direct to the buying points in order to circumvent the lower prices offered by the middlemen, but this was obviously contingent upon ownership of (or access to) donkey transport. Not all households owned donkeys of their own, and in any event the new buying policy had caused a tremendous price inflation for donkey hire and purchase.

As these prices have not been fixed with close regard to the actual peasant transport costs, a wholesale inflation in the price of donkeys has occurred and money which should go to the farmers is drained off to donkey dealers cashing in on the situation. [NAK SNP 17 6800/1947]

The important point I wish to make is simply that after 1939 a slight change in pricing and buying policy enormously expanded the village- and hamlet-level activities of yan baranda and middlemen. The advance and crop mortgaging systems thrived and, if anything, pushed further into the countryside, coeval with the enlarged village operations of the buying agents. The marketing boards, then, may have dampened the massive price fluctuations of the past but did very little to lessen the ills of the advance system, and if anything actually promoted it.

However those at the bottom that fall into debt suffer badly and it seemed estimated that about a fifth or a quarter of the smaller farmers become indebted during the *damuna*. This local estimate of rural indebtedness seems to bear some relation to the proportion of the crop that is sold in advance at less than scale price. Advances are occasionally asked by groups of villagers but the advances actually before October apparently come from Hausamen, little capital being available from the larger buyers at this time. Apart from those that fall into complete insolvency there seems to be an extensive credit system run as a sideline by the Syrian agents in the loan of cloth in exchange for promise of nuts, presumably at considerable profit to the trader. [NAK SNP 17 6800/1947]

The introduction of the scale as a replacement for the traditional bucket measure only served to compound the problem of underpayment for export commodities at the point of sale. M. G. Smith (1950), working in Zaria Province in the early 1950s, illustrated the devaluation of peasant labor through underpayment at the scale, in this case by the marketing board cotton mallams (table 6.19). Smith estimated that the total loss to direct producers who frequented twenty local cotton markets was in the

TABLE 6.19
COTTON SALE AT SCALE POINTS IN ZARIA, 1951

Cotton price per lb		Weight (pounds)	Town	Gift to cotton mallam (shillings)	Cash value		Amount paid		Percentage underpayment
s	d				s	d	s	d	
15	4	44.5	Saminaka	1–2	12	6	9	6	24.4
12	9	42.5	Saminaka	1–2	11	9	8	9	25.4
10	9	46.5	Saminaka	1–2	13	1	8	1	38.4
13	6	43.5	Dutsen Wai	1–2	12	1	7	6	38.6
15	6	52.5	Soba	1–2	15	0	10	1	33.0
14	6	56.5	Soba	1–2	16	4	9	9	40.0

SOURCE: M. G. Smith (1950, p. 317).

order of £73,000! In a sense, the favorable postwar prices[90] were nonetheless a vast material improvement over the depression. Furthermore, some peasants in resisting the clutches of the middlemen smuggled their produce into French territory, where groundnut prices were considerably higher than the artificially depressed offerings of the marketing boards (Collion 1981).[91] But on balance, the war had irrevocably sealed the hegemony of a Nigerian commercial class whose origins lay deep in the political economic changes wrought by complex and contradictory tendencies within the process of capital accumulation. The war also marked a watershed in the history of the peasantry, for the penetration of capital into the countryside had clearly operated to further differentiate rural producers. Commoditization had irrevocably transformed the conditions of peasant reproduction.[92]

POSTWAR FAMINE AND PEASANT WELFARE

[The famine] situation has arisen, as both you and I know, not merely because of the corn crop . . . but because certain traders . . . have cornered the market by buying up all the available corn in order to [resell] at exorbitant prices at a time when they know that the shortage was bound to occur.

—Resident Maiden, Katsina Province, 1951

Stimulated once again by the aversion of a near disaster in 1943 and the self-evident shortcomings of ad hoc relief, the colonial government resurrected the storage and famine reserve policy toward the end of the war. The new proposal subsumed two rather distinct storage programs: a "provincial system" to meet local, immediate crises arising from seasonal inflation and localized shortage; and a "strategic system" designed to fulfill long-term Nigerian needs in light of widespread crop failure or military insecurity. Both the governor and the secretary to the northern provinces believed nonetheless that a famine reserve was out of the question.

[For] there is not the requisite amount of grain in the Northern Provinces to make the formation of such a reserve possible. [NAI C50 26 36289/S.18]

The food controller, Dr. Bryce, opted for small reserves to cover what he referred to as "sensitive districts" and was able to effect under this general rubric a government reserve system of ten thousand tons of grain to be purchased at harvest time from surfeit regions. The reserve was city-based, designed to control urban food inflation and the threat of "city-famine." To this end, five permanent stores were erected in four northern provinces with a total capacity of 10,000 tons. In practical terms a reserve could only function on requisitioned grain, for government bulk purchases on the open market would have immediately hoisted cereal prices; yet by 1946, requisition was already subject to much criticism. Among the peasantry requisitioning had always been unpopular, and for many bureaucrats any talk of granaries was colored by their assumption that NA reserves bred smallholder complacency. Amid much relief, during November 1947 the policy of grain requisition was abandoned and with it the short-lived reserve system. As the secretary of the northern provinces put it, the time had come when "the laws of supply and demand should again be permitted to function." Two years later, however, two poor harvests in Katsina and Daura—and again during 1954 in Sokoto and Bornu—showed the folly of the government's ways.

The 1949 wet season was poor throughout the northern divisions, and the sorghum harvest in particular was at least 50 percent below normal. District officers in Kazaure reported a higher than usual cin rani, and by January 1950, almost one-third of all adult male taxpayers had departed from Yankwashe and Amaryawa districts (NAK Kanoprof. 398/S.1 1951). Households steadfastly refused to sell grain but increasingly turned to the consumption of wild fruits, large-scale cassava planting and a massive decapitalization of small livestock.[93] By February with conditions deteriorating rapidly the Kano Resident estimated that 20,000 people required a minimum of three months' food relief. In Daura, the situation appeared worse still. District Officer Cooke calculated that no less than 30,000 were in desperate need in the five northern districts (NAK Kanoprof. 398/S.2 1951). In Katsina, all of the northwestern reaches of the emirate had experienced some form of crop failure; millet prices leaped by 100 percent shortly after the 1949 harvest to 1/- per *tiya*, and a local medical officer reported a growing dependence on leaves and wild foods, most especially the *cidiya* tree (Kat. Cent. Off. W468/1951).

The very real possibility of NA intervention had been raised during late 1949 by the Katsina Council but was unanimously rejected in favor of a propagandist strategy that would "encourage farmers to stand on their own feet." When relief finally became inevitable, only a miserly 200 tons of sorghum could be bought at £20 per ton, a price that demanded a large NA subsidy to reduce market rigged prices to a level within the limited purchasing power of the popular classes. To have avoided financial loss the NA would have had to sell grain at 1/2d per tiya, only slightly less than the "free market." The Kazaure administration was forced to borrow £20,000 from its wealthier Kano sister, while Daura could only stand to cover 250 tons of millet, which would only provide a ridiculous twelve days' relief for the 30,000 victims. Problems of finance aside, however, grain was virtually unobtainable anyway, especially at the price that the administration was prepared to pay. Certainly bulk purchase in the open market was impracticable.

Buying from District Heads has now reached its limits, and only leads to
competitive price rises with corn being brought by lorry from other areas. Corn
is even re-exported from Kano to rural markets, from which areas it was first
bought. The corn surplus [of the north] is now largely in the hands of the
Syrians of Kano. [Kat. Cent. Off. W468/1950]

This was quite predictable in view of the fact that several months prior a
Mai'aduwa district officer had remarked on the appearance of merchants,
traders, and buying agents collecting outstanding debts in corn in the
hope of cornering the market and preempting the seasonal price rise.
Resident Maiden in Katsina concurred with Grey's analysis of Mai'aduwa,
placing the burden squarely on the shoulders of the grain trade.

This has its same root cause as in Katsina emirate. Areas with surplus corn have
disposed of it to traders and it has found its way to Kano and into the hands of
the leading Syrian traders. Localities of bad crops, to purchase corn, have to
offer higher prices than those prevailing in Kano to entice corn back. An added
reason this year for the shortage of corn is that advances received in anticipation
of the groundnut crop were paid off to a large degree in corn. [Kat. Cent. Off.
W468/1950]

By April 1950 the shortage of staple commodities was reputedly as
severe as the famine of 1943 with the millet harvest still five months away.
Yet in spite of the repeated claims of the Katsina Resident for direct
assistance—to the tune of 5,000 tons for four Katsina districts alone—a
skeptical secretary to the northern provinces in Kaduna concluded that
"before government funds can be used for famine relief, it must first be
shown that a real famine exists. . . . His Honor is not persuaded that relief
measures are necessary" (Kat. Cent. Off. W468/1950). A rightly frustrated commentary by the district officer concluded that the Katsina and
Daura administrations were thus powerless to assist "unless the situation
deteriorates." Although grain began to appear in the rural districts, only
the mixed farmers and the relatively well-to-do peasantry could afford
the inflated prices. By June a tiya of millet had exceeded 2/-, five times
greater than the year before and clearly well beyond the reach of the
ordinary farmer.[94]

By July, livestock including poultry were almost entirely disposed of
at the lowest imaginable prices. Heavy debts were incurred since a bag of
corn could be borrowed only at £8, to be repaid at harvest. Prices rose
steadily (figure 6.7) fueled by the erratic rainfall of 1950, which promised
another mediocre harvest. Many resorted to wet-season laboring at the
expense of their own farms, but wage rates actually fell from 1/- to 9d per
day, barely enough to cover the grain requirements of a small child. By
mid-August a point was reached where no grain could be obtained on
credit and "many had to live on leaves for five to seven days consecutively"
(Kat. Cent. Off. 732/S.1/1951). Farms were neglected, some left the

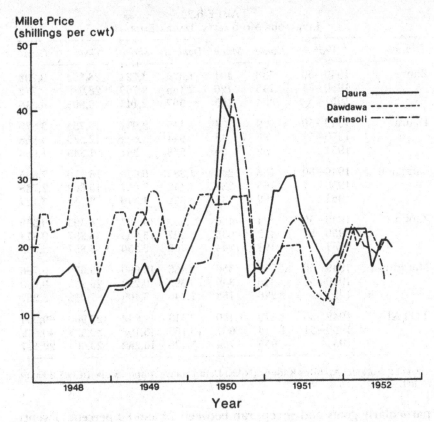

Figure 6.7. Millet prices, Katsina area 1948–52. Adapted from A. T. Grove
(1955, p. 68).

emirate entirely, and women and children were seen in large numbers begging in the larger marketplaces. Even where planting had been possible the palliative effect of the groundnut crop proved to be chimerical since the bulk of the harvest had already been acquired by middlemen prior to maturity. Most householders had borrowed either money or seed (*malkem sampiri*) from local merchants early in 1950, promising to repay one bucket of groundnuts at harvest (then worth 7/-) for every 3/- borrowed. When the groundnut crop failed corn was sold to pay off debts and fulfill tax obligations.

Any estimation of physical or social costs remains highly conjectural. A local survey in Daura emirate is of some value insofar as it at least sketches the contours of demographic dispersion and livestock sale between 1949 and 1951 (tables 6.20 and 6.21). It seems that the total population was reduced by almost one-third while small livestock losses,

TABLE 6.20
LIVESTOCK MORTALITY, DAURA EMIRATE

District	Year	Horses	Mares	Donkeys	Sheep	Goats	Cows
Baure	1949–50	738	401	1,826	3,724	28,893	9,208
	1950–51	743	426	2,156	9,766	28,988	9,772
	1951	384	155	507	2,143	5,905	3,216
Daura	1949–50	99	64	1,145	2.951	13,786	3,876
	1950–51	85	43	944	3,002	12,389	3,568
	1951	52	24	538	361	1,345	1,988
Sandamu	1949–50	168	233	1,285	6,040	18,156	7,695
	1950–51	165	234	1,442	7,067	16,668	7,738
	1951	102	148	832	1,819	2,713	5,124
Zango	1949–50	324	406	2,589	13,427	33,395	9,339
	1950–51	422	635	3,227	15,065	33,237	9,874
	1951	191	244	1,703	2,550	3,857	6,033
Mai'aduwa	1949–50	350	336	2,466	10,090	33,670	9,786
	1950–51	326	349	2,392	10,298	29,255	9,860
	1951	226	183	1,246	3,409	7,086	6,267
TOTAL	1949–50	1,679	1,440	9,313	41,232	127,900	39,904
	1950–51	1,714	1,667	10,163	45,198	120,537	40,812
	1951	955	754	5,426	10,282	20,904	22,517

SOURCE: National Archives Kaduna (NAK) Daura Native Authority File DCO/S.2 Famine Relief.

particularly goats and sheep, ran between 75 and 80 percent. Twenty-seven mixed farmers, by definition wealthier peasants, were forced to sell oxen to cover food purchases. Tax figures in Bindawa, to the west of Daura, indicate a 10 percent decline in 1950–51, and 6,000 people are reported to have migrated from Durbi District (Katsina) alone (Grove 1952). Physical displacement and decapitalization rather than human mortality again seems to have been characteristic of 1950–51 but the obvious flimsiness of the data do not bear the load of generalization. Nonetheless, it is of some consequence that the Katsina medical officer reported fifty deaths due to starvation in three small hamlets in Sarkin Bai District in Daura. Equally indeterminate is the degree of property exchange, particularly land, which from the depression onward had become increasingly commoditized in the densely settled zones. In Bindawa, at any rate, where population densities exceeded 300 per square mile, farms did change hands; one large trader acquired thirty-five acres in 1950 in the northeast part of the village from eight different owners, all of whom were forced into distress sales (Grove 1957). According to Grove, the famine in Bindawa, "increased the disparity between the well-to-do and the poor" (p. 35).

TABLE 6.21
DEMOGRAPHIC DATA, DAURA EMIRATE

District	Year	Adults	Children	Infirm	Blind	Lepers	Total
Baure	1949–50	20,487	9,712	1.687	150	16	32,052
	1950–51	21,016	9,636	1,790	157	16	32,615
	1951	12,346	5,494	1,690	46	6	18,982
Daura	1949–50	8,405	6,795	926	273	9	16,408
	1950–51	7,988	5,765	917	107	6	14,783
	1951	6,378	3,964	649	9	1	11,001
Sandamu	1949–50	10,407	7,438	1,109	46	21	19,021
	1950–51	10,388	7,771	1,012	57	19	19,247
	1951	7,291	5,083	817	22	6	13,219
Zango	1940–50	17,997	13,267	1,904	253	68	33,489
	1950–51	17,973	14,455	2,157	344	55	34,984
	1951	14,524	7,564	1,436			
Mai'aduwa	1949–50	17,621	13,202	1,687	81	22	32,613
	1950–51	17,051	12,893	1,625	97	17	31,683
	1951	11,155	6,766	750	44	7	18,722
TOTAL	1949–50	74,917	50,414	7,313	803	136	133,583
	1950–51	74,416	50,520	7,501	762	113	133,312
	1951	51,694	28,871	4,742	222	45	85,574

SOURCE: National Archives Kaduna (NAK) Daura Native Authority File DCO/S.2 Famine Relief.

Even the administrations in Daura and Katsina recognized that the poor upland harvest in 1950, in spite of their proselytizing to a "thriftless peasantry," cast a long shadow over the following year. In Daura alone, a survey conducted during September estimated that 25 percent of all households would be without grain four months prior to the millet harvest of 1951; at least 22,000 persons would require direct assistance. From the government's perspective, however, they were about to plunge into another year of inspissate gloom; as one district officer put it, "the grain surplus, such as it is, is in fewer hands." In May 1951, Greig estimated that in Marusa District, 37 percent of the populace had no corn at all and 6 percent held 39 percent of the corn in the whole district (Kat. Cent. Off. W468/1951). Faced with an oligopolistic control of local grains, mass purchase on the open market was out of the question and Katsina again found itself as one among several provincial administrations competing for the somewhat slim pickings of an altogether unfavorable year.

Since Kano are purchasing one thousand tons from Niger Province [for relief] it is also unlikely that they can supply us [Katsina] . . . we might try Lafiya. . . . I do not think any nearer neighbor can help. [Kat. Cent. Off. W419/S.1 1951]

Seven hundred and fifty tons of cereals were finally purchased in Lafiya (largely through market rigging and direct assistance)[95] for distribution in the worst hit districts. The relief effort, however, was hardly a runaway success. Aside from simple quantitative limitations, it was unusually difficult to keep track of disbursements and the DOs in Marusa and Mani were rightly skeptical that relief distribution was at all equitable. Large amounts of grain were missing due to short measuring, inaccurate paperwork, and outright embezzlement by district heads. Market rigging often failed to bring down local prices and in Kazaure so-called "subsidized corn" still lay well beyond the means of the average hand farmer. On the brighter side, grain did at least reach the districts; some 250 tons in Daura and a little less in Katsina. In Mani District some 12,000 received direct assistance and 875 paupers were supported for several weeks (Kat. Cent. Off. W461/ 1951). But this is, in a profound sense, eyewash. For with the advent of motorized lorry transport, and after half a century of experience, a small emirate like Daura lost, through death and migration, 48,000 people and 151,000 small livestock over a two-year period.[96] The administration in contrast spent £10,000, the majority of which (transport costs notwithstanding) was redeemed as short-term credit. To use the Katsina Resident's words, the relief program was "an unqualified success." But this was a Pyrrhic victory; it was no news to the Hausa peasantry that they, yet again, bore the hefty burden of famine.

The anxiety over potential or actual food shortage was raised by Governor Sir John Macpherson in 1953 in an address to Kano officials, appropriately in a province in which rapid urban growth, high population densities, and expanded postwar groundnut production prevented anything like self-sufficiency in grain. Macpherson was reluctant to advocate compulsory planting of staples but preferred a "nationwide drive for increased production" for what he saw as true self-help (NAK Kanoprof. 5/1 7552/1953). Perhaps as a response to the governor's concern and the food scare in 1954,[97] the minister of natural resources and the director of agriculture raised the issue of long-term storage.[98] The colonial orthodoxy saw the two pillars of grain security as, on the one hand, the dampening of seasonal price fluctuations and, on the other, price parity between food and export crops. The director of agriculture echoed the views of many others in his ideological preference for the self-equilibrating market which "automatically increased food production" as a particular commodity was in short supply. The governor conversely cajoled the ministers into nominally accepting a 50,000 ton reserve system subject to the acquisition of relevant information from other colonies. The colonial office contacted FAO for advice on corn storage, while the northern region approached the Indian and East African High Commissions. To their chagrin the agricultural officers discovered that the East

African Commission had, in actual fact, never held a reserve against famine, while the Indian famine codes were "no more than detailed instructions for methods of sanitation" (NAK Kadminagric. 1/1 6040/ 1955).[99] Not discouraged, the government earmarked £1.75 million for grain reserves in the 1955–1960 development plan, though little materialized in practical terms until Baldwin's report in 1957. Finally, five stores were to be constructed capable of holding 20,000 tons involving an outlay of £700,000.[100]

But this was not before time. A slightly hysterical Agriculture Department in Bornu wrote to the director of agriculture in 1954 complaining of what he called the normal overconcentration on cash crops. Buoyant groundnuts prices and the legacy of the wartime groundnut campaign had transformed the food-to-export ratio among Kanuri households. The Acting Resident in Bornu was equally distressed; grain almost disappeared from the Maidugarui market in 1954 and even a light harvest "now causes distress and anything worse . . . results in something like famine" (NAK Kadminagric. 36534/1954). In a desperate attempt to regulate grain movement, Sokoto Province—faced with a similar crisis—attempted to institute a Kafkaesque donkey permit system, which would have required each donkey trader to acquire at least three passes to move goods fifty miles from Sokoto to Gwandu (NAK Sokprof. C.87 Vol. II/1956). But the situation was probably even worse than the administration admitted or recognized. In a study of six villages in northern Katsina at the time of Independence, Luning's (1963) survey determined that between one-fifth to one-third of household acreage was devoted to groundnuts.[101] Since Baldwin's estimates in 1950 the net deficit of grain production for the province as a whole had actually increased from 8 to 22 percent.[102]

Luning's study is of singular importance because it captures both the fragility of the food economy and the cumulative changes wrought by commoditization in the twilight years of colonial rule. As subsequent studies were to document, Katsina villages were marked by pronounced socioeconomic inequality.[103] Mean income statistics are, of course, difficult to interpret but Luning's material on six farming families established that at least three were only marginally above a poverty datum line; conversely, the gross income of two mixed farmers was respectively 1,000 and 1,500 percent greater than village mean annual incomes (1963, pp. 113–117). The extent to which commoditization had proceeded was shown both in the emergence of dry- and wet-season wage laboring, in which almost 20 percent of all adult males participated, and the proliferation of land sale. By 1960 an acre of manured land could command £4 to £5, roughly half of an average farm income; at least one-quarter of the farm holdings were acquired by purchase, pledge, or lease[104] (1963,

p. 79). Further, of fifty-four recorded cases of land sale, thirty-eight were attributed to poverty and indebtedness. The insecurity of simple reproduction was above all encapsulated in the credit relation itself; in four communities, average debt per family constituted between 30 and 40 percent of gross income, roughly two-thirds of which was taken from merchants, village heads, and produce buyers. Of all credit lines, one-quarter were consumptive, principally for foodstuffs, and 15 percent for farming expenditures, at least half of which covered seed acquisition. Luning (1963, p. 101) also established that some 50 percent of the grain loans carried short-term interest rates of at least 100 percent. The structural crisis of the peasantry was clear; rural producers were obliged to borrow at usurious rates to secure simple reproduction, and increasingly, to offer food as security. Yet this was also a cyclical debt trap.

> To repay this rate of interest often means that the farmer will be short of corn again next year . . . [but] he must have corn and may be glad to take 5 bundles for 10. [NAK Zariaprof. 1486 A/1958]

The impoverishment of the rural poor and their vulnerability to harvest failure was thrown into stark relief in Vigo's (1958) credit survey. In what was admittedly a poor year in Katsina, 68 percent of the population surveyed sought loans; the average debt amounted to an extraordinary £13 per individual.[105] Table 6.22 refers to Bornu and Bauchi, two provinces that did not suffer from harvest shortfalls; it shows that by the planting rains, between half and four-fifths of all farmers had exhausted their domestic grain supplies. In a sense, then, *every* wet season was a moment of crisis in the cycle of peasant reproduction.[106] The transformation of a light harvest into a famine was structurally inevitable and, as the Bornu Resident remarked, simply a matter of time. Fortunately, the favorable postindependence weather conditions and sturdy export markets postponed the next tragedy for a decade. But when it materialized in the early 1970s there had been nothing quite like it since the great famine of 1914.

ECOLOGICAL DEGRADATION AND MARKET CRISES

> Let us not flatter ourselves overmuch on account of our human victories over Nature. For each such victory it takes its revenge on us . . . at every step we are reminded that we by no means rule over Nature like a conqueror over a foreign people.
>
> —F. Engels

Since the logic of the household economy is to be distinguished from the rationale of the capitalist enterprise, its requirements for simple reproduction can be severely compromised by a deterioration of trade.

TABLE 6.22
HOUSEHOLD GRAIN SUPPLY BY MONTH, 1957

BAUCHI PROVINCE (village)	No. of households	Exhaustion of domestic grain supply by month (% of households)											
		J	F	M	A	M	J	J	A	S	O	N	D
Liman Katagum	100	–	–	4.9	–	43.0	54.8	–	54.8	–	–	–	–
Kwankiyal	50	–	–	–	–	24.8	19.4	33.3	19.4	–	–	–	–
Korori	50	–	9.1	31.7	29.3	4.7	6.4	–	9.7	–	–	–	–
Jarkasa	50	–	63.6	43.9	20.7	4.0	–	–	3.3	50.0	–	–	–
Nassiru	50	–	27.3	14.6	29.1	7.4	9.7	66.7	6.4	–	–	–	–
Tulu	50	–	–	4.9	21.9	16.1	9.7	–	6.4	50.0	–	–	–
Total	350	–	7.9	14.9	38.3	80.9	89.7	90.6	99.4	100%	–	–	–

BORNU PROVINCE (village)	No. of households	Exhaustion of domestic grain supply by month (% of households)											
		J	F	M	A	M	J	J	A	S	O	N	D
Hasba Talbaro	50	–	–	–	5.8	–	19.2	21.0	5.6	–	–	–	–
Mafa	50	–	–	–	5.8	10.2	8.3	10.0	11.1	–	–	–	–
Babban Gida	50	–	9.1	6.8	5.8	11.2	10.2	2.2	11.1	–	–	–	–
Jawa	100	–	–	–	–	13.2	6.4	7.8	5.6	–	–	–	–
Shame Kura	100	–	54.6	–	30.2	25.9	3.7	5.6	5.6	–	–	–	–
Langawa	50	–	27.2	20.0	15.1	5.9	8.3	4.5	11.1	–	–	–	–
Kwajefa	50	–	9.1	20.0	19.8	8.8	3.2	4.5	11.1	–	–	–	–
Gwoza (Plain)	50	–	–	–	1.3	3.4	9.6	17.7	27.7	57.1	100	66.7	–
Kala	100	–	–	26.6	4.7	6.8	21.0	20.0	11.1	42.9	–	33.3	100
Total	600	0.5	2.3	4.8	19.2	53.3	79.5	94.5	97.5	98.7	99.0	91.5	100.0

SOURCE: Report on Survey of Agricultural Credit: Katsina, Sokoto, Bauchi and Bornu Provinces 1958. National Archives Kaduna (MSWCD 1358/S. 5A).

Falling prices, market crises, inflation of marriage costs or an additional tax burden can be felt as a deterioration in exchange entitlements, which "means a reduction in levels of consumption or an intensification of commodity production or both" (Bernstein 1977, p. 64). I have tried to chart the genesis and evolution of this simple reproduction squeeze among the northern peasantry. But the squeeze did not operate only at the level of exchange or increased drudgery for the farmer compelled to raise his labor time; these pressures can also be transmitted to the physical environment and given, as it were, an ecological expression. It was not only that Hausa peasants were barely able to secure their material needs, but the strains of debt, tax, and an irreducible domestic consumer demand threatened primary production and the long-term productivity of the land itself.

Ecological change has been very much part of Sahelian prehistory. Even contemporary droughts cause reversible short-term changes in local biota; tree mortality during the 1971–74 drought was for example quite pronounced, depending on their relative resilience and topographical situation. Three species (*Acacia senegal, Commiphora africana* and *Guiera senegalensis*) suffered especially high mortality and pasture production fell from nearly one ton of dry matter per hectare in the northern savannas to practically zero. This is only to be expected and, in any case, it now seems clear that these degraded plant associations, and the "*brousse tigrée*" generally exhibit high resiliency upon the return of favorable rains. Throughout the colonial period, however, large areas of uncultivated bush were brought under cultivation, which changed the face of hitherto relatively pristine savanna grasslands. In many cases, this expansion was a function of both demographic growth and the demands of the colonial state on peasant labor.

During the first thirty or so years there was an almost constant influx of immigrants from the French territories who usually settled in the northern divisions and contributed to the unusually high population growth in some of the emirates. Any demographic estimates, whether based on tax receipts or census materials, are notoriously unreliable. But Katsina emirate, which may not be at all representative, grew by almost 300 percent between 1908 and 1952 (table 6.23). To the extent that many of these new farmers cleared new farmland, we can assume that the vast expanses of open bush that Barth so vividly described rapidly disappeared. But this has little to do with ecological instability since, in spite of the claims of colonial officers like Lamb, shifting and long fallow systems of cultivation were not environmentally maladaptive. In this sense landscape alteration is not necessarily synonymous with long-term environmental degradation. Yet Scott (1979, p. 6) confidently claims that "the 60 years after 1910 witness[ed] a progressive decline in the overall produc-

TABLE 6.23
POPULATION GROWTH, KATSINA DISTRICTS

District	1908	1948	1952	% change (1908–1952)
Kaura	40,403	66,616	76,754	94.5
Durbi	43.240	88,091	90,694	104.5
Danja	no data	73,617	99,960	–
Galadima	45,727	85,501	107,637	117.5
Kankiya	17,983	65,586	76,587	325.8
Yandaka	25,727	76,904	119,899	366.0
Ingawa	62,664	61,700	61,836	0
Maska	no data	59,285	88,393	–
Kaita	16,422	58,217	68,190	315.2
Dan Yusufa	28,744	34,478	37,186	29.3
Mashi	19,330	45,748	54,208	180.4
Kankara	no data	38,144	60,946	–
Ruma	4,251	52,897	75,257	1670.3
Marusa	13,959	24,957	26,841	92.9
Tsagero	no data	15,665	16,942	–
Jibiya	1,014	22,156	31,529	3100.0
Dankama	3,745	7,428	9,738	162.1
Kogo	no data	22,858	32,976	–
Tsaskiya	no data	33,539	56,653	–
Magajin Gari	no data	40,486	52,267	–
Mallamawa	no data	10,642	11,122	–
Musawa	17,572	72,411	83,997	378.0
Totals	354,076	1,056,926	1,339,998	278.4

SOURCE: Nigerian National Census, 1952. Native Authority Statistics, Katsina Central Office.

tivity of the [West African] harsh lands and an increasing desertification of their previously fertile land." Since, to my knowledge there is little empirical information in Hausaland pertaining either to yields or ecology with sufficient time depth to substantiate Scott's claim, any discussion of environmental deterioration must necessarily be prudent. The question becomes, then, whether in view of demographic pressures on land and the effects of increasing commoditization one can logically assume serious ecological consequences.

The socioeconomic changes during the colonial period elicited three distinct agronomic responses: (i) an extension of the cultivated area, (ii) a shortening of fallow periods, and (iii) a growth of permanent cultivation through the intensive use of organic manures. To the extent it understood them at all, the colonial administration constantly vacillated over the empirical consequences of these changes. The senior conservationist of forests, for example, wrote in 1915 that the Sahara Desert was rapidly extending southward, that the greater part of the country was "practically desert," and the "natives secured food with great difficulty."[107] Others like Lamb, the agricultural director, believed the Hausa to be simply bad farmers who "made no attempt to induce fertility" (cited in Hill 1972, p. 304). The pastoral Fulani were, needless to say, inveterate arsonists. The creeping desert–incompetent farmer syndrome reached rather hysterical proportions in the 1930s with a report by Stebbing (1935), a forestry officer with limited West African work experience. Stebbing, a devotee of theories of secular climatic change, held to the rapid extension of the southern frontier of the Sahara Desert, which had stabilized three miles north of Maradi! His report cataloged extensive dune systems, a fallowing water table and other symptoms of desertification. Stebbing's work was roundly demolished by a Sokoto district officer, a verdict subsequently upheld by the Anglo-French Forestry Commission of 1936–37, which discredited any mechanical advance of the desert.[108] The Commission, and a subsequent report on sylvan conditions in Katsina and Kano by Fairburn (1937), did however draw attention to the "potential danger" of shifting cultivation and the need for considerable forestation to the tune of 25 percent of each provincial territory.

By the 1940s the prevailing opinion had shifted. It was no longer a question of farming technique as much as numbers; the Malthusian specter apparently haunted the northern emirates, especially along the French boundary where, in any case, expanded groundnut production and aeolian erosion were organically linked. This purely quantitative view of the ecological threat also extended to livestock: Kano, and Katsina in particular, were seen as hopelessly overpopulated in relation to pasture availability. These pressures in fact provided an important justification for the postwar resettlement programs and community development projects that contained renewed efforts at soil conservation, bunding, and mixed farming. The difficulty here, from a theoretical perspective, is that the close settled zones had supported huge farming populations since at least the eighteenth century. Sustained yield agriculture based on increased applications of organic manure and peasant labor time was certainly no passport to an ecological Armageddon. Furthermore, groundnuts actually fixed nitrogen and were not, like cotton, a massive drain on soil nutrients. To make sense of what is an obviously complex human ecological situation requires, I believe, a local-level perspective that brings into focus the spatial patterns of land use, of the *terroir* as the French so aptly put it.

The traditional agricultural production system was based on two types of land use, extensive and intensive. The village land-use system contained gradations of farming intensity that corresponded spatially to several concentric rings of cultivation centered on the village. The closest ring, known in Hausa as *karakara,* was permanently cultivated, its fertility restored through the intensive application of animal manure, and compound droppings. The second ring, known as *gonar daji* (literally bush fields), or *maiso,* was extensively cultivated, soil fertility being maintained through medium-term fallows of six to seven years. The peripheral rings, daji, or bush land, was only sporadically cultivated and constituted a reserve for firewood and pastures for village livestock. The intensification of peasant production transformed this spatial equilibrium of the terroir. Koechlin's (1977) work in Maradi confirms that, irrespective of local ecological conditions, as land demand grows there is a process of parallel evolution of agricultural systems. Long fallowing techniques are supplanted by land intensive, short fallowing methods, which quite rapidly develop into what Koechlin terms a *"blocage du system."* Fallowing is no longer practicable, or can only be effected during a very short period (often in particular cases where the cultivator does not have the time to weed his field). The area cultivated is simply too large to be manured. The negative consequences of this pattern have been frequently emphasized: destruction of plant cover, soil exhaustion, and the deterioration of arable lands. With the subsequent decline in agricultural yields, farmer revenues are accordingly reduced. The principal avenue open to the farmer at this point is a further expansion of cultivated area or intensive manuring. A vicious cycle of intensification is thus complete.

The cycle certainly reached critical proportions in the close settled zones, where even short-term fallow had long disappeared. Persistent demographic growth in the Kano region had in any case resulted in a significant decline in the size of average family holdings. Between 1932 and 1964

the number of separately occupied plots on the 448 acres which were surveyed increased by 42% to 185. . . . During the same period the cultivated area increased by 26 acres [of] mostly marginal land. . . . Of all plots registered in 1932, 41% had been subdivided by 1964 while only 16% had been consolidated. . . . Fragmentation is also increasing. The average plot decreased in size by 22% between 1932 and 1964, [and] the average holding by 11%. [Mortimore 1970, p. 385]

Yet as Mortimore observes, the permanence and productivity of Kano agriculture on holdings of barely three acres has not been achieved through massive land deterioration. An assessment of Dawaki ta Kudu District (table 6.24) in the Kano close settled zone in 1938 showed that population densities of almost 400 per square mile had been sustained over many decades by huge grain yields from often small (average 4.6 acres) but heavily manured holdings. The more fertile jigawa soil received at least two tons of droppings per acre provided by some 40,000

TABLE 6.24
MILLET YIELD, DAWAKI TA KUDU DISTRICT, KANO PROVINCE 1937

Soil Type	Millet yield lbs per acre	Manure loads per acre*
Jangargari or Jigawa	1469	56
Dabaro or Tsakuwa	1021	30
Shabuwa	826	27
Fako	503	10

SOURCE: NAK SNP 17 30361/1938.
*One load is roughly 120 lbs.

small livestock, roughly twelve animals per household. Even in the closely populated districts not all fields were, of course, equally maintained, weeded, or seeded; peripheral farms or low fertility maiso holdings were especially vulnerable. But of this point, environment deterioration is not to be posed in a spatially indiscriminate manner. Raynault's (1977b) study in Serkin Haussa concluded that 40 percent of family heads held no farmland within a one-mile radius of the village; many families, conversely farmed only small peripheral plots on the maiso land where yields fell by between one-fifth and two-thirds (Miranda 1979, pp. 37, 38). These poor peasants had limited access to donkey transport or animal droppings,[109] which impaired their ability to upgrade the quality of their marginal holdings. The marked disparity in yields between farms held by peasants of different economic status is quite well documented,[110] but the ecological pressures on smallholdings that receive few inputs are necessarily considerable. Declining commodity prices and the burden of state taxes unquestionably forced peasants to extract more from their Lilliputian holdings, principally by working harder and longer hours. The ecological implications of this reproduction squeeze were especially problematic for marginal producers.

I do not wish to paint an entirely Panglossian picture of the environmental conditions of peasant production. As marginal scarp lands were brought under the hoe they became vulnerable to wind erosion, especially in the northern districts (Mortimore 1968). Sokoto, with densities in excess of 700 people per square mile, suffered from severe soil problems; Prothero (1958) reported the abandonment of low-fertility holdings in northern Sokoto, and the high incidence of seasonal migration has been generally interpreted as a response to the poverty of the agrarian sector. Perhaps the most striking case of ecological collapse during the colonial era, however, occurred among the Birom on the plateau. The Birom land-use system was a complex pastiche of long- and short-term fallow systems, crop rotation, intensive manuring, and terracing, which sustained quite high densities on the relatively poor plateau soils. The Birom economy was profoundly ruptured by the mine operations; land was directly appropriated after 1908, wooded areas cleared, and the plateau opened up to Fulani pastoralists who, by the 1930s, had made heavy inroads into the montane pastures. Birom men, unable to cover their tax obligations through food production, were increasingly drawn into the orbit of the mine wage economy. Population growth, the demise of terracing, and the erosion of communal forms of labor control all took their toll. In 1942, a survey of Gyel District identified the crux of the ecological crisis.

> Shifting cultivation . . . has disappeared, and farmers now find their farms limited, often to a ridiculously small acreage, and are therefore unable to leave them fallow for sufficient periods. Lang Git of Gyel, for instance, has been planting one farm on poor soil continuously for 15 years with acha and millet because, as he says, if he leaves it fallow he would have to go hungry and he prefers the certainty of at least a small crop. . . . The essence of the system is carried on in fallow periods which become shorter and shorter, until, instead of being four or five times as long as the cultivated periods as they should be, they become an odd year or two at the end of a five to six years' cultivation period. [cited in Freund 1981, pp. 160–61]

Average holdings of 4.4 acres per adult were incapable of providing sufficient food without "gross over-usage of the land."[111] Many Birom peasants rented farms in distant districts, but by 1947 the Birom as a whole were obliged to purchase 20 percent of their domestic food consumption.

Government policy in Birom land was based largely on soil conservation, reclamation, reforestation, the adjustment of livestock numbers, and terracing schemes, which turned out to be model failures that the administration attributed to the Birom mentality. When the geographer A. Grove (1952) completed his important study in the early 1950s little had changed. Sheet erosion and gullying were in evidence, for which Grove blamed "the backwardness of the indigenous inhabitants" (p. 2) in spite of the fact that "effective methods of . . . bench terracing and basin listing are used by the Pagans" (p. 39). Like so much of colonial pedagogy, the scapegoat for the structural frailty of peasant systems resided in native intelligence—or the absence of it—and a standard proclivity for uncontrolled reproduction.

An important source of ecological disequilibrium also stemmed from the growth of pastoral herds, particularly after the setback of the 1919 rinderpest epidemic. The 1920s and 1930s were probably periods in which herd size and composition declined,[112] but rough estimates suggest that cattle numbers increased from about 2.8 million in 1926 to between 7.8 and 9.7 million in 1960 (Werhahn et al. 1964).[113] Table 6.25 estimates

TABLE 6.25
Cattle Grazing Capacity

Province	Cattle population[1]	Estimate of total[2] (%)	Optimal graze per animal unit (acres)	Grazing area available per animal unit[3] (acres)
Kano	672,000	60	30	7.2
Katsina	477,000	60	30	5.6
Sokoto	718,000	60	30	16.0
Bornu	1,679,000	75	30	12.0
Bauchi	453,000	50	30	21.0
Plateau	199,000	?	10–15	21
Zaria	195,000	unreliable	10–15	75
Niger	130,000	unreliable	10–15	82
Adamawa	428,000	90	10–15	41

[1]From 1960 cattle vaccination figures.
[2]Demographic estimates made by Werhahn et al. (1964).
[3]Figures computed on the basis of available forested and "residual" areas in each province (Werhahn et al. 1964, p. 88).

grazing capacity in 1960 in relation to these animal numbers. The pressure on pasture was far from fictive; it was not uncommon to see 1,500 animals around dry-season wells, with the inevitable consequence that sealing and trampling were severe. Conflicts over dry-season pasture, particularly the fadama, escalated as the moist floodplains were brought under cultivation by Hausa farmers. As sedentary populations grew, impinging on village grazing territories and traditional cattle routes, crop trampling increased and court cases against the Fulani grew markedly (van Raay 1975). In the close settled zones, the dry-season visitation by herders disappeared altogether and cattle-owning farmers evacuated their livestock (usually by entrustment to Fulani shepherds) to less populated districts in Bauchi, Jos, Bornu, or even the French territory.[114]

The net effect of the growth of animal and human numbers was not simply over-grazing, soil erosion, and interethnic conflict but also a geographic displacement. Many pastoral Wo'daa'be moved northward into Niger only to discover similar pressures;[115] groundnut production in French territory increased from less than 5,000 tons in 1942 to over 100,000 tons in the early 1960s (Collion 1981).[116] In 1954, the French established a "northern limit of cultivation," beyond which cultivators did not have the legal right to collect crop damages from herders whose animals trampled crops. However, this measure was only selectively enforced and crop cultivation continued to expand northward. In 1961, the independent Nigerian government had to move the limit farther northward, a de facto recognition of what had long been the case. While this northward movement possibly eased grazing pressures in the moister savannas, the disequilibrium between numbers and pasture in the Sahel was exacerbated still further (Bernus 1973). All this was of course thrown into tragic relief in the Sahelian famine of the early 1970s.

CIRCUITS OF LABOR AND FOOD

There can be no single economist of sound mind and good memory who does not attach importance to the annual migrations.

—V. I. Lenin

Wherever capitalism is introduced its immediate effect is to produce a rural exodus which tends to prevail over rotating migration . . . and rapidly exhausting the resources of the domestic economy.

—C. Meillassoux

As one moment of the labor process, migration has been crucial to the development of capitalism. Vast population movements provided the driving force in capitalist growth, a process Marx described under the rubric of primitive accumulation. Labor mobility has, of course, arisen in widely different epochs, and I have shown how seasonal trade, dry-season migration (cin rani), and the peripatetic scholar tradition are all intrinsic to nineteenth-century Hausaland. Permanent migration (kaura) of individuals and entire families is not only of great antiquity but was very probably central to the genesis of the Hausa state itself. But colonial conquest opened a new chapter in labor mobility, one that detailed the progressive proletarianization of rural producers, the creation of a "floating population" at least partially sustained by the wage relation, and a permanent rural-to-urban exodus of considerable magnitude, fueling the rapidly growing northern cities.[117] This whirlpool of seasonal and permanent migration was inevitable "to the extent that capital can only develop by continually decomposing those sectors which are backward compared with the most profitable forms" (Castells 1979, p. 355). These qualitatively and quantitatively new patterns of mobility were, in the first instance, derivative of a deliberate and coercive state policy; forced labor was transported to the minesfield and the railways, usually on a short-term basis for seasonal but intensive employment. By 1914, there were 17,800 monthly recruits on the plateau, while during the famine of the same year 14 percent of all male householders in Bauchi were compelled to spend the rainy season laboring on the Bauchi Light Railway (Freund 1981, pp. 76–77). Unlike southern Africa, the minesfields never relied on organized recruitment, but drew on a "voluntary" system; to this extent labor supply was closely aligned with the development of individual cash taxes on rural producers. Cash hunger and tax obligations were blunt instruments for labor control and presented mine capital with continuous problems of year-round recruitment. Migration, whether to the mines on the plateau, or in Ashante, or as casual labor in the southern cities, was at any rate a rational individual response to cash demands and went hand in hand with the breakup of rural households, the commoditization of the countryside, and the monetization of social reproduction (Meillassoux 1981).

In northern Nigeria the historical origins of a pool of poorly paid migrants (what Marx called the light infantry of industrial capital) are obscure. From the first decade of colonial rule, political labor was of some consequence; further, local migration—usually by whole families—was a regular form of peasant resistance to excessively high taxes. Almost 2,000 individuals migrated from Kano Province to southern Katsina in 1908 to escape the ludicrously high land taxes imposed by Resident assessment.[118] There was also a regular influx of Hausa migrants from the French territory fleeing the dreaded colonial capitation taxes; this drift rapidly populated the sparsely settled northern Sokoto districts. Gwadabawa District, for example, grew by 31 percent between 1911 and 1916, while the densities of Gada and Tangazer leaped from 22 per square mile in 1910 to in excess of 100 in 1935 (Prothero 1958). Local and regional food shortage added yet another component to this migratory vortex. Here I am interested in two aspects of labor circulation; the development of seasonal migration (cin rani) for wage labor, and permanent migration (kaura) to the older cities and the "new towns" like Funtua and Gusau. These two categories of migratory behavior were organically linked since it is clear that regular season visitations to Kano, Katsina, and Gusau for petty trade or casual labor often developed into permanent residence.

In spite of the dearth of references to large-scale seasonal migration during the first thirty years of colonial rule, it was very much in evidence by the First World War. In 1915 considerable numbers of men regularly left Gwandu in Sokoto Province for the Gold Coast. But the impact of migration was markedly uneven; the demands for cash could obviously be met locally through cash-crop production, and seasonal mobility was accordingly most intense in areas where off-farm income sources and groundnut cultivation was relatively undeveloped. Freund (1981) observed that mine labor in 1914 contained an usually high proportion of Hausa and Kanuri migrants from Sokoto and Bornu where these conditions were clearly met. The further intensification of commodity production, however, undermined food production to the extent that cash incomes from groundnuts and cotton required supplemental income from casual labor. Indeed, one motive for cin rani was to conserve domestic grain; migrants spoke of "hiding" (*b'oye*) their household staples in a manner that conveys the poverty of those who were thrust into the labor market. By the 1930s, dry-season labor had developed apace; 3,500 migrants passed Yelwa each month en route to Oshogho, Ibadan, and Ilorin. The Annual Report for Sokoto Province in 1936 reported "a large seasonal migration to the Gold Coast in search of money to pay tax and support their families" (cited in Prothero 1958). Migrant workers supplied the dry-season labor power for the fledgling cotton gins in Gusau and southern Katsina; and of course the demand from the plateau mines grew steadily. During the period of forced wartime labor, the mines drew upon 92,000 conscripts alone, channeled to Jos from the nine northern provinces.

The scale of seasonal wage labor was highlighted by Prothero's (1976) important study in Sokoto Province conducted between October 1952 and March 1953. The survey recorded almost a quarter of a million migrants, roughly 44 percent of the total adult male population according to the 1952 census. The vast majority of those interviewed were en route to Ghana, the southwest of Nigeria, and the then eastern region (figure 6.8).

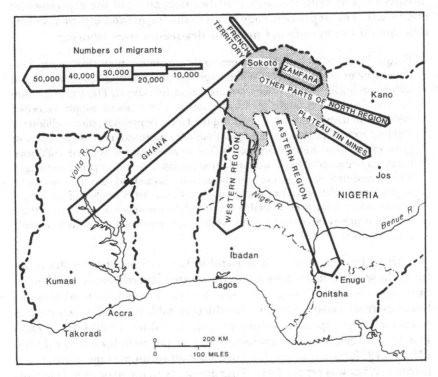

Figure 6.8. Destinations of migrants, Sokoto Province 1952–53. From Prothero (1957).

Of the total number 45 percent were laborers and 24 percent petty traders; just over half sought money and 16 percent food. From the northern divisions almost one-quarter had left in search of food, which led Prothero to conclude that

> all evidence points to the fact that even in good years the return from the land in crops for local consumption and for sale, in order to provide a cash income for necessary purchases and the payment of tax, is not sufficient for the whole population. [Prothero 1976, p. 17]

A study conducted much later by Olofson (1976) in Funtua reached similar conclusions; of 48 migrants interviewed, 15 were water carriers, 15 laborers, and 10 petty producers. Almost 60 percent of those polled came to earn money for tax, marriage costs, debt repayment or food.

The explosion of seasonal migration was a particular manifestation of the crisis within the peasant economy. Its geographic unevenness was partly a reflection of the manner in which commodity production and off-farm income sources had developed in the northern provinces. The massive migratory dislocations caused by famines were amplifications of already existing patterns, and a further deepening of the reproduction crisis itself. The depressed wage levels in the formal and informal sectors only served to intensify the need for dry-season wage laboring:

> Before World War I, a day's wages could buy more grain than at any time thereafter until the present. While wages crept up during World War I and immediately afterwards, prices mounted more quickly yet. The 1921–2 slump for the first time brought about a situation where labour supply exceeded demand on the minesfield. . . . During the Great Depression, the conditions of 1921–2 were repeated for a longer time on a more extended scale. Peasants grew groundnuts more than ever before to meet the needs of tax-collectors, taxes not being reduced so substantially as the fall in producer prices and wages. This intensified the pressures on the peasant household. On the minesfield, wages were reduced to one-third and less of the 1928 levels and yet labour continued to make itself available for a declining number of jobs. From 1933, world tin prices recovered rapidly while wages remained as low as 2s a week. [Freund 1981, p. 82]

After the war, costs of living and inflation experienced a sharp upturn; these price incursions were transmitted directly to the rural economy, not only as declining real wages for partly proletarianized peasants but as increased costs of social reproduction (table 6.26). Marriage costs in particular were especially vulnerable; M. G. Smith's (1950) work in Zaria Province revealed that on average marriage payment for a first wife was £10 to £12, between one-third and one-half of an average annual cash income. What was especially striking among both the male marriage costs and the dowry sent by the brides family (*gara*) was the proportion of cash

TABLE 6.26
MARRIAGE COSTS

Year	Source	Location	Marriage costs (range)	Index of consumer prices 1960 = 100 (%)
1937	Giles	Zaria	15s–£3	20
1949–50	Smith	Zaria	£3–£80	70
1955	Kirk-Greene	Adamawa	£30	90
1956–57	Vigo	Northern States	£5–£15	95
1967	Hill	Katsina	£30–£40	115

exchanges and the strategic function of imported cloth.[119] Cloth valued at £9 and cash gifts of £12 to £18 were quite common. This reinforced the demand for cash, which in the Zaria communities studied by Smith was met from cotton, petty commodity production, and trade. In Adamawa, conversely, seasonal migration, known locally as *tafiyar dandi*, was widespread and entered into explicitly for purposes of tax and bride-price (Kirk-Greene 1955, p. 376). Such ceremonial expenditures were not simply vehicles by which money and commodities penetrated into the household economy; they projected peasants into the web of commodity relations, which for many involved wage laboring. But the absence of a fully proletarianized class of wage laborers meant on the one hand a subsidization of reproductive costs by the household economy and on the other the subjection of peasant livelihood to the vagaries of changing real wages, inflation, and changing terms of trade.[120]

The emergence of a migrant labor force did more than articulate a precapitalist household economy with the agents of international capital, it actively contributed to the decay of social relations in the countryside. Migrants were, as Kautsky (1976) observed, "tremendous agents of progress in their own villages." Migration undermined customary labor relations, injected cash into the local circuits of exchange, and stimulated wage employment (Standing 1980). Most importantly, it created, by an industrial labor reserve, a source of cheap labor power that gravitated to the large urban centers. As conditions deteriorated in the villages, and as regular visitations to the cities bred a familiarity with urban conditions, many seasonal migrants became permanent urban dwellers, filling in the interstices of a saturated informal sector.[121] The new towns like Jos, Kaura Namoda, Gusau, and Funtua catered to the rural exodus but the interwar period also witnessed a major immigration of Yoruba and Ibo clerks, traders, and administrators into the large northern cities. The vast majority of southern migrants were, of course, segregated residentially from their Hausa brethren in the Sabon Gari townships. The colonial famines boosted the influx of additional migrants into the Hausa cities, though it is quite impossible to estimate the numbers involved. By 1943 at any rate, the Commissioner of Labour was referring to an urban crisis (Department of Labour 1943, p. 3), and a decade later the problem of urban underemployment was distressingly uncontainable, even to a colonial administration loathe to admit the emergence of a lumpen class. The critical point, however, is that seasonal migration and urban growth must be lent a historical specificity that sees both as the obverse of the "malaise paysanne." Crises of simple reproduction among the peasantry were part of the very same process by which the "veritable whirlpool of geographical and occupational mobility," as Castells (1979) calls it, flourished.

Patterns of labor mobility also generated a distinctive geography of food (figure 6.9). Some of the close settled districts imported cereals on quite a large scale prior to the colonial conquest but the rapid growth of the minesfield and of the northern cities generated significant new demands. For the most part they were met by highly commercialized food production in areas such as Zamfara, southern Katsina, Bornu and parts of the Middle Belt. The growth of motorized transport and all-weather roads after 1945 markedly improved the scope and efficiency of the food system and the extent to which urban merchant capital could encompass the peripheral areas. But the source of wage foods was necessarily

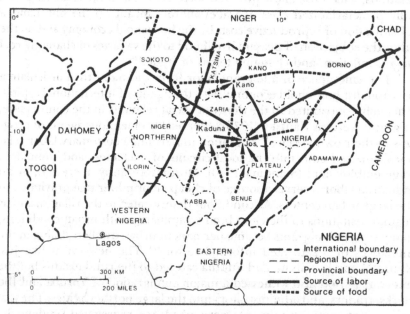

Figure 6.9. Sources of food and labor, 1945.

dynamic and changeable, reflecting in large measure producer responses to price incentives. Outward railings of grain from Dutsen Wai (Zaria) for example between 1927 and 1939 fluctuated annually from almost nothing (in 1938) to 2,700 tons per year (in 1928), signaling farmers' estimates of wage food profitability in relation to groundnuts and cotton.

STATE, FAMINE, AND PEASANT RESISTANCE

> No more taxes, no more slaves, no more laws
> and each to do as he pleases.
>
> [Peasant epithet in Kano, ca. 1908]

> [The Europeans] cheat us behind our back,
> They are rubbing shit in our calabash,
> Flies crawl over our food
> If we cut down a tree we will be arrested
> They will imprison our families
> They fence off the forest in our farms
> They say our property is the Governor's farm
> When they find a leaf in our hand
> They arrest us and fine us.
>
> —A yau ba maki NEPU sai wawa, c. 1955

I have tried to suggest that the colonial state in northern Nigeria was neither a "Great White Umpire" (Hopkins 1973) nor a crushing leviathan that simply consumed huge peasant surpluses, later digested by metropolitan capital.[122] Life, and colonial political economy in particular, is much more complicated than that. The colonial state is conceptually impoverished by abstracting it from the contradictory forces within which it operated and over which it presided and attempted to maintain some semblance of cohesion. Colonialism preserved the form of peasant production yet transformed the conditions of reproduction. It opened up avenues for the appropriation of an expanded surplus product by European firms; but to accomplish this class alliances were sealed, which ensured that the sarauta elites and indigenous merchants also appropriated part of a product that was not readily expanded. The state, then, was the distillation of forces involved in the confrontation of European capitals, indigenous modes of production, and local patterns of resource endowment (Berman 1980, Lonsdale 1981).

The peasantry clearly emerged as the bedrock of the colonial state, but it was less evident how their surplus product was to be appropriated and divided. The enormous expansion in commodity production was achieved by a preservation of household production, even though the purpose of production underwent a radical transformation. But the state did not necessarily always back the interests of individual capitalists, or always intercede with more onerous tax burdens to increase revenue and stimulate export crop production.[123] As Freund (1981, p. 75) notes, the government generally promoted conservative policies toward precapitalist social forms in the interests of stability. It was scarcely a rarity for the state to receive sharp criticism from the firms, who complained that direct taxes crippled trade. Moreover, the state occasionally attempted to regulate the advance system of the middlemen and to actively support peasant interests.

That is to say that the state, the firms, the Nigerian middlemen, and the sarauta all wrestled over the appropriation of the surplus product. But ultimately the entire edifice rested on the millions of peasants doing what they were suposed to do; namely produce and consume commodities in a predictable way. But smallholders everywhere have been remarkably ornery and this is why the issue of labor control was so central to state operations. Taxation was a fundamental but blunt mechanism for compelling peasants to contribute to the cash economy. Monetary demands might be met through craft production, labor migration, or borrowing as well as by planting groundnuts. Excessive taxation ran the risk, in the early years at least, of resistance or massive emigration. In this limited sense, the partial incorporation of Hausa smallholders gave them breathing space; a farmer who owned four acres and produced millet was given room to move. He was, in part, uncaptured (Hyden 1980); he was able to hold the market at arm's length. Markets did not necessarily place peasants in straitjackets; they presented alternatives for some that avoided either wage labor or cash-crop production. Of course, the Great Depression revealed that even the market could not be avoided entirely. As Fred Cooper (1981a) observes, taxes were obligatory and new items of consumption indispensable.[124] From colonial perspective, the depression revealed the great virtue of partial commercialization in agriculture that ensured cheap commodity production and subsidization of peasant welfare and reproduction. But as Cooper also notes, a system of production that does best in a depression leaves something to be desired. Because commodities could not be secured simply through conditions of exchange, merchant capital increasingly employed credit to bind peasants, and to assert itself at the point of production.

The whole arena of labor control was characterized by constant struggle and peasant resistance, if not revolt, against explicit coercion by the state, taxes, or the voracious appetites of the buying agents. The evidence suggests that localized opposition, withdrawal, tax evasion, flight, desertion, sabotage, robbery, and religiously inspired revolt were a vital chapter in the history of the Hausa peasantry. Popular protest often assumed a Mahdist bent, as one might fully anticipate in a context of social disorder, political crisis, and the ostensible release of captive labor (Tahir 1975). Lugard felt that Mahdist movements surfaced almost every year between 1900 and 1906, culminating in one of the last violent reactions to imperial incorporation at Satiru. The insurrection at Satiru village in 1906, occasioned by the proclamation of a jihad against the British and the emergence of the village head (Mallam Isa) as a Mahdi, reached critical mass following the death of the Acting Resident at Sokoto, two officers, and twenty-five mounted infantry at the hands of a motley group of peasants armed with bows and arrows. The rebels, including a new-found leader who succeeded Mallam Isa after his death in combat, captured a Maxim gun and rifles and accrued a good deal of prestige in the process (Adeleye 1971, Tukur 1979). The slaying of a British officer elicited a particularly brutal response from the colonial state, but *only* with the complicity of the sarakuna. Indeed, Satiru in all its bloodiness marked the first real instance of class collaboration between the British and the Hausa-Fulani elites.

Satiru was the highwater mark of semiorganized peasant military, but rural dissent of a lesser form was commonplace. Two years after Satiru, Yola was apparently threatened by "propagandist mallams," (Tukur 1979, p. 331) and delayed guerrilla resistance was widespread in the swamps of Hadejia and, more persistently, by pagans in and around the plateau. Protest was certainly sporadic but also strategic, frequently taking the form of cutting telegraph wires. Significantly, some of the early popular protest was directed against the new sarauta class who, insofar as they were British electives replacing the deposed emirs and hakimai, were seen as wholly illegitimate. By the 1920s many of the emirs were identified directly with the British and as a consequence lost the strategic support of the influential ulema (Tahir 1975). Rural hostility toward the new district heads who, as NA salaried officials, stood arm in arm with the British was especially marked when district reorganization projected the hakimai into their rural domiciles. The physical presence of the district heads was not only a burdensome affront, but severed already existing patron and chaffa ties, which were a legacy of the nineteenth century. The early hakimai were treated at best indifferently; in Bornu, the head of Marte District was actually killed in the course of jangali collection (NAK SNP 15/1 19/1906).

Taxation elicited some of the most sustained peasant reaction. Perhaps the most spectacular manifestation of rural discontent surfaced in Dawakin Tofa District in Kano in 1908 in direct response to a new system of assessment (NAK SNP 7 1974/1908). A spontaneous rejection of the new imposition culminated in the outright condemnation of all taxation and the deposition of several village heads, who were summarily booted from their communities. Resident Cargill overreacted and dispatched seventy-five mounted troops and a Maxim gun to Dumbulum; he was met with complete diffidence, although he effected a large number of arrests. This was not unusual; early tax collection in Katsina was conducted with military support and occasional punitive expeditions. Several "ring-leaders" from Gwadabawa District in Sokoto were arrested in 1909 for tax evasion and imprisoned for six months (NAK Sokprof. 78/1909); and blood was spilled in Adamawa in 1909, and again in 1911 in communities that refused to submit to assessment (Tukur 1979, p. 672). Not all of this popular demonstration was particularly "popular." MacBride (NAK SNP 17 30261/1937) for example reported considerable agitation in Dawaki ta Kudu District (Kano) against the adoption of the Revenue Survey Assessment, but it was propagated among large landowners, by "interested persons residing in Kano" (p. 2). The previous lump-sum system computed by village headmen almost certainly undertaxed influential kulaks; the revenue assessment, conversely, carried a much heavier burden for the rich; hence the protest "by these classes with vested interests in the present system, particularly the village headmen" (p. 4).

The outbreak of the First World War, in which the Turkish Caliphate entered on the side of the Central Powers, prompted new fears of a pan-Islamic revolt. Paranoia among British administrators in the northern emirates sustained the view that wartime insecurities could early turn a malleable talakawa into visionary jihadists (Osuntokun 1977). H. R. Palmer presumed, quite correctly as it turned out, that British survival ultimately depended on the support of the emirs whom they had attempted to co-opt:

> Native rulers and *Ulema* are not an absolute guarantee against fanatical outbreaks but they are the most effective buffer that can be devised . . . the judicial councils of the Emirs, the Cadis and Imams are in receipt of substantial salaries from the Native treasuries. [Palmer, cited in Osuntokun 1977, pp. 143, 144]

There was an upsurge of popular unrest in 1914–16; a rebel district head from Fika emirate actually captured Potiskum town in 1915 and a group of peasants—"disorganized and yelling war cries"—were slaughtered near Dambam. Other disquiet was reported in Bornu, Fika, Yola, and Sokoto; but in what might have been a difficult period the emirs and Hausa bureaucrats were steadfast in their loyalty to the British. The Mahdist scare in the 1920s and the slight colonial hysteria over Islamic propaganda and radical ulema, also proved to be unnecessary and unfounded (Tribenderana 1977).

Much of what passed as resistance to capitalist penetration was, however, of a wholly different order. It was grounded in a long-standing tradition of "dissent from within," to use Last's (1970, p. 356) adage, in which relations between peasant and state were defensive and evasive. For didactic purposes I refer to these as (i) deformation, (ii) withdrawal, and

(iii) implicit resistance. In the case of deformation I include the plethora of communicative devices by which peasants attempted to wriggle from the clutches of colonial officers. The colonial ledger and district notebooks, in particular, are littered with reference to farmers ignoring or "forgetting" local ordinances and provincial dictates; this was especially pronounced in the attempts to hide children and disguise granaries, or in the process of tacit agreement (*sai abinda ka ce*) and, of course, outright deceit (Spittler 1979). It is no accident that Resident Temple devoted a wonderfully endearing chapter in his book, *Indirect Rule in Northern Nigeria*, to "the art of lying," which "has reached a very high state of perfection among the natives of the Northern Provinces" (1918, p. 103). Tax collection, according to Temple, could reduce the unwary political officer to a "condition of bewilderment and bemusement so as to render [him] incapable" (p. 113).[125] By withdrawal, I refer largely to the process of tax avoidance by migration and evasive tactics, or of the Fulani herders in hiding animals, leasing cattle to kin in French or German territory, or simply increasing their mobility (see NAK SNP 10 169p/1915). The decision to flee was very much rooted, as Last (1970) shows, in traditions of nineteenth-century dissent, though in the twentieth century land scarcity and the costs of mobility effectively limited its efficacy. And finally, there was implicit resistance, which included smuggling (the illicit groundnut trade to Niger), occasional theft (tin stealing on the plateau), highway robbery (witness the grain thefts in the famines of 1914 and 1927), and dissident religious affiliation, perhaps most conspicuously seen in the growth of the Tijaniya (Paden 1973).

In much of this peasant dissent, quietism and diffidence is to be understood as effective protest (Last 1970). Much protest, such as it was, centered on parochial issues but illuminated hidden forms of political consciousness, including cultural forms of protest—poetry, praise epithets, verse and so on. Though barely understood by the colonial officers, they constituted a symbolic opposition, as Scott (1977a) calls it, representing "the functional equivalent of class consciousness in pre-industrial agrarian societies" (p. 284). In this sense, the activities of the peasantry were part of a long historical record of struggles over the disposition of their product. The colonial period ushered in a new social field of force in which the surplus was appropriated and fought over in profoundly new ways.[126] Famines indicated that these struggles had been decisively lost by the peasantry in spite of their dogged resistance.

CONCLUSION

The fundamental material contradiction about which much resistance centered was the simple reproduction squeeze. In the cycle of household economy this was given effect as the struggle to secure simple reproduction under regularly deteriorating conditions of production or exchange (Bernstein 1979). The historical engagement of state and peasantry, in other words, hinged on the conditions of their reproduction. For rural producers, colonial incorporation ruptured the household cycle in which commodity production subsequently became "internalized." Commoditization actually proceeded along three fronts; the conversion of the products of surplus peasant labor into commodities, the conversion of the means of production into commodities, and the transformation of labor itself into a commodity (Kitching 1980). But the unevenness of capitalist penetration meant that these processes expanded differentially; not all households adopted export crops, not all males migrated to the mines, and only some profited from commerce. The result was a highly heterogeneous matrix of rural labor situations predicated on different commoditization.[127] Distilling this heterogeneity to manageable proportions reveals that the expansion of commodity production was undertaken by a broad stratum of a middle peasantry, for whom more and more of household labor time was directed to commodity production. If they avoided the hardships of labor migration, the middle peasants were irregularly dependent on the market for subsistence. In addition, a phalanx of the rural poor secured simple reproduction only through the sale of their labor power, in the dry season to the mines and the urban informal economy, and in the rains laboring on the farms of their wealthier brethren. Some eked a living from low-return crafts and petty trade, as is clear from M. G. Smith's (1955) study in Zaria. At any rate, among this quasi-proletarianized class a large proportion, perhaps 30 to 50 percent, of subsistence needs were met through purchase. And finally, a strata of well-to-do farmer-traders developed, who probably devoted a greater proportion of their holdings to export commodities but still remained largely self-sufficient in food. They were deeply engaged in trade and, in a general sense, acted as agents of commodity relations. In all of this, monetization (which was a necessary corollary of generalized commodity production) provided a fertile ground for the proliferation of the credit mechanism that allowed merchant capital to exercise indirect control over production.

I have argued that commoditization had profound implications for food security and famine. In an aggregate sense, food production per capita declined and many rural producers confronted annual grain purchase to fulfill an irreducible domestic demand. These periods of grain shortage corresponded to those in which preseason loans were distributed. Further, harvest shortfall or price fluctuations were felt as household crises, which could lead to an intensification of the cycle of indebtedness. As Marx observed, the mere death of a cow might render the small peasant incapable of renewing his production. The intensification of commodity production subjected the rural poor to "all the horrors of producing for an increasingly demanding market and none of the benefits of capitalism over other modes of production" (Mueller 1980, p. 203). At best, local shortage was an annual occurrence.

The changed conditions of peasant reproduction also peeled away the tissues of a moral economy. Commodity production and the participation in market relations had individuated household production, but the agency of the colonial state was also critical. New systems of administration, improved communications, and the bureaucratic questions of a centralized state enhanced effective control over elites and peasant alike.

> This process greatly reduced the opportunities for collusion and evasion that had provided such an effective buffer against elite exactions in the pre-colonial era. Detailed and increasingly accurate censuses and cadastral surveys conducted by trained bureaucrats, whose loyalties were directed to the administrative corps and colonial system as a whole rather than a local patron or powerful minister, made it possible for the government to collect that share of the produce which it claimed as its due. [Adas 1980, p. 539]

Taxes were seen by the peasantry (with good reason) as a loss of their *rights* (Tahir 1975, p. 333). Even a low assessment by colonial reckoning far exceeded the flexible and customary exactions of the precolonial period. In short, the incorporative process bred a sort of endemic vulnerability among a large segment of rural producers who, to use Marx's phrase, had increasingly come to live a "vegetable existence." Vigo (1958, p. 36) was very much to the point when he noted that "producers are made up of millions of peasant farmers whose livelihood is easily upset by reverses of weather, the effect of which may be felt for more than a single season," and which resulted in a series of devastating colonial famines (table 6.27).

The progressive incorporation of areas like northern Nigeria into a world economy altered the face of famine itself. It had the contradictory effect of rendering grain available in the marketplace but without sufficient means to procure it. Those who came to regularly depend on grain purchase were necessarily vulnerable to a volatile grain trade sustained by the regularity of regional and local deficits. More generally, the partial transformation of Hausa peasants made them vulnerable to capitalist market crises, and also subject to the precapitalist limitations of the selective development of the means and forces of production. The intervention by the colonial state through relief, in a situation in large measure of its own making, was ineffective.[128] In part this reflected the sheer magnitude of the problem, the mathematics of the gross numbers at risk; in part, it also represented a misconception of the etiology of the problem (peasant lethargy or overpopulation) and the bureaucratic incompetency

TABLE 6.27
A CHRONOLOGY OF FAMINES IN
NORTHERN NIGERIA

Year	Katsina-Daura	Kazaure, Hadejia, Kano	Sokoto	Bornu
1904	1904			
	1906			
1908		1908		
	1911			
1912				
	1914 1915	1914	1914	1914
1916				
				1919
1920		1920		
			1921	
1924				1924
1928	1927	1927	1927	1927
1932				
1934				
1938				
1942				
	1943	1943	1943	1943
1946				
1950	1950			
	1951	1951		
1954	1954		1953*	1953*
		1956*		
1958	1958*	1958		1958

*Of local significance

of a sometimes comatose administration. But it was also not in the material interest of the state to regulate the merchant relationships upon which it also depended. Here lay the root of the contradiction between state and peasantry.

The political economy of colonialism in northern Nigeria was, to paraphrase Keith Hart (1982, p. 85), a preindustrial combination of indigenous smallholders and large European trading monopolies. As in all state systems in which a good deal of revenue came from the land because the majority of people lived there, the maintenance of centralized political control in Nigeria was invariably problematic. The advent of modern transportation alleviated this somewhat, but such a decentralized system necessarily meant a good deal of local revenue leakage and difficulties of labor control. Up to a point, then, the peasant had an exit option. But I have shown that the deepening of commodity relations indeed limited the extent to which peasants could either revert to subsistence production or lessen the effects of overproduction of export commodities in the face of a volatile climate. The colonial state was instrumental in the proliferation of commodity production. Yet like all states, the colonial state in northern Nigeria confronted the possibility of fiscal and legitimation crises. Ironically, in its attempt to deepen commodity relations through taxation, monetization, and local merchant capital it often eroded its own fiscal and political stability. Famines in this regard were not only crises of production but were equally seen as consumption crises—in particular the market for European manufactures was reduced—and direct threats to political legitimacy. In her study of colonial Tanganyika, however, Bryceson (1981) argued the converse, that without colonial commodity production the peasant "would have [been] prone to sporadic food shortfalls" (p. 94) while the colonial state actually enhanced and regularized food supply through famine relief. I have argued conversely that the retarded form of capitalist development in Nigeria blocked any form of accumulation based on increased rural productivity and a transformation of the forces of production. Furthermore, commoditization weakened in a variety of ways the position of rural producers in the face of harvest variability. The colonial state was again critical in this process of siphoning peasant labor largely through absolute surplus extraction. Yet there were obvious limits to this system as the famines testify. Under these circumstances the state did indeed intervene with relief to regularize supply, but I have attempted to show that the magnitude of the problem was far beyond the means of the colonial government while the administrative incapacity of the state apparatus left rural producers with little but their poverty. In contrast to Bryceson's suggestion, there were no regularizing functions since expanded commodity production was achieved without raising peasant productivity and without a state capable of provisioning requisite food relief. As a result, the peasantry entirely shouldered the burden of famine. I would argue, however, that this can only be understood as a result of the contradiction between the stagnation of the productive forces and the development of productive relations, with the result that the form of production remained precapitalist while circuits of food—and social life in general—became increasingly commoditized.

State relief unquestionably assisted some; famine mortality was almost certainly less in 1943 than 1914; and the advent of the motorized lorry evened out gross price differentials. But technological intervention proved to be a two-edged sword.

> Before the improvement of road communication [local] deficiency was made up by supplies, cheap in price, brought in by donkey. . . . [Now] in a bad year the surplus . . . is attracted quickly to the big town by speculative traders. . . . [It] can only be secured by offering a price sufficient to attract the corn back. [NAK Daura NA 6/S.2/Vol. II 1952]

Famine, then, needs to be posed structurally, as a reflection of "the tragic and absurd organization of society" (de Castro 1977, p. 22). On balance, the costs of this absurdity and the tragedy of famine were borne almost wholly by the peasants. Popkin's (1980, p. 81) claim that material improvements under colonialism "helped keep peasants alive" and "improved the quality of the minimum subsistence floor" is, for Nigeria at least, highly dubious. The lone voice of a Daura district officer captured the colonial dilemma in 1959 with his observation that "it is the height of complacency to report month after month food supplies adequate when in fact there is a permanent chronic shortage" (Kat. Div. Off. KAT/FOO-2 1959, p. 2). This was silent violence in all its ghastly ugliness.

7

CLIMATE, FAMINE, AND SCARCITY IN THE 1970s

*Le paysan était maintenant tombé sous la dépendance du marché,
qui était pour lui encore plus capricieux et plus incertain que la
temperature.*

—*Karl Kautsky*

The successive drought years of the early 1970s are things of the past, but the effects of the poorest rainfall since 1913 extend far beyond the immediate drought period.[1] The exceptional meteorological conditions that precipitated the crisis were continental in scope, embracing much of Sudano–Sahelian West Africa, parts of Ethiopia and the Horn, and the East Africa savannas. The Sahelian famine itself has, of course, become a cause célebre. Many thousands of herders and farmers died a slow and painful death. Many more thousands faced forced sedentarization, massive asset depletion, and awful squalor in the ad hoc relief camps; countless other refugees piled up in the swollen southern cities eking out a pathetic existence in the interstices of the informal urban economy.

The 1969–74 drought severely affected Chad, the Gambia, Mali, Mauritania, Niger, Senegal, and Upper Volta in West Africa, an area close to 5.5 million square kilometers. With a total population of about 23.6 million, it is estimated that over 6 million were at risk in the Sudanic and Sahelian regions alone. Poor rainfall, well below the long-term averages, was sustained over a 4- to 5-year period; it was this cumulative quality that rendered the crisis of the 1970s so debilitating. In Mali and Senegal, for instance, staple upland crops in 1972–73 yielded an average of only 40 to 50 percent of the expected harvest (Berg 1975). These shortfalls translated into massive household deficits for populations already made vulnerable by a postindependence export commodity boom and, in the case of pastoralists, by an ecological marginality induced in large measure by growing land-use competition and a startling increase in the number of animals. Yet because the Sahel was so terribly peripheral (from a geopolitical perspective at least) remarkably little is known about the genesis or the consequences of the famine, despite the voluminous writing on the subject.[2] In what is the most speculative sort of quantitative deception, it is estimated that at the very least 100,000 people died; the livestock toll for cattle alone was in the order of 3.5 million head.[3] The number of small ruminants that perished was probably double that figure.[4]

Perhaps because of this empirical indeterminacy, the body of literature on the origins and dynamics of the Sahel famine is conspicuously diverse and contradictory. There is certainly something here for everyone. Corrupt administration, a tardy and ineffective relief effort, expanded export commodity production, overpopulated and degraded animal pastures, multinational agribusiness schemes, desertification, albedo change and, to use the words of one of John Updike's characters in his novel *The Coup*, "bad ecology" have all surfaced with some academic regularity.[5] In one sense such eclecticism makes for healthy debate and a critical consciousness, but in another it reflects the acute poverty, and interminable recycling of very limited data. It has also bred a somewhat hysterical, if not morbid, concern for what are seen to be decaying or dying cultures and the need for a salvage anthropology.[6] And not least, the publicity of starving thousands in the Sahel prompted a massive foreign assistance commitment to the West African drylands. The United Nations Conference on Desertification in 1977, Henry Kissinger's pledge of several billion dollars to "roll back the desert," and the huge twenty-five-year reconstruction effort by the Club du Sahel were very much part of the discovery of Sahelian poverty, which in the last five years has become a thriving business.[7] All this is not to lessen the burden and the suffering of the famine or to delegitimize Sahelian poverty. But it is now clear that answers to many critical questions that pertain to conditions in the early 1970s are political and many more ultimately unknowable.

AGRICULTURE, WAR, AND FAMINE, 1960–1975

While a great deal of attention during the 1970s was focused on the plight of the pastoral sector and the demise of nomadic systems of livelihood, there has been a general reluctance to identify the far greater numbers at risk, and the profound consequences of famine in the sedentary farming zones to the south of the Sahel proper. Much of Nigerian Hausaland falls within this Sudanic belt, which in 1973 may have had a population in excess of 25 million. In 1973 when the federal government defined a "disaster area" north of 12° latitude, perhaps as many as 8 million were directly experiencing the effects of a major food crisis. Both in terms of the magnitude of food shortage and the degree of social and economic dislocation, the famine of 1972–74 was by local and official opinion at least as severe as the great famine of 1914. Animal mortality was reportedly as high in 1973 as in any period in the recent past, although statistics on human mortality and disease are wholly lacking. As Michael Mortimore (1973, p. 107) noted, "people said that in Kakalaba [1914] there was money but no food to buy with it; in 1973 people had no money but there was food." One may choose which is the worse situation.

The fifteen-year period after 1954 was generally one of favorable harvests in the North. There had been localized shortages in Katsina and Daura in 1954, in Bedde Division in 1958 and 1960 and in the Sokoto-Illela area in 1959 and 1966.[8] But on reflection, during a time in which household commodity production expanded enormously rainfall conditions appeared consistently favorable. In Sokoto, Maiduguri, and Kano over the period 1950 to 1970, for example, annual rainfall fell significantly below the long-term annual mean only on a couple of occasions. But this fortuitous meteorological record should be situated in the broader context of postwar relations between state and peasantry.

The postwar marketing boards, which were statutory export monopolies to finance "development," accumulated huge trading surpluses up until the mid-1950s. Export prices were extremely favorable following the Second World War and the Korean War, and by 1952 the export volume was roughly 50 percent higher than the 1945 level; the export price index stood at four times its 1945 counterpart (Helleiner 1966, p. 30). Since import prices lagged behind the buoyant export sector, the net barter terms of trade moved sharply in Nigeria's favor. At the zenith of the postwar boom, the 1954 constitutional changes proved a major boost to the devolution of fiscal powers to regional authorities. Accordingly, the boards were also regionalized and bequeathed accumulated financial surpluses of £87 million, which were gradually run down as each regional government encouraged infrastructural, welfare, and industrial investment. The newly regionalized boards then commenced upon a deliberate policy of rebuilding trade surpluses to further finance regional development and party political expenditures (Forrest 1981).

The importance of the constitutional developments of the 1950s was precisely that the material basis of three discrete regional economies in Nigeria, each dependent on a different source of peasant surplus, was further intensified. In the 1954 constitution, the financial autonomy of the regions was vastly augmented through a major overhaul of the entire revenue allocation system. It specifically assigned increased roles to the regions, which were granted the responsibility of education, health, agriculture, industrial development, and secondary roads. The federal government retained exclusive control over external affairs, defense, currency, exchange rates, and major infrastructure. However, as the regions availed themselves of new forms of finance—produce sales tax, personal income taxes, and indirect taxes—so was the regional political economy of Nigeria deepened and an aspiring bourgeoisie further fragmented along ethnic, religious, and geographic lines. The stark regionalization of the economic base of the state not only tied each subeconomy differentially into the world economy (based in large measure on prevailing commodity prices) but also highlighted the fiscal vulnerability of each region, the strains of which were ultimately transmitted through the federal structure as interethnic tension.

The newly independent and politically fragile Nigerian state confronted precisely this fiscal crisis in the early 1960s. In fact, since 1954 export prices had been stagnant or declining (though the value of total exports rose steadily) while the value of imports had regularly outstripped exports. As the new barter terms of trade turned downward, the foreign exchange reserve plummeted from £260 million in 1955 to less than £70 million in 1964. In the early 1960s, however, a sharp recession in export prices was felt through the marketing boards raising their effective rate of surplus appropriation. Since increases in direct taxes were politically unpalatable, the export recession was transmitted as a significant deterioration in real produce prices. In 1964, export price indices were *below* the levels that prevailed during the Great Depression of the 1930s. As import prices rose gradually, the balance of merchandise trade slumped and the terms of trade deteriorated markedly. Faced with necessary importation of capital goods for the industrialization programs initiated in the 1950s and the burden of debt repayments, the balance of payments in visible and invisible accounts moved into deficit and external assets declined.

In sum, the fiscal crisis of the early 1960s marked the dissolution of economic regionalism. Costs of rural production were rising, real export prices slumped and the question of cheap food for a growing and increasingly volatile urban poor (who had successfully organized a national strike in 1964) assumed strategic significance. The question of what would happen to the attractive new source of revenue—petroleum—naturally occupied the center of the political stage in relation both to the structural problems within the agrarian sector and also the balance of payments to which it was already a significant contributor (£4 million) by 1960. This was, of course, answered smartly with the collapse of the First Republic and the succession of Biafra. But the outbreak of civil war must ultimately be seen in relation to the contradictory centripetal and centrifugal forces that were generated by the disintegration of the regional economic base and the centralizing tendency provided by the rise of petroleum production.

The civil war actually broke out in 1967 and naturally further aggravated the fiscal situation. Planned economic development ground to a halt and federal defense and security expenditure increased by almost 800 percent over a two-year period (World Bank 1974, p. 138). Resources to finance the war were drawn from increased import duties coupled with a massive withdrawal of funds from social services and considerable internal borrowing (£468.9 million by 1970). Yet ironically, the growth of oil production throughout the difficult war years enabled Nigeria to emerge quite financially, if not politically, solvent. Nonetheless the structural problems in the agricultural sector that had been partially responsible for the fiscal crisis of the 1960s still confronted an admittedly expanded federal system at the termination of the civil war. In some respects there had been a significant deterioration in agricultural performance due to wartime dislocation, and by 1970 staple food imports and relief stood at over a quarter of a million tons. Gazetted producer prices of cocoa, palm oil and groundnuts fell steadily. Groundnut production, however, in 1970 was still higher than in 1960 even though producer prices had fallen by 56 percent.

By the early 1970s, two principal canons of rural development were firmly in place; the employment of tax policies by the commodity boards to finance development, and, to use the words of the Joint Planning Committee, "the belief that food production activities can take care of themselves" (cited in van Apeldoorn 1978, p. 44). The First (1962–68) and Second (1970–74) National Development Plans did nothing to transform this fundamental equation. The rural sector was posed as an economic receptacle from which agricultural surpluses were canalized; rural-urban wage and income differentials widened markedly. Farmers became, in Olatunbosun's (1975) words, "Nigeria's neglected rural majority." By 1970, Nigeria imported over a quarter of a million tons of wheat. According to a Sokoto farm survey in 1967, 24 percent of the entire sample of rural peasants, and 51 percent of the poorest stratum, were not self-sufficient in millet (Norman et al. 1976, p. 125). When M. G. Smith (1955) conducted his Zaria study in 1949 roughly 10 percent of total household cash expenditures were devoted to grain purchases; when Matlon (1977) completed a similar survey in the mid-1970s the figure was well in excess of 20 percent.[9]

The crucial drought years (1972 and 1973) did not, then, occur at a propitious moment. Though the 1969 wet season was not unfavorable, with perhaps the notable exception of the northeast, conditions in the succeeding years worsened progressively up to 1973. Taking the 1969–73 period as a whole, only southwestern Nigeria received average rainfall (Oguntoyinbo and Richards 1977). Kowal and Adeoye's (1974) regression functions derived from twenty-three climatic stations between 11° and 15°N show clearly that total rainfall in 1972 was only 25 to 70 percent of the long-term annual means.[10] The northern synoptic stations of

Nguru, Maiduguri, Katsina, and Kano all received less than two-thirds of expected precipitation (figure 7.1). The rains began far later than normal north of 11.50°N, and in some locations were four to five decades (10 day periods) late. Most of the northern states experienced severe dry periods in late June and early July, and an early termination of the monsoon. The growing seasons in Katsina, Potiskum, Sokoto, Kano, and Zaria were all between two and three decades below expectation (Kowal and Knabe 1972). The 1973 rainfall pattern proved to be equally, if not more, anomalous (figure 7.1). All stations received less than expected; Nguru and Kano were particularly badly hit (less than 50 percent of normal) while most other stations reported between 60 and 80 percent of long-term annual means.[11] The onset and termination of the rains stand in sharp contrast to the 1960s, with the length of both the wet and growing seasons severely truncated (table 7.1). June and July were appalling drought months; Katsina received barely more than four inches in June and July together, roughly one-third of the anticipated total.

While the crop and weather reports of the various states provide some of the best sources for an evaluation of food availability and crop losses, the information is still pitifully vague and inaccurate (table 7.2).[12] It seems clear that the 1973 season experienced the harshest shortfall. All of the northern districts, Sokoto, Kano, Katsina, Daura, and Bornu, lost between 50 and 100 percent of normal harvests. In a survey of 631 village heads in Kano during 1973, 90 percent reported that yields were one-

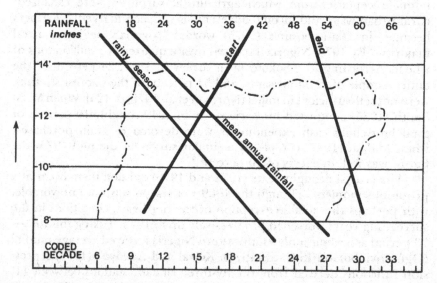

Figure 7.1. Regression of annual rainfall in northern Nigeria. From Kowal and Knabe (1973).

TABLE 7.1
LENGTH OF RAINY SEASONS

Station	Rainfall (inches)			Duration of rainy season (decades)			Duration of growing season* (decades)		
	av.	1972	1973	av.	1972	1973	av.	1972	1973
Nguru	21.7	9.7	10.1	10	3	6			
Katsina	29.1	18.7	17.4	12	12	7	15	13	8
Potiskum	31.6	27.1	17.5	12	10	6	15	12	8
Sokoto	29.6	21.6	15.3	12	11	5	15	12	7
Kano	34.8	23.4	16.3	13	12	8	16	14	7
Bauchi	43.4	35.6	28.3	15	15	10	18	18	13

SOURCE: Kowal and Knabe (1972).

*Assuming 4.0 inches in storage

quarter of normal or less (Mortimore 1977). In Danbatta District, which suffered a 50 to 90 percent loss in 1972, the majority of households had consumed all their subsistence grain by July of the following year. The superior performance of early millet was evidenced by the fact that only 16 percent of the villages reported a near complete failure in 1973, in contradistinction to the poor performance of sorghums. In the Northeast, crop losses were severe in both 1972 and 1973; an area of 57,000 square kilometers was severely affected and the average cereal loss in 1972 alone amounted to 1.1 million tons (North East State 1974). Khalil (1974) estimated that 3.8 million were directly at risk.

Following close on the heels of the poor harvest of 1972, the severe drought of the succeeding year dealt a crushing blow to household subsistence. The water table fell markedly in most districts causing excessive well deepening or outright abandonment. The wet-season rice crop along the Rima and Kebbi floodplains in Sokoto failed entirely; dry-season fadama production in Daura and Katsina was threatened by the complete absence of riverine water sources. A survey of twenty-three drought-affected districts in Sokoto Division and six in Argungu revealed massive losses of guinea corn and millet; 373,140 tons of cereals were lost in these districts, with total crop failure. Some 2.5 million confronted the very real possibility of acute hardship. In five Daura districts and four in Katsina, crop failure was 100 percent; the total loss of guinea corn and millet in Daura, Dutsin Ma, and Katsina (north) totaled 160,000 tons. In Kano, the harvests of the northern divisions were deplorable, at best 20 percent of normal; Hadejia, Gumel, Kazaure, and Jahun were in dire straits by early 1974. The permanent secretary for agriculture in the state estimated that

TABLE 7.2
Estimates of Crop Losses

State	Worst affected areas		Percentage crop loss (millet)		Number of persons affected	
	1972–73	1973–74	1972–73	1973–74	1972–73	1973–74
Sokoto	North of Sokoto	Six northern districts	20	90–100	1.2 million severely affected	1.4 million in areas of total failure 650,000 in 14 districts
	Argungu Birnin Kebbi	Fourteen other Sokoto districts	30 15	80		
Kaduna	Daura Katsina (North) Dutsin Ma	Daura Katsina (North) Dutsin Ma	30 35 20	90 50 40	no estimate	1.85 million
Kano	Hadejia Gumel Danbatta Kazaure	Hadejia, Gumel		85		±1.2 million
		Danbatta, Bichi	50–90	66	no estimate	±2. million
		Southern district		50		
Borno/ Bauchi	Disaster area north of 12°30′N	Severely affected north of 11°N	80	75	2 million	3.8 million
	Severely affected 11°–12°30′N	Dikwa, Katagum	20	no estimate	1.8 million	3 million

SOURCE: Adapted from van Apeldoorn (1978, p. 89).

1.2 million people were directly affected. According to the *New Nigerian* (November 23, 1974), crop losses in Northeast State exceeded 800,000 tons, the disaster area then subsuming all territory north of the 11° parallel. As a surrogate measure of the agricultural devastation wrought by the drought years, groundnut exports, which stood at 199,000 tons even in 1972, fell to 30,000 tons in 1973–74 and to nothing the following year. By the rains of 1974 perhaps as many as 4 million peasants faced a stunning food crisis.[13]

The performance of the grain marketing system between 1972 and 1974 is of some consequence because, with very few exceptions, no major rural markets ever had suffered absolute failure. Large quantities of cereals were carried through commercial channels from Benue and the plateau to northern consumers, and this in spite of the attempts by state governments after March 1974 to control interstate food trading by heavily policed border checks. Prices, nevertheless, rose continuously from the dry season following the harvest failure of 1972;[14] guinea corn and millet prices moved in parallel with only minor discrepancies at harvest time. Mean prices for staples in Kano (table 7.3) indicate that cereal price levels were several times higher by the hungry season of 1974. According to van Apeldoorn (1978, p. 132), based on what is admittedly patchy information, the highest price levels and the most violent price perturbations occurred in Sokoto and Niger states; from a predrought price of ₦50 per ton, millet soared to in excess of ₦200 per ton in April 1973 and hovered at that level until government relief destabilized the market in March 1974. In the northern zone, at least half of the markets surveyed by van Apeldoorn (1978) had broken the ₦100 per ton threshold by February 1973; conversely, the markets to the south of Jos only intermittently peaked at ₦100, in July 1973, and again in March and June of 1974. By June 1973 the majority of markets in the North reported prices over ₦150; specifically, birnin Kebbi, Argungu, Gusau, and Kat-

TABLE 7.3
CEREAL PRICES, KANO DISTRICTS
(per 100 lb bag)

Crop	Predrought 1972 (naira)	Preharvest 1973 (naira)	Postharvest 1973 (naira)	Preharvest 1974 (naira)
Guinea corn	4–5	11.50	11.70	16.45
Early millet	4–5	11.50	11.80	16.45
Beans	no data	20.90	23.50	31.30
Rice	no data	26.20	28.70	39.00

SOURCE: Mortimore (1977), Crop and Weather Reports (1972–74).

sina were all subject to millet prices in excess of ₦200 per ton during May and June 1973, and again in the early months of 1974. I suspect, however, that Mortimore (1977, p. 20) is quite mistaken in his claim that "prices maintained a high degree of homogeneity" throughout the North; village prices (which are wholly unavailable for the period under consideration) tend to be notoriously volatile, and the incomplete penetration of international capital had not smoothed out an uneven regional price surface. In December 1974 for instance, guinea corn fetched over ₦200 per ton in Argungu, ₦120 per ton in Gusau, and less than ₦100 in Gumel. In any event, the transportation infrastructure and an active merchant capital kept grain markets plied with foodstuffs, even if prices were both spatially heterogeneous and often beyond the meager purchasing power of the average talakawa. It is quite safe to assume that throughout the twelve northern divisions grain prices held steadily at double predrought levels for at least fifteen months (figure 7.2).

It is to be expected that the massive socioeconomic dislocation of the Sahel famine generated complex patterns of human mobility. This vortex of movement was complicated further in Nigeria for the very good reason that internal mobility was overlaid by a huge international influx of refugees from Niger, Chad, Upper Volta, and Mali. An oil-rich Nigeria constituted a much better economic prospect for destitute Sahelian herders than the already swollen capital cities along the desert edge. Faulkingham and Thorbahn's study (1975) near Madaoua in the Niger Republic estimated that male dry-season migrants between the ages of fifteen and forty-four years increased from 37.3 percent in 1969–70 to 75 percent in 1973–74. At least 30 percent of the cin rani migrants headed for Lagos, and another fifth to urban destinations in northern Nigeria. In the vicinity of Madaoua, some hamlets lost between 55 and 80 percent of their populations to northwestern Nigeria as permanent out-migrants. For the most part, however, the detail of this transnational exodus must remain forever lost.[15] There were isolated reports of large numbers of Malian and Nigerian refugees in Bornu and Daura, and an unfortunate ethnic conflict between local farmers and Malian herders at Dikwa. Madhi (1976) also interviewed seventy-eight foreign migrants in Maiduguri, three-quarters of whom were Touareg herders; 60 percent of those surveyed were males in their twenties working as watchmen, tea sellers, gardeners, and laborers. At least half of the migrants in Maiduguri intended to stay permanently. Beyond these skeletal insights we remain thoroughly ignorant.

The number of Nigerian villages that reported emigration after the poor harvest of 1972 rose sharply, though there was nothing like a regional or even district survey to document the trend fully. In the northern Kano divisions, communities that lost migrants rose from 140 prior to the drought to 483 in 1974 (Mortimore 1977, p. 29). Destinations

Price per Ton (naira)

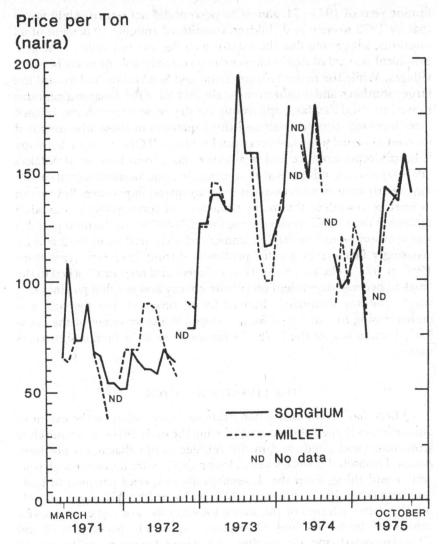

Figure 7.2. Grain prices in Katsina, 1971—75. From crop and weather reports.

within Kano State apparently became proportionately less frequent; 29 percent departed for Zaria and Kaduna, 22 percent to Gombe, 6 percent to the southern states, and 10 percent left Nigeria altogether. In one of the few available migration studies conducted in an area with a history of cin rani, Abdu (1976) documented a progressive increase in personal and familial mobility in three Illela villages (Sokoto) after 1971. The total number of seasonal migrants expanded from 171 in 1971 to 394 in 1972, and 329 in 1973, roughly 32 percent of all the taxpayers; during the peak famine year of 1973–74, almost 50 percent did not return. Abdu noted that by 1972 women and children constituted roughly 10 percent of all migrants, suggesting that the exodus included entire families. The geographical pattern of destinations exhibits considerable diversity between villages. While the majority from Tozai and Sonnani drifted toward the larger southern and northern cities, almost half of the Amarawa migrants moved to rural Zamfara, apparently for dry-season agriculture. In each case, however, between half and three-quarters of those who migrated worked as casual wage laborers ('yan kwadago).[16] Of course, such a study is hardly representative and in any case has its own lacunae. If Ndaks's (1976) study in Sandamu is at all accurate, in some locations migration was apparently neither a necessary nor a widespread imperative. But we can at least be confident that many thousands of (principally) young adult males left their rural abodes during the early 1970s; for the most part this was temporary and probably commenced with herders in 1972 and increasingly farmers in greater profusion during 1973 (van Apeldoorn 1980, p. 57).[17] The vast majority of refugees and migrants flocked to the cities to become dependent on private charity and the slim pickings of a wage economy fortunately buoyed by oil revenues. For the rest, it is embarrassing to admit that we are as thoroughly ignorant of the peculiarly human side of the 1972–74 famine as its sister famine sixty years earlier.

THE LIVESTOCK SECTOR

There has been much, often dramatic, speculation on the extent of animal losses in the Sahelian states during the early 1970s. It is quite clear from interviews conducted in the refugee camps that many northern pastoral households were leveled, losing their entire herds through starvation and thirst; even the drought-resilient species perished in large numbers (Laya 1975; Horowitz 1976). In Niger Republic alone, possibly not the worst affected of the states, total numbers of cattle, sheep, and camels fell by 64, 83, and 82 percent, respectively, between 1972 and 1976. In comparison, the northern Nigerian savannas probably escaped relatively unscathed. Of course, this is all subject to the huge caveat that much of what passes as hard, quantitative data on livestock numbers are, in reality, little more than window dressing. In the case of Hausaland, aggregate figures vary seasonally; nomadic herds are present for only part of the year, and to my knowledge there is no reliable estimate of the proportion of cattle held by sedentary farmers, though the figure of 40 percent is frequently cited (de Leeuw 1975). Under famine conditions, with no baseline statistics to boot, drought casualties are not readily assessed; absolute numbers categorically declined but the relative proportion of drought-induced starvation versus forced sale is wholly incalculable. Import cattle from Niger and Chad account for the swollen slaughter statistics in 1972–74, but the proportion of total loss they represent is equally unknowable. The huge turnover in small ruminants at the village level, which constituted a major source of famine liquidity, is naturally unknown. Total losses amounted to perhaps ₦200 million in value.

The poverty of aggregate data is reflected in the contradictory conclusions of some northern states that numbers of cattle were considerably higher after 1974, due presumably to the influx of Sahelian herds. The federal commissioner for agriculture reported to the *New Nigerian* in September 1973 that 300,000 cattle had died of starvation; Khalil, the head of an Expert Committee on Livestock Losses in Northeastern State, felt that 450,000 head had died and 150,000 were slaughtered for salvage in that state alone (Khalil 1974). The absolute number of livestock units in the northeast fell from eight to six million. In Sokoto, Argungu, and Gwandu Divisions in the Northwestern State, mortality due to starvation ran at 30, 21, and 9 percent respectively (Jiya 1974). It is of course difficult to know what to make of all this. A little more meaning is conveyed by the slaughter and trade statistics; between 1968 and 1973 total trade cattle ran between 800,000 and 900,000, rising by 10 percent in 1974 and dropping sharply by one-third in 1975. Slaughtered stock rose sharply from 0.91 million head in 1972 to 1.2 to 1.3 million between 1973 and 1974, falling to 1 million in the following year.

These statistics suggest what one might anticipate intuitively. Herders faced with weak and starving animals during the drought liquidated their assets and tried, as much as possible, to retain fertile animals for breeding when favorable conditions returned. The pressures on herd off-take, however, were quite extraordinary during the drought years. Millet prices more than tripled in many rural markets while animal prices plummeted as herders were forced to rapidly destock (through sales and slaughter) if they wished to recoup any capital at all from their dying animals (table 7.4). Cash was required for taxes and millet purchase. Aliyu's (1976, p. 25) estimates of animal losses between 1971 and 1974 among thirteen Fulani families in northern Sokoto varied from 71 percent for cattle, 64 percent for sheep and 57 percent for goats; these statistics indicate consistently high losses in the face of escalating millet prices. The burden of the changing terms of trade is reflected in the different amounts of millet obtained from the sale of a cow in the year immediately preceding the drought (1971, 3,690 pounds) and two years into the drought (1973, 390 pounds). In fact among the Shuwa Arabs of Borno, prices slumped to ₦2 per head at one point, while a bag of millet could fetch N20. In an important study in Niger, Sutter (1980) established

TABLE 7.4
HERDER TERMS OF TRADE IN BORNU

Type	1971		1973		1975	
	Price per head (naira)	Millet equivalent	Price per head (naira)	Millet equivalent	Price per head (naira)	Millet equivalent
Cattle	90	3,690 lbs	30	390 lbs	180	3,600 lbs
Sheep	15	615 lbs	10	130 lbs	30	600 lbs
Goats	7	287 lbs	4	52 lbs	20	400 lbs

that the sale of sheep, camels, goats, and cattle by Wo'daa'be herders increased by up to 40 percent in 1972 and fell by 60 percent in the immediate aftermath of the famine. But a critical factor in the recovery of the pastoral sector after a drought is the shift in terms of trade in favor of pastoral products. Between 1973 and 1975 the millet equivalent rose by roughly nine times due to the postdrought scarcity of animals. This shift in the terms of trade enabled herders to sell fewer animals as animal prices increased, and to begin the arduous task of herd reconstruction. However, the quadrupling of cattle prices from 1973 to 1975 also had the practical effect of making it very expensive, and in many cases impossible, for stricken herders to buy cattle on the open market as part of their herd reconstitution strategies.

The treacherousness of reconstitution is highlighted by an examination of drought culling practices in 1972–73 (table 7.5). Normally, mature bulls and old females constitute the current account, namely, animals to be sold for marriage, tax, or millet purchase. This fact, coupled with the low calving rates of nomadic herds, accounts for the normally low percentage of females in slaughtered stock. During the 1960s, for example, female livestock accounted for less than 20 percent of total slaughter cattle; mature or calving females were obviously rarely sold and the offtake rate was usually in the order of 9 percent. During 1972–73 the proportion of female sales skyrocketed to 40 percent, which included a massive increase in immature females. Indeed, almost 20 percent of slaughtered females were apparently pregnant. The outcome was a significant decrease in herd numbers and a major distortion in herd composition; breeding cows, heifers, and young stock were all projected onto the market in a desperate attempt to confront rapidly deteriorating terms of trade. The disequilibrium in age and sex composition takes a generation to self-correct, and inevitably leads to herd vulnerability during the reconstitution phase itself.

It seems unlikely that animal mortality was particularly high among sedentary communities, though Mortimore (1977) documented the death of 4,423 cattle in forty-eight villages in Danbatta District (Kano), between 30 and 50 percent of the total herd. Much more widespread was the conscious liquidation of animals, especially goats and sheep (table 7.6), which were often the property of women. The marginal evidences on animal demography indicate that the 1972–73 season was probably the most severe in terms of capital turnover; perhaps two-thirds of all losses occurred in that year. With the exception of remote districts where buyers were not to be had, losses through death and distress sales featured less prominently than progressive liquidation. Either way, small livestock clearly provided an economic buffer of enormous consequence for household survival.

TABLE 7.5
CULLING RATES AND HERD COMPOSITION

	Bulls				Cows			
	1963[1]		1973[2]		1963		1973	
Age	% of all bulls	% of all animals	% of all bulls	% of all animals	% of all cows	% of all animals	% of all cows	% of all animals
Under 4 Years	11.9	9.8	40.6	24.9	5.5	16.3	36.9	14.2
Over 4 Years	88.1	71.9	59.4	36.3	94.5	2.0	63.1	24.3

SOURCE: Kano (1974), Federal Meat and Livestock Authority statistics.

[1] A survey of 9 urban cattle markets; sample size of 135,000 animals.
[2] A survey of 16 largely rural markets in Daura and northern Katsina 1972–73; sample size of 148,000 animals.

TABLE 7.6
LIVESTOCK DEPOPULATION

	% Decline 1971–74			
Stock	Daura[1]	Daura[2]	Hadejia[3]	Sokoto[4]
Cattle	67	63	71	71
Sheep	75	62	73	64
Goats	75	60	64	57
Donkeys	58	64	71	67

[1]Sandam village, Daura (Ndaks 1976)

[2]Rijiyar-Tsamiya village, Daura (Ahmed 1976)

[3]Five Mungurun villages, Hadejia (Daudu 1977)

[4]Illela village, Sokoto (Aliyu 1976)

THE RELIEF EFFORT

Unlike their response to previous famines, the government—both federal and state—launched major relief schemes in 1973 and 1974 that were unprecedented in scale and scope. In sharp contrast to the experience of the Sahelian states, grain distribution, well-digging, and the provision of livestock feed in Nigeria was self-financed, administered, and implemented by widely differing local and state bureaucracies. It remains a matter of some debate just how well the relief effort accomplished its task, and more specifically whether the Nigerian political leadership rose to the occasion. To my knowledge, there has been no thorough evaluation of famine relief, either by the relief committees or by federal inquiry; the various official investigations after July 1975 closed with yet more recommendations for further investigations.[18] But the crisis of the 1970s revealed what had been glaringly apparent to the colonial state in 1927; namely, that the vulnerability of peasant producers to crises of simple reproduction demanded massive state intervention to secure the survival of perhaps ten million farmers and herders. In 1973, by virtue of a quirk of geological history, Nigeria could at least afford to devote some of its newfound oil wealth to this enormous but ultimately futile task.

Throughout the drought period the Federal Military Government (FMG) made significant fiscal allocations to the northern state governments. The Federal Livestock and Agriculture departments had already pushed for direct assistance by October 1972, and approximately ₦10 million was granted early in the new year (*New Nigerian*, January 16, 1973). After the poor harvest of 1973, the FMG announced a further ₦12 million grant for grain stores and free cereal relief, ₦5 million (through the Ministry of Mines and Power) for livestock feed, and N20 million for grain purchase. Following a somewhat dramatic visit to the North by General Gowon in December 1973, a N30 million federal grant prompted the formal establishment of state relief committees. In actual fact only half of the federal allocation was released in 1973–74. The budget of that year made no mention of drought expenditures and the Nigerian government was conspicuously absent from the regional drought meetings in Ouagadougou, organized ostensibly to chart a comprehensive relief program for the affected West African states. An additional N1 to N1.5 million came from voluntary contributions.[19]

The state relief organizations, which bore the brunt of the practical problems surrounding food distribution, varied in bureaucratic form and functions. I have no intention of pursuing this theme in any detail; it has been admirably summarized by van Apeldoorn (1978, pp. 63–91). I simply wish to identify some of the principal attributes of relief operations in Northcentral (now Kaduna) State, and more specifically of the administrative performance in Daura and Katsina emirates, two divisions probably not unrepresentative of the northern states as a whole. Relief operations began in March 1973 with the supply of 4 million bundles of hay, 15,000 bags of livestock feed and (in the same month) the sale of grains at subsidized prices.[20] Twelve hundred tons of guinea corn were to be sold at 5 kobo per mudu (3 lbs), while 2,500 tons of rice and 2,000 more tons of guinea corn were to be acquired and sold by June 1973. All this was conducted amid wild rumors of all livestock fodder relief being consumed in three days and the smuggling of relief grain into Niger (*New Nigerian*, April 23, 1973). By July almost 5,000 tons of grain had been sold.

The sale of subsidized cereals was orchestrated, and it seems ultimately impaired, by the district heads. Grain was distributed to the peasantry on the presentation of a current tax receipt, which entitled each tax payer to three tiya (roughly 15 pounds) of grain. The system was shortly abandoned as it became clear that the talakawa were not capable of covering even subsidized grain costs, and so sale monies were not recovered in full.[21] In January 1974 the distribution system was changed. Each community nominated four village elders to assume the responsibility for what became, from May onward, free distribution. Between May 13th and August 31st, 1974, a total of 49,600 bags were distributed among seventeen Katsina districts. But the new system still suffered from the old failings; district heads underestimated local needs, relief requests to Kaduna elicited sluggish responses, bags of grain were regularly reported mysteriously missing (fifteen in Dankama, Kaita District for instance), and short-measuring flourished. Two local village studies conducted in Daura (Ndaks 1976; Ahmed 1976) were especially ascerbic in their criticisms of the free-relief exercise. In Rijiyar-Tsamiya, total relief did not amount to more than one week's domestic consumption; many of the *masu hali*, the wealthier peasants, received two and half times the stipulated quota, and much of the local distribution was embroiled in village politics; district and village heads and the relief committee bureaucrats appeared equally culpable. The Justice Mohammed Commission, which delved into relief purchases, uncovered yet more suspicious dealings, which implicated provincial secretaries.[22]

A preoccupation with corruption is itself quite specious. It is true for example that in Kano State N1 million allocated to water supplies simply vanished. But in Niger and Sokoto states irregularities amounted to less than 1 percent of total tonnage. What is of greater strategic significance is the enormity of the reproductive crisis that the famine represented, and the magnitude of the relief effort that it theoretically required. Table 7.7 suggests that while considerable quantities of grain did indeed reach the talakawa, the enormous federal expenditure (almost $100 million) was, in practical terms, quite insignificant. In aggregate, the average drought victim could have benefited only marginally from food relief. In comparison, the Sudano-Sahelian populations of some 6 million were the recipients of 1.4 million tons of grain relief; in Nigeria at least an equal number of victims received only one-tenth of that quantity. The costs of survival, then, were seemingly incurred by a rural populace who, in

TABLE 7.7
PER CAPITA FOOD RELIEF

	States			
	Northwest	Northcentral	Kano	Northeast
Maximum relief Nov. 1972–Nov. 1974 (in tons)	26,700	20,000	14,000	84,000
Maximum population affected 1973–74 (in millions)	2.05	1.85	1.2	3.8
Grain relief per capita (max. pop., in kilos)	13	11	12	22
Minimum population affected 1973–74 (in millions)	1.00	0.9	0.6	1.9
Grain relief per capita (min. pop., in kilos)	26	22	24	44

keeping with the colonial era, met the crisis through migration, asset sale, and what one might legitimately refer to as "self-exploitation."

In the following section I report a case study to examine both the current response to drought and food shortage and the conditions of peasant and herder production that rendered the agrarian economy so fragile in the first place.

CASE STUDY: KAITA VILLAGE, KATSINA

When Barth passed through Kaita District over a century ago he said it was "one of the finest landscapes I ever saw in my life." I see little reason to alter that judgment now. Situated amid the manicured parkland of baobab, borassus palm, and locust bean, Kaita village is a large, nucleated settlement (*gari*) of some 400 compounds (pop. 2,809). Roughly twelve miles to the northeast of birnin Katsina, Kaita occupies an upland site slightly to the east of a poor laterite track (which accommodates a goodly measure of illicit trade to and from Niger), and about one mile to the west of the floodplain of the *gulbin* Kaita, a tributary of the river Tagwai (figure 7.3). The presence of a lowland (fadama) riverine environment has become a hallmark of the area because the seasonally inundated watercourses and alluvial floodplains are now intensively cultivated and occupy a large segment along the eastern flank of the district. The ribbonlike band of lowland foliage is in fact a highly differentiated riparian habitat in spite of considerable human modification during the last fifty years,[23]

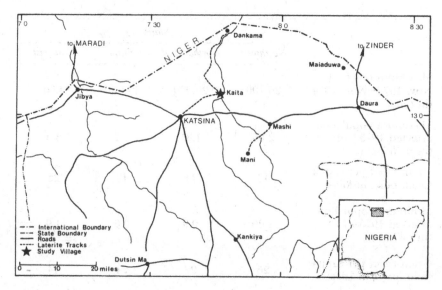

Figure 7.3. The study area: northern Katsina.

which has reduced some of the riverine ecology to a floodplain parkland dominated by useful tree species.[24]

Unlike the vast majority of Hausa villages, Kaita is the locus of a prestigious and influential district head (hakimi), the Sarkin Sullubawa, related by blood to the current emir of Katsina.[25] Although the concept of a statistically modal Hausa village is absurd, it bears reiteration that the presence of a hakimi, and the proximity to a seasonally damp bottomland and to an emirate capital, do not in themselves make Kaita village a notably atypical Hausa community. As Hill (1972) discovered in Batagarawa as well, Kaita's identity is in some measure distinct from an urban ambience in spite of its close sociological ties through the three masu sarauta families and several large merchants.[26] Kaita is more unrepresentative in its historic intercourse with the emir's palace, and in particular the considerable landholdings which are, in part, attached to the office of district headship. At the same time, it is assuredly representative of a class of relatively large and accessible market garuruwa, which have become almost synonymous with much of contemporary Nigerian Hausaland.[27]

The prejihad origins of Kaita village remain obscure but seem associated with Gobirawa immigrants from southern Niger who fled during a period of internecine strife in the mid-eighteenth century.[28] The fortunes of the village took a new turn following the jihad, for the newly inaugurated sarkin Katsina, Umaru Dallaji, established a large estate (gandu) in Kaita under the jurisdiction of his eldest son Mohammed Bello. The ruling Fulani aristocracy also installed a replacement for the deposed village head (Mallam Maigeza), a client and close friend of the Katsina emir. From this point onward Kaita became a favored rest place (*nassarawa*) of the Katsina aristocracy.

Throughout the nineteenth century, territorial administration in what is now Kaita District was diffuse and discontinuous. Despite the establishment of a royal estate (gandu) in the early 1800s, the construction of a rampart by the Sarkin Katsina Ibrahim (1870–1882) and an elaborate "summer palace," formal administration and birni control remained vague and decentralized. Large tracts of territory to the north of Kaita consisted of dense, uncultivated bush (daji) while to the south the sparsely settled plains had been progressively depopulated during the Katsina-Maradi wars of mid-century. Local political power resided among an officeholding clique, most conspicuously the four *magaji* of Kaita, Gulbi, Sauri, and Gafiya, all of whom were resident in Kaita village for the majority of the year. In practice, large numbers of villages and hamlets were held in fiefs—or at least in chappa allegiance—by absentee aristocrats, principally the high-ranking palace officeholders in Katsina town, notably the Durbi, Kankiya, and Kaura.

The northern settlements remained decidedly peripheral, markedly so during periods of political insecurity, fulfilling defensive functions as frontier outposts (*dakaru*). It was not until the territorial reorganization by the British that Kaita District emerged as a geographically contiguous entity, coterminous with Sullubawa authority. Between 1903 and 1905, Kaita, Girka, Dankaba, Sawarya, Yanhoho, Gafiya, and Gande villages constituted the small district of *Kankiya Fadama*, which was given to Bello, son of Emir Yero. At that time, the precolonial territorial system remained largely intact, for Yandaki and Matsai were in the hands of the Durbi, Alemi under the Marusa, and Dancaffa, Kefin Mashi, and Bada with the Kankiya. Bello was, however, quickly replaced by Sarkin Sullubawa Yerima Abdu who resided in the district on an isolated estate at Tarkama near Abdallawa. The traditional home of the Sullubawa clan was, nevertheless, Zandam and Bugaje, two villages directly west of birnin Katsina, both of which had been granted to leaders of the Katsina Sullubawa—Umaru Dunyawa and Na'Alhaji—for assistance during the jihad. Sarkin Sullubawa Shehu who held Bugaje, Kusa, and Kanwa in his own right at the turn of the century, was elected as district head of the newly consolidated Kaita District in 1908, and accordingly moved the administrative headquarters from Bugaje to Kaita.[29] From this point until the present, the office of hakimi has remained largely in the hands of the ruling Sullubawa.

When Barth passed through in the 1850s, Kaita was of some regional significance and, like its sister towns of Dankama, birnin Kuka, and Mai'aduwa, was a member of a select group of rural marketplaces that marked the commercial interface between the desert edge and the savannas. Asbenawa, Agalawa, and Gobirawa merchants and long-distance traders (*fatake*) brought livestock, salt, and natron from the Sahel proper to these northerly markets in exchange for millet, tobacco, craft goods, and in the nineteenth century, slaves. Kaita was one of the northern termini of this long-distance trade, and several respected and influential caravan leaders (*madugai*) resided in the Kaita-Gafiya area. Kaita and the other fringe settlements were served by grain traders (yan kwarami), principally Bugaje and Maguzawa, who brought grain from the (then) surplus producing "arewa" communities, in exchange for kola, tobacco, and cloth. Kaita was, in addition, an important slave market, which in conjunction with Ajiwa and Makurda was fully integrated into a prosperous rurally based exchange network that largely bypassed birnin Katsina itself.

Throughout the colonial period, Sullubawa District remained an economic and administrative backwater, ignored by the provincial administration in favor of the richer, more fertile laka districts that held much more commercial promise for cotton and groundnut production. An early assessment of Shinkafi, several miles to the southwest of Kaita, by Palmer in 1906 is of some significance only because of Palmer's horror at the economic marginality of most households (NAK Katprof 1 #36).

Kaita occasionally surfaces in colonial reports as an unwieldy, under-populated district economically compromised by the taki taxation system. However, the district remained spectacularly nondescript, populated by large numbers of settled Fulani, scattered communities of non-Muslim maguzawa, and an ever burgeoning population of Nigerian Hausa, who had fled heavy French capitation taxes to settle in the northern Katsina districts.

According to an entirely unreliable assessment by Palmer in 1908 (NAK SNP 7/10 1512/1909), the population of Kaita District (including Dankama) was 20,187 and saddled with a wholly unrealistic tax burden of 3/11d per adult male. By 1925 the figure was 36,432 and continued to double every twenty-five years. Some areas grew even faster at the village level; between 1947 and 1977 the population of Dankaba, Gafiya, Abdallawa, and Kusa—areas where land scarcity had not been a serious constraint—grew by almost 200 percent.[30] By the mid-1970s, the population density for the entire district had risen to 242 per square mile and some of the southern village areas, now legitimately part of the Katsina close settled zone, stood in excess of 400 per square mile (figure 7.4).[31]

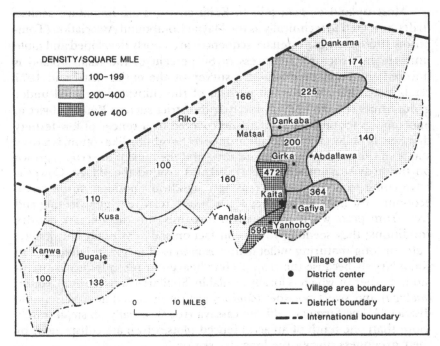

Figure 7.4. Population densities (per square mile), Kaita District by village area. From local government statistics 1977, Katsina provincial office, Katsina.

In 1977 Kaita village consisted of 473 discrete households (gidaje). Although almost 100 gidaje were classified as nonfarming, almost 90 percent of the village population were farming families (table 7.8).[32] Among households engaged directly in agriculture, 70 percent consisted of less than 10 individuals; the mean size of farm units was 6.7 persons, each householder having an average 1.5 wives and a little more than 3 children (table 7.9). The proportion of married men who presided over their own households and did not have direct access to privately owned land was very low, less than 2 percent.[33] The agricultural economy is marked by a striking opposition between rainfed upland farms, consisting of permanently cultivated sorghums and millets, and a lowland, riparian system which, though it occupies only 5 percent of the total cultivated area, is intensively farmed for dry-season irrigated crops (lambu), wet-season sorghum and rice, and flood-retreat tobacco cultivation.[34] The vast majority of peasant producers harnessed the fruits of the land through their own familial labor and a remarkably simple agricultural technology.[35]

THE UPLAND (JIGAWA) SUBSYSTEM

Most upland or *tudu* soils in Kaita environs are immature aeolian drifts, referred to technically as the Matsai Compound Association (Tomlinson 1960),[36] whose catenary sequences are poorly developed and quite uniform in structure. In excess of 80 percent of the Kaita upland is devoted to cereal production; a survey of the entire district in 1977 established that less than 10 percent of the cultivated area fell under groundnuts (FADP 1978).[37] In an arid district such as Kaita, subject to enormous variability in rainfall and covered by a veneer of low-fertility drift, early millets are especially attractive. Sorghum, like cotton, is a risky staple in the northern Sudan savannas and the bulk of the crop is grown on the heavily manured lands (karakara) around the village. Cowpeas have come to occupy an increasingly significant position in the cereal economy, for not only are they leguminous, relatively high yielding and free from pests when cultivated in mixtures, but can tolerate hot-dry conditions; they seemingly thrive in fact on soil of virtually any quality. Late- or long-maturing millet (*dauro, maiwa*) is of no great significance in Kaita largely because the crop prefers heavier or recently cleared farmland, neither of which is locally available. Similarly yams (*gwarzo*), cotton (*auduga*) and sweet potatoes (*dankali*) are rarely found anywhere in the district. A few farmers cultivate cassava (rogo), usually on small (rarely more than one-tenth of an acre) fenced plots, which are conspicuous by their greenness during the long dry season.

Permanently cultivated upland farms are rarely monocropped but are usually planted in complex crop mixtures involving quite varied

TABLE 7.8
KAITA DISTRICT: DEMOGRAPHIC SURVEY

Social unit	Males			Females		Children		General population	
Type	Number	Total	% of total pop.	Total	% of total pop.	Total	% of total pop.	Grand total	% of total pop.
Masu sarauta*	4	8	.3	18	.6	56	2.0	82	2.9
Other farming units	371	544	19.4	831	29.6	1,069	38.8	2,444	86.9
Nonfarming units	98	42	1.5	141	5.0	100	3.4	283	10.2
Totals	473	594	21.2	990	34.6	1,225	43.6	2,809	100.0

*Traditional ruling elite who occupy the principal political and administrative offices in the community.

TABLE 7.9
KAITA VILLAGE: FARM UNIT SIZE

No. of persons per farm unit	No. of units	% of total farm units	Population	% of total farm population
1	9	2.4	9	0.4
2	24	6.4	48	1.9
3	32	8.5	96	3.8
4	56	14.9	228	9.0
5	53	14.1	265	10.5
6-10	148	39.5	1,102	43.6
11-15	42	11.0	520	20.6
16-20	4	1.1	67	2.6
Over 20	7	2.1	191	7.6
Totals	375	100.0	2,526	100.0

genetic materials; a bewildering array of cereal varieties have evolved in (and are suited to) local geographical conditions. Almost 80 percent of all fields are planted in crop mixtures. The proportion of single cropping is in fact higher than in both Zaria (16.6 percent) and Sokoto (7.1 percent),[38] reflecting not so much the extent of rural commercialization, though this is certainly considerable, as the riskiness of sorghums in extreme northerly latitudes. The most popular crop mixture is sorghum and millet, followed by millet and cowpeas, and sorghum-millet-cowpeas.

During the depression, limited bush and light settlement in the Kaita village area permitted short-term fallowing. But population growth has rapidly transformed the prewar fallow systems, and the majority of the jigawa upland is now permanently cultivated. In lieu of fallow some smallholders, especially those with limited access to organic manure, rotate (*juya*) crops, preferring to monocrop the less demanding millets after several seasons of sorghum production. The sharp distinction drawn by Hill (1972) between infield and outfield systems is, in fact, of very limited utility in Kaita for the good reason that most holdings are permanently cultivated and receive considerable applications of organic manure (taki).[39] Each farming household owns an average of about six goats and three sheep, but the rate of fertilizer application varies from less than one ton per acre to in excess of ten tons. Local opinion expressed a preference for 100 *mangala* per acre as an optimal input, that is, roughly five to seven tons.[40] The average rate of application per farm, however, is thirty-five mangalas (1.5–2.0 tons) per acre, a figure congruent with Mortimore's (1971) estimate in the close settled zones of Kano but considerably less than Schultz's (1976) 5.5 tons per acre in Zaria. Upland holdings are rarely manured every year since the effectiveness of livestock dressings are reputed to last at least three years. Indeed, excessive application of manure renders the jigawa soils too "hot" and unsuitable for most early millets. In any one year it is unlikely that more than 15 percent of all holdings will be intensively dressed prior to the wet season.

While there is a distance decay effect in the application of manure— the peripheral holdings tend to receive lighter inputs in view of the transportation costs—the enormous pressures on landholdings and the fact that many households have access to only one upland farm mitigate against a sharp infield-outfield division. Since uncultivated bush is wholly unavailable in Kaita, and in view of the almost perpetual demand for land borrowing (aro) or leasing (*haya*), less than 2 percent of upland farms are under fallow in any one agricultural season.[41] Each farming household owns 1.5 upland farms, each roughly three acres in size.

THE LOWLAND (FADAMA) SUBSYSTEM

The riparian environment is highly variegated, consisting of quite discrete microenvironments located between the streambed and the peripheral terraces (figure 7.5). The parent material of the lowland soils is recent alluvium but aeolian and colluvial movement of sandy materials from adjacent higher ground forms surface deposits at the floodplain margins. The soils are structurally complex, exhibiting a wide range and combination of textures. The soil series are best considered as outcomes of several different, though frequently concurrent, processes of deposition. These depositional forms have given rise to a tripartite soil se-

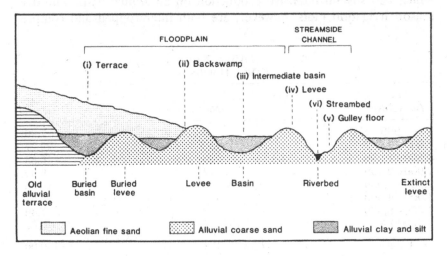

Figure 7.5. A classification of Kaita fadama.

quence; a light gray, sandy Dankabba series; a gray, silty Gafiya series in
the basins; and a brown or gray clay-loam along the river margins (Kadandani series). This division corresponds closely to the Hausa classification
of hydromorphic soil distinctions.[42]

The suitability of the riparian niche for farming varies tremendously
according to the shape and curvature of the fadama, the soil and moisture
conditions, the flood level and alkalinity, and the sophistication of local
agronomic practice. Wet-season crops, long-maturing sorghums, and rice
(shinkafa) are grown either on the floodplain proper or in the silty basins
beyond the levees of the river. Tobacco (taba), which demands quite
specific soil conditions, is always planted on the fadama margins; cowpeas
are occasionally cultivated in the damp basins, being planted, like tobacco,
at the end of the rains and harvested four or five months later. Dry-season
irrigation (lambu) is confined to the margins of the streambed, though
increasing pressure on riparian resources has necessitated the cultivation
of small basins well beyond the watercourse itself. During 1977 forty-
seven farms were devoted to wet-season cultigens such as tobacco, sorghum, and rice. These nonirrigated holdings were without exception
much smaller than their upland counterparts. The lambu plots, conversely, were diminutive with respect to both upland and nonirrigated
lowland farms; the mean size of lambu holdings was 2,383 square yards
(table 7.10) although 40 percent were less than 1,500 square yards.

Unlike the jigawa environment, lowland holdings—with the notable
exception of lambu plots—are not manured. Floodplain sites are annually inundated and receive a new input of fertile alluvial material. Both
rice and sorghum are monocropped on the heavy hydromorphic soils,
which can sustain intensive production on an annual basis. The dry-
season irrigation plots, however, are both intercropped and compre-

TABLE 7.10
LAMBU HOLDINGS

Size (sq. yards)	No.	% of total
0–999	9	7.46
1,000–1,499	36	29.77
1,500–1,999	20	16.53
2,000–2,499	12	9.92
2,500–2,999	20	16.53
3,000–4,000	8	6.61
4,000–6,000	9	7.46
6,000 +	7	5.62
Totals	121	100.00

hensively manured with a variety of specialized organic fertilizers.[43] At the onset of the harmattan, the wells (*riyiya*) are redug and small seedbeds prepared around the lip of the well that are planted with tomatoes, peppers, onions, and lettuce during December. When the entire holding has been leveled and the earth graded, a matrix of small beds are constructed (fangali), interconnected by a network of small channels (*korama*) and waterways (figure 7.6). During January and March the irrigated crops (*jaguga*) are transplanted to the fangali in complex crop mixtures, the more delicate vegetables occupying precise locations within the irrigated beds.

The main irrigation channel (*doki*) generally divides into several smaller canals (*kworama*) about ten inches and six inches deep, which follow the sides of the fangali; water is admitted to each individual bed by a sluice.[44] Within each bed, onions, tomatoes, and peppers tend to be intercropped while lesser cultigens like sorrel, gourds, squashes, and leafy vegetables are planted along the borders and occasionally in the pathways (*mabiyar*) separating the beds. After transplanting, weeding and thinning is almost continuous, and manure is applied at least three times during the

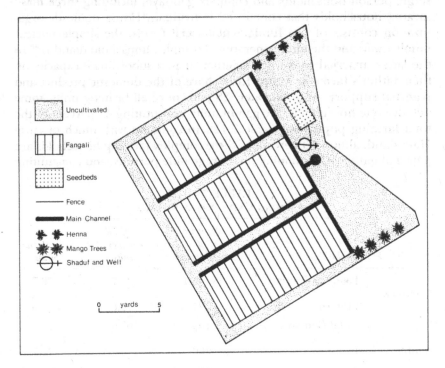

Figure 7.6. A lambu farm.

growing season. The periodicity of water distribution fluctuates with climatic conditions; during the cool harmattan water may be required only once each four to five days, while at the height of the hot season daily watering, consuming four to five hours labor time, is an absolute necessity. By the hot season, farmers lift in the order of several hundred calabashes of water per hour. The farms are fenced in December to prevent the (then) free-ranging ruminants from invading the plots. By February the first harvest of onions appears, followed successively by tomatoes and peppers, which extend into the early rainy period.[45] Commencing at roughly the same time as the onion harvest, the first leaves of the fadama tobacco harvest are collected, tied into bundles, and stored for price rise, usually being sold during the rains to specialized traders who export much of the crop to Niger.

LABOR MOBILIZATION AND SCHEDULING

The majority of peasant labor in Kaita is mobilized through the domestic group, which varies considerably in size and complexity. The average farm unit in 1977 consisted of 6.7 persons, but there were also single-person households and complex gandaye, including three masu sarauta households that contain 82 individuals. Hausa domestic organization consists of two fundamental social forms; the simple nuclear family (*iyali*) and the multigenerational complex household (gandu).[46] In the latter, married sons work together or in a subordinate capacity on their father's farms in return for a share of the domestic product and paternal support. Approximately 28 percent of all farming units, some 106 discrete households, are gandu units, constituting 41 percent of the total farming population (table 7.11). In common with much of rural Hausaland, almost 80 percent of these complex farming households are paternal gandaye, containing on average nine persons, and constituting

TABLE 7.11
FARMING UNITS, KAITA VILLAGE

	Household Type	Number of households	% of all complex units	% of all units
Complex	Paternal Gandaye	85	80.2	22.7
	Fraternal Gandaye	21	19.8	5.6
	Total Gandaye	106	100.0	28.4
Simple	Iyali	269		71.7
	Totals	375		100.0

33 percent of the farm population (table 7.12). Among the 269 simple farm units, the mean household size is significantly smaller, averaging 5.5 individuals per nuclear family.

Several caveats are in order, however. The 106 gandaye in Kaita are far from uniform with respect to the classical model of gandu structure and authority described by Hill (1972) and M. G. Smith (1955). At least 80 percent are loosely "cooperative" gandu in which the autocratic familial authority exercised by the mai gida has been significantly decentralized. In Kaita, as in Sokoto, almost three-quarters of sons in gandu paid their own tax, and the authority invested in the mai gida was, in view of off-farm income opportunities, often quite nominal. Also, the percentage of gandaye units is quite high in relation to other research that established the incidence of gandu in Katsina, Zaria, and Sokoto as, respectively, 29, 23, and 19 percent.[47] Indeed, if one considers the proportion of married sons in gandu in relation to total number of married males who could be part of complex farm units, the incidence of gandu is high, in excess of 50 percent. In view of the general claim that the last quarter century has witnessed a gradual dissolution of gandu in Kaita, the institution is nevertheless far from moribund.[48]

In Kaita village the increasing pressures exacted by demographic growth and smaller landholdings have generated a socioeconomic context in which it makes much economic sense to remain in gandu—indeed in fraternal gandu—not only as a security device but to exploit the scarce lambu lowlands. In an area where viable secondary occupations are not readily available, especially for the poor and newly married sons, and where the poor spend much time searching for casual labor to consume the long dry season, the lambu sector has much to commend it. The fact that lambu agriculture minimally requires two individuals to orchestrate the water allocation process confers a further advantage on cooperative activity, and hence on some form of loose economic union, whether paternal or fraternal. Though married sons tend to receive individual plots (*gayauna*)[49] at marriage from their fathers, the diminutive size of lambu holdings (and hence their relative indivisibility) and their economic

TABLE 7.12
POPULATION OF FARMING UNITS

Household type	Average size	% of total farming population
Paternal Gandu	8.9	8.1
Fraternal Gandu	8.6	33.2
Total Gandu average	8.75	41.3
Iyali	5.5	58.7

attractiveness, is conducive to a certain degree of resiliency among
gandaye quite unlike other communities where possibilities of off-farm
income are somewhat different. Not surprisingly, then, a high proportion
of lambu farms are cultivated by either paternal or fraternal gandu work
groups.[50] Table 7.13 illustrates that over 70 percent of all lambu plots are
farmed by gandaye farming units, of which over 60 percent are fraternal;
that is, married brothers working and cultivating the gardens together.

   While labor supply is overwhelmingly provided from within the
domestic unit there are two other forms of labor provision. First, communal work groups (gayya) while still fairly common among isolated
communities in Kaita District, are moribund in Kaita village and held in
low esteem.[51] Wealthy householders occasionally call a gayya for house
repair or for ceremonial reasons, but their function in the agricultural
economy is of no consequence since they are generally regarded as an
inefficient, poor quality systems labor supply. And second, wage labor
(kwadago) hired by the day (*yan kwadago*) or by contract (*yan jinga*). The
wage relation is principally geared to the provision of labor power on the
farms of wealthier farmers, especially during the critical periods of planting and weeding. Some men actually migrate locally during the wet season
as casual farm laborers, making use of the local variation in rainfall onset,
and hence planting times. These laborers (*dan barima*), and wage laborers
generally, are always poor farmers or their sons, who have insufficient
capital for dry-season trading and frequently find themselves short of
wet-season cash, principally for grain purchase. A wealthy household
might hire perhaps thirty man days of farm labor during the year,
peaking between June and September for upland weeding and again in
December and January for the arduous tasks of lambu field preparation
and well construction.[52]

   One final component of domestic organization that impinges directly
upon labor supply is the incidence of wife seclusion (auren kulle), what
Hill (1977, p. 84) mysteriously refers to as an "anxiety syndrome." In
sharp contrast to the earlier part of the century when purdah was largely
the preserve of notable malamai and aristocracy, virtually all married,
premenopausal women in Kaita village were secluded in 1977. Although
the nature of wife seclusion is subject to personal interpretation, it was not
uncommon for recently married girls to find themselves restricted to the
confines of their husband's compound and unable to leave except under
supervision. The profound shame associated with wives working on their
husband's fields is sufficient to remove the majority of women from the
agricultural labor force even though they may, and increasingly do, own
farmland. The impoverishment of the poorer peasantry is unquestionably exacerbated by their steadfast refusal to permit women to labor on
domestic farms. The fact that women are economically active within the

TABLE 7.13
LABOR ORGANIZATION ON IRRIGATED HOLDINGS

Farm size (sq. yds)	Paternal gandaye (i)			Fraternal gandaye (ii)			Single adult plus child (iii)			Friends: abokin aiki (iv)			Other (v)		
	No.	% of (i)	% of all lambu farms	No.	% of (ii)	% of all lambu farms	No.	% of (iii)	% of all lambu farms	No.	% of (iv)	% of all lambu farms	No.	% of (v)	% of all lambu farms
500–999	2	5.5	1.7	3	5.8	2.5	2	8.3	1.6	1	1.3	0.8	1	33.3	0.8
1000–1499	9	15.0	7.4	15	29.4	12.4	9	37.8	7.4	3	42.9	2.5	—	—	—
1500–1999	3	8.3	2.5	9	17.7	7.4	8	33.3	6.6	—	—	—	—	—	—
2000–2499	5	13.9	4.1	6	11.8	5.0	—	—	—	1	14.3	0.8	—	—	—
2500–2999	4	11.2	3.3	13	25.5	10.7	2	8.3	1.7	1	14.3	0.8	—	—	—
3000–4000	5	13.9	4.1	1	2.0	0.8	1	4.1	0.8	1	14.3	0.8	1	33.3	0.8
4000–6000	3	8.3	2.5	4	7.8	3.3	1	4.1	0.8	—	—	—	1	33.3	0.8
Over 6000	5	13.9	4.1	—	—	—	1	4.1	0.8	—	—	—	—	—	—
Totals	36	100%	29.7	51	100%	42.1	24	100%	19.7	7	100%	5.7	3	100%	2.4

limits set by seclusion—indeed their earnings and ownership of small livestock is crucial to domestic reproduction—does not alter the fact that the rural poor generally suffer from chronic labor constraints that can only be aggravated by wife seclusion.

COMMODITIZATION, INCOME, AND INEQUALITY IN KAITA

[The owner of labor power's] natural wants, such as food, clothing, fuel, and housing vary according to the climatic and physical conditions of this country. On the other hand, the number and extent of his so-called necessary wants, as also the modes of satisfying them, are themselves the product of historical development.

—K. Marx, *Capital*, Vol. I

The fact is that peasantries nowhere form a homogenous mass or agglomerate, but are always and everywhere typified by internal differentiation along many lines.

—Sidney Mintz

A major thread running through the historical warp and woof of the Hausa peasantry has been the deepening of commodity relations within the reproduction cycle of the peasant household. This process was given its particular motion by the specific character of state intervention after 1900, but all recent studies of household expenditures underline the general extent to which purchased commodities, especially items of personal consumption (food, manufactures, clothing) have become fully incorporated into the household budget. Many of the currently purchased use-values were, of course, formerly produced within the local economy. Historically these trends are reflected first in an increase in domestic monetary expenditures, that is, an increase in real terms in annual cash expenditures, which is a necessary concomitant of the commoditization process; and second, in the relative increase in food expenditure, a point to which I shall return. Whatever the proportion of produced to purchased items, however, the needs of simple reproduction emerge from the historically and socially defined subsistence level within the region.

Commoditization and the proliferation of exchange transactions in money not only proceeded through consumer items but also embraced the means of production and labor power itself.[53] The genesis of a market in land is seen in the means of acquisition of land in Kaita (table 7.14), which reveals that almost 20 percent of holdings were bought or rented.[54] Among fadama farms, which are much sought after but limited in number, almost two-thirds were either purchased or rented. Yet in spite of the antiquity of farm sale, land transactions in Kaita village are something of

TABLE 7.14
FARMS: MEANS OF ACQUISITION

Type	Upland	Lowland	Total	%
Purchase (saye)	62	60	122	13.6
Inheritance (gado)	638	56	694	77.4
Borrow-Rent (aro)	6	46	52	5.8
Gift (Kyauta)	18	0	18	2.0
Trust (Amana)	11	0	11	1.2
Totals	735	162	897	100.0

a rarity except under conditions of extreme deprivation or personal calamity. The great scarcity of land in relation to population combined with the enormous inflation in farm prices since 1972, have determined that even those most likely to sell (namely, the poorer households) will only do so as an act of last resort. In light of the progressive increase in upland farm prices,[55] the possibility of reacquisition is necessarily slight. The price trends on lambu farms are equally pronounced; a half-acre plot, which brought ₦40 in 1940, can now demand twenty times that figure.

The land question in Kaita has, however, become increasingly involuted and complex, due principally to land scarcity in relation to population, farm prices, and household needs. As land became the primary economic and social asset so did patterns of land ownership become more diffuse. All land is certainly recognized as individually owned, and all farm property has a remarkable degree of security with regard to disposition and retention. But to the extent that inheritance serves to fragment and subdivide holdings and inflated farm prices mitigate against ready purchase, patterns of land ownership and use have become increasingly separated. More specifically, almost half of all farms in Kaita are not worked by their owners even though farmers with usufructuary rights refer to these holdings as gado. These inherited holdings are in fact subject to additional claims by others (usually kin) and hence can not be sold by the cultivator. Historically in Kaita there has been an increase in the assignation of usufructuary rights thereby facilitating the circulation of land. This emerging pattern reflects a heightened frequency of heir postponement of claims to land though these rights are not relinquished and indeed are frequently maintained by individuals not resident in the village (and in some instances actually live far afield in Lagos, Kaduna and Ibadan). As I shall argue, this has simultaneously served to limit land sales, to deflect land accumulation, to involute patterns of ownership and use, and to magnify the awareness among both men and women of heir eligibility and property allocation. When the poor do sell land it is largely irreversible and the general effect is to transfer land resources from the less well-off to the rich.[56] A sample of farm sales over the last twenty years in Kaita reveals that the volume of commercial transactions is still quite small, and that sales generally arise from extenuating circumstances, often due to famine, personal calamity or high social expenditures, notably marriage.[57]

Most farmers participate in the market nexus not through labor sale or farm transactions but almost on a daily basis in the procurement of reproductive needs. In spite of the conventional wisdom that poses food subsistence as a major goal of peasant production in Hausaland, self-sufficiency is increasingly rare (table 7.15). The extent to which households must procure their means of subsistence on the market magnifies the high demand for cash as a percentage of total income, and specifically for reliable cash-earning opportunities whether on or off the farm. Norman's (1967) work in Zaria estimated that at least one-quarter of the total value of farm production was marketed, but the manner in which cash income is earned depends in large measure on local opportunities. In Kaita, dry-season lambu, and the wage labor demand that it generates, sustains the local appetite for cash to supplement locally produced subsistence. In remote Sokoto villages, seasonal migration (cin rani) provides this monetary vent for 65 percent of all adult males between fifteen and forty-nine years (Goddard 1973). Though many aspects of social life are

TABLE 7.15
SELF-SUFFICIENCY IN CEREALS

	Percentage of farmers				
Degree of self-sufficiency	Sokoto	Zaria	Bauchi	Kaita	Overall average
Not self-sufficient	17.1	61.9	32.1	47.0	37.0
Production Less than 75% of needs	13.8	35.3	20.5	37.4	20.8
75–125% of needs	13.9	40.2	28.8	26.2	28.8
125–200% of needs	28.7	17.9	23.5	20.6	23.6
More than 200% of needs	43.6	6.6	27.2	15.8	27.2

SOURCE: Norman, Pryor and Gibbs (1979, p. 71); field data, 1976–78.

not directly mediated by the market relation, even the gift networks between households may stimulate and demand market participation and monetization.

> The gift requires the participation of the market.... To offer one, it is necessary to produce, sell, borrow, sell one's labor, buy imported products and thus participate in commercial circuits on the international scale. Far from constituting a whole body of archaic customs, the gift thus appears as an activator of the most modern exchange currents. [Nicolas 1967, p. 152]

A constitutive element of the moral economy has been transformed, then, into an agent of its own demise.

Aggregate statistics that pertain to a model Hausa family may, of course, be highly spurious. Hausa villages are not (and probably never have been) undifferentiated entities. Households vary markedly in terms of the life chances of their members, which reflect the resources each may command in their lifetimes. Landholding and income tends to vary with the demographic structure of households; the large farm units till more land and earn higher incomes than the smaller households. Income and farm statistics on a per capita basis, however, tend to reduce the equalities that emerge from more aggregate figures based on the household. Either way, most village research in Hausaland has not failed to notice the pronounced differences in economic and material welfare between households (table 7.16). Simmons's (1976) work in Dan Mahawayi (Zaria) estimated that six households spent between £500 and £2,400 per annum, while the remaining thirty-four in her sample spent between £40 and £340. Matlon (1977) reported the annual net income of six households in southern Kano averaged ₦2,715, eight times the mean income per household and three times the average per resident.[58] While the degree of interhousehold landholding equality is markedly reduced when a per consumer equivalent statistic is computed, it remains evident nonetheless that there are quite high levels of landholding concentration, particularly in the closely settled zones.[59] Equally, however, the ability of the wealthy to accumulate plots is mediated by (i) heir postponement and new forms of land circulation that limit sale, and (ii) the tendency among the rich polygamous families to partition large holdings among married sons. In this sense, gini coefficient statistics (were they available) might actually indicate a historical ambiguity in landholding inequality in some of the densely settled districts.[60]

In her seminal work in Katsina and Kano, Polly Hill (1972; 1977) distinguishes four distinct economic strata, which she defined by "their ability to withstand the shock of a very poor harvest." The rich ones are able to make loans, distribute gifts, and perhaps even prosper through trade and off-farm income. The poor, conversely, borrow, incur debts,

TABLE 7.16

INCOME, EXPENDITURE AND LANDHOLDING: HAUSA HOUSEHOLDS

Date	Source	Location	Description	Sample size	Mean farm holding size (acres)	Percentage earned, expended or owned		% of farm holdings below 4 acres
						By poorest 40% of households	By wealthiest 10% of households	
1949–50	Smith (1955)	Zaria	Income per resident	139		24	29	
			Mean holding size	167	5.1	16	25	51
1966–67	Norman (1967)	Zaria	Income per household	103		19	27	
			Mean holding size	320	8.2	13	30	43
1968	Goddard (1976)	Sokoto	Income per household	100		19	22	
			Mean holding size	371	7.3	15	27	41
1970–71	Simmons (1975)	Zaria	Expenditure per household	120		18	29	–
1974–75	Matlon (1971)	Kano	Income per household	100		28	19	–
1967	Hill (1972)	Katsina	Mean holding size	171	5.6	13	33	42
1970	Hill (1977)	Kano	Mean holding size	544	2.2	6	40	85
1978	Clough (1979)	Katsina	Mean holding size	118	7.4	11	40	49

migrate, decapitalize, and perhaps sell farms. Hill shows that wealthy farmers are more likely to be older men with large households and sons in *gandu*; they own and farm more land per household, per working male and per resident. They manure their land more intensively, and are more likely to buy land and hire labor than smaller farmers. The wealthy produce more grain and groundnuts and, in Batagarawa, are more likely to cultivate high-value crops such as tobacco, to own ploughs and groundnut decorticators, and to keep cattle. They generally engage in intervillage trade in grain and other commodities, store grain for resale, and lend money. Each of these resources and activities provides the means to accumulate other resources and to permit the wealthy to consolidate their advantaged position.

The poor, conversely, are most likely to be found among the old and in households headed by young men on small lightly manured holdings. The poor have smaller households and their married sons are less likely to remain in gandu. Heads of poor families usually engage in menial, often transient, occupations that yield low returns. They engage in wage labor and borrow heavily to buy grain in the rainy season. The worst off are those with no credit worthiness; at best they beg a little land to farm (aro), or borrow cornstalks to make beds for sale. It is common for poor men to sell both their farm manure and their farms. The poor are not only short of land but also lack the means (cash, manure and family labor) with which to farm effectively. They dispose of their few resources to meet their reproductive needs, trapped in a vicious cycle of impoverishment.

The conflation of variables that define poverty and wealth is of more general applicability in Nigerian Hausaland. Indeed, the simple quantitative measures of interhousehold inequality in Kaita village were established using a local Hausa classification of economic status similar to that derived by Polly Hill. Farmers generally recognize three distinct economic strata. First, (Group I) is the big farmer (*manyan noma*) or trader (*madugu*) who is generally referred to under the generic term of masu arziki. Among this strata the conjunction of trade, petty commodity production, and large holdings permits accumulation greatly in excess of domestic subsistence requirements. Extensive use of hired labor and especially investment in cattle are also closely associated with the wealthy households. Second, (Group II) is a broad middle strata of farmers who are successful in the sense that they adequately fulfill domestic food demands and engage in relatively lucrative dry-season occupations and trade. And third, (Group III) is a group of poor—often desperately poor—households (*matalauta*) who are barely self-sufficient in grain from their small upland holdings; they rarely have access to the capital necessary to participate in petty trading or to acquire the lowland plots suited to dry-season lambu, both of which might alleviate their appalling economic circumstances.

Table 7.17 clearly indicates that among farming units the three economic groupings exhibit distinct demographic characteristics at the household level. Of the fifty-six rich households—which constitute 14 percent of the farming population—the average number of dependents per mai gida is three times larger than the Group III counterparts. Similarly, the incidence of gandu is much more pronounced in Groups I and II; 50 percent of all rich farm units are gandu households compared with 3 percent in the poorest category. Almost 100 percent of Group III households are small nuclear families unable to provide the sort of economic security in numbers characteristic of complex farming units.

TABLE 7.17
FARMING UNITS: CHARACTERISTICS BY ECONOMIC CLASS

| | Economic class | | | |
Variable	I	II	III	Total
No. of farming units	56	226	93	375
% of all farming units	14.9	60.3	24.8	
Women	191	515	130	836
Average no. of women per farm unit	3.4	2.3	1.4	
Children	285	686	132	1,103
Average no. of children per farm unit	5.1	3.0	1.4	
Dependents	559	1,324	268	2,151
Average no. of dependents per farm unit	9.9	5.8	2.9	
Average no. of wives per householder	1.9	1.4	1.0	
Total no. of granaries	205	450	98	753
Average no. of granaries per farm unit	3.7	2.0	1.0	
Population	615	1,550	361	2,526
Small livestock per unit	12.1	6.6	2.6	
Cattle per unit	2.1	0.12	0	

Among the nonfarming units (table 7.18) the overwhelming proportion (in excess of 70 percent) are chronically poor; 80 percent are unmarried female householders residing alone or with small children. The unmarried females are practically landless since their farm holdings are invariably lent on trust; they are dependent for the most part on the income derived from the sale of cooked foodstuffs and support from close kin.

Other aspects of village inequality can be gleaned from a consideration of secondary occupations and the lambu sector. With regard to the former it is clear that most householders and their sons make every attempt to have some form of dry-season occupation, and in some cases have two or three.[61] Indeed it is evident that off-farm income has become the critical component in the relative prosperity of individual households. In contrast to the majority of Hausa communities, the occupational structure of Kaita is broadened by the irrigated farm sector that provides economic opportunities for both lambu farmers and casual agricultural wage work, particularly land preparation and well construction. Excluding dry-season agricultural occupations (*noman rani*), over 50 percent of all principal secondary occupations pertain to trade or crafts (sana'a). However, of the 318 occupations, 229 were exclusively the preserve of Groups I and II. Not all occupations are equally lucrative or economically viable, and only a small number of low status, unproductive occupations are available to the rural poor. The lucrative occupations associated with trade, local government salaried positions, and the artisanal skills such as smithing, carpentry, and butchering, are closely correlated with the Group I households. For poor families low-status occupations such as collecting fodder, mat making, washing clothes, and honey collection predominate, supplemented by casual wage labor (kwadago).[62] Kwadago is not, however, a particularly lucrative endeavor, though labor is scarce at critical periods and rural wage rates accordingly volatile. During 1977—

TABLE 7.18
NONFARMING UNITS: CHARACTERISTICS BY ECONOMIC CLASS

	Class		
Variable	I	II	III
Households	1	27	70
Average no. of women	4	1.8	1.4
Average no. of children	8	1.7	0.8
Average no. of dependents	13	3.0	1.3
Average no. of livestock	—	3.5	1.6
Population	14	109	160

78 the prevailing wage rate per hour varied from ten (April) to thirty (July) kcbo per hour, which, for a usual day's labor would barely cover the cost of a tiya of millet. When lambu occupations are included, the pattern of occupations is further skewed, for 107 of the 121 lambu farmers in 1978 belonged to Groups I and II. Indeed, the distribution of lambu holdings is markedly uneven.[63] Of the 121 lambu horticulturalists who cumulatively farmed 282,174 square yards of fadama, 51 percent of land area was occupied by the largest 24 market gardeners. Conversely, the sixty-five smallest lambu plots—two-thirds of which are rented, not owned—constitute more than 60 percent of the total population of market gardeners, yet they occupy less than 30 percent of the cultivated area (table 7.19). The mean size of lambu holdings belonging to Group I is 4,856 square yards, compared with 1,289 square yards for Group II.

This brief sketch hardly purports to be a comprehensive survey of inequality in Kaita. Indeed it is clear that what marks these simple quantitative distinctions between strata is the complexity of their interrelations; the poor suffer from few livestock, lower landholding per consumer equivalent, less attenuated domestic organization, distress grain sales, low-return secondary occupations, wet-season wage laboring, chronic indebtedness and so on. These are issues to which I shall return. Here I simply wish to identify the broadest contours of economic inequality. Suffice to say that irrespective of strata the search for cash has become a critical element in the domestic economic calculus; and household production generally has a pronounced seasonal timbre that corresponds to the ebb and flow of cash abundance and scarcity (Raynault 1977*b*). The pulsed character of crop sale and purchase, of agricultural work and wage laboring, and of craft and trade endeavors is of great consequence in understanding the periods of crisis in simple reproduction that threaten the economic security of the poorest households.

DROUGHT AND ADAPTIVE FLEXIBILITY

> They [the Hausa] know that drought can come again in any year and that its occurrence cannot be predicted. . . . When faced with drought or other natural disasters . . . their chief response is to pray to God.
>
> —Roder and Dupree

Odious images of Islam have an embarrassingly long-standing lineage in the West. It is, then, entirely appropriate that Roder and Dupree (1974), in a study of drought among Hausa peasants in Muslim northern Nigeria, should only see fatalistic farmers mercilessly crushed by the elements, and their fate wholly in the hands of a benevolent Allah. But in an area in which at least 85 percent of the economically active population is directly involved in agriculture, rainfall variability—both spatial and

TABLE 7.19

IRRIGATED FARM HOLDINGS

Farm size (sq. yds)	No. of farms	% of total no. of farms	% of total farmed area	Average no. of adult workers per farm	Average no. of child workers per farm	Average no. of shaduf per farm
0–499	9	7.6	2.5	1.5	0.4	1.0
500–999	36	29.8	17.4	1.6	0.7	1.0
1,000–1,499	20	16.5	10.8	1.5	0.9	1.0
1,500–1,999	12	9.9	11.0	2.0	0.6	1.2
2,000–2,499	20	16.5	17.4	2.1	0.4	1.2
2,500–2,999	8	6.1	9.0	2.3	0.6	1.1
3,000–4,000	9	7.5	14.1	2.8	0.3	1.9
4,000–6,000	7	5.6	16.8	3.4	0.8	1.9
Totals	121	100%	100%	2.2	0.6	1.3

temporal—is a matter of acute public concern. Unlike the more temperate climes where the growing season is largely determined by the temperature regime, in Kaita where temperatures rarely fall below 42°F (the critical threshold for plant growth) the length of the growing season is dependent upon the distribution of annual rainfall. Farm preparation, seed germination, and early crop growth in particular are contingent upon an adequate quantity and frequency of precipitation since the predominantly aeolian soil carries a large water deficit at the onset of the growing season. Cereals cannot rely, at least during their early stages of development, on moisture stored in the soil and are therefore dependent on rainfall alone. The value of rainfall to Hausa agronomy is as much related to its distribution and reliability as to absolute quantity.

All parts of northern Katsina are markedly seasonal. Superimposed upon the seasonal cycle of wet and dry are epicycles of enormous variability; periodically the onset of the monsoon is delayed, the totals may be poor, monthly distributions skewed, or the termination of the rains unseasonally early. In view of its northerly location (latitude 13°05'), the onset of the rainy season in Kaita is late in relation to most of northern Nigeria, usually commencing sometime in late May with a pronounced monomodal distribution, and peaking in August and July (figure 7.7). The ITCZ, however, does not act like a temperature region front for there is no direct correspondence between its surface and rainfall. Furthermore, the advance of the ITCZ is irregular, proceeding in a series of surges, halts, and retreats. For the Kaita farmer, then, the regular round of the seasons is presented at the local level as tremendous irregularity, by discontinuities, false starts, and extreme patchiness. To talk of averages or mean statistics is somewhat spurious. The actual empirical incidence of rainfall is at the farm level rather than with ideal patterns or statistical trends. As the Hausa proverb has it, "Ruwan da ya daki, ka shi ne ruwa" ("Rain which falls on the hut, that's real rain which matters").

Some measure of local variability in rainfall can be gleaned from figure 7.7. Mean monthly totals for the period 1951–68 vary considerably, precipitation in April and October being generally unreliable. July and August tend to be less subject to major perturbations. The effective growing period for most of Kaita District is about 120 days, but this needs to be weighed against the common occurrence of "false starts," which necessitates replanting.[64] Throughout the North, false starts followed by at least two-week dry spells occurred in approximately half of the recorded years. The severe drought in Kaita during 1973 was such a case; a heavy early rain in April was followed by an appalling drought that extended into mid-June.[65] The rains generally terminate in an abrupt and dramatic fashion, usually in mid-September and the dry season is well

Rainfall (inches)

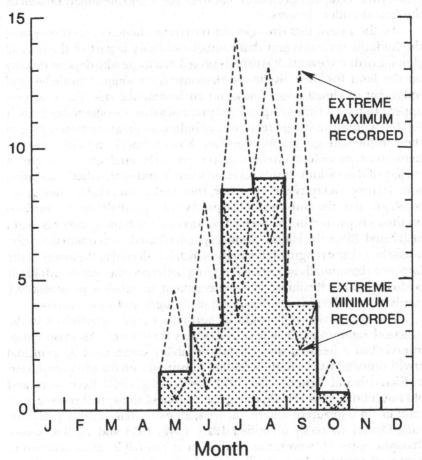

Figure 7.7. Average monthly rainfall, Kaita village. From local climatic data, provided by Kaita village, district office.

established by the end of October. Relative humidity falls markedly to less than 20 percent and winds persist from the northeast, bringing a haze of fine harmattan dust, which as Ekwensi puts it "veils the walls and trees like muslin on a sheik." Grasses and valuable fodder quickly wither, many trees shed their foliage, and lakes, ponds, and marshes rapidly disappear. From November to March temperatures are relatively cool with daily maxima of 75–90°F although during the harmattan nighttime temperatures can plunge sharply, and ice has been known to form in low-lying hollows. Through April and May temperatures climb steadily, and immediately prior to the appearance of the monsoon the climate is stiflingly oppressive. Daily temperatures soar over 100°F and are finally broken by the first thunder showers.

To the extent that drought is a recurrent phenomenon throughout the Sudanic savannas and that rainfall variability is part of the normal climatic order of events, it is to be expected that those who depend directly on the land for their livelihood demonstrate a sound knowledge and judgment of climatic variability and environmental risk. Kaita farmers appear to have a firm grasp of local processes that are observable in their totality within the village territory, including an acute understanding of their immediate geographical milieu. Kaita farmers had little comprehension of, or indeed intellectual interest in the etiology of drought. A variety of discussions simply revealed a vague and ill-specified association with Islamic metaphysics. However, they had a remarkable, almost visceral, grasp of the empirical consequences of rainfall deficits (or surfeits) on their crops, and of the prescribed ways in which the symptoms might be treated. Since the Hausa farming system is based on manual cultivation it has the great strength of flexibility, which is reflected in the ability of the farmer to continually adjust his cropping pattern as the season unfolds. It is this adaptive flexibility and management in relation to subsistence needs that underpins my discussion of drought and food shortage.

The recursivity of drought in northern Katsina is reflected in the practical significance it is lent by farmers themselves. All masu gidaje interviewed reiterated that rainfall variability constituted *the* principal environmental risk in Kaita, a finding consistent with the work conducted by Richards and Oguntoyinbo (1974) and Luning (1963). Both young and old householders can recall, with great readiness, individual years of poor rainfall. In a group of elderly farmers, all more than seventy years old, each farmer correctly identified 1926, 1942, 1953 and 1959 as severe drought years. However, the recall of poor rainfall is rarely matched in historical accuracy by a recollection of excessively wet years. With the notable exception of 1908 (referred to locally as *gizgabo*), which is a historic landmark of some regional significance, most wet years beyond five or six seasons from the present were only irregularly committed to memory. Kirkby (1974) argued on the basis of her Oaxacan experience that recollection of past climatic events is a function of recency and magnitude, but that extreme hazards tend to block the recall of earlier events and act as fixed points with which to calibrate others. In Kaita this did not appear to be the case, for the drought-famine of the 1970s did not erase either the memory of prior droughts or the manner in which they were ranked, while wet years were generally rather transient.

As regards the perception of drought periodicity, 73 percent of the informants felt that occurrence was random, 21 percent that bad years occur in clusters or pairs, and 6 percent thought droughts were cyclical, although an important caveat here pertains to the high probability that the concept of cyclicity was misinterpreted. These statistics demand a certain modesty in their explication, however, since randomness is not so much a statistical concept for the Kaita farmer as an expression of the unknowable will of Allah. In spite of the preference for randomness as a descriptor of drought occurrence, elder householders pointed to at least two trends in secular climatic change. First, farmers unanimously agreed that early rains, the March showers (*ruwan tofan geza*), had disappeared entirely; and second, that the seasonal distribution of precipitation had become increasingly capricious. Not only was the onset, termination, and distribution of the rains more erratic but the peak months of July and August (*tsululun damana*) were seen to be less reliable than in the past. Plentiful late rains (*ruwan tsira*) to terminate the growing season were, in the words of one farmer, a luxury. Sixty-five percent of all informants nevertheless believed that a good early rain (*kiri, mashariya*) bode well for the entire wet season.

Most farmers prefer rain that increases gradually throughout the growing season, terminating in September or October. Drought interludes may have a serious impact, especially if they occur in early June (germination of the cereals), late July (heading of millets), or September (heading of sorghum). Drought spells at other times may not be problematic and some farmers cherish a dry spell in early September, which facilitates the millet harvest. Particularly intense rain, conversely, can result in waterlogging and arduous farmwork. Of course, at the microlevel as all farmers reiterate, there is no model wet season but only seasons appropriate for a specific crop. Within these limits a sample of twenty Kaita farmers assigned the following probabilities to four typical states of nature. The frequency of "very bad" years (like 1972–73) was estimated at 8.3 percent and that of "very good" years (such as 1978) at 12 percent. "Good" and "bad" years were assigned probabilities of 44.3 and 35.4 percent respectively.

Memory of specific rainfall events, then, and the understanding of local climatic processes in relation to general crop requirements is consistently astute. In this sense one can quite legitimately argue that the Hausa "cognized environment," to use Rappaport's (1971) terminology, is isomorphic with our "operational model," that is to say, it is congruent with empirical measurements of rainfall and Western crop ecology. In some respects, of course, Hausa explanations seem spurious, particularly those concerning drought causation and the mechanics of weather. Rainfall is ultimately arbitrated by Allah and drought is refracted through the prism of religion; as a consequence extreme rainfall variability may be a decidedly moral issue. In fact, during the severe 1973 drought the emirs of Kano, Katsina, and Bauchi all held public prayers in which Imams demanded a refrain from "acts of immorality." Concurrently, prostitutes in Sokoto, Zaria, Katsina, and Jos were strongly advised to take husbands within three months; and in Katsina landlords actually evicted many women, who migrated to Datsun Ma thirty miles to the south (whereupon incidentally it promptly rained!). Yet if these abstract theorizations of climate are draped in religion, they are not necessarily bad or wrong-headed for the criterion of adequacy for a cognized model is not its theoretical accuracy but its functional and adaptive effectiveness. More-over, to cloak nature in Islamic divinity and to lend drought a peculiarly moral etiology, may simultaneously provide protection for a fragile ecology and highlight the critical significance of rainfall through its sanctification.

Rainfall, then, is variable, and Kaita farmers are acutely concerned with the nature of this variation. In Hausaland, as in much of the semiarid tropics, the prevailing agricultural system can be viewed as specifically adapted to the limiting factors of low and uncertain precipitation, high rates of evaporation, and low biological productivity. First, farming behavior is best seen as sequential adjustments (or response strategies) to time-honored adaptations, what Bennett (1978) calls a "rational-choice" model. In view of the uncertainty of each year, Hausa farmers make daily decisions as the season develops. This close supervision and management revolves around two critical moments: the start of the rains and the first weeding. The process of adaptive management can be simplified by decomposing each wet season into five artificial stages (see figure 7.8), which roughly correspond to discrete decision-making segments. At stage 1 the farmer has little idea of what state of nature will prevail except his subjective estimates based on past experience. Some farmers may undertake the risky venture of dry planting (bizne) during this first stage in the hope of germinating large acreages of millet early on and hence bringing forward the harvest date. At stage 2 (planting of millets), the farmer still cannot predict rainfall and generally plants millet followed later by sorghum, possibly altering spacing and sown area in response to the lateness of the planting rains to compensate for the possibility of reduced yields. At stage 3 the rains are (or are not) established and plants germinated. On this information farmers can begin to form definite expectations of their cropping patterns. Poor germination demands re-planting or resupplying and perhaps crop substitution; this may develop into stages 4 and 5 for late maturing crops such as sorghum and cowpeas. Conversely, if germination is good farmers can be more confident that some or all subsistence requirements will be met since their crop mix will probably be able to withstand a midseason drought. This stage model is an obvious simplification of an almost infinitely complex decision-making

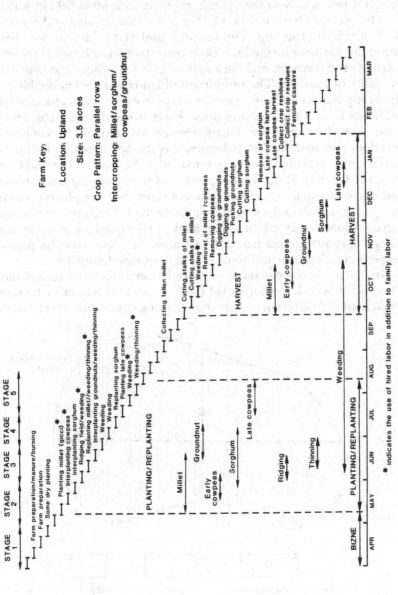

Figure 7.8. Sequential decision making on an upland farm.

process; figure 7.8 gives a vivid indication of this sequential complexity though it refers only to the operations on an individual field in Kaita.

The second characteristic of Hausa dryland farming is the prevalence of mixed cropping. The research undertaken at Ahmadu Bello University has documented the close correspondence between the incidence of crop mixtures and the length of growing season (and hence the variability of rainfall). The proportion of cultivated area in double and triple crop mixes clearly increases as the probability of drought is amplified (table 7.20). Crop mixtures provide a secure and dependable return in the face of a capricious climate, though Norman and his colleagues have demonstrated that risk reduction may also be compatible with profit maximization and high returns per man hour (Norman, Pryor, and Gibbs 1979, pp. 62–63). However, the practice of intercropping is inseparable from the sequential patterns of farm management since plot crop mixes emerge temporally as the season unfolds. In the 1977 season for example, Mallam Hamisu planted an entire field in millet and some weeks later planted sorghum across half the field area. At a later date, he planted cowpeas creating four different crop enterprises (figure 7.9).

In Kaita, the arrangement of crops in mixtures varies considerably between farmers. Indeed a World Bank survey in Gusau in 1979 identified at least 300 different combinations during one season. Several of the

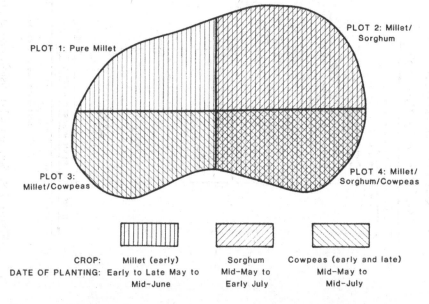

Figure 7.9. Evolution of crop enterprises. Adopted from World Bank (1981), vol. 1.

most common forms of spatial arrangement of crops in northern Katsina are displayed in figure 7.10. Within this diversity, however, it is possible to identify three broad patterns (World Bank 1981, vol. 1, pp. 66–67). First, interplanting on the same rows, which includes the placement of later crops between stands of earlier seedings but on the same ridges. Second, inserting at regular intervals a row of one crop between two rows of another (for instance groundnuts between millet). And third, mixtures in which the second or third crops are planted between the ridges of the earlier crop, either in the furrow or on the side of the ridge. These latter mixtures, especially in the more humid areas in southern Katsina, can become extraordinarily complex if six or seven different cultigens are involved.

In all upland systems in Kaita the *gicci* system prevails, which consists of sowing wide-spaced early millets in the furrows of the previous year's ridges immediately after the first rains, subsequently splitting the ridges and sowing other crops between the millets, usually sorghum and cowpeas when the rains are established. The rationale of gicci is to produce an early millet crop as soon as possible after the long dry season to defray or offset the expenditure on highly inflated grains. Early sowing would not be possible unless plant populations were sparse enough to minimize competition for the scant soil moisture during the early wet season. The wide spacing thus permits subsequent interplanting of less drought-tolerant cultigens when the probability of the stop-start phenomenon is less likely.[66]

The simple intercropping model developed by Norman requires careful specification, however, since he (like Farrington [1976] and Low [1974] working in other parts of Africa) develops an immutable "standard farm plan" that is apparently instituted grosso modo every year. Crop mixtures appear as static, ready-calibrated agricultural programs that are run automatically year after year. All that changes interannually, it seems, is output. Yet what characterizes Kaita agriculture above all else is its flexibility, and a crucial property of most Hausa farming systems is their ability to be continuously adjusted and tuned. Kaita farmers attempt

(i) Millet-Sorghum   (ii) Millet-Cowpeas   (iii) Millet-Cowpeas-Sorghum

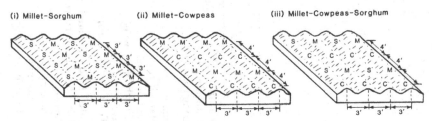

Figure 7.10. Common intercropping systems in Kaita.

TABLE 7.20

CROPPING PATTERNS, LATITUDE, AND RAINFALL IN NORTHERN NIGERIA

Variable	Sokoto area	Malumfashi area	Zaria area	Omu-Aran area
Location:				
Latitude (N)	13° 01′	11° 55′	11° 11′	8° 09′
Longitude (E)	5° 15′	7° 45′	7° 38′	5° 10′
Climate				
Start of rains	June 1–10	May 1–10	May 11–20	Mar 21–31
End of rains	Sept 21–30	Sept 25–30	Oct 1–10	Oct 1–10
Length of growing season (in days)	150	170	180	260
Total rainfall (cms)	76	97	104	126
Rainfed land cultivated:				
Total hectares surveyed	353.1	184.7	360.5	84.3
Percent in:				
Sole crops	7.1	55.4	16.6	40.4
Crop mixtures	92.9	44.6	83.4	52.8
Double cropping				6.8

Percent of crop mixture area in:				
Two crop mixture	23.5	18.1	50.5	72.7
Three crop mixture	51.0	9.1	28.5	24.5
Four crop mixture	23.8	11.0	14.5	2.8
Five or more crops	1.7	5.5	6.5	
Percentage of adjusted acres in:				
Early maize		1.0		17.3
Late maize				10.6
Millet	36.6	8.7	20.4	18.5
Sorghum	20.0	39.0	31.6	
Groundnuts		16.3	11.7	
Cowpeas	30.7	7.2	12.0	
Cassava		0.3		11.2
Yams				30.1
Cotton		22.8		
Total devoted to major crops:	87.3	95.3	75.7	87.7

SOURCE: Longhurst (1977), Norman (1976).

wherever possible to preserve this flexibility and do not adopt a rigid minimax strategy. They adjust agricultural practice in accordance with the objective local level (farm) occurrence of rainfall. In sharp contrast to Roder and Dupree's Yelwa peasantry (who apparently labored under the Tolstoyan load of Islamic doctrine and simply prayed, suffered, and starved) Kaita farmers were neither passive nor arbitrary but executed a series of drought adjustments.

Of course, the detail of each individual cropping mix and planting schedule is enormously complex. Farmers have innumerable (often non-commensurable) objectives, and it is probably denigratory to suggest that they can be entirely distilled into a single objective such as "safety-first," or indeed that such a monolithic goal has a generality across socioeconomic strata. The multidimensionality of cropping behavior is a function of the amount and nature of land the farmer has been able to acquire, family labor and funds for hired labor, complementary inputs and off-farm income, the level of grain in store, the nature of the early rains, and how he perceives the profitability and associated uncertainty of the different mixtures (Longhurst 1977), and doubtless much more. In spite of the specific contingencies of individual decision making, it is clear that one can talk meaningfully of the "goal of subsistence" for all farmers. In Kaita all smallholders and large farmer-traders ranked millet and sorghum as the most critical crops in order of perceived importance. This lexical ordering of priorities is reflected in the primary attention lent to the timely planting and weeding of foodstuffs above all other activities. While farmers aim at a minimum food target each year, the temporal element is also significant because farmers are especially sensitive to the production of millet at the right time. Particularly among cereal-deficient households, farmers place a premium on an early millet harvest. This preference is explained in the comments of two Kaita farmers. As Mallam Isa told me, "there is a need to fill the hungry period (lokacin yunwa) in August when stocks are low, prices are high, and when there is still heavy farm work to be done." And in the words of Mallam Hamisu, the head of a poor farming household, "if there is a drought later in the rainy season, I want to be assured of at least *some* corn."

To return to the stage model, we can infer that through adaptive flexibility farmers gradually switch from subsistence concerns to income and cash demands. By stage 3, farmers are (i) able to devise concrete expectations based on the prevailing state of nature, and (ii) estimate with some confidence the food production outlook. Based on these calculations, farmers will also decide whether to sell domestic grains from the previous year (at relatively favorable seasonal prices), assuming of course that such surfeits exist. What concerns me here, however, is the sort of flexibility that farmers possess in this sequential decision process. Specifically, I examine indigenous knowledge of moisture conservation and crop substitution as means to mediate the possibility of debilitating droughts that threaten the minimal subsistence demands.

Responses to rainfall variability generally consist of two broad strategies: (i) the control of microclimates, and (ii) the sequential use of crop varieties and management of lowland microenvironments.

(i) *Control of Microclimate.* As one would anticipate in an area where rainfall is erratic and evaporation rates high, the majority of drought responses refer to the control of microclimate and the *preservation* of local soil moisture. Of particular significance is the increase in ridging (*huda*), especially cross-ridging (*kadada*), to conserve surface moisture, and an intensification of weeding to reduce weed-crop competition. Respondents reported that ridging (68 percent) and increased weeding (84 percent) were preferred strategies during a period of erratic rainfall. As a general rule plant spacing tends to be much more compact on the heavily manured holdings near settlements, but three-quarters of the farmers interviewed believed that stands should be thinned and spacing widened when rains appear patchy or badly distributed.[67]

The other category of adjustments attempts to *reduce moisture requirements*, principally through the replacement of long-maturing cereals by drought-tolerant varieties. Sixteen percent of the sample took the precaution of planting cassava (*rogo*) during July as a "hunger breaker" if the upland crop prospects looked bleak by the midrains. The limited number who resorted to cassava is largely a reflection of land limitations, inability to procure cassava cuttings, and a general demand for early cereals to defray the cost of grain purchase. On the other hand, the crop substitution of drought-resistant millets and sorghums was much more widespread, being preferred in slightly over 70 percent of all cases. While almost no research has been undertaken on the varietal makeup of indigenous cereals and pulses in Hausaland, it is evident from the terminology alone that farmers have a long-standing record of genetic experimentation, and a subtle knowledge of crop types, particularly millets, in relation to moisture tolerances, pedological requirements, and maturation rates.[68]

Many of the northern Katsina varieties predate the European presence, while others are complex hybrids of local and introduced high-yield grains. The most commonly planted cereal varieties have drought tolerances that are carefully determined; millets are generally able to withstand a twenty-day drought when about one month mature (six to nine inches high), in contrast to fifteen days for sorghum and nineteen days for beans. By midseason when the plants are three or more feet high, drought tolerances among the cultigens are much more equitable, usually between twenty-five and thirty days. Groundnuts are much more susceptible to water shortage and tend to be removed altogether from the planting schedule should replanting be required. In Kaita during 1973 after a very poor start of the rains, almost three-quarters of farmers either substituted short-maturing sorghum for the traditional *jar dawa* variety or replaced sorghum entirely with millets and quick-maturing beans (*dan arbain*).

On balance, then, it appears that during and after droughts Hausa cultivators attempt to maximize food production at the expense of cash crops such as groundnuts, and shift cropping patterns in favor of short-maturing, drought-resistant millets. Sorghums tend to be deemphasized or partially substituted with less moisture-demanding, if more frugal, varieties.[69]

(ii) *Sequential Use of Crop Varieties and Management of Lowland Micro-environments.* The inventory of drought adjustments constitutes only one dimension of the human ecology of drought. A more recondite picture includes the manner in which individual coping mechanisms are orchestrated and conjoined to real meteorological conditions. In this respect it is apposite to recall that the environmental context within which Kaita farmers conduct their agronomic affairs is not homogeneous but consists of four cognitively discrete microenvironments; a broad jigawa upland and three fadama niches. The broad sandy alluvial floodplain adjacent to the *gulbi* is devoted to rice and sorghum, the basins of laka soil to wet-season sorghum or dry-season irrigation, and the levees to tobacco or market gardening. The precise manner in which these niches are exploited and articulated each year depends in large measure on the pattern of local precipitation. As a general rule, the fadama niche expands during drought years to compensate for the decline in food availability.

This expansion-contraction model is, however, deceptively simple, and individual cases reveal a management of fadama environments in which the role of crop varieties is critical. Figure 7.11 indicates how cropping patterns, crop varieties, and the lowland biomes are articulated in a sequential process of decision making in accordance with the demands of the rainfall regime.

Case 1, Favorable Rainfall (1978). The first rains appear in early May and are plentiful, so Mallam Hamisu plants his upland farms with a short-maturing, relatively high-yield millet (*zongo*). Two or three weeks later, during which time the rains are consistently good, the wide-spaced (gicci) millets are interplanted with long-maturing, high-yield sorghum (jar dawa or kaura) and cowpeas (*gamagori*), in conjunction with groundnuts. Lowland plots adjacent to the gulbi may be planted with rice and sorghum (jar dawa) immediately afterwards. At the termination of the rains, fadama areas with a red clay horizon are devoted to tobacco. After

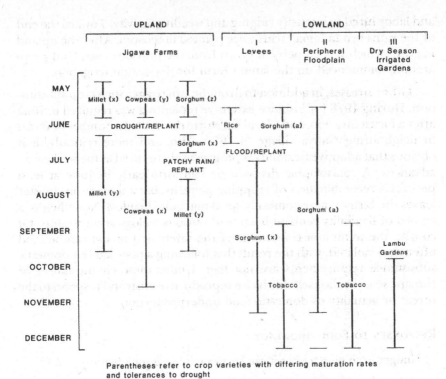

Parentheses refer to crop varieties with differing maturation rates
and tolerances to drought

Figure 7.11. A model of farmer response to rainfall variability.

the upland harvest, householders may turn to dry-season irrigation if
there is sufficient labor or domestic interest.

Case 2, A Drought Year (1973). The planting rains began in early May
and Alhaji Musa planted zongo millet, followed shortly afterward by
farafara sorghum and cowpeas. Rainfall throughout most of May was
poor which necessitated replanting during early June. Accordingly,
zongo millet was substituted by a shorter-maturing variety (*dandigale*) and
farafara sorghum replaced by a less moisture-demanding *yar bazenga*
variety. Cowpeas were replanted with a hardy dan arbain type reputed to
mature in two months. The fadama plots that had been planted in rice
and jardawa sorghum were ruined by a severe flood during June; replanting neglected rice altogether and concentrated on yar bazenga guinea
corn. Upland sorghum failed in one of the farms and was replaced by
short-maturing millet (dandigale) in the hope that at least a small harvest
might be gleaned given the shortened growth period. Kaura sorghum
grown on a moist fadama plot required no replanting. Spacings were
widened on all upland farms, no manure added during the rainy period,

and labor hired to intensify ridging and weeding activity. Toward the end of the rains two fadama farms were planted in tobacco. After the upland harvest, which was 25 percent down from the previous year, land preparation commenced on the lambu farm for dry-season irrigation.

Other stresses, in addition to drought, can trigger such crop substitution. During 1978 for instance extensive replanting was required in June after a locust invasion, and a local hailstorm devastated a number of farms in neighboring Gafiya village in 1977. Also, and more critically, it is obvious that adaptive flexibility is progressively reduced as the wet season advances. A catastrophic drought or hailstorm early in June at least permits a recombination of cropping patterns, but a midseason disaster leaves the farmer, agronomically speaking, quite helpless. Nonetheless, a record of flexibility remains in spite of obvious biological constraints. Of course, the minimum constraints of the safety-first model can be (and often are) violated, with the result that following a poor harvest domestic subsistence requirements are not met. Under these circumstances of climatic severity, households face a reproductive crisis and respond to the threat or actuality of domestic food underproduction.

RESPONSES TO FOOD SHORTAGE

Hunger is no disgrace but it can compromise a person's honor.

—African Proverb

Notwithstanding former flexibility in relation to rainfall variability, the minimum constraints of the safety-first model can be broken; indeed for some households such a transgression has become a recognized part of peasant life. A major drought simply projects the reproduction crisis onto a larger segment of peasant society. But because a subsistence crisis (or a severe harvest shortfall) is in some respects an intensification of existing cycles and is recursive over the long term, households do not respond arbitrarily to food shortages. Most families schedule their grain consumption during a normal year, ensuring as far as possible an adequate caloric supply for the wet season. All masu gidaje are sensitive to the seasonal fluctuations in millet prices and the debilitating effects of wet-season purchase when prices are perhaps 1 to 200 percent above normal. Households in Kaita are also fully able to compute their domestic needs in relation to harvest quality. Following the poor harvest of 1973 when the drought reduced millet yields by roughly 25 percent, Kaita farmers certainly knew when their granaries would be exhausted. Households make preemptive decisions following a drought in an attempt to mitigate the somewhat predictable effects of a severe shortage or market distortion perhaps six months distant.

Most response strategies to actual or potential food shortage are in fact extensions of practices conducted in some measure during a normal year. The vast majority are in situ and can be broadly classified as self-help. The precise constellation of responses during a crisis, and in particular the decision to migrate, reflects in large part local income-earning opportunities. A vast array of money-making enterprises are of course pursued; secondary occupations are expanded, livestock and personal possessions sold, and property pledged. Cash and grain are borrowed from kin, patrons, and traders. Wage labor expands enormously and many migrate to the cities in search of casual employment. Under conditions of labor oversupply, the wage rate may fall as it did in Daura in 1973–74. The less fortunate turn to kinsmen and patrons for charity, scramble for wild foods to supplement an already meager diet and ultimately face the real possibility of huge decapitalization, and most drastically land sale and permanent out-migration.

Response to the 1973–74 crisis in Kaita is probably representative of many communities in which local employment opportunities afforded some economic flexibility (table 7.21).[70] The lambu sector is an attractive and lucrative means of generating much needed cash, but there is always a frenetic scramble for plot rental around harvest time because lowland holdings are clearly limited in number in relation to total demand, emphatically so in drought years. During 1978 after the mediocre grain harvest of 1977, the number of lambu farmers increased by 56 percent over the previous season; as one acquaintance put it, "[this year] we're even making lambu in our *zaure* [entrance hut]." The increase of market gardening correspondingly inflates the demand for casual labor—notably for well construction and farm preparation—although many tenants are seasonally deficient in cash for hiring labor. Nonetheless, during both 1974 and 1978 migrant laborers actually came to Kaita in search of (and for the most part obtaining) rather sporadic farmwork, even though wage levels fell by 20 percent in 1974. For this reason, cin rani did not constitute a major strategy in Kaita by virtue of the local employment opportunities. Only eleven individuals left on cin rani on 1973–74, principally to Kano where they worked in construction.[71]

Other secondary occupations flourished with new vigor, but with less money in circulation the demand for consumer commodities and services tends to be highly elastic. Some traders (not least the grain merchants who were able to dispose of old stock at high prices and the livestock buyers who bought at excessively depressed prices) were actually the beneficiaries of huge profits. Other trades like blacksmithing, weaving, and butchery are apparently lucrative irrespective of harvest quality. For individuals without access to a usual dry-season occupation the situation was necessarily more bleak, partly because the craft sector in Kaita has a

TABLE 7.21
RESPONSE TO FOOD SHORTAGE: KAITA, 1973–74

Response	Frequency n = 74
Food purchase	70
Intensify secondary occupation	68
Support from kin, friends	58
Borrow grain, money	52
Sale of other assets	44
Wage laboring	37
Sale of livestock	35
Government relief	21
Dry season irrigation	20
Cin rani (seasonal migration)	11
Land pledging	9
Sale of land	3

"closed shop" quality; even wage laboring requires a modicum of political acuity to tap the local government resources that trickle down to some of the larger district communities like Kaita. As a consequence the rural poor tend to be individuals who are without profitable secondary occupations and resort to the low-status trades such as collecting fodder or firewood, selling manure, or perhaps weaving mats, all of which are inconsistent and paltry in their pecuniary rewards.

Women are important economic agents and contribute significantly to the household cash inflow. In spite of their socially subordinate status and the constraints imposed by purdah, rural women remain economically active—and frequently prosperous—through their domestic trading activities. In Kaita, the entire cooked food industry is the preserve of women, though much of the footwork is undertaken by children.[72] Almost two-thirds of all married women are engaged, at some level, in the food trade which, if the work of Longhurst (1977) and Simmons (1976) is at all representative, brought a return of 3 kobo per hour for fura and 9 to 15 kobo per hour for *kuli* (fried groundnuts). Nearly all women are also members of rotating savings institutions (*adashi*), contributing between 10 kobo and ₦1 per week, and drawing out deposits for critical expenses. A large proportion of small livestock are also owned by wives, and increasingly farms and trees, though farm holdings are invariably loaned. However, the wife is relatively autonomous in her economic affairs, a condition that is reinforced by polygamy and easy divorce. From the wife's perspective nothing would be so counterproductive as to assist her husband without repayment. Divorce leaves the wife out of pocket, while economic assistance makes it easier for the husband to take a second wife.

In any case all women, assist their husbands in one form or another, even if only through the purchase of soap which is, strictly speaking, the prerogative of the husband. In many cases, however, wives made short-term interest-free loans to their husbands, usually during the wet season, to be repaid at harvest. Significantly, almost half of the small livestock sold during 1973–74 belonged to women.

The critical period following a severe drought is the six- or eight-week hiatus prior to the new millet harvest. The consumption of wild foods increased markedly in June and July 1974,[73] and consanguinal support had clearly reached its limits. The majority of households already felt the pinch of empty granaries and high millet prices, and reciprocal kin support was slight. Grain gifts and exchanges contracted in what Laughlin (1978) calls an "accordion effect." By June 1974, almost 60 percent of all households reported empty granaries; in early August millet reached ₦160 per ton, almost 90 percent above the prevailing January price (figure 7.12). Small livestock appeared on the market with great regularity after May; goats in particular were liquidated for grain purchases. Each household sold an average five animal units during the year; almost half were sold between May and August.[74]

As the crisis deepened in the wet season of 1974, grain and cash loans became a regular mechanism for survival, usually taken as short-term credit from village merchants and grain dealers. Farmers prefer loans in grain for the very good reason that cereal prices may double over the loan period. Cereal loans (*falle*) tend to be highly usurious; one bundle of sorghum or millet borrowed during May or June (when most loans were contracted during 1974) was repaid by two and occasionally three bundles at harvest. Loans repaid in cash or borrowed in money form, which are referred to generically as *bashi da ruwa* in Kaita, carried less irksome interest, usually about 50 percent over a three- to four-month period. During periods of hardship when the demand for credit is great, creditors are less sanguine about any form of loan outside of a circle of friends and associates, and interest rates reflect this general lack of confidence.[75] In these conditions the rural poor have no credit worthiness to call upon.

In Kaita, interest on grain loans was reported as 50 percent higher than normal during 1973–74. At the same time the proclivity to intensify obviously usurious rates of interest were mediated by a variety of social relationships. The fifteen clients attached to the households of the four Kaita *masu sarauta* families, for instance, were supported on free grain distributed by their respective patrons. In another case a householder who was a tractor driver received a low-interest grain loan in return for ploughing services pledged to the creditor for the following year. Onerous interest rates can be further offset by debt repayment in labor or by offering farm property as collateral. Since pledging of holdings is invari-

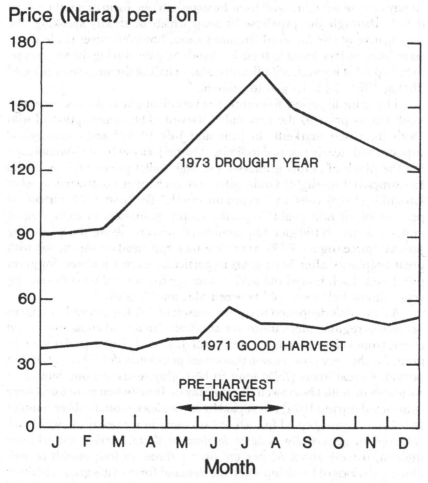

Figure 7.12. Interseason millet prices. From Kaita District office.

ably a precursor to outright sale, and in view of the scarcity of land in Kaita itself, only the desperately poor resort to (or even contemplate) pledging. Outright sale therefore represents a somewhat hopeless cul de sac. There were only six cases of farm sale in Kaita during 1973–74, 50 percent of which were associated with subsequent migration from Kaita village.

All this suggests that households do not respond arbitrarily to food crises for which they are in some sense conceptually prepared; rather they do so serially, with respect to the intensity of what one might call famine "signals." Their behavior, in an aggregate sense, is graduated with respect to time and the proportion of domestic resources they commit (figure 7.13). Low-order responses, such as planting changes, borrowing food from kin, or wage laboring are relatively flexible and pliant. To the extent that these coping mechanisms are incapable of securing reproduction, slower and deeper responses follow, such as the sale of livestock, grain loans, liquidation of assets, or pledging. The terminal strategies in this sequence may be, as in the case of farm sale, largely irreversible. Food crises, then, have episodic careers that apparently possess a logical structure and, within limits, are quite predictable. Households restructure their farm activities to maximize the availability of products, minimize current commitments by suspending unnecessary allocation of resources (for instance ceremonial expenditures) and begin the painful process of the disposal of goods, livestock, borrowing, mortgaging, and perhaps ultimately out-migration. The government often intervenes toward the end of this sequence of events.[76]

The restructuring of household budgets during food crises is, however, more complex than aggregate patterns might indicate. Put rather differently, it would be counterintuitive in a society distinguished by marked landholding and income inequalities to assume a parity among responding households. Farmers in Kaita know how to ridge and space; equally, they understand the theoretical avenues open to them in the event of a poor harvest. But the majority of Group III households were obviously constrained by capital shortage and access to land. For the likes of Mallam Audu, who holds roughly two acres of upland and little else, the substitution of long-maturing cereals or the orchestration of lowland farms is irrelevant. Millet and sorghum varieties may be in the granaries of the rich but rarely anywhere else. Some well-off farmers can afford to purchase the requisite seed, clients may call upon the benevolence of their patrons, and still others may borrow a tiya of seed until harvest time. But the chronically poor suffer desperately from a lack of purchasing power and their low credit worthiness. During the 1977 wet season, when two replantings were necessary, no Group III farmers substituted short-maturing millets and sorghums for the usual long-maturing varieties.

The most vulnerable households quite naturally wish to bring the harvest date of upland cereals as far forward as possible. The demand for an early harvest fulfills the need not only for tax payment (N6 during 1978), which is collected at the termination of the rains, but also for the minimization of grain purchase at highly inflated price levels. The imperative of early millet tends to offset the more productive cultivation of sorghums, a dilemma compounded somewhat by the recent demise of groundnuts as a major cash earner. A late harvest can have equally disastrous consequences for households dependent upon borrowed or purchased grain during the preharvest hunger period. Large farmers, then, have the luxury of being able to choose a cropping pattern on the

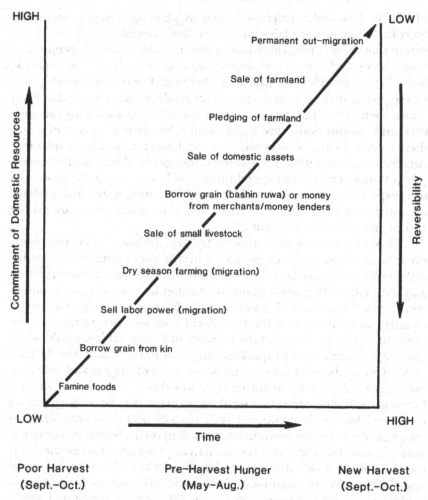

Figure 7.13. Temporal sequence and organization of responses to food shortage.

basis of the early rains. Members of Group I can confidently run the risk of monocropping sorghums, gambling on a massive yield should the rains prove favorable, yet still preserve flexibility through the option of short-maturing millets and access to the wet bottomlands should the early rains fail.

All households have fixed postharvest costs, notably tax, house repair, and ceremonial expenditures, which exact a heavy toll on families who are pressed to cover these costs through the sale of foodstuffs at relatively low prices. Some householders with sufficient capital make large-scale purchases at harvest time to avoid wet-season purchases, a strategy wholly unfeasible for the less opulent. But even during the crisis of 1974 at least 20 percent of all households were not compelled to purchase their means of subsistence and at least 5 percent actually sold grain. Cereals were never totally absent from the local market, but prices rose sharply and exposed all consumers to the vicissitudes of a volatile exchange economy. But in a market nexus, the bulk of adjustment to reduced food supplies is borne by low-income consumers. In light of the low initial level of food consumption, rising millet prices impose very great privation. In Kaita where food substitutability is low—other than an increasing dependence on low caloric wild leaves and fruits—high prices are transmitted to domestic budgets as an exclusion of highly nutritive oils and meat and a reduced caloric intake.

While there tends to be a minimization of current financial commitments in a drought year, secondary occupations assume a critical role in postharvest recovery. The fact that most adults engage in some form of productive activity during the dry season should not obscure the stratified basis of occupational access. I have already implied that the lucrative trades such as brokerage, petty commerce, local government employment and dry-season irrigation are denied to the poor through capital shortage, a low credit standing, minimal political influence, or because the occupations have an exclusionary structure. This is noticeably the case with the evanescent state resources that filter down to the village level and are creamed off by a phalanx of rural elites and their clients. In this respect, information is a valued and precious commodity denied to those who need it most. The lower incidence of gandaye among Group III households also constrains the material benefits that size can confer.

I have emphasized how dry-season irrigation constituted a major buffer mechanism in the event of a mediocre upland harvest, and how during 1978 after one such shortfall, the number of lambu farmers increased by 55 percent. Though fadama land is decidedly scarce, the expansion in lambu production can only occur because of the existing pattern of holdings. During some years, only a proportion of the lambu farms are cultivated, perhaps because the prior upland harvest was good or because potential lambu farmers have insufficient capital or labor. After a drought, however, the demand for fadama rises and large plots are subdivided and rented. A large proportion of the drought year market gardeners are, therefore, tenants who compete and negotiate for plot rental. The landlord-tenant system is, of course, colored by all sorts of personal, kin, or patronage relationships. But this should not disguise the fundamental constraints under which poor families labor. First, they generally don't have the political, familial, or economic capital to lubricate the rental process. Second, from the perspective of the landlord, a poor householder is an unattractive tenurial proposition in relation to a middle peasant with a larger gandu labor supply and available capital. And third, participation in the market garden sector presupposes some start-up capital for seed, manure, labor, capital equipment (the shaduf), and perhaps tractor hire. Table 7.22 indicates the expansion of lambu market gardeners between 1976–77 and 1977–78, the latter following a drought year. Of the 121 farms cultivated during 1977–78, 44 were new additions, of which 37 were rented. For the reasons I have hinted at, however, many are precluded from participating in irrigated agriculture, for as Early Scott observed in neighboring Ajiwa "farmers who rent land are often not poor or even lacking la.d. Instead they are themselves well off farmers who wish to expand [production]" (1976, p. 124).

During 1978, only 7 percent of all lambu tenants were Group III households, while 70 and 23 percent were Group II and I, respectively. Yet even those who could gain access to fadama property faced high risks, if not dubious tenurial arrangements. At a superficial level, many of the land transactions are referred to as aro (loan), and Hill (1972) apparently believes that such agreements are personal, interest-free transactions. In Kaita the lambu tenure system is, however, recondite involving a great many land dealings (subsumed under the generic term aro), which are clearly quite formal, transitory, and above all, interest-bearing. There is a Hausa term meaning rental (*haya* or *goro*), but there are also social and ideological reasons for denying its existence. As Wood discovered in a Muslim region of Bangladesh, exploitative relationships are concealed and institutionally disguised at the level of village social relations.

TABLE 7.22
DRY SEASON IRRIGATION DURING DROUGHT YEARS

Size (sq. yards)	No. of farms	No. owned	No. rented	No. of farms cultivated 1976–77**	No. of farms cultivated 1977–78*
0–999	9	3	6	6	3
1,000–1,499	36	17	19	11	25
1,500–1,999	20	12	8	10	10
2,000–2,499	12	10	2	3	9
2,500–2,999	20	15	5	10	10
3,000–4,000	8	7	1	1	7
4,000–6,000	9	6	3	3	6
Over 6,000	7	5	2	0	7
Totals	121	75	46	44	77

*A drought year
**A fair harvest

Both consciously through verbal agreements and informal arrangements backed by sanctions; and more pervasively through the class-based management of the hegemonic, egalitarian Muslim kinship ideology which denounces interest rates and the like [Wood 1978, p. 42].

The point I wish to make is that for farmers who rent small gardens, a potentially profitable enterprise is modified by local systems of surplus appropriation and high-risk marketing. Rental payments generally assume two forms. Some landlords prefer payment in labor time because it avoids the troubled waters of interest-bearing capital, but also because a guarantee of wet-season labor has enormous practical value. The second system is credit-based, referred to as "*kantahuda*," in which the renter customarily agrees to pay the owner in kind. During 1978 a small quarter-acre lambu plot could command a rent of one or two mangalas of onions, or ten to twenty baskets (*kwondo*) of tomatoes or peppers. The approximate retail value of such payments vary between ₦25 and ₦50. The rent burden is complicated by the riskiness of the marketing sector that deals in irrigated produce. Suffice to say, that structural defects in the long-distance market garden commercial network, principally between Kaita and the southern urban centers, such as Ibadan and Lagos, frequently conferred heavy financial losses on some unfortunate gardeners during 1978.[77]

In view of the limited opportunities for off-farm or market-garden income, it is the poor who first begin to feel the squeeze of empty granaries and inflated cereal prices in the marketplace. The limits of personal charity, kin support, and asset liquidation are quickly exceeded and the vulnerable families have to resort to widespread borrowing. It is hardly original to point out that indebtedness is endemic in Hausa society; as Nicolas (cited in Hill 1972, p. 329) put it "la société [Hausa] peut apparaître comme un reseau extrèmement touffu de prêteurs et d'emprunteurs." The credit system is of course closely correlated with, and a necessary prerequisite for, the normal functioning of the agricultural system; for as the Kaita farmer says "bashi hanje ne, yana cikin kowa" ("debt is like intestines, everyone has them"). But the universality of debt, and the fact that there are few institutional or juridical means for creditors to press their debtors, does not alter the fact that credit standing is of great economic significance. Most moneylenders will not lend to the obviously destitute for the very good reason that repayment is unlikely, but they can be assured that debtors will make every attempt to repay in order to maintain some credit standing in a wholly unpredictable future. Those who can locate a creditor necessarily face stiff interest charges. Further, it is not always to the detriment of the moneylender that a postponement of capital repayment be renegotiated by a debtor because of high interest. Indeed Bhaduri (1977, p. 352) has shown that default is "the very essence of the economic phenomenon of usury." Long-term debts, in other words, can become semi-institutionalized and debtors quasi-clients. The creditor may have to write off full debt recovery (*biyo bashi*), but in lieu he has claims on the borrower, not least on his labor power. Either way, there is no such thing as a free lunch when it comes to borrowing money or grain.

This is not simply a recognition of the fact that the poor are "too poor to farm" (Hill 1972, p. 193), shackled by their own poverty. But rather that village political economy structures drought or famine responses in wholly different ways; indeed during 1973–74 Groups I and III responded in a polar, if complementary, fashion (table 7.23). Crudely put, while the poor resorted to the sale of livestock, pledged farms, incurred debts, sold their labor power, and borrowed grain at usurious rates, their wealthy counterparts bought stock at deflated prices in conditions of oversupply, sold or lent grain to needy families, purchased wage labor at depressed rates (the wage rate actually fell in Kaita during 1973–74), and purchased the scarcest resource of all on their own terms, namely land. The dynamic of rich-poor relations is perhaps captured most eloquently by the fact that the masu arziki could support horses during 1972–74 in Kaita while the talakawa could barely support themselves.[78]

This exposition of famine response in the context of rural inequality is explicitly stark and stereotyped. The broad strata of middle peasantry,

TABLE 7.23
RESPONSE TO FOOD SHORTAGE BY CLASS, 1973–74

	Economic class		
Response	I (n = 56)	II* (n = 75)	III (n = 93)
Purchase grain	3	37	91
Sell grain	26	3	
Sell labor		17	87
Buy labor	51	17	
Sell livestock	4	29	61
Buy livestock	21	2	
Sell assets		8	47
Borrow from traders or merchant		18	39
Lend money or grain	8	12	
Pledge farm			11
Sell farmland			6
Buy farmland	6		
Migrate			5

*This is a 30% sample of all Group II households.

in Kaita at least, seems able to withstand the onslaught of both a fickle climate and a rapacious commercial elite. Nevertheless it is at the extremes of the economic spectrum, as Marc Bloch noted, where the dynamics of the entire system are thrown into brightest illumination. In this respect it would be a mistake to see wet and dry years simply as cycles of accumulation and disposal; rather, during a subsistence crisis epicycles of accumulation and decapitalization can occur simultaneously within a single community, intensifying extant patterns of differentiation and immiseration. In Kaita village the success of households to accommodate drought depended largely on access to land, capital accumulation during nondrought years, and the facilities for capital restoration in the aftermath of a period of asset depletion. As I have attempted to demonstrate these three variables are all structurally constrained among the rural poor, and hence the disposal-accumulation model is decidedly lopsided. As Jodha put it,

> the only element of certainty in the process of adjustment is that owing to the specific conjunction of demand and supply factors the affected [poor farmer] is a loser both while selling assets during the drought year and buying the same during the post drought [period] [Jodha 1975, p. 1615].

Because this is the case, much of what I have termed responses to food deprivation is, among the poor at least, a series of highly individual scavenging tactics in a vain bid to stabilize subsistence. It represents what Scott (1976, p. 121) quite admirably refers to as "a ransacking of the social and economic environment from the sidelines." In this sense Amartya Sen is only partly right when he says that a famine is a breakdown of an economic system. It is, I argue, the further breakdown of an economic system already in the process of breaking up.

SEASONALITY AND SOCIAL REPRODUCTION IN HAUSALAND

> The answer is we're in a trap
> we don't have seasons on our map
> Our disciplines aren't trained to see
> the range of seasonality

> —Robert Chambers

> Cereals commerce does not indicate the existence of a surplus. . . . Everything points to its origin in the economic vulnerability of certain family heads and it operates to accentuate their weakness and dependence.

> —Claude Raynault

The vast majority of African peasantries live in tropical environments with a pronounced wet-dry seasonality.[79] Under conditions of rainfed agriculture, almost any agricultural production is seasonal to the extent that it involves a sequencing of labor and biological processes that are dependent, in large measure, upon the temporal pattern of precipitation. The precise conflation of these climatic and biological cycles with specific agronomic practice frequently involves the alternation of periods of intense agricultural labor—the timing of which is productively critical—with other periods in which peasants may have to wait out the processes of plant growth and maturation. The complexity of these seasonal cycles[80] is, of course, not simply reflected in the fact that variations in rainfall, temperature, or growing season can influence patterns of labor demand or product availability, but also that such periodicities are dependent upon the particular constellation of crops, techniques of production, form of the labor process, and social relations of production.

In Hausaland the seasonal cycle of household reproduction has its own unique timbre. Toward the end of the dry season the labor and energy requirements for fetching water, gathering food, and off-farm activities to earn cash to purchase food tend to increase. Food becomes scarcer and less varied as domestic granaries run down and millet prices climb steadily in the marketplace. Poorer families, strapped by their small holdings and limited familial labor, begin to suffer earlier than other households. They have less food in view of the lower productivity of their farms and their labor, a shortage of capital, and miserly nonfarm occupations. Some seasonally migrate, others undertake casual and poorly paid wage labor. The rains denote a crisis in the reproductive cycle. Heavy and urgent agricultural demands have to be met promptly and the precise timing of labor mobilization is imperative. Intense physical labor—for land preparation, planting and weeding—comes at the time when food is scarcest. Food prices tend to be inflated and rural communications difficult. Many of the lower income groups are in a negative energy balance, losing weight as their work output exceeds calorie intake; the quality of nutrient intake declines. The wet season is also the least healthy period of the year with maximal exposure to infections. Government health services are often restricted at the period when poor food quality and the stresses of physical work combine to lower immune response. Future food supplies and the securement of subsistence for a new cycle of reproduction depend upon the farmer's ability to work or hire in labor during the crisis period. Births tend to peak at this period, making it strenuous for women and small families. Afflicted by sickness, birth and pregnancies, food shortage, poor diet, and high grain prices, the six or eight weeks of the soudure represent quasi-crisis conditions. The pressures to borrow, mortgage crops, or sell labor are necessarily acute. The seasonal energy crisis shifts the terms of trade against wage labor. When the harvest comes, debts have to be repaid along with tax. Food is abundant, prices are low, and debts are repaid in a buyers market. As the dry season progresses, conditions improve, risk of infection declines, caloric intake rises, and diets become more varied. Those who lost weight may regain it. Marriages, ceremonies, and social activity increase and there is a peak in conception rates. Gradually the cycle of seasonality commences all over again.

There is obviously no sense in which this cycle of climatic periodicity is attributed to a sort of causal primacy, for seasonality no more generates poverty than it does wealth (Chambers, Longhurst, Pacey 1981). But the low development of productive forces in Hausa agriculture subjects social reproduction to the obvious temporal patterns of rainfall and biological development. In short, the period prior to the first millet harvest constitutes, even under normal conditions, a major hiatus in the reproduction cycle. A poor harvest and the onset of famine simply expands and intensifies what is, in any case, a period of some anxiety and stress. This climatic juncture is readily appreciated through labor mobilization. According to Norman (1967), an average of 241 man hours are spent on the family upland farm during the peak wet-season month, more than 80 percent above the mean monthly input. The four busiest months from June to September account for 53 percent of the total annual labor. Even in Kaita where dry-season irrigation occupies one-quarter of farming household time between January and June, the significance of labor mobilization during wet-season bottlenecks, most especially planting and weeding, cannot be overemphasized. Timing and getting the requisite workers in the right place at the right time strikes to the very heart of tropical agronomy.

The gravity of the soudure crisis is further illuminated by the temporal sequencing of other epidemiological and socioeconomic variables (table 7.24). In Kaita, the incidence of malaria, diarrhea, guinea worm, and skin infections all peak in the mid and late wet season. The breeding cycle of malaria in northern Nigeria (Ross and Etkin 1982) is interrupted by the onset of the dry season in October; the main breeding sites begin to evaporate within 8 weeks of the onset of the harmattan. During the dry season the mosquitoes spend most of their time in deep cracks, rock crevices, and animal burrows; transmission is accordingly low, evidenced by a 0.5 percent parasitaemia rate in newborns during the dry season. But the early rains of April and May create the sunlit hydrological conditions suitable for rapid reproduction, and the preparation of the soil for the new millets creates many additional small breeding sites. The behavioral and physiological activities of the vector now return to normal, and the renewed growth of vegetation in the pools of water allow for the breeding

TABLE 7.24
SEASONALITY AND STRESS IN KAITA

	Dry Season			Wet Season			
				Crisis period			
Variables	Early	Mid	Late	Early	Mid	Late	Harvest
C-S Meningitis			H				
Malaria				H	H	H	
Diarrhea				H	H	H	
Guinea worm				H	H	H	
Skin infections				H	H	H	
Filariasis	H						
Agricultural labor demand			H	H	H	H	H
Food stocks	H	H		L	L	L	
Food prices	L	L		H	H	H	
Food consumption	H	H	H	L	L	L	H
Body weight and energy balance	H	H		L	L	L	
Debt repayment							H
Tax							H
Ceremonial expenditures	H	H					H
Deaths		L	L	H	H	H	H
Conceptions		H	H				
Births						H	H

Note: H = high; L = low.

of important secondary vectors. Malaria transmission is intensified; the wet season incidence in newborns may reach 25 percent.[81] Faced with excessively high agriculture labor demand, the opportunity costs of work loss that accompany this wet-season resurgence are clearly enormous.

Subsistence production and seasonal grain availability should be situated within the cycles of labor mobilization and disease patterns. A considerable body of nutritional work suggests that the onset of the rains coincides with diminished food availability in contrast to the immediate postharvest period (Schofield 1979). Protein calorie malnutrition among children rises significantly and adult body weight declines (Hunter 1967). In spite of limited nutritional data, however, work on seasonal undernutrition in Nigerian Hausaland is hardly equivocal. Simmons (1976) working in villages near Zaria computed an average daily per capita intake for the whole year of 2,264 calories, varying from a low of 1,949 calories in December and January, after the main upland harvest, to a high of 2,458 calories in April and May, the first two months of the planting season. Protein intake was similarly distributed, peaking in August and September with a trough in December and January. Average protein intake generally met recommended requirements. Simmons speculated that these departures from conventional wisdom reflected changes in body needs rather than available supply; the greater needs for farmwork during the planting and first weeding (between April and May) and the reduced calorie needs of the postharvest period. In Kaita, where dry-season irrigated agriculture demands heavy labor input, households are nonetheless highly sensitive to wet-season grain demands, and will make all possible efforts to carefully schedule millet consumption. Simmons, however, prefaced her Zaria findings with the serious caveat that the upland harvest during her research year was good, but even when total caloric intake rises, energy needs may still exceed consumption with the result that people still may be, in an energetic sense, hungry.

In any case, a rather different image is brought into focus when consumption and sale data are disaggregated (table 7.25). Simmons made a crude economic distinction between rich and poor predicated on cattle ownership. On the basis of this dichotomy, it is clear that during the critical preharvest months, grain consumption per capita per day was almost 30 percent higher among cattle owners. Further, the average grain purchase (in pounds per month) between April and September, when prices were 90 percent higher than the harvest level, was at least one-third greater among poor farming households.[82] By the January following the 1970 harvest, poor households had already disposed of 100% of their total annual grain sales at roughly 5 kobo per kilogram. The rich, conversely, sold 49 percent of their sorghum between April and August 1971, during which period it fetched, on average, 6.9 kobo per kilogram.

The social relations of trade specifically generate conditions in which considerable grain "surpluses" circulate in the food economy, fueled by a complicated interdigitation of debt, cash hunger, and the seasonal timing of cereal sale and purchase. Of course food prices are seasonally volatile in Hausa markets; in Hays's (1975) study of seventeen urban markets, wet-season peak prices were on average 30 to 32 percent higher than immediate postharvest levels. In Kaita village the 1977–78 season was unusually freakish in this regard; following a mediocre harvest, the price of a tiya of millet leaped from 60 kobo in September 1977 to a record price of ₦1.20 in July 1978. By May 1978, almost 80 percent of Group II and III households reported empty granaries.[83] I have suggested that a critical element in the local food economy is the timing of crop purchase and disposal in relation to class position. There is in fact a direct inverse relationship between cash outlay on millet and economic situation; Group

TABLE 7.25
GRAIN AVAILABILITY, ZARIA 1970−71

Variable	Rich cattle owners	Poor noncattle owners
Grain consumption in cal/cap/day (April−September)	2,597	1.949
Grain consumption in lbs/cap/month (April−September)	41	31
Average grain purchase in lbs per month (April−September)	59	82
Guinea corn sale as % of total sales		
Sept−January	50.3%	100%
April−August	49.7%	—

SOURCE: Simmons (1976); Hays (1975).

III households spend at least three times as much per consumer as their Group I counterparts.[84] Much of this buying activity in 1977−78 did not occur in the marketplace at all but represented private grain transactions between peasant and village-based food merchants, usually during June and July. Households projected onto the grain market procured millet in a variety of ways (table 7.26), but short-term cereal loans (falle) repaid in kind at high interest and the sale of small livestock were of signal importance. These same households had paradoxically sold some of their millet and cowpeas after the harvest of 1977, principally to cover tax, for debt repayment and necessary social expenditures, most critically house-repair and consumer items for ceremonial gift-exchange. The complementarity of postharvest distress sales (at low prices) and wet-season purchase (at inflated prices) defines the structural parameters of a cycle of impoverishment in which poor households must operate[85] (figure 7.14). Many of the better-off Group II households also contributed to the postharvest millet glut because of heavy social consumption associated with ceremonial, especially marriage, costs.[86] However they sold proportionately less and were generally able to borrow more[87] and to finance the hiring of wage labor in the rainy season, principally from their irrigated agriculture incomes.

The majority of the wealthy farmers consciously withheld grain in 1977−78 for the wet-season price rise; those with surpluses sold millet in June, July, and August in order to buy wage labor and invest in cattle,

TABLE 7.26
MILLET PROCUREMENT STRATEGIES IN KAITA, 1978

Strategy	No.	%
Livestock sale	14	28
Borrow grain	12	24
Wage labor	11	22
Trade or crafts	9	18
Kin support	3	6
Other (including lambu)	3	6
Totals	50	

Note: Data are responses from fifty household heads from Groups II and III who were asked in May, 1978, to state their principal means of acquiring millet until the new harvest.

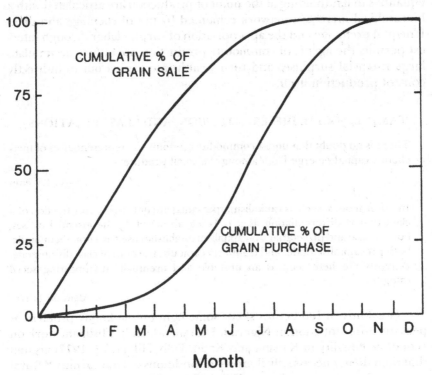

Figure 7.14. Grain sale and purchase among poor households.

which since the early 1970s have become sources of huge speculative profits.[88] Several among Group I are grain dealers who are active in wet-season lending operations. During 1978 a bundle of millet borrowed in May was repaid in kind at harvest time with a very minimum of 50 percent interest. Most *falle* loans characteristically demand two bundles for every one borrowed. In September and October, then, debt repayments in kind provide a means by which rurally-based wholesalers can canalize large stocks of undervalued millet, which are promptly evacuated to urban consumers in Katsina, Kano, and Daura. In Kaita, six large grain traders were agents for urban-based merchant's capital; the urban merchants were huge food wholesalers who fronted capital to their rural clients to facilitate postharvest buying operations.

An examination of the social relations of trade and the seasonal cycle of household reproduction reveals that many households are barely able to provide their own means of subsistence. They are obliged to sell grain at depressed prices, liquidate stock, incur high-interest debts, or pursue wage labor at the expense of their own farms to enable them to procure millet for domestic consumption. In this conjuncture, fundamental inequalities in landholding at the point of production are articulated with a hierarchical merchant network cemented by ties of clientage and debt. Unequal exchange and the appropriation of surplus labor through interest permits the agents of commodity production not only to accumulate large financial surpluses and turn wealth into capital but to indirectly control production itself.

FAMINE, SOCIAL DIFFERENTIATION, AND CLASS RELATIONS

There is no doubt that under commodity economy . . . representatives of merchant's capital emerge from among the small producers.

—V. I. Lenin

In other modes, such as capitalism, [peasants] are only a *transitory* fraction of a class that is differentiating as it is being absorbed by the essential classes, bourgeoisie and proletariat. As capitalism establishes itself as a dominant mode, both precapitalist modes and transitory capitalist fractions of class disintegrate. Peasants are here seen as an unstable and eventually disappearing social category.

—Alain de Janvry

The study of food crises sheds some light on the knotty problem of peasant differentiation in Nigerian Hausaland. In her brilliant work on economic equality in Katsina and Kano, Polly Hill (1972, 1977) argued that men do not necessarily flourish in conditions of land surplus.[89] Rural communities are, according to Hill (1977, p. 165), innately inegalitarian and the poor specifically "inhabit a looking-glass world of contrariety . . . [making] worst use of available resources, who 'import' more than they 'export' and who have few influential friends." In Batagarawa, the conditions of individual impasse were explicable principally in terms of "the general workings of the rural economic system." Poor households applied less manure, sold more grain at lower prices, had unremunerative off-farm occupations, and were too poor to borrow; "a conspiracy of circumstances operated against him" (Hill 1977, p. 165). Yet, even in these conditions, households were upwardly and downwardly mobile; in fact, in a sense rural Hausa was almost a vindication of untrammeled Henry Fordism because Hausaland appeared saturated with competitive capitalists who, in spite of the general workings of the economic system, could still succeed. The Schumpeterian logic is glimpsed in Hill's reference to the close association between economic status and innate energies and inabilities.[90] More specifically,

> in a society where a man has no choice but to strive to be a working farmer on his own account . . . and where organising ability, good judgement, financial aptitude, timing, man-management and so forth are just as important as in business life, it is obvious that innate characteristics, such as intelligence, will bear some relationship to farming efficiency. [Hill 1972, p. 174]

Quite so. Hill does acknowledge that some of the poor suffer from misfortune and a mediocre start in life but in their origins, the poor are a "representative cross-section" of the population. Many sons of rich farmers die in abject poverty and many sons of impoverished fathers flourish as wealthy trader-farmers. In short, "there is nothing to prevent an energetic, efficient and intelligent man . . . who has inherited no land and has no working sons, from becoming a notable farmer" (1972, p. 153).

Hill's work is in fact a rather complex admixture of the Chayanovian theory of peasant economy[91] and postulates derived from neoclassical economics. Chayanov's project was to develop a microeconomic theory of peasant farming in which inequities in farm income and landholding were not socially determined but arose from demographic differentiation. Crudely put, farm size expands and contracts in keeping with family age and sex composition. The demographic life cycle has its own trajectory, which results in transformations in farm size; production is accordingly determined by (i) total family size, (ii) age and sex composition of the family, (iii) the socially accepted minimum standard of living and (iv) the subjective evaluation of consumption work beyond (iii). The first two determine the consumer-worker ratio, the third translates minimum consumption into farm size (without use of hired labor), and the fourth establishes interhousehold variations in income about a mean household constitution. Family size is, then, an independent variable that determines access to the means of production and the magnitude of economic activity. The inequalities of income and farm holdings are reproduced statically between generations, accounting for observed patterns of household mobility. Hill's work showed empirically that there was a remarkably close association between the wealth classification and size of farming holdings, that "older men have a much greater chance of being rich than younger men" (1977, p. 113), and that "the average number of dependents of all categories is greater for [the] rich" (1977, p. 115). This model of "cyclical kulakism" is lent an intergenerational quality in northern Nigeria through patterns of Muslim inheritance by which the wealth of large families is dissipated upon the death of the household head.

Like Shanin's (1972) analysis of the Russian repartitional commune, Hill recognizes that a more complex Chayanovian model is required which incorporates chance,[92] and what are variously referred to as leveling-up-and-down mechanisms. This theoretical pluralism is mediated in Hill's work by her appreciation that the rural economy can be viewed structurally (i.e., material advantages can be systematically reproduced), but this is not actively pursued.[93] Instead, Hill concludes that some measure of exploitation of the rich by the poor is inevitable in any community where inequality is pronounced. Extreme poverty, even in Kano where the village is "incipiently if not actually stratified" (1977, p. 100), is apparently debilitating but not calamitous. Rather "village responsibilities for providing social security are much wider [than the cities] and inhibit capital growth" (1972, p. 198). There is no class and the moral economy survives.

Another phalanx of related research armed with farm management surveys and the weaponry of marginalist economics attempts to measure peasant efficiency. David Norman (1967, 1976) and his colleagues at the Rural Economy Research Unit conducted several village studies in Zaria, Sokoto, and Bauchi, which purport to show that farmers allocate resources "in a manner consistent with the goal of profit maximisation" (Norman et al. 1979, p. 67). More specifically, indigenous crop enterprises by economic strata show that resources are efficiently allocated; the marginal value products of land and labor estimated by Cobb-Douglas production functions are not significantly different from factor costs.[94] Norman derives from these statistics that "there is little potential for increasing incomes by recombining existing inputs and enterprises" (1970, p. 11). Recent work in this vein by Matlon (1977) and Crawford (1980) comes close to Hill's findings; Matlon specifically argues that income differentials in southwest Kano were due to differences in the physical productivities of land and labor, which approximately reflected interpersonal differences in aptitude and work motivation (p. 432).[95]

Matlon sees poor households as being strapped by cash constraints that derive from their lower productivities, limited access to intensive crops (peppers and onions), and poor management; farmers short of cash were unable to achieve a high degree of technical efficiency.[96] Choice of crop mix, the timing of crop sales, and the cost of credit did not, however, explain income differentials to any significant degree.[97]

Most of Norman's peasants were relatively poor but efficient; Matlon's were impoverished because they were managerially inefficient. But this is ultimately predicated on the view of Hausa farmers as heads of family firms who confront one another as individual (capitalist) cells in a larger organic (market) structure. This view of peasant production is mirrored by studies of local exchange and circulation. Some work in Hausaland has attempted to show how traditional local marketing systems approximate effective competition, specifically the lack of entry conditions, large numbers of traders, a risky selling environment, and so forth. This clearly argues for low seasonal price swings and no distress sales. However, much of the testing of market performance is ambiguous, and the statistical data are highly suspect (see Harriss 1978). Hays's work (1975), for instance, in northern Nigeria on the structure and performance of the grain trade in a rural-urban distribution system shows that larger farmers sell more grain and sell it later at higher prices than do small farmers, yet he concludes that intermediaries generally provide productive marketing services at "reasonable cost," given their technical environment. Actually, the purportedly competititve structure of his markets belies the fact that spatial arbitrage is acknowledged as inadequate and temporal price differences excessive. Berg (1977) nonetheless interprets Hays's work as a crushing condemnation of the "imprudent peasant-monopolized market" model; rather "these Nigerian studies suggest that a 'prudent peasant-competitive market' model is more applicable [and] there are structural reasons for believing this to be so" (1977, vol. 1, p. 11). Hays concludes that resource allocation in marketing is "approximately optimal" given the particular income distribution; however, he does not question the role performed by the rural-urban exchange systems in changing this income distribution.

In the course of accounting for the historical changes in the rural sector I have covered ground that suggests a somewhat different interpretation of economic inequality than those that emphasize personal attributes. In *Rural Hausa*, Hill points to the fact that the system is "sticky" and indeed much of the high-quality empirical work collected in Hausa villages over the last decade could support a radically different theoretical architecture. Matlon (1977, p. 427), for example, mentions that a small group of village elites appropriated 20 percent of government resources (mostly seed and fertilizer) for resale or personal consumption. King

(1976) and Clough (1981) report similar involvements by masu sarauta, large traders in the village cooperative societies and the cotton-buying networks. In spite of her claim that rural wage laboring was seldom undertaken at the expense of farming, Hill (1972, p. 118) estimates that one-third of the laborers in Batagarawa lacked farmland, and one-third needed wages to finance farming. What she called "self-perpetuating poverty" meant quite simply that "those who are penniless and whose granaries are empty early on in the farming season have no time to work on their own farms" (Hill 1969a, p. 32). In sum, merchant capital seemingly occupies a strategic position in the perpetuation of rural inequality: the well-to-do have better connections outside the village, debt and inheritance practices ensure that the poor cannot break out of the food-shortage–wage-laboring cycle, and migration appears as the termination of a gradual slide into desperate impoverishment.

These evidences do not constitute good reason to wholly abandon the rationale of the life cycle. The demographic trajectory of households is of great consequence in understanding both household labor allocation by sex and age and the timing of some critical household expenses associated with the marriage of girls and adult men. But the particular options available to each household unit are "determined by its access to the means of production and its form of interaction with the wider economy" (Deere and de Janvry 1981, p. 364). In this light, the Chayanovian model stands in sharp contrast to its historic protagonist, namely, Lenin's theory of social differentiation, according to which capital gradually transforms direct producers into wage laborers, their labor being captured by a class of progressive rural capitalists (Lenin 1964). Lenin develops indices of differentiation based on the *concentration* of the means of production in which the better-endowed households not only have access to more land but have greater numbers of livestock, more capital equipment, better access to nonfarm income, and are, in a general sense, agents of commodity production. This class relates to land as a commodity, their production is highly commoditized and they make extensive use of wage labor. Unfortunately, much of the intellectual sclerosis that afflicts peasant studies derives from the mechanical application of Lenin's insights; but the strength of his insight is that it beckons us to examine the variety of paths or roads associated with capitalist development in agriculture.

The development of commodity production in rural Hausaland has presented four areas in which social differentiation runs counter to the orthodoxy of innate attributes, managerial competency, and household life cycle. First, the genesis of wage labor is an expression of the gradual tendency toward socioeconomic polarization. The pattern of poor farmers engaging in wet-season laboring on the farms of the well-to-do is well documented in Hausaland, and it is difficult to imagine that the son or household head who labors twenty days during the growing season—and sometimes migrating to local villages to do so—is not delaying or foregoing his own farm operations. Norman's data show that 36.1 percent of total labor supplied to large farms was nonfamily in origin. A similar study in Gusau and Funtua shows that over a two-year period almost one-third of all farm labor was hired (World Bank 1981, p. 55). In Kano, farmers have actually become commuter workers in the industrial sector (Lubeck forthcoming) and it is clear that many of the very poor households are reproduced in large measure through the wage relation. If there is no developed landless class, even in the Kano close settled zone, it is quite ridiculous to argue, as Hill (1977) does for Dorayi, that the village is separate from the city wage economy; her own data reveal that fifty-one individuals migrated daily as laborers, and sixty or so as "spasmodic laborers," while 10 percent of farmland was owned by Kano residents. The massive growth of Kano city is stark testimony to the impoverishment of rural households who are pushed from the countryside by debt and personal destitution, and whose departure as *yawon dendi* (children of the world) is quite frequently shrouded in mystery and shame. The absence of a rural class of full-wage laborers—and hence in its place the gradual process of permanent out-migration—is a subject to which I shall briefly return, but it is connected with quite specific ecological and political economic conditions that have not encouraged to date land concentration as Lenin predicted.

Second, inherited wealth seriously modifies the Chayonovian predilection for the dissipation of household assets upon the death of the mai gida. In spite of the rather obvious fact that individuals may squander their inheritance from a well-to-do father, data from Kano and Kaita (table 7.27) show clearly that in many cases the sons of wealthy peasants start off in life with huge material advantages and prosper accordingly. Hill's example of Mallam Tukur is a case in point. Even if it is true that the farmholdings of farmer-traders are fragmented by inheritance among a large number of married sons, these same individuals also inherit access to lucrative trades or extravillage opportunities that have become the sine qua non of local accumulation. Conversely, for many of the land-poor households the rising value of land and increasing demographic pressures have enhanced sensitivity to inheritance issues. The result has been a marked increase in heir postponement and deferred land claims. In Kaita, for instance, this has had the effect of increasing the amount of land in circulation but simultaneously generating a diffuse landholding pattern in which many poor farmers who hold gado land are in fact joint owners; that is to say, they possess usufructuary rights. Many of these land

TABLE 7.27
FATHER'S WEALTH IN RELATION TO ECONOMIC STATUS OF MARRIED SONS

| | Son's Wealth | | | | | | |
| | Rich | | Neither | | Poor | | |
Father's Wealth	Dorayi	Kaita	Dorayi	Kaita	Dorayi	Kaita	Total
Rich	8	12	18	6	1	1	46
Neither	3	2	28	27	5	3	68
Poor	–	–	6	3	17	25	51
Totals	25		88		52		165

SOURCE: Hill (1977, p. 142), and Kaita village survey, 1977–78.

claims are held by individuals resident outside of Kaita itself. From a recent study by Ross (1982) in a heavily populated area near Kano, the pattern of land circulation appears extraordinarily diffuse.

In Hurumi 96 people from 54 households cultivated a total of 378 plots. Only 16 individuals farmed solely the land which they owned. At the other extreme, 28 farmed only land they did not own. Fifty-two others farmed land they owned supplemented by land received from others. Of the 92 who owned land 31 gave land to others, 33 simultaneously gave and received plots, and 47 only received land. . . . Excluded from the participation in circulation were those hamlet residents who did not claim shares . . . also excluded were individuals residing outside of the hamlet. Sixty-nine of the absentees had deferred claiming and disposing of their land which constituted 75% of the area otherwise held by local residents designated as principal owners. Another 44 absentees owned and maintained land rights and provided Hurumi residents with approximately 18% of the land they cultivated. [Ross 1982, p. 17]

While this land situation may indeed mitigate against land accumulation and dispossession, it is clear nonetheless that the tenurial position of many farm households is tenuous. In this regard, the apparent ability of small-holders to reproduce themselves on their own holdings is quite spurious; it is only permitted by a rapid circulation of land that is fostered by a multitude of deferred claims and extensive borrowing.

Third, the patterns of unequal exchange that bind rural producers to local merchant capital and to regional economic systems more generally, acts to structurally reinforce a cycle of peasant reproduction that severely limits the ability of the rural poor to accumulate. Seasonal timing of crop sale and purchase conflated with the pressures of postharvest cash needs, wage laboring, and indebtedness project the rural poor into exchange relations that perpetuate and deepen their own poverty. Conversely, merchants prosper through unequal exchange. Clough (1977), in a southern Katsina study on intervillage grain wholesalers, estimated that net weekly profit on dry-season buying operations was 15 to 23 percent, on long-term storage between 70 and 148 percent and on falle repayments (returns on investment) as high as 223 percent.

Local village or hamlet trade, however, is inseparable from large-scale urban-based merchant capital, the role of rural officeholders, and increasingly the activities of the state governments. In Kaita, for example, which has become a grain exporter in view of the demise of groundnuts since 1975, urban merchants in Kano, Katsina, Daura, and Jibiya advance capital to village wholesalers who trade with these advances several months prior to the delivery of grain to their patrons. The local traders accordingly benefit in several ways.

> Firstly, large advances enable him to participate actively in harvest grain marketing. Secondly, they provide him with money to store his own grain. Thirdly, urban merchants pay him a commission per sack when they collect the stored grain. Fourthly, there is an element of 'acceptable cheating'. The rural wholesaler will pay carriers to fill the sacks of grain with 38 instead of the 40 normal measures. Finally, part of the profits which he earned on selling grain stored from harvest until the peak prices of July, will be distributed through his clients to farmers as *falle*. These are 100 per cent interest loans repayable in kind. Much in the manner earlier described for cotton, these loans will be repaid with grain at the harvest in November. Merchant capital, based in the towns, thus finances a 'cycle of accumulation' for the inter-village wholesaler. Urban advances enable him to store grain against inter-seasonal price rises; grain collected as repayment of loans is stored and further augments profits. Urban merchants benefit because they are able to use the rural trader's client network and his storage facilities. [Clough 1981, pp. 278–79]

Since local authorities and state governments also employ this same system for necessary grain purchases, village traders can benefit from the expanded oil boom expenditures and the inflated domestic food prices that have accompanied the rapid circulation of oil rents. At the lowest orders of the trade network, the client-traders working with capital fronted by larger assemblers can accumulate by buying cheap (at harvest) and selling dear (in the wet season) and through interest-bearing falle loans to smallholders. Trade, then, is a major avenue for accumulation by virtue of its association with state-derived oil rents and through surplus appropriation from direct producers. Much of the trading profits are reinvested in expanded trade, in transportation and (in Kaita at least) in cattle.

Finally, there is the peculiar rural dynamic of indebtedness in relation to the cycle of reproduction, most especially marriage and postharvest expenses. Unfortunately, there is no way of reconciling the few, contra-dictory reports of rural indebtedness (table 7.28). Vigo (1957) and Luning (1963) calculated high-interest rates in Katsina, but Hays (1975), King (1976), and Matlon (1977) working in Zaria, Bauchi, and Kano recorded few debtors and low-interest rates. Matlon (1977) estimated that cash loans to the poorest households were actually interest-free and loans received from commercial sources carried an average interest of 30 per-cent, which was apparently a reasonable reflection of the high costs of administering short-term loans to farmers without collateral. Because debt is such a sensitive issue—it is almost impossible to systematically collect data on it—these differing views are perhaps to be expected. But I am not convinced that the more winsome writings on the credit relation approximate real conditions;[98] in spite of the oft cited claim that there is no class of professional moneylenders in Hausaland, in a de facto sense there is.[99] In Kaita six individuals are recognized as regular creditors—one mai sarauta, four trader merchants, and one wealthy woman. Their activities have flourished with the growth of a rural salaried class, who are referred to locally as *yan bashi* (sons of debt). These nonfamilial sources of credit become important after poor harvests, when a depression in the local economy reduces the amount of money in circulation and the effi-cacy of mutual or kin support. Accordingly, the money market assumes a distinctively oligopolistic quality. The borrowing of foodstuffs (falle) during most years invariably carries usurious interest rates; 72 percent of all loans carried interest of over 70 percent during one wet season. Though interest on cash loans (bashi da ruwa) is markedly less, debtors much prefer grain in periods of dearth because the market for grain tends to be so unstable.

In Kaita falle loans are very much part of the village economic fabric. Working in another grain exporting region in southern Katsina, Clough's (1980) study of Marmara also established that in a community in which 20 percent of all households held two-thirds of the land, in excess of 60 percent of farming households had no grain by August, and 50 percent met this deficit through falle loans. Short-term, high-interest loans of this sort are calculated during July—stage 3 of my planting sequence—when a reasonable estimate of harvest quality (and hence grain price) can be made. Based on this calculation, Kaita creditors speculate on the likely harvest price of millet and sorghum and then give half of this amount to debtors in return for a full sack (either in money or kind) at harvest. In 1976 for instance, the peak July grain price was ₦16 per sack and cred-itors estimated a 25 percent drop in price by harvest time and hence gave ₦5−6 in return for a full sack. In view of the variability of falle rates between creditors and the differential rates of repayment among debtors, the rates of return on three-month loans was generally between 50 and 100 percent.

TABLE 7.28
SUMMARY OF CREDIT-LOAN DATA IN NORTHERN NIGERIA

Area	n	% in debt	Source % of loans from kin	% of loans from traders	Interest (% of all loans) Under 50%	Over 50%	Use (% of all loans) Food	Farming	Trade
Katsina[1]	600	48	20	50	1	99	27	25	n.d.
Katsina[2]	4881	69	21	73	34	66	24	15	36
Kaita[3]	35	68	33	67	30	70	51	36	20
Maradi[4]	6172	40	16	84	70	30	27	13	n.d.
Borno State[5]	232	35	60	40	90	10	5	76	n.d.
Kano State[6]	119	35	68	32	90	10	16	70	n.d.

SOURCES:

[1] H. Luning (1963)

[2] A. Vigo (1957)

[3] Author's survey (1978)

[4] G. Nicolas (1967), in Niger Republic

[5] R. King (1976)

[6] R. King (1976)

Note: n.d. = no data

Furthermore, credit markets are clearly linked to other factor markets in the context of a poor agrarian economy. In Kaita this is clearest in respect to labor; the ideological impurity of high-interest rates can be avoided through various forms of labor obligation. Some farmers who gained access to lambu farms as aro (loan) were oftened obliged to work on the landlord's farm during the following wet season. Recycling of debts frequently evolves into a type of client relationship in which the creditor has claims on the debtor's wet-season labor. Under conditions of wage labor shortage and variable wage rates, debt relations fulfill a critical function in labor mobilization among prosperous households.

The function of credit in the household economy is not simply captured by those families unable to secure their own means of subsistence on a regular basis. Indebtedness has to be understood in terms of necessary postharvest costs, which include not only the payment of taxes but house and fence repair and socially necessary gift and ritual exchanges. For an average farming family these expenditures might amount to ₦50 to ₦70. When added to debt repayment, these postharvest costs not only explain the intensity of market transactions in November, December, and January but also highlight the patterns of seasonal budgetary instability that makes borrowing a necessary part of the cycle of reproduction. Direct taxation, however, is currently of lesser significance in household expenditures than in the past. In grain equivalents, the six naria flat rate per head in 1978 constituted only one-third of a sack of millet; in 1955 the prevailing tax burden was equivalent to 1.75–3.0 sacks per adult, and in the early 1930s 1–8 sacks. Marriage costs conversely have come to be of signal importance. Marriage is not only ideologically central in Hausa society but constitutes perhaps the principal vehicle for securing social, and hence material, ties within the community. The extension of the household, then, is essential to economic success. At the same time— average marriage costs for a first wife[100] have risen markedly—from roughly ₦1 to ₦2 in 1900, to ₦60 in the late 1960s to almost ₦400 in 1977—fueled by the postcivil war inflation in social commodities like cloth and enamel bowls, which occupy a significant role in ceremonial exchanges (table 7.29). Between 1930 and 1978 the consumer price index rose by twenty-five times; over the same period, marriage costs leaped by a factor of seventy. In grain equivalents, the costs of first marriage in the late 1930s approximated twelve sacks of millet; by 1978 this had risen to a minimum of twenty sacks. The timing of these huge expenditures is naturally correlated with the specificities of the household life-cycle but it is entirely possible that in middle age a household head might face the marriage costs of his son(s) and daughter(s) in addition to taking an additional wife of his own.[101] A second wife and the marriage costs of two sons and a daughter might, over a ten-year period, run in the order of

TABLE 7.29
MARRIAGE EXPENSES IN KAITA VILLAGE, 1977–78

Exchange	Cost (Naira)
Groom's marriage costs*	
Alama: sign of affection	10.00
Gaisuwa and greetings gifts	5.00
Discussion with girl's parents (*Jin Magana*)	10.00
Na gane ina so: "I desire her"	50.00
Tashin Sallah: presents for religious festivals	20.00
Baiko: confirmation ceremony[1]	50.00
Lefe: clothes and cloth for the bride[2]	100.00
Dauren aure: marriage ceremony	60.00
Tarewa: gifts for the bride's arrival at the groom's house	30.00
Walima: marriage feast[3]	30.00
Total	390.00
Bride's parents marriage costs	
Parents have to match the *lefe* price of the groom's parents to provide property for the new wife.	100.00
Kayan gara: money given to the groom and his parents at the wedding feast plus properties carried by the wedding procession.[4]	150.00
Total	250.00

[1] Includes salt, sugar, pillows, rush mats, water jugs, cotton mattress, head ties, metal pots, sandals, jewelry, perfume.

[2] Includes also enamel bowls and dishes.

[3] Millet, chickens, goats.

[4] Decorative brass basin, enamel bowls and money.

*Met by the groom's parents for the first wife, assuming he is living and farming with his family.

₦1,500 to ₦2,000. These expenses clearly compound the debt cycle among rural poor for whom the consolidation and extension of the household is critical.

I have argued that the historic changes in Nigerian Hausaland over the past eighty years have seen the transformation of a peasantry into a class of simple commodity producers. The household remains the fundamental unit of production and reproduction; increases in productivity are generally achieved through an extension of labor time, but the wage relation has not become the source of individual reproduction. However, commodity production is the dominant element in the cycle of household reproduction, and is increasingly secured through market mechanisms and the circuits of capital (Boesen and Mohele 1979). I have suggested that differentiation among commodity producers is grounded in these mechanisms and circuits. More specifically, commodities are exchanged below their value in a systematic relation of unequal exchange. Because households are concerned with the costs of securing the reproduction of labor and the means of production, the exchange value of their products may plummet without forcing them out of production. For many, however, reproduction can be secured only through credit, which becomes the vehicle for further impoverishment.

As Harriet Friedmann has shown, however, all the conditions of commodity reproduction are also conditions of capitalist reproduction, which raises the question of the stability of the household economy (Kongstad and Monsted 1980). In other words, are Hausa producers only a transitory social stratum under capitalism? Clough (1981) for example believes that the relation between the household and the capitalist economy is structurally stable. There are, I think, three tendencies that go some way toward explaining the short-term persistence of small-scale household commodity production within Nigerian capitalism. First, the hegemonic role of merchant capital established unequal exchange as a logical precondition for the survival of the household:

> The petty commodity mode of production would be open for replacement by capitalist [agriculture] . . . if the exchange value of the product was high enough to cover both the reproduction and capital and normal [profit]. [But] here is the basis of the real competitiveness of peasant agriculture. [Boesen and Mohele 1979, p. 164]

Merchant capital opportunities have expanded enormously following the oil boom of the early 1970s; the increased circulation of commodities has opened new trade avenues that provide a relatively high rate of return in relation to upland agriculture. And of course merchant capital thrives in its parasitic role, though incapable of revolutionizing the system of production itself. Since the Nigerian state has made no sustained effort to transform the relations of production in the countryside until very recently, the hegemonic position of merchant capital has gone unchallenged.

Second, technical and biological conditions mitigate against the emergence of a local agrarian capitalist class or the intervention of productive (international) capital based on dryland and upland agriculture. No convincing technological package has yet emerged that makes it profitable for producers to divert capital into dryland farming. Indeed the biological and seasonal constraints in the semiarid tropics present a series of labor supply problems—not least the smoothing out of periodicities in year-round production—that have provided considerable resistance to capitalist agriculture (Mann and Dickinson 1978; Vergopoulos 1974). Indeed, it is significant that the major interventions by state and international capital have emerged in the realm of large-scale irrigation projects precisely where some of the biological and technical constraints can be circumvented.

And third is the resistance of the household economy itself. Because of the attraction of the merchant realm and the logic of unequal exchange, rural producers have been able to maintain their smallholdings. Indeed as a swollen commercial sector becomes more competitive, the provision of low-interest credit may actually assist the reproduction of the rural poor. Nonetheless, the 1970s have witnessed a plethora of petty trade or laboring opportunities as the circuits of capital have expanded, and there has been enough economic slack to allow even the rural poor to cling tenaciously to their Lilliputian holdings. Delayed division of land because of the security afforded to individuals who postpone claims has also assisted the small farmer. The persistence of noncapitalist social relations—limited reciprocal support, extended kin assistance, patronage, and so forth—have also provided the wherewithal for the reproduction, or more accurately survival, of impoverished households. It is this conjuncture that makes a capricious climate so problematic, because large numbers are hypervulnerable to small fluctuations in income or harvest quality.

Historically, small-scale commodity production has been remarkably persistent even in the face of primitive accumulation properly defined. Indeed, de Janvry (1981) has observed that the farmer and merchant roads to capitalist development in agriculture are frequently slow and uneven. The question still remains, however, why in a society such as northern Nigeria in which merchant capital has a dominant position in the rural sector, mercantile interests have not directly penetrated, controlled, and transformed the point of production itself. I have hinted that for this to occur the rate of profit from agricultural production must be at least equal to that of trade and usury. But once again the conditions under which these profitability conditions have been met in the past have been synonymous with, and often demanded, the direct intervention of the state. It is to the expanded role of the state in agriculture since the oil boom, and its implications for small-scale agricultural commodity production, that I turn in the final chapter.

CONCLUSION

We only dimly realise how dependent we are in every way in all our decisions. There's some sort of link-up between it all, we feel, but we don't know what. That's why most people take the price of bread, the lack of work, the declaration of war as if they were phenomena of nature: earthquakes or floods. Phenomena like this seem at first only to affect certain sections of humanity, or to affect the individual only in certain sectors of his habits. It's only much later that normal everyday life turns out to have become abnormal in a way that affects us all.

—Bertolt Brecht

Famines are social crises that represent the failures of particular economic and political systems. In what must now seem like a wholly morbid fascination with why peasantries starve to death, I have charted the genesis and evolution of subsistence crises in northern Nigeria in relation to climate. There has been a close association between rainfall deficits and human starvation along the desert edge; I have tried to show however that there is no simple causal determinacy. The relations between climate and society are unfortunately not so readily contained. Rather, I have pursued Marx's dictum that a specific relation of man to nature arises from a specific form of material production. In viewing peasantry and food systems through this optic, it becomes readily apparent that a famine must be posed historically; it projects onto the screen of society the very inner workings of social systems. I believe that the successive famines in Hausaland following colonial conquest revealed the contradictory fashion in which international capital confronted peasants and progressively transformed their conditions of reproduction. These famines afford an insight into the violence, and the massive burden, that such a confrontation imposed.

In drawing together the theoretical threads of famine genesis and effect, there are three items that require comment. First, a historical analysis permits us to distinguish between various types of famine, which (though they share common existential conditions) do not share similar developmental attributes (Sen 1980). A typology of famines would, then, not only address obvious differences in the technological conditions of production, communications systems, and the structure of the agrarian economy but would also identify the strategic importance of the market, changing terms of trade, commoditization, and exchange entitlements. In this way, the etiology of famine is neither a neo-Malthusian inevitability nor the mechanical outcome of a decline in food availability, but may emerge from discrepancies between price and purchasing power. In Nigeria, the role of the market entitlement system and the progressive commoditization of foodstuffs are of significance in grasping the changing character of colonial and postcolonial hunger, in spite of the relative smallness of the rural and urban proletariat.

Second, the resiliency of food systems, and more specifically their ability to perform adequately in relation to environmental and economic perturbations, is embedded in the very fabric of political-economic relations. Famine at the local level can be understood as the collapse of subsistence security. Climatic risk for example is not given by nature, but as Porter (1965, p. 409) puts it, by a "negotiated settlement" since each society has institutional, social, and technical means for coping with risk. I have argued that food shortage is, in this sense, grounded in the prevailing social relations of production. In precapitalist society, subsistence security can be understood in terms of the moral economy of the peasantry. The moral economy was distorted as new relations of production emerged and the cycle of reproduction was commoditized. The erosion of subsistence security was a complex and uneven phenomenon in northern Nigeria because of the contradictory role of merchant's capital, which simultaneously ossified and corroded elements of material and social reproduction. The essence of these corrosive forces with respect to food security is captured by Bernstein in his observation that

> [through colonialism] the relations of production of the domestic mode are destroyed, leaving its individual cells, the peasant households, to confront capital . . . the search for cash incomes to meet the needs of simple reproduction is precisely to individualise the basis of simple reproduction, to substitute the household for the community. [Bernstein 1976, cited in Kongstad and Monsted 1980, p. 23]

This individuation exposed producers to both economic and environmental threats. In a sense, then, the relation between nature and society was transformed, a transformation encapsulated in the succession of major food crises. It is into these emerging capitalist relations in the countryside that human adaptation to climatic stress is deposited.

And third, famine was seen to possess a logical structure. In the same way that Hausa farmers are prepared for local variation in rainfall so are they cognizant of the necessary coping mechanisms when confronted by a poor, drought induced harvest. Household members respond serially through characteristic modes of famine behavior. As Jodha (1975) discovered in western Rajastan, rural producers hope to neutralize the effects of bad years by accumulation during favorable periods. Peasants specifically responded to shortage by (i) restructuring their household activity to maximize food and income during the year, (ii) reducing current commitments by decreased consumption, (iii) disposing of inventories, (iv) selling or mortgaging assets, and (v) migrating to find wage labor. The case study of a Katsina community revealed, however (as did Jodha's research in India), that response strategies are refracted through the prism of peasant differentiation and indeed may actually contribute toward its further development. A proper understanding of famine requires, however, that we move beyond simple quantitative measures of inequality to the determinate structure of the social relations of production. For the rural poor, the precariousness of the material and technical conditions of production in conjunction with the pressures exerted by commodity production, debt, seasonal grain sale and purchase, and the sale of labor, lends itself to a simple reproduction squeeze. The household is obviously vulnerable to failure in any of its material elements of production. In his Kano study Crawford (1980) specifically analyzed the impact of stochastic variability, such as weather, on household resiliency and determined that eleven poorly endowed households (roughly 30 percent of the sample) accumulated capital more slowly, purchased more grain, and sought more emergency loans than their wealthier counterparts.[102] Crawford's simulation also established that small, poorly endowed families were "less able to alter their farm plan effectively in the face of changing weather" (p. 242);[103] annual incomes among these households fluctuated more from year to year than those of the rich, and there was evidence of a steady slide into debt. It is, of course, the constellation of these social relations, which bind households together and project them into the marketplace, that determines the precise form of the household vulnerability. It is also these same social relations that have failed to stimulate or have actually prevented the development of the productive forces that might have lessened this vulnerability. The critical point is that severe food shortage may have a type of ratchet effect in which disposition of assets, especially land, may be irreversible for the poorest strata.

My arguments concerning household fragility raise the question of whether one can legitimately talk of a relative or absolute increase in vulnerability through time. In comparing 1913 and 1974 it may well be that human mortality among pastoralists and farmers alike was massive in 1913–14; the loss of animals, in spite of the purported growth of livestock after the 1920s, may have been greater. This has led several authors to conclude that there has been a "lessening in the impact of climate fluctuation upon populations" (Bowden et al. 1981, p. 508). I have suggested, however, that such a proposition is highly specious. Indeed, the question of relative dislocation or vulnerability is politically irrelevant. Perhaps a quarter of a million people died in the Sahelian famine of the 1970s; many thousands in Nigeria were quite literally forced to abandon their homes; many more thousands liquidated their Lilliputian assets with minimal government relief. In this context the question is more appropriately, Why, after half a century of colonial "development" and a decade of independence in a much richer world economy, did such a disaster occur in 1973? Furthermore, Why, after a huge commitment of foreign aid to reconstruct the desert edge, is the threat of another massive famine almost omnipresent? Why has a huge increase in Nigerian revenue since the oil boom done nothing to alleviate the food crisis in a rural sector that is crippled by limited inputs, and millions of desperately poor peasants?

To pose these questions is to move beyond simple chronological comparisons and to look for very different, and often political, answers.

I hope that I have also given some cause to think carefully about much that passes as geographic natural hazards research, or cultural ecology. The evidence adduced from contemporary villages indicates that, in spite of a conceptual and practical preparation for drought, the political economy of farm production constituted the necessary starting point. This was so, not in some simple quantitative sense—there are rich and poor peasants who exhibit different adaptive capabilities—but rather because the social relations of trade and production define what is and what is not possible. Social relations are, as Adam Przeworski notes, given to a historical subject as realms of possibilities and structures of choice. Households do not suffer intrinsically from usurpation, hypercoherence, linear thinking, or bad values, as much geographic and anthropological work implies; rather these pathologies emerge from the existing social relations of production. A political economy approach identifies the constraints under which many poor households labor. In relation to their obvious absence of choice, partial control over the productive process, and limited flexibility and autonomy, these farming units are maladapted; that is to say, they are households constrained in their ability to respond to threats, disturbances, and perturbations. The content of this maladaptation, perfectly captured by the plight of the rural poor in Kaita, is revealed in two discrete senses. First, had these households been informed in 1971 that two successive harvest failures were about to occur, it is unlikely that they could have critically altered the actual event of 1972–74. And second, drought occurrence now almost automatically brings hardship for the rural poor. Currently, political economy does indeed determine a direct and necessary linkage between minor climatic change and individual hardship.

Like all theory natural hazards theory is not ready-made, but like any intellectual artifact it has its material and ideological conditions of existence. Conventional hazards theory is also ideological in that it sustains historically specific views of nature, of society and of change. Timpanaro's comment that economic inequities for which the structure of society is responsible are often attributed to nature is, I believe, an especially apposite commentary on much hazard work. In this sense, the Hausa view of drought and famine as essentially moral and political, and therefore grounded in human practice, is perhaps much more to the point.

8

FOOD, AGRICULTURE, AND THE OIL BOOM, 1970–1980

Our literature frequently contains too stereotyped an understand-ing of the theoretical proposition that capitalism requires the free, landless worker. This proposition is quite correct as indicating the main trend, but capitalism penetrates into agriculture particu-larly slowly and in extremely varied forms.

—*V. I. Lenin*

          For the uninitiated, a visit to Lagos, Kano, or Kaduna can be deeply traumatic. Most visitors are baffled by what seems like massive chaos and poverty in the midst of apparent material plenty. Nigeria is one of the world's ten most populous nations: it is of great strategic significance, rich in petroleum, and, for some at least, a potential industrial giant in a continent generally wracked by abject poverty and limited economic potential. And yet in spite of the huge surge of petro-leum revenues in the 1970s, Nigeria operates in constant failure mode. As a highly critical *Economist* report (January 23, 1982) lamented, "How can so much money and such high hopes engender such chaos?" The massive importation of consumer goods over the last decade and the rapid growth of the public sector tends to obscure both the impoverishment of the popular classes in the oil boom era and the extent to which the material benefits of petroleum have been inequitably distributed. A closer examination of contemporary Nigeria quite starkly reveals the social strains imposed by an economy firmly ensconced on a laissez-faire roller coaster. In 1979 two million man-days were lost due to industrial disputes. At least two hundred peasants were reported killed in 1980 during a violent confrontation on a large, state-funded irrigation scheme near Sokoto. A basic needs report by the International Labor Office talks of a significant deterioration of living conditions among the rural and urban poor since the oil bonanza. And this was concurrent with the release of the Annual Report of the Central Bank of Nigeria, which at the time of publication had "no actual data on federal government and expenditure"!

What is to be made of all this? It is all too facile to leave an explanation of these conditions at the level of "corruption," of predatory statism, or as the *Economist* put it, of "Nigeria's chucking it away." I situate the last decade of Nigerian development in terms of the leading role of state expenditure in capitalist development and class formation. More specifically, I examine (i) the impact and distributional effects of this oil-funded capitalist transformation on the agricultural sector and the rural popular classes, (ii) the state response to the agrarian crisis of the mid-1970s, and (iii) the prospects for agrarian transformation and capital accumulation in the next decade.

ECONOMY, SOCIETY, AND THE OIL BOOM

The material basis of the Nigerian colonial economy was provided by export commodity production from an indigenous peasantry, principally cocoa in the West, palm produce in the East and groundnuts and cotton in the North. A foreign-owned extractive industry, most notably tin, was of lesser significance. A small number of European and Levantine merchant firms dominated the import-export trade; this merchant capital presided over a huge substratum of Nigerian traders and transporters who operated in the countryside in a profitable symbiosis with local bureaucrats and political officeholders. The entire commercial edifice was cemented through ties of clientage and credit. Manufacturing, conversely, was markedly underdeveloped, although small-scale petty commodity production flourished in the expanding urban informal economy.

I explained how, for complex historical reasons, colonial capital did not radically transform preexisting social relations of production, but rather provided political and commercial pressures (for example, taxation or forced production) to redirect and intensify export commodity production. The early "nationalization" of land by the colonial state prevented (or rather limited) massive land accumulation and large-scale agrarian production by either Nigerian or European farmers. Since the household remained the dominant form of production, both the commercialization of land and labor progressed unevenly and slowly. The colonial state was accordingly limited in scope and forged an alliance with precapitalist ruling classes who were transformed into native authority bureaucrats. At least until the outbreak of the Second World War, colonial investment outside of fundamental infrastructure was sharply constrained.

No significant change took place in the economic base of the colonial state during the period of decolonization (1945–60) since it remained founded on peasant export production. Nonetheless, a shift occurred in the manner in which the peasant surpluses were disposed of and allocated. In the context of the British war economy and postwar metropolitan reconstruction, the colonial state intervened directly in the produce trade through government export monopolies, accumulating surpluses through depressed produce prices. The postwar boom in primary commodities provided an exceptionally favorable world market situation for this transformation, and hence for state accumulation. Under the influence of the new political arrangement, state activity increased dramatically. Peasant export earnings were redirected to finance an expansion of public services, including the central administrative functions of the state itself. The number of wage earners in the economy rose quickly as the major towns and urban centers expanded. While many public services were diffused regionally, the principal effect was a general centralization of commodity earnings at the regional state level. It provided a sufficiently distinct home market for a modest level of import-substituting manufacturing for which the state offered subsidies and incentives to foreign capital. Participation by private Nigerian capital was not seriously considered and local "entrepreneurship" was rather encouraged by various small-scale schemes.

Independence and the consolidation of Nigerian control over the state did not, however, fundamentally alter this postwar colonial pattern. Naturally, a class of Nigerian bureaucrats and politicians were now capable of utilizing the state apparatus for personal accumulation but the nascent bourgeoisie was divided along regional and ethnic lines. The weak federal structure was precisely a reflection of this crude regionalization of the Nigerian economy, but its shaky political and fiscal foundations were rocked by the crises of the 1960s. On one hand, the decline in global commodity prices in the immediate postcolonial period undermined the fiscal stability of the state, compelling the state marketing monopolies to raise the effective rate of surplus appropriation from peasant producers by lowering already depressed produce prices. And on the other hand, rising costs of production, the threat of massive rural dissent and regional political divisions placed the petroleum sector, which had only effectively begun operations in the late 1950s, at the center of the political stage. Indeed, the collapse of the First Republic can be seen in part as a by-product of this decomposition of the regional economic base, the fiscal crisis of the early 1960s, and by the emergence of petroleum as a powerful centralizing force.

The civil war marked a watershed in the course of Nigerian development. From its prewar mercantile basis and a wholesale dependence on several agrarian export commodities, Nigeria emerged in the 1980s as a robust and outspoken member of a semi-industrial, capitalist periphery. In the North this transition is perhaps best captured in the remarkable transfiguration of Kano. In 1963, with a population of just over a quarter of a million, Kano was a classically mercantile city specializing in the export of groundnuts. By 1980, its population was estimated to be well in excess of 1 million, with an industrial labor force of some 50,000. Kano has experienced a rapid proliferation of multinational investments in manufacturing, the internationalization of consumption styles among the urban rich, the commoditization of urban social relations, a sharp upturn in the numbers of a disenfranchised and militant "floating population," new waves of rural migrants from the close settled zone, and not least a corresponding increase in urban violence.

The petroleum economy has been a critical element in this transformation. The huge growth in oil revenues since 1973—which amounted to ₦10 billion, almost 15 percent of the Nigerian gross national product (GNP)—not only permitted the reconstruction of a war-devastated economy but also provided the means to support increased state centralization at the federal level. The proliferation of states further deepened local and regional economic dependence on a kitty of centrally administered oil revenues, which naturally fluctuated in accordance with prevailing petroleum prices and the demand for Nigerian oil in a world economy. In this sense, the end of the civil war not only marked a sort of federal consolidation but also a much closer integration of the states into a capitalist world economy.

From the early 1950s until the breakdown of civil authority in 1966, Nigeria pursued an import-substitution path, foreign owned for the most part and catering to the consumer habits created by Western capital. Nonetheless the industrial proletariat constituted a small proportion of the actively employed, and manufacturing represented only 4.8 percent of Nigerian national output in 1960. Agriculture, conversely, accounted for 58 percent of GNP in 1964 and employed 70 percent of the active workforce. Furthermore, between 1960 and 1967 the volume of export crops grew at an annual compound rate of growth of 4 to 6 percent. Staple food output expanded more or less in tandem with population growth. Food and live animal imports amounted to £12 million in 1954 (10 percent by value of total imports), and £21.2 million in 1967 (9.5 percent by value of total imports). The food production index grew from 82 in 1960 to 89 in 1967, and the food importation index over the same period actually fell from 105 to 99. Three-fourths of the food imports in 1966 and 1967 were processed forms of nutritionally "superior" food items: fish, wheat and flour, milk and sugar. Indeed, based on the experience of the previous decade, FAO projections in the mid-1960s estimated food surpluses for the seventies simply by letting the food sector take care of itself.

All this proved, however, to be quite transitory and chimerical. Following the termination of the war in 1969, growth of the Nigerian econ-

omy has been rapid. Between 1970 and 1976 GNP grew at a real annual
rate of 7.4 percent, and GNP per capita at 5.4 percent per annum.
Moreover, growth has been accompanied by a significant sectoral transformation (table 8.1). By 1975 agriculture accounted for only 28 percent
of national output, while the proportion of the labor force remained high
at 64 percent (Matlon 1981, p. 324). Conversely, the contribution of
petroleum to federal revenue and to GDP between 1964 and 1974 increased from 4 to 80 percent and from 3 to 46 percent, respectively
(Oyediran 1979, p. 69). These changes in sectoral constitution reflected
not simply a growth in nonfarm activities (notably mining and manufacturing) but a stagnant agrarian economy (table 8.2). Between 1970 and
1976 total farm output in Nigeria fell by −0.2 percent. This may be
accounted for in part by the severe harvest shortfall in 1972 and 1973, but
as I explain in the following section it is also a reflection of labor demand
in other sectors, pricing policy, and changing forms of production in the

TABLE 8.1
COMPARISON OF NATIONAL OUTPUT
(in percentages)

Sector	1960	1963	1970	1975	1979
Agriculture	64.1	55.4	43.8	28.1	22.4
Oil & mining	1.2	4.8	12.2	14.2	25.0
Manufacturing	4.8	7.0	7.6	10.2	5.1
Building & construction	4.0	5.2	6.4	11.3	9.7
Others	25.9	27.6	30.0	36.2	37.8
Totals	100.0%	100.0%	100.0%	100.0%	100.0%

SOURCE: Federal Office of Statistics, National Accounts of Nigeria 1960/61−1975/76,
Lagos, World Bank Annual Report, 1980.

TABLE 8.2
SECTORAL GROWTH RATES IN THE NIGERIAN ECONOMY IN CONSTANT PRICES
(in percentages)

Period	Agriculture	Oil & mining	Manufacturing	Building & construction
1960−65	2	38	15	10
1966−69	−1	8	6	1
1970−75	−1	12	14.5	21

SOURCE: Federal Office of Statistics, National Accounts of Nigeria 1960/61−1975/76,
Lagos.

countryside. In 1974 the food production index stood at the same level as 1960; over the same period the food import index tripled.

Growth patterns in the 1970s also generated substantial income disparities between sectors. According to Matlon (1981, p. 324), between 1970 and 1975 per capita GNP measured in constant 1974–75 prices in agriculture remained virtually constant at ₦61 per capita, compared to the increase in the national average from ₦137 to ₦189. Per capita farm incomes fell, therefore, from roughly 45 to 32 percent of the national average. Relative to per capita GNP in all nonfarm sectors, average agricultural output per capita fell 34 percent during the first half of the 1970s. With the possibility of continued expansion in nonfarm employment, a high income elasticity, and a population growth of perhaps 3 percent per annum, food deficits have been projected to a staggering 8 million tons by 1985 (IFPRI 1976).

It is ironic, then, that the Consortium for the Study of Nigerian Rural Development (see Eicher and Liedholm 1970) should have suggested export crop expansion and a Green Revolution package "to provide lead time to feed the projected 90–100 million people in Nigeria by 1985" (p. 385) as the development strategies for the 1970s. By the end of the Second Development Decade neither projection had been met. The agricultural export commodity sector had quite literally disintegrated (table 8.3); equally, the index of total food production, which stood at 100 in 1969, had increased to only 107 in 1975 and was barely at 113 by the end of 1978. In 1974 less than 1.5 percent of federal capital expenditures in agriculture (roughly ₦300,000) was spent on research into improved food crop production (Ogbonna 1979). In fact, only in April 1980 was a National Council on Green Revolution established by President Shagari (*West Africa*, Feb. 11th). This is not to suggest that state policy had not changed between 1967 and 1975. Taxation through regional marketing boards was substantially reduced, and ultimately the regional boards were dismantled and replaced by national commodity boards. But in spite of (and perhaps in part because of) these efforts, by the mid-1970s the Nigerian food economy was in complete disarray.

OIL, STATE, AND THE REGIME OF CAPITAL ACCUMULATION

At the time of Independence in October 1960, Nigeria had become self-sufficient in crude oil, producing rather less than 20,000 barrels per day (Pearson 1970). Petroleum self-sufficiency had not been easily won. Exploration began in the late 1930s but, following its suspension during the Second World War, drilling operations were not undertaken until 1951. The first significant discovery was made at Oloibiri in the Niger Delta in 1956 and oil production on a commercial scale commenced in

TABLE 8.3
AGRICULTURAL EXPORTS
('000 tons)

Commodity	1961	1972	1973	1974	1975	1976	1977	1978	1979	1980
Groundnuts, (decorticated)	494	106	199	30			8			
Cocoa, raw	777	228	211	180	202	231	165	205	125	157
Palm kernels	411	212	137	185	173	257	169	63	72	50
Palm oil	165	2								
Cotton, raw	35	1	5				9	8	2.8	2.6
Rubber	55	41	49	59	57	39	18	29	34	31

SOURCE: Quarterly Economic Review of Nigeria, 1981, Helleiner (1966).

1958. At Independence there were four fields in the eastern region and two in the western; by 1980 in the Niger Delta alone there were 150 producing fields connected by a lattice of pipelines to five export terminals (Ogbonna 1979). By virtue of its light gravity and low sulphur content, Nigerian crude was an attractive proposition for the oil companies, and accordingly acquired a handsome premium. In 1961 production was 46,000 barrels per day (b/d); with the construction of the trans-Niger pipeline in 1965 and the exploitation of offshore fields, production leaped to 275,000 b/d and to 420,000 b/d prior to the civil war. Despite the total logistical and administrative breakdown entailed by the civil war, the million barrel daily mark was passed in 1970 and by 1973 had doubled to 2.06 million b/d.

When Nigeria joined OPEC in 1971, a Nigerian National Oil Corporation—subsequently renamed the Nigerian National Petroleum Corporation (NNPC) in 1977—was created as a vehicle for partnerships with foreign oil companies. The government's share in the companies was 35 percent after 1973, raised to 55 percent in 1977, and to 60 percent in July 1979. By late 1979, NNPC had title to 1.7 million b/d from its joint ventures, making it one of the world's largest sellers. By 1972, in fact, oil constituted 83 percent of Nigerian exports, but after OPEC's 1973 initiative, which raised the price of crude oil, Nigeria's terms of trade improved threefold (World Bank 1980)—a windfall gain roughly equal to 15 percent of 1974 GNP (table 8.4). Oil's share in federal government revenue rose from 17 percent in 1971 to 71 percent in 1973, and to 86 percent in 1975. Total public spending rose from less than 20 percent of GNP in 1970–73 to 35 percent in 1974–77. By 1976–77, however, the federal budget was in deficit.[1]

Prior to the civil war, the political and fiscal strength of the federal center was relatively weak in relation to the regions. The state apparatus was certainly open to foreign capital and charged with the support of private Nigerian enterprise but, in practical terms, state patronage favored the merchant capitalists, the buying agents, the contractors—those actively engaged in primitive accumulation (Forrest 1981). The number of economic institutions (such as the Central Bank) were limited, and the federal plan was in reality a conflation of individual regional plans. Federal activity was most important in the realms of infrastructure and public utilities.[2] Following the civil war, however, the state was expanded, centralized, and increasingly involved in production. The emergence of oil revenues not only permitted a measure of autonomy from foreign aid but allowed a consolidation of state ownership, the restructuring of the Nigerian economy, and the genesis of a powerful, centralized bureaucracy. The growth of the federal budget (table 8.5) in conjunction with the creation of new states in 1967 and the transforma-

TABLE 8.4
PETROLEUM PRODUCTION AND REVENUE
(1975 = 100 b/d and 100 million nairas)

Year	Index of crude petroleum production (million b/d)	Index of crude petroleum exports (million nairas)	Index of volume of crude petroleum exports (million b/d)	Index of crude petroleum export price (nairas)
1973	115	1,933	116	33
1974	126	5,665	128	94
1975	100	4,593	100	100
1976	116	5,894	116	108
1977	117	7,046	120	122
1978	106	6,033	108	118
1979	129	10,034	130	174

SOURCE: International Financial Statistics, Vol. XXXIII #12 (1980, p. 288).

Key: b/d = barrels per day.

TABLE 8.5
FEDERAL GOVERNMENT FINANCES
(N million)

	1973/4	1974/5	1975/6	1976/7	1977/8	1978/9	1980
Revenue	1848	4325	4870	5628	6274	9805	12055
Current expenditure	755	1058	2220	2040	2697	2800	4687
Capital expenditure	767	1850	4131	5332	5939	7320	9102
Surplus (+) or Deficit (−)	+326	+1435	−1481	−1744	−2362	−405	−1734

SOURCE: World Bank Country Economic Memorandum, p. 42.

tion of revenue allocation, made the state governments increasingly dependent on transfers from a vastly enlarged federal pool. The level of statutory grants to the state governments grew from ₦323.8 million in 1974 to ₦2,534 million in 1979–80 (Rupley 1981, p. 266). Following the Revenue Allocation Act of February 1981 the revenue-sharing system was as follows: total federal revenue ₦15,773.5 million; statutory grants to state governments ₦4,968.7 million (31.5 percent of the total); statutory grant to local governments ₦1,577.4 million (10 percent); and retained as federal revenue ₦9,227.5 million (58.5 percent).

If one examines the impact of petroleum revenues on the recurrent revenue of Kano State, the fiscal contribution to state centralization becomes quite obvious. In 1971–72, total revenue amounted to ₦33.2 million of which ₦7.2 million (21.9 percent) was derived from local Kano State sources and ₦25.9 million (78.1 percent) from the federal government. By 1975/76 the corresponding statistics were as follows: total revenue ₦133.25 million of which ₦17.36 (13 percent) was derived from Kano State, and ₦115.5 million (87 percent) from the federal government. Since this trend is likely to continue, it is probable that at this time (1982) well over 90 percent of Kano's revenue is federally provided.

Revenue from virtually all federally collected sources since 1979 has been shared, stabilizing state and local government budgets. However, heavy federal reliance on petroleum—75 percent in 1979–80—is a potential destabilizing element "inasmuch as the States . . . will also find themselves adversely affected by downward fluctuations in the quality and price of oil exports" (Rupley 1981, p. 275). Following the 1973 price hike, state revenues comfortably exceeded expenditures; but since that time there have been budget deficits, inflation, external overspending and borrowing, cuts in government spending and a severe recession. In

1981, President Shagari faced the prospect of massive fiscal surgery in government expenditure, merely one year after the Okigbo Commission reported on revenue sharing, and coinciding with the ₦82 billion Fourth Development Plan (1980–85). Oil production actually slumped by 63 percent between January and August 1981, being little more than 60,000 b/d in early September compared to an average of 2.06 million b/d in 1980 (*African Business*, November 1981).

The tremendous boost in oil revenue nevertheless provided the material basis for the ₦30,000 million Third Development Plan (1975–80), a project that Schatz (1977) aptly described as "euphoric planning." Real per capita consumption was projected to grow at no less than 10.5 percent per annum "so that the average Nigerian would experience a marked improvement in his standard of living" (cited in Rimmer 1981, p. 57). But national accounts reveal total per capita consumption lagged significantly behind the rate of inflation between 1970 and 1977. Further, the Third Plan included not only an increase in real income but a more even distribution; a reduction of unemployment; a substantially expanded public role in banking, refining, and manufacture; and, through a series of indigenization decrees, support of a nascent Nigerian capitalist class. Although many of these projections did not materialize, Nigeria—like other OPEC states, particularly Indonesia and Venezuela—was able to invest its newfound revenues in a plethora of infrastructural projects in joint production ventures with foreign capital, and in urban-based construction, that sustained a burgeoning state bureaucracy and upper-income contractors (Lubeck and Burke 1981). As a necessary preface to my discussion of the impact of state revenues on agriculture, I briefly sketch the consequences of this massive transfer of petro-dollars to the Nigerian state treasury in terms of (i) state centralization and its expanded productive functions; (ii) urban-based investment, including construction and manufacture; (iii) the internationalization of consumption and import growth; and (iv) the worsening of income distribution.

As I have already described, the growth of oil revenue provided for increased centralization of state functions and the emergence of a federal state as a type of central development agency in its allocation of these burgeoning revenues. Much of the development spending was channeled into defense, infrastructure, education, and the oil industry.[3] By the late 1970s the standing army was estimated at 200,000 and in the 1978 budget the federal police budget alone stood at ₦193.2 million. Huge sums were devoted to middle class housing for an expanded bureaucracy; university expansion bordered on the extravagant, creating seven new campuses; and the Universal Primary Education (UPE) program absorbed ₦1,000 million by 1977 though, as Freund (1978, p. 94) put it, "without any clear sense of purpose." The massive program of public works construction geared to domestic and foreign contractors,[4] was particularly costly; the O'Kene–Kaduna and Benin–Shagamu roads cost roughly ₦100 million each.

The centralization process was given expression (in an allocative sense) through an expanded system of state patronage—that is to say, federally administered contracts—and in its commitment to direct productive involvement in the national economy. In the seventies, the range of public corporations and companies was significantly extended with the addition of the Nigerian National Oil Corporation (1971), the Nigerian Steel Development Authority (1971), and the Nigerian Mining Corporation (1972). An integrated iron and steel industry began in 1979 with the signing of a ₦1.2 billion contract for a blast-furnace steel works at Ajaokuta.[5] Federal capital expenditures on industry also grew rapidly between 1970 and 1978 (table 8.6), which has given the state a monopoly in some important areas (fertilizer, pulp, and paper). Many of the projects are

TABLE 8.6

FEDERAL CAPITAL EXPENDITURE ON INDUSTRY 1970–1977/78
(million naira)

Product	Amount
Oil	1329.1
Joint ventures	(514.6)
Refineries	(506.0)
Other	(308.5)
Industrial development banks	282.2
Cement	169.5
Iron & steel	161.4
Sugar	97.5
Pulp & paper	96.6
Mining	38.6
Car assembly	26.9
Fertilizer	17.8
Small-scale industries	10.9
Salt	8.3
Industrial development centers	3.7
Other	44.3
TOTAL	₦2286.8

SOURCE: Forrest (1980, p. 14).

joint ventures with foreign capital, the state providing security, infrastructure, and a protected market. This is clearly the case with the car assembly plants—Peugeot in Kaduna, Volkswagen in Lagos, and Leyland in Ibadan.[6] In this sense, the state does not constitute a dominant force in manufacturing as a whole, but its expanded functions in the realm of finance capital has permitted the federal government to direct resources to productive investment and to support large-scale projects owned publicly or privately by Nigerians (Forrest 1977). By 1979 the Nigerian Industrial Development Bank and the Nigerian Bank for Commerce and Industry had equity in the order of ₦140 millions and had sanctioned 439 projects.

In spite of the rapid growth of domestic manufacturing output in the 1970s (table 8.7), much of the new productive activity was undertaken by multinational firms.[7] In many instances existing Asian and Levantine capital was bought out, but after Imperial Chemical Industries and the Bank of America were established, Dunlop, Bata, Lonrho, Fiat, and Union Carbide all invested heavily (Lubeck 1978). Sales and profits for international capital increased sharply; UAC sales grew from ₦201,560 in 1972 to ₦788,500 in 1978. Profit over the same period increased by almost 700 percent (Fadahunsi 1980). Although the proportion of paid-up capital held by private non-Nigerian sources declined following the indigenization decrees—it stood at 58.2 percent in 1972 (Bierstecker 1981, p. 82)—the oil boom has not ushered in a dramatic increase in Nigerian industrial investment.[8] Paradoxically, indigenization (by encouraging Nigerian investment with foreign capital) may have actually discouraged local investment; in any case, as the 1975–80 Third Plan noted, "trading activities normally represent the quickest means of increasing income" (p. 152).[9]

Although the growth of federal revenue has not generated something like a fully developed state capitalism in Nigeria, it has in a more general sense supported private accumulation through the establishment of conditions for the reproduction of capital. This sort of physical and infrastructural development, managed by a centralizing state, generates a construction boom on an enormous scale. Much of the construction, especially of office, residential, and small-scale industrial buildings, is ideally suited to the local Nigerian bourgeoisie, who in the act of contracting to the state or to private consumers are directly incorporated into petroleum rent seeking. The principal beneficiaries of the construction boom have been the state bureaucrats and the firms, but urban construction has also become the hallmark of Nigeria's OPEC status. The bias of state expenditure toward the major cities, and the construction sector demand for vast numbers of unskilled laborers, fueled the process of rural-urban migration, particularly from the land-scarce close settled

TABLE 8.7

INDEX OF MANUFACTURING OUTPUT FOR NIGERIA

(Average Annual % Growth)

Period	Index for total manufacture	Vehicle assembly	Roofing sheets	Paints and allied products	Soap and detergents	Cotton textiles	Other textiles	Sugar confectionary	Soft drinks
1964–74	8.9	4.5	–1.1	15.6	9.5	17.1	–	16.8	16.8
1974–78	15.3	51.1	26.2	25.5	22.7	7.9	27.0	21.6	21.6

SOURCE: *African Business*, Dec. 1980, p. 49.

zones.[10] The spectacular growth of Kano for instance has drawn young productive men out of the agrarian sector; and the spatial expansion of the city and the growth of new working class areas have encroached upon the densely populated periurban districts (Frischman 1977). Spatial expansion and the commoditization of land has spawned a volatile secondary land market and a good deal of real estate speculation.

Attempts to regulate land appropriation through a modification of tenurial arrangements have not been successful. Peasant land appropriated by the state is compensated at levels far below the prevailing market price, generating a good deal of vocal dissent on the part of dispossessed peasants. Indeed, speculative housing and the demand for land has been, in part, stimulated by state housing subsidies, which has placed further pressures on land sale to urban speculators.[11] In Kano, Lubeck found that

> informants report with concern a previously unknown practice of enclosing land in the peri-urban area with barbed wire. In this way the urban land market expands outward devouring the peasantry who migrate . . . [and] are forced to pay high rents for crowded rooms in hastily constructed buildings. [1978, p. 39]

The urban crisis extends, of course, far beyond Kano. The southern cities have very probably mushroomed at even faster rates. Ogbonna's (1979) study of Port Harcourt, which grew from roughly 200,000 in 1969 to 800,000 in 1977, identified similar patterns of rural exodus, land speculation, and urban decay. Warri has grown still faster; it is the fastest-growing city in Nigeria, after Lagos.[12] In all cases, however, middle class residential expansion and the provision of urban services could not possibly accommodate the massive rural influx. In Port Harcourt, Lagos, and Warri 63, 72, and 60 percent, respectively, of urban households occupy only one room, one-third of which are without tap water; the average number of persons per room in each of those cities is, according to recent federal statistics, 3.7, 3.9 and 2.6 persons respectively.

Perhaps the most obvious aspect of the oil boom has been the dramatic surge of imports, transforming Nigerians into what one author has seen as a nation of cargo cult adepts. In 1973, Nigerian merchandise imports stood at ₦1.1 billion,[13] and by 1981 were ₦14.6 billion. Of course, almost 50 percent by value reflected capital expenditures (table 8.8) but the importation of consumer goods experienced a meteoric growth. By the mid-1970s luxury manufactures seemed to fill the shelves of every store; high fidelity equipment imports increased from ₦1.5 million in 1973 to ₦15 million in 1976.[14] In the same year Nigeria imported 216,000 motorcycles and scooters at a cost of ₦67 million. Car imports, boosted by state subsidized low-interest loans for government employees, reached the 100,000 mark by the mid-1970s. The burst of commodity fetishism was closely linked to ostentatious state-sponsored projects such as large-scale hotel construction, the second World Festival of African Culture

TABLE 8.8
NIGERIAN IMPORTS
(million naira)

Principal imports	1974	1975	1976	1977	1978	1979 (Jan.–Aug.)
Food and live animals	155.2	232.0	441.8	790.3	1,108.6	699.0
Drink and tobacco	9.1	19.6	63.7	146.8	57.7	5.0
Crude materials	63.4	67.0	79.3	70.7	113.6	92.5
Mineral fuels, etc.	50.9	92.0	181.2	136.8	181.2	111.6
Oils and fats	3.6	6.8	24.7	46.8	81.8	60.2
Chemicals	188.7	284.0	398.4	464.9	680.4	392.0
Manufactured goods	512.1	888.0	1,135.7	1,581.9	1,970.2	973.6
Machinery and transport equipment	608.3	1,306.0	2,447.4	3,528.8	3,759.4	1,720.6
Misc. manufactures	113.4	208.0	351.4	516.8	668.2	197.8
Other	10.7	8.2	8.5	13.0	13.8	12.0
Total imports	₦1,715.0	₦3,717.0	₦5,140.0	₦7,100	₦6,524	₦4,264.5

SOURCE: Quarterly Economic Review of Nigeria, 1980.

(FESTAC), which cost in the order of ₦140 million, and huge public works.[15] All this bred a sort of fanatical acquisitive ethos; everyone wanted (to use Richard Joseph's adage) a cut of the action.

The impact of the oil boom on Nigerian economy and society must ultimately be situated in relation to the internationalization of capital and the internal regime or mode of capital accumulation. I have suggested that petroleum revenues expanded and centralized the Nigerian state. The centrality of the state apparatus, however, transcends simple administrative capability; since the onset of military rule a burgeoning state capitalist sector has emerged, which controls basic industries and places technocrats in a position to directly manage industrial enterprises. Equally, state controlled oil rents have been used to encourage accumulation among Nigerian industrialists albeit in conjunction with foreign capital. In this sense, the oil boom has intensified the import-substitution that was already in place after the civil war, and further integrated Nigeria into a network of global Fordism. In the words of Beckman,

> the transition reflects the growing strength and organisational capacity of the domestic bourgeoisie in its handling of the state apparatus. It is the outcome both of the systematic grooming of this class by international capital and its emergence in the process of accumulation itself. It corresponds to the requirements of international capital for a local support system capable of managing local contradictions and provides the appropriate conditions for international accumulation. [Beckman 1981, p. 17]

Nevertheless, state expansion, rent seeking, and petroleum-inspired accumulation has not generated a national bourgeoisie that has seized control of the Nigerian state. Rather the state has taken over large segments of the economy—often well beyond its technocratic and administrative capacity to manage—and internalized the class forces within Nigeria as a whole. Most commentators agree that the Nigerian state sector is corrupt and chaotic but this must be seen in relation to the dominant political alliance of civil servants, merchant capitalists, politicians, and nascent industrialists that is maintained through an elaborate system of state patronage funded by petro-dollars. This fragile alliance is not compatible with rational state-capitalist planning; indeed, expanded oil revenues simply permit the alliance to flourish through a parasitic growth of clientism. In the private sector, individual accumulation rests on the largesse of the rentier state rather than on the direct control of the state apparatus.

FOOD, AGRICULTURE, AND THE POPULAR CLASSES

This ruinous inflation is, in fact, the only thing the Nigerian producer gets from the "oil boom . . ." the farmers in these parts say "Nairan na ba ta da albarka," meaning, this naira has no blessing, no weight! The petro-naira has not blessed them with the essentials of existence, rather its abundance is part of the process of denying them the benefits of what they produce. They continue in their poverty.

—Yusufu Bala Usman

Some classes benefited materially from the commodity boom, as measured by the consumption of purchased imports, but the majority of the urban and rural poor found any hard-won gains rapidly eroded by inflation. The Nigerian government, in overvaluing the naira and reducing import controls, actually intensified the inflationary spiral; the Adebo and Udoji wage claims, which were intended to mediate rising costs of living, also contributed to the surge of inflation. Though wages increased by 159 percent between 1971 and 1978, the price level of wage goods leaped by as much as 800 percent. In Port Harcourt, price indexes (using a base-line of 100 in 1960) in December 1977 for accommodation, clothing, food, fuel, and transport stood at 168, 479, 670, 333 and 268, respectively (Ogbonna 1979, p. 214). The composite cost of living index for Nigeria as a whole (based on the same 1960 figure) rose to 215 in 1970, 349 in 1974, 377 in 1976, 493 in 1978 and to almost 600 in March 1980. Over the period 1960–1978 the government minimum wage rate rose by 200 percent (Williams 1980).[16] Price indexes in rural and urban areas were equally bleak (table 8.9).

The post-oil boom political economy of Nigeria is perhaps made even more distinctive by the sluggish performance of agriculture, more specifically the collapse of export production, the stagnation of food production, and spiraling food imports. Between 1976 and 1978 food production, in relation to population, was 89 percent of that between 1960 and 1970 (*West Africa*, December 1, 1980). Over the period 1970–78, real food output per capita declined by 1.5 percent per annum; total food output has also been a splendid failure (table 8.10). Food imports have risen dramatically; in 1977 total food imports stood at ₦790 million (almost 11 percent of total imports), while in 1965 the bill was ₦46.4 million (8.8 percent of all imported commodities).[17] The dependence of Nigeria on externally produced staples has grown markedly since 1972 (table 8.11);[18] in 1980 the federal government spent ₦1.5 billion on imported cereals alone (*West Africa*, September 7, 1981).[19] Furthermore, the staple imports have been subject to the galloping inflation of the 1970s, which in 1978 was running at 16 percent per annum. In addition, the likelihood of closing the import food gap, which is currently running at 15 percent of gross caloric supply, seems slight. According to the World Bank, the projected deficits for 1985 and 1990 are 6.6 and 10.6 million tons of staple foodstuffs respectively. This would require an astonishing 11 percent growth rate in domestic food production to close the food gap by 1985. The 1980 Green Revolution strategy of the federal government estimates that a 4 percent growth rate is "realistic."

TABLE 8.9
CONSUMER PRICE INDEX
(1975 = 100)

Expenditure group	Urban low-income wage earner		All rural groups	
	December 1979	March 1980	December 1979	March 1980
Food	214.5	218.3	183.7	182.5
Staples	205.1	214.0	178.1	174.9
Proteins	249.7	252.2	205.1	207.3
Oils and fats	191.9	184.7	156.3	156.0
Vegetables and fruits	237.8	244.5	185.2	186.5
Others	163.3	159.6	177.0	175.4
Drinks	202.4	201.4	179.0	186.7
Food and drinks	213.6	215.8	183.5	182.8
Tobacco and kola	176.9	177.6	207.4	212.6
Accommodation, fuel, and light	191.4	199.4	170.7	187.0
Household goods and other purchases	171.9	176.3	166.1	175.9
Clothing	189.3	195.5	236.2	246.6
Transport	185.7	186.1	209.2	198.1
Other services	198.4	209.3	180.8	194.3
All items	201.6	206.6	187.2	189.1

SOURCE: Federal Office of Statistics, Nigeria 1980.

TABLE 8.10
OUTPUT OF MAJOR FOOD CROPS
(in '000 tons)

Crop	1972	1973	1974	1975	1976	1977	1978	1979
Guinea corn	5794	2298	3125	4738	3325	3700	3770	3785
Millet	2835	2391	3794	5554	4737	2950	3060	3100
Rice	279	447	487	525	515	579	842	1000

SOURCE: Federal Office of Statistics, Nigeria Quarterly Economic Review (Nigeria), 1980.

TABLE 8.11
FOOD IMPORTS

Year	Total food imports (N millions)	% of total imports	Wheat Quantity[1]	Wheat Value[2]	Rice Quantity[1]	Rice Value[2]	Barley Quantity[1]	Barley Value[2]	Maize Quantity[3]	Maize Value[2]	Fish Quantity[1]	Fish Value[2]	Meat Quantity[1]	Meat Value[2]
1965	46.4	8.8	55.6	7.6	1.2	0.2	no data		no data		34.3	14.3	0.5	0.3
1970	57.7	7.6	258.7	15.4	1.7	0.1	no data		no data		6.6	2.9	n.a.[4]	n.a.
1972	95.1	9.6	296.7	22.0	5.8	1.0	no data		no data		20.8	5.3	n.a.	n.a.
1974	154.8	8.9	318.3	50.7	4.8	1.4	9.7	0.009	20,171	0.6	14.7	7.4	0.4	0.3
1977	790.3	10.9	720.0	96.0	413.0	155.0	94.9	0.04	2,440	3.4	100	71.0	23.0	21.6
1980	1560.0	11.0	n.a.	231.6	n.a.	132.0	n.a.	n.a.	n.a.	23.1	n.a.	n.a.	n.a.	n.a.

SOURCE: Forrest (1981), Federal Office of Statistics, Central Bank of Nigeria (1980).

[1] In '000s of metric tons
[2] Millions of naira
[3] In '000s of kgs
[4] not available

The expanded food import trade also reflected a change in urban diet and specifically the eclipse of traditional staples such as millet, sorghum, and gari, by cheap white breads and imported rice. The growth of wheat (principally imported from the United States) has been especially dramatic since it has increasingly become the staple of the urban poor. Between 1970 and 1981, imports of wheat leaped from 250,000 tons to 1.5 million tons; the value of U.S. wheat in 1981 alone ran at over $1 billion. Wheat appeared doubly cheap throughout the 1970s in relation to the price of oil (table 8.12) because the barter terms of trade moved sharply in favor of imported staples. Similarly, price ratios moved favorably for rice in relation to local foodstuffs such as gari, which suffered from a rapid rate of domestic inflation. While the government attempted to stabilize wheat and rice prices—the price of wheat flour for instance was officially maintained at ₦241 per ton between 1974 and 1980—the low cost of landed imports was not in fact passed on to the Nigerian consumer and resulted in superprofits for those able to obtain import licenses through state patronage.[20] Thus in August 1980, the officially controlled price of wheat flour was ₦276 per ton but open market prices in Kaduna and Lagos were in excess of ₦560 per ton. In 1977 the landed cost of rice was ₦15 per bag but fetched in excess of ₦100 per bag due to merchant speculation (*Washington Post*, December 27, 1980). In this re-

TABLE 8.12

INTERNATIONAL WHEAT PRICES IN RELATION TO OIL PRICES AND WHEAT IMPORTS

Year	No. 2 Dark Gulf Wheat (price index)	Nigeria food price index	Oil/Wheat Terms of trade (bu./bbl.)*	Wheat imports (volume index)
1962/3	100	100	/	100
1970/1	95	138	1.10	218
1971/2	94	179	1.30	395
1972/3	138	183	1.23	357
1973/4	283	190	0.96	310
1974/5	297	267	2.34	317
1975/6	279	311	2.77	307
1976/7	202	377	3.18	415
1977/8	192	407	4.41	747
1978/9	225	438	3.66	949
1979/80	277	493	3.96	999
1980/81	278	500	6.10	1340

SOURCE: Federal Office of Statistics, World Bank Economic Memorandum, 1980 United States Department of Agriculture, *Wheat Situation* (1970–1981).

*Wheat prices refer to average annual wheat export price per bushel (No. 1/2 Hard Red Winter). Oil prices refer to the posted price of Arabian light per barrel.

gard, foodstuffs were part of the inflationary spiral and clearly under-mined some of the urban wage settlements of the 1970s. Lubeck's (1978) work strikingly illuminates how Kano wage workers were confronted with rapidly rising prices of wage goods (table 8.13); cereals increased in price by five to six times over a nine-year period. This material contradiction and the fall in real wages goes some way toward explaining the increased militancy of the Nigeria Labor Congress which, in February 1980, de-manded a minimum wage of ₦300.00 per month. Between 1976 and 1979 the number of man-days lost to industrial disputes leaped from 14,141 to 200,374 (Central Bank of Nigeria; 1979).

From the perspective of the popular classes, then, the decay of the food sector combined with the high inflation of wage foods has unques-tionably contributed to a stagnant and impoverished standard of living, even in the face of massive oil rents. Matlon's (1981) survey of three Kano villages in 1975–76 for example estimated that 20 percent of all house-holds experienced caloric deficits of 15–29 percent, and that there was a "serious degree of absolute impoverishment among the poorest 30–40 percent of households" (p. 339). The recent basic needs report by the International Labor Office estimated that 4 million families were below the poverty data line in 1978, an increase of over 25 percent since 1973. In the urban sector, the quality of life among lower income groups is equally bleak; the proportion of households living in one room has grown signifi-cantly since 1970 and rents have soared to the extent that they now absorb a minimum of 30–40 percent of domestic incomes. The generalized filth, disease, and crime in such cities as Lagos and Ibadan have become almost legendary. It is no surprise, then, that Bienen's (1980) recent work confi-dently concludes that "oil emerges as a critical factor in producing income inequality through a sharp increase in the differentials of labor productiv-ity and per capita income between rural and urban populations" (p. 6). Interpersonal income distribution nationwide moved from a gini index of

TABLE 8.13
FOOD PRICES AND WAGES IN KANO

Commodity	Price				% increase 1971–80
	1971 (₦)	1975 (₦)	1978 (₦)	1980 (₦)	
Millet (measure)	.17	.50	1.10	1.20	605
Rice (measure)	.83	1.6	2.5	5.5	562
Sorghum (measure)	.21	.5	1.00	1.00	376
Starting wage per day	₦.87	₦1.75	₦2.25	₦3.85	342%

SOURCE: Lubeck (1978, 1981).

roughly 0.5 in 1960 to 0.7 in 1975.[21] According to Bienen the Udoji wage review also produced a worsening of income distribution in the public sector. The swollen urban informal sector unquestionably benefited little from the newfound oil wealth. The deepening discrepancy in intraurban income distribution was mirrored by severe rural-urban differences (Diejomaoh and Anusionwu 1980).[22]

In summary, the impact of oil rents on the Nigerian agricultural sector has been catastrophic. As de Janvry (1981) has shown, in a disarticulated economy such as Nigeria in which wages appear only as a cost in the accumulation process, there are powerful forces at work to support a cheap food policy. Faced with a sluggish domestic supply response in the face of increased incomes and a rapidly growing urban populace that accompanied the construction-manufacturing boom, the Nigerian government provided cheap-wage foods through importation. As it turned out, the issue of import licenses was simply a way of distributing oil rents and as a consequence local foods were anything but cheap. Oil revenues could have been used to raise domestic producer prices but the fear of exacerbating inflationary pressures effectively prevented this. Furthermore, a shortage of labor in the countryside and steadily rising costs of production in many instances that local production could not compete with underpriced imports, particularly since the Nigerian naira was probably overvalued by at least 50 percent. Throughout the 1970s producer prices offered by the government for foodstuffs were consistently below producers' costs; in the case of millet and sorghum, the prices offered by the National Grains Board in 1977−78 were 20−50 percent below estimated production costs (World Bank Economic Memorandum 1979). Prices for the traditional export commodities such as cotton, groundnuts and cocoa were in fact raised in the mid-1970s, but by that time cost of production increases and labor shortage blocked a positive supply response. In the case of cotton which is an input into local manufacturing, powerful interests opposed sharp producer price increases. Some commercial foodstuff producing areas such as Zamfara and southern Katsina unquestionably participated in the expanded government demand for staples, but as shown in chapter seven, there is no reason to expect that all small-scale producers necessarily benefited from high sorghum prices. By the mid-1970s, accumulation through rent seeking and access to the state had resulted in a stagnant agrarian sector incapable of generating either export revenues through traditional means or large quantities of competitively priced wage foods.

Against this backdrop of an oil boom political economy I propose to sketch the recent efforts of the Nigerian state at agrarian transformation. For purposes of brevity I concentrate on its critical components: the new Green Revolution Program (including the National Accelerated Food

Production Program), the integrated rural development projects, the state involvement in agrarian production frequently in conjunction with international finance capital, and ideological efforts to inspire domestic production, such as Operation Feed the Nation (OFN). In short, I argue that faced with the food crisis that has emerged during and after the 1972–74 famine, the Nigerian state has embarked upon a new project of public investment, which stands in sharp contrast to the peasant-based strategies of the colonial period. In spite of the government's populist and smallholder rhetoric, every indication is that the persistence of small-scale commodity production is in question.

THE AGRARIAN QUESTION AND RURAL DEVELOPMENT

Dependence on imported foods was no solution to the Nigerian crisis since it was contingent upon ever expanding oil revenues and was ultimately politically dubious. Cheap imports further depressed local foodstuff production,[23] and the low prices offered by the marketing boards had all but quashed export commodity production.[24] In this sense, the famine of 1973–74 simply highlighted an already crisis-ridden agrarian economy. The civil war and the consecutive drought years (and an outbreak of groundnut rosette disease in 1975) had certainly dislocated production, but structural problems clearly lay at the heart of the sluggish agricultural performance. The health of the food economy in the long term had to be markedly upgraded, which meant confronting noncapitalist relations of production in the countryside.

The federal government directly addressed the food crisis in the Third Development Plan (1975–80), which gave pride of place to agriculture, specifically food. The proportion of government spending in agriculture remained low—roughly 5 percent—but oil revenue permitted a huge increase in actual spending (table 8.14).[25] In spite of the priority of "ensuring food supplies in adequate quantity and quality to keep pace with increased population and urbanization" (Third Development Plan 1975, p. 65), it was clear that the agricultural sector was still to be the bedrock of the cheap food policy and a source of foreign exchange revenue. Moreover, the vast majority of rural smallholders were profoundly marginal to revenue allocation. Of the total allocated capital of ₦3.1 billion, 23 percent went to massive irrigation schemes, 14 percent to direct production schemes under state management, and 10 percent to extension service and input (Etuk 1978; van Apeldoorn 1981).[26] The Third Development Plan provided nonetheless the means for a radical transformation of Nigerian agriculture, ostensibly to increase food supplies without increasing food prices. Broadly speaking, the Nigerian state's project is a two-pronged strategy. The first involves various state

TABLE 8.14
EXPENDITURE ON AGRICULTURE, BY MAJOR EXPENDITURE CATEGORY
(in ₦ million)

	1977/78 estimates (Recurrent & capital)				3rd plan 1975–1980 (Capital exp.)	
	Federal	States	Total	Percent	Total	Percent
Extension service and input supply[1]	34.0	89.1	123.1	(16.0)	305.6	(10.0)
Fertilizer purchases		43.0	43.0	(5.6)	313.3	(10.2)
Mechanization	0.9	33.7	34.6	(4.5)	71.5	(2.3)
Direct production schemes	11.1	47.2	58.3	(7.6)	432.6	(14.1)
Seed multiplication	2.8	18.9	21.7	(2.8)	62.9	(2.1)
Credit	16.0	11.2	27.2	(3.5)	194.9	(6.4)
Irrigation	182.4	45.2	227.6	(30.0)	701.5	(22.9)
Training	1.2	15.9	17.1	(2.2)	47.3	(1.5)
Marketing and storage	15.4	15.5	30.9	(4.0)	73.1	(2.4)
Miscellaneous	5.1	13.7	18.8	(2.4)	132.8	(4.3)
TOTAL CROPS	268.9	333.3	602.3	(78.8)	2335.8	(76.4)
Livestock	20.3	77.4	97.7	(12.7)	487.7	(15.9)
Forestry	7.6	35.1	42.7	(5.5)	135.7	(4.4)
Fisheries	8.5	15.2	23.7	(3.1)	99.4	(3.3)
TOTAL AGRICULTURE	305.3	461.1	766.4	(100.0)	3058.3	(100.0)
Less federal grants to states			12.6			
TOTAL (net)			753.8			

SOURCE: *The Green Revolution*, vol. 2.
Lagos: Federal Ministry of Agriculture.
[1]Includes special programs – Operation Feed the Nation (OFN), National Accelerated Food Production Project (NAFPP), Agro Service Center Programs (ASC) and Agricultural Development Projects (ADP).

production schemes, often in concert with international finance capital and multinational agroindustrial concerns. And the second involves expanded parastatal marketing and subsidized input systems which (i) encourages the emergence of a larger scale mechanized agriculture and (ii) promotes differentiation within the countryside by attracting urban and administrative elites into production, or appealing to rural "progressive farmers." This, then, marks a new phase of capital accumulation in Nigeria and agriculture is a direct threat to the future of small-scale peasant production.[27]

Specifically I shall examine four state and private responses to the food crisis. First, direct state intervention in production (for the provision of wage foods) and distribution, the latter subsuming national price and marketing policy and also the establishment of a federal strategic grain reserve in an attempt to regularize the conditions of rural production. Second, state (and foreign) investment in large-scale irrigation schemes and river basin development authorities (RBDAs) principally for the production of wheat and rice. Third, a Green Revolution strategy centered on Agricultural Development Projects (ADPs) that are based loosely on the prototypical integrated rural development projects of the World Bank. These efforts are geared toward simultaneously improving rural productivity through heavily subsidized inputs of credit, fertilizer, and seed and enhancing the provision of cheap wage foods (especially maize and sorghum in the North) from a prosperous middle peasantry. And finally, what de Janvry (1981) refers to as the merchant road to capitalist development, namely merchant-bureaucrat food enterprises, characteristically in luxury foodstuffs such as poultry and small livestock, and often as joint ventures with foreign capital. What emerges, I argue, is a complex and contradictory attempt at agrarian transformation through expanded public intervention and foreign capital. Nigeria is following several quite different roads to agrarian capitalism: a classically farmer road as Lenin defined it, in which the seeds of accumulation are sown among petty commodity producers; a merchant path oriented toward middle income foodstuffs; an open-door policy for foreign agribusiness; and, not least, a huge investment in irrigation which appears as an elaborate mechanism to redistribute oil rents through state patronage and to therefore cement critical class alliances within the state itself.

STATE PRODUCTION AND DISTRIBUTION

The Third National Development Plan initiated increased involvement by federal and state governments in the direct production of agricultural products, especially wage foods. In the early 1960s the Farm Settlement Schemes in western Nigeria established 1,500 acre farms for

TABLE 8.15
CAPITAL ALLOCATION TO GOVERNMENT FOOD PRODUCTION PROGRAMS,
1974/75–1979/80

| | | Allocation to government programs | |
States	Total food crop allocation (million naira)	Amount (million naira)	Percent of total
Benue Plateau	3.03	2.30	76
East Central	35.62	30.16	85
Kwara	24.84	12.72	51
Midwest	16.55	16.55	100
North Central	4.57	2.00	44
South East	14.49	11.64	80

SOURCE: Third Development Plan 1975–80, Vol. II.

similar purposes; but by 1971 the Western Region Government had spent ₦16.4 million—55 percent of total capital expenditure for agriculture—with almost no productive success. The new efforts are vastly expanded (table 8.15); government food companies for example were allocated ₦114.2 million. In the southern states government plantations and food companies were granted ₦67.35 million from a total of ₦131.38 million for food crops. Three parastatals—the National Livestock Production Company, the National Grains Production Company (NGPC) and the National Rootcrop Production Company—were charged with accelerating food production through large-scale heavily mechanized productive units.[28] The NGPC has established 4,000 hectare farms, which include storage and processing facilities.[29] By 1980 food production farms had been established at Mokwa (Niger), Jema (Kaduna), and Ilero (Oyo); similar enterprises are under construction in Bauchi and Kano, and should be completed in all the remaining states by 1982. The Livestock Company engages in cattle, pig farming, and dairy production; three poultry hatcheries produce 5.4 million chicks annually, and state-funded broiler factories are under construction at Agege and Port Harcourt.

In addition, the NGPC and its sister organization the Nigerian Grains Board (NGB) are responsible for the purchase and large-scale storage of cereals. The two organizations have essentially complementary tasks, the NGB being mainly concerned with short-term and seasonal rather than long-term, strategic functions. Since 1977, the NGB has assumed responsibility for the provision of all strategic grain reserves, while the NGPC acts as a storekeeper. Both institutions attempt to secure grains in private markets through a guaranteed minimum pricing policy. The federal strategic reserve program provides for 250,000 tons of stored grain, although only an 82,000 ton nominal capacity has been constructed to date at twelve northern locations. A further 80,000 ton capacity has been under construction since 1978 while each state has a regional reserve system to fulfill more local public demands and market rigging. At present this state capability is insignificant though projected to be 350,000 tons by the end of the decade.

Whether the grains boards can effectively and efficiently manage the tasks which they have been assigned, however, is another question entirely. The minimum price policy has been a fiasco since its inception in 1975; the guaranteed price is invariably announced after planting and has been set well below prevailing market levels. In 1977–78, the prices offered per ton for millet and paddy rice were respectively N110 and N240, yet producer prices on the open market were N207 and N267! Not only has a ridiculously small amount of grain actually been purchased—and hence the grains trade remains wholly in the hands of influential urban and rural merchants—but storage has been remarkably shoddy. In 1978–79, 68,000 tons of assorted grain were bought yet the entire amount was subsequently sold at a huge loss as livestock feed in 1980 due to its poor condition following storage.

The outlook for large-scale mechanized farming is also not especially sanguine. An earlier state effort in Nigeria—the Niger Agricultural Project at Mokwa—proved to be an unmitigated disaster, being abandoned in 1954 after a loss of one million pounds. Recent state schemes seem equally unsatisfactory; several of the settlement schemes have been scaled down in Ondo State and others, such as the Warlo scheme, transferred to other authorities (in this case the Hadejia River Basin Development Authority). A more recent and glaring failure is the mechanized farm at Agenbode in Bendel State. Originally planned to cultivate about 85,000 hectares at three different sites, only 3,000 hectares have been developed at the astronomical cost of N11.7 million. Low yields of maize and rice coupled with insurmountable managerial and technical obstacles led to its demise in 1976 unless the Bendel State government could supply the new management with another N11 million.

Perhaps for these sorts of reasons, foreign capital has been notably reticent to invest in Nigerian mechanized farm projects in spite of the highly attractive conditions offered by the state. The expense of land clearing, seasonal labor shortages, and the high costs of mechanized farm operations (especially weeding) have all translated into low profitability thresholds for agribusiness. The World Bank estimated in fact that mechanized maize and groundnut production was not commercially viable without massive government subsidies (1979, p. 112). United States corporations have accordingly shown far greater concern for market widening rather than for direct production; Andrew Young has recently waxed eloquent on the transformation of Sokoto into an African San Joaquin valley, a conversion "that is profitable for U.S. farm methods" (*Washington Post*, March 9, 1981).

The Nigerian government has, nevertheless, continued to encourage investment by private foreign capital in the agricultural sector. Nineteen joint ventures are already planned by companies from Brazil, Canada, and Europe[30] (*African Business*, November 1981), and in July 1980 the U.S. government and Nigeria established a Joint Agriculture Consultative Committee (the JACC) to encourage American agribusiness, in conjunction with the U.S. Department of Agriculture, to invest heavily (*Foreign Agriculture*, June 1981). This agreement included the opening of Nigerian trade and investment centers in the U.S., and the installation of a new U.S. Department of Agriculture trade office in Lagos. The memorandum of understanding on agriculture also provided for the establishment of an intergovernmental working group to design and implement specific agricultural projects in Nigeria. The first project undertaken as a result of this agreement consisted of a soil survey of Nigeria conducted with the assistance of a team of U.S. Department of Agriculture experts sent to Nigeria by the Reagan administration. The U.S. members of the Committee represent giant agribusiness and financial concerns, including farm equipment manufacturers (FMC Corporation, Allis-Chalmers, Ford Motor Company); fertilizer, pesticide, and seed producers (Pfizer, Occidental Petroleum, Whittaker); food processing operations (Carnation, Pillsbury, Ralston Purina); and financial institutions (Chase Manhattan, First National Bank of Chicago). Earlier this year, U.S. Agriculture Secretary John Block promised extensive support for the JACC (*West Africa*, No. 3323, April 6, 1981, p. 763). More recently, Assistant Secretary for African Affairs Chester Crocker specifically hailed the fledgling JACC as the administration's prime model "of the contributions and benefits of private sector involvement in Africa to which we are giving encouragement." By the mid-1970s, European firms had also begun to invest in luxury foodstuff production: the Bokko poultry farm in Plateau State was a joint venture between the state government and the German firm Rau Imex, and Danish and British companies had established pig farms near Kuru. In both instances, investment had encouraged vertical integration principally through the encouragement of hybrid maize among local farmers as livestock feed.

In light of these new trends, the Land Use Decree of March 1978 has important implications for the social transformations I have mentioned. The decree is a complex document with many fuzzy areas and has accordingly been claimed as a triumph by right- and left-wing factions alike. It covers a wide range of matters pertaining to tenure, trusteeship, rent, rights of alienation, revocation of rights, and compensation (see

Igbozurike 1980; Uchendu 1979). Part I of the decree is radical insofar as it vests all land in the state. Accordingly the legal status of the Nigerian user becomes one of statutory occupancy, not ownership, and the interests and benefits of these statutory rights are tightly circumscribed by law. In practice the state has wide powers of intervention, and tenurial principles have been radically shifted.

First, the corporate character of the traditional tenure has been eliminated. In its place we have a contractual system of tenure validated by a certificate of occupancy which sets out terms of tenure, including access, succession, duration, and rents. Second, the new tenure system limits enjoyment of interest in land to one single holder who "shall have the sole right to and absolute possession of all the improvements on the land." Third, the proprietary rights which were exercised under the traditional tenure have been replaced by possible claims to improvements on the land. Fourth, by breaking the local sovereignty in land, access to land, under a uniform system of rules, may be gained by any Nigerian anywhere in the country [Uchendu 1979, p. 70].

While the full implications of these changes seem unclear, it appears that a prime purpose of the decree is to permit widespread state acquisition of land for large-scale agricultural schemes, whether directly funded or as joint ventures with foreign capital. By broadening the eminent domain for state production or acquisition, the Nigerian state restricts the right to hold land without developing it, makes undeveloped land available, and prevents land withholding for speculative purposes. Federal intervention to reform land rights has, then, provided the wherewithal for the state to self-consciously direct the social transformation of agriculture.

IRRIGATION AND RIVER BASIN DEVELOPMENT AUTHORITIES

In conjunction with the Green Revolution strategy, the most important pivot about which much agrarian development rotates is the massive commitment to irrigation and large-scale water management. The case for irrigation appears quite self-evident in an area subject to limited rainfall, recurrent drought and open, irrigable floodplains. The colonial state fostered local water control in the Sokoto-Rima valley from a very early period but irrigation has become a major source of federal revenue—and of political conflict—since 1960. The growth of the schemes has been quite spectacular; from £1.37 million (of a total capital expenditure on agriculture of £4.01 million) in the period 1962–68, irrigation currently accounts for ₦2.26 billion out of ₦8.98 billion in the Fourth Development Plan (1981–85). While 1.5 million hectares have been identified by the 11 RBDAs as potentially irrigable, only 15,000 are currently under irrigation, with the possibility of perhaps 100,000 by 1985. Huge expenditures of this magnitude have been roundly criticized by the World Bank in view of the low yields, limited benefits, and high opportunity costs in relation to smallholder schemes (World Bank 1979). Irrigation has been justified in terms of drought defense, wheat import-substitution, and its linkage effects, but its real value to the Nigerian state resides in its political expediency. Its continued fiscal priority in the face of low yields, salinization, poor drainage, technical difficulties and the like is a direct reflection of the attractiveness of RBDAs as unencumbered mechanisms to distribute oil rents and hence develop a political constituency.

The major studies of the northern river basins were undertaken by international donor organizations in the late 1960s. These reports recommended basin development through dam construction and large-scale irrigation, and feasibility studies were smartly commissioned for three major developments: the Kano River Project, the Bakalori Project in Sokoto, and the South Chad Irrigation Project. The decision to move ahead with dam construction and pilot projects began in 1970 and hence predates both the famine and the oil boom-food crisis. The consultancy and construction contracts became lucrative sources of patronage both for Nigerian elites and foreign firms. A Yugoslav company is involved in Kano, Dumas (France) at Hadejia, Impresit/Fiat (Italy) at Bakalori and Edok-Eter (Greece) at South Chad. As the RBDAs were established between 1973 and 1976, top civil servants, military personnel and private businessmen appeared with remarkable consistency on the governing boards. In some instances design and construction were not even put out to tender.

The recently completed Bakalori irrigation project 150 kilometers southeast of Sokoto provides a blueprint for these sorts of partially state-funded enterprises. The impetus for Bakalori came from a Fiat-based bank consortium which is now in the hands of an Italian contractor (IMPRESIT). Two contracts for construction totaled ₦154 million to be completed by March 1980; but by January of that year costs stood at ₦350 million and construction was blocked by farmer opposition (*West Africa*, May 12, 1980). The total irrigated area will be 25,000 hectares, involving the displacement of forty villages, the loss of 20,000 hectares of fadama land, and the resettlement of 13,000 people.[31] To construct the canal and sprinkler systems, extensive land leveling was required, costing ₦81 million (Oculi 1981).[32] The original plan envisaged small farms of roughly 12.5 acres and multicropping systems of wheat, rice, maize, sugar cane, tobacco, tomatoes, and local cereals (*West Africa*, August 28, 1978). However, encouraged by a consulting company (MASDAR) to develop a wealthy farmer class, the state established 350-hectare "development farms." Within a year of completion some indebted farmers sold out to teachers, businessmen, and officials.[33]

The Bakalori experience is not unusual. Wallace (1979) and Palmer-Jones (1977) showed how the first phase of the Kano River Project at Kadawa, which involved the construction of the Tiga dam in 1974, suffered from similar defects.[34] The resettlement of 12,000 farmers at Tiga resulted in a deterioration of material conditions for 43 percent of all settlers, most particularly felt as a lack of good farmland (Voh 1980). Like Bakalori, downstreamers on the Hadejia valley lost access to fishing and lucrative vegetable production (Stock 1978). At Kadawa, south of Kano, tenure, labor, and technical shortcomings severely constrained the operation of the project; the project functions ineffectively but to the benefit of project workers, locally influential trader-farmers, and rich outsiders (Palmer-Jones 1977). The production of wheat on the Kano River project costs much more than imported wheats. It will probably require high subsidies even to cover recurrent costs. The production of wheat and tomatoes for urban markets conflicts with the farmers' wish to produce guinea corn, which is harvested after wheat should be planted. Production is further constrained by untimely provision of tractor ploughing and fertilizers, and inadequacies in the flow of water and maintenance of canals. The project authorities do not own the land and are therefore unable to direct the farmers to comply with their wishes. All this needs to be seen against the massive costs per hectare of irrigation agriculture: ₦2,000 in Bakalori, ₦1,750 in Chad (Phase 1), ₦1,200 in Chad (Phase II), and ₦8,000 in Kadawa (Kano).

The state has also become heavily committed to estate sugar production; the Third Development Plan budgeted ₦350 million to three integrated projects in Gongola, Kwara, and Niger states. In most cases, sugar production is closely linked to irrigation and dam construction; the huge Savanna sugar project at Numan is tied to the ₦144 million Kiri dam on the Gongola River. Here too, however, the performance of estate agriculture has been poor; inflated technology prices, infrastructural bottlenecks, and poor management and financing account for huge delays and massive overspending. Expenditure on the Savanna Sugar Company alone stands at $412 million,[35] although the irrigation remains uncompleted and "there appears little likelihood of the sugar ever being competitive on the world market" (*Quarterly Economic Review*, 3rd Quarter 1981, p. 20). Undeterred by these difficulties, the Nigerian government is going ahead with the $568 million Sunti sugar estate,[36] which will employ 4,000 people and ultimately produce 50,000 tons per year. The government's decision to acquire 90 percent of the equity from Tate and Lyle has halted production, however.

Despite the claims by the Federal Ministry of Agriculture that the irrigation schemes are capable of producing 300,000 tons of cereals and vegetables, the RBDAs have not resulted in significant increases in food production. In 1981–82 only 40,000 tons of grain were produced on irrigated land. Production and productivity problems are particularly debilitating in the case of wheat; the FAO quoted yields of 3–4 tons per acre in the mid-1960s in Nigeria but a decade later yields of two tons are optimistic. According to Palmer-Jones (1980), salinity, poor management, and water control problems plague even the new projects, with significant farmer losses as a result. Huge federal subsidies are incurred in order to sustain and facilitate continued wheat production (see tables 8.16 and 8.17) which cannot, in view of the overvalued naira, compete with North American imports. According to the World Bank (1979, p. 20), the rates of return for large irrigation projects in the north are 2–3 percent at best; the development costs are between six and forty thousand naira per family.

High production costs and subsidization does not mean, of course, that influential and large irrigators cannot make handsome profits. Indeed the frequency with which merchants, politicians, and businessmen are moving onto the schemes suggests a high profitability. And not surprisingly, further developments at Challowa, Gronyo, Hadejia (stage I), Zauro in Sokoto, and Mada in the Benue valley are all in process. Whether these schemes actually transpire, and whether irrigation will continue to receive favored treatment, will ultimately be a political question.[37] Ironically, the World Bank's smallholder emphasis must in this regard appear quite radical to some members of the Nigerian state and the criticism that the Bank has received of late, both from the political right and left, is singularly instructive. Conflicts are currently brewing over the proposed capital expenditures of the federal Ministry of Water Resources, which funds the RBDAs, in light of the fiscal crisis of the state. The outcome of this struggle will, however, not only be dependent on future oil prices and domestic production but more critically on the changing class forces within Nigeria itself.

THE GREEN REVOLUTION STRATEGY

In addition to a direct involvement in production, the Third Development Plan provided for a huge expansion of capital expenditure for raising rural productivity and food production. The allocation of ₦750 million to finance agricultural development since 1975 has seen an explosion of parastatal organizations concerned directly with subsidized credit, fertilizer, mechanization, integrated rural development, and land tenure changes (Essang 1977).[38] A major impetus for parastatal expansion was the food crisis, and the early efforts—specifically Operation Feed the Nation (OFN) established in 1976 and the National Accelerated Food Production Program (NAFPP) founded in 1972—were designed to boost

TABLE 8.16

Wheat Production Costs to Farmers in Northern Nigeria

	Gamboru I farmers 1976–7 (₦)	Gamboru II farmers 1976–7 (₦)	Yau farmers 1976–7 (₦)	Hadejia farmers 1976–7 (₦)	Kadawa farmers 1976–7 (₦)	Kadawa farmers 1976–7 (₦)	Tungan Trudu 1976–7 (₦)	Jekarade farmers 1976–7 (₦)
Water charges	17.29	42.00	49.41	29.64	24.70	24.70	4.94	24.70
Tractor charges	24.71	–	–	32.11	18.78	39.38	14.82	48.80
Seed	27.17	27.17	32.93	37.05	16.92	24.01	17.93	40.00
Fertilizer	19.81	14.82	12.97	17.29	59.86	25.07	8.65	22.50
Labor	102.83	261.91	132.15	110.58	84.57	142.65	262.99	245.00
Activity preparation	1.37	20.00	49.40	–	–	32.29	74.10	–
Planting	–	20.00	24.70	–	11.02	13.54	14.82	20.00
Fertilizing	–	4.94	14.82	–	–	–	9.99	80.00
Weeding	28.70	24.70	12.35	–	–	15.00	61.75	80.00
Irrigating	14.55	20.00	21.00	–	14.07	54.94	29.64	25.00
Harvesting	19.36	8.00	9.88	–	14.88	–	34.58	20.00
Threshing	26.85	34.58	–	–	41.51	17.32	2.40	–
Winnowing	–	–	19.76	–	–	9.56	11.12	?
Transport	?	8.65	4.94	–	3.09	–	24.70	–
Others	–	–	–	–	–	–	–	–
Sacks	12.00	17.29	–	11.20	16.00	28.00	11.00	20.00
Other	–	–	–	68.27	–	–	–	–
Total cash costs	191.27	302.67	252.16	306.09	220.83	283.81	320.45	381.00
Average yields t/ha	1.22	1.73	1.98	1.12	1.64	3.11	1.11	2.00
Cost per ton	156.78	174.95	127.35	273.29	134.65	91.26	288.30	190.50
Price N ton	280.00	280.00	300.00	280.00	280.00	230.00	340.00	230.00
Gross revenue	341.60	484.40	594.00	313.60	295.20	715.30	377.40	460.00
Net revenue/ha	150.33	181.73	341.84	7.51	74.37	431.49	56.95	79.00

SOURCE: Report on Wheat Production and Marketing in Nigeria (1979), p. 60.

TABLE 8.17
ESTIMATES OF SUBSIDIZED AND ACTUAL COSTS OF WHEAT PRODUCTION

| Location | Costs of production | | | | Government subsidy | |
| | N per hectare | | N per tonne | | per | |
	Farmer	Actual	Farmer	Actual	Ha	Ton
Gamboru (I)	191.27	355.79	156.78	291.63	164.52	134.85
Gamboru (II)	302.67	459.13	174.95	265.39	156.46	90.44
Yau	252.16	444.27	127.35	224.32	192.11	97.03
Hadejia	306.90	376.72	273.29	336.36	70.63	113.79
Kadawa 1975/6	220.83	328.08	134.65	200.05	107.25	65.40
1976/7	283.81	464.94	91.26	149.50	181.13	57.24
Tungan Tudu	222.29	446.19	202.08	405.63	223.90	203.55
Goronyo	234.81	452.81	237.18	457.48	218.10	220.30
Jekarade	381.00	579.09	190.50	289.55	198.09	99.05

SOURCE: Report on Wheat Production in Nigeria (1979), p. 69.

and mobilize individuals around the food issue. Operation Feed the Nation was largely a propagandistic strategy directed at mass motivation and incentives (Ekhomu 1978). Almost 30,000 postsecondary students were paid ₦96 per month to participate in rural production schemes, though with very little effect; in view of the minimal logistical and institutional support by the government there is little evidence to suggest that OFN significantly raised food production.[39] The NAFPP, conversely, was aimed to stimulate production of rice, maize, sorghum, millet, wheat, and cassava through the integrated use of high-yielding seed varieties, chemical inputs, credit, and improved marketing. The program has concentrated on "packages of improved practices," or production kits, ostensibly for small-scale producers. In addition the state constructed 380 agro-service centers to improve input delivery and technology transfer.[40] Seed laboratories have been completed in Ibadan and Kaduna, and a National Mechanization Center is in progress at Ilorin.

In spite of the huge logistical difficulties, tractor and fertilizer inputs rose steadily (tables 8.18 and 8.19); by 1980 Nigeria was using in excess of 1 million tons of fertilizer. In 1979 a further ₦18 million was allocated for short-term mechanical improvements in all of the states,[41] and several rice projects were established covering 6,000 hectares in Anambra, Imo, and Cross River states (*West Africa*, January 14 and 21, 1980). The entire program received further support in April 1980 with the establishment of a coordinating body, the National Council for Green Revolution, which aims to "boost agricultural production and to ensure rural development through . . . agro-based industries [and] the construction of feeder roads" (*Africa Now*, October 1981, p. 181).

TABLE 8.18
FERTILIZER IMPORTS

Year	Import value (million naira)	Import quantity (1000 MT)
1970/71	1.6	34.1
1971/72	1.8	52.0
1972/73	4.0	83.0
1973/74	3.1	84.4
1974/75	6.1	83.7
1975/76	12.3	150.9
1976/77	20.4	207.8
1979/80	34.6	339.8
1980/81	n.a.	513.8

SOURCE: World Bank (IBRD), 1978, 1979. Federal Ministry of Agriculture, Lagos 1980.

TABLE 8.19
TRACTOR IMPORTS
(in million naira)

Year	Tractors: wheeled, <40 hp No.	Value	Tractors: wheeled, >40 hp No.	Value	Total value farm machinery
1973	397	1.3	468	1.4	6.1
1974	319	1.5	319	0.9	10.8
1975	2576	13.8	1196	5.1	46.7
1976	2066	13.2	349	3.1	58.3
1977*	806	9.9	120	2.2	n.a.

SOURCE: International Bank for Reconstruction and Development, Agricultural Sector Review, 1979, Paper 9.

*January–June only.

The new Green Revolution initiative is in fact building upon the prototypical integrated rural development projects (IRDPs) initially sponsored by the World Bank in the early 1970s. Following MacNamara's famous 1973 speech in Nairobi, Bank lending increasingly supported agriculture and "reaching the rural poor"; this was a "new style" of rural development project providing an integrated package of technological and service inputs, ultimately to raise rural productivity and "increase production for the market" (World Bank 1975, p. 3).[42] Since 1963 the World Bank has eclipsed USAID as the principal donor to Nigeria, and by

1978 had loaned $295 million to agricultural projects (Olinger 1978, Williams 1980).[43] By the late 1970s there were nine integrated rural development projects, each catering to 60,000 to 80,000 farmers. During 1980 other loans were negotiated with the World Bank for projects in Sokoto ($168 million), Bauchi ($132 million), Kano ($142 million), and Ondo (₦59.6 million);[44] the Federal Director of Rural Development has apparently been assured that the Bank will assist the multiplication of such projects to all states by 1983 (*West Africa*, April 6, 1981).

The first IRDPs began in the North in 1975 on some of the richest farmland at Gombe, Funtua, and Gusau, with a combined expenditure of ₦98 million funded by the International Bank for Reconstruction and Development (IBRD), and the state and federal governments.[45] Each project posed rural stagnation as a function of inadequate infrastructure, inputs, or price incentives, which it provides. As Forrest noted, however,

> in terms of the IBRD policy paper, rural Hausaland appears to represent an "intact" social structure with well defined communities, authority structure and [without] gross inequalities of wealth or access to land [Forrest 1981, p. 234].

In the case of the Funtua project this working assumption covered 7,590 square kilometers and included 80,000 families spread over five districts in Funtua and Malumfashi local government areas. Ironically, however, the project distinguishes between traditional, progressive, and large-scale farmers who actually receive different treatment and different government subsidies.[46] In 1976–77 almost ₦1 million in inputs and credit were supplied; village heads assessed and identified credit-worthy farmers. In the following year, fertilizer was distributed on a first-come–first-serve basis, and distribution focused on large farmers who benefited from ox ploughs, tractors, sprayers, and insecticides. By 1978–79 sorghum accounted for 67 percent of the estimated value of production but cotton and maize had reached only 50 percent of projected estimates.

In spite of the purported smallholder focus of NAFPP and the IRDPs, the new Green Revolution package has important social and economic consequences for the countryside that threaten the future of the Nigerian peasantry. In attempting to capture rural producers through parastatal functions and subsidized inputs, the Nigerian government has actually encouraged large-scale production and promoted the participation of urban and rural elites in agricultural operations. In attempting to transform the forces of production by subsidization, the high demand for inputs discriminates against the rural poor, irrespective of their appreciation of fertilizer or insecticide utility. The scarcity of input works in favor of the bureaucratic elites, influential merchant-traders, and traditional aristocracies, in spite of the claims by the World Bank (1981) that individual rather than structural factors determine productivity (p. 20), and hence that "class" differences reflect "individual farming aptitudes" (p. 19). The expansion of rural credit for instance by the Agricultural Credit Guarantee Scheme entailed ₦30.9 million in 1980 but only 42.5 percent was approved; 68 percent went to livestock and poultry production and 10 percent to mixed farmers, both of which exclude the vast majority of small farmers (*African Business*, November 1981). Of the ₦5.2 million available for food production, credit worthiness stipulations favored wealthy peasants. The experience of the cooperative movement in Nigeria over the last twenty years clearly shows how such potential benefits are characteristically usurped by influential kulaks. In his study of three villages in Kano State, Matlon (1981) documents the substantially higher participation rate among village elites (sarauta, traders and bureaucrats) in government programs (table 8.20).

TABLE 8.20
VILLAGE ELITE'S SHARE OF GOVERNMENT REVENUE

Resource	Village elite	Tenth decile	Entire random sample
Household size			
Family size (av. no. of persons)	19.5	6.3	6.7
Number of wives	2.5	1.2	1.4
Av. size of farm (ha.)			
per household	11.4	3.2	2.5
per capita	0.58	0.51	0.37
Incomes			
Income (₦)			
per household	2,715	626	346
per capita	139	99	52
Participation in government programs			
No. of contacts with extension agent in last 5 years	5	0.3	0.3
Has bought fertilizer directly from gov't stores (% of heads)	50%	10%	1%
Kilograms of groundnut seed rec'd. in state gov't. relief program	277	24	6
Kilograms of improved groundnut seed rec'd. in seed multiplication program (Zoza only)	122	5	7
Kilograms on fertilizer received on credit (Zoza only)	145	13	17
Percent of household heads who attended adult literacy classes	50%	10%	8%
Percent of school-aged children in school	27%	11%	6%

SOURCE: Matlon (1981, p. 351).

In much of the North, village and district heads have huge discretionary powers in the selection of program participants and Matlon estimates that of total supplies to the three villages "20% was diverted for the personal use of selected members of the elite" (Matlon 1981, p. 352).

The agricultural development projects, in spite of their populist rhetoric, are actually oriented to larger-scale mechanized production.[47] The average farm size in the Funtua project is 4.1 hectares but the project aims to transform "all progressive farmers into large scale [100 hectare] farmers" (D'Silva and Raza 1980, p. 285).[48] In 1979 there were 186 large-scale farmers, 19,562 progressive farmers, and 66,438 traditional cultivators. Sixty percent of all extension visits concentrated on the progressive class, while the large-scale producers received intensive advice on design, implementation, and supervision of farm plans.[49] As the FADP observed in response to local criticism,

> I think your paper underestimates the influence of vested interests and the local hierarchy. A project on the scale of F.A.D.P. would not take off at all unless we had their support. This in turn means working through the system, rather than outside it. . . . It is not our job to start social revolutions. . . . Instead we prefer the "trickle down" approach from farmer to farmer, accepting that some will thereby benefit later than others. As a consequence, we concentrate on our notorious "progressive" farmers. [*New Nigerian*, March 10, 1978]

In any event, the project has actually failed to provide many of the purported service benefits; in 1980 only 520 kilometers of road had been built, and few villages had significantly improved their water or electricity supply, postprimary schools, or maternity centers since 1966. Additionally, if crop production has increased it has not occurred in the projected fashion, and prices have often been terribly depressed. In 1978–79 maize markets were saturated and farmers faced falling prices, while cotton lagged behind expected growth trajectories. Sorghum, conversely, dominated local production contrary to expectations.

The project has also been hampered by cash flow problems, budgetary overexpenditure on construction, poor marketing,[50] and low disease resistance in high-yield varieties (HYVs). More critically for the small farmer, heavily indebted and incapable of obtaining inputs, the possibility of further impoverishment is high. A class of "overnight" farmers from urban businessmen, civil servants, and district heads have been created by the strategic provision of subsidized inputs. As D'Silva and Raza put it, "the emergence of a landless class is a possibility for the first time in the area" (1980, p. 295).[51] According to the World Bank data (1981, vol 1), between 1976 and 1979 the percentage of farm holdings less than two hectares on the Funtua and Gusau projects increased from 36 to 47 percent and from 36 to 41 percent respectively, while the adopters of the integrated package were overwhelmingly "large, land-rich households" (p. 210).

The new Green Revolution strategy proposed in 1980 envisages a massive expansion of these schemes; between 1980 and 1985 a fivefold increase in cropped area by large-scale irrigation, a threefold increase in sugar estates and a fourfold expansion of large-scale mechanized farms. The World Bank projects—known officially as Agricultural Development Projects—will grow from 629,000 families (1980) to 3,831,000 (1985). A modified Green Revolution package will be supplied to so-called residual Accelerated Development Areas (ADAs) which will cover two-thirds of all Local Government Areas by 1983. The recently published Berg Report, moreover, sees these northern Nigerian prototypes as great successes in view of their size, incentive structure and effect. On these projects

> Trickle down theory worked because large farmers proved to be greater risk takers. [Berg Report 1981, p. 53]

It has been argued, however, that interventions by international finance capital such as the World Bank act less to foster agrarian capitalism properly defined than to stimulate expanded household commodity production and to consolidate a prosperous and politically quiescent middle peasant bulwark in the countryside (see Cowen 1981, Beckman 1981). In this regard de Janvry (1981) is right to point to the political content of integrated rural development projects insofar as they attempt to stabilize the functional dualism of peripheral capitalist economies. It is also reasonable to assume that World Bank projects expand commercialization in the widest sense. On the Funtua project for example fertilizer use doubled between 1976 and 1978, constituting 32 percent of total sales in Kaduna State; sales of mechanized equipment leaped as the number of service centers increased from eleven in 1977 to seventy-one in 1980. Moreover, the marketed surplus as a percentage of household production on the FADP grew from 0.1 percent in 1975 to 13.3 percent in 1979. And yet the Nigerian projects clearly exhibit the contradictions of such a purportedly smallholder emphasis, for on one hand political elites are able to establish large-scale enterprises with the support of the project bureaucracies, and on the other the projects themselves *establish the conditions for local accumulation through agricultural production.* Middle peasants in other words can and, as the World Bank data indicate, are becoming something else; namely, large-scale, capitalized agrarian producers. State intervention on ADPs lays the foundation stones for primitive accumulation; that self-sufficient, commercialized middle peasants may be transitory beneficiaries is perhaps to be expected.

THE MERCHANT-BUREAUCRAT ROAD

Although this trend remains relatively undeveloped, urban traders and bureaucrats are beginning to invest in agricultural production of typically high-value crops such as livestock and poultry. The high income elasticity of these products guarantees a rapidly growing market during the oil boom and they have the additional advantage of requiring little labor. Seasonal labor shortages, an overvalued naira, government subsidies, and the relative wealth of the merchants, dictate that such schemes are highly mechanized. This is especially clear in the growth of chicken farms in the immediate vicinity of Kano, and the tomato paste and livestock industries on the plateau. In the short run, of course, luxury food production does little to contain either wage food inflation or spiraling food imports, and indeed creates a powerful lobby strongly in favor of keeping feed grains such as maize and sorghum at depressed price levels. Ultimately, however, this particular mode of development is constrained by its relative profitability in relation to other rent-seeking activities (contracting, expanded trade, state patronage). The weak and contradictory nature of the private response strongly suggests that the food gap must be a state responsibility. The new flush of joint ventures between merchant capitalists and foreign agribusiness would not fundamentally alter this state of affairs since metropolitan capital also appears singularly interested in market widening and luxury food commodities.

AGRARIAN TRANSFORMATION AND CRISES OF THE STATE

The Fourth National Development Plan (1980–85) represents a new and expanded initiative in Nigeria's transition to capitalism. The general focus of the Plan is "increased self-reliance and considerable reduction of our dependence on the external sector" (Fourth Plan 1980, p. 20) through a massive commitment of federal funds. Total expenditures over the five-year period are estimated to be ₦82 billion of which ₦10.66 billion (roughly 13 percent) will be invested in the agricultural sector. A centerpiece of the new state intervention is a national food plan that aims at national self-sufficiency by 1987; to this end more than ₦2.3 billion have been allocated to the ADP/ADA projects alone, and anticipated purchases of fertilizer between 1981 and 1985 are in the order of ₦850 million. The strategy intends to further upgrade rural productivity—to systematically introduce farm machinery as the Minister of Agriculture put it—and rests on four short-term objectives. First, a targeting of smallholder production units through parastatal intervention. Second, an immense expansion of the ADP/ADA programs. Third, the encouragement of private sector development in production and private input provision. And fourth, the coordination and development of rural infrastructure. In 1981, the Shagari administration allotted ₦1.16 billion to achieve these ends, second only in magnitude to industry and roughly double the capital expenditure of the 1975–79 period.

The strategy of the Fourth Plan is inseparable, however, from several key assumptions, which underscore the fiscal basis of expanded state intervention. In particular, increased oil production and rising crude prices, the diversification of public revenue sources, a ceiling on recurrent government expenditures, and a revision of trade policies (especially imports) in relation to foreign exchange earnings, are all critical components for successful implementation. In the context of these obvious constraints, agrarian transformation in Nigeria must be situated in terms of the relative strengths and weaknesses of state power. I should like to consider in conclusion, then, the capability of the Nigerian state to manage the transition that it has initiated and to contain the contradictions thrown up in the process of capital accumulation. To pose the question in this way is to appreciate that the state and the class alliances that sustain it are subject to fiscal, legitimation, and administrative crises. What follows is a simple examination of possible sources of conflict that the Nigerian state may have to confront in the 1980s in view of its anticipated political and economic project.

First, there is the question of the managerial capacity of the state, the necessity of a disciplined, technocratically competent bureaucracy to plan and execute production (*the administrative crisis*). Most commentators note the gross inefficiency, mediocrity and corruption of state enterprises and administrative bureaucracies. In the course of two weeks in 1982 for example stories on the following subjects appeared in the Nigerian press: a not inconsiderable number of public officials high in the federal government were deeply involved in hemp-smuggling using diplomatic pouches; a Nigerian citizen left £0.5 million in a London taxi, while another made a present of £3 million to an Englishwoman; Dr. Olosola Saraki donated a total of ₦695,000 to various charitable institutions in his constituency, Ilorin, having accepted a ₦50,000 bribe from Leyland Motors; Richard Akinjide (Attorney General, Ministry of Justice) took a ₦120,000 bribe from Jamal Engineering Company under the First Republic, and stayed eighteen months in Ikoyi Hotel at government expense, running up a bill of ₦113,234; two senators awarded a contract for a new aircraft to a British firm and asked the firm to add ₦9 million to the bill paid by the Nigerian government, the sum to be split between the senators and the middlemen who arranged the deal; Governor Ibrahim of Niger State was found to be carrying ₦3 million on him when he visited London recently.

The 1970s were a huge spending spree, thoroughly disorganized and chaotic, in which civil servants, technocrats, and merchant capitalists canalized state revenues into their own coffers. In the course of events, millions of naira have mysteriously disappeared or surfaced in Swiss bank accounts. In 1979, for example, the Public Accounts Commission reported that the Nigerian Customs and Excise could not account for ₦8 million missing vouchers, that the Ministry of Finance had no listing of ₦2 billion of state investments (1970–74), and in a condemnation of bureaucratic management, that high-ranking civil servants had completely ignored the direction of routine duties (*West Africa*, November 9, 1981). In 1981 the Central Bank of Nigeria had no actual data on revenue and expenditure during 1981 (*Economist*, January 23, 1982). The problem is, as Lubeck (forthcoming) concludes, organizational and motivational, and the solution demands a structural transformation at the political level in terms of class discipline and at the bureaucratic level for reasons of efficiency.

Second, is the whole problem of resistance and class struggle in relation to state weakness (*the legitimation crisis*). This is perhaps most explicit in the urban areas, not only with rising crime and violence among the popular classes but the recurrent successes of the Nigerian labor movement in securing significant wage increases through the Adebo and Udoji commissions. In the rural sector, peasant resistance to the state is grounded in the individualized nature of household production, and already violent rural responses to étatist intervention have surfaced. In April and May 1980, 200 farmers were reported killed on the Bakalori irrigation project after they blocked roads and occupied offices following a compensation dispute (*West Africa*, May 12, 1980). Further, the success of the populist Peoples Redemption Party (PRP) in the 1979 elections in Kano and Kaduna states suggests that the 1970s has seen a broadening of the sociological basis of peasant resistance. The PRP governor of Kano State, Governor Rimi, has already claimed that his party has enabled the rural producer to remove the shackles of "the traditional [rulers], the Alkali [and] the police, who have been the state instruments of this oppression" (*West Africa*, October 20, 1980).[52] In addition, the PRP governor of Kaduna State, in direct opposition to the federal Minister of Agriculture, voiced his untrammeled opposition to the World Bank rural development projects that

> merely serve a handful of large-scale farmers who are basically urban dwellers, but who have taken away most of the benefits at the expense of the small peasant farmers in the villages. [*New Nigerian*, November 21, 1980]

Perhaps the most startling example of popular dissent was the 'Yan Tatsine millenarian movement of December 1980. An Islamic sect under the leadership of their prophet Alhaji Mohammed Marawa attempted to take over the Friday Mosque in the old city of Kano with the intention of seizing control of Kano. Blocked from reaching the Friday Mosque by the police, the 'Yan Tatsine took over a school, fought with and killed at least two policemen and then retreated into the 'Yan Awaki section of the old city. There they fortified their area, seized from fifty to sixty-five hostages and prepared to fight the authorities. After ten days of widespread disorder marked by vigilante groups seizing alleged followers, protracted fire fights between the police and the 'Yan Tatsine, and the breakdown of public order, the Nigerian army was called in on December 28. The army leveled the area and drove the rebels to a village outside of town where their leader died and a large number of his followers were either killed or captured. A tribunal of inquiry has gathered evidence and testimony from hostages and followers; estimates of the loss of life vary from 1,000 to 10,000.

The social and political views of the movement are related to the name "tatsine" which in Hausa means "to damn," in this case invoking the leaders' preaching style during which he damned all those who concerned themselves with modern materialism. His followers were told to carry only enough money to satisfy their needs for one day. During his stay in Kano (he had been expelled from the city around 1962 as well as from other Nigerian cities) he and his followers verbally and sometimes physically attacked merchants and landlords, and seized property in the area of 'Yan Awaki prior to the confrontation of December. In sum, 'Yan Tatsine involved an overt critique of the crude materialism and inequality that accompanied the petroleum boom in Nigeria. The movement was not solely a lower class revolt, but it was directed against the wealthier classes of Kano, especially those who ostentatiously flaunted Western life styles and consumption. The followers of the movement were largely *gardi*, a Hausa term meaning an unmarried man who wanders from community to community studying the Koran. The same institution also served as the base of the recruitment of industrial labor in Kano.

The social conditions that provided the underlying material causes for the 'Yan Tatsine movement are clearly critical. Prior to the petroleum boom the means of subsistence (food and housing) in the cities of Kano were cheap and available to the younger gardi Koranic students. Since 1973, inflation, drought, and the beginnings of a capitalist transformation of agriculture, have all exerted pressure on peasant households and undermined the traditional rural economy. These changes increased the flow of the rural poor through Koranic and other Islamic networks into cities like Kano. Once in Kano, however, the gardi found the climate much less hospitable than had been the case in the past, less because of a decline in charity and morality, but rather because of the high price of food and housing in a booming petroleum economy. Also, many of the jobs performed by Koranic students were eradicated by new techniques. Cement construction is replacing traditional mud and sun-dried brick construction, mostly because of the rise in the price of labor, and motorized transport is replacing cart pushing and head porterage. But most importantly, Kano has become a semi-industrial city, not merely a groundnut exporting center with household production units. Capitalism is developing alongside overcrowding and increased migration from the countryside; traditional charitable institutions find difficulty in maintaining aid as in the past. Though the system is overwhelming, at the same time there are visible changes in attitude toward the indigent. Violent crime and theft have increased enormously since 1970. 'Yan Tatsine, in this context, was expressive of the despair and frustration arising from the ashes of the oil boom, and indicates the extent to which the Nigerian state must directly confront and contain glaring class antagonisms.

The third aspect of state weakness is the dependence on oil revenue (*the fiscal crisis*). The 1978 oil cutback is instructive in this regard. Price and market conditions for petroleum were depressed and production dropped to less than two million barrels per day. Between 1977 and 1978 total government revenues declined by 10.9 percent and the proportion of direct taxes raised from oil profits plummeted by 25.3 percent. As a result the overall balance of trade worsened from a 1977 surplus of ₦537 million to a deficit of ₦2.147 billion. In real terms, capital expenditures declined by 28.1 percent between 1977 and 1978, but even more serious in welfare terms was the 39 percent reduction in education and the 56 percent cut back in health. These federal constraints were passed onto the states, reflected in a 14.3 percent cut in recurrent expenditures and a huge 44 percent drawdown in capital outlays between 1977–78 and 1978–79. The implications for balanced economic growth were, of course, quite disastrous.

The recent slump, however, due to an oil glut related to economic recession in the European Economic Community and North America, is much more serious. Production fell from 2.09 billion b/d in January 1981 to 0.64 billion b/d in August (table 8.21); the loss in oil revenues is expected to be about ₦4.3 billion for 1981 (*West Africa*, September 28, 1981). In August, Nigeria actually reduced the price of its oil by $4 per barrel, by which time foreign exchange reserves were supporting the import bill. By March 1982 Nigeria's external reserves had fallen from ₦5.7 billion to ₦1.2 billion over a nine-month period. The bulk of the Fourth National Development Plan is, of course, expected to come from the oil sector. Not surprisingly, the fiscal crisis has resulted in an austerity budget for 1982, and President Shagari has already forced the government to prune ₦1.0 billion from planned expenditures (*African Economic Digest*, Oct. 30, 1981). Most publicity has been given to the possible civil service cuts, and the import regulations of the April budget but the larger cuts must come from delaying capital projects; one-third of the planned projects are likely to be withheld. Significantly, the River Basin Development Authorities have already been cut from ₦1.55 billion to ₦0.21

TABLE 8.21
OIL PRODUCTION IN NIGERIA

Year	Barrels per day
1960	0.017 million
1961	0.046 million
1965	0.27 million
1966	0.42 million
1968	1.1 million
1969	0.54 million
1970	2.1 million
1971	1.53 million
1972	1.82 million
1973	2.3 million
1974	2.3 million
1975	1.81 million
1976	2.0 million
1977	2.25 million
1978	1.45 million
1979	2.4 million
1980	2.06 million
1981 (January)	2.09 million
1981 (February)	1.95 million
1981 (March)	1.86 million
1981 (April)	1.62 million
1981 (May)	1.16 million
1981 (June)	1.4 million
1981 (July)	0.77 million
1981 (August)	0.64 million

SOURCE: *Nigeria Trade Journal, Africa Confidential,* September 30, 1981.

billion (*African Economic Digest,* October 2, 1981). Though Nigeria is considered to be underborrowed internationally, it remains unclear what the vulnerability of oil dependence might mean for continuing the agrarian transformation.[53]

CONCLUSION

In a sense, at the time of Independence Nigeria lacked a national economy. Since agrarian household petty commodity production provided the material basis of the state, this form of production is only partially reproduced through the circuits of capital at the level of the national division of labor. Since capitalism was retarded, the state appeared as the only set of social relations at the national level (Bernstein 1980). At the same time, in 1960 the state class that had emerged since the Second World War had no organic connection with production, and hence had no base in civil society in terms of class fractions to whom it could specifically appeal. Up to the civil war, then, the postcolonial period witnessed the persistence of the agrarian economy with little qualitative development.

I have suggested that since the famine of the 1970s, this political economy has changed markedly, not least with respect to the agrarian basis of the postcolonial state. The petroleum boom permitted a strengthening of the state apparatus in a fiscal sense, with an ability to expand the bureaucratic class, and a capacity to regulate production through parastatals. The inability of the state, however, to effectively manage the process of capital accumulation resulted in a catastrophic stagnation of the agrarian sector, a process that had actually been developing throughout the 1960s. Because the state was relatively weak—if fiscally robust—in the face of a growing and militant urban working class, the provision of cheap food from 1972 onward was increasingly sustained by oil revenues, which permitted huge staple imports. Nevertheless, the food crisis could only be temporarily ameliorated by massive imports; since the Third Development Plan the state has embarked upon a somewhat contradictory strategy to prevent the wholesale erosion of the agrarian basis of the Nigerian postcolonial state. First, it has by-passed the peasantry altogether by state food production, although it is unclear how competitive (in global terms) these wage food schemes will actually be. Second, it has encouraged capitalist farming through irrigation projects and joint ventures with private foreign capital; the prime beneficiaries have been businessmen, bureaucrats, and wealthy traders, all with relevant contacts to banks and state institutions.[54] And third, a progressive farmer strategy in which subsidized inputs initiate a self-propelling transformation, reinforcing and accelerating processes of differentiation and concentration whose origins lay deep in the colonial period.[55]

The implications of the oil boom and the agricultural transformation for famine and famine relief are rather murky. Following 1974, the Third Development Plan made no specific commitment to food security per se though several state governments received support from an ineffectual National Committee on Desert Encroachment, principally for afforestation. A Federal Grain Reserve Scheme was expanded in 1981 to accommodate 250,000 tons of relief, but the national drive toward self-sufficiency and the river basin projects are seen as the real basis for future Nigerian food security. In actual fact, it is entirely unclear how large-scale irrigation projects perform under drought conditions, and whether they can indeed supply staples at competitive prices. There is every reason to expect that the rural development projects serve only to marginalize further the smallholders, who are most vulnerable to climatic perturbations (van Apeldoorn 1981).

It remains to be seen whether the Nigerian state can control and regulate the social contradictions it has unleashed. Material conditions remain highly explosive; gross domestic output stagnated in 1980, agriculture was "slow paced," and staple food prices continued to skyrocket, increasing by 82 percent between January 1980 and January 1981. In these circumstances of increased polarization and antagonistic social classes it seems possible that the Nigerian state may resort to sheer repression, managed under the ideology of a bureaucratic-authoritarian regime. In the last months of 1981 Peoples Redemption Party spokesmen were arrested and newspaper editors were placed in detention (*West Africa*, August 10, 1981). For the peasants, however, Barrington Moore is probably right when he says that under capitalism "sooner or later they are its victims." I suspect that what we are witnessing in Nigeria is the beginning of what John Berger refers to as a final act of historical elimination.

APPENDIX

HAUSA VERSE PERTAINING TO FAMINE

The following oral verse (*kirarai*) was collected by the author with the assistance of Mallam A. Saulawa during the summer of 1977 in Katsina town. The two informants were Sarkin Tabshi of Katsina, the emir's official praise singer, and Mallam Gumuzu, an ex-ward head in the eastern section of the town. All verse collected pertained to the famines of the twentieth century and have been elaborated with the use of footnotes to explicate the more subtle points. The references referred to in the Appendix are Reverend G. Bargery, *Hausa-English Dictionary* (London: Oxford University Press, 1934) and J. Dalziel, *A Hausa Botanical Dictionary* (London: Allen and Unwin, 1916). I would like to acknowledge the assistance provided by Professor Neil Skinner in the translation of these pieces. As in the body of the text, the verse presented here does not include the diacritical marks sometimes employed in the Hausa language.

Gyallare 1913–1914: Sarkin Tabshi, Katsina, 26/7/77

Gyallare, yunwa cikin ciki taka nisawa
Gyallare, ta shekara tana warin jakkai
Ba ni zuwa Yantumaki, ba ni zuwa Tsafe
Wa da kane na fada saboda kunun dussa.

Gyallare! Hunger that groans in the stomach!
Gyallare! That has a year long stink of (dead) donkeys!
I am going neither to Yantumaki nor Tsafe
Senior brother and junior brother are fighting over gruel made of bran.

Kakalaba 1914: Sarkin Tabshi, Katsina, 26/7/77

Kakalaba, bakar yunwa
Gyallare, mai sa maza kuka.

Kakalaba, black famine
Gyallare, making brave men cry.

515

'Yar Balange 1942: Sarkin Tabshi, Katsina, 26/7/77

'Yar Balange yunwar 'yan birni
Ba ka shuka gyeda ba ka ja gindi
Yau wani ya yi gabas bai karya ba
Mai dan Sanho[1] ta bi da maza !Sarkin Barna!

'Yar Balange! Famine of the townspeople!
You did not plant any groundnuts yet you move on your
buttocks!
Today one person went to the east without breakfast
Time of the little bag! Subduer of brave men! Supreme
destroyer!

[1] Another name for the famine throughout Kasar Katsina. *Sanho* is a "two handled bag of woven grass something like a workman's tool bag" (Bargery, p. 899); this refers to the bag people took to obtain relief.

'Yar Balange 1942: Sarkin Tabshi, Katsina, 26/6/77

Ina sarakuna? Ku dangina
'Yan Cikin Gida ku rage yanga
Kowa shi yi yamma[1] da sanhonai
Ba a kwalkwasa[2] sai an koshi
Abin tausayi na can kauye
Yandaki, Gafiya, Abdalawa,
Sun bi goriba[3] sun fyade ta
Dattijai suna fada Haben Birni
Yaran sun je wurin awo ba su samu ba
Ca suke rashin karfi ne wai
Abin ba rashin karfi ne ba
In takamark karfi mai taushi
Boran[4] Tagimba zaki mai karfi
Ya je bidar awon bai samu ba
Mun yi godiya Sarkin Yaki[5]
Garin rogo shi ne Kaura[6]
Madawaki goje gaban gayya
Bai bar mu mu kwana da yunwa ba
Sanho ne dari sai kai rogo
Don na ga taliyar Kaura an yi
Kuma na go tsattsafar[7] rogo an yi
An yi dambunai[8] da burabusho[9]
In an sa nono duk daya ne
Balle a yi teba[10] a gyara shi
Mun gode Tambara[11] matar Kaura
Da ta yi kwalkwasarta ta mowanci
Ta kashe bakwai ba su haura ba
Ga sarakuwa ga surukinta ana jan gindi[12]

Allah shi saukaka jam'a taro
Wannan shekara duk mun gurzu.

Where are you, princes? My kinsmen
You inhabitants of the palace you had better reduce your
   swaggering
Go to the West with your woven basket
You cannot show off on an empty stomach
Something pitiful is there in the country
Yandaki, Gafiya, Abdallawa,
Going from one dum-palm to another knocking down the nuts
Elderly men are fighting at Haben Birni
The children went to get relief but there was none
The elders were thinking that it was due to the children's
   lack of strength
But the whole issue is not concerned with strength
Even if strength is your boast, (you become) soft
Borau, husband of Tayimba, who has lion's strength
We went to get relief but could not get any
We thank the Chief of the Warlords
Cassava flour is the Kaura
Because I see macaroni made from the Kaura
Madawaki, lynch-pin, in the front rank of the army
He did not leave us to go to bed hungry
Only you can fill 100 baskets
And I have seen *tsattsafa* made of cassava
Similarly it is turned into *dambu* and *burabusko*
If you add milk, there's no difference[13]—still less if you
   prepare *teba* with it
We thank you Tambara wife of Kaura
For showing off, like the favorite wife she is
She (who) killed seven, not more[14]
Here is a mother-in-law and here her son-in-law pulling
   themselves along on their buttocks,
May God bring alleviation to the people, the whole lot of
   them
This year we have all suffered.

[1]Not geographically west, but refers to the market area where grain was distributed.
   [2]Flamboyance, provocative gesture (Bargery, "The character of a spoilt child" [Kats.]
p. 675).
   [3]*Goriba: Hyphaene thebaica*, Mart., (Palmeae), Dum Palm, *Kwalshi* is the edible kernel of
the unripe nut, eaten raw (see Dalziel, p. 40).
   [4]Borau was strong-man of the emir's court who had recently died.
   [5]The reference here is to *garin rogo*.
   [6]Chief of the war lords.
   [7]*Tsattsafa* (Bargery, "Thin wheaten cakes," pp. 1036–37).
   [8]*Dambu* (Bargery, "Flour with a small quantity of onion or Indiana hemp leaves
admixed and the whole steamed," p. 205).

[9]*Burabusko* (Bargery, "A Bare-bari form of *tuwo* made with coarsely ground flour," p. 132).

[10]*Teba*: paste made from *garin rogo* (cassava flour).

[11]Refers to the dorawa tree (locust bean tree, *Parkia filicoides*) the seeds (kaluwa) are made into fermented black cakes *daddawa* (see Dalziel, pp. 25–26). Due to lack of *garin rogo* for several days people ate *dorawa* products.

[12]*Jagindi* is another Katsina name for the famine; derived from *gindi* (buttocks) and *jagindi* (Bargery, "sort out groundnuts left in the ground after the plants have been pulled up"). The image is of people pulling themselves along on their buttocks (reminiscent of *jagindi*), associated with queuing up for relief. (See Bargery, pp. 1384–85.)

[13]That is, from millet food.

[14]This is an obscure reference.

Kwana 1927: Told by Mamman Gumuzu, age 87 years 5 months, Katsina, 25/7/77

Kwana bakar daga[1] hana jere[2]
Auren da ta kashe ya yi zambar goma

Kwana, evil charm, that prevents weddings, that dissolved
marriages to the number of 10,000

[1]*Daga*: word was unknown, possibly as suggested from Bargery (p. 188). Informant suggested it meant "suffering."

[2]*Jere*: according to Bargery this means "arrange all things in a row." In this context it refers to the decorative arrangement of calabashes by housewives on the inside of rooms.

Gyallare 1914: Mamman Gumuzu, Katsina, 28/7/77

Ayye iye raye,yeraiye iye raye raraye,
Allah ya sani Gyallare yunwa ce
Gyallare, dawar arewa mai dadin daka
Ina ka gano Gyallare?
Cikin dajin Dambo[1] tana karyar faru[2]
Allah ya sani ba ni zuwa Yantumaki[3] na ga abin tausayi
Uwa da diya na fada saboda kunun dussa
Allah ya sani ba ni zuwa Ketare[4] in ketare dangina
Allah ya sani ba ni zuwa Koda, yunwa na koda[5] tana ta fure
har tana zuba 'ya'yaye
Katakiri[6] ya sha tuwon bado har ya yi santi[7]
Ya ce ashe masara na cikin ruwa ba a gane ba
In dai Allah na ruwa talaka Bature[8] ne
Samari ku dau galma[9] ku huda kabewa[10] da yakuwa[11] a sha tafshe.

Allah he knows Gyallare is a famine
Gyallare! Northern guinea corn which is nice to pound
Where did you discover Gyallare?

In the bush of Dambo she is breaking neem branches
God knows I will not go to Yantumaki because the sight is
 so pathetic.
Mother and daughter are fighting over gruel made of bran
God knows I will not go to Ketare, to run away from my
 kinsfolk
God knows I will not go to Koda
Extreme hunger is abundant, is blossoming, is bearing fruit
Katakiri, ate *tuwo* made of water-lilies and said how good it
 was
He said "so maize grows in water and we never knew it!"
If God brings rain the peasant is a white man
Boys, take your hoes and ridge up pumpkin and sorrel so that
 we may drink *Tausche* soup

[1]Dambo is a village in Jibiya District to the northwest of Katsina, near the border with Niger.

[2]*Faru: Odina barteri*, indigenous neem. "A large tree with pinnate leaves and small berries" (Dalziel, p. 29).

[3]Yantumaki is a town about 30 miles south of Katsina now on the Malumfashi road.

[4]Ketare and Koda are two small and now rather unimportant emirate villages.

[5]*Koda* (Bargery, "Repair and sharpen the edge of a tool by beating; Roughen the surface of a millstone by beating," p. 617).

[6]Katakiri was a local Katsina character who was partially paralyzed.

[7]*Santi, fanya* (Bargery, "Passing complimentary remarks on food one is eating [considered very bad manners and as showing that the speaker is unaccustomed to good or well cooked meals]," p. 300).

[8]*Bature* is here associated with zaki (lion) and therefore strength, power and *wealth*.

[9]*Galma (garma)*: "The hand plough used for ridging . . . it is perforated being made of metal strips" (Hill 1972, p. 242).

[10]*Kabewa: Cucurbita pepo*, pumpkin or pompion. "A large cultivated gourd with harsh foliage and yellow flowers . . . gundar kabewa = the small immature fruits used in soups" (Dalziel, p. 52).

[11]*Yakuwa: Hibiscus sabdariffa*, red sorrel, rosella. "A cultivated plant with acid leaves and succulent calyx (usually red in color, used as a vegetable . . . daudawar beso = seeds boiled and crushed and the oil extracted, used in soup" (Dalziel, pp. 103–104).

Gyallare 1914: By Sarkin Tabshi; 26/7/77, Katsina town

Ayye iye raye, iye raye,
Ayye iye raye,
Kadan Sarki ya zo garin kallon rahi
Ayye iye raye, inna Sarki zai sauka?
Ayye iye raye, gidan baban kunu[1]
Kaura[2] ma ya taho garin kallon rahi
Ina zai sauka? Gidan baban kunu
Durbi ma ya taho garin kallon rahi
Ayye iye raye, ina zai sauka? Gidan baban kunu

Galadima ya taho garin kallon rahi
Ayye iye raye, ina zai sauka? Gidan baban kunu
Yandaka ma ya taho garin kallon rahi
Ayye iye raye, ina zai sauka? Gidan baban kunu
Sai ka dau hakuri dauki dangana kai ne babba.

If the king goes to visit the garden
Where will he lodge?
In the house of the giver of gruel
Kaura, too has come to visit the garden
Where is he going to lodge?
In the house of the giver of gruel.
Durbi too has come to visit the garden
Where is he going to lodge?
In the house of the giver of gruel
Galadima has come to visit the garden
Where is he going to lodge?
In the house of the giver of gruel.
Yandaka has come to visit the garden
Where is he going to lodge?
In the house of the giver of gruel.
Be patient, be resigned. You are the most senior.

[1]Literally "gruel-daddy"; refers to one household opposite what is now the Nassarawa primary school but was formerly the emir's lodge, which had large granaries and was supporting destitute children for some time.

[2]Kaura, Durbi, Galadima, Yandaka are traditional *sarauta* of Katsina emirate and refer to the district heads of the respective districts.

NOTES

CHAPTER 1

1. Officially, agriculture's share of GDP in most sub-Saharan countries is between 30 and 60 percent. But insofar as agricultural production is valued in relation to government producer prices (which are invariably below export or import parity prices) this is almost certainly a significant underestimation.

2. The index of per capita food production (1969–71 = 100) in the developing countries (excluding Africa) grew from 95 in 1966 to 102 in 1977 (FAO Yearbook 1977).

3. Total grain consumption per capita (kilograms) in sub-Saharan Africa fell from 142.5 in 1969 to 131.6 in 1975 (IFPRI 1977).

4. Over the period 1960–80, the growth of the 30 principal commodity exports in agriculture was 1.8 percent by value and zero percent by volume. Sisal, timber, and oil seeds experienced marked declines.

5. Wheat and rice were the fastest growing imports (roughly 11 percent per year). Food imports were especially high in Ethiopia, Ghana, Nigeria, Sudan, Tanzania, Zaire, Ivory Coast, Senegal, Congo, and Zambia.

6. See for instance the Berg Report (1981), otherwise referred to as the World Bank's *Accelerated Development in Sub-Saharan Africa: An Agenda for Action*, in particular chapter 5.

7. See Sorokin (1975), Cahil (1978), and Masefield (1963).

8. Some of the better recent work on the political and economic derivation of famine includes UNRISD (1977), Seaman and Holt (1981), Sen (1980), Laughlin and Brady (1978), Currey (1978), Shepherd (1980), Bhatia (1967), many publications in the Indian journal, *The Economic and Political Weekly*, and the work of the famine group of the East-West Center, University of Hawaii.

9. See Jodha (1975), Alamgir (1980), and Sen (1976, 1977) for excellent discussions of these issues in India.

10. By food production systems, I refer to complexes of human activity and interaction that affect the production, consumption, appropriation, trading, and circulation of food. Involved are a sequence of physical events—namely, the incorporation of energy, labor, and raw materials into food and the circulation of foodstuffs in circuits up to the point

of consumption—which are not static and immutable but constantly changing in response to ecological and socioeconomic influences (see UNRISD 1975).

11. For a representative sampling of geographic hazards work see White (1974, 1973), White et al. (1978), Kates (1971), Hewitt (forthcoming), and Torry (1979). Relevant writing on human or cultural ecology and ecological anthropology includes Clarke (1977), Grossman (1977), Clarkson (1970), Rappaport (1979), Bennett (1976), Orlove (1980), and Moran (1978).

12. See Anderson (1979), Anderson et al. (1977), Bartlett (1980), Lipton (1968), Moscardi and de Janvry (1977), and Roumasset (1976).

13. See Roumasset et al. (1979) and an excellent review of this book by Chibnik (1981).

14. See Binswanger (1978) and Jodha (1978a, 1978b).

15. In this sense social life is wholly overdetermined and it is denigratory to suggest that peasant economy can be reduced to a simple rationality.

16. For discussions of the purely climatic aspect of the Sahelian crisis see Winstanley (1973), Lamb (1974), Bryceson (1973), Newman and Pickett (1973), and Otterman (1974).

17. Similar arguments have been made by Meillassoux (1974), O'Keefe and Wisner (1977), Derriennic (1978), Wisner (1978), and Copans (1978). In much of this work, however, little attempt is made to specify the precise form of the relation between political economy and starvation.

18. This is implied by Sen (1977) when he states that the possibility of famine increases with the emergence of labor as a commodity, with neither the protection of the household system of peasant agriculture nor of social security.

19. Most Africanist writing on peasants would probably follow Shanin's (1971, p. 240) simple definition that "the peasantry consists of small agricultural producers who, with the help of simple equipment and [family] labor . . . produce mainly for their own consumption and for the fulfillment of obligations to the holders of political and economic power." For a critique of peasantries as a separate mode of production, see Ennew et al. (1977), Bernstein (1979), Friedmann (1978a, 1979b) and de Janvry and Deere (1979).

20. See for example Bundy (1979) and the Kenya debate, especially Cowen (1976, 1980) and Njonjo (1977).

21. See Harrison (1977), Kautsky (1899), Lenin (1964), and Tribe and Hussain (1981).

22. For a sophisticated variant of this view see de Janvry (1981).

23. See Amin (1974), Bernstein (1976), and Banaji (1973).

24. See Rey (1973), Post (1978), Taylor (1979), Foster-Carter (1977), Bradby (1975), and Bartra (1979).

25. Raikes (1978) has argued that the growth of middle peasants was (i) confined to Central Province and (ii) restricted to certain crops like tea. See also Peterson (1982).

26. As Foster-Carter (1977, p. 74) argues, to allow any empirical variation to define a new mode produces "inevitable inflation and debasement of the coinage: each Andean valley has its own mode of production, and individuals may change them two or three times a week like underwear."

27. For a similar argument with respect to Ghana, see Howard (1980). For northern Nigeria see Clough (1981).

28. See Wallerstein and Martin (1979), Braudel Centre (1978), and Friedmann (1979*b*).

29.

In simple commodity production the ownership of the enterprise and the provision of labor are combined in the household. As a result there is only one class directly involved in production and in the distribution of the product. Production and consumption are organized through kinship instead of market relations. The household purchases means of production, puts them in motion with its own labor, and owns the final product. The latter is sold to renew all elements of the productive process, which consist exclusively of productive and personal consumption. The basic condition for simple commodity reproduction therefore, is the continued re-creation of the integrity of the household as a unit of productive and personal consumption. [Friedmann 1979*b*, p. 559]

Also see Boesen (1978) and Kelly (1878).

30. Dattawa are expected to know the history of their communities; Usman noted that it was from them that basic information for resolving issues on land, housing, succession to office, and a variety of sociopolitical problems, were derived. See Y. B. Usman (1974, p. lvi).

31. In Great Britain the following sources were used: the Public Records Office, Kew; Rhodes House Library, Oxford University; the British Museum, London; the Commonwealth Society Library, London; and the University of London, School for Oriental and African Studies. In Nigeria the sources were: the National Archives, Ibadan and Kaduna; the libraries of the Universities of Ibadan and Ahmadu Bello; Nigerian Institute for Social and Economic Research; the Palmer Papers, Jos Museum; the Katsina Museum; the Katsina Divisional and Provincial Offices; and Kaita District Office. Various materials were also kindly supplied by the Institute for Agricultural Research Library and the Northern Nigeria History Project, both of Ahmadu Bello University.

32. Perhaps the assessment report to end all assessment reports was that compiled by D. MacBride, on Dawaki ta Kudu District, Kano Province, in 1937.

33. Many of the points raised here emerged from discussions with Sam and Jay Jackson, Richard Palmer-Jones, Paul Clough, and Louise Lennihan. See also C. Jackson (1978) and Palmer-Jones (1978).

CHAPTER 2

1. I have no idea whether Hausaland was *the* great unexplored region, as Polly Hill (1972, XIV) claimed in 1972, but it certainly cannot lay claim to that description one decade later.

2. See for example Triulzi (1981), and Bernstein and Depelchin (1978/1979). Much of this work has drawn heavily from the French Marxism of Godelier, Suret-Canale, Meillas-soux, Rey, and Coquery-Vidrovitch; see also Crummey and Stewart (1981) for an overview of this materialist work. For a recent review of the old genre see Curtin (1981) and more generally Zerbo (1981). The best work from a Nigerian historian in this regard is unques-tionably the spectacular writing of Yusufu Bala Usman (1977, 1978); in particular see his condemnation of the epithet "traditional" as a cover term for precapitalist formations in Africa, and his powerful epistemological treatise on historical recovery from European primary sources, such as Barth.

3. Of great relevance here are the vibrant, if polemical and fractious, debates among British historians centered on people's history and the new social history. See Thompson (1978), Anderson (1980), Samuel (1981), and various contributions to the journal *History Workshop*.

4. In this chapter I omit any detailed exegesis on the ecology and geography of the Hausa plains, which constitutes the primary emphasis in chapter 3.

5. As Sutton (1979, p. 104) aptly put it in describing the implications of Hausaization "[b]eing Hausa implied belonging to a wider, more open and receptive system, rural . . . but not rustic, one in which the countryside could support and interact with semi-urban centers where markets gradually developed and political power was increasingly focussed." See also Usman (1973) and Tahir (1975).

6. I draw heavily in this section on the brilliant work of Y. B. Usman who has charted the contours of the *sarauta* system in Katsina. In addition, I found H. F. C. Smith (1971), Greenberg (1946), Tahir (1975), and Nicolas (1975) useful.

7. These forms of worship were "naturalistic" in the sense that their peculiar meta-physic embraced the force of nature and the spiritual or cosmological powers surrounding the cycle of agricultural production. For a discussion of the *iskoki* pantheon among con-temporary non-Muslim communities see Faulkingham (1971), Nicolas (1975), and Barkow (1973).

8. The social division of labor between town and country in the Hausa states is, then, of considerable antiquity. Surpluses channeled to the capitals as tribute, taxation, or corvée labor were expressive of the new dynastic centralism. In the case of Kano, Sarki Tsaraki (1136–94) demanded tribute from rural dwellers, while his son Jaguji (1194–1267) col-lected a poll tax levied on each household to the tune of one-eighth of the domestic product. By the time of Muhammed Rumfa (1463–99), a regular revenue system had been formal-ized by a central treasury system.

9. For general introductions to the context of the jihad see Hiskett (1973), Last (1974), and Adeleye (1971); and for a discussion of the social roots of reformism see Waterman (1970), Stewart (1977), Waldman (1968), M. G. Smith (1966), and Usman (1973).

10. The malamai were given juridical and religious posts; territorial posts fell largely to the clan leaders and the Caliph's kinsmen who were given titles like "waziri," "galadima" and so on. Usman (1973) suggests, however, that the scholarly relatives of the Shehu, the *sarakunan yaki*, politically overshadowed all other offices.

11. "The Shari'ah was supported by deep-rooted public sentiment. The Islamicate social order presupposed a widespread loyalty to Islam, to the Muslim Ummah community. . . . This loyalty was not only a spiritual but a social virtue, in one sense a political virtue." (Hodgson [1974], 2: 119).

12. For an interesting Weberian analysis of the so-called Middle period of Islamicate history and the 'yan amir system see Hodgson (1974, pp. 91–135).

13. The palace cadre in Kano at the turn of the century consisted, in descending order of status, of the emir, twenty-three aristocratic sarakuna, twelve free nobility (hakimai), eleven military slave officials, the court ulema and the emir's men (the jekadu, the police, the clients). See Tahir (1975, p. 229).

14. "By virtue of the military and economic assets which these slave *hakimis* controlled through their official lieutenants, by 1893 it had become virtually impossible to effect any important measure without their concurrence. This was a new state of affairs attributable to the centralizing policies of Mohammed Bello, more especially his taxation reorganization which enhanced the power and influence of the *cucunawa*" (Fika 1973) cited in Lubeck (1977, p. 17).

15. Amin (1974, p. 74) makes a similar point:

In every pre-capitalist mode of production, the generation and the use of the surplus are *transparent*. The producers therefore cannot accept the extraction of the surplus they produce and of which they know they are the producers unless they are *alienated* so as to consider this extraction necessary for the survival of the social and natural order. The politico-ideological lever therefore necessarily takes a religious form and dominates the social life.

16. In my insistence on the centrality of the state I wish to dissociate myself from the so-called mosaic theory of classical Orientalism (see Turner 1978, p. 40). The mosaic theory poses Islamic society as despotic, factionalized, and presided over by circulating elites; the entire edifice is miraculously held together by the institutional mechanisms, values, and beliefs of Islam. What emerges is a tradition of intrigue, stagnation, and mosaic stratification in which class is unimportant in relation to tribe, ethnicity, and religion.

17. H. R. Palmer, NAK Katprof 2076 1905, no pagination.

18. For a fascinating analysis of the historically changing character of the dialogue and interchange between Arne and Muslim Hausa as "fractions ethniques" in Niger see Nicolas (1975).

19. It is worth recalling Weber's (1968, p. 1016) hypothesis on prebendalism; namely, that centralized patrimonialism is vulnerable to fiscal crisis unless the state can maintain central loyalty through economic growth and/or conquest. The Caliphate, insofar as it prospered in the second half of the century, did not face the possibility of decentering due to a financial inability to pay off imperial armies and state officialdom. See Weber (1968) and Turner (1978).

20. Last (1970) argues that a free bureaucracy was more developed in Sokoto than in palace-centered emirates like Kano, where personal slaves performed state functions. Fika's work (1978) has shown that Kano slaves were allocated specific responsibilities and the chief slave (*shamaki*) directed 50 titled subordinates.

21. Following Turner (1978, p. 50), by "prebendalism" I mean a system in which land is allocated to state officials, not as heritable property, but as a transient right to siphon tribute from the peasantry. See Weber (1968, p. 259).

22. Tukur (1979, pp. 341–42) makes the point eloquently in discussing Gwandu: "there were single towns which had no single overall sarakuna, an example being Ambersa which had no less than six headmen. Similarly in the emirate of Kano [in Kura district] . . . the town of Chiromawa contained 309 compounds or families of which 179 paid taxes to the headmen of Kadama, 30 to the headman of Ringimawa, 21 to the headman of Gorwa Baba and 16 to the headman of Mallam."

23. Bargery (1934, p. 146) in his famous Hausa dictionary defines chaffa as "attaching oneself to a person of influence for the advantage of his protection and in return being to a certain extent at his call."

24. Mr. Glenny, Kano Province, Barde District Assessment Report, 1909, NAK SNP 7 6166/1901. In Gumel emirate, Mr. Dupigny notes that the chaffa system is appropriation by a privileged class, usually resident in large towns, of the taxes of the talakawa who owe allegiance to them. He gives four examples of towns of 83, 84, 41, and 34 compounds of which 54, 43, 28, and 19 respectively paid chaffa. (Kano Province, Dawaki Tsakkar Gida District Assessment Report, NAK SNP 7/10 5570/1909, par. 78.).

25. For an intriguing discussion of this subject in Baure in the late nineteenth century see M. G. Smith (1978, pp.241, 242). Smith points out that both tarayya and sarauta systems operated simultaneously, though the latter was dominant: "At Baure tarayya patrons collected the tax and grain tythes from scattered subjects whose affairs they administered. . . . If the people of a town were dispersed under different [tarayya] officials . . . each [official] dealt with his subjects through a local headman (mai gari) who they elected. . . . Masu ga'i were expected to report relevant local developments to their lord as his jekada . . . they served as channels of communication" (M. G. Smith, [1978], p. 242). This is not unlike the *kofa* system described by Tukur (1981, p. 355) and Last (1967, p. 5), which according to Bargery (1934, p. 618) refers to an intermediary between two persons of different status.

26. In any case an entirely different picture could have been gleaned by Hill through a careful reading of Low's (1972) research in Hadejia: "There existed in short, a clearly defined hierarchical edifice, built of successively articulated clientage relations between men of government rank, with all free officials (but the meanest and the emir) at once patrons and clients, and hence a chain of command along which orders, requests and intelligence could move in culturally familiar ways. Cementing the layers of this pyramid were messengers (jekadu, sing. jakada), themselves either clients or slaves and often bearing a title, who lived much of the year in the settlements they were assigned to as agents of their superior" (Low 1972,p. 17).

27. Hausa describe hereditary occupations as *karda*, and achieved or adopted crafts as *shigege*. For a discussion see M. G. Smith (1978, pp. 37–40).

28. Whether secluded or not women were certainly active in petty trade (especially cooked foodstuffs), spinning and weaving, pot making, gathering, tree crops, and so on. Under customary law women could not own compounds, land, or other major capital assets, certain trees notwithstanding. To my knowledge almost nothing has been written on the political economy of women in the precolonial period. Useful summaries are contained in Ferguson (1973), Hill (1972), Pittin (1976), and M. .G. Smith (1978).

29. To enter into a statistical refutation of slave to free ratios is a relatively futile exercise in view of obvious measurement problems, save perhaps to note (i) the rather preposterous exaggerations by the European explorers, and (ii) the not inconsiderable geographic variability between high density emirates like Kano and low density counterparts like Daura. For detailed discussions of these and other institutional parameters see Lovejoy (1978), Hill (1975, 1977), Tambo (1976), M. G. Smith (1954), Hogendorn (1978), and Lovejoy and Hogendorn (1979).

30. Lugard commented specifically on slave rights and redemption.

Slaves were usually given opportunities of earning money, either by trading, or by cultivation, or by hiring out their labor after paying a fixed sum to their master; in other cases they were allowed to retain all of their earnings of a similar periodic payment; but from these earnings they had usually to provide their own food and clothing. They were generally allowed to purchase their redemption on the system known as Murgu under which a slave either paid a certain fee as earnest of his intentions, and was then free for a year (retaining his house and land) to work off his ransom money, or he paid off his board and lodging and could pay off the ransom by installments in his own time. . . . Self-redemption and ransom are of course only applicable to slaves born or long held in servitude and not to newly captured slaves or to others held illegally. [1918, p. 233]

31. Female slaves could marry other slaves in which case their children, though of slave status, became part of the owner's household, while children born of a slave woman and a free man were free on their owner's death. M. G. Smith (1978, p. 45) suggests, however, this may not have been the case in Daura, and in any case Hausa, as opposed to Islamic, practice is ambiguous on this count. M. G. Smith (1978, p. 421) gives an example of a sarkin bai (chief slave) in Daura who in 1900 left the following property in his estate: twenty slaves, twenty-three horses, thirty-five cows, thirty-seven boxes of robes, and twenty silver anklets.

32. Patterson actually goes on to argue that his definition of slavery is "represented legally as a condition of propertylessness and symbolically as a state of social death" (1979, p. 40). At this point, palace slaves become marginal to his rubric but, by the same token, I am entirely convinced by his argument that the Ottoman *ghilman*—a position not unlike the *bayan sarki* in the Caliphate—was fully slave in status. Like all other social processes "slavery is fluid, transitory and antithetical" (Patterson 1979, p. 47).

33. Economic structure does not denote a "mode of production" and is not synonymous with it. The latter I employ in the specific sense of the social properties of the production process: namely its purpose, the form of surplus labor appropriation, and the mode of exploitation (Cohen 1980, p. 80). I return to this nexus of properties later in this chapter.

34. Any economic structure can consist of a heterogeneous collection of production relations; society is never constituted solely by serfs, slaves, proletarians, cooperative laborers, or independent producers. But as Cohen (1980, p. 78) observes "there will be no unordered melange of slaves, serfs and proletarians." Rather, there will be a dominant relation binding immediate producers.

35. In any social formation, there is a variety of labor processes by means of which the appropriation of nature is organized. Under feudalism, for example, labor processes based on cooperation, labor service, wage labor, and tenancy can coexist while subsumed within a dominant relation.

36. Yet the Hausa birane were wholly urban no matter how protean the term. The demographic estimates of birnin Kano in the nineteenth century vary from a realistic 30,000 to a rather unrestrained flight of fancy by Robinson who, in 1894, flaunted a figure of 100,000 (see Frischman 1977). By all other canons the Caliphal cities were genuinely urban; encouraged by a firm if discrete urbanization policy, the birane were creators of effective space, nodes in a central place hierarchy, loci in webs of administered trade, and imbued with the cosmo-magical symbolism of Muslim urbanity (see Wheatley 1972). The Hausa cities were labyrinthine and aleatory in the classical tradition of Islam; they constituted the cells of a political community and maintained a corporate and relatively autonomous existence. For a discussion of the urban economy of jihadi Kano see Lubeck (forthcoming).

37. Imam Imoru's inventory of fadama crops is enormous, including rice (*Oryza glaberrima*), wheat (*Tritium vulgare*), indigo (*Indigo arrecta*), cotton (*Gossypium* spp.) and a plethora of fruits like pawpaw, mango, and lime.

38. Perry Anderson (1975, p. 501) in his exegetical remarks on Islamic civilization remarks that "horticulture always occupied a special position within Islamic agrarian systems. . . . [Because] the gardens . . . were exempt from the state ownership of soil . . . [h]orticulture formed . . . a 'luxury sector' in industry, patronized by the rich and powerful."

39. Foureau's comments on turn-of-the-century Zinder are revealing and insightful.

the irrigation ditches diverging from the well are well taken care of; each small garden is enclosed by a fence made of dry branches, or by a thicket hedge. Here and there I saw three or four date palms, numerous papaya trees, tobacco, pimentos, onions, hemp, pumpkins, watermelons, castor-oil plants, and finally a few beds of cotton. The natives carefully manure these gardens and I observed manure in perfectly groomed heaps, waiting to be spread. [1902, p. 499]

40. The chemical fundaments of the tanning process, various textile dyes, silk industry, artisan practices such as mat making, and a complex Hausa pharmacopaeia were all sustained by wild and semicultivated plants and grasses endemic to the Hausa plains.

41. I am aware of the existence of large-scale manufacture—gandu and slave-based leather production for instance described by Tahir (1975, p. 29217) in Kano—but the presence of merchant-ulema enterprises and a highly developed exchange economy is not incompatible with my judgment that both remained subordinate to household production. In fact these "corporations" were large patrimonial households.

42. Cohen (1980, pp. 80, 81) has an excellent discussion of gradations in the production of commodities for exchange. There is, for instance, an important distinction between an item produced for exchange, for exchange-value, for maximum exchange-value, and for capital accumulation.

43. This is the basis of Hill's preposterous claim that Dorayi, located within walking distance of birnin Kano, has few ties with one of the most robust and rapidly growing metropolises in West Africa. In doing so she not only neglects information to the contrary in her own text but also completely misrepresents the economic social texture of the Kano close settled zone. See Shea (1981) on historical ties between Dorayi and the city economy, and Lubeck (forthcoming) on rural-urban commuters.

44. This sentiment has been admirably expressed by Tahir in his discussion of Kano.

We note that for Kano almost every *Ulema* family has a dual-Scholastic aspect. Individuals generally, particularly among the numerically large base of struggling and middle levels of Society, tend to treat the commercial and scholastic roles as alternatives depending on the greater profitability of each and the general climate of competition in both. [Tahir 1975, p. 27]

45. Nicolaisen (1963, pp. 209–13) estimates that millet consumption among Touareg is 150 kilograms per person per year, a quantity far exceeding the domestic production of northern or southern estates and gardens.

46. Hausa-organized caravans brought millet, leather goods, and cloth to Agadez in exchange for livestock and salt. The Touareg sent clients to Bilma in October and November returning with salt and dates, and were then joined by Touareg men and their livestock. These caravans terminated in the Hausa birane and the large rural markets of the northern emirates (Collion 1981; Baier 1980).

47. See Stenning (1959), Hopen (1958), Dupire (1962), and Sutter (1980) for a discussion of these patterns of exchange among contemporary Ful'be.

48. Usman (1973, p. 13) observes that

The importance of pastoralism in the commerce of the Kasar Hausa, for example, is reflected in the position that the *sarakunan pawa* occupy in market organization from an early period. The *runji* or *mahauta* were not only butchers but also livestock brokers involved in all types of commercial livestock transaction. Wealthy Fulani clans like the Yerimawa of Ingawa in Katsina and some of the Wodabe had their own *runji*."

49. "The division of labor as the aggregate of all the different types of productive activity constitutes the totality of all the physical aspects of social labor as labor producing use-values" (Marx 1971, p. 51).

50. The gida consisted of a core of males descended in a patrilineal line from a common ancestor, usually the first man to have cleared land in the vicinity of the village. Residence in the gida was almost exclusively patrilocal: wives on marriage move to their husband's compound and daughters born in the gida marry into other gidaje. Two basic types of household organization can be distinguished that relate to the cycle of growth and segmentation of the gida's patrilineal core. The nuclear household (*iyali*; pl. *iyalai*) denoted a man, his wife or wives, children (real or adopted) and other dependents. Composite household units (*gandu*; pl. *gandaye*) contained two or more male adults and their respective families. Strictly speaking, gandu may be either paternal (between fathers and sons) or fraternal (under control of the eldest brother upon the father's death). Clearly the detail of each gandu form and the predominance of each type has changed historically. Fraternal gandu was much more prominent in the nineteenth century but is now seen as a transient and temporary phenomenon. See Imam Imoru's useful historical discussion in Ferguson (1973, pp. 199–244).

51. In return for family labor on collective gandu fields, the mai gida had well-defined responsibilities, including the payment of tax, the provision of subsistence, shelter, marriage expenses, and an obligation to give personal plots (*gamana*) to married sons and brothers (see Greenberg 1947; M. G. Smith 1955; Hill 1972; Nicolas 1965; and Raynault 1972).

52. Gayya, according to Bargery, is the "collecting together of a number of people to assist another in some piece of work" (1934, p. 375), and in the past included nonagricultural tasks such as house construction and well digging.

53. The Katsina Resident reported that "it is apparently usual for large groups of . . . Asbenawa . . . to move south to Galadima District and hire themselves out for work on cotton farms. . . . They are known as "wawan Kanawa" (NAK Reports, 1909). Also early reports from Yabo and Silame Districts of Sokoto Province indicate an extensive hired labor system of some antiquity in which laborers from Wurno and Gwadabawa went to the Gulbin Kebbi region for rice cultivation. Known locally as "yanga aiki" or "yanga lada," they worked from 6 a.m. to 2 p.m. and received 3d per day plus food. See NAK SNP 10 230/1913 Silame District Assessment Report, Sokoto Province, Capt. Foulkes, par. 121, and NAK SNP 10 Yabo District Assessment Report, Sokoto Province, p. 70. Shea (1975) and Tahir (1975, pp. 277, 278) both reported the use of hired labor in the Kano textile and leather industries, the latter being paid 500 cowries per unit of *sanwa* (processed skin). At the turn of the century Imam Imoru described masons (*magina*) and construction workers (*yankwaba*) who were fed by their employees and paid respectively 1,000 and 300 cowries at the end of the task (Ferguson 1973, p. 337). Porters (*yan alaso*) were also de facto wage laborers who, as the Hausa epithet has it, "yan alaso baka asara sai gamno" ("[have] nothing to lose but their head cushions"). See also Bello (1978, p. 22) and Freund (1981) for other information.

54. This was obviously not an economy of individualized private producers where every producer must exchange in order to reproduce. In the Caliphate there was no massive separation of direct producer from the means of production, and doubtless those who labored in the dry season were in any case wet season farmers. Furthermore, the process of proletarianization is, as Marx observed (1973, p. 502), one of gradual dissolution. In this sense Tahir (1975, p. 277) is probably correct in his surmise that kwadago in Hausaland maintained a patrimonial quality insofar as wage laborers were attached to big men who lent grain and acted as patrons though there was no formal client relation. In this sense labor was not entirely "free," but what Marx called "potentially free."

55. Jigawa cultivation relied on locally produced hoes (*fartanya*), hand plows (*galma*) and axes (*masassabi*). Last (1978, p. 44) implies that the distribution of these simple iron implements was far from universal even in the nineteenth century.

56. Last (1978, p. 27) has noted that the introduction of the shaduf for fadama cultivation in Sokoto and a small sugar refinery were important technical innovations in the nineteenth century.

57. Ownership confers a range of rights with respect to the use of an object, to appropriate income generated by it, to destroy or transfer it as property and so on. The spectrum of rights over labor and the means of production held by serf, slave, proletarian, and independent producer clearly vacillate along a gradient of ownership (see Cohen 1980, pp. 63, 64).

58. Hindess and Hirst (1975, p. 189) point out that this nonseparation results from the limited development of the wage labor relation, a retention of a portion of the household's domestic product, a low level of division of social labor, and the reproduction of the economic conditions of production within the unit of production; these conditions were all met in the Caliphate.

59. In Kano at the turn of the century, kharaj was 4,000 cowries near the city walls and 1,170 cowries in the less populated peripheral districts; see Kano Province Economic Survey 1909, p. 8 (provided by Dr. P. Lubeck).

60. *Jisi'ah* was a legitimate poll tax on conquered non-Muslims, while death duty (gado) in Hausaland had, in Buxton's words (1916, p. 371), "a perfectly lawful foundation."

61. Hodgson (1974, I, 98) points out that revenues were levied by no means in accordance with Shari'a but according to "decrees and formal contracts," "local custom," and a "balancing of multiple interests," which was characteristic, he feels, of the 'yan amir system. But it is clear from his discussion that Shari'a provided the legitimacy for tax appropriation.

62. Labor rent supposes the separation of necessary and surplus labor time and is the basis of Lenin's corvée economy. Rent in kind does not presuppose the separation of the land of the direct producer from that of the landlord, but surplus assumes the form of a part of the domestic product. Money rent supposes the existence of a form of money, a commoditization of the economy, and a social division of labor between town and country. For a useful discussion see Hindess and Hirst (1975, p. 191).

63. According to Cargill (cited in Paden 1968, p. 1010) zakkat was the "granary of the Emir. . . . The ruling class and more especially the Emir and his huge following practically subsist on the zakka, the whole Emirate forming a sort of granary from which they drew supplies as they wanted."

64. Cargill's minute on shuka and rafi taxes in Kano is fascinating.

There is a general principle underlying all *Shuke* and *Karofi* assessments, *viz* that rates are heavier for towns near markets, than for towns who have to bring their produce a long distance to market or are in the bush. At Bagwoi where nearly all the alkamma (wheat) is grown there is a special custom regarding alkamma. Once a man has planted wheat, he must continue to pay the assessed tax on his first crop, (which varies according to size) each succeeding year, whether he plants or not; the tax becomes in fact a permanent ground rent on that plot, so long as he continues to hold it. [Kano Province Economic Survey 1909, Resident Cargill, p. 12]

This supports Shea's belief that, through taxes on petty commodity production, the state was able to directly regulate local production.

65. Barth estimated that in 1851 the total tribute levied by the emir of Kano amounted to 100 million cowries, nine-tenths of which came from the kudin kassa at a rate of 2,500 per household (see Gowers 1921, p. 50).

66. Morel also mentions the preferential tax system in manufacture.

The Hausa system provided that taxes be levied upon basket and mat makers, makers of plant for cotton spinners, bamboo door makers, carpenters, dyers, blacksmiths, and white smiths as well as upon bee keepers, hunters, trappers, and butchers. Exemption from taxes was granted to shoe makers, tailors, weavers, tanners, potters, and makers of indigo. [Morel 1911, p. 120]

67. Zaria's rate of kudin kassa rose from 2,000 cowries per hoe in 1860 to 6,000 in 1890 (Lubeck 1968, p. 14).

68. "The theory of Islamic law has thus developed only a few rudiments of a special law of real estate; conditions of land tenure in practice were often different from theory, varying according to time and place" (Schacht 1964, p. 142).

69. The colonial administration was obviously confused over the land tenure issue. Much of the testimony given to the Northern Nigeria Lands Committee in 1908 was vague, misleading, contradictory, and often pure speculation. Resident Temple at least conceded that he simply did not know and was in "deep water." The confusion stems in part from the enormous variation in local custom, in part from the rigid adherence to property concepts of

bourgeois origin that were not directly applicable to Hausaland, and in part to the colonial insistence that no form of private property could possibly exist in Hausaland (see Northern Nigeria Lands Committee 1910).

70. Strictly speaking most land following the jihad was territorial wakf by right of conquest: this consisted of (i) Sokoto and Gwandu as tithes in the sense that they constituted the Islamic heartland during the jihad and hence were tax exempt; and (ii) tributary or *kharaj* lands, namely the remaining emirates, which were juridically under jihadi hegemony by right of conquest, and were therefore subject to kharaj taxes. See Ega (1980, p. 89).

71. In this sense it is critical to distinguish between *possession* (the ability to put the means of production into operation) and legal *ownership* (the power to appropriate the means and dispose of the object of production). See Taylor (1979, p. 284) and Corrigan (1980, pp. 3, 4). Cargill was very much to the point in his observation that kharaj (or kudin kassa) was an ancient family tribute for the right of cultivation on hereditary property, "it implies that a man possesses land" (Kano Province Economic Survey 1909, p. 6).

72. Marx went on to point out that property is nothing other than an exposition of the social relations of production.

73. Land known as "hurum" refers to rights of occupancy based on some former services rendered to the state by ancestors of the occupiers. "Haraji" holdings or official farms (gandu) were attached to most of the political offices. Chaffa holdings were those in which an individual could extract bribes above the taxation level in lieu of protection and other services from the tenant. See Shea (1975, p. 41).

74. Many of these practices enabled a farmer to raise money on (or dispose of) land without a *de jure* sale! Loans and rental occurred but over short duration fearing loss of possession. Pledging existed but land was redeemable in perpetuity. As Frischman (1977, p. 72) observes, the latter was a form of sale but "the fact that the land could always be bought back by the original owner made it distinct."

75. Palmer (NAK SNP 4846/1908) admitted as much for the Kano zone which he saw as an "Arab influence." Withers Gill (NAK SNP 17/8 2252/1909) quotes turn of the century farm sales in Zaria as follows: 30,000 cowries (18/6d) for an upland farm yielding 100 bundles; 300,000 (£3.–2.6) cowries for a sugar holding.

76. Cargill (Kano Province Economic Survey 1909, pp. 6, 7) felt that in Kano where "no new land is available" the kudin kassa had become a fixed rate (*kai-ida*), which implied "a fixed tax associated with certain family property" regardless of the original owners. These farms, which were by definition regularly traded (i.e., the historical familial connection had been ruptured) were called *gonar kurdi*. I take this to be indicative of the changing and indeterminate quality of property relations under conditions of land scarcity and widespread commoditization.

77. Following Taylor (1979, pp. 106, 107) I take social formation to refer to the totality of economic, political, ideological, and theoretical practices in a concrete historical context. While the economic structure is my analytic starting point, the peculiar correspondence of the labor process with the social relations of production provides an illumination that colors the entire formation.

78. This is what Cohen refers to as the "social mode of production."

79. These authors actually continued the theoretical lineage spawned by Godelier (1978, pp. 240–43), who argued that the great Sudanic kingdoms were essentially Asiatic in form though the material basis of the state rested on aristocratic domination of long-distance trade rather than on an interposition in peasant production.

80. Coquery-Vidrovitch specifically argued that

The taxes raised with the aid of ruling classes by the sovereigns who here and there assumed power were hardly levied on the peasants since Africa was precisely the place where agriculture was least able to produce a surplus . . . the prestations or other economic obligations had primarily the symbolic role of guaranteeing the social structures. [Coquery-Vidrovitch 1976, p. 105]

81. For a critique of the exchange-dominated view see Brenner (1977).

82. The Asben and Bornu circuits involved trading livestock, salt, leather, ivory, gold, cloth, ostrich feathers, and the like northward while importing cloth, beads, swords, blades, brass, copper, scent, paper, horses, and utensils. The Gwanja trade was dominated by kola, livestock, and cloth, largely organized by Kano-based merchants of Beriberi and Agalawa origin. See Usman (1973), Baier (1980), and Lovejoy (1972).

83. As the nineteenth century progressed, international trade items increasingly entered local exchange circuits. With the expanded commoditization of the Caliphate economy, the dominance of merchant capital, and the growth of agricultural production this is to be expected. But it does not alter my argument concerning the extent to which trade per se sustained the entire state system.

84. "On the basis of every mode of production, trade *facilitates* the production of surplus products destined for exchange. . . . Hence . . . all development of merchant's capital tends to give production more and more the character of production for exchange-value and to turn products more and more into commodities" (Marx 1967, I, 326, 327).

85. Lovejoy and Klein (1979, p. 208) feel that in a statistical sense it is hard not to talk of a slave mode of production where half to three-quarters of the populace is enslaved. See also Terray (1974), Kilkenny (1981), and Roberts (1981). Parenthetically, I am not aware of any evidence, save for the confused speculation of Richardson and Clapperton. that hazards a free to slave ratio of 1:1 for the Caliphate *as a whole.*

86. I remain unconvinced by the arguments of Padug (1976), Anderson (1974), and Hindess and Hirst (1975) on the slave mode except in a very limited sense of a material way of producing things. There is nothing in the nature of slavery that implies a given economic organization (see Patterson 1979, pp. 47–52).

87. See M.G. Smith (1978, p. 44) for Daura. In Kaita where I lived during 1976–78, historical reconstruction revealed that just less than 10 percent of the community was captive in about 1900. The vast majority (80 percent) were held by the resident hakimi and several Fulani merchants and traders.

88. "The transition from slave to free labor was achieved without widespread economic and social dislocation" (Hopkins 1973, p. 227).

89. Smaldone (1977, pp. 160, 161) suggests that slave acquisition may have been prohibitively costly by the last quarter of the nineteenth century. This would suggest

perhaps tighter labor control, reduced manumission, or new forms of quasi clientage that masters might exercise over their ex-slaves.

90. As Cooper (1981, p. 22) suggests, slave rights emerge as a result of struggle and resistance; "slaves tested the limits of exploitation by working poorly, disobeying orders." Manumission helped prevent the crystallization of a self-conscious slave class but required continual importation of slaves. Last (1967, p. 199) states that the Caliphal viziers' most common complaints pertained to "slave problems," and Tahir (1975, p. 330) speculates that on the slave estates passive resistance was widespread. Until we know more of these pressures in the Caliphate the dynamics of slave development and manumission must remain obscure.

91. M.G. Smith (1965) refers to Rowling's Kano land tenure study in which he suggests that ex-slaves working on gandun sarauta work their own portion in exchange for their labor on the part the officeholder retains himself.

92. Sutter (1981) has situated Damagaram within a lineage mode of production in which relations of production are materialized through systems of prestation, redistribution, and reciprocity (see Meillassoux 1978). In this system, there is less control over the means of material production than of human reproduction (i.e., subsistence and women). However, I fail to see the utility of this formulation; in the Hausa emirates corporate lineages and the lineage concept were not widespread, and in any case it treats the agrarian economy in splendid isolation from the state apparatus.

93. For an excellent discussion of this point see Poulantzas (1978, p. 18) and Corrigan (1980, pp. 1–25).

94. This is, of course, a thoroughly Gramscian notion in which "The state is the entire complex of practical and theoretical activities with which the ruling class not only justifies and maintains its dominance but manages to win the active consent over whom it rules" (Gramsci 1934, p. 244).

95. Hindess and Hirst (1975, p. 195) point out that under these conditions the level of exploitation, the number and character of exploiters, and the mode of consumption of the surplus product (conspicuous consumption, monumental architecture) is politically-ideologically determined. In the Caliphate, I tend to believe that Last (1978, p. 25) is near the mark in his suggestion that levels of consumption by official households were relatively low though the number of consumers may have been high.

96. As Marx (1973, p. 858) observed, "Trade will naturally react back in varying degrees upon the communities between which it is carried on. It will subjugate production more and more to exchange value. . . . [It] dissolves the old relations. Thereby increases money circulation. First seizes hold of the overflow of production; little by little lays hold of the latter itself. *However the dissolving effect very much depends on the nature of the producing communities between which it operates*" (emphasis mine).

97. "In the commercial sphere, sheer financial and material superiority supported by acclaimed mystical powers obtained through commerce with the *ulema* and *baraka* from Allah sustained the dominance of big *attajirai* (merchants)" (Tahir 1975, p. 268). The ulema could be significant merchant-producers in their own right. Tahir (1975, pp. 308–11) describes the case of Mallam Ibrahim who was the centerpiece of a craft-ulema network embracing seven slave gandaye and thirty independent clerics.

98. Brenner (1977, p. 37) makes the point that:

[W]here the direct application of force is a precondition of ruling class surplus extraction . . . economic surplus is diverted from reproductive to unproductive labor. Correlatively, where the family [form] predominates . . . [it] hinders even the elementary steps toward the development of the specialization of labor.

As I have tried to elucidate, the peculiar conjunction of class forces in Caliphal society had in fact loosened these constraints.

99. In light of this resumé, Amin's (1972, p. 507) formulation of a tributary mode of production—"the persistent parallel existence of a village . . . and a socio-political structure [which] exacts tribute"—greatly impoverishes the socioeconomic texture of Caliphate society."

CHAPTER 3

1. Paradoxically, Le Roy Ladurie is skeptical of the long-term impact of climate since "in the long term the human consequences of climate seem to be slight, perhaps negligible, and certainly difficult to detect" (1971, p. 119). However, it appears to me that this is not a conclusion readily derived from his own work and perhaps reflects an emphasis on the impact of discrete climatic *events* rather than on climatic *trends*.

2. "The reason that the harm done, over longer time periods, is often . . . slight is that in the long run societies adjust. Even primitive technologies have some capacity for adaptation. In measuring the human consequences of climate change our attention should be focused on those processes of adaptation" (de Vries 1980, p. 630). Speaking as a historian, de Vries's comments are entirely legitimate and certainly accord with this book. Reading his remarks as a geographer or ecological anthropologist is, however, a little discomforting since adaptation has been the focus of both of these disciplines for over twenty years (Sauer 1957; Alland 1975; Robson 1978).

3. See Post (1973), Claxton and Hecht (1978), Alexandre (1977), and Lamb and Ingram (1980) for a representative sampling.

4. For relevant discussions of annual fluctuations on economic and social life in Europe see de Vries (1977), Post (1977), and Alexandre (1977).

5. The identification and impact of periodic climatic cycles has a long standing and impressive intellectual pedigree from Malthus and Jevons to Lord Beveridge. At worst, the identification of periodicities is Rorschach testing under another name. On British data alone, 7, 11, 22, 80 and 100 year cycles have been identified. In the West African context where meteorological data are, at best, eighty years young, this sort of exercise is in my opinion preposterous.

6. What matters here is climatic variance in relation to survival and livelihood. This may be conceived, in part, as a problem of risk; it directs attention for example "away from measuring the change in the average yield of wheat toward identifying alterations in the crop mix" (de Vries 1980, p. 625).

7. The types of information utilized by Nicholson (1979) include lake-level variations; vegetation and landscape; changes of stream regime and river levels; reports of famines,

droughts, and floods; climatic descriptions; and meteorological reports from colonialists and early European travelers in Africa. Early geographical journals, historical chronicles, archives, travel journals and settler's diaries, ships' logs, maps, and colonial records as well as geological and palynological studies are useful sources.

8. Because the principal intent of this chapter is not a rainfall chronology or climatic reconstruction, the limitations of historical sources are not critical. I wish to show, from admittedly limited materials, that spatiotemporal variation in precipitation has been a recursive feature of Sudano-Sahelian climate. There have clearly been short periods of greater or lesser dryness—periods of climatic anomaly as Nicholson refers to them—but the broad climatic contours have been relatively stable since 4500 B.P. Nicholson has rightly emphasized the complex and varied forms of rainfall instability (i.e., to depart from simple notions of wetness-dryness or north-south oscillations of climatic systems). But my concern here is not the etiology of rainfall anomalies as much as a simple documentation of their historic antiquity and a correlation of the regularity of drought occurrence in the recent past.

9. Rainfall "is undoubtedly the most significant climatic factor in Africa as a whole as temperature has a relatively small annual range and wind is [of] low speed" (Griffiths 1972, p. 7). It is significant that the Hausa view drought as *the* most significant environmental hazard, and that it is cognitively inseparable from its most extreme effect, famine. Many Hausa farmers, in the course of discussion, reiterated that "yunwa da fari, duk daya ne" ("drought and famine, it's the same thing").

10. In a recent book two anthropologists have posited this relationship in the following way: "if a decremental shift in basic resources is due to recursivity in the environment of an individual organism, society will at all times be organized to respond and adapt to that eventuality" (Laughlin and Brady 1978, p. 47).

11. Sahlins (1976, p. 88) referred to this view as a type of "ecology fetishism" in which marriage becomes genetic interchange and cannibalism a subsistence activity. Jonathan Friedmann (1979, p. 259) is correct in pointing out that systems (especially the social variety) need not be cybernetic in order to be systems.

12. "Chaque niveau d'organisation sociale a des effets spécifiques sur le fonctionne-ment et le reproduction de l'ensemble de la société et par voie de conséquence sur les rapports de l'homme avec la nature . . . c'est seulement en tenant compte du jeu spécifique de tous les niveaux du fonctionnement d'un système économique et social que l'on peut découvrir la logique du contenu et des formes des divers modes de réprésentation, des diverses formes de perception de l'environnement" (Godelier 1974, p. 124).

13. See Keay (1953), Clayton (1960, 1962), and Buchanan and Pugh (1955) for a general description of Sudanic savanna vegetation.

14. See Pullan (1974) for a discussion of farmed parkland in West Africa.

15. The term "fadama" has been employed in a number of contrasting and contra-dictory ways (see Bargery 1934; M.G. Smith 1955; and Buchanan and Pugh 1955). I follow Turner's (1977, p. 35) characterization.

The *fadamas* then are low lying relatively flat areas sometimes streamless depressions and sometimes areas adjacent to streams. They are waterlogged or flooded in the wet season. At the very beginning of the wet season they may be marked by a flush of new vegetation`. . . but are most conspicuous at the end of the rains.

These riverine niches are characteristically well wooded, populated with *Fypha australis, Saccharum spontoneum, Mitragyna inermis, Borassus aethiopum, Hyphaene thebaica*, and a plethora of moisture-loving grasses and forbs, especially *Ipomoea repens, Cyperus dives*, and *Oryza barthii*.

16. See Cocheme and Franquin (1967), Kowal and Knabe (1972), and Oguntoyinbo and Richards (1977) for a technical discussion of this point.

17. The ITCZ assumes over its surface a WNW-ESE orientation. The rate of movement is irregular being on average in the current period between 1.9° and 4.9° per month.

18. According to Kowal and Adeoye's (1974) regression equations, the relation between mean annual rainfall and latitude proves to be a significant one: distance from the source of moisture is a dominant factor and accounts for about 60 percent of the variation in total rainfall. In the equation annual total rainfall decreases on average by 5.1 inches for every degree of latitude. Start and end of the rains also follow a north-south pattern. About 75 percent of the variation in the start of the rains, and about 76 percent of the variation in the end of the rains can be attributed to latitude.

19. Current mean annual precipitation for stations in northern Hausaland is in the order of 20 inches (Katsina 29.1, Nguru 21.7) and for the southern margins of Kasar Hausa roughly 50 inches (Kaduna 50.6, Minna 52.3). In all cases rainfall peaks in July and August.

20. A rough measure of this variance can be gleaned from the rainfall data for Kaita village where I lived, covering the period 1951–68. Mean monthly precipitation for July and August (the most *reliable* months) were respectively 8.5 and 8.7 inches; the variance (i.e., the amplitude between extreme maximum and minimum recorded) for both months were respectively 11 inches and 9.5 inches. Over the period 1969–77, the onset and termination of rains at birnin Katsina was as follows; earliest onset April 17th, latest onset June 3rd; earliest termination September 13th, latest termination November 1st. (See Kowal and Knabe 1972; Watts 1979).

21. Termed the Ogolien episode in West Africa, this era witnessed the formation of dunes and ergs and aeolian deposits in regions that are much wetter today, stretching ENE-WSW from Senegal to Chad (see Nicholson 1976, p. 32 ff.) Rognan and Williams (1977) suggests that this period saw a weakening or absence of the summer monsoon system associated with the advance of the ITCZ.

22. Over the period 11,000–8,000 B.P., lacustrine deposits were laid down in the Ténéré and eastern Niger, while the Ogolien dune system was stabilized by vegetative growth. The lakes of the Ténéré reached their maximal extent about 8,000 B.P. (Nicholson 1976, p. 41). Sudanian vegetation probably reached into northern Mauritania.

23. Lacustrine histories from Lake Chad and the inland Niger delta depict these patterns with some clarity (Oguntoyinbo 1981).

24. Muslim Hausa often explicitly associated poverty (*talauci*) and famine (*yunwa*) with evil. The peculiar cultural perception of famine is no doubt related to the social stigma that attaches to its consequence, namely, poverty and destitution.

Poverty is a black man with a dirty, matted hair.
With a hump on back, spinal curvature, covered with sweat.
With eczema, stench, bad smell and dirt . . .
If it follows a boy it makes him old;
It bends him into an aged man resembling a fishhook.
If it follows an old man it finishes him off;
He becomes thin, like a bowstring.
He becomes bewildered [and] confused.
[Imam Imoru, "The Song of Poverty and Wealth," see S. Pilaszewicz 1974, pp. 67–117]

25. Oral testimony, collected from Sarkin Tabshi, August 1977, Katsina. The entire verse, with a detailed exegesis, appears in the Appendix.

26. See Sa'id (1978, p. 39). According to Abdullahi Mahdi (1978) tradition has it that the first farmers to cultivate this area accumulated considerable wealth in slaves and horses when a famine forced people to come and buy grains from them.

27. In my opinion, Nicholson's (1978) data rely too heavily on the chronicles for this early period. The dendrochronological and palynological evidences are less equivocal and, in any case, the data on lake and river levels more often than not reflect moist conditions in the watershed areas to the south of the northern savannas and the Sahel.

28. Chad, Sudan, northern Niger, and parts of Senegambia certainly suffered dry conditions. A seven-year drought hit Bornu, but the Bornu Chronicles situate it sometime in the period 1690–1720, somewhat later than Nicholson's designation.

29. This episode is recorded as one of massive social and economic dislocation along the length of the desert edge.

30. Baier (1980, p. 30) reports that only one drought of a single year's duration (1855) was reported in travelers' accounts. A radically different image is brought into focus from even a cursory discussion with elderly Hausa farmers in the provinces.

31. Nicholson (1978, pp. 105, 106) believes that the period 1828–39 was one of "severe drought" in much of tropical Africa and the Sahara. Other dendrochronological research pertaining to Lake Chad levels delimits a 12-year drought.

32. The droughts of the mid and late eighteenth centuries (particularly in the 1850s, 1870s and 1880s) were not as Baier (1980, p. 30) believes of "localised" shortage.

33. Nicholson's (1978, pp. 108, 109) own precipitation anomaly maps actually indicate drought occurrence over the period 1870–90 in Hausa territory. My own oral data collected in Kano, Katsina, Daura, and Sokoto support this conclusion.

34. I do not include the arid episode of the early nineteenth century associated with low lake levels in the eastern Chad basin.

35. Much of the groundwork was in fact prepared by the School of Oriental and African Studies (SOAS) African Drought Seminar organized by Dr. H. Fisher in the immediate aftermath of the massive Sahelian drought and famine of the early 1970s. See also Nicholson (1976, 1978), Cissoko (1968), Curtin (1975), and Lovejoy and Baier (1975).

36. In Cissoko's (1968, p. 814) words,

cette instabilité politique accéléra la régression économique. Le commerce perdit ses moyens de défense et d'expansion. L'agriculture était rendue difficile par les brigandages et les guerres. Les famines dans ces conditions étaient fréquentes et la moindre disette était ressentie gravement. La fréquence des grandes famines est de sept à dix ans environ au XVIIè et de cinq au XVIIIè siecle. Deus famines, l'une au XVIè siecle, de 1639 a 1643, l'autre un siècle après, de 1738 à 1756, marquèrent profondément le déclin de la Boucle.

Timbuctoo, which at the birth of the sixteenth century was a city of 80,000, plummeted to a little over 10,000 in 1800.

37. In most studies (see Nicholson 1976; Lovejoy and Baier 1975) this is principally confined to the Bornu, Agadez, Tichitt, Nema, and Oualata Chronicles and the Tarikhs of the Niger Bend. In Hausaland I also employed other pieces of didactic and/or historical verse such as the "Song of Bagauda," but have not examined any of the major Arabic sources and documents.

38. Lovejoy (1978, p. 350) confidently claims that the great drought "forced the evacuation of most of the Sahelian states and villages so that plantations had to be abandoned." Since he cites no written or oral testimony in support of this speculation it is difficult to know how to interpret his remarks.

39. In my oral reconstructions the following individuals were especially helpful: Galadiman Daura, Alhaji Sule (November 28, 1977), Alahaji Bala Nebi and Alhaji Abe, Mallam Abubakar (July 20, 1977), Sarkin Makada, Daura (May 25, 1977), and Mallam Mammam Gumuzu, Katsina (July 25, 1977). A complete listing appears in the Bibliography.

40. To assume a priori that there is an inescapable linear causality between famine and drought is risky, even in the Sahel where the two are coterminous in the eyes of most desert-edge dwellers. Yet it is worth recalling that Agadez was evacuated in 1780 due to flooding. Nicholson (1976) comes very close to this mechanical inevitability in the construction of her "drought-famine chronologies."

41. See Cissoko (1968, pp. 806–21), Aliyu (1974, II, 735), and St. Croix (1944, p. 27). The rinderpest outbreak, called *jakirji* in Bauchi, was dated as 1895 by Aliyu, while St. Croix fixes the time as 1887–91. On balance, excessive wet episodes and/or floods appear in 1615–25, about 1820, about 1850, and 1865–75.

42. The tension between the exiled Katsina Hausa (based in Maradi) and their Ful'be conquerors who presided over the emirate can be traced through the military squabbles following the jihadi victory.

43. The information on which this is based was provided by the Galadiman Daura (Nov. 28, 1977), Dunbar (1971), and Salifou (1971).

44. In these instances, informants emphasized that a mediocre harvest reflected badly distributed rainfall during the wet season (*budi*)—"a disruption of the normal order" as Bargery put it—or a short drought (*bushi*) during crucial periods of the growing season, which stunted regular processes of maturity. Oral testimony in fact suggests that crop losses due to pest infestation, crop diseases, and locusts were, by comparison, quite infrequent.

45. Typically the peasant cultivator avoids high-cost failures that attempt a big but risky killing; he "minimizes the subjective probability of the maximum loss" (Scott 1976, p. 5).

46. Scott (1976, p. 5), describing the Southeast Asian peasantry, says, "The use of more than one seed variety, the European traditional farming on scattered strips, to mention only two, are classical techniques for avoiding undue risks often at the cost of a reduction in average return."

47. Gouldner (1960, p. 171) calls these attributes of village sociology and exchange the "norm of reciprocity." It has been a prominent line in substantivist thought that social exchanges were universal in precapitalist societies, part of a moral commitment to the ideal of collective rather than individual suffering (see Polanyi 1957). See also Sahlins (1972) for a discussion of patterns of reciprocities.

48. Patron-client relations are dyadic ties that encompass a "broad but imprecise spectrum of mutual obligations" (Popkin 1980, p. 419). The terms of exchange depend on the relative bargaining power of each party but its legitimacy rests upon the provision, among other things, of subsistence rights (see Scott 1972). As Patterson (1979, p. 36) aptly notes, "patron and client may have unequal power but the relationship is freely established and they are moral equals."

49. Much anthropological work conducted in the ethnographic present is quite consistent with this view though not couched in peculiarly moral or ethical terms. From the ethnographic literature it is possible to distinguish five strategies to lessen vulnerability to risk: (1) resource diversification, (2) famine foods, (3) storage, (4) conversion of food into tradable exchange items, and (5) social relations that emphasize sharing. See Colson (1979).

50. For specific critiques of Scott, see Adas (1980, 1981), Popkin (1979, 1980), Cummings (1981) and Bates (1978). The "moral economy" debate has also been conducted in the pages of *Past and Present* in response to Thompson's original piece; see Coats (1972), and Genovese (1973).

51. Popkin never explains quite what he means by "political economy" but it appears to be an amalgam of public choice theory and Adam Smithian economics. In this work—and in much contemporary social theory—I take political economy to be Marxian in form, that is "to do with the specific social forms of wealth or rather of the production of wealth" (Marx 1973, p. 853).

52. Popkin (1980, p. 413) observes that "I cannot be sure that any of the moral economists . . . would either recognize or agree with my statement of their assumptions." In my opinion this is a major understatement since in aggregating the work of Wolf, Migdal, Scott, Hobsbawm, Barrington Moore et al. he has constructed a specious model of peasant society that certainly bears little resemblance to, let us say, Scott's exegesis of the moral economy of the peasantry.

53. It is not the case that precapitalist society is intrinsically more moral, but rather that certain welfare functions were assumed by customary patterns of law and social relations and were morally enforceable. I have no idea what Popkin means by the efficiency (with respect to what?) of the moral economy; to my knowledge few if any of the moral economy school have posited precapitalist formations as "stable" though much of Scott's historical discussion is certainly slight.

54. Popkin (1980, p. 50) argues that the moral economy approach sees stratification as originating with capitalism and markets and that "if there is truly a moral economy, it is not clear that classes and strata emerge at all" (1980, p. 466). His first claim is quite preposterous since, to my knowledge, none of the Marxist-influenced authors make this claim; Scott (1976, pp. 5, 35–40) is explicit on this point. And as regards the second, Thompson's original formulation emphasized that the moral economy did not level socioeconomic differences; rather it helped reproduce them. The moral economy grew out of the tension and struggles between plebs and patriarchs, two "classes" that were mutually inter-dependent (see Thompson 1977).

55. It is difficult to place Popkin's argument temporally; he attempts to derive universal peasant traits (i.e., they are "self-interested") (1980, p. 430) yet one is frequently left wondering whether the precolonial "peasant" and the rural producer in contemporary Thailand are at all different beings.

56. From this working principle Popkin lends analytic priority to self-interest subject to the assumption that "at different times, peasants care about themselves, their families and their friends"! (1980, p. 432). Because I have failed to grasp the theoretical significance of "rationality" I have also had great difficulty with the questions he poses (1980, pp. 421, 422) which seem obvious or rather redundant (i.e., how are needs ranked, why don't peasants scatter ties among patrons, why do peasants aspire to village office?).

57. I address Popkin's arguments on the impact of the colonial state and the market in the following chapters.

58. This is the ecological fallacy under another guise. As Bates (1978, p, 141) suggests, there is little reason to assume that individual rationality or preference can attain rational social outcomes or the eventuality of a particular institution.

59. "Whatever the level of specialisation in production of commodities, if household reproduction is based on reciprocal ties, both horizontal and vertical, for renewal of means of production and subsistence, then reproduction resists commoditisation. If access to land, labour, credit, and product markets is mediated through direct, non-monetary ties to other households or other classes, and if these ties are reproduced through institutionally stable reproductive mechanisms, then commodity relations are limited in their ability to penetrate the cycle of reproduction" (Friedmann 1979*b*, p. 163).

60. In short, it does not make much political sense to starve those upon whom you ultimately depend for surplus appropriation.

From the elite side, the notion of a subsistence guarantee also has something of a self-evident equality to it. Except for transitory and excessively rapacious tax farmers and psychotics who reveled in cruelty to others, administrators and local notables would have seen little point in extracting so much revenue from the peasantry under their control that their subjects were unable to survive [Adas 1980, p. 526].

61. Franke and Chasin's (1980, p. 61) work on the precolonial Sahel is, it seems to me, open to this criticism. They ultimately opt for a subsistence affluence view, "a series of adaptations to environmental zones in which the overall picture that emerges is one of relatively prosperous and stable communities in which the balance was clearly on the side of environmental preservation" (pp. 61, 62). Kjekshus on precolonial Tanganyika is equally as subject to this type of idealist gloss (1977, pp. 1–8).

62. I do not want to enter into the Humpty-Dumpty world of the semantics of drought. For my purposes, I take drought to refer to "a rainfall-induced shortage of some economic good . . . brought about by inadequate or badly timed rainfall" (Sandford 1979, p. 34). Future incidence of drought therefore depends not only on rainfall but also on trends in demands and other supply-side perturbations.

63. To quote Chayanov (1966, p. 6),

the degree to self exploitation is determined by a particular equilibrium between family demand for satisfaction and the drudgery of labor itself. . . . As long as the equilibrium is not reached between the two elements being evaluated (i.e. the drudgery of the work is subjectively estimated as lower than the significance of the needs for whose satisfaction the labor is endured), the family, working without paid labor, has every cause to continue its economic activity. As soon as the equilibrium is reached, further labor expenditure becomes harder . . . to endure than is foregoing its economic effects.

64. The idea of subsistence security is an important concept and requires some comment. It implies, of course, an objective, minimal level below which households cease to be fully paid by members of society; obligations are not met, savings are nonexistent and the continuity of the household, in a biological sense, is at stake. This base level is in practice a zone rather than a threshold, below which fundamental physiological demands—in the order of 600 pounds of millet per adult male per annum for the Hausa peasant (Simmons 1976; Nicolas 1965)—are not met. The determination of the subsistence level presupposes culturally determined patterns of food preference and distribution, for concepts such as hunger and food shortage are culturally shaped, reflecting historical circumstances and previous experience. To be sensitive to the cultural dimension is not, however, to undermine the utility of the subsistence-level concept. To fall below this zone is to endure *famine* conditions where biological survival is threatened. To hover continually within the zone, is to experience food shortage that threatens health and personal welfare.

65. An early colonial district assessment, which is one of the very few to have attempted a demographic survey, estimated child mortality in the first two years at 55 percent. See NAK SNP 10 347p/1915 District Assessment of Maradu, Sokoto Province, 1915.

66. There are, to my knowledge, no precolonial yield statistics for Nigeria Hausaland but some of the earliest information from farm assessment reports appear below:

		Yield (threshed lbs per acre)					
		1911		1912		1914	
Sokoto District	Area measured (acres)	Millet	Sorghum	Millet	Sorghum	Millet	Sorghum
Mariki	6.5	497	165	497	209	–	–
Maradu	75	–	–	–	–	594	308

SOURCE: NAK SNP 10 472p/1913, NAK SNP 10 347p/1915.

NOTE: These yields are between 10% and 30% higher than current Agriculture Department estimates.

67. I am aware of the absence of any consensus about the definition and measurement of risk or risk aversion. There appear to be two broad denotations of risk: one refers to a measure of the dispersion of possible outcomes associated with a particular economic alternative; the other as the probability that returns will fall below a critical disaster threshold (see Roumasset 1979). However ill-defined, small and middle peasants nevertheless consider variations of outcomes when making agricultural decisions (Chibnik 1981).

68. For a similar argument for precolonial India see McAlpin (1979) and Morris (1974).

69. Risk preference at higher income levels is not inconsistent with the formulation.

70. Morris (1974, p. 1856) in discussing a similar system among traditional Indian dryland farmers points out that if rainfall conditions are not the best, a farmer is forced to start making rather difficult choices. Assuming that his preferred mix can be produced in the face of some variation of onset, quantity, and timing of rains, he probably plays a complicated game of estimating the chances he is taking as he decides whether he should hold firm to his preferred crop mix or shift to an alternative.

71. H.R. Palmer made the important observation that fadama crops were especially relevant to famine: "Another point perhaps worth noting is that these special [fadama] crops are an insurance against famine," NAK SNP 10 3035/1909 Katsina Division, Kano Province, Half Yearly Report 1909, par. 256.

72. A Hausa epithet says, "We have discovered the locust's secret, you whose stomach is foul. We have discovered rizga [tuber] and cassava for you do not betray a rizga farmer."

73. Imam Imoru made the following notation:

There are small and large bins. Some hold 40–70 bundles while others hold 100 to 500 bundles. There is one which holds 1000 bundles but a commoner does not build one this big. . . . I saw bins in Talata Mafara, Zamfara, which were said to store 2,000 bundles each, and they were for the rulers. [Ferguson 1973, p. 65]

74. For a description of the opening and closing of the granary and its ritual significance see Nicolas (1975, p. 282).

75. "After the harvest the seed destined to be planted the next year as well as the quantity of grain necessary for the subsistence of the group during the planting season were placed by the clan head in a large granary which could not be opened until after the first rains. Religious rites placed these reserves under the divinity of agriculture, Uwar Gona" (Raynault 1975, p. 12).

76. Rowling (1949, p. 16) noted, for example, that in Kano Province, "in order to conserve its food supply the entire family goes off elsewhere leaving only an old member or two to look after their home; the total exodus varying between 10 percent when there is a good harvest to 60 percent in a [bad] year."

77. There is now a huge literature on Sahelian pastoral economies but very little good historical research. For a representative sampling see Monod (1975), Dahl and Hjort (1976), Swift (1977), Baier (1980), MAB (1975), and the Pastoral Network (Overseas Development Institute, London).

78. Camels for instance are more drought resistant than cattle, and do not suffer from rinderpest. Species diversity also assists in the temporal distribution of milk availability through staggered lactation rates.

79. Stock alliance referred to the transfer of irrevocable rights to specific animals and their offspring among close kin. The donor could not reclaim the same animal but possessed reciprocal rights on another beast. Stock clientage referred to the temporary transfer of use rights over specified animal products to cover temporary food shortage. See Dahl and Hjort (1979, pp. 21, 22).

80. Palmer described this system as holding "in nearly every Katsina town before 1905" (NAK Katprof 1289/1909). He also noted that *unguwa* (i.e., wards within villages) had no real corporate identity and did not fulfill suprahousehold functions along the lines of lineage segments in non-Muslim communities.

81. Maradu District Assessment for example in Sokoto Province revealed that one-tenth of Gara township (population about 5,000) farmed in Mafara village area. See NAK SNP 10 347p/1915.

82. Hill (1977, p. 71) estimates that in about 1900 only a very small proportion of the population of Kano Province resided in settlements over 1,000 persons. She implies that the majority of the rural populace lived in dispersed homesteads and small hamlets.

83. I cannot accept, however, Hill's judgment (1977, p. 130) that "impoverished households in the nineteenth century stood in much the same plight as they do today" since it apparently denies the change wrought by the colonial state after 1900. See chapters 4, 5, and 6.

84. In spite of Popkin's (1979, p. 132) emphasis on individual peasant self-interest, given the prevalence of use-value production subject to environmental risk and the vulnerabilities imposed by limited technological development, it is surely in the interest of most households to share losses (i.e., it is beneficial to cooperate) irrespective of the distrust and envy which he emphasizes.

85. Other gifts include *kudin godiya* (gifts of thanks), *alheri* (health), *kori* (a gift for a service rendered such as praise singing), *toshi* (a complimentary gift), *kudin goro* (kola money usually given at most ceremonies), and *gindimi* (a communitywide gift exchange system). The vocabulary points to complexity and subtlety of the gift nexus but the dominant aspect is, as Nicolas puts it, its "caractère expressif."

86. Biki as a contribution system linking partners is an important institution especially associated with major ceremonial events. Since it often involves poor people, patterns of contribution and return are frequently small and flexible (see Hill 1972, p. 211).

87. *GIDA* is capitalized to distinguish it from *gida*, meaning household.

88. Strictly speaking, barantaka refers to political clientage, *baranci* to menial domestic clientage, and *mutumci* to commercial or business clientage.

89. Although ties of primary clientage are of less significance in contemporary Nigeria Hausaland, Faulkingham (1971) working in an isolated non-Muslim community in Nigerian Hausaland in the 1960s discovered that 75 percent of all married men were either patrons, clients, or both. *Barantaka* thus extended outward in complicated bifurcating chains in which "patrons are clients to other patrons who [are clients] to other patrons" (p. 158).

90. Tahir (1975, pp. 277, 278) points out that wage laborers were in fact quasi clients, sustained during the dry season by free or noninterest loans of grain. The leather manufacturer Sharuk-na Tsakuwa controlled 70 clients and 150 slaves, the latter being sustained by their own "moral economy" (see Roberts 1981).

91. Shea (1975) notes that Koranic wage labor was used in the dyed cloth industry since, as strangers, they were ideally suited to casual employment.

92. Nicolas (1969, p. 228) makes the point that "un desástre, la sécheresse, . . . la famine on l'abondance peuvent reinforce l'autorité d'un souverain." But the recurrence of these phenomena can be used to stimulate dynastic competition.

93. Imam Imoru wrote that "There are very many towns where the ruler has a big farm. When it is going to be cleared, the common people, talakawa, gather from different towns and do the work because they beg cereals from him when there is famine. Likewise, the blind, makafi, and cripples, guragu, beg from him" (Ferguson 1973, p. 61). See also the Imoru's description of elite functions in "The Song of Poverty" (Pilaszewicz 1971, p. 87).

94. I believe that the Sarkin noma was a widespread institution in the nineteenth century even among communities nominally Muslim. It is to be recalled in any case that the jihad was a reform movement not a process of massive conversion and the maguzawa community remained quite large (see Last 1976, who estimated the contemporary maguzawa population in the northern states as 250,000).

95. M. G. Smith (1978, p. 70) described this situation among pagan Hausa in Daura during the early nineteenth century.

96. The dubu was inseparable from the more embracing spiritual universe of maguzawa communities, the iskoki pantheon. Among Kano maguzawa the Inna is the mother of all spirits although in Kazaure *Inna* is apparently referred to as *Uwar Gona* (the farm mother); in both cases, her principal concerns are the fertility of the farm and protection of property. Her two sons, Gajimari and Kure, are more or less universal. This triad tends to dominate the la: ge and complex local pantheon of spirits each of which had an appropriate sacrifice. See Greenberg (1946) and Barkow (1970). In Kazaure the dubu ceremony was called *taral rugga*. Each community had two or three sarakunan noma, titles that were inheritable (NAK Kanoprof HIS/5, p, 101).

97. In nineteenth-century Zamfara, the bukin dubu and the Sarkin noma were institutional means for raising agricultural productivity and were an integral part of the flourishing Zamfara grains trade, which was so crucial during severe food crises in the Hausa plains (Na Dama 1976). Occasionally a second dubu was held in conjunction with the election of a *Sarkin Hatsi* who, in Kazaure at least, was a prominent official within the hierarchy of Sarakunan noma. Several other maguzawa rituals, including the female potlatch, the (*kan*

kworiya), the initiation of *bori* adepts (*girka*), and intervillage youth exchanges (*wasan Kara*) all served, in varying degrees, redistributive purposes.

98. [The Sarkin Noma] is the ultimate defense against famine;

when the grain in any gida is exhausted the residents may obtain an interest free loan of grain from the Sarkin noma's bins to be repaid at harvest. Finally, the Sarkin noma provides seed for any who may have consumed his own supply as food. [Faulkingham 1971, p. 81]

99. Imam Imoru described a drought "salla" during the nineteenth century in which common folk searched for rain without the gaiety of usual salla festivals (see Ferguson 1973, p. 81).

100. The following is a description of a maguzawa rain ritual from Kano province by a colonial officer in the 1930s:

When the rain is required for the crops the [leaders] collected the inhabitants at the tsafi in front of the . . . house who in turn made their sacrifices of goats, chickens and rams, each according to his wealth. There is feasting, drumming and dancing amidst libations of [beer]. Women put on their husbands clothes. . . . All Maguzawa are emphatic that these dances will produce rain. [NAK Kanoprof HIS/5 1937 p. 89]

101. Among the Kano maguzawa there appears to have been a pestilence ritual in which the wife of the Sarki collected the local inhabitants, who were given grain and engaged in mass prayer outside the village or town walls. See NAK SNP 9 257/1921 Assessment Report, Kano Province, Districts of Sabon Birni, Isa, Zurmi, and Moriki.

102. C. Laughlin and I. Brady (1978, p. 42) state that "We would expect the control of the ritual to form a subset of power resources for leaders in societies confronting deprivation. It is precisely through ritual that leaders may demonstrate their capacity for appropriate action—action that is perceived by all concerned as necessary and sufficient for the return to abundance."

103. Raynault for instance notes in his discussion of Damagaram that "this region, which at the beginning of the century exported large quantities of grain both to the North, to the nomads, and to the South, to the more densely populated areas of northern Nigeria, had a deficit (of grain) in 1960" (cited in Campbell 1976, p. 61). See also NAK SNP 7 4055/1912 for a similar view by Mr. Webster.

104. Many conversations in Katsina revealed that grain production and the grains trade was an important (and commonplace) avenue to financial success in the nineteenth century.

105. From interviews conducted with the following at Rafin Dadi, birnin Katsina July 13th, 1977: Wakilin Kudu Alhaji Ilyasu Rafin Dadi; Alhaji Hamza Yankyaure; Alhaji Lawal; Mallam Gurshe Darma; Mallam Samaila; Alhaji Mohammedu; Mallam Danjuma; Mallam Isa; Alhaji Umaru; Mallam Tata; Mallam Magaji.

106. The Sarki ruled less by fiat than through skillful manipulation of factions, cliques, and lineages, which consumed much time and energy in the birni. Hakimai, anxious to maintain their position in webs of dynastic politicking, often spent much time in the capital, devolving responsibility, including tax collection, to the jekadas and *masu garuruwa*, individuals who were not only knowledgeable of local affairs but had much reason to (1) avoid

central overseeing and (2) maintain close relationships with rural residents. This is not to suggest the collectors were neither self-interested nor rapacious, but it was in their interest (since they illicitly appropriated a proportion of peasant rents) to avoid local dissent and migration, which ultimately filtered back to the palace courtiers.

107. Adas (1981, p. 234) observed that in both Java and Burma "cult movements that coalesced around mystics and holymen and seers also provided . . . outlets for peasant protest."

108. For a useful discussion of the limits to exploitation and peasant refuges in the classical period of Islam see Hodgson (1974, I, 102).

109. Scott (1976, p. 53) identified this trait among the Southeast Asian kingdoms. "[In] *bad years the collection of taxes fell off substantially and, reluctantly, remissions were granted for whole districts hit by floods, pests, or drought.* This lenience may in part have been due to a symbolic alignment of the traditional court with the welfare of its subjects but it was also surely a reflection of the traditional state's inability to reliably control much of its hinterland" (emphasis mine).

110. Cohen and Brenner in their work on precolonial Bornu discovered that "some groups by virtue of service to the throne at an earlier date, might be wholly or partially tax exempt and would generally possess a document (mahram) to prove it. . . . Tax exemptions could also be used as patronage to increase or maintain a political following. There are also traditions suggesting that they were temporarily applicable during times of drought or disaster so that a local community could direct all its efforts to the resuscitation of its productive capacities and then later return to full participation in the taxation system" (Cohen and Brenner 1974, p. 122).

111. H.R. Palmer (NAK SNP 15 ACC. 374 1907 p. 9) noted that "the Hausa have a bitter repugnance of a capitation tax" which explains in some measure the massive defection of Hausa from the French Sudan in the first decade of colonial rule, where rigid capitation tax had been instituted.

112. Hewby (NAK SNP 10 111/1908) felt that one-third of zakka was lost in transit due to "robbery" or consumption by the collector. In any case, there is little evidence to suggest that zakka, insofar as it was optional and graduated with respect to economic status, was onerous.

113. Using prevailing prices, I have estimated that the tax levy ca. 1900 for a nuclear family without adult sons was equivalent to roughly twenty-five-days grain supply for one person (i.e., 2,500 cowries in toto or roughly the price of a small sheep). This tax computation includes kudin kassa and an estimated levy of 1,500 cowries for trade, industrials, or shuka crops. The entire village of Dankaba (300–400 compounds), for example, contributed only two bags of cowries as its kudin kassa contribution (NAK Katprof 1789/1904). Kudin kassa in Kano was purportedly 4,000 cowries in the 1890s, at least in the central districts, which according to Cargill was "moderate" (NAK SNP 10 7173/1909). In the border districts the rate was much lower, about 1,100–3,200 cowries.

114. In 1851 the exchange rate was 2,500 cowries to the dollar; by 1895 Marie Theresa dollars were exchanging hands at 5,000 cowries. See Lubeck (1968). In Zaria, however, the land tax increased from 1,200 cowries per hoe in 1846 to 4,000 in 1863, and finally to 7,200

in 1901, though cowry devaluation over the same period was probably not more than 150 percent (NAK SNP 10 236 p./1919).

115. Hewby (NAK SNP 10 111/1908) felt that shuka and rafi taxes accounted for between 25 and 40 percent of total revenue in Kano at the time of conquest. In Zaria, the constitution of taxes had increased from a single levy of 200 cowries per hoe in 1804–21 to 7,200 cowries per hoe plus shuka-rafi levies of between 5 and 8,000 cowries in 1881 (NAK SNP 10 236p/1919).

116. Stewart (1968, p. 269) concurs with this synopsis in her review of the northern emirates. She concludes that "the system of taxation seemed well regulated and fairly apportioned in the nineteenth century. To what extent abuses existed . . . is not known but the increase in taxation . . . is not sufficient evidence of the existence of such practices."

117. Sa'ad Abubakar, describing the eastern emirates of the Caliphate, suggested that "it was customary to plan for disaster and so there would be crops available every year that the community could consume. . . . In regard to the sadaqat [zakka] the essence of the collection was for the upkeep of the poor and destitute. Long before the coming of the British, the poor and the destitute in society looked to the emirs for all their needs and these were at all times satisfied" (Abubakar 1975, p. 34).

118. Millet was so stored in the village of Yandaki, eight miles north of birnin Katsina, though it was at this time (about 1900) a fief of the Durbi, a principal officeholder in the central emirate administration.

119. M.G. Smith (1967a, pp. 112, 113), referring to the Hausa Kingdom of Maradi, notes that "the bundled grain was then stored in special granaries and recorded by the ruler and the hakimi separately. From these stores, the ruler made annual distributions to his officials, in amounts which varied with rank. As Secretary, the Magajin Bakebi recorded the ruler's donations and reserves, the latter being kept as security against famine or loss through war."

120. I have taken this from a quotation by a Hausa informant referring to nineteenth-century Kano, in Yusufu (1976, p. 58).

121. During the Babban Yunwa, household granaries were often exhausted by the early hot season (four to five months after harvest) with the result that many families had fled their villages by the onset of the new rains. Sacrificing the harvest made reconstitution and recovery doubly difficult (Mallam Sani, Alhaji Gambo, Mallam Mohammed Gimba, in Katsina town, June 24, 1977).

122. The Katsina famine of 1888 for instance followed on the heels of two or three below average harvests. It "crept upon us" one informant put it (Mallam Ibrahim Ladan, Cikin Gida, Katsina April 14, 1977).

123. In discussion with elderly farmers, the prevailing consensus was that in the aftermath of a severe famine, it required five to seven good harvests to reconstitute household granaries to "acceptable levels" (Alhaji Bala Datuhudu, Mallam Audu Hitiya, Mallam Maitaba, Mallam Danburadi, in Kaita village, August 15, 1978).

124. See Jodha (1975) and Morris (1974) for a discussion of famine response in India.

125. The most common famine food were

Yadiya	(*Leptadenia lancifolia*)
Kauci	(*Loranthus spp.*)
Dorowa	(*Parkia filicoidea*)
Kuka	(*Adansonia digitata*)
Dinya	(*Vitex doniana*)
Tafasa	(*Cassia tora*)
Goriba	(*Hyphaene thebaica*)
Giginya	(*Borassus flabellifer*)
Gamji	(*Ficus abutifolia*)
Aliyara	(*Euphorbia balsaminifera*)
Kawuri	(*Ficus kawuri*)
Zogale	(*Moringa oleifera*)
Yakuwa	(*Urena lobata*)
Chediya	(*Ficus capensis*)

126. This sequence builds upon the excellent work of Jodha (1975) who has worked extensively on contemporary famine responses in Rajastan.

127. In any case, the collection of oral data on famine is not particularly easy in view of the sensitivity of familial origins in Hausa society.

128. I am grateful to Mr. M. Duffill for this piece of information.

129. Mallam Anyo Kaita, interview in Kaita village, February–March 1978.

130. Oral testimony, Katsina town June 24, 1977. Mallam Kadabo, Alhaji Gambo, Mallam Mohammed, and Mallam Sani; in Kaita village, September 5, 1977, Alhaji Bala, and Mallam Audu Hitiya.

131. Hausa men complain bitterly that it is they who suffer during times of dearth for they rarely, if ever, prepare cooked food. Strangely enough a colonial officer made the same observation during the famine of 1914 (NAK Katprof. 1/1 3148/1914 p. 2).

132. Following a two-year drought, Dahl and Hjort (1976, p. 13) estimate that an ox herd of "normal" sex-age diversity would take roughly 28 years for a complete recovery of fertile cows, heifers, and female calves.

133. At the peak of the famine of the late 1880s in Katsina, a bull exchanged for 2–3 *taiki* of grain; in 1903, a nonfamine year, a cow commanded 19–20 *taiki* of millet (see NAK Katprof. 1769/1903).

134. For a useful discussion of the impact of famines and the constraints imposed by technological underdevelopment, see Wright (1979) and Jodha (1975) on precolonial Zimbabwe and India, respectively.

135. Imam Imoru writes that "if there is a famine, people go abroad to bring macaroni for the wealthy man," while the "poor man eats leaves and Indian Hemp" (see S. Pilaszewicz, 1974, pp. 94, 95).

136. Famines can obviously occur without an absence of foodstuffs in the marketplace (i.e., availability). Famine is characteristic of some people not having enough food, which may arise because of an absolute decline in food supply or through declining exchange entitlements (i.e., consumers are incapable of acquiring what exists). During the Irish Famine of 1846 markets were "plentifully supplied with meat, bread [and] fish" (Wodham-Smith 1957, p. 159).

137. "Some people produce the food they eat and a failure of production . . . would directly expose them to starvation" (Sen 1980*a*, p. 617).

CHAPTER 4

1. See A. G. Hopkins (1973, pp. 124–57). Also M. Klein (1971) and G. Williams (1976, pp. 13–17) for more detailed analysis.

2. See K. O. Dike (1956) and Okime (1968) for an elaborate discussion of the role of merchant capital in the Niger Delta.

3. More precisely, the exchange of industrial commodities for the produce of rural producers mediated by European merchants' capital realized a part of the peasants' surplus product through unequal exchange. This surplus product when converted into money took the form of merchants' profits.

4. For a comprehensive discussion of these changes see E. Hobsbawm (1968), and D. Landes (1972).

5. I have taken this term from P. Ehrensaft and E. Brown (1973).

6. See S. H. Frankel, *Capital Investment in Africa* (1938, especially pp. 158–60); for a description of the monetary boards see A. Hopkins (1970).

7. Myint in his *The Economics of the Developing Countries* (1967, pp. 42, 43) accordingly characterized precolonial formations as follows (in case his myopic vent makes any sense whatsoever):

> this suggests that initially there must have been a considerable amount of under-employed or surplus labour in these [peasants] families. . . . There was abundant wasteland waiting to be cultivated, but labour remained underemployed because there was a lack of effective demand for its potential increase in output. In the initial situation, with the available surplus land and surplus labour, and with the traditional methods of cultivation, a peasant family could have produced a much larger agri-cultural output than it was actually producing for its own subsistence consumption. But it chose not to do so, for the simple reason that every other peasant family could do the same and there would be no one in the locality who would want to buy the surplus output. With the poor transport and communications, and the rudimentary exchange system which existed before the opening up of the export trade, the local and domestic market of the underdeveloped countries was too narrow and unorga-nized to absorb their potential surplus agricultural output.

8. G. Heilleiner (1966, pp. 11, 12) has made a similar argument:

> The appearance of external markets for the products of the Nigerians' land and labour broke the traditional terms of trade (price) between leisure and goods; greater

prizes, in the form of cloth, weapons and salt, could be obtained for their products than ever before. The Nigerian peasant producer responded by increasing his labour (and land) inputs so as to raise his output. These peasant producers could thus be induced, with unchanged preference functions, to abandon still more of their leisure in favour of the labour required to produce exportable output.

9. I use this term as a historical abstraction that simply refers to an agrarian social formation characterized largely by simple reproduction; in other words the cycle of household production is dominated by the production of use-values. Clearly, colonialism did not introduce either the commodity form or merchant capital; rather the colonial state extended and intensified commodity production pushing peasants toward fully fledged petty commodity production (see Friedmann 1979, pp. 71, 72). In this sense the presence of merchant capital is not incompatible with what I refer to as natural economy. As Marx (1967, I, 328) put it,

> capital can, and must, form in the process of circulation, before it learns to control its extremes—the various spheres of production between which circulation mediates. Money and commodity circulation can mediate between spheres of production of widely different organization, whose internal structure is still chiefly adjusted to the output of use-values.

10. I am particularly indebted to Robert Shenton's (1982) work which concerns the development of capitalism in northern Nigeria.

11. The necessity of violence in colonial overrule pays testimony to the ideological conflict in the process of incorporation of the Caliphate. The categorization of Lugard and his imperial brethren as "Christian dogs" as the Caliph put it, effectively negated any possibility of "peaceful" conquest (see Lubeck 1979, pp. 194, 195).

12. The most well-known examples of this debate are R. Milliband (1969), and N. Poulantzas (1973). For extensions of the debate in the realm of African studies, see C. Leys (1976), N. Swainson (1980), M. von Freyhold (1977), and S. Langdon (1977).

13. I lean heavily for this exegesis on the work of Berman and Lonsdale (1980) who are clearly influenced by the work of Holloway and Piccioto (1978).

14. The same point is made by Jack Wayne (1981) when he points out that the state in Tanganyika was not simply a mechanism for increasing exploitation since it was also concerned with its own reproduction (i.e., revenue and law and order).

15. For an excellent discussion of these issues in the context of British paternalism at the turn of the century, see P. Hetherington (1978).

16. Lugard (1922, p. 204) in fact believed that West African Sudanic peoples were not "pure negro" and hence were afforded higher qualities by the "mixing of blood": "Alien immigrants in the northern tropical belt (of Africa) afforded better material for social organization, both racially and through the influence of their creed, than the advanced communities of negro stock."

17. For a good discussion of the purported wealth of northern Nigeria and the place occupied by cotton see J. Hogendorn (1978).

18. As is well known, the density of European political officers in relation to the indigenous population in the northern provinces was extraordinarily light. In 1903 the entire protectorate was administered by fifty-two political officers.

19. I have drawn heavily on the work of Hetherington (1978) and from a lecture delivered by Thomas Hodgkin at Stanford University and University of California at Berkeley on the antiimperial tradition.

20. Many of Temple's influential ideas are laid out in his *Native Race and Their Rulers*, and also in his testimony to the Northern Nigeria Lands Committee (1910), which constituted almost one-quarter of the evidence presented.

21. Temple (1918, p. 145) expressed this fear most directly.

It is the mental condition of the African . . . which constitutes the principal danger [for] . . . the emergence of title to land [would mean] the peasant may be driven from his holding . . . and large blocks of land may fall into the control of a small number of individuals.

22. After amalgamation in 1914 the majority of state revenue (51 percent in 1929 and 46 percent in 1939) came from import duties. Direct taxation constituted 38 percent and 43 percent, respectively.

23. This information actually refers to Katsina Division. The information is culled from Hull (1968, pp. 260–62), Hill (1977, pp. 49–54), NAK Katprof 1858/1910, NAK Katprof 1836/1909.

24. Girouard had written to Lugard, "I favour the complete nationalisation of the land on a landholder's not a landlord system [to protect] against the land grabber" (NAK SNP 15/3 390/1908). (See also NAK SNP 15 374 A8.)

25. Both Orr and Palmer fell into the collectivist camp; the latter did not want to give the masu sarauta the power to sell land, which he felt would reaffirm their privilege as "landholders and princes" (NAK SNP 15/3 377/1907).

26. As Mary Bull (1963, pp. 62, 63) put it,

the views of this committee derived as much, if not more, from collectivist theories current in England at this time than from northern Nigerian experience; the theorists saw in northern Nigeria the field in which their theories could be applied.

27. As Palmer observed in his testimony to the Lands Committee,

In northern Nigeria, generally speaking, it commands no such value in the open market. Nobody will buy when there is plenty of land available for practically no cost. The land is to the cultivator what his tools and iron are to the blacksmith. For assessment purposes the value of the crops and stock and fruits of industry are, therefore, the only basis on which taxation can be calculated, because it is only they that have a market value. [Lands Committee 1910, p. 89]

28. Rowling (1949, p. 9) in a review of land tenure in Kano reported that "the present theoretical ban [on land sale] is quite pointless." He noted that the sale of rights is known by everyone to be "universal and common" (p. 49). Prices varied with size and fertility and had doubled over twenty years.

29. The unpopular taki tax was the brunt of much peasant abuse and it is ironic that the word taki in Hausa, in addition to its colonial use as pace, also means manure. As many informants pointed out, kudin taki was indeed shit money. In Katsina, the tax actually began in 1911.

30. With the institution of the taki system, Emir Dikko was able to replace district heads with his own allies and supporters and by 1916 25 percent of all hakimai were relatives or servants of the emir.

31. Until 1927 the old Katsina emirate, consisting of nineteen districts covering 8,106 square miles, was a division within the province of Kano. Between 1927 and 1934, Katsina emirate was absorbed by Zaria Province but the deep-rooted political rivalries between the two necessitated a dissolution in 1934 by which both Zaria and Katsina were conferred full provincial status. Even though Katsina was a division of Kano during the first quarter century of British rule, it possessed a large measure of administrative autonomy, particularly during the Palmer period.

32. An excellent discussion of administrative change in Katsina emirate is provided by R. Hull, "The Development of Administration in Katsina Emirate, Northern Nigeria 1887–1944" (Ph.D. dissertation, Columbia University, 1968). See also A. M. Saulawa, "British Colonial Administration Policies and Migrations in the Birnin Katsina 1903–54" (B.A. thesis, Department of History, Ahmadu Bello University, 1977).

33. The BCGA, desperate to penetrate the local market, had even suggested in 1905 that people be forced to pay taxes in cotton and later in 1922 that settled cotton growing "colonies" be established along the rail line. See Shenton and Lennihan (1981).

34. As Lugard (RO CO 879/119 #1070) put it,

the Hausa . . . when faced with inflated prices, or . . . the absence of the cheap class of cloth he desires, no longer exports his raw cotton but reserves it for his own looms . . . it is earnestly to be hoped that interference with the economic laws of supply and demand will soon be no longer necessary.

See also Shea (1975, pp. 87–90), and S. Smith (1979).

35. For a discussion of the genesis of extensive groundnut cultivation in the North see Hogendorn (1975, 1978).

36. To my knowledge, there has been no major study of the role of Levantine capital in northern Nigeria. See NAK SNP 9 386/1918, NAK Kanoprof 4455/n.d., NAK SNP 17 38133. Also Hogendorn (1978, pp. 139–42), and Baldwin (1956).

37. Merchant firms offered imported cloth to secure agricultural commodites; the cloth was then sold to realize money to pay taxes. Particularly after 1927, the advance system penetrated deep into the countryside, and growers could not curtail production even in the face of falling prices. See NAK SNP 17 10199 Vol. II. This system is discussed in detail in chapter 5.

38. See P. Bauer (1954), who provides a wealth of information pertaining to the commercial and banking structures in colonial West Africa.

39. In Kano Province for instance revenue rose from £61,000 in 1907 to £124,000 in 1909 and to £215,000 in 1913. All administrative estimates were continually exceeded by actual receipts.

40. In Kay's (1975, p. 95) words,

merchant capital is trading capital and the surplus value that it seizes is used to expand trade not the forces of production. In fact it drains part of the surplus product out of the sphere of production, and the more it develops the more enervating its effects. . . . The history of underdevelopment is the fullest expression we have to these contradictory tendencies of merchant capital to both stimulate and repress the development of the forces of production and to both open and block the way for the full development of capitalism.

41. In practice, however, they were income taxes computed as 10 percent of gross individual income levied on all adult males over sixteen years.

42. To my knowledge there is no adequate treatment of agricultural policy in colonial northern Nigeria, and in particular of the role of the experimental stations. For a good introduction see Forrest (1981).

43. Interest-bearing capital serves a specific purpose.

Usurer's capital employs the method of exploitation characteristic of capital, yet without the latter's mode of production. This condition also repeats itself within bourgeois economy in backward branches of industry, or in those branches which resist the transition to the modern mode of production. [Marx 1967, I, 597]

For a good discussion of merchant and interest-bearing capital in a peripheral formation, see Keyder (1980).

44. One of the basic difficulties of seasonality in a rainfed agriculture is that (1) machinery is idle, (2) the climatic uncertainty makes for high-risk production, and (3) the temporal variation in labor requirements present scheduling problems. In this sense, agricultural operations are sequential not simultaneous; hence the use of machinery can transform the biological cycle into a mechanical flow process. Mann and Dickinson (1978) have made a similar argument; they suggest that the nonidentity of production time and labor time that is characteristic of certain agricultural commodities is shown to have an adverse effect on the rate of profit, the efficient use of constant and variable capital, and the smooth functioning of the circulation and realization process. They reason that the persistence of family farms is to be located in the unattractiveness of agricultural production for capital, for in the case of many agricultural products there is a considerable period during which "labour time is almost completely suspended as when the seed is maturing in the earth." These periods are "unproductive" in the sense that, while necessary to the production of the commodity, they do not keep labor working and hence do not create value. In the North, it is entirely conceivable that large-scale labor-intensive farming could have been undertaken on the "labor reserve" model, but the constant spectre of underproduction of foodstuffs implied that a seasonal labor force drawn out of agricultural production might have devastating consequences. Interestingly, the African Ranches Scheme (Dunbar 1970) and the infamous Katsina ostrich farm which was devastated by a tornado (both attempts at large-scale "livestock" production) were complete failures.

45. This is, of course, the Amin (1974) and Vergopoulos (1974) thesis; namely, the capitalist mode of production dominant in urban areas articulates with simple commodity

production in the countryside. Big-landed property, by taking advantage of the rigidity of land supply, constitutes an obstacle to industrial capitalism. Small producers, with little power, can be easily forced to work not for profit but for survival. Conditions are created in which prices of agricultural products are low, imported manufactures are expensive, and hence capital can afford to shun the countryside exploiting through the realm of circulation.

46. The development of a fully capitalist agriculture necessitates the replacement of land ownership by specifically capitalist relations of production. Landowners and land as a critical factor in production would be eliminated in the sense that agriculture would become *industrial*, both in terms of technology and the relations of production. Historically, industrial capitalism has developed alongside agriculture rather than in production per se.

CHAPTER 5

1. Much of the best work on peasant economy and commodity production has emerged from a group of scholars who are (or have been) attached to research institutions in Nairobi and Dar-es-Salaam. See the work of Bernstein (1978, 1979), Cowen (1981, 1976), and Bryceson (1980). In addition, the recent publications of Friedmann (1978a, 1978b, 1979a), Elwert and Wong (1980), Kelly (1979) and Boesen (1979), are especially useful. Much of this discussion was, of course, preempted by the Kautsky and Lenin debate at the turn of the century.

2. Commoditization may be measured by the proportion of goods purchased at market-determined prices for productive and personal consumption. Mobility of labor, land, and credit may be estimated by the uniformity of wages, rents, and interest rates given differences in skill, fertility, location, and so on (see Friedmann 1979b, p. 13).

3. For Necker, famine revealed the workings of a society divided between powerful landowners and a mass of landless, or near landless, laborers. Hunger was a particular form of violence which derived from institutions, and particularly from the laws governing property rights. See Spitz (1978, pp. 874–875).

4. There were of course other exports during the early colonial period, notably hides and skins (research currently in progress by R. Shenton), shea nuts, ostrich feathers, and tin (W. Freund 1981). However, with the exception of tin ore, most other export commodities did not make an impact on either colonial or Nigerian revenue.

5. See the dissertation by P. Shea (1975) on the development of an export–oriented dyed cloth industry. Also Barth (1965, II, 423 or 424) and Staudinger (1889, p. 623).

6. The groundnut (*Arachis hypogaea*), although a dry neutral plant, is sensitive to both temperature and precipitation. It is relatively more difficult to produce in the deprived southern Guinea savanna than in the areas farther north because of greater incidence of pests and leaf spot. Ideal rainfall is in the order of 25–30 inches per annum, and the most suitable soils are the well-drained, light, sandy loams preferably slightly acid. Cotton (*Gossypium hirsutum*) is grown under a wide range of climatic conditions, but most of the crop is grown in the northern Guinea and Sudan savanna zones with a rainfall of 30–45 inches and a 120- to 180-day rainy season. Another minor area of production is in the extreme north of the Sudan savanna—the groundnut zone par excellence—where in spite of low rainfall and a short season (100 days), cotton can be grown on riverine alluvial soils. For further details see A. Kassam (1976).

7. Hogendorn (1978, p. 105) makes a similar argument. "The key to the growth of groundnut production in these early days was more intensive interplanting. The groundnut with its shallow roots draws on soil nutrients at a higher plane than guinea corn or millet. Planted between them and adding nitrogen . . . the nuts could be harvested with little sacrifice of foodstuffs."

8. Shea (1975, p. 66) makes a similar point. He argued that grain was regularly imported into Kano emirate in the nineteenth century and that food deficits occurred around the birni long before conquest.

9. In a manner not unlike that described by Geertz (1971) among Asian wet-rice cultivators, Hausa peasants procured additional increments of grain and groundnut production by the intensive application of manure. Reductions in fallow and ultimately the appearance of permanent cultivation was accompanied by the increased application of organic manure. For a study of the relations between manuring, productivity, and population densities in Hausaland, see J. Schultz (1976). A typical guinea corn (threshed) yield is 350 to 400 pounds per acre without manure, and 650 pounds intensively manured. Manure outputs are approximately 12 goats = 7 donkeys = 2 cattle = 2.5 tons of manure. See J. King (1939) and K. Hartley and Greenwood (1933). MacBride estimated that manure costs in Kano varied from 2 to 30 percent of the value of grain crops. On heavily manured *jangargari* soils an average of fifty-seven ass loads of manure per acre constituted 21 percent of the value of the grain yield (roughly 1,209 pounds unthreshed).

10. It was estimated that the cost of an adequate daily diet, including beans but not meat and excluding the cost of firewood and cooking, was 2½d per adult per day, or 4/4½d per week for a household including a man, wife, and two children. The current wages of 4d to 6d per day for regular labor were thus insufficient to provide an adequate diet for a small household (see table below).

	Weekly wages		Food		Firewood		Total	
	s.	d.	s.	d.	s.	d.	s.	d.
Case B.	4	8	3	1½	1	2	4	3½
Case S.	4	6	3	5	1	2	4	7

11. By 1937 the production of cattle, sheep, and goat skins was as follows: 10.17 million, 1.69 million, and 4.80 million pounds, respectively, at a collective value of £876,214. The export head of beef cattle increased from 25,000 in 1917, to 84,878 in 1952. The cattle trade was, of course, considerably larger since the southern cities constituted the principal consumer demand for pastoral products. In 1936, 100,847 cattle crossed the Jebba bridge on the hoof, a further 23,590 by rail. The Dantata family in Kano were instrumental in the evolution of this cattle trade. See Baier (1974), Forde (1946), Okediji (1975), and Dunbar (1970).

12. See "Report on the Sylvan Conditions and Land Utilization in Northern Kano and Katsina Provinces, 1939" (NAK Kanoprof- 5/1 File 4048). In the close settled zones pastur-

age was at a premium by the turn of the century, and in 1912 H. R. Palmer noted that in Kano Province "there is hardly enough pasturage for existing cattle" (NAK Kanoprof. 5/1 108/1916).

13. To my knowledge, no historical work has been undertaken on conflicts between pastoral and sedentary communities under conditions of limited graze and high population density. For a recent work see T. Eddy (1979), and van Ray (1975, pp. 36, 37); the latter showed that between 1962 and 1967 the number of court cases against Fulani pastoralists in Safana Native Court, Katsina, due to crop damage had increased by 20 percent.

14. In comparison with Dupire's 1947 estimates of Wo'daa'be expenditures—20 percent of which was for food, and 35 percent for clothing—Sutter's 1977–78 data show that, respectively, 66 percent and 15 percent of monetary expenses were incurred on food and clothing. Sutter conducted his study during a period when the terms of trade had moved sharply against the pastoral economy.

15. Grain prices in Kano were generally higher than those prevailing in Damagaram and hence attracted foodstuffs southward into the savannas. Prices per pound of millet in Kano (k) and Zinder (z) were as follows: 1909, 0.1d (k) and 0.1d (z); 1920, 1.1d (k) and 0.5d (z); 1926, 0.7d (k) and 0.4d (z); 1936, 6.0d (k) and 0.3d (z). See Baier (1980), Sutter (1981), and Watts (1979). After the 1930s, as groundnuts made inroads into the Damagaram food economy, much of Nigerian Hausaland also became a food-deficit area.

16. Cattle taxes were collected from July to October. In spite of the widely held belief that Wo'daa'be could easily avoid *jangali*, "this may not be open to any considerable number of Fulani since, despite their migratory life, they are tied to a fairly rigid cycle of movements and returns for a particular area are checked by the district head and any marked discrepancy or anomaly is investigated by the administration" (Forde 1946, p. 209).
  The somewhat more flexible, not to say chaotic, system in Niger may have been a further inducement for some Wo'daa'be to flee northern Nigeria.

17. For many of us who have worked in rural Hausaland and are convinced that yields have declined historically (see Raynault 1977; Collion 1981) the absence of good-quality yield data from the colonial period is highly problematic. Assessment reports did estimate yields but unless the type, quality, and manure input to the farm is known, any historical comparison is dubious. Since weather conditions fluctuate on an annual basis anyway, the task is doubly difficult. A comparison of crop productivity (pounds per acre) on manured holdings in Sokoto derived from the same district is perhaps of some value. (See D. Norman et al. 1976, p. 96; and NAK SNP 472p/1913.)

Year	Millet	Guinea corn	Peas
1967/8	689	111	56
1913	704	304	100

18. The entrustment system has been almost wholly ignored throughout the Sahel and the West African savannas. Village cattle are increasingly nonresident in Hausa villages, and appear only when the owner wishes to make a sale. While on lease, the Fulani have total

rights over milk production but not over offspring. One impact of the drought in northern Katsina was the exchange of ownership between pastoralists and agriculturalists; however the entrustment system has ensured that many Fulani stayed in business, though their *ownership* of herds within their jurisdiction declined markedly. See C. Delgado, "Southern Fulani Farming Systems in Upper Volta," *USAID Report, 1978*, Center for Research on Economic Developments, University of Michigan, Ann Arbor. Research is currently in progress on this issue by Tom Bassett, University of California, Berkeley.

19. Working in Nigerian Hausaland Raynault (1976, 1977a), Nicolas (1965), Miranda (1979), and Sutter (1981) have all commented on the historic decline of large family farming units and estates.

20. Goddard (1973, p. 214) discovered that the incidence of gandu was highest in the densely populated, land-scarce riverine areas where the requirements of mutual security were apparently high. Goddard argued however that some of the needs for collective security could be met within a loose gandu structure, though the traditional authority and decision-making roles have changed. See also Tina Wallace (1979).

21. Hill's work revealed that 38 percent of 717 married men lived in houses containing at least 7 married men (i.e., big houses).

22. The average wage rate per laborer per week in the tin mines was as follows: 1912, 3/-; 1918, 4/-; 1924, 5/9d; 1930, 4/- (Ndama-Egba 1974, p. 85).

23. Forde (1946, p. 168) commented that

[farm laboring] is felt to be a shameful sign of distress and, if undertaken at all, is generally done in another village. Moreover, the needs for labour on a man's own farm are at their maximum at this time and on this labour will depend his own harvest and later income. Such labour is also said to be very poorly paid, money or corn to the value of 3d. per day being a good reward.

24. Nicolas put it this way, using the role of praise singers (*makada*) as a measure of cultural change, "in days gone by they sang of the exploits of warriors, the fecundity of the genitors, richness in millet, the beauty of women. Today they sing of wealth, piety, wearing apparel and a house of *banco*" (1962, cited in Collins 1974, p. 86).

25. Roseberry's work on merchant capital in nineteenth-century Venezuela provides an excellent blueprint for the commercial activities of European, Levantine, and Hausa merchants in northern Nigeria and is worth citing at length.

It is through usurers' capital that merchant capital can move beyond the sphere of circulation into production. While the two types of capital (merchant and usurers') can be separated conceptually, in practice they are often united in the same persons. Both require the accumulation of money wealth. The merchant/money-lender may use one form of capital to aid in the accumulation of capital through the other form. For instance, the merchant as money lender may use credit and interest relations to buy cheap and sell dear, thus establishing what Marx called a "system of robbery." Where scattered producers own or control means of production and are producing commodities and the merchant/money-lender enters into direct relations with the producers rather than with upper class members, the merchant may loan money for the production or consumption expenses of the production unit (i.e., for its reproduction). [Roseberry 1978, pp. 8, 9]

See also C. Keyder (1980, pp. 579–97).

26. Giles (NAK Zariaprof. 1486A) commented on borrowing for food as follows: "For food, 'that is the great reason.' . . . It is easy for a good farmer to run short of guinea corn . . . if it is not caterpillars, it is locusts, or fire, or the farmer was ill last season, or had to sell some of his corn to pay a debt, or he repaid in corn for a loan of corn taken last season. . . . You *must* have corn, till the (early) maize or millet is ripe" (pp. 23, 24). On borrowing for marriage, "'for your boy's marriage you borrow without hesitation or patience; an unmarried son in the compound is a horse which had not been tethered.' More men than not, except in unusually wealthy towns, borrow to make up this amount: it is 'the common debt' or even 'the only cash debt.' A man raises all he can himself first then borrows 7/-to 30/-; 10/- is the most ordinary people borrow. . . . A gown which fetches 10/- (is resold by the borrower), repaid at 15/- is a typical loan. But you can even take a 7/- gown at 20/-, 10/- at 30/- if necessary" (pp. 27, 28).

27. References to shortweighting are quite numerous. See M. G. Smith (1951) for an excellent discussion of this in Zaria. (Also NAK SNP 17 22185 Vol. III; NAK SNP 1 2218E Vol. II.)

28. Giles's comments on interest rates, quoting local opinion in Zaria, are worth quoting in view of the prevailing opinion that interest tends not to be onerous in the countryside.

"There is not one righteous man in ten villages who lends corn without interest." The usual rate is 1 for 2 ("hansaku") or 2 for 3; even 1 for 3, if you are pressed [p. 24]. A man needing money during the rains may raise money by selling so many bundles of corn at 4d or 6d. The money is paid now, the corn only delivered at harvest. Such corn is largely bought by women. Or he tries to borrow: a merchant says he will lend him so much, and hands him a sack or a bowl: the loan is to be repaid by so many measures at a certain price. Future corn was sold at Agaji at 7½d a bundle and 3/6 a sack; it was only 3/6 on the "spot" market at its cheapest, but buyers are willing to give the same price for "futures," in order to secure a supply at the cheap rate. [pp. 43–44]

29. In spite of the fact that any information on rural indebtedness and moneylending is difficult to obtain since usury and interest are such ideologically charged issues in Muslim society, there is every reason to take seriously Vigo's findings. Vigo was a long-term civil servant in northern Nigeria with a vast amount of local-level experience. Giles acknowledged the invaluable work of Vigo in his 1937 report; furthermore Vigo's fluency in Hausa language and the respect he commanded in the districts adds considerable legitimacy to his survey.

30. Prior to the Second World War, the competition between produce buyers in the countryside was often intense, particularly when the firms were under pressure to maximize exports. The result was cut-throat competition between the Syrians, UAC, and their agents, which occasionally exploded into outright violence (NAK Kanoprof. 4455). Under these circumstances of competitive buying, advances flourished and farmers could afford to be selective in their creditors. In 1945 rural producers not only benefited from buoyant commodity prices but repaid loans to middlemen in cash not in produce, preferring to sell to other buyers who offered still higher prices (NAK Kanoprof. 2401 Vol. III).

31. There were in fact several attempts by the colonial administration to regulate moneylending during the 1930s and 1940s, which met with little success in the rural areas since some of the most active creditors were invariably the local-level bureaucrats. In 1945 N.A. Ordinance No. 17 prohibited the mortgage of standing crops, penalizing each agent to

the tune of £15 for the first offense. Yet in the same year, the Katsina Resident observed that a major moneylender in the province was a prominent member of the emir's household (NAK SNP 17 38133). It is ironic that in the same year as Vigo's report, Alhaji Ahmadu Dantata proposed to the executive committee in the northern region (NAK MSWD 1358/S.1) that

> the practice by certain unscrupulous people especially Syrians and Lebanese of advancing money and goods to farmers at exorbitant prices during the wet season and requiring them to pay with their crops at harvest time be stopped.

32. Forde (1946, p. 244) commented on the producer response to price unpredictability.

> Should the season end with a rising price level, the tendency to increase the area of production will be visible in the following season; on the other hand, in many areas on the fringes of the ground-nut country, cotton is a competing export crop, and if the price of ground-nuts is depressed throughout the months of sale in relation to that of cotton lint, there will be an increase of the acreage under cotton at the expense of ground-nuts in the next year.

CHAPTER 6

1. To my knowledge no systematic effort to estimate regional food deficits and surfeits was ever made. Local or district data are patchy, inconsistent, and doubtless horribly inaccurate at the level of yield per unit area. Even in the 1960s the weakest macroeconomic information pertained to the food sector.

2. Much of this information is derived from the Colonial Blue Books covering the years 1904–1910 (PRO CO 446 ref. 19358, April 30th 1905; Tukur (1979, pp. 903–907; and NAK Yolaprof. Vol. I 1904). In all these early cases, though there was great loss of life, "the government was unable to assist" (Annual Report Northern Nigeria 1904).

3. "The famine which devastated the country so terribly in 1904 still continues. It is estimated that fully 50 percent of the riverain pagan tribes in the Gongola Valley have died from starvation. To quote two cases: the towns of Banjeran and Shillem originally contained 8,000 and 4,000 apiece, but now only 336 and 676 respectively." Cited in R. Kuczynski (1948, I, 696).

4. According to Mallam Gunuzu (interview, Katsina, July 25, 1977), after the deposition of Emir Abubakar by the British in 1904 for subversion, the election of his successor Yero—an aged and partly blind head of a junior Dallaji family—prompted much political squabbling, and finally a rejection of British overrule by Yero himself. Prior to his removal from office, however, Yero demanded that all farmers in and around the birni should not plant their farms, ostensibly to complicate the accession of Emir Dikko.

5. Interviews with Mamman Gumuzu, July 25, 1977, Katsina. Also Mallam Ibrahim Nakara, July 14, 1977, Katsina; and Alhaji Bala Dantahudu, Mallam Danburadi, and Mallam Audu, Kaita village, September 1977.

6. The majority of the information on 1908 is abstracted from NAK Kadminagric File 14429, Famine relief, no pagination.

7. In actual fact southern Katsina was also affected, though to a lesser degree, and Palmer (NAK SNP 7 4691/1909) observed in 1909 that "there are few sheep and goats . . . in the more southern villages owing to the failure of 1908." The northern Katsinawa were actually selling grain surpluses to "the hungry Kanawa" (NAK Katprof. 1289/1909).

8. In a pathetic commentary, Festing remarked that the new district heads "will not even report [the refugees] less they should suffer. . . . The gates of most towns in these particular districts are shut against the wretched people who have supplied what little food is inside their walls" (NAK SNP 7 5490/1908 p. 3).

9. Oral testimony, Mallam Sani, Alhaji Gambo, and Mohammed Saulawa, Katsina town, June 24, 1977. Also NAK Katprof. 1388, Katsina Division, Quarterly Report, 1907, no pagination; NAK Katprof. 1821 Annual Report Kano Province,1907 par. 126; NAK SNP 7/10 3035/1909, Kano Province Annual Report, 1909, par. 166.

10. See NAK SNP 7, 3835/1912 Kano Province, Gumel Emirate, Mohamon Na Keta Assessment, 1912, pp. 1, 2. Also Kanoprof 5/1, 1708 Vol. 1, Revenue Survey in Kano, n.d., p. 8.

11. Mallam Abdu Yarsiba, Katsina, July 4, 1977; and Alhaji Abe. Interviews with Bala Rabi and Alhaji Abdullahi, Katsina town, July 20, 1977. See also NAK SNP 15 ACC. 162/1908–09, p. 3.

12. Between 1903 and 1907, the total levy on the three principal taxes rose from 6,400 ·to 12,000 cowries, payable in kind. In 1908 this was collapsed into a single farm tax and commuted into cash at the minimum rate of 3/-per holding; that is to say, a direct, fixed annual levy of approximately 10 to 15 percent of the total production of "an average holding." The special taxes were abolished in 1920. For a discussion of these changes see R. Hull (1968, pp. 252–276). (Also NAK SNP 7/10 3035/1909, par. 238; NAK Katprof. 1 1849, 1865, 1842; Katsina Division, Quarterly Reports, 1910, Reports #50, 51, and 52.)

13. For a discussion of the tax revolt in Madawaki District see NAK SNP 7 1974/1908 and Tukur (1979, p. 662).

14. See NAK SNP 10 567p/1915, Tukur (1979, p. 568 ff.), and Shenton (1982).

15. The canoe tax, for instance, was absurdly high, ranging from 5/- to £3 per canoe per annum in spite of the fact that five shillings would buy a canoe outright (Tukur 1979, p. 595; and NAK Sokprof 756/1905).

16. By comparison, in Katsina emirate in 1908 the tax per adult male varied between a low of 2/5d (Dan Yusufu District) and 5/5½d in Galladima (NAK SNP 7/10 1512/1909).

17. The British felt that the early tax rates were low and could be raised to higher flat rates when the threat of popular protest was eradicated and military hegemony established (see NAK Sokprof 315/1905).

18. Birdwistle commented that "when I was in Sokoto an attempt was being made by the brokers who had large stocks of cowries to force the exchange, which had been unduly inflated up to 600 cowries for 3d down to 300. This situation was caused by the scarcity of silver in the province at the time the annual collection of tribute was made, the Government

ruling that this . . . should not be accepted in either cowries or kind but only in cash. Holders of silver this position, naturally took advantage of it to get possession of cowries at a very cheap rate with a view to putting them back on the market at a very dear one" (NAK SNP 7/8 1765/1907).

19. District Head salaries, which in Zaria and Kano ranged from £100 to £1,000 per annum, were used to support staff which (according to Resident Goldsmith) should have numbered in the order of twenty to function adequately (see NAK SNP 10 51p/1915; NAK SNP 10 98p/1914; NAK SNP 10 107p/1914).

20. The talakawa shouldered the additional drudgery of house construction for their new hakimai and entourage (NAK SNP 7 1114/1912) and the continuation of precolonial cheppa payments, which the colonial officers neither controlled nor fully grasped (see Tukur 1979, p. 440; NAK Yolaprof A12/1912).

21. Within eleven months of British occupation in Sokoto, forced labor had constructed the court house, the Resident's billets, an army camp, and a government jail (NAK Sokprof 5/1904).

22. Railway construction was described by Lugard in 1903 as "forced levies of carriers guarded by bayonets" and, not surprisingly, many households migrated for fear of conscription (NAK SNP 10 107p/1914).

23. At the time, there was a local peasant epithet which captured the tenor of peasant discontent. "No more taxes, No more slaves, No more laws and each to do as he pleases."

24. See R. Hull (1967, pp. 262–65). (Also NAK SNP 10/6 134p/1912; Kano Province Annual Report, 1912, pp. 5–26.)

25. See NAK Katprof, 1/1 1216, Katsina Division, Quarterly Report #64, 1913, Resident Mathews, par. 21, who argued that households were reducing the size of their holdings.

26. Production rose from 2,000 tons in 1912 to 19,000 tons in 1913 (Hogendorn 1978).

27. See Grove (1973), Schove (1977), and Nicholson (1976) for detailed meteorological information on the 1913 drought.

28. Other regional names for the 1914 famine are *Kakalaba* (derived from the ache of hunger inside one's stomach), *Gyallere* (meaning suffering of an intense sort), *Kumumuwa* (derived from *Kukumi* meaning hardship), *Kankamo* (meaning tight in the sense of constrained) and *Sude mu Gaisa* (meaning to lick ones hands). (Mallam Kadabo, Mallam Sani, and Alhaji Gambo, Katsina town, June 24, 1977; Wakilin Kudu, Lahaji Hamza Yankyaure, Alhaji Lawal, Mallam Gurshe Darma, Mallam Samaila, and Alhaji Mohammedu, Katsina town, July 13, 1977.) For relevant oral verse see the Appendix.

29. Oral data, Alhaji Urwatu and Alhaji Alyasu, Katsina town, April 7, 1977.

30. See NAK Katprof. 1. 3146, Northern Division, Kano Province; Quarterly Report, March 1914, p. 5; NAK SNP 389p/1915 Kano Province Hadejia Emirate; Assessment Report, Mr. Hall, par. 73.

31. NAK Kanoprof. 4/2 447/1914 Kano Province Half Yearly Report, June 1914, p. 2. Also NAK SNP 9 321p/1914 Kano Division Food Prices, p. 1.

32. The peasantry withheld nuts in the hope of a price rise, but the firms were able to extract small quantities which were sent south for export and then brought north again to be sold to the peasantry at inflated prices when the famine was at its most intense. (See NAK Kanoprof 4/2 447/1914 Kano Province Half Yearly Report, June 1914, p. 25.)

33. See NAK SNP 10 102/1915 Sokoto Province Annual Report #11, 1914; the Resident observed that three classes were affected by high prices, the poorer classes (mainly agricultural, and also urban poor), the Fulani cattle owners who do not farm, and the chiefs (and those engaged in administrative work), who to some extent depended on purchases of grain, p. 19.

34. As irony would have it, one of the local explanations for the outbreak of war was the idea that Germany refused to provide foodstuffs for relief when called upon by Britain to do so.

35. NAK Kanoprof. 4/2 447/1914, p. 2. See PRO CO 583 17, ref. 30585, Food Supplies, 1914, p. 304.

36. NAK Kanoprof. 4/2 447/1914, pp. 2, 3. Also PRO CO 583, 7, ref. 28655, 1914 Food Reserves, p. 43.

37. A similar holdup was staged the previous month in Babban Mutum where local reserves were raided (NAK Katprof. 1/1 3148/1914).

38. Prior to their departure, destitute households became increasingly dependent upon wild or "famine" foods. A Northern Division officer reported that "the talakawa resort to wild herbs and roots . . . at first *tsaido* later *kinchia* then *karangia*" (NAK Katprof. 1 3148/1914).

39. According to Resident Buxton, Bornu experienced a total decrease of 142,312, roughly 29 percent of the 1913 population (NAK SNP 10 109p/1915).

40. Alhaji Dankalu, Mai-aduwa, March 10th 1978.

41. Tukur (1979, p. 16) estimates the famine mortality of Bornu alone as 84,000.

42. Several residents in Katsina town described to me how their nascent trade interests were irrevocably terminated by the 1914 famine.

43. Freund believes that even at the inflated grain prices of 1913 the real income of mine workers prior to the First World War was higher than at any time since (1981, p. 66).

44. See *The Mining Journal*, 97, 4 (1912), pp. 424, 425.

45. The Shuwa Patrol originated because the Arabs were "truculent," "they refused to stop burning grass," "ignored Game Preservation laws" and were "criminals" (NAK SNP 10 95/1914).

46. See Baier (1977, p. 50) for a discussion of the pastoral economy about 1914 in Niger.

47. According to official jangali estimates there were 4 million head of cattle in 1913 and 3.53 million in 1918 (NAK Katprof 1/1 1329/1925).

48. Many herders were undoubtedly forced into a sedentary life-style until herds were reconstituted, but those with large, diverse herds were able to resume their nomadic existence quite quickly. Reduced herd size and distorted age-sex composition limited the extent to which Fulani families could participate in the postfamine price boom; but it seems clear that, for those with animals, high prices and high demand shifted the terms of trade in favor of the pastoral sector. By 1918 cattle prices were between five and ten times higher than prewar levels (see Baier 1980, p. 244).

49. NAK SNP 9 2846/1918 Annual Report Northern Provinces, 1918, par. 85. "The shortage of corn is . . . due to the increased cultivation of groundnuts and cotton and increasing non-farm communities."

50. Dispossessed talakawa received uncultivated bush in lieu of their farms.

51. According to Swainson (1938, p. 8) "[farmers] were not energetic until spurred by the threat of dispossession."

52. In 1935, of thirteen mixed rice farmers, ony two were "peasants"; the Annual Report mentions in passing that several Sokoto sarauta, including the Sultan and the Wazir, held acreage on the scheme.

53. NAK SNP 10 105/1920, Annual Report Sokoto Province #16, 1919, par. 60. The extension of cotton had progressed very rapidly in southern Katsina, and by 1924 almost one-third of the cultivated area in Maska District was devoted either to cotton or groundnuts.

54. By 1925, in Tudun Wada District, Kano Province, where the average holding was 2.7 acres per adult man, each household "grows as much cotton as grain" (NAK SNP 9 2949/1925).

55. Poor rainfall in Sokoto Province during 1918 pushed up grain prices until they were far in excess of the purchasing power of the administration to fulfill the needs of institutions. As a result grain was compulsorily obtained from farmers at deflated prices. (See NAK SNP 10 289p/1919; Half Yearly Report Sokoto Province, 1919, par. 63.)

56. This discussion is largely based on NAK Biudist. #260 1919, and Katsina Museum, manuscript #109, 1920.

57. The Kano Resident preferred moral and political pressure on the "improvident Kano farmer," while in Bornu the risk of shortage was "not so great." The Governor felt inclined to argue that any famine expenditure could be met from the NA treasury since, as he pointed out, only £3,000 had been spent on relief in 1914. I can only assume that the Governor was apparently unaware that some 150,000 people had died as a consequence.

58. Interview, Mamman Gumuzu, Katsina town, July 25, 1977.

59. McCullogh observed an extraordinarily high incidence of amoebic dysentry due to the overconsumption of famine foods.

60. McCullogh observed that

the famine foods of the Hausa were carefully inquired into . . . and it appears that in the towns some . . . grain can be obtained . . . from the rich. The grain is pounded in the usual way but the husks are not winnowed out. A porridge is made of the whole grain called "daka duka." The small quantities of grain are [filled] out with large quantities of leaves. . . . It is remarkable that the price of meat does not increase much. As the crops fail so fodder gets scarce and animals are slaughtered for food. In the . . . districts the same remarks apply with the addition that more leaves are eaten. [NAK Katprof, 1 2098, p. 3]

The plants referred to are *giginya (Borassus flabellifer), dinya* (Vitex Cienkowskii), *cediya (Ficus Thannengii), ciciva (Maerua angolensis).*

61. The price data are taken from: NAK SNP 10/9 120p/1921 Kano Province for the fifteen months ending March 1921; NAK SNP 10 181/1925 Kano Province Annual Report, 1924, p. 63; NAK Kano LA 28/1927, Food Prices.

62. "It is important that grain should be put freely on the market when the new crops are ripening so that people may not be tempted to eat unripe millet. There were many deaths . . . from this cause" (Report on Famine Relief 1927, p. 55).

63. According to the ordinance, the food controller had the power to prohibit food import and export. Imported foodstuffs were to be supplied in bulk to the NAs who were then responsible for the organization and distribution of relief (Famine Relief 1927, p. 5).

64. The emirs supported Butler to the extent that the sale of crops prior to maturity and crop mortgaging were prohibited. Yet through these mechanisms the agents of the European firms acquired produce in the face of stiff competition.

65. Between 1928 (when groundnuts fetched £12 per ton) and 1933 (when the prevailing price was £2.–13.0) total peasant production increased by almost 300 percent.

66. "During the last few years the activities of middlemen have increased enormously. . . . The situation reached a climax in the last buying season when the greater part of the crop was marketed by middlemen and commissions offered by the firms reached unheard of levels . . . which meant that .1d to .2d per pound was lost to the producer" (NAK SNP 22185 Vol. II/1939).

67. "Cotton is the chief money crop but is not available as cash until the end of December and in order to pay their tax the farmers have to borrow on their crops. . . . Later in the season the farmer is more or less at the mercy of the middleman and has to accept whatever price he cares to offer" (Katsina Museum, #234/1934).

68. In the event of nonpayment, the peasant stood to have his farm holdings confiscated. For this reason, most taxpayers resorted to borrowing from local creditors rather than run the risk of confiscation and incurring the wrath of local bureaucrats.

69. The firms accordingly attempted to regulate competition by merchandise agreements in 1934 and 1937 that maintained market shares among the companies based on past performance (Shenton 1982).

70. See NAK Ministry of Natural Resources 12805 Vol. I, Famine Relief, 1930; 10233A Locust Destruction, 1932; 16474 Locust Infestation 1938; 10233B Locusts 1939; NAK Kadminagric. 14429 Famine Relief, 1930; NAK Katna 1 403 Famine Relief, 1930; NAK Kanoprof 5/2 Locust Destruction, 1930.

71. Flying swarms first appear in early May and lay eggs. The first generation of hoppers appears four weeks later, but the more numerous second generation hatches in mid-September and continues to be troublesome for two months.

72. "[T]he Bichi colony . . . appeared for a long time to be doing well but at the end of the season it was found that . . . farmers were not free men . . . but were retainers of the local District Heads and were farming the land for his benefit" (Agricultural Report 1929, p. 4).

73. Between 1932 and 1945 526 mixed farmers started in Daura emirate, and over the same period there were 261 failures (NAK Daura NA 1/1 60/1946).

74. Mixed farming permitted farming households to expand their cultivated area but generated additional labor demands—for weeding, manuring, harvesting—which could not be met from existing familial sources.

75. For a discussion of the Nigerian cooperative movement see Strickland (NAK Kadminagric. 621/1934), King (1976), and Adeyeye (1978).

76. The cooperative movement had always been more successful in the southern provinces. By 1952, there were 690 registered in the western and eastern regions, compared to 69 in the northern emirates (Adeyeye 1978, p. 73).

77. See NAI 37909//S.14/C.1 Food Control: West African War Council, 1939, p. 3. The following discussion of the intrawar period is based largely on the following archival materials: NAI CSO 26 38983 Food Control, Miscellaneous; 37909/S.14/C.2 West African War Council, Food Control; 36378/S.24 vol. 1, Food Production During the War 1940–42; 36289/S.4/C.8, Food Reserves in the Northern Provinces 1944; 36289/S.4/C.2 Vol. II–IV, Millet and Guinea Corn Purchases 1940–45; 37909 vol. 1–2, Supply of Foodstuffs to HM Forces, 1940–41; also NAK Kadminagric 1/1 3712, Food Supplies: Government Grain Reserves, Katsina; NAK Kadminagric 1/1 72691 vol. 1, Corn Storage; NAK Kadminagric 37228 vol. 11, Kano Food Supplies 1943; NAK Kadminagric. 31657/S.3 Vol. II, Economic Organization and Grain Production; NAK KatNA 1/1 403 Grain Reserves 1940; NAK KatNA 1/1 349 Food Control During Wartime, 1939.

78. See NAI DC/11 4038/vol. 1, Food Control, pp. 2–6. Also NAK Kadminagric. 1/1 72263 Vol. II, Sale of Foodstuffs, p. 1.

79. NAK KatNA 1/1 403, p. 71: "That NAs whose people tend to concentrate on export crops . . . should maintain reserves at their headquarters of 1000 tons of corn . . . according to circumstances."

80. The 1942–43 famine is known variously as 'Yar Gusau, 'Yar Balange, and 'Yar Dikko. The latter is an appellation confined to Katsina and refers to the significance attached to Emir Dikko's grain requisition in 1942.The prevailing opinion on 'Yar Balange seems to be that during 1943 a poverty-stricken peasant attempted to sell his sister in exchange for food.

81. "[T]he Great Bengal famine of 1943 was a *boom* famine. Food output did not fall very much. . . . But the economy—fed by immense war-related expenditures—was subjected to powerful expansion of demand in general and demand for food in particular" (Sen 1980, p. 618).

82. The method of computation for potential grain surpluses available for requisition was remarkably suspect. For Daura for instance each adult male was assumed to have 3.5 acres yielding 500 pounds of threshed millet per acre—an optimistic figure even for the more fertile districts of Kano. The mean grain consumption per adult male plus dependents (presumably one wife plus a child) was 30 pounds, that is to say well below 2 pounds per person per day. After a magical sleight of hand, the food controller concluded that 2,000 tons of grain was "surplus" in Daura for the 1942 season.

83. NAK SNP 17/4 34327 Annual Report, Katsina Province 1941, p. 27. The average tax burden was raised by 3d.

84. The data are taken from NAI CSO 26 37909/S.5 Vol. III, Grain Supplies for the Military; NAI CSO 26 36289/S.6, Grain Bulk Purchases: Allocation and Distribution, 1943, p. 12.

85. Frequent claims were made that peasants who failed to meet groundnut quotas as part of the wartime campaign were summarily shipped off to the mines.

86. The death rates among Bornu recruits during the early 1940s ran at roughly twenty-five per thousand.

87. The Resident concluded in a minute that the root causes of the trouble were (i) 10,000 tons of requisitioned grain exceeded local capacity, (ii) insufficient attention to village capacity, and (iii) irregularities by NA officials. The latter involved illicit sale of relief grain and the prosecution of several NA bureaucrats in the emir's household (NAK Kat. NA VI 403/1944).

88. According to Cowen (1980) the postwar drive to increase commodity production in the colonies arose out of a national response by the Labour Party in Britain in the face of American economic hegemony.

89. Weeks (1977) estimates (using supply and demand elasticities that took account of "real" prices in the event of no Board price regulation) that effective tax rates of groundnuts and cotton were 27 and 30 percent respectively.

90. Groundnut prices were buoyant throughout the postwar period and production grew from 250,000 tons in 1940 to 428,000 tons in 1954.

91. Collion (1981) estimates that considerable quantities moved into Niger in 1947–49 and 1954–56, approximately 7,000 tons in an average each year.

92. This was obvious from M. G. Smith's (1950) household study in Zaria Province in 1949.

93. "An indication of the seriousness . . . is to be found in the small numbers of goats and sheep. . . . The possessor of 3 goats may be counted a wealthy man. Horses are selling for as little as £5" (NAK Kanoprof. 398/S.1 1951).

94. As is the case throughout much of the North, the size of the wet season tiya is roughly 20 percent smaller than the postharvest tiya (which is about five pounds).

95. The issue of grain on credit to farmers to tide them over the "hungry season," six tiyas per householder and two tiyas for each family member per week.

96. The provincial administration estimated 250 deaths in Daura, and for the first time invoked overpopulation as a major cause of the famine (NAK Katprof 1/1 4028/S.1 1951).

97. After a poor harvest in 1954, the price of sorghum in many of the northern emirates leaped by £16 per ton.

98. See NAK Kadminagric. 72691/1955; NAK Kanoprof 2/2 AGR/46 1956; NAK Kadminagric. 1/1 6040/1955.

99. In an extraordinary statement, the UK Trade Commission in New Delhi reported that "storage methods in India have been rather primitive consisting mainly of digging pits . . . pushing grain into them and hoping for the best."

100. The stores were to be located at Gusau, Funtua, Kano, Zaria, and Bukuru.

101. The highest proportion, just over 30 percent of domestic farm acreage, was found in Bindawa, a district with little uncultivated bush, only 3 percent under fallow, and population densities of almost 350/square mile.

102. Southern Katsina was a surplus producer of grain, which suggests that the dry northern districts were in massive deficit.

103. In Bindawa village, 50 percent of the farmers owned less than five acres of upland, while almost 20 percent cultivated in excess of ten. Luning's (1963) simple stratification indicates that in Ilale and Bugasawa villages between 30 and 40 percent of farmers were forced to labor during the wet season.

104. In Bindawa and Kadandani the proportion of purchased fields was closer to 40 percent.

105. Vigo's survey in Katsina established that 60 percent of all loans were taken from traders, canteens, and village heads; 22 percent of the loans were for food, 15 percent for marriage, and 15 percent for labor. In four Katsina villages, the proportion of loans taken for food constituted 43 percent of the total.

106. "Under normal circumstances the purchase of grain becomes one of the principal components in the budget of the average farmer, especially in cotton and groundnut areas" (Vigo 1958, p. 16).

107. H. R. Palmer, in response, was of the opinion that the savannas had changed little since the time of Ibn Battuta. "Bornu, almost treeless as it has been for many decades is a perfect reservoir for cattle and produces millet in abundant quantities" (NAK Katprof. 1 1389/1916).

108. "It is not appreciated by those who have visited parts of the northern emirates at the height of the dry season what this country looks like after the rains" (NAK Sokprof. 2/1 4094/1935).

109. MacBride pointed out that manure, when available, cost ¾d to 1½d per assload, and donkey hire was 2d per day.

110. See Sutter (1981), Hill (1972), Raynault (1977*b*), and M. G. Smith (1950).

111. By 1942, 13 percent of all arable land had been alienated for mining purposes and 73 percent was on license or lease.

112. According to surveys by de St. Croix and Sharwood-Smith in the 1930s, the percentage of male animals among 1,000 enumerated cattle was 16 percent, somewhat less than optimal. See Dupire (1962) and Dahl and Hjort (1976) for a comparison. In 1931–32 a large herd in Kano Province lost 29 of its 132 animals due to mortality and sale (NAK SNP 9 18783/1932).

113. Jangali receipts indicate 4.4 million in 1960–61; Werhahn et al. (1964) estimate 7.8 million based on output rates and 9.7 million on hide statistics.

114. With the resultant loss of manure (see E. Scott 1979). For practical and legal reasons the dry-season grazing of Fulani herds on crop residues has become less popular, particularly in populated districts.

115. "The first victims of this evolution were the herders, progressively forced towards the desertic zone; when a sudden halt of the rains come, they cannot advance the date of their migration towards the southern grazing lands, now under cultivation. The number and violence of the conflicts between herders and farmers reflects the growing tension between the two groups during the last decades" (Raynault 1975, p. 10).

116. This also meant a significant decline in food production in an area that had become a major grain supply area for Katsina, Kano, and Sokoto.

117. See Freund (1981), Olofson (1976), Osoba (1969), Prothero (1957), and Saulawa (1977).

118. NAK SNP 9 472/1909. This was certainly not exceptional and flights of this form recurred throughout the period up to 1945 (see Hull 1967; Fika 1973; Tukur 1979).

119. M. G. Smith's example of a salt-seller's marriage is instructive; of the total expenditure incurred by the groom's family (£9.15.5), roughly £5 involved cash gifts and £2.10.0 for European cloth.

120. This is the essence of Meillassoux's (1981) argument concerning the partial engagement of rural producers in the modern sector. The actual wage per laborer covers only the (short-run "variable") costs of sustaining the labor power spent by the individual laborer, but not the ("total average") costs necessary to maintain and reproduce capitalist workers as a group. This difference is what Meillassoux calls "labor rent." For a further discussion see Amin (1974), and Plange (1979).

121. Some of the "surplus" population migrated to take up farming in areas of land surplus. This was particularly the case in Gombe emirate where voluntary settlement by Fulani pastoralists and immigration by Hausa farmers after 1949 were instrumental in postwar development in that area (Tiffen 1976).

122. For a discussion of the state as least-effort principle see Hopkins (1973), for the instrumental view see Suret-Canale (1971) and Brett (1973).

123. "It was the contradictory purpose of accumulation . . . within a local framework. It demanded the creation of a local political system . . . governed not by the "needs of capitalism" but rather by crisis-driven efforts to contain social conflicts . . . generated by them" (Lonsdale 1981, p. 109).

124. I have no idea why Milewski (1975, p. 44) should argue that "the greater part of society, living outside the money economy, remained virtually unaffected."

125. Though Temple's diatribe on the science of lying and the native mind sometimes reads like Thomas Pynchon, any fieldworker in Hausa society knows precisely what he means. M. G. Smith's (1955) anecdotal remarks on his reception in a Zaria village in the late 1940s are especially instructive.

126. For a discussion of peasant protest in relation to the Little Tradition and colonial hegemony see Scott (1977*a*, 1977*b*, 1977*c*) and Ranger (1977).

127. One could envisage (i) a peasant who grew only foodstuffs in a relatively self-sufficient manner, part of which was sold; (ii) a peasant who grew food for domestic consumption and also export commodities; (iii) a peasant as in (ii) but who was forced to purchase local grains; (iv) a peasant who supplemented grain and export crops through sale of labor (a) to mines or (b) to local farmers; (v) the household as in (iv) but which was a year-round petty commodity producer (blacksmith, weaver); and (vi) the wealthy farmer who purchased little food, grew large quantities of cotton and groundnuts, but generated the great proportion of cash income from trade.

128. For a strikingly similar instance of colonial predation and ineffective relief see the accounts of the 1930–31 famine in Niger (Fugelstad 1974; Saifou 1975; Derriennic 1977).

CHAPTER 7

1. For a discussion of Sahelian rainfall anomalies in the late 1960s and early 1970s see Bernus (1973), Oguntoyinbo and Richards (1977), Dalby et. al. (1974, 1977), Charney (1975), and Bryceson (1974). On the long-term socioeconomic effect of the famine see Berg (1975).

2. See Baker's (1977) discussion of what he calls the "Sahel information crisis."

3. See Sheets and Morris (1974),Ware (1975), and Caldwell (1975). It was, however, quite frightening how quickly these figures were adopted unconditionally by the United Nations and other agencies.

4. In Niger, for instance, between 1972 and 1976 animal losses were as follows: cattle (64 percent), sheep (83 percent), goats (94 percent) and camels (82 percent). See Sutter (1980).

5. The literature is huge but for a representative sampling see Copans (1975), Comité Information Sahel (1974), Glantz (1976), Derriennic (1977), Franke and Chasin (1980), Galais (1977), Lofchie (1975), Meillassoux (1974), Shephard (1975), Richards (1975), Ormerod (1976), and Rapp (1974).

6. See Thurston Clarke (1978) and Franke and Chasin (1980, pp. 5–15).

7. The proliferation of Sahelian research and rural development efforts over the past five years has been quite extraordinary. The list of acronyms is itself astonishing. Much of the academic research and report writing—and here one might single out some of the AID-sponsored work—has however been of the most primitive quality.

8. The 1954 famine in Katsina is referred to as "*Uwar Sani*," and in Daura localized shortages in 1967 and 1970 as "*sololo*" ("it lasted too long") and "*Mai dan buhu*" ("everyone hunted grain with a small sack"). In 1959 the Resident of Sokoto reported that there was a famine "but no one died" (Provincial Annual Report 1959, p. 155).

9. Sutter (1981) working in Zinder (Niger Republic) discovered that household food expenditures also increased from 5 percent in 1961 to 34 percent in 1977–78.

10. In Yola 1972 was quite wet, and close to average in Jos, Minna, and Kaduna.

11. Kaduna, Zaria, and Bida received close to the long-term average rainfall.

12. For a review of available data see van Apeldoorn (1978, Vol. I).

13. Several papers on drought effects and consequences appear in the Proceedings of the Conference on the Aftermath of the Drought in Nigeria, Kano, 1977. See van Apeldoorn (1978a, 1981).

14. Although it is something of a platitude among researchers in Hausaland, it bears reiteration that price data are notoriously varied in quality. The spatial heterogeneity of local prices, equally varied differences in local grain measures, and volatile prices between seasons all testify to the difficulty of confident generalizations.

15. Mortimore (1977, p. 35) reported that 26.7 percent of all immigrants into seventy-one Kano villages over the period 1972–74 were "international," almost wholly from Niger.

16. Of the total migrants from the three villages, 53 percent were occupied as laborers, 13 percent as farmers, 12 percent participated in trade and 5 percent as butchers (Abdu 1976, tables viii–x).

17. For what little empirical data exist on famine-induced migration, see van Apeldoorn (1978), Ndaks (1976), Kura (1976), Ahmed (1976), Abdu (1976), and Mortimore (1977).

18. A considerable amount of work on the relief effort was conducted by the Centre for Social and Economic Research of Ahmadu Bello University, from which I benefited greatly. See van Apeldoorn (1981), Hassan (1976), and Saulawa (1976).

19. The *Daily Times* fund reached over three-quarters of a million naira by February 1974; the southern states also contributed significant quantities of gari.

20. Daura received 350 tons for this purpose.

21. Saulawa (1976, p. 38) cites eleven officeholders in Daura who owed ₦61,358 in total.

22. See the White Paper on Kaduna State Judicial Commissions of Inquiry, Kaduna State, 1976, p. 27.

23. The two floodplain woodland communities, to the northeast and southeast of the gari, are heavily inundated during the wet season and their hydromorphic soils are sufficiently heavy and poorly drained to prevent dry-season cultivation. As a consequence, these two bottomland niches remain relatively well wooded with *Typha australia, Saccharum spontaneum*, a sprinkling of goriba and giginya, an occasional community of *Mitragyna inermis* and a plethora of moisture-loving grasses and forbs, most especially *Ipomoea repens, Cyerus dives, Oryza barthii, Acroceras amplectens* and *Echinochloa acolonium*.

24. Lemon, mango, guava, dum palm, shea-butter, Christ's thorn and desert date all thrive along the riverine margins.

25. In 1976 the district head of Kaita was the second son of Emir Usman Nagogo who died in 1981.

26. This is not to argue, of course, that Kaita is not part of the economic hinterland of Katsina, which it clearly is; the flourishing periodic market located in garin Kaita attracts merchants from well beyond a twenty-mile radius. Indeed, I argue that the penetration of urban merchant capital into the countryside, articulated through rural trading networks, is critical for any understanding of the processes of rural differentiation and impoverishment. Masu sarauta refers to the three households that can be said to constitute the ruling class, a traditional elite. As I document later, these households are much larger than average and clearly wealthier than other families, with perhaps the notable exception of several village-based merchants and grain traders. The district head, Sarkin Sullubawa Hussaini, is the brother of the current emir of Katsina and a person of regional importance. The district scribe, the brother of a well-known northern politician and the son of the former district head, is a large landholder and prosperous rural businessman. The village head, the galadima, assumed his position from his father during the late 1960s and the headship has remained within his family for at least three generations. These three individuals are uniformly recognized as masu sarauta by the Kaita populace and are distinguished not so much by their wealth, which in two cases is enormous, but by their blood and their political connections with both the traditional Muslim elite in Katsina and the current local government cadre based in birnin Katsina, of which they are part. From the perspective of the peasant (talakawa) the masu sarauta are individuals in which wealth, political influence, and traditional Muslim-based legitimacy have all simultaneously congealed.

27. Kaita village is to be distinguished from the entire district of which it is the administrative center; from the Kaita *village area*, which subsumes five lower-order territorial units (*unguwa*), namely Girmawa, Daba, Dabawa, Gande, and Kaita itself, and finally from Kaita *unguwa*, which embraces the gari and several smaller hamlets and dispersed homesteads within a radius of roughly two miles.

28. The formative period is generally associated with two rather mythical figures, Dindin and Baree, who seem to have appeared during the 1780s, and an enormous baobab

tree that possessed certain magical attributes and ritual significance. The first village head (magaji) of garin Kaita, which was then located adjacent to the fadama approximately one mile to the east of the current site, was one Danpapa. He was succeeded by his son Kalu, who was deposed by the jihad forces during the early 1800s.

29. The territorial extent of Kaita District has historically been quite stable with the exception of the incorporation of a diminutive Dankama district (ninety square miles) in the early 1950s. Kaita District is currently 814 square miles, constituted by twelve village areas (ungawa).

30. Dankaba village area grew by 240 percent and Gafiya by 225 percent (statistics provided by Katsina Provincial Office).

31. According to a survey of Kaita District by the Funtua Agricultural Development Project in 1978, 68 percent was cropped, 5 percent fallow, 14 percent forest, 8 percent uncultivated, and 5 percent "not available" (i.e., tracks, roads, rivers).

32. The nonfarming category subsumed the desperately poor landless men, many of whom were clients (baraori) for the village masu sarauta; a large number of single or multiple female units who quite frequently possessed farmland but generally entrusted it to others; and a wealthier group of local government salaried employees, many of whom were posted to Kaita and were landless though they often retained and cultivated farmland in their home communities. The average size of nonfarm households was 2.9 persons; 70 percent were presided over by women.

33. Ninety-five percent of all adult males were either landowners or part of complex farm holding units (gandaye).

34. Of 896 individual farms, 168 were fadama holdings.

35. Kaita is very much a hoe culture based on the *fartanya* (small hoe) and *galma* (hand plow). In 1977 there were only six registered mixed farmers in Kaita village, four of whom were, in practical terms, no longer active. While there is a limited market for plough hire among the wealthier households, the potential value of oxen and plough units has been largely undermined by the presence of three tractors owned by one sarauta family and two merchant-trader households. Either way, the deceptively simple technology of the precolonial epoch prevails among smallholder grain producers, who constitute the core of the Kaita agricultural economy. A sample of Kaita farmers interviewed during 1977 revealed that only 5 percent make use of a plough or other forms of mechanical cultivation on upland farms, and less than 15 percent employ artificial fertilizer.

36. Matsai soils consist principally of several feet of fine, pale sand and quartz over yellow looms and coarse sands (see Tomlinson 1960).

37. Following the rosette epidemic in 1975, and the depressed prices offered by the marketing boards, only 3 percent of farm households planted groundnuts in 1977.

38. See Norman (1967) and Norman et al. (1976).

39. Among a sample of thirty-seven farmers, 30 percent used ashes (toka), 37 percent goat, donkey, or sheep manure (takin dabobin gida), and 35 percent household refuse (takin juji).

40. Between January and June most livestock are free-ranging, consuming local fodder, principally *sabara, dilo,* and *kalgo* leaves, but during the period of upland cultivation they are tethered and fed on legume weeds and grasses collected from arable farms. The manure is accrued from these tethered holdings throughut the dry season. The piles of manure are then spread thinly immediately prior to the rains, in spite of the fact that much material is questionably lost through aeolian drift. The rate and periodicity of application of fertilizers varies enormously between households. Successful farmers with small cash surpluses often purchase manure, generally from poor or destitute households who are desperately short of money for dry-season consumption and ceremonial activities.

41. I am highly skeptical of Hill's (1972) claim that Batagarawa was land surplus in 1967. A decade later there is almost no cultivated bush in northern Katsina, as one might deduce from the population densities.

42. The Dankabba series is referred to locally as *yashi,* which Bargery (1934, p. 112) defines as "coarse sand usually applied to river sand." The heavy poorly drained basin soils of the Gafiya series, on the other hand, are subsumed by the general term "*laka*" or "*allaka.*" The terminology surrounding these finely divided alluvial materials is complex since they were variously referred to as "*kalankuwa,*" *lallakiya,*" and "*babbarkiya.*" And finally, the Kadandani subset (the aeolian and colluvial deposits overlaid on basin sediments) is identified as a discrete pedological category but is usually unnamed, except perhaps in a generic sense as "*kasar fadama*" or occasionally as "*dandori.*"

43. The prized but rather elusive white egret manure (*balbela*) and pigeon deposits (*dan tattabara*) are priority items for onion cultivation, while ashes and limited quantities of goat manure appear well suited to tomatoes, pumpkin, gauta, datta, and peppers. Cattle manure is never used and donkey wastes only rarely on these items.

44. There are in fact three different water distribution systems. First, the *fangali* system is preferred for the cultivation of onions and salad vegetables. Each bed is a rectangular depression usually five feet by three feet, surrounded by a small embankment (*kege*) about three inches wide. Second, the *jakki* system generally employed for spices and cotton, which consists of a long, narrow channel—perhaps twenty feet long and one foot wide—which feeds widely spaced depressions in which the cultigens are planted. And third, the *korama* system is a lattice of long canals separated by meter-wide, shallow platforms on which cultigens with relatively narrow moisture tolerances, such as tomatoes, are grown (for a discussion in Niger see Raynault 1969).

45. Yields are difficult to compute but from data collected during 1978, the average output per fangali was as follows: onions, 20 lbs per bed; peppers, 3 baskets (*kwondo*) per bed amounting to 15 to 20 pounds; and tomatoes, roughly 50 pounds per bed. At 1978 prices, an acre (1,000 fangali) of tomatoes would be valued at roughly ₦500.

46. Domestic organization can really be studied processually only as a tendency, not as a state. Gandaye and iyalai intersect cyclically on the death of a father, sons may remain together in a fraternal gandu, or they may set out on their own and establish their own independent nuclear unit. When their sons marry, and continue to work with their fathers, the domestic structure once again becomes a paternal gandu. In addition, there are numerous other factors besides stage in the household development cycle (such as the manner in which households participate in larger economic networks) that influence the size, composition, and functions of gandaye. The household, to use·Medick's (1976) term, is "contextually identified."

47. See Hill (1972) and Goddard, Mortimore, and Norman (1976) for comparable work.

48. See Goddard (1973) regarding gandaye in Sokoto, and for similar arguments in Nigerian Hausaland see Sutter (1981), Miranda (1979) and Raynault (1977*b*).

49. Under conditions of land scarcity gamana plots tend to be small and masu gidaje are increasingly reluctant to divide up the collective fields. In Niger, according to Raynault (1977*b*, p. 24), women produced 25 percent of total cereals on their gamana fields, but very few fields are held in this manner in Kaita. Yields on these individual farms are generally about one-quarter less than their collective counterpart (see Miranda 1979).

50. In relation to the upland, fadama cultivation is labor intensive. In Sokoto, man hours per cultivated acre of upland was 195; fadama conversely required 389 man hours per acre (Norman et al. 1976, p. 74).

51. Sutter's (1981) work in Yelwa indicates, conversely, that the average number of man days of gayya labor per household was 40 per annum; the corresponding figure for wage labor was seven.

52. According to Norman et al. (1976, p. 30), in Sokoto, average family labor per farm holding was 266 man days per year, excluding 48 man days of hired labor. In Kaita, almost 50 percent of families hired in wage labor at some period of the year; the prevailing wage rate was between ₦1 and ₦1 20 kobo per day (six hours). An average household hires in between four and five days of wage labor during June, July, and August.

53. Rural wages rose from roughly 3d per day in the 1930s to 1/- in 1948 (Pedler 1949), 2/- to 5/- in 1957 (Vigo 1957), 6/- in 1971 (Hill 1977), 60 kobo (6/-) in 1974 (Matlon 1977), ₦1.50–₦2 in 1978 (Watts 1979), and ₦3 in 1979 (Clough 1979).

54. In Zaria and Sokoto the figures were respectively 3.7 percent and 22.1 percent (Goddard, Mortimore, and Norman 1976, p. 324).

55. In Kaita the rough and ready purchase prices (per acre) of jigawa farmland were as follows: 1900, 1/-; 1935, 7/-; 1950, 30/-; 1960, £7; 1970, £40; and 1976, ₦150–300.

56. Among the wealthy households, one-quarter of all farms were purchased; in contrast only 8 percent of the remaining farms were acquired through purchase.

57. According to a sample of thirty farm sales over the last thirty years, the reasons for sale were as follows: famine and food shortage (6), taxation (4), marriage costs (3), migration of owner (2), confiscation (2), no inheritor other than wife (2), owner too old to farm (2), landholding too small to be subdivided (2), personal financial predicament (cause unspecified) (6), farm pledged then finally sold (1).

58. Gini coefficients on net farm income in Kaura Kimba (Sokoto), Dan Mahawayi (Zaria), and Naboyi (Bauchi) were 0.4043, 0.5004, and 0.3873, respectively. See Norman, Pryor and Gibbs (1979, p. 127). The gini coefficient is a concentration ratio between 0 (total equality for any distribution) and 1 (total inequality).

59. Gini coefficients on landholding distribution were highest (i.e., high landholding inequality) in an isolated Bauchi community with a high land per resident ratio and lower

population densities (gini coefficient 0.5577) and in a densely settled Sokoto fadama village (0.4319). Coefficients were lowest in a high density nonfadama village in Sokoto near birnin Sokoto (0.1987).

60. This seems to be the case in Takatuku, Sokoto State. In Dawaki-ta, Kudu District, Kano, a revenue assessment report shows that over a ten-year period (1937–47) landholdings changed as follows:

| Size | 1937 | | 1947 | |
	Dawaki	*Ruma*	*Dawaki*	*Ruma*
Less 2 acres	16.3%	12.1%	20.1%	14.5%
2–5	50.1%	40.0%	53.3%	39.1%
6–10	20.3%	27.3%	16.5%	26.1%
10+	13.4%	22.2%	10.1%	20.3%

61. In absolute terms the most common nonfarm occupations were local government employees (12 percent), petty trade (7.2 percent), large-scale trade and contractors (6.6 percent), Koranic scholars (6.6 percent), butchers (4.8 percent), weaving (4.8 percent), mat making (4.8 percent), and brokerage (3.3 percent).

62. Of Group I, 50 percent of the total occupations were trade-related compared to 11 percent in Group III. Eighty percent of Group III occupations were craft or wage-related.

63. No systematic effort was made to measure upland farms but the results of landholding measurements of eight Group I, seventeen Group II and nine Group III households revealed the following average acreages: Group I, 10.1 acres; Group II, 4.5 acres; and Group III, 2.0 acres.

64. The dates of onset (O) and termination (T) of the rains in Kaita 1969 to 1975 were as follows: 1969 O = May 19th, T = October 20th; 1971 O = April 17th, T = September 30th; 1973 O = June 2nd, T = October 2nd; 1975 O = May 12th, T = September 15th.

65. Annual totals vary over very short distances; in 1962 the total precipitation in Kaita, Dankama, and Yandaki was respectively 20.1, 38.2, and 28.1 inches.

66. Occasionally farmers dry-plant (*bizne*) prior to the onset of the damana but timing is critical for seed cannot be left in the soil ungerminated for more than ten to fourteen days. Further, the probability of a false start during the early part of the wet season is very high. Householders who dry-plant tend to be those with relatively large holdings and planting is related to domestic labor supply, their financial capacity to purchase casual wage labor, and their ability to complete planting within one or two days of the onset of the rains.

67. Daudu (1976) and Ndaks (1976) reported no change in crop spacing in Katsina and Daura in 1973; Aliyu (1976) however, working in Sokoto, established that 84 percent actually reduced spacing.

68. The principal millet varieties used are zongo, dandigali, wuyan bijimi, maigashi, dan barno, and tamajen hatsi; growth cycles vary from 80 to 120 days. Sorghum varieties include farfara, kaura, yar bazenga, jar dawa, babada, kama, and kerama.

69. These trends are noticeably different from those gleaned from a hastily conducted survey of a small sample of farmers near Katsina by Richards and Oguntoyinbo (1978) who established that 10 percent increased their acreage, 20 percent used tractors, 10 percent employed more labor, 60 percent "farmed cooperatively" (?), and 20 percent instituted new agricultural methods (unspecified).

70. In Daura emirate during the same year (Ahmed 1976, p. 25), responses to food shortage among a sample of 150 households were as follows: 80 percent sold labor, 60 percent sold animals, 60 percent collected fodder, 4 percent sold land, 37 percent sold manure, 33 percent sold wood, 26 percent borrowed money or food, and 6 percent sold other property.

71. Similarly in a Daura study only fifteen individuals left on *cin rani* (Ahmed 1976). Conversely, Mortimore (1977) estimated that in Kano State almost one-half of all household heads left for some period following the 1973 harvest.

72. Women reported that during 1973–74 the production of luxury items like *kadi* and *nakiya* was minimized but the production of cheap cooked foods such as kuka and gari actually increased significantly since many poor families substituted cooked foods for grain.

73. The most common foods were yadiya (*Leptadenia lacifolia*), kauci (*lorathus* spp.), kuka (*Adansonia digitata*), tafasa (*Cassia tora*), aliyara (*Euphorbia balsaminifera*), yakuwa (*Urena loborta*), and chediya (*Ficus capensis*).

74. According to Ahmed (1976, pp. 23, 24) working in Rijiyar-Tsamiya village (Daura) the average household holding of sheep and goats fell from 4.5 and 8.7, respectively, in 1972 to 1.8 and 3.4 in 1975.

75. Almost two-thirds of all households reported borrowing grain or cash with some form of interest, although any estimate of mean interest rates is almost impossible to derive.

76. The state relief effort distributed 500 tons of grain in Kaita District, roughly seven pounds per person, between June and August 1974.

77. The riskiness of marketing pertains to the decision whether to sell one's produce to wholesalers in the Kaita market at relatively low prices, or to risk sending the vegetables south in the hope that price levels are much higher. Because of the poverty of the communications system, producers send vegetables from Kaita with no prior knowledge of Ibadan prices other than those prevailing during the prior week.

78. In one of the few village studies that explicitly address the impact of the 1973 famine in household inequality, Ahmed (1976, pp. 23, 24) determined that in Rijiyar-Tsamiya (Daura) the holdings of the "rich" increased from an average of 5.3 farms to 6.0 between 1972 and 1975. Those of the "poor" fell from 3.0 to 2.2. Ahmed estimated that 17 percent of the talakawa's holdings were pledged.

79. I am especially indebted to the Institute of Development Studies at Sussex for participation in a Conference on Seasonality and Rural Poverty in 1978, from which I

gleaned many of the ideas in this section. See Chambers (1979), and Chambers, Longhurst and Pacey (1981).

80. Climatic seasonality can obviously be measured in a variety of ways; Walsh (1978) distinguishes relative seasonality (the degree of contrast between rainfall at different times of the year) and absolute seasonality (the length of the dry period).

81. During the 1977 wet season, the average number of days on which the mai gida could not work due to illness was May to June, 2.0 days; July to August, 2.8 days; September to October, 2.9 days; and November to December, 3.2 days.

82. In his study of Yelwa village, Sutter (1981) estimated that all economic groups fulfilled 100 percent of their domestic needs from their own production in November 1977. By June 1978 the two poorest segments supplied only 48 and 37 percent of their needs from home-produced grain.

83. During the same period, in a similar area in Nigerian Hausaland (Sutter 1981) only fifty miles from Kaita, the price of millet rose from 28 to 80 CFA per kilo. By February 1978 half of the monthly consumption of millet of the poorest households was purchased.

84. For similar conclusions on the time of grain purchase and sale see Raynault (1976, 1977b) and Sutter (1981).

85. Sutter (1981) also discovered that in Yelwa the poorest households purchased 28 percent of total cereals between September and December at a mean price of 35.5 CFA per kilo, and 72 percent after January at an average price of 62.5 CFA per kilo.

86. An "average" expenditure for a first wife in Kaita in 1977 was ₦250, at least half of mean annual income.

87. That is to say, they simply had greater credit worthiness.

88. Between March and July 1978 the only individuals who sold millet or cowpeas were wholly from Group I households.

89. I reserve judgment on whether Batagarawa was in actual fact land surplus.

90. Hill was unable to provide scientific evidence that farmers varied greatly in their efficiency.

91. See Chayanov (1966). For an examination of the Chayanovian model and its shortcomings see Harrison (1975, 1977), Hunt (1979), Patnaik (1979), Shanin (1972).

92. "[There] is much truth in the philosophical attitude . . . that it was only if he also had luck on his side that he could fight back" (Hill 1977, p. 165).

93. As she admits, it is ridiculous to analyze the causes of *individual* poverty (1977, p. 164).

94. In my opinion there are critical methodological weaknesses in the farm survey methods (Palmer-Jones 1978a, Watts 1980) to say nothing of the interpretation of differences in factor productivities.

95. According to Crawford (1980, p. 240) the overall inferior performance of poorly endowed households to accumulate was their inability to (a) carry out crop fertilization and (b) engage in profitable off-farm occupations.

96. Matlon admits that the masu sarauta do not readily fall into his theoretical frame.

97. I cannot discuss here the methodological problems of Matlon's work, not least the use of income as a stratification device, difficulties in aggregation, the causes of different factor productivities, and the estimation of incomes where input and output markets are not well developed. See Palmer-Jones (1978*b*).

98. Hill (1972, p. 122) talks of "choosing" credit and "granting" falle loans.

99. "At Dan Alhaji, six farmers were quoted straight away as well-known money-lenders. . . . In other words, moneylending comes near to being a recognized profession" (Giles 1933, p. 72).

100. Saunders (1978) estimated that in south-central Niger, a first marriage cost, on average, $250 in 1971.

101. A marriage of kinsmen auren gida or marriage to a widow or divorcée (*zawara*) is less costly (perhaps 40 to 50 percent less) than taking a young, never-married girl (*buduruwa*).

102. Crawford (1980, p. 241) estimated that poorly endowed households accumulated net capital at less than one-third the rate of the better endowed.

103. Matlon (1977) shows how cash constraints on the poor are an obstacle to optimal timing of farm operations with the result that income and output are correspondingly low.

CHAPTER 8

1. In 1975 there was a significant decline in oil output; annual production fell by as much as 20 percent due principally to a world recession and overpriced crude (Ogbonna 1979, p. 77). Also the NNCP ordered a 10 percent reduction in output in August 1979 to extend the life of known reserves—which at the present level of production would last at least 25 years. This cutback followed an earlier complete relaxation of oil production ceilings in 1978, when at one point production dropped to 1.5 million barrels per day (b/d). It had recovered to 2.4 million b/d by July 1979 (*New Africa Yearbook* 1979, p. 275).

2. The first statutory corporations included the Electricity Corporation of Nigeria (1951), the Nigeria Coal Corporation (1961), the Railway Corporation (1955), Nigeria Airways (1959), and so on.

3. The military government's development budget for 1979–80 indicates the priorities of the era, with ₦2,092 million (32 percent of the budget) allocated to the oil industry and manufacturing, ₦962 million (14.5 percent) to transport, ₦602 million (9 percent) to defense, ₦540 million (8 percent) to power, and ₦391 million (6 percent) to education. In the same financial year the major recipients of recurrent, or operational, expenditures were education with ₦874 million (30 percent of the recurrent budget), and defense with ₦520 million (18 percent) (*New Africa Yearbook* 1979, p. 270).

4. "The synonym for a wealthy Nigerian became 'contractor,' symbolising a new . . . symbiosis between two rapacious partners, expatriate business and a swelling Nigerian class of compradore contractors" (Freund 1978, p. 98).

5. The steel works would initially produce 1.3 million tons a year and eventually 2.5 million tons. To complement the blast furnace, West German firms are building a direct-reduction plant at Warri, due for completion in 1981 at a cost of N1.26 billion. Steel rolling mills are to be built at Katsina, Jos and Oshogbo.

6. Both Bierstecker (1978) and Hoogvelt (1979) argue that the indigenization legislation of 1972 and 1977 (Nigerian Enterprises Promotion Decrees) did not increase Nigerian participation in the control of production. It simply shifted the financial risk of investment onto Nigerians without any increased control. It also seems unlikely that any local accumulation has been promoted by indigenization, but rather conspicous consumption, real estate speculation, construction, and mercantile projects.

7. The growth of manufacturing investment principally involved low-technology production (textiles, cement, soap), which constituted 75 percent of paid-up capital in 1972. The greatest concentration of manufacturing in Nigeria is in Lagos-Ikeja (33 percent), and Port Harcourt, Aba, Kaduna, and Kano (37 percent in all). Almost 300,000 people are employed in the modern manufacturing sector (*Africa Now*, October 1981, p. 147).

8. Using an industrial production index of 100 in 1972, the Central Bank reported that by 1981 the indexes for a variety of industries stood as follows: soft drinks (443), roofing sheets (274), pharmaceuticals (143), cotton textiles (182), beer (214), sugar (210) and vehicle assembly (3,515). See *Quarterly Economic Review of Nigeria*, Annual Supplement, 1980 and *Africa Economic Digest*, May 1982.

9. According to Bierstecker (1978) 41 percent of "large, local capital" (i.e., an annual turnover exceeding N2 million) in Nigeria is commercial and trading capital.

10. In the three periurban districts of Gezawa, Kumbotso, and Ungogo adjacent to Kano city the proportion of total taxpayers participating in the formal sector taxpayer system (PAYE—pay as you earn) increased from zero in 1963 to 6 percent in 1973 (involving over 3,000 individuals).

11. Within the cities the older established urban wards have also felt the real estate speculation. Increased rates, upgrading of property, and high tenant turnover has gentrified some of the traditional working class areas, pushing long-time community residents to peripheral and unstable neighborhoods.

12. Lagos is something else altogether. With a population of roughly 4 million it has been referred to as "the dirtiest capital in the world" by the United Nations. The massive growth of the city has not been matched by a transformation of urban services, and the extent of squalor, urban congestion, and disease is quite appalling. Following the Udoji wage increase, a standard room of N8.10 rocketed to N25 per month with an advance of 1–2 years, and it was estimated in 1976 that Lagos required 50,000 housing units for the laboring poor (*African Development*, October 1977). According to Fapohunda (1977) unemployment in 1974 was not less than 8 percent; a 1971 survey estimated unemployment at 21 percent.

13. In 1964 food, manufactures, and machinery constituted 8.1, 35.5 and 29.5 percent, respectively, by value of total imports. In 1978 the statistics were 12.8, 22.8 and 43.6 percent (Central Bank of Nigeria, 1979).

14. Between 1970 and 1977 importation of ready-made garments increased from ₦2.0 million to ₦68.8 million, TV sets and air conditioners from ₦1.1 million to ₦39.1 million, and passenger cars from ₦7.0 million to ₦249 million.

15. The import extravaganza reached its Kafkaesque zenith with the 1975 cement scandal in which 20 million tons of cement (eight times the capacity of Lagos port) sat in 400 ships outside Lagos harbor.

16. Based on the relationship between the government minimum daily wage and the consumer price index, real wages lagged noticeably over the 1960–76 period. The real wage index stood at 100 in 1960 (see table below).

Year	Lagos	Northern States
1960	100	100
1965	113	142
1970	87	115
1975	120	227
1976	100	186

17. Food import price indexes (1960 = 100) for wheat (55) and fish (43) in 1966 increased to 115 and 289, respectively, in 1975. The composite food import price index rose from 100 in 1960 to 308 in 1975.

18. Total U.S. exports to Nigeria reached $1.1 billion in 1980; U.S. farm exports grew from $23 million in 1972 to $301 million in 1978 (*Foreign Agriculture*, 1981 June). Wheat constituted almost half of food exports, being $61 million in 1975 (Oculi 1978, p. 64).

19. In 1978 Nigeria imported 248,785,985 kilograms of wheat flour at a cost of ₦55.1 million; 60 percent was imported from the United States.

20. A five-man task force on the "ricegate" affair documented a considerable involvement in illegal licensing and hoarding by members of both Houses in the National Assembly (*West Africa*, December 1, 1980).

21. In a study using data from the income tax returns of 1966–67 in the former western state, the concentration coefficient was put at 0.47. A survey of 1,635 households conducted in 1967 in all states except three of the then eastern region, found a concentration ratio of 0.58. Another study using personal income tax data (which include self-employed as well as PAYE taxpayers), calculated before-tax gini coefficients for the state of Bendel of 0.39 in 1965–66, 0.525 in 1970–71, and 0.39 in 1971–72. For the western state the corresponding figures were 0.37, 0.28, and 0.31. See Bienen and Diejomach (1981).

22. The Bienen volume concluded that income distribution *within* the agricultural sector was "relatively" equal in comparison to the urban sector, but was characterized by "prevailing generalized poverty" (p. 8). From a national perspective, the income levels in agriculture were so low that the richest households would be placed among the relatively poor (see Matlon 1981).

23. During the 1970s the International Institute for Tropical Agriculture (IITA) developed a HYV maize, which in 1977 was distributed to 2,500 pilot villages. In the same year, the abolition of all import duties on maize meant that U.S. corn could be imported at ₦150 per ton, ₦100 below the cost of local production.

24. Faced with low producer prices, low productivity of existing trees, rising labor costs, government neglect, and inefficient organization of the commodity boards, cocoa and palm oil production plummeted. Cotton and groundnut prospects were equally bleak (see *African Business*, November 1981). By the mid-1970s no palm oil, groundnuts, or cotton were being exported.

25. Capital expenditure by the state governments on agriculture amounted to 18 percent of total state capital expenditure for the two years 1975–77. However, state government recurrent expenditure on agriculture was less than 7 percent of total state recurrent expenditures in 1973–74 and 1975–76. Expenditure on agriculture has not exceeded 3 percent of the federal government's recurrent budget since Independence, and since 1975 has not exceeded 2 percent of that budget. The federal government's actual capital expenditure on agriculture for 1975–77 was only 3 percent of its total.

26. According to a critique by the Central Planning Office, the Third Development Plan was "overambitious" not least because so little was stipulated in planned form. In one year, ₦600 million went to nonplan projects.

27. The Fourth Development Plan (1981–85) represents a major expansion of state policy in the agrarian sector, allocating an anticipated 15 percent (₦4.5 billion per annum) of all capital resources to agriculture (*African Economic Digest*, November 13th, 1981). The 1981 budget allocated ₦1.62 billion to agriculture (*Quarterly Economic Review*, 1st Quarter 1981), four times the allocation of the preceding budget.

28. In conjunction with the food companies, the Bush Clearing and Land Development Program has cleared 45,845 acres of land for expanded state farming operations (*Africa Now*, October 1981).

29. The NGPC is also intended to "encourage Nigerian entrepreneurs to invest in large-scale farming" (CSER 1978, p. 219).

30. Nigerians must have at least 40 percent equity interest in (a) the manufacture of agricultural machinery and (b) plantation agriculture. In agro-industrial concerns (milling, processing, poultry, etc.) Nigerians must control 60 to 100 percent of equity interest.

31. The scheme employs about 500 Italians, 55,000 Nigerians and 600 Portuguese workers.

32. Much criticism has been leveled at the project on the grounds of ecological degradation through leveling, the unresponsiveness of some of the projected crops (especially wheat), the loss of locally valuable trees in clearing, inadequate resettlement, and the effective loss of huge quantities of local fadama.

33. Irrigated farming also meant the abandonment of dry-season crafts and the demise of wet-season sorghum production. The poor, however, cannot forgo these occupations and therefore tend to lease land (Williams 1981).

34. The Plan anticipated a productive capacity of 80,000 tons by 1980.

35. The Commonwealth Development Corporation holds 5.6 percent of the equity.

36. Management is currently in the hands of Poland's Polimex Corporation, Cuba's Imexpal, and the Soviet Prommash Export (*Africa Now,* November 1981).

37. The 1982 federal budget allocated capital expenditure on water resources of N471.3 million, only 66 percent of last year's nominal appropriation of N710.5 million (*African Economic Digest,* February 12, 1982).

38. The ministry's eight departments are: the Federal Departments of Agriculture, Fisheries, Forestry, Livestock, Rural Development, Agricultural Co-operatives, and Pest Control Services, and the Planning, Monitoring, and Evaluation Division. The parastatals are: National Livestock Production Company, National Grains Production Company, National Rootcrops Production Company, Nigerian Rubber Board; Nigerian Palm Produce Board; Nigerian Grains Board; Nigerian Groundnuts Board, Nigerian Cocoa Board; Nigerian Cotton Board; Nigerian Agricultural and Cooperative Bank; and the Nigerian Beverages Production Company.

39. The launching of OFN coincided with the huge handling problems in Lagos port with the result that fertilizer imports recommended for OFN were not available (Ekhomu 1978).

40. The allocation for this purpose in the 1981 budget was N5.2 million.

41. This consisted of 200 tractors, 50 trucks, 250 mobile threshers, 250 irrigation pumps, 250 cereal threshers, and 1,800 maize shellers (*Africa Now,* October 1981).

42. For critical discussions of the new-style projects see van de Laar (1980), Feder (1976), and Williams (1981).

43. The Bank participated in only agrarian programs in Nigeria in 1974, with a $20 million loan for cocoa rehabilitation, followed successively by five loan agreements for seven state-owned ranches, integrated development projects, palm estates, and river valley development totaling $110 million.

44. The Bank has also agreed to loan N21.6 million for smaller agricultural development projects and rural management training institutes in Ilorin, Oyo, and Ekiti-Okoto (*Quarterly Economic Review of Nigeria,* 2nd Quarter 1981). The Bank is appraising projects in Borno, Imo, Bendel, Ogun, and Cross River states.

45. Two other projects at Ayangba and Lafiya started later in 1977 at a cost of N116 million.

46. The broad objectives of the project were 1,500 kilometers of road, 85 earth dams, 5 development centers per district, 77 farm service areas, an administrative and evaluation unit, and the provision of credit, extension, and marketing services (D'Silva and Raza 1980).

47. Clarke (1979) discusses the efforts of the Cocoa Development Unit which requires participating smallholders to provide one hectare to obtain HYVs, fertilizers, and sprays.

But one hectare is more than farmers plant in one year, and for the rural poor is more than 50 percent of land available for cocoa and food.

48. Small-scale producers on the FADP owned 3.9 hectares, utilized 31.9 man days per hectare and spent ₦8 per hectare on inputs. The large-scale farmer owned 94 hectares, used 70 man days per hectare and spent ₦15 per hectare on inputs.

49. Large-scale farmers receive subsidized tractors, additional extension visits and preferred fertilizer distribution. In 1979 each large farmer had a guaranteed ten tons of fertilizer in contrast to traditional farmers who, if they were lucky, received three bags (see van Apeldoorn 1981, p. 140; and Jackson 1979).

50. In 1977–78 poor marketing arrangements for cotton resulted in farmers selling to middlemen at low prices; according to an FADP report (1978 Quarterly Report) the situation was "pathetic and explosive."

51. Ruttan (1975) pointed out the possible regressive income effects of IRDPs.

52. In Kano the Rimi administration has taken a strong antisarauta line—abolishing tax, reducing the authority of district heads, and even trying to remove the emir—which has gained support among the urban talakawa. But the PRP leadership is petit bourgeois in outlook and unlikely to represent the material interests of the industrial workers (Lubeck 1981).

53. In March 1982 the Central Bank of Nigeria temporarily banned the issued letters of credit to importers. This was followed by new import regulations and tariffs on consumer goods, rice, cereal flour, and passenger cars (*African Economic Digest*, April 30 1982).

54. For a discussion of similar effects in Ghana see Shepherd (1981).

55. Cowen (1976, 1980) argued that the intervention of international finance capital in Kenya served to expand a middle peasantry rather than hasten its dissolution. While the aims of the World Bank projects in Nigeria may be populist, their effects are clearly contradictory, accelerating the disappearance of small peasants (de Janvry 1981).

BIBLIOGRAPHY

UNPUBLISHED SOURCES

GOVERNMENTAL ARCHIVES, NORTHERN NIGERIA

Records of the Northern Nigeria Secretariat Group. National Archives, Kaduna (NAK SNP).

Reference	Description
NAK SNP 15 acc 7a	Major Festing's Report, 1899–1900
NAK SNP 1/1 vol. 1 #130	Currency Questions, 1901
NAP SNP 98/1901	Barter, 1901
NAK SNP 1/1 vol. 1 #264	Currency in Northern Nigeria, 1901
NAK SNP 1/1 vol. 3	Notes on Cotton Growing, 1903
NAK SNP 6 4286/1905	Plantations, 1905
NAK SNP 6 64/1907	Political Agent Kiara
NAK SNP 6 81/1907	Intelligence Report
NAK SNP 6 102/1907	Land Tenure and Revenue in Northern Nigeria
NAK SNP 6 136/1907	Kano Provincial Assessment
NAK SNP 6 162/1907	Memorandum on Land Tenure
NAK SNP 7 881/1907	Customs Revenue
NAK SNP 7 1765/1907	Tour of Commercial Intelligence Officer, Birdwhistle
NAK SNP 7 1859/1907	Proposed Transport Policy

NAK SNP 7 1867/1907   Kano Province Annual Report, 1907

NAK SNP 7 2390/1907   Katsina Division, Fawa District Assessment Report

NAK SNP 7 2410/1907   Possibilities of Cotton Growing in Northern Nigeria

NAK SNP 7 2442/1907   Salt Rates

NAK SNP 7 2732/1907   Enquiries Regarding Cotton Growing

NAK SNP 7 2813/1907   Native and Resident Assessment

NAK SNP 7 2968/1907   Kano and Katsina, Assessment Summary, 1907

NAK SNP 7 2978/1907   Cadastral Survey of Northern Nigeria

NAK SNP 7 3095/1907   Kano Province, Half Yearly Report (June), 1907

NAK SNP 15 acc 369   Land Tenure in Hausa States, 1907

NAK SNP 15 acc 372   Salaries for District Sarkis, 1907

NAK SNP 15 acc 374   Memorandum on Land Tenure, 1907

NAK SNP 15 acc 376   Native Administration Proposals, 1907

NAK SNP 15 acc 380   Native Administration Proposals, 1907

NAK SNP 16 4002   Memorandum on Land Tenure, 1907

NAK SNP 10 111/1908   Report on Kano Emirate, 1908

NAK SNP 7 656 5/1908   Memorandum on Land Tenure, 1908

NAK SNP 1538/1908   Kano Province Annual Report, 1907

NAK SNP 2949/1908   Kano Province Annual Report, 1908

NAK SNP 7 3120/1908   Ostrich Farming by the London and Kano Company

NAK SNP 7 5490/1908   Kano Migration Report

NAK SNP 7 6350/1908   Sokoto Province, Argungu Division, Tribute Assessment

NAK SNP 6565/1908   Land Tenure and Assessment

NAK SNP 9 472/1909   Kano Province Annual Report, 1909

NAK SNP 7/10 1512/1909   Kano Division Assessment, 1908–09

NAK SNP 7/10 3035/1909   Kano Province Half Yearly Report (June), 1909

NAK SNP 7 3272/1909   Kano Province Assessment, 1909

NAK SNP 7 5263/1909   Kano District Assessment, 1909

NAK SNP 1/10 6166/1909   Kano Province, Barde District Assessment Report, 1909

NAK SNP 5252/1909   Taxation in Zaria Province

NAK SNP 10/6 3835/1909   Kano Province Quarterly Reports, 1909

NAK SNP 15 acc 384 a18   Correspondence Regarding Indirect Rule in Kano, 1909

NAK SNP 16 0109   Documents of Historical Interest, 1909

NAK SNP 1515/1910   Kano Notes

NAK SNP 3635/1910   Kano Province Annual Report, 1910

NAK SNP 6242/1910   London and Kano Company Litigation

NAK SNP 6255/1910   Muri Province Quarterly Report

NAK SNP 17 50897   Native Land Proclamation

NAK SNP 1114/1912   Kano Province Annual Report, 1911

NAK SNP 7 1140/1911   Sokoto Province, Wurno District Assessment

NAK SNP 7 1354/1911   Kano Province, Kiru District Assessment, 1911

NAK SNP 7 2384/1911   Kano Province, Yerima and Galadima District Assessments

NAK SNP 7 2715/1911   Kano Province, Dutse District Assessment, 1911

NAK SNP 7 2991/1911   Gonyoro District Assessment

NAK SNP 7 3973/1911 Trade in Sokoto Province

NAK SNP 7 2793/1912 Kano Province, Makama District Assessment, 1912

NAK SNP 7 3835/1912 Kano Province, Gumel Emirate, Mohaman Na Keta Assessment, 1912

NAK SNP 7 4055/1912 Kano Province, Dan Iya District Assessment, 1912

NAK SNP 7 5785/1912 Kano Province, Dan Buram District Assessment, 1912

NAK SNP 7 6689/1912 Industrial Taxation

NAK SNP 7 6249/1912 Katagum Division, Azare District Assessment

NAK SNP 10 134p/1913 Kano Province Annual Report, 1912

NAK SNP 10 135p/1913 Kano Province, Madaki District Assessment

NAK SNP 10 152p/1913 Sokoto Province Annual Report, 1912

NAK SNP 10 182p/1913 Bornu Province Annual Report, 1912

NAK SNP 10 230/1913 Sokoto Province, Silame District Assessment, 1914

NAK SNP 10 379/1914 Sokoto Province, Dundaye District Assessment, 1913

NAK SNP 10 430p/1913 Kano Province Quarterly Report (March), 1913

NAK SNP 10 448p/1913 Kano Province Final Assessment, 1913

NAK SNP 9 1147/1914 Report for Northern Provinces, 1913

NAK SNP 10 92p/1914 Bornu Province Annual Report, 1913

NAK SNP 10 104p/1914 Report on Argungu for 1913

NAK SNP 10 105p/1914 Sokoto Province, Talata Mafara District Assessment

NAK SNP 10 134p/1913 Kano Annual Report, 1914

NAK SNP 10 260p/1913   Creation of Sub-District Heads

NAK SNP 10 261p/1913   Hired Labour

NAK SNP 10 262p/1913   Emir's Relations with Non-Natives

NAK SNP 10 363p/1913   Baiawa District Assessment

NAK SNP 10 364p/1913   Sokoto Province, Argungu District Assessment

NAK SNP 10 366p/1913   Sokoto Province, Argungu District Assessment

NAK SNP 10 410p/1914   Zaria Province Annual Report, 1914

NAK SNP 10 414p/1914   Katsina Division, Sulibawa and Ingawa
                        Districts Assessment

NAK SNP 10 567p/1913   Sokoto Province, Denge District Assessment

NAK SNP 10 631p/1913   Kano Division, Jemaari District Assessment

NAK SNP 10 689p/1913   Sokoto Province, Kebbi District Assessment

NAK SNP 10 705p/1913   Sokoto Province, Kaura Namoda District
                        Assessment

NAK SNP 10 743p/1913   Northern Division, Dambam District
                        Assessment

NAK SNP 10 769p/1913   Dogondaji District Assessment

NAK SNP 10 770p/1913   Sokoto Province, Jega District Assessment

NAK SNP 16 c4002   Land Tenure in Northern Nigeria, 1913

NAK SNP 8 55/1914   Native Labour

NAK SNP 9 98p/1914   Kano Province Annual Report, 1913

NAK SNP 9 1147/1914   Report for Northern Provinces

NAK SNP 10 102p/1915   Sokoto Province Annual Report, 1914

NAK SNP 10 175p/1915   Zaria Province Annual Report, 1914

NAK SNP 10 221p/1914   Northern Provinces, Crop Season Report,
                        1914

NAK SNP 10 231p/1914   Kano Food Prices

NAK SNP 10 250p/1914   Nassarawa Province Reports

NAK SNP 10 476p/1914   Sokoto Province Reports

NAK SNP 10 494p/1914   Kano Province Half Yearly Report (June), 1914

NAK SNP 10 609p/1910   Sokoto Province, Raba District Assessment

NAK SNP 10 681p/1914   Zaria Town Assessment

NAK SNP 8 139/1915   Non-Natives in Native Areas

NAK SNP 9 1885/1915   Northern Provinces Agricultural Department, Annual Report, 1914

NAK SNP 10 54p/1915   Sokoto Province, Kwiambana District Assessment

NAK SNP 10 55p/1915   Sokoto Province, Bondugu District Assessment

NAK SNP 10 93p/1915   Katsina Division, Kaura District Assessment

NAK SNP 10 102p/1915   Sokoto Province Annual Report, 1914

NAK SNP 10 139p/1915   Kano Province Annual Report, 1914

NAK SNP 10 152p/1916   Bornu Province Annual Report, 1915

NAK SNP 10 170p/1916   Kano Province Half Yearly Report (December), 1915

NAK SNP 10 274p/1915   Sale of Land

NAK SNP 10 382p/1915   Kano Province Half Yearly Report (June), 1915

NAK SNP 10 389p/1915   Kano Province, Hadejia Emirate Assessment Report, 1915

NAK SNP 10 465p/1915   Gummi District Assessment

NAK SNP 10 474p/1915   Kano Reports

NAK SNP 10 536p/1915   Sokoto Province, Jega District Assessment

NAK SNP 10 553p/1915   Gwangwan and Karaye District Assessment

NAK SNP 10 795p/1915   Village Heads' Share of Excess Tax

NAK SNP 10 254p/1916   Deposition of Certain Sub-District Headmen

NAK SNP 10 419p/1910   Sokoto Province, Kwarre District Assessment

NAK SNP 10 511p/1916   Sokoto Province, Gando District Assessment

NAK SNP 10 518p/1916   Kano Province Half Yearly Report (June), 1916

NAK SNP 10 567p/1916   Sokoto Province, Tureta District Assessment Report, 1915

NAK SNP 10 637p/1916   Sabon Birni District Assessment

NAK SNP 10 768p/1916   Taxation of Private Property of Emirs

NAK SNP 10 97p/1917   Zaria Province Annual Report, 1916

NAK SNP 10 145p/1917   Bornu Province Annual Report, 1916

NAK SNP 10 148p/1917   Sokoto Province Annual Report, 1916

NAK SNP 14 2742/1916   Undesirability of Touts and Middlemen

NAK SNP 8 189/17   Intelligence Report

NAK SNP 9 386/1918   Kano Middlemen Engaged in Trading, 1918

NAK SNP 9 2846/1918   Northern Provinces Annual Report, 1918

NAK SNP 10 203p/1917   Comparison of Taxes Paid in Sokoto, Katsina, Zaria, and Bida

NAK SNP 10 162p/1918   Zaria Province Annual Report, 1917

NAK SNP 10 179p/1918   Kano Province Annual Report, 1917

NAK SNP 10 200p/1918   Sokoto Province Annual Report, 1917

NAK SNP 10 45p/1918   Zaria Town Assessment

NAK SNP 10 481p/1918   Kano Province, Tudun Wada Village Assessment

NAK SNP 10 44p/1918   Kano Division, Barde District Assessment

NAK SNP 10 511p/1918   Sokoto Province, Illo District Assessment

NAK SNP 10 93p/1919   Kano Province Annual Report, 1918

NAK SNP 10 95p/1919   Zaria Province Annual Report, 1918

NAK SNP 7 236/1919   Zaria Province, Soba District Assessment

NAK SNP 8 6/1919   Cash Shortage

NAK SNP 9 2846/1919   Northern Provinces Report

NAK SNP 10 273p/1919   Zaria Province Annual and Quarterly Reports, 1919

NAK SNP 10 289p/1919   Sokoto Province Half Yearly Report (June), 1919

NAK SNP 318p/1919   Kano Province Half Yearly Report (June), 1919

NAK SNP 10 370p/1919   Principles of Taxation

NAK SNP 9 1609/1920   Attitudes Toward Cotton Growing

NAK SNP 9 3329/1920   Cotton

NAK SNP 10 105/1920   Sokoto Province Annual Report, 1919

NAK SNP 10 211p/1920   Dan Marusa District Assessment

NAK SNP 10 105p/1920   Zaria Province Annual Report, 1920

NAK SNP 10 120p/1921   Kano Province Annual Report, 1920

NAK SNP 10 126p/1921   Sokoto Province Annual Report, 1920

NAK SNP 10 316p/1920   Kano Province Half Yearly Report (June), 1920

NAK SNP 7 387/1923   Zaria Province Annual Report, 1922

NAK SNP 9 73/1923   Zaria Province Annual Report, 1922

NAK SNP 10 26/1922   Sokoto Province Annual Report, 1921

NAK SNP 10 548/1922   Kano Province Annual Report, 1921

NAK SNP 9 98/1924   Sokoto Province Annual Report, 1923

NAK SNP 9 100/1924   Zaria Province Annual Report, 1923

NAK SNP 9 1044/1923   Kano Province, Maska District Reassessment, 1923

NAK SNP 9 603/1924   Kano Province, Sumaila District Assessment, 1924

NAK SNP 9 705/1924   Report on Groundnut Trade in Kano Province

NAK SNP 635/1925   Kano Province Annual Report, 1924

NAK SNP 9 1458/1924   Kano Province, Kiyawa District Assessment, 1924

NAK SNP 9 2909/1924   Kano Province, Tudun Wada District Assessment, 1924

NAK SNP 10 181/1925   Kano Province Annual Report, 1924

NAK SNP 7 1460/1925   Dutse District Assessment

NAK SNP 17 K102 Vol. I   Bornu Province Annual Report, 1925

NAK SNP 17 K111   Zaria Province Annual Report, 1925

NAK SNP 17 K105 Vol. II   Kano Province Annual Report, 1926

NAK SNP 17 K111 Vol. III   Zaria Province Annual Report, 1926

NAK SNP 17 K2151   Principal Famines of Hausaland, 1926

NAK SNP 17 Vols. I, II   Sokoto Province Annual Report, 1926–27

NAK SNP 17 K1653   Zaria Province Annual Report, 1927

NAK SNP 17 K5093   Kano Province Reassessment, 1927

NAK SNP 17 6808 Vol. I　　Bornu Province Annual Report, 1927

NAK SNP K6892　　　　　　Kano Province Annual Report, 1927

NAK SNP 17 9159　　　　　Zaria Province Annual Report, 1928

NAK SNP 17 K8823　　　　Katsina Division, Yandaka District
　　　　　　　　　　　　　Assessment, 1929

NAK SNP 17 1894 Vol. I　　Zaria Province Annual Report, 1929

NAK SNP 17 12004　　　　Kano Province Annual Report, 1929

NAK SNP 17 KC Series　　Katsina Division, Yandaka District
　　　　　　　K8833　　　Assessment Report, 1929

NAK SNP 17 6800　　　　　Groundnut Middlemen, 1930

NAK SNP 17 14603 Vol. I　Bornu Province Annual Report, 1930

NAK SNP 17 14818 Vol. I　Sokoto Province Annual Report, 1930

NAK SNP 17 14830　　　　Zaria Province Annual Report, 1930

NAK SNP 17 14868 Vol. I　Kano Province Annual Report, 1930

NAK SNP 17 25673a　　　　Kano Food Prices, 1930

NAK SNP 17 18921 Vol. I　Sokoto Province Annual Report, 1932

NAK SNP 17 18939 Vol. I　Zaria Province Annual Report, 1932

NAK SNP 17 19187　　　　Bornu Province Annual Report, 1932

NAK SNP 17 29652a　　　　Kano Food Prices, 1932

NAK SNP 17 21303 Vol. I　Sokoto Province Annual Report, 1933

NAK SNP 17 21304　　　　Zaria Province Annual Report, 1933

NAK SNP 17 21325 Vol. I　Bornu Province Annual Report, 1933

NAK SNP 17 21326 Vol. I　Kano Province Annual Report, 1933

NAK SNP 17 11703　　　　Mixed Farming, 1934

NAK SNP 17 19378a　　　　Groundnut Prices, 1934–38

NAK SNP 17 20070 Vol. I   Cooperative and Advances, no date

NAK SNP 17 23562   Zaria Province Annual Report, 1934

NAK SNP 17 11703 Vol. II Agricultural Extension, 1935

NAK SNP 17 21336   Arewa Gabbas Assessment, 1935

NAK SNP 17 25673   Kano Province Annual Report, 1935

NAK SNP 1486a   Giles Credit Report, 1937

NAK SNP 17 11703 Vol. III Agricultural Extension

NAK SNP 17 29615   Zaria Province Annual Report, 1937

NAK SNP 17 30862   Zaria Province Annual Report, 1938

NAK SNP 17 11159   Farm and Family Budgets, 1938

NAK SNP 17 30847a   Kano Province Annual Report, 1938

NAK SNP 17/4 30876   Katsina Province Annual Report, 1938

NAK SNP 17 29652   Kano Province Annual Report, 1937

NAK SNP 17 29664   Sokoto Province Annual Report, 1937

NAK SNP 17 20007   Farm and Family Budgets, 1939

NAK SNP 17 1864   Advances

NAK SNP 17/4 34327   Katsina Province Annual Report, 1941

NAK SNP 17 31183   Zaria Province Annual Report, 1943

NAK SNP 17 30007   Grain Prices, 1943–46

NAK SNP 17 31079   Relative Cost of Groundnut and Guinea Corn Production, 1943

NAK SNP 37005   Kano Province Annual Report, 1943

NAK SNP 17/4 37094   Northern Provinces, Chiefs Conference, 1945

NAK SNP 17 41986   Kano Province Annual Report, 1946

NAK SNP 43599   Kano Province Annual Report, 1948

Records of Provincial Administrations, Local Authorities, and Departments Pertaining to the Northern Provinces and the Secretariat Group. National Archives, Kaduna

Katsina Province (NAK KATPROF)

NAK KATPROF 1/1   Katsina Division Quarterly Reports, 1903
1769

NAK KATPROF 1/1   Katsina Division Monthly Reports, 1904
1789

NAK KATPROF 1/1   Katsina Division Monthly Reports, 1905
1797

NAK KATPROF 1/1   Katsina Division Quarterly Reports, 1907
1388

NAK KATPROF 1/1   Katsina Division Annual Report, 1907
1813

NAK KATPROF 1/1   Kano Province Annual Report, 1907
1821

NAK KATPROF 1/1   Katsina Division, Report on
1289   Taxation, 1908

NAK KATPROF 1/1   Katsina Division Quarterly Reports, 1908
1828

NAK KATPROF 1/1   Katsina Division Quarterly Report
1836   (March), 1909

NAK KATPROF 1/1   Katsina Division, Yandaka District
1898   Assessment, 1909

NAK KATPROF 1/1   Katsina Division Quarterly Reports
1849, 1842   (March and June), 1910

NAK KATPROF 1/1   Katsina Division Quarterly Report
1865   (December), 1910

NAK KATPROF 1/1   Katsina Division Quarterly Report
1216   (December), 1913

NAK KATPROF 1/1 Kano Province, Northern Division
3146−48 Quarterly Reports, 1914

NAK KATPROF 1/1 Katsina Division Annual Report, 1914
1978

NAK KATPROF 1/1 Katsina Division Annual Report, 1916
1242

NAK KATPROF 1/1 Katsina Forest Reserves, 1916
1389

NAK KATPROF 1/1 Mai'aduwa District Reassessment, 1925
611

NAK KATPROF 1/1 Katsina Division Quarterly Reports, 1926
1853

NAK KATPROF 1/1 Katsina Division Annual Report, 1927
2098

NAK KATPROF 1/1 Katsina Division, Kaita District
1323 Assessment, 1928

NAK KATPROF 1/1 Katsina Division, Kaura District
1503 Assessment, 1928

NAK KATPROF 1/1 Katsina Division Quarterly Reports, 1928
1928

NAK KATPROF 1/1 Katsina Division, Kaita District
Acc. 1299 Assessment, 1931

NAK KATPROF 1/1 Moneylenders, 1942
128

NAK KATPROF 1/1 Katsina Province Annual Report, 1942
3276

NAK KATPROF 1/1 Migration from Katsina Province, 1942
5277

NAK KATPROF 1/1 Katsina Division Annual Report, 1943
3333

NAK KATPROF 1/1 Famine Relief, 1944
403

NAK KATPROF 1/1 4028/S.1	Katsina Province Annual Report, 1950
NAK KATPROF 1/1 4145	Katsina Province Annual Report, 1951
NAK KATPROF 1/1 4183	Katsina Province Annual Report, 1952
NAK KATPROF 1/1 4	Katsina Division, Dankama District Assessment Report, no date
NAK KATPROF 1/1 36	Katsina Division, Kaita District Assessment Report, no date
NAK KATPROF 1/1 Acc. 162	Taxation, no date
NAK KATPROF 1/1 K2076	History of Katsina, no date

Katsina Native Authority (NAK KATNA)

NAK KATNA 2/36 403	Famine Relief and Corn Reserve, 1930
NAK KATNA 1 349	Food Control During Wartime, 1939
NAK KATNA 1 403	Grain Reserve, 1940
NAK KATNA 2/36 W9	Kaita District File, no date
NAK KATNA 2/36 W762	Durbi District File, no date
NAK KATNA 2/36 W763	Ingawa District File, no date
NAK KATNA 2/36 768	Dan Yusufa District File, no date
NAK KATNA 2/36 W8 Vol. IV	Jibiya District File, no date

Kano Province (NAK KANOPROF)

NAK KANOPROF 5/1 95/1913	Kano Province Annual Report, 1913
NAK KANOPROF 5/1 717/1913	Kano Province Quarterly Report (September), 1913

NAK KANOPROF 5/1   Kano Province Annual Report, 1914
95/1914

NAK KANOPROF 4/2   Kano Province Half Yearly Report
447/1914   (June), 1914

NAK KANOPROF 5/1   Kano Province Half Yearly Report
412/1916   (June), 1916

NAK KANOPROF 1   Kano Province, Daura Emirate
3267/1923   Assessment Report, 1923

NAK KANOPROF 1   Kano Province, Kumbotso District
761/1932   Reassessment Report, 1932

NAK KANOPROF 5/1   Locust Destruction, 1930
564

NAK KANOPROF 5/1   Groundnut Prices and General Tax, 1937
20007

NAK KANOPROF 5/1   Requisitioning of Grain, 1945
5853A

NAK KANOPROF 5/1   Famine Relief, 1950
398 Vol. II

NAK KANOPROF 5/1   Famine Relief in Jahun and Dutse, 1951
398 S.4

NAK KANOPROF 5/1   Famine Relief Kazaure Emirate, 1951
398 S.1

NAK KANOPROF 5/1   Famine Relief Scheme: Danbarta, 1951
S.5

NAK KANOPROF 2/2   Crop Failure Precautions, 1956
AGR 46

NAK KANOPROF 2/2   Northern Division Agricultural Reports,
AGR 78   1958

NAK KANOPROF 5/1   Revenue Survey in Kano, no date
1708 Vol. 1

NAK KANOPROF 5/1   Pagan Communities in Kano, no date
HIS/5

Kano Local Authority (NAK KANOLA)

NAK KANOLA 28/1927   Food Prices, 1927

NAK KANOLA 8/1929   Food Prices, 1929

Zaria Province (NAK ZARIAPROF)

NAK ZARIAPROF 7/1   Zaria Province Annual Report, 1927
2575

NAK ZARIAPROF 1   Agricultural Co-operation, 1933
1480 Vol. I

Sokoto Province (NAK SOKPROF)

NAK SOKPROF 12/1911   Wababi District Assessment

NAK SOKPROF 69/1911   Salame District Assessment

NAK SOKPROF 265/1911   Chafe District Assessment

NAK SOKPROF 385/1911   Badawa District Assessment

NAK SOKPROF 387/1911   Bazai District Assessment

NAK SOKPROF 542/1911   Gumi District Assessment

NAK SOKPROF 553/1911   Bukwium District Assessment

NAK SOKPROF 3/1 793   Famine Relief in the Northern Provinces, 1927
Vol. II

NAK SOKPROF 2/1 4094   The Approaching Sahara, 1937

Biu District (NAK BIUDIST)

NAK BIUDIST 260   Famine, 1919

Gwandu Native Authority (NAK GWANDUNA)

NAK GWANDUNA   Food Price Control, 1942
1253d

Ministry of Agriculture (NAK KADMINAGRIC)

NAK KADMINAGRIC   Famine Relief, 1927
12805 Vol. I

NAK KADMINAGRIC   Strickland Report, 1934
621

NAK KADMINAGRIC   Famine Relief, 1935
14429

NAK KADMINAGRIC   Famine Relief, 1937
9900

NAK KADMINAGRIC   Time of Tax Collection and Its Effect
3503   on Agricultural Production, 1937

NAK KADMINAGRIC   Locust Destruction, 1932
10233A

NAK KADMINAGRIC   Locust Infestation, 1938
16474

NAK KADMINAGRIC   Locusts, 1939
10233B

NAK KADMINAGRIC   Food Supplies: Government Grain
1/1 3712   Reserves, Katsina, 1943

NAK KADMINAGRIC   Kano Food Supplies, 1943
37228

NAK KADMINAGRIC   Purchase of Wheat and Other Grains, 1944
33485 Vol. I

NAK KADMINAGRIC   Motion by Emir of Gwandu, 1944
72263

NAK KADMINAGRIC   Famine Relief, 1955
1/1 6040

NAK KADMINAGRIC   Corn Storage, 1955
1/1 72691

NAK KADMINAGRIC   Food Supplies, no date
1/1 3712

NAK KADMINAGRIC   Servants or Employees of Trading Firms
19735   Advancing Money to Natives, no date

NAK KADMINAGRIC   Economics Organization in Grain
1/1 3165/S.3   Production, no date

NAK KADMINAGRIC   Grain Reserves Policy, no date
36667

NAK KADMINAGRIC   Corn Storage, no date
37228 Vol. II

Ministry of Social Welfare and Cooperatives (NAK MSWC)

NAK MSWC 1358/S.1   A Survey of Agricultural Credit in the
Vol. I   Northern Region, 1958 (Vigo Report)

NAK MSWC 1358/S.2   Agricultural Credit, 1958–60
S.6

Miscellaneous: Special Reports

NAK C Series G.25   Groundnut Campaign, Kano, 1944

NAK C.83   Forced Labour, 1931–34

NAK NDC 103   Groundnuts, 1933–34

*Records of Federal Departments and Ministries. Interregional Correspondence and Some
Miscellaneous Northern Region Archival Material. National Archives, Ibadan (NAI),
C.S.O. 26 series.*

NAI CSO 06083   Katsina Division, Dankama, Zandam and
                        Ruma Districts Assessment Reports, 1922

NAI CSO 03949   Katsina Division, Galadima District
                        Assessment Report, 1922

NAI CSO RG/X89   Report on Famine Relief in the Northern
                        Provinces, 1927

NAI CSO AR4/1   Northern Region Annual Reports, 1900–11

NAI CSO AR5/A3   Department of Agriculture Annual
                        Reports, 1915–1963

NAI CSO 24887 Vol. II   Locust Control, 1930

NAI CSO 24887 Vol. IX   Locust Control, 1946–48

NAI CSO 26570   Locust Investigation, 1931–41
Vols. I-III

NAI CSO 23542   Committee of Civil Research, 1929–38
Vols. I–III

NAI CSO 37909   Supply of Foodstuffs to HM Forces,
Vols. I, II   1940–46

NAI CSO 37909/S.14/   West Africa War Council: Food Control,
C.1   1942–43

NAI CSO 36378   Local Food Production, 1942

NAI CSO 36378/S.24   Local Food Production in the Colonial
Vols. I, II   Emirates During the War, 1942–45

NAI CSO 36289/S.11   Grain Supplies for the Minefields, 1943

NAI CSO 36289/S.15   Grain Bulk Purchases, 1943

NAI CSO 37909/S.5   Grain Supplies for the Military, 1942–45
Vols. III, IV

NAI CSO 36289/S.4/C.2   Millet and Guineacorn Purchases, 1944–46
Vols. II-IV

NAI CSO 36289/S.4/C.8   Food Reserves, Northern Provinces, 1943

In addition,
Series CSO 23 #15   Northern Nigeria Minute Papers, 1914, 8 vols.

Series CSO 4 #1   Governors Inspection Notes, 1886–1937,
6 vols.

Series CSO 1 #26   Northern Nigeria Despatches to and from
the Colonial Office, 1912–13, 8 vols.

Series CSO 1 #32   Nigeria Despatches to the Colonial Office,
1912–51, 250 vols.

Records in the Katsina Museum (KM)
KM #109   Scheme for Action Against Famine in
Northern Nigeria, 1920

KM #234   Mortgaging of Cotton Crops, 1922

KM #2329   Tax List Katsina NA, 1936–37

KM #452   Half Yearly Cotton Reports, 1937–47

KM #2255   Trade Relations with French Territory, 1939

Records in the Katsina Central Office (KCO) and the Katsina Divisional Office (KDO) of the Katsina Local Government Authority

KCO #W414	Groundnut Plots, 1942
KCO #W229	Groundnut Campaign Propaganda, 1944
KCO #W715	Food Prices: Returns of 1947–50
KCO #W732/S.1	Agricultural Reports, Daura, 1949–51
KCO #W24	Births and Deaths: Returns of 1948–49
KCO #W468/S.1	Famine Committee Minutes, 1951
KCO #W468	Famine Relief Measures, 1950–51
KCO #W461	Famine Relief Measures, 1949–51
KCO #W419/S.1	Purchase of Corn for Relief, 1949–51
KCO #W419 Vol. II	Purchase of Corn for NA, 1950
KCO #395 Vol. III	Food Prices, 1949–52
KCO #W40 Vol. IV	Market Prices, 1952
KCO #PUB/136	History of Katsina, no date
KDO #KAT/CRO 27 Vol. I	Crop Failure Precautions, 1954
KDO #KAT/FOO-2	Food Supplies, 1956
KDO #KAT/CRO-19	Farm and Shade Trees, 1957
KDO #KAT/CRO-7	Crop Damage by Storms and Floods, 1964
KDO #KAT/ MISC-2 Vol. II	Droughts, 1973–74
KDO #KAT/ECON-8	Economic Plants, no date
KDO #KAT/CRO-17	Cowpeas, no date
KDO #KAT/FAR-18 Vol. II	Gawo Trees, no date

Records in the Jos Museum, Nigeria. Principally Catalogue 116, Concerning the Correspondence of H. R. Palmer—The Palmer Papers—and His Enthnographic Notes Concerning the Kano Maguzawa.

Item No. 137	Katsina, no date
Item No. 138	Kano Maguzawa, no date
Item No. 152	Kano Taxes Pre-1900, no date

Records in the Kaita District Office, Kaita Village, Katsina (KD). Largely Uncataloged Local Administrative Paperwork between 1939 and 1960, Including a Kaita District Notebook.

KD #21	Rangadin Hakimai, 1939–54
KD #56	Jimolin Harajin, 1943–61
KD #(?)	Labarun Kudin Tiya a Kasuwar Kaita, 1947
KD #6	Dankama Monthly Reports
KD #133 Vol. III	Census, no date
KD #45	Littafin Jangalin Kasar Kaita, no date
KD #3 Vol. II	Haifuwa da Mutuwa, no date

GOVERNMENT ARCHIVES, GREAT BRITAIN

Public Records Office, London. The Colonial Records (PRO CO), which Consist Largely of the Following:

PRO CO 446	This series (115 volumes) contains the most comprehensive documentation of the development of the Protectorate of Northern Nigeria, 1897–1913.
PRO CO 583	Colonial correspondence to and from Nigeria (228 volumes) between 1914 and 1940
PRO CO 587	Proclamations of the Northern Nigeria Government (2 volumes) covering the period 1900 to 1913
PRO CO 879	Miscellaneous confidential material, from about 1875 to 1920

PRO CO 465   Blue Books of Statistics, Northern
Nigeria, 1900–13 (14 volumes)

PRO CO 586   Northern Nigeria Government Gazettes,
1900–13 (4 volumes)

PRO CO 660   Annual Reports 1900–13 and Trade
Statistics, 1913–41, Northern Nigeria
(41 volumes)

PRO CO 554   West Africa, Original Correspondence,
1911–40 (125 volumes)

PRO CO 763   Register of Correspondence, 1912–40
(13 volumes)

Parliamentary Papers

Cd. 1433   Correspondence Relating to Kano, 1904

Cd. 2875   Mineral and Economic Products Reports,
Northern Nigeria, 1906

Cd. 3309   Memorandum on the Taxation of Natives
in Northern Nigeria

Cd. 5101, 5102   Report of the Northern Nigeria Lands
Committee and Minutes of Evidence, 1910

Cd. 8247, 8248   Committee on Edible and Oil Producing
Nuts and Seeds, Minutes of Evidence

Cd. 1600   Report of a Committee on Trade and
Taxation for British West Africa, 1920

Manuscript Collections

Manuscripts Held by Rhodes House, Oxford University (RH)

Anderson, P.   Mss. 710 17s 4/2, Royal Niger Company
Administration

Arnett, E. J.   Mss. Afr. s952, Northern Nigerian
Exports, etc., 1902–40

Backhouse, M. V.   Mss. Afr. s601, Birniawa Assessment

Baker, J. E. D.   Mss. Afr. s312, Kano Revenue Survey

Brice-Smith, M.	Mss. Afr. s230, Kano Province Reports
Bushwacker	Mss. Afr. s177, Nigerian Reminiscences
Carr, F. B.	Mss. Afr. s546, Nigerian Reminiscences
Carrow, J. H.	Mss. Afr. s1443, Nigerian Reminiscences, Correspondence with Heussler
Clifford, H. C.	Mss. Afr. 1149, Correspondence with Gowers
Cragg, V. E.	Mss. Afr. 1588, Memoirs of a Wife of a Political Officer in Northern Nigeria, 1924–33
Crocker, W. R.	Mss. Afr. s1073, Touring Diaries
Davies, J. B.	Mss. Afr. s1428, Service with the United Africa Company
de Forest, D.	Mss. Afr. 354, Letters
Edwardes, H. S. W.	Mss. Afr. r106, Diaries, 1905–15
Edwardes, H. S. W.	Mss. Afr. s769, Papers, 1906–24
General Secretariat Office	Mss. Afr. s1585, Kola Trade
Giles, L. C.	Mss. Afr. s887, The Hausa Village and Co-operation, 1937
Gowers, W. F.	Mss. Afr. s662, Notes on Trade in Sokoto Province
Grier, S. M.	Mss. Afr. s1043, Service in Nigeria, 1905–25
Guy, J. C.	Mss. Afr. r95, 96, Touring Diaries
Jacob, S. M.	Mss. Afr. t16, Report on Taxation and Economics of Nigeria in 1934
Kirby, H. M.	Mss. Afr. r44, Notes of the Wife of a Director of Agriculture
Lugard, F. D. L.	Mss. Afr., Lugard Papers

Mackie, J. B.   Mss. Afr. s822, 823, Personal Correspondence

Matthews, H. de   Mss. Afr. s1557, Notes of the Resident
                             of Katsina, 1919

Nicholson, R. P.   Mss. Afr. r8, Northern Nigerian Notes

Rosedale, W. O.   Mss. Afr. s582, Northern Nigerian Memoirs

Royal Niger Company   Mss. Afr. s85–101 Papers, 1898–1930
                             (18 vols.)

Sharwood-Smith, B. E.   Mss. Afr. s984, Report on the Fulani and
                             Assessment of Jangal (Gwandu), 1933

Smith, J. H.   Mss. Afr. s1232, Touring Reports

Stevens, T. J.   Mss. Afr. s834, Papers

Temple, O.   Mss. Afr. 1531, Notes for a Nigerian
                             Handbook

Turner, R.   Mss. Afr. 424 ff325–29, Proposal for
                             10-Year Development Plan for Niger
                             Province

Walker, C. R.   Mss. Afr. s433–45, Diary of an Assistant
                             District Officer in Northern Nigeria, 1915–20

Ward, J. F.   Mss. Afr. s1036, Diary of an Agricultural
                             Officer, 1928–30

Watt, L. S.   Mss. Afr. s1412, Diary of an Agricultural
                             Officer in Northern Nigeria, 1939–59

Wilson, G.   Mss. Afr. 2549, Touring Diaries

Woodhouse, C. A.   Mss. Afr. s236–66, Diaries, 1908–33

Manuscripts in Possession of the Royal Commonwealth Society Library, London

Papers Relating to Colonial Administration in Northern Nigeria

Manuscripts in Possession of the Guildhall Library, London

Minutes of the Africa Section of the London Chamber of Commerce

Manuscripts in Possession of the Liverpool Public Library

Minutes of the African Trade Section of the Liverpool Chamber of Commerce

Manuscripts in Possession of the Manchester Public Library

Minutes of the Manchester Chamber of Commerce

London and Kano Company Papers

Lugard, F., Political Memoranda (1906)

UNPUBLISHED THESES AND DISSERTATIONS

Abdu, P. "Drought Caused Migration Around Illela (Sokoto)." B.S. thesis, Ahmadu Bello University, Zaria, 1976.

Abdullahi, M. "Traditional Elites and Political Modernization: Local Government Reforms in North West State of Nigeria." Ph.D. dissertation, University of Chicago, 1977.

Ahmed, M. L. "Socio-Cultural Organization and the Sharing of the Impact of a Natural Hazard in Rijiyar-Tsamiya, Daura." B.S. thesis, Ahmadu Bello University, Zaria, 1975.

Aliyu, A. "The Establishment and Development of Emirate Government in Bauchi 1805–1903." 2 vol. Ph.D. dissertation, Ahmadu Bello University, Zaria, 1974.

Aliyu, M. "Modification of Agricultural Techniques in Response to Drought, Illela, Sokoto." B.A. thesis, Ahmadu Bello University, Zaria, 1976.

Baier, S. "African Merchants in the Colonial Period: A History of Commerce in Damagaram, Niger 1880–1960." Ph.D. dissertation, University of Wisconsin, 1974.

Barkow, J. "Hausa and Maguzawa: Processes of Differentiation in a Rural Area of North Central State, Nigeria." Ph.D. dissertation, University of Chicago, 1970.

Bashir, M. "The Economic Activities of Secluded Married Women in Kurawa and Lallokin Lemu, Kano City." B.S. thesis, Ahmadu Bello University, Zaria, 1972.

Campbell, D. "Strategies for Coping with Drought in the Sahel." Ph.D. dissertation, Clark University, 1976.

Charlick, R. "Power and Participation in the Modernization of Rural Hausa Communities." Ph.D. dissertation, University of California, Los Angeles, 1974.

Clarke, J. "Agricultural Production in a Rural Yoruba Community." Ph.D. dissertation, University of London, 1978.

Collins, J. D. "Government and Groundnut Marketing in Rural Hausa, Niger; the 1930s to the 1960s in Magaria." Ph.D. dissertation, Johns Hopkins University, 1974.

Collion, Marie-Hélène. "Market Integration and Socio Economic Evolution of a Peripheral Region: The Case of Damagaram, Niger." Ph.D. dissertation, Cornell University, Department of City and Regional Planning, 1981.

Crawford, E. W. "A Programming Simulation Study of Constraints Affecting the Long-Run Income-Earning Ability of Traditional Dryland Farming Systems in Northern Nigeria." Ph.D. dissertation, Cornell University, 1980.

Daudu, I. "Modification of Agricultural Techniques in the Drought Situation, Mungurun." B.A. thesis, Ahmadu Bello University, Zaria, 1975.

Dunbar, R. "Damagaram (Zinder, Niger) 1812–1906: History of a Central Sudanic Kingdom." Ph.D. dissertation, University of California, Los Angeles, 1971.

Ega, L. "Status, Problems and Prospects of Rural Land Tenure in Kaduna State." Ph.D. dissertation, Cornell University, 1980.

Faulkingham, R. "Political Support in a Rural Hausa Village, Niger." Ph.D. dissertation, Michigan State University, 1971.

Ferguson, D. "Nineteenth Century Hausaland, Being a Description by Imam Imoru." Ph.D. dissertation, University of California, Los Angeles, 1973.

Fika, A. "The Political and Economic Reorientation of Kano Emirate, Northern Nigeria 1882–1940." Ph.D. dissertation, University of London, 1973.

Frischman, A. "The Spatial Growth and Residential Location Pattern of Kano." Ph.D. dissertation, Northwestern University, 1977.

Grossman, L. "Cash, Cattle and Coffee: the Cultural Ecology of Development in the Highlands of Papua New Guinea." Ph.D. dissertation, Australian National University, 1979.

Hogendorn, J. "The Origins of the Groundnut Trade in Northern Nigeria." Ph.D. dissertation, London University, 1966.

Hull, R. "The Development of Administration in Katsina Emirate, Northern Nigeria, 1887–1944." Ph.D. dissertation, Columbia University, 1967.

Idi, M. "Organisation, Operation and Administration Problems of Drought Relief Committees in Kano State." B.A. thesis, Ahmadu Bello University, Zaria, 1976.

Jackson, J. "A Socio-Economic Survey in the Kano River Project Area, Northern Nigeria." M.A. thesis, University of East Anglia, 1980.

Kura, A. G. "Social and Economic Adaptation to Drought in Bedde Division, Bornu." B.A. thesis, Department of Sociology, Ahmadu Bello University, Zaria, 1976.

Lennihan, L., "The Origins and Development of Agricultural Wage Labor in Northern Nigeria, 1886–1980." Ph.D. dissertation, Columbia University, 1982.

Malton, P. "The Size, Distribution, Structure and Determinants of Personal Income Among Farmers in the North of Nigeria." Ph.D. dissertation, Cornell University, 1977.

Mshelia, S. "The 1913 Drought in Bornu Province." B.S. thesis, Ahmadu Bello University, Zaria, 1975.

Ndaks, G. "The Effects of the 1972–73 Drought on the Agricultural Community of Sandamu in Daura Emirate, Kaduna State." B.A. thesis, Ahmadu Bello University, Zaria, 1976.

Nicolas, G. "Circulation des Richèsses et Participation Sociale dans une Société Hausa du Niger." Unpublished dissertation for the Doctorat de Troisième Cycle, Université de Bordeaux, 1965.

Nicholson, S. "A Climatic Chronology for Africa: Synthesis of Geological, Historical, and Meteorological Information and Data." Ph.D. dissertation, University of Wisconsin, 1976.

Njonjo, A. "The Africanisation of the White Highlands." Ph.D. dissertation, Princeton University, 1977.

Oculi, O. "Colonial Capitalism and Malnutrition, Nigeria, Kenya, and Jamaica." Ph.D. dissertation, University of Wisconsin, Madison, 1977.

Ogbonna, O. D. "The Geographic Consequences of Petroleum in Nigeria with Special Reference to the Rivers State." Ph.D. dissertation, University of California, Berkeley, 1979.

Okediji, F. "An Economic History of the Hausa-Fulani Emirates, Northern Nigeria 1900–1939." Ph.D. dissertation, Indiana University, 1972.

Ola, R. F. "The Evolution of Local Government Institutions in Kano Emirate, Northern Nigeria." Ph.D. dissertation, Carleton University, 1974.

Olofson, H. A. "Funtua: Patterns of Migration to a New Hausa Town." Ph.D. dissertation, University of Pittsburgh, 1976.

Paden, J. "The Influence of Religious Elites on the Community, Culture and Political Integration in Kano, Nigeria." Ph.D. dissertation, Harvard University, 1968.

Peterson, S. "The State and the Organizational Infrastructure of the Agrarian Economy: A Comparative Study of Smallholder Development in Taiwan and Kenya." Ph.D. dissertation, University of California, Berkeley, 1982.

Sa'id, H. I. "Revolution and Reaction: The Fulani Jihad in Kano and its Aftermath 1807–1819." 2 vols. Ph.D. dissertation, University of Michigan, 1978.

Saulawa, A. "British Colonial Administrative Policies and Migration in the *Birnin* Katsina 1903–1954." B.A. thesis, Ahmadu Bello University, Zaria, 1977.

Saulawa, L. "1973–74 Drought: Source and Distribution of Relief Materials in Katsina Emirate." B.S. thesis, Ahmadu Bello University, Zaria, 1976.

Saunders, M. A. "Marriage and Divorce in a Muslim Town (Mirria, Niger Republic)." Ph.D. dissertation, Indiana University, 1978.

Schultz, J. "Population and Agricultural Change in Nigerian Hausaland." Ph.D. dissertation, Columbia University, 1976.

Shea, P. "The Development of an Export Oriented Dyed Cloth Industry in Nineteenth Century Kano Emirate." Ph.D. dissertation, University of Wisconsin, 1975.

Shenton, R. "The Development of Capitalism in Northern Nigeria." Ph.D. dissertation, University of Toronto, 1982.

Smith, M. G. "Social and Economic Change among Hausa Communities, Northern Nigeria." Ph.D. dissertation, University of London, 1950.

Steward, M. "The Political Structure of Northern Nigeria Emirates." Ph.D. dissertation, University of Ibadan, 1968.

Sutter, J. "Economic Integration and Peasant Economy: A Case Study of Two Hausa Villages in Niger Republic." Ph.D. dissertation, Cornell University, 1981.

Tahir, I. "Scholars, Sufis, Saints and Capitalists in Kano 1904–1974: Pattern of a Bourgeois Revolution in an Islamic Society." Ph.D. dissertation, Cambridge University, 1975.

Tukur, M. M. "The Imposition of British Colonial Domination of the Sokoto Caliphate." 2 vols. Ph.D. dissertation, Ahmadu Bello University, Zaria, 1979.

Turner, B. "The Fadama Lands of Central Northern Nigeria: Their Classification, Spatial Variation and Present and Potential Use." 2 vols. Ph.D. dissertation, University of London, 1977.

Usman, Y. B. "The Transformation of Katsina ca. 1796–1903: The Overthrow of the Sarauta System and the Establishment and Evolution of the Emirate." Ph.D. dissertation, Ahmadu Bello University, Zaria, 1974.

Voh, J. "Resettlement Adjustment Patterns to Rural Development: the Case of Tiga Dam, Kano." Ph.D. dissertation, Iowa State University, 1980.

Wisner, B. "The Human Ecology of Drought in Eastern Kenya." Ph.D. dissertation, Clark University, 1978.

Watts, Michael. "A Silent Revolution: The Changing Character of Food Production and the Nature of Famine in Northern Nigeria." Ph.D. dissertation, University of Michigan, 1979.

Yusufu, Y. "Slavery in Nineteenth Century Kano." B.A. thesis, Ahmadu Bello University, Zaria, 1976.

Unpublished Papers and Manuscripts

Abubakar, S. "A Survey of the Economy of the Eastern Emirates, Sokoto Caliphate, during the Nineteenth Century." Paper presented to the Sokoto History Seminar, June 1975.

Anthony, K., and Johnson, B. "Field Study of Agricultural Change in Northern Katsina." Preliminary Report no. 6, Food Research Institute, Stanford University, 1968.

Beckman, B. "Oil, State Expenditure and Class Formation in Nigeria." Paper presented to the Nordic Association of Political Scientists, Turku, August 1981.

Berg, E. "The Recent Economic Evolution of the Sahel." Center for Research on Economic Development, University of Michigan, Ann Arbor, 1975.

Berman, B. "Articulation, Class and the Specificity of the Colonial State." Paper presented to African Studies Association, Philadelphia, October 1980.

Bernstein, H. "State and Peasantry in Tanzania." Paper presented to the Institute of Commonwealth Studies, London, Peasant Studies Seminar, 1980.

Bernus, E. "Case Study of Desertification: the Gyhazar and Agawak Region of Niger." United Nations Conference on Desertification, Nairobi, 1977.

Chambers, R. "Seasonal Dimensions to Rural Poverty." Paper prepared for a Conference on Seasonality and Rural Poverty, University of Sussex, July 1978.

Chambers, R. "Shortcut Methods in Information Gathering for Rural Development Project." Paper presented for the World Bank Agricultural Sector Symposium, Washington, D.C., 1980.

Clarence-Smith, G. "Drought in South Angola and Northern Namibia, 1837–1945." Paper presented to the School of Oriental and African Studies, London, 1974.

Clayton, W. "A Preliminary Report on the Vegetation and Soils of Northern Nigeria." Institute of Agricultural Research, Samaru, 1957.

Clough, P. "Farmers and Traders in Rural Hausaland." Manuscript, Oxford University, Queen Elizabeth House, 1977.

———. "Indebtedness among the Rural Hausa: a Case Study." Manuscript, Oxford University, Queen Elizabeth House, April, 1980.

Cooper, F. "Africa and the World Economy." Paper presented for the Social Science Research Council, delivered to the African Studies Association, Bloomington, Indiana, 1981.

Cowen, M. "Notes on Capital, Class and Peasant Household Production." IDS Discussion Paper, Nairobi, 1976.

———. "The British State and Agrarian Accumulation in Kenya after 1945." Paper presented to the Social Science Research Council Conference on the African Bourgeoisie, Dakar, December, 1980.

de Leeuw, P. N., and Van Raay, H. G. T. "Fodder Resources and Grazing Management in a Savanna Environment: An Ecosystem Approach." ISS Occasional Papers, The Hague, 1974.

Ehrensaft, P., and Brown, B. "The West African Mode of Production in Colonial Nigeria, 1884–1945." Manuscript, McGill University, Montreal, 1973.

Ekhomu, D. O. "National Food Policies and Bureaucracies in Nigeria." Paper presented to African Studies Association, Baltimore, November 1–4, 1978.

Etkin, N., and Ross, P. "Malaria, Medicine and Meals: plant use among the Hausa and its impact on disease." Manuscript, Department of Anthropology, University of Minnesota, 1982.

FADP. "Land Use, Cropping Patterns and Area Covered by Individual Crops in Kaduna State." Funtua Agricultural Development Project, Funtua, 1978.

Fapohunda, O. "Employment and Unemployment In Lagos." ISS Occasional Paper no. 60, The Hague, 1977.

Fisher, J. "Famine in Africa." Paper presented to the School of Oriental and African Studies, London, 1974.

Forrest, T. "State Capital in Nigeria." Paper prepared for a Conference on The African Bourgeoisie: The Development of Capitalism in Nigeria, Kenya and Ivory Coast, Dakar, December 2–4, 1980.

———. "The Economic Context of Operation Feed the Nation." Manuscript, Department of Economics, Ahmadu Bello University, Zaria, 1977.

Freund, W., and Shenton, R. "The Incorporation of Northern Nigeria into the World Capitalist System." Paper presented to the Institute of Commonwealth Studies, London, December 1978.

Friedmann, H. "Peasants and Simple Commodity Producers: Analytical Distinctions." Paper presented to Peasants Seminar, University of London, 1979c.

Harris, D. "Traditional Systems of Plant Food Productivity and the Origins of Agriculture in West Africa." Paper delivered to the IXth International Congress of Anthropology and Ethnological Sciences, Chicago, 1973.

Horowitz, M., ed. "Colloquium on the Effects of Drought on the Productive Strategies of Sudano-Sahelian Herdsmen and Farmers." Institute for Development Anthropology, New York, 1976.

IBRD. "Nigeria: Country Profile." International Bank for Reconstruction and Development, Washington, D.C., 1978.

Jackson, C. "A Study of Rural Hausa Women." Paper presented to the Institute for Agricultural Research, Ahmadu Bello University, Zaria, 1978.

Jiya, M. "Report on the Effects of Drought Conditions on Livestock Production in NW State (1972/73)." Nigerian Society of Animal Production, Bagauda Lake, March 25–27, 1974.

Kadzai, A. "Operation Feed the Nation as an Aspect of Nigeria's Economic and Social Strategy for Industrialization." Manuscript, Ahmadu Bello University, Zaria, 1976.

Khalil, I. M. "The Effect of Droughts in the Northeastern State." Nigerian Society of Animal Production, Bagauda Lake Hotel, Kano, March 25–27, 1974.

King, R. "Farmer's Cooperatives in Northern Nigeria: A Case Study Used to Illustrate the Relationship Between Economic and Institutional Change." Department of Agricultural Economics, University of Reading, 1976.

Koechlin, J. "Rapport de Mission d'Etude sur le Milieu Naturel et l'Utilisation du Sol dans la Région de Maradi." Mimeographed. Programme de Recherches sur la Région de Maradi, Université de Bordeaux, 1977.

Kungwai, N. "The Political Economy of Rural Development in Nigeria: A Case Study of FADP." Ahmadu Bello University, Zaria, 1977.

Last, D. M. "The Sokoto Caliphate and Bornu 1820–1880." Paper delivered to Bayero University, Kano, postgraduate history seminar, November 1978.

Longhurst, R. "Calorie Expenditure and Cropping Patterns." Institute of Development Studies, Sussex, 1977.

———. "The Provision of Basic Needs for Women: A Case Study of a Hausa Village." Report prepared for ILO, London, 1977*a*.

Lonsdale, J. "State As Social Process." Paper prepared for the Social Science Research Council, presented to the African Studies Association, Bloomington, October, 1981.

Lubeck, P. "The Revenue System of Pre-Colonial Kano Emirate." Manuscript, Northwestern University, 1968.

————. "Islam and Resistance in Northern Nigeria." Manuscript, Sociology Board of Studies, University of California, Santa Cruz, 1977.

————. "External Development and the World System: Kano in the Nineteenth Century." Manuscript, Comparative History Seminar, University of California, Santa Cruz, 1979.

————. "Islamic Networks and Urban Capitalism." Paper presented to the African Studies Association Meetings, Philadelphia, October 1980.

Lubeck, P., and Burke, E. "Islam, Oil and Nationalism." Paper prepared for a Conference on Global Crises and Social Movements, University of California, Santa Cruz, October 1981.

Mahdi, A. "The Genesis of Kano's Economic Prosperity During the Nineteenth Century." Paper delivered to the Annual Meeting of the Historical Society of Nigeria, Ahmadu Bello University, Zaria, 1978.

Mahdi, M. "Migration into Kano and Maidurguri." Interview data, Centre for Social and Economic Research, Ahmadu Bello University, Zaria, 1976.

Mortimore, M. "A Report on Farmer Responses to Drought in Northern Kano State 1973–74." Department of Geography, Ahmadu Bello University, Zaria, 1977.

Miranda, E. "Etude des Déséquilibres Ecologiques et Agricoles d'une Région Tropicale Semi-Aride au Niger." Institut de Recherche et d'Application des Méthodes de Développement, Université de Bordeaux II, 1979.

Na Dama, G. "Legends, Rituals and Ceremonies Connected with Agricultural Activity and Craft Production in Zamfara During Nineteenth Century." Seminar paper, Ahmadu Bello University, Zaria, 1976.

Nicholson, S. "A Climatic Chronology for Africa." Paper presented to the Xth INQUA Congress, Birmingham, U.K., 1977.

Nkom, S. "Class Formation and Rural Development: A Critique of Rural Development Programs in Nigeria." Paper presented to the Social Sciences Staff Seminar, Ahmadu Bello University, Zaria, 1978.

Oguntoyinbo, J., and Richards, P. "Peasant Farmer Responses to Drought Conditions in West Africa." Paper delivered to the Conference on the Aftermath of the Drought in Nigeria, Bagauda Lake, Kano, 1977.

Palmer-Jones, R. "Irrigation Development and Irrigation Planning in the North of Nigeria." Manuscript, Ahmadu Bello University, Zaria, 1977.

————. "Field Research Methods Used in Farm Management Studies." Paper presented to the Institute for Agricultural Research, Zaria. 1978*a*.

————. "Peasant Differentiation in Rural Hausaland." Manuscript, Institute of Agricultural Research, Ahmadu Bello University, Zaria, 1978*b*.

Palmer-Jones, R. and Baker, E. "The *Gicci* System of Intercropping." Paper presented to the National Seminar on Groundnut Production, Bagauda Lake, Kano, 1978.

Pask, G. "Some Mechanical Concepts of Goals, Individuals, Consciousness and Symbolic Evolution." Paper presented at the Wenner-Gren Institute Symposium on the Effects of Conscious Purpose on Human Adaptation, New York, 1968.

Pittin, R. "Social Status and Economic Opportunity in Urban Hausa Society." Manuscript, Department of Sociology, Ahmadu Bello University, Zaria, 1976.

Raikes, P. "The Development of a Middle Peasantry in Kenya." Paper no. A78.3, Centre for Development Research, Copenhagen, 1978.

Richards, P. and Oguntoyinbo, J. "Drought and the Nigerian Farmer." Paper presented to the Social Science Research Council (SSRC) Conference on Environmental and Spatial Cognition in Africa, Capahosic, Virginia, 1974.

Ross, P. "Land as a Right to Membership." Paper presented to a Workshop on State and Agriculture in Nigeria, Berkeley, 1982.

Scott, E. "The Ecology of Sedentary Farming in Northern Nigeria." Paper presented to the Association of American Geographers Annual Meeting, New York, April 1976.

Shea, P. "Approaching the Study of Production in Rural Kano." Paper presented to the International Conference on the History of Kano, Bayero University, Kano, September 1981.

Simmons, E. "A Case Study of Seasonal Variation in Food and Agriculture." Paper presented to the Conference on Seasonality and Rural Poverty, University of Sussex, July 1978.

Standing, G. "Migration and Modes of Exploitation: The Social Origins of Immobility and Mobility." Mimeograph. International Labor Office, Geneva, 1980.

Starns, W. "Land Tenure Among the Rural Hausa." LTC Paper no. 104, Land Tenure Center, University of Wisconsin, 1974.

Stewart, C. "Shehu Usman dan Fodio's Social Revolution Reassessed." Paper presented to the Symposium on the Cultivator and the State in Africa, Urbana, Illinois, 1977.

Sutter, J. "Commercial Strategies, Drought and Monetary Pressure: Wo'daa'be Nomads of Tanout, Niger." Manuscript, Cornell University, March 1980.

Tomkins, A. "Defining Health Problems of a Rural Area." Paper presented to the Conference on Seasonality and Rural Poverty, University of Sussex, July 1978.

Tomlinson, P. "Report on the Detailed Soil Survey of the Livestock Investigation Center, Katsina, and the Reconnaissance of the Surrounding Area." Bulletin no. 11, Institute of Agricultural Research, Samaru, 1960.

Tribenderana, P. K. "British Educational Policy in Northern Nigeria 1906–1928: A Re-assessment." Social Science Staff Seminar paper, Ahmadu Bello University, Zaria, 1977.

Tukur, M. "The Role of Emirs and District Heads in the Imposition, Assessment and Collection of *Kudin Kassa* and *Jangali* in the Emirates, 1903–14." Paper presented to Ahmadu Bello University History Seminar, Zaria, 1977.

USDA/AID. "Food Problems and Prospects in Sub-Saharan Africa: The Decade of the 1980's." USDA, Washington, D.C., September 1980.

UNRISD. "Food Systems and Society: Project Proposal." Mimeograph. UNRISD, Ref. UNRISD/76/C.19 GE.77–1621, Geneva, 1976.

Usman, Y. B. "Some Conceptual Problems in the Study of the Economy of Political Communities of the Central Sudan." Paper presented to the Nineteenth Annual Congress of the Historical Society of Nigeria, Zaria, 1973.

———. "The Transformation of Political Communities; Some Notes on the Perception of a Significant Aspect of the Sokoto Jihad." Paper presented to the Sokoto Seminar on the History of the Central Sudan, Sokoto, 1975.

———. "Some Notes on the Three Basic Weaknesses in the Study of African Cultural History." Department of History, Ahmadu Bello University, Zaria, 1977.

———. "The Assessment of Primary Sources: Heinrich Barth in Katsina 1851–54." Paper presented to Department of History, Ahmadu Bello University, Zaria, 1977a.

van Apeldoorn, J. "Drought In Nigeria." 2 vols. Mimeographed. Centre for Social and Economic Research, Zaria, 1978.

van Apeldoorn, J., ed. "Proceedings of the Conference on the Aftermath of Drought in Nigeria." Mimeograph. Centre for Social and Economic Research, Zaria, 1978a.

Walker, D. J. R. "Groundnut Production in Nigeria: An Economic Consideration." Manuscript, Course Study, London School of Economics,1949.

Walsh, P. "Climatic Seasonality in the Tropics." Paper prepared for a Conference on Seasonality and Rural Poverty, Institute of Development Studies, University of Sussex, July 1978.

Ware, H. "The Sahelian Drought: Some Thoughts on the Future." United Nations, ST/SSO/33, New York, 1975.

Waterman, P. "The Jihad as an Episode in African History." Manuscript, School of Basic Studies, Ahmadu Bello University, Zaria, 1970.

Watts, M. "Peasantry, Merchant Capital and International Firms: Colonial Capitalism in Northern Nigeria." Paper presented at Social Science Research Council (SSRC) Conference, The African Bourgeoisie: State and Entrepreneurial Classes in African Capitalism, Dakar, December 2–4, 1980.

Wayne, J. "Structural Contradictions of the Colonial State: The Case of Tanganyika in the Early Years." Working Paper no. 23, Sociology Department Structural Analysis Programme, Toronto University, 1981.

Weeks, J. F. "Extraction of the Agricultural Surplus and the Burden of Financing Economic Growth in Nigeria." Mimeograph. Institute of Development Studies, Sussex, 1974.

Williams, G. "Rural Inequalities in Nigeria." Report prepared for the International Labor Office (ILO), Geneva. Oxford University, St. Peter's College, 1980.

Werhahn, H., et al. "The Cattle and Meat Industry in Northern Nigeria." Mimeograph. Frankfurt, 1964.

World Bank, Agricultural Sector Assessment for Nigeria, World Bank, Washington, D.C., 1979.

ORAL INTERVIEWS IN NORTHERN NIGERIA

Between 1976 and 1978, during the course of field research, I interviewed roughly fifty individuals in Katsina, Daura, and surrounding villages concerning drought, famine, and other relevant issues pertaining to the nineteenth century. The following individuals in particular provided invaluable information:

Wakilin Kudu Alhaji Ilyasu Dadi, 73 years, Katsina town, July 13, 1977.

Alhaji Hamza Yankyaure, 88 years, Katsina town, July 13, 1977.

Alhaji Lawal b. Rashidu, 74 years, Katsina town, July 13, 1977.

Mallam Badamasi, 69 years, Katsina town, June 23, 1977.

Alhaji Bala, 78 years, Kaita village, September 5, 1977.

Mallam Danburadi Bakani, 79 years, Kaita village, September 5, 1977.

Galadiman Daura Alhaji Sale, 103 years, Daura, November 28, 1977.

Alhaji Urwatu b. Abdullahi, 99 years, Katsina town, July 7, 1977.

Alhaji Gambo b. Isa, 82 years, Katsina town, June 24, 1977.

Mamman Gumuzu, 87 years, Katsina town, June 25, 1977.

Mallam Ibrahim, Sarki Makada, 115 years (?), Daura, November 28, 1977.

Mallam Gandu, 85 years, Dan Gamji, November 10, 1977.

PUBLISHED SOURCES

OFFICIAL GOVERNMENT PUBLICATIONS

AERLS. *Report on Wheat Production and Marketing in Nigeria.* Zaria: Ahmadu Bello University, 1979.

Baldwin, K. D. *Report on the Movement of Locally Grown Foodstuffs.* Kaduna: Government Printer, 1957.

———. *Groundnut Marketing Survey.* Kaduna: Ministry of Agriculture, 1956.

de St. Croix, F. W. *The Fulani of Northern Nigeria.* Lagos: Government Printer, 1944.

Fairburn, W. A. *Report on the Sylvan Conditions and Land Utilisation in Northern Kano and Katsina Provinces.* Kaduna: Ministry of Agriculture, 1937.

Famine Relief. *Report on Famine Relief in the Northern Provinces.* Lagos: Government Printer, 1927.

Federal Government of Nigeria. *Third National Development Plan 1975–1980.* Lagos: Government Printing Office, 1975.

————. *The Green Revolution: A Food Production Plan for Nigeria.* 2 vols. Lagos: Federal Ministry of Agriculture, 1980.

Grove, A. T. *Land and Population in Katsina Province.* Kaduna: Government Printer, 1957.

————. *Land Use and Soil Conservation on the Jos Plateau.* Bulletin no. 22 of the Geological Survey of Nigeria. Lagos: Government Printer, 1952.

Keay, R. *An Outline of Nigerian Vegetation.* Lagos: Government Printer, 1953.

Luning, H. *An Agro-Economic Survey in Katsina Province.* Kaduna: Government Printer, 1963.

Meek, C. G. *Land Tenure and Land Administration in Nigeria and the Cameroons.* Colonial Research Studies no. 22. London: 1957.

Nash, T. A. *The Anchau Rural Development and Settlement Scheme.* London: HMSO, 1948.

Nigerian Census. *Nigerian Population Census.* Vol. V. Medical Census Northern Provinces. London: Crown Agents, 1941.

Northern Nigeria Agriculture Department. *Annual Report,* 1914–1955. Kaduna: Government Printer.

Northern Provinces. *Northern Provinces Advisory Council.* Record of the Proceedings. Kaduna: Government Printer, 1932.

Prothero, R. *Migrant Labor From Sokoto Province.* Kaduna: Government Printer, 1958 (reprinted by University of Liverpool, Department of Geography, African Population Mobility Project, 1976).

Rowling, G. *Report on Land Tenure, Kano Province.* Kaduna: Government Printer, 1949.

Smith, M. G. *The Economy of Hausa Communities in Zaria.* Colonial Research Series, no. 16. London: HMSO, 1955.

Tiffen, M. *The Enterprising Peasant: The Economic Development in Gombe Emirate, Northeastern Nigeria 1900–1968.* London: HMSO, Overseas Research Publication, no. 21, 1976.

Vigo, A. H. "A Survey of Agricultural Credit in the North of Nigeria." Mimeograph. Kaduna: Ministry of Agriculture, 1957.

Nongovernment Serial Publications

Africa Now (London)

African Business (London)

African Economic Digest (London)

Economist (London)

Foreign Agriculture (Washington, D.C.)

Gaskiya Ta Fi Kwabo (Zaria)

International Financial Statistics (Washington, D.C.)

The Mining Journal (London)

New African (London)

New Nigerian (Kaduna)

Nigerian Newsletter (London)

Pastoral Network (London, Overseas Development Institute)

Quarterly Economic Review of Nigeria (London)

Washington Post (Washington, D.C.)

West Africa (London)

Published Books and Monographs

Abraham, R. C. *Dictionary of the Hausa Language.* London: Hodder and Stoughton, 1946.

Adeleye, R. *Power and Diplomacy in Northern Nigeria.* Ibadan: Oxford University Press, 1971.

Adeyeye, S. O. *The Co-Operative Movement in Nigeria.* Gottingen: Vandenboeck and Ruprecht, 1978.

Ahn, P. M. *West African Soils.* London: Oxford University Press, 1970.

Alamgir, M. *Famine in South Asia: Political Economy of Mass Starvation.* Cambridge, Mass.: Oelgeschlager, Gunn, and Hain, 1980.

Allan, W. *The African Husbandman.* Edinburgh: Oliver and Boyd, 1965.

Altman, L., and Dittmer, D. *Metabolism*. Bethesda, Md.: Federation of American Societies for Experimental Biology, 1968.

Amin, S., ed. *Modern Migrations in West Africa*. London: Oxford University Press and the International African Institute, 1974.

Amin, S. *Le Developpement Inégal*. Paris: Editions de Minuit, 1972.

Anderson, J. *Islam in Africa*. London: Cass, 1970.

Anderson, J. R., et al. *Agricultural Decision Analysis*. Ames: Iowa State University Press, 1977.

Anderson, P. *Arguments Within English Marxism*. London: New Left Books, 1980.

————. *Lineages of the Absolutist State*. London: New Left Books, 1975.

————. *Passages From Antiquity to Feudalism*. London: New Left Books, 1974.

Baier, S. *An Economic History of the Central Sudan*. London: Oxford University Press, 1980.

Baldwin, K. D. S. *The Niger Agricultural Project*. Oxford: Basil Blackwell, 1957.

Bargery, G. *A Hausa-English Dictionary*. London: Oxford University Press, 1934.

Barth, H. *Travels and Discoveries in North and Central Africa*. 3 vols. London: Cass, 1858 and 1859 (reprinted 1965).

Bartlett, P., ed. *Agricultural Decision Making: Anthropological Contributions to Rural Development*. New York: Academic Press, 1980.

Bates, R. *Markets and States in Africa*. Berkeley, Los Angeles, London: University of California Press, 1981.

Bateson, G. *Steps to an Ecology of Mind*. New York: Ballantine, 1972.

Bauer, P. *West African Trade*. Cambridge: Cambridge University Press, 1959.

Bennett, J. *The Ecological Transition*. Oxford: Pergamon, 1976.

Berg, E., et al. *Marketing, Price Policy and Storage of Food Grains in the Sahel*. 2 vols. Ann Arbor: Center for Research on Economic Development, University of Michigan, 1977.

Berger, J. *Pig Earth*. London: Reader's and Writer's Co-operative, 1979.

Bhaskar, R. *The Possibility of Naturalism: A Philosophical Critique of Contemporary Human Sciences*. Sussex: Harvester Press, 1979.

Bhatia, B. M. *Famines in India*. New Delhi: Asia Publishing House,1967.

Bienen, H., and Diejomaoh, V., eds. *The Political Economy of Income Distribution in Nigeria*. New York: Holmes and Meier, 1981.

Bierstecker, T. *Distortion or Development?: Contending Perspectives on the Multinational Corporation*. Cambridge, Mass.: MIT Press, 1978.

Boesen, J., and Mohele, A. T. *The "Success" Story of Peasant Tobacco Production in Tanzania*. Uppsala: Scandinavian Institute of African Studies, Centre for Development Research, no. 1, 1979.

Bottomore, T. B., and Rubel, M., eds. *Karl Marx: Selected Writings in Sociology and Social Philosophers*. Harmondsworth: Penguin, 1963.

Braudel, F. *Capitalism and Material Life*. New York: Harper and Row, 1973.

—. *The Mediterranean and the Mediterranean World in the Age of Philip II*. New York: Harper and Row, 1972.

Brett, E. A. *Colonialism and Underdevelopment in East Africa: The Politics of Economic Change 1919–1939*. New York: Nok, 1973.

Buchanan, K., and Pugh, J. C. *Land and People in Nigeria*. London: London University Press, 1955.

Buell, R. *The Native Problem in Africa*. New York: Macmillan, 1928.

Bundy, C. *The Rise and Fall of the South African Peasantry*. Berkeley, Los Angeles, London: University of California Press, 1979.

Calvert, A. F. *Nigeria and its Tinfields*. London: E. Stanford, 1912.

Carter, I. *Farm Life in Northeast Scotland*. Edinburgh: John Donald Publishers, 1979.

Chambers, R., Longhurst, R., and Pacey, A., eds. *Seasonal Dimensions to Rural Poverty*. London: Frances Pinter, 1981.

Chayanov, A. V. *The Theory of Peasant Economy*. Homewood, Ill.: American Economic Association, 1966.

Clarke, T. *The Last Caravan.* New York: Putnam, 1978.

Cocheme, J., and Franquin, P. *A Study of the Agroclimatology of Semi-Arid West Africa South of the Sahara.* Rome: FAO, 1967.

Cohen, G. *Karl Marx's Theory of History: A Defense.* Princeton: Princeton University Press, 1980.

Comité d'Information Sahel. *Qui se Nourrit de la Famine en Afrique?* Paris: Maspero, 1974.

Copans, J., ed. *Sècheresse et Famine du Sahel.* 2 vols. Paris: Maspero, 1975.

Corrigan, P., ed. *Capitalism, State Formation and Marxist Theory.* London: Quartet Books, 1980.

Crowder, M. *West Africa Under Colonial Rule.* London: Hutchinson, 1968.

Crummey, D., and Stewart, C., eds. *Modes of Production in Africa: The Pre-Colonial Era.* Beverly Hills: Sage, 1981.

Curtin, P. *Economic Change in Pre-Colonial Africa: Senegambia in the Era of the Slave Trade.* Madison: University of Wisconsin Press, 1975.

Dahl, G., and Hjort, A. *Having Herds: Pastoral Herd Growth and Household Economy.* Stockholm: Studies in Social Anthropology, 1976.

Dalby, D., and Harrison-Church, R. J., eds. *Drought in Africa 1.* London: International African Institute, 1974.

Dalby, D., et al., eds. *Drought in Africa 2.* London: International African Institute, 1977.

Dalziel, J. *A Hausa Botanical Vocabulary.* London: Fisher Unwin, 1916.

de Castro, J. *The Geopolitics of Hunger.* New York: Monthly Review, 1976.

de Janvry, A. *The Agrarian Question and Land Reformism in Latin America.* Baltimore: Johns Hopkins University Press, 1981.

Delgado, C. *The Southern Fulani Farm System in Upper Volta: A New Old Model for the Integration of Crop and Livestock Production in the West African Savannah.* Monograph, Livestock Production and Marketing in the Entente States of West Africa Series. Ann Arbor: Center for Research on Economic Development, University of Michigan, 1978.

Derriennic, H. *Famines et Dominations en Afrique Noire.* Paris: Editions l'Harmattan, 1978.

Dike, K. O. *Trade and Politics in the Niger Delta.* London: Oxford University Press, 1956.

Dupire, M. *Peuls Nomades: Etude Descriptive des Wodaabe du Sahel Nigerièn.* Paris: Institut d'Ethnologies, 1962.

Echard, N., Adam, J., and Lescot, M. *Plant Medicinales Hausa de l'Ader.* Paris: Laboratoire d'Ethnobotanique, 1972.

Eddy, E. D. *Labor and Land Use on Mixed Farms in the Pastoral Zone of Niger.* Monograph III in the Livestock Production and Marketing in the Entente States of West Africa Series. Ann Arbor: Center for Research on Economic Development, University of Michigan, 1979.

Eicher, C., and Liedholm, C. *Growth and Development of the Nigerian Economy.* East Lansing: Michigan State University Press, 1970.

Faulkner, O. T., and Mackie, J. R. *West African Agriculture.* Cambridge: Cambridge University Press, 1933.

Feierman, S. *The Shabaa Kingdom.* Madison: University of Wisconsin Press, 1974.

Fika, A. *The Kano Civil War and British Overrule 1882–1940.* Ibadan: Oxford University Press, 1978.

Fisher, A. G., and Fisher, H. G. *Slavery and Muslim Society in Africa.* London: Clarendon Press, 1970.

Forde, D., and Scott, R. *The Native Economies of Nigeria.* vol. 1. London: Faber, 1946.

Foureau, F. *Mission Saharienne Foureau-Lamy.* Paris: Masson, 1902.

Franke, R., and Chasin, B. *Seeds of Famine: Ecological Destruction and the Development Dilemma in the West African Sahel.* Montclair: Allanheld and Osmun, 1980.

Frankel, S. H. *Capital Investment in Africa.* Oxford: Oxford University Press, 1938.

Freund, W. M. *Labor and Capital in the Nigerian Tin Mines.* London: Longmans, 1981.

Galais, J. *Pasteurs et Paysans du Gourma.* Paris: CNRS, Centre d'Études de Géographie Tropicale, 1977.

Garcia, R. V. *Nature Pleads Not Guilty.* Oxford: Pergamon Press, 1981.

Geertz, C. *The Social History of an Indonesian Town.* Berkeley, Los Angeles, London: University of California Press, 1971.

————. *Agricultural Involution: Processes of Ecological Change in Indonesia.* Berkeley and Los Angeles: University of California Press, 1963.

Gervis, P. *Of Emirs and Pagans.* London: Cassell, 1963.

Glacken, Clarence. *Traces on the Rhodian Shore.* Berkeley and Los Angeles: University of California Press, 1967.

Glantz, M. *Desertification.* Boulder: Westview Press, 1977.

Glantz, M., ed. *The Politics of Disaster: the Case of the Sahelian Drought.* New York: Praeger, 1976.

Gowers, W. F. *Gazetteer of Kano Province.* London: Waterlow, 1921.

Gramsci, A. *Prison Notebooks: Selections.* 1934. Reprint. London: Lawrence and Wishart, 1971.

Greenberg, J. *The Influence of Islam on a Sudanese Religion.* New York: J. J Augustin, 1946.

Griffiths, J. F., ed. *Climates of Africa.* World Survey of Climatology, vol. 10. London: Elsevier Publishing Co., 1972.

Hart, K. *The Political Economy of West African Agriculture.* Cambridge: Cambridge University Press, 1982.

Hastings, A. *Nigerian Days.* London: Bodley Head, 1925.

Helleiner, G. *Peasant Agriculture, Government and Economic Growth in Nigeria.* Homewood, Ill.: Irwin, 1966.

Hetherington, P. *British Paternalism and Africa 1920–1940.* London: Cass, 1978.

Heussler, R. *The British in Nigeria.* London: Oxford University Press, 1968.

Hewitt, K., ed. *Interpreting Calamities* (forthcoming). London: George Allen and Unwin.

Hill, P. *Population, Prosperity, and Poverty: Rural Kano, 1900 and 1970.* Cambridge: Cambridge University Press, 1977.

————. *Rural Hausa: A Village and a Setting.* Cambridge: Cambridge University Press, 1972.

Hindess, B., and Hirst, P. *Pre-Capitalist Modes of Production.* London: Routledge and Kegan Paul, 1975.

Hiskett, M. *A History of Hausa Islamic Verse.* London: School of Oriental and African Studies, 1975.

————. *The Life and Times of Shehu Dan Fodio.* London: Oxford University Press, 1973.

Hobsbawm, E. *Industry and Empire.* Harmondsworth: Penguin, 1968.

Hodgson, Marshall. *The Venture of Islam.* 3 vols. Chicago: University of Chicago Press, 1974.

Hogendorn, J. *Nigerian Groundnut Exports.* Zaria: Ahmadu Bello University Press, 1979.

Holloway, J., and Picciotto, S. *State and Capital: A Marxist Debate.* London: Arnold, 1978.

Hopen, C. *A Pastoral Fulbe Family in Gwandu.* London: Oxford University Press, 1958.

Hopkins, A. G. *An Economic History of West Africa.* London: Longmans, 1973.

Hussain, A., and Tribe, K. *Marxism and The Agrarian Question.* 2 vols. Atlantic Highlands, N.J.: Humanities Press, 1981.

Hyden, G. *Beyond Ujamaa in Tanzania.* Berkeley, Los Angeles, London: University of California Press, 1980.

IFPRI. *Meeting Food Needs in the Developing World: Location and Magnitude of Task in the Next Decade.* Washington, D.C.: International Food Policy Research Institute, 1976.

Igbozurike, M. *Nigerian Land Policy: An Analysis of the Land Use Decree.* Nsukka: Department of Geography, University of Nsukka, 1980.

Ikime,O. *Merchant Princes of the Niger Delta.* London: Heinemann, 1968.

ILO. *Nigeria: First Things First.* Addis Ababa: International Labor Office, 1981.

Johnson, D. G. *World Agriculture in Disarray*. London: Macmillan, 1973.

Johnston, H. A. *The Fulani Empire of Sokoto*. London: Oxford University Press, 1967.

———. *A Selection of Hausa Stories*. Oxford: Clarendon Press, 1966.

Kassam, A. H. *Crops of the West African Semi-Arid Tropics*. Hyderabad: ICRISAT, 1976.

Kautsky, K. *Die Agrarfrage*. 1899. Published in French as *La Question Agraire*. Paris: Giard and Brier, 1900.

Kay, G. *Development and Underdevelopment*. London: Macmillan, 1975.

Kesner, R. *Economic Control and Colonial Development*. Westport, Conn.: Greenwood Press, 1981.

Kirk-Greene, A., ed. *Political Memoranda by Lord Lugard*. London: Cass, 1970.

Kirk-Greene, A. *Barth's Travels in Nigeria*. London: Oxford University Press, 1962.

Kirk-Greene, A., and Rimmer, D. *Nigeria Since 1970: A Political and Economic Outline*. London: Hodder and Stoughton, 1981.

Kitching, G. *Class and Economic Change in Kenya: The Making of an African Petite-Bourgeoisie*. New Haven: Yale University Press, 1980.

Kjekshus, H. *Ecology Control and Economic Development in East African History*. Berkeley, Los Angeles, London: University of California Press, 1977.

Klein, M. *Peasants in Africa*. Beverly Hills: Sage, 1980.

Kongstad, P. and Mönsted, M. *Family, Labour and Trade in Western Kenya*. Uppsala: Scandinavian Institute of African Studies Centre for Development Research, no. 3, 1980.

Kowal, J. M., and Kassam, A. H. *Agricultural Ecology of Savanna:A Study of West Africa*. Oxford: Oxford University Press, 1978.

Kowal, J., and Knabe, D. *An Agroclimatological Atlas of the Northern States of Nigeria*. Zaria: Ahmadu Bello University Press, 1972.

Kriedte, P., Medick, H. and Schlumbohm J. *Industrialization Before Industrialization* Cambridge: Cambridge University Press, 1981.

Kuczynski, R. R. *Demographic Survey of the British Colonial Empire.* vol. 1. London: Oxford University Press, 1948.

Ladurie, L. E., *Times of Feast, Times of Famine: A History of Climate Since the Year 1000.* New York: Doubleday, 1971.

Landes, D. *Prometheus Unbound: Technological Change and Industrial Development From 1750 to the Present.* Cambridge: Cambridge University Press, 1972.

Last, D. M. *The Sokoto Caliphate.* London: Longmans, 1967.

Laughlin, C., and Brady, I., eds. *Extinction and Survival in Human Societies.* New York: Columbia University Press, 1978.

Lenin, V. I. *The Development of Capitalism in Russia.* Moscow: Progress Publishers, 1964.

Lis, C., and Soly, H. *Poverty and Capitalism and Pre-Industrial Europe.* Atlantic Highlands, N.J.: Humanities Press, 1979.

Low, V. *Three Nigerian Emirates: A Study of Oral History.* Evanston: Northwestern University Press, 1972.

Lubeck, P. *Islam and Urban Labor: The Making of a Muslim Working Class in Northern Nigeria* (forthcoming).

Lugard, F. D. *Political Memoranda.* Nos. 1–12, 1918. Reprinted in *Political Memoranda by Lord Lugard,* edited by A. Kirk-Greene. London: Cass, 1970.

————. *Amalgamation of Northern and Southern Nigeria (1919) and Administration (1912–1919).* Reprinted with an introduction in *Lugard and the Amalgamation of Nigeria: A Documentary Record,* edited by A. Kirk-Greene. London: Cass, 1968.

————. *The Dual Mandate in British Tropical Africa.* London: George Allen and Unwin, 1922.

————. *Political Memoranda.* London: Waterlow, 1906.

MAB. *Management of Natural Resources in Africa: Traditional Strategies and Modern Decision-Making.* Paris: UNESCO, Man and the Biosphere Program, 1978.

————. *The Sahel: Ecological Approaches to Land Use.* Paris: UNESCO, Man and the Biosphere Program, Technical Notes, 1975.

————. *The Impact of Human Activities on the Dynamics of Arid and Semi-Arid Zone Ecosystems.* Paris: UNESCO, Man and the Biosphere Program. 1975a.

McPhee, A. *The Economic Revolution in British West Africa*. London: Cass, 1926.

Marks, S., and Atmore, A., eds *Economy and Society in Pre-Industrial South Africa*. London: Longmans, 1980.

Marx, K. *Grundrisse: Foundations of the Critique of Political Economy*. Harmondsworth: Penguin Books, 1973.

————. *The 18th Brumaire of Louis Bonaparte*. New York: International Publishers, 1972.

————. *A Contribution to the Critique of Political Economy*. London: Lawrence and Wishart, 1971.

————. "Wage, Labor and Capital," 1849. Reprinted in *Selected Works*. Moscow: Progress Publishers, 1968.

————. *Capital*. 3 vols. New York: International Publishers, 1967.

Masefield, B. *Famine: Its Prevention and Relief*. London: Oxford University Press, 1963.

Mauny, R. *Les Siècles Obscurs de l'Afrique Noire: Histoire et Archéologie*. Paris: Fayard, 1971.

Meillassoux, C. *Maidens, Meal and Money: Capitalism and the Domestic Community*. Cambridge: Cambridge University Press, 1981.

Meillassoux, C., ed. *L'Esclavage en Afrique Précoloniale*. Paris: Maspero, 1975.

Miers, S., and Kopytoff, I., eds. *Slavery in Africa: Historical and Anthropological Perspectives*. Madison: University of Wisconsin Press, 1977.

Migdal, J. *Peasants, Politics and Revolution*. Princeton: Princeton University Press, 1974.

Milliband, R. *The State and Capitalist Society*. London: Weidenfeld and Nicolson, 1969.

Mischlich, A. *Uber Die Kutturen Im Mittel-Sudan*. Berlin: Andrews and Steiner, 1942.

Monod, T., ed. *Pastoralism in Tropical Africa*. London: Oxford University Press, 1975.

Monteil, P. L. *De Saint-Louis à Tripoli par le la Tchad*. 1895. Reprint. Paris: Alcan, 1939.

Moore, B., Jr. *The Social Origins of Dictatorship and Democracy.* Boston: Beacon Press, 1966.

Moran, E. *Human Adaptability.* Belmont: Duxbury Press, 1978.

Morel, E. *Nigeria: Its People and Problems.* London: Cass, 1911.

Mortimore, M., and Wilson, J. *Land and People in the Kano Close Settled Zone.* Zaria: Department of Geography, Ahmadu Bello University, 1965.

Murray, M. *The Development of Capitalism in Colonial Indochina 1870–1940.* Berkeley, Los Angeles, London: University of California Press, 1980.

Myint, H. *Economic Theory and the Underdeveloped Countries.* London: Oxford University Press, 1971.

————. *The Economics of Developing Countries.* London: Hutchinson, 1967.

Nadel, S. F. *A Black Byzantium: The Kingdom of Nupe in Nigeria.* London: Oxford University Press, 1942.

Ndama-Egba, B. *Foreign Investment and Economic Transformation in West Africa 1870–1930 with Emphasis on Nigeria.* Lund: Economic History Association of Lund, Vol. XV, 1974.

Necker, J. *Sur la Legislation et le Commerce des Grains.* Paris, 1775. Cited in P. Spitz, "Silent Violence: Famine and Inequality," *International Review of Social Science,* XXX, 4 (1978), 867–92.

Nicolaisen, J. *Ecology and Culture of the Pastoral Tuareg.* Copenhagen: National Museum of Copenhagen, Ethnological Series, no. IX, 1963.

Nicolas, G. *Dynamique Sociale et Apprehension du Monde au Sein d'une Société Hausa.* Paris: Institut d'Ethnologie, 1975.

Okonjo, I. *The British Administration in Nigeria 1900–1950.* London: Nok Publishers, 1974.

Olatunbosun, D. *Nigeria's Neglected Rural Majority.* Ibadan: NISER, 1975.

Ollman, B. *Alienation: Marx's Concept of Man.* Cambridge: Cambridge University Press, 1974.

Orr, C. *The Making of Northern Nigeria.* London: Macmillan, 1911.

Osuntokun, A. *Nigeria in the First World War.* Ibadan: Longmans, 1977.

Oyediran, O., ed. *Nigerian Government and Politics Under Military Rule 1966 – 1979*. New York: St. Martin's Press, 1979.

Paden, J. *Religion and Political Culture in Kano*. Berkeley, Los Angeles, London: University of California Press, 1973.

Palmer, H. R. *Bornu, Sahara and the Sudan*. London: Cass, 1936.

————. *Sudanese Memoirs*. 3 vols. Lagos, 1928. Reprinted. London: Cass, 1967.

Palmer, R., and N. Parsons, eds. *The Roots of Rural Poverty in Central and Southern Africa*. Berkeley, Los Angeles, London: University of California Press, 1977.

Pearson, S. *Petroleum and the Nigerian Economy*. Stanford: Stanford University Press, 1970.

Perham, M. *Native Administration in Nigeria*. London: Cass, 1937 (reprinted 1962).

Polanyi, K. *The Great Transformation*. Boston: Beacon Press, 1957.

Popkin, S. *The Rational Peasant*. Berkeley, Los Angeles, London: University of California Press, 1979.

Post, J. D. *The Last Great Subsistence Crisis in the Western World*. Baltimore: Johns Hopkins University Press, 1977.

Post, K. *Arise Ye Starvelings: The Jamaican Labour Rebellion of 1938 and its Aftermath*. The Hague: Martinus Nijhoff, 1978.

Poulantzas, N. *State, Power, Socialism*. London: New Left Books, 1978.

————. *Political Power and Social Classes*. London: New Left Books, 1973.

Rappaport, R. *Ecology, Adaptation and Religion*. Richmond, Calif.: North Atlantic Books, 1979.

Raynault, C. *Structures Normatives et Relations Electives—Etude d'une Communauté Villageoise Haoussa*. Paris: Mouton, 1972.

Reuke, I. *Die Maguzawa in Nordnigeria*. Freiburg: Bertelsmann Universitatsverlag, 1969.

Rey, P.-P. *Les Alliances de Classes*. Paris: Maspero, 1973.

Richardson, J. *Narrative of a Mission to Central Africa*. Vol. II. London: Chapman and Hall, 1853.

Rodinson, M. *Islam and Capitalism*. Harmondsworth: Penguin, 1974.

Rodney, W. *How Europe Underdeveloped Africa*. London: Bogle-L'Ouverture Publications, 1972.

Roumasset, J., et al., eds. *Risk, Uncertainty and Agricultural Development*. New York: Agricultural Development Council, 1979.

Roumasset, J. *Rice and Risk*. Amsterdam: North Holland Press, 1976.

Ruxton, F. H. *Maliki Law*. London: Luzac and Co., 1916.

Sahlins, M. *Culture and Practical Reason*. Chicago: Aldine, 1976.

———. *Stone Age Economics*. Chicago: Aldine, 1972.

Samuel, R., ed. *People's History and Socialist Theory*. London: Routledge and Kegan Paul, 1981.

Schacht, J. *An Introduction to Islamic Law*. Oxford: Clarendon Press, 1964.

Schatz, P. *Nigerian Capitalism*. Berkeley, Los Angeles, London: University of California Press, 1977.

Schmidt, A. *Marx's Concept of Nature*. London: New Left Books, 1971.

Schofield, S. *Development and the Problems of Village Nutrition*. Montclair, N.J.: Allanheld and Osmun, 1979.

Schon, J. *Magana Hausa*. London: Society for Promoting Christian Knowledge, 1885.

Scott, E. *Indigenous Systems of Exchange and Decision Making among Smallholders in Hausaland*. Ann Arbor: Michigan Geographical Publications, no. 16, 1976.

Scott, J. *The Moral Economy of the Peasant*. New Haven: Yale University Press, 1976.

Sen, A. *Poverty and Famines*. London: Oxford University Press, 1980.

Sennett, P., and Cobb, J. *The Hidden Injuries of Class*. New York: Vintage, 1972.

Shanin, T. *The Awkward Class*. Oxford: Clarendon Press, 1972.

Sharwood-Smith, B. *But Always As Friends*. London: Allen and Unwin, 1969.

Sheets, J., and Morris, R. *Disaster in the Desert*. Washington, D.C.: Carnegie Endowment for International Peace, 1974.

Shephard, J. *The Politics of Starvation*. Washington, D.C.: Carnegie Endowment for International Peace, 1975.

Smaldone, J. P. *Warfare in the Sokoto Caliphate: Historical and Sociological Perspectives*. Cambridge: Cambridge University Press, 1977.

Smith, M. *Baba of Karo*. London: Oxford University Press, 1954.

Smith, M. G. *Affairs of Daura*. Berkeley, Los Angeles, London: University of California Press, 1978.

———. *Government in Zazzau*. London: International African Institute, 1960.

Sorkin, P. *Hunger as a Factor in Human Affairs*. Gainesville: University of Florida Press, 1975.

Sourdel, D. *La Civilisation de l'Islam Classique*. Paris: Arthaud, 1968.

Staudinger, P. *Im Herzen der Haussa Länder*. Berlin: Landsberger, 1889.

Stenning, D. *Savanna Nomads: A Study of the Wodaabe Pastoral Fulani of West Bornu Province*. London: Oxford University Press, 1959.

Suret-Canale, J. *French Colonialism in Tropical Africa: 1900–1945*. London: C. Hurst and Co., 1971.

Swainson, N. *The Development of Corporate Capitalism in Kenya 1917–1977*. Berkeley, Los Angeles, London: University of California Press, 1980.

Taylor, J. *From Modernization to Modes of Production*. New York: Humanities Press, 1979.

Temple, C. *Native Races and Their Rulers*. London: Cass, 1918 (reprinted 1968).

Thompson, E. P. *The Poverty of Theory*. New York: Monthly Review, 1978.

———. *The Making of the English Working Class*. Harmondsworth: Penguin, 1963.

Timpanaro, S. *On Materialism*. London: New Left Books, 1978.

Tomlinson, G., and Lethem, G. *History of Islamic Propaganda in Nigeria.* London: Waterlow, 1927.

Trimingham, S. *Islam in West Africa.* London: Oxford University Press, 1958.

Turner, B. S. *Marx and the End of Orientalism.* London: Allen and Unwin, 1978.

Urvoy, Y. F. *Histoire de l'Empire du Bornou.* Paris: Larose, 1949.

Usman, Y. B. *For the Liberation of Nigeria.* Boston: New Beacon Press, 1978.

van Apeldoorn, J. *Perspectives on Drought and Famine in Nigeria.* London: Allen and Unwin, 1981.

van de Laar, A. *The World Bank and the Poor.* Boston: Martinus Nijhoff, 1980.

van Raay, H. G. T. *Rural Planning in a Savanna Region.* Rotterdam: University Press, 1975.

Vischer, I. *Croquois et Souvenirs de la Nigèrie du Nord.* Paris: Freres, 1915.

von Grunebaum, G. *Islam: A Study in Cultural Orientation.* New York: Barnes and Noble, 1961.

Wallerstein, I. *The Modern World System: Capitalist Agriculture and the Origins of the European World Economy in the Sixteenth Century.* New York: Academic Press, 1974.

Weber, M. *Economy and Society.* vol. 1. Berkeley, Los Angeles: University of California Press, 1968.

Wells, J. *Agricultural Policy and Economic Growth in Nigeria.* Ibadan: NISER, 1974.

Wheatley, P. *The Pivot of the Four Quarters.* Edinburgh: University of Edinburgh Press, 1972.

White, G., ed. *Natural Hazards: Local, National, and Global.* London: Oxford University Press, 1974.

White, G., Burton, I., and Kates, R. *Environment as Hazard.* London: Oxford University Press, 1978.

Williams, G., ed. *Nigeria: Economy and Society.* London: Rex Collins, 1976.

Wolf, E. *Peasants.* Englewood Cliffs, N.J.: Prentice-Hall, 1966.

Woodham-Smith, C. *The Great Hunger*. New York: Harper and Row, 1962.

World Bank. *World Development Report 1980*. New York: Oxford University Press, 1980.

————. *Assault on World Poverty*. Baltimore: Johns Hopkins University Press, 1975.

PUBLISHED ARTICLES, PAPERS, AND PERIODICALS

Abalu, G. "A Note on Crop Mixtures Under Indigenous Conditions in Northern Nigeria," *Journal of Development Studies* 12 (1976), 212–20.

Abalu, G., and D'Silva, B. "Nigeria's Food Situation," *Food Policy* 5, 1 (1980), 49–60.

Adas, M. "From Avoidance to Confrontation: Peasant Protest in Pre-Colonial Southeast Asia," *Comparative Studies in Society and History* 23, 2 (1981), 217–47.

————. "Moral Economy or Contest State?: Elite Demands and the Origins of Peasant Protest in Southeast Asia," *Journal of Social History* 15 (1980), 521–46.

Alexandre, P. "Les Variations Climatiques au Moyen Age," *Annales* 32, 2 (1977), 183–97.

Al-Hajj, M. "Hayatee B. Sa'id: A Revolutionary Mahdist in the Western Sudan." In *Sudan in Africa*, edited by Y. Hasan. Khartoum: University Press, 1971. Pp. 128–41.

Alland, A. "Adaptation," *Annual Review of Anthropology* 4 (1975), 59–73

Amin, S. "Capitalism and Ground Rent: The Domination of Capitalism Over Agriculture in Tropical Africa." Mimeograph, IDEP, Dakar, 1974. Reprinted in Amin, S. *Imperialisme et le Développement Inégal*. Paris: Minuit, 1976. Pp. 45–83.

————. "Underdevelopment and Dependence in Black Africa: Origins and Contemporary Forms," *Journal of Modern African Studies* 10, 4 (1972), 503–24.

Anderson, J. "Nature and Significance of Risk in the Exploitation of New Technology." In *Proceedings of the International Workshop on Socioeconomic Constraints to Development of Semi-Arid Tropical Agriculture*. Hyderabad: ICRISAT, 1979. Pp. 297–303.

Anderson, J. N. "Ecological Anthropology and Anthropological Ecology." In *Handbook of Social and Cultural Anthropology*, edited by J. Honigmann. Chicago: Rand McNally, 1973. Pp. 179–239.

Baier, S. "Long Term Structural Change in the Economy of Central Niger." In *West African Culture Dynamics*, edited by B. K. Schwartz and R. E. Dummett. The Hague: Mouton, 1980. Pp. 587–602.

———. "Trans Saharan Trade and the Sahel," *Journal of African History* XVIII (1977), 37–60.

Baier, S., and Lovejoy, P. E. "The Tuareg of the Central Sudan: Gradations in Servility at the Desert Edge." In *Slavery in Africa: Historical and Anthropological Perspectives*, edited by S. Meirs and I. Kopytoff. Madison: University of Wisconsin Press, 1977. Pp. 391–411.

Baker, R. "The Sahel: An Information Crisis." Development Studies Reprint no. 12, University of East Anglia, 1976.

Banaji, J. "Capitalist Domination and the Small Peasantry: Deccan Districts in the Late 19th Century." In *Studies in the Development of Capitalism in India* (no editor). Lahore, Pakistan: Vanguard Books, 1978. Pp. 351–429.

———. "Modes of Production in a Materialist Conception of History," *Capital and Class*, Autumn 1977, 1–44.

———. "Summary of Selected Parts of Kautsky's Agrarian Question," *Economy and Society* 5, 1 (1976), 2–49.

———. "Backward Capitalism, Primitive Accumulation and Modes of Production," *Journal of Contemporary Asia* 3, 4 (1973), 393–413.

Barkow, J. "Muslims and Maguzawa in North Central State, Nigeria: An Ethnographic Comparison," *Canadian Journal of African Studies* VII (1973), 59–76.

Barr, T. N. "The World Food Situation and Global Grain Prospects," *Science* 214 (1981), 1087–95.

Bartra, R. "Modes of Production and Agrarian Imbalances," *International Social Science Journal* XXXI (1979), 27–38.

Bates, R. H. "Food Policy in Africa—Political Causes and Social Effects," *Food Policy* 6 (1981), 147–57.

———. "People in Villages: Micro-Level Studies in Political Economy," *World Politics* 31 (1978), 129–49.

———. "States and Political Intervention in Markets," Social Science Working Paper, no. 345, California Institute of Technology, 1978*a*.

Bauer, P. T. "British Colonial Africa: Economic Retrospect and Aftermath." In *Colonialism in Africa 1870–1960*. Vol. 4, edited by P. Duignan and L. H. Gann. Cambridge: Cambridge University Press, 1975. Pp. 632–54.

Bennett, J. "A Rational-Choice Model of Agricultural Resource Utilization and Conservation." In *Social and Technological Management in Dry Lands*, edited by N. Gonzales. Boulder: Westview Press, 1978. Pp. 151–86.

Berger, J. "Toward an Understanding of Peasant Experience," *Race and Class* XIX (1978), 345–59.

Berman, B., and Lonsdale, J. "Crises of Accumulation, Coercion and the Colonial State," *Canadian Journal of African Studies* 14, 1 (1980), 37–54.

Bernstein, H. "African Peasantries: A Theoretical Framework," *Journal of Peasant Studies* 6, 3 (1979), 420–43.

———. "Notes on Capital and Peasantry," *Review of African Political Economy*, no. 10 (1978), 60–73.

———. "Underdevelopment and the Law of Value," *Review of African Political Economy* 7 (1976), 53–59.

Bernstein, H., and Depelchin, J. "The Object of African History: A Materialist Perspective," *History in Africa*, vol. 5, pt. 1 (1978), 1–19; and vol. 6, pt. 2 (1979), 17–43.

Bernus, E. "Drought in Niger Republic," *Savanna* 2 (1973), 129–32.

Berry, S. "Rural Class Formation in West Africa." In *Agricultural Development in Africa: Issues of Public Policy*, edited by R. Bates and M. Lofchie. New York: Praeger, 1980. Pp. 401–24.

———. "Cocoa and Economic Development in Western Nigeria." In *Growth and Development of the Nigerian Economy*, edited by C. Eicher and C. Lidholm. East Lansing: Michigan State University Press, 1970. Pp. 15–33.

Bettelheim, C. "Theoretical Comments." In *Unequal Exchange: A Study of the Imperialism of Trade*, by A. Emmanuel. New York: Monthly Review Press, 1972. Pp. 271–322.

Bhaduri, A. "On the Formation of Usurious Interest Rates in Agriculture," *Cambridge Journal of Economics* 1 (1977), 341–62.

Bienen, H. "The Political Economy of Income Distribution in Nigeria." In *The Political Economy of Income Distribution in Nigeria*, edited by H. Bienen and V. P. Diejomach. New York: Holmes and Meier, 1981. Pp. 1–27.

Binswanger, H. P. "Risk Attitudes of Rural Households in Semi-Arid Tropical India," *Economic and Political Weekly* 13 (1978), 49–62.

Boesen, J. "On Peasantry and the Modes of Production Debate," *Review of African Political Economy*, 15/16 (1979), 154–61.

Bowden, M. J., et al. "The Effect of Climatic Fluctuations on Human Populations: Two Hypotheses." In T. M. Wigley, M. J. Ingram, G. Farmer, eds, *Climate And History*. Cambridge: Cambridge University Press, 1981. Pp. 479–513.

Bradby, B. "The Destruction of Natural Economy," *Economy and Society* 4, 2 (1975), 127–61.

Brenner, R. "The Origins of Capitalist Development: A Critique of Neo-Smithian Marxism," *New Left Review* 104 (1977), 3–42.

Bryceson, D. F. "Colonial Famine Responses—the Bagamoyo District of Tanganyika, 1920–61," *Food Policy* 6, 2 (1981), 78–90.

———. "Changes in Peasant Food Production and Food Supply in Relation to the Historical Development of Commodity Production in Pre-Colonial and Colonial Tanganyika," *Journal of Peasant Studies* 7, 2 (1980), 281–311.

Bryson, R. "Climatic Modification by Air Pollution; the Sahelian Effect," Report no. 9, Institute of Environmental Studies, University of Wisconsin, Madison, 1973.

Bull, M. "Indirect Rule in Northern Nigeria 1906–1911." In *Essays in Imperial Government*, edited by K. Robinson and F. Madden. London: Oxford University Press, 1963. Pp. 59–67.

Buntjer, B. "Rural Society: The Changing Structure of *Gandu*." In *Zaria and Its Region*, edited by M. Mortimore. Zaria: Department of Geography, Ahmadu Bello University, 1970. Pp. 157–69.

Cahill, G. "Famine Symposium," *Ecology of Food and Nutrition* 6 (1978), 221–30.

Cain, M. "Risk and Insurance: Perspectives on Fertility and Agrarian Change in India and Bangladesh," *Population and Development Review* 7, 3 (1981), 435–74.

Caldwell, J. "The African Drought and Its Demographic Implications," New York, Population Council, 1975.

Cardew, M. "Gobir Granaries," *Nigeria Magazine* 67 (1960), 216–23.

Castells, M. "Immigrant Workers and Class Struggles in Advanced Capitalism: the Western European Experience." In *Peasants and Proletarians: The Struggles of Third World Workers*, edited by R. Cohen, P. Gutkin, and P. Brazier. London: Monthly Review Press, 1979. Pp. 350–69.

Charney, J., et al. "Drought in the Sahara: A Biogeographical Feedback Mechanism," *Science* 187 (1974), 364–65.

Chibnik, M. "Small Farmer Risk Aversion," *Culture and Agriculture*, 10 (1981), 1–5.

Cissoko, S. "Famines et Epidémies à Timuctoo dans le Boucle du Niger du XVIIe Siècle," *Bulletin de l'Institut Francaise d'Afrique Noire*, B., 30 (1968), 806–21.

Clarke, J. "Peasantization and Landholding." In *Peasants in Africa*, edited by M. Klein. Beverly Hills: Sage, 1980. Pp. 177–220.

Clarke, W. "The Structure of Permanence." In *Subsistence and Survival: Rural Ecology in the Pacific*, edited by T. Bayliss-Smith and R. Feachem. San Francisco: Academic Press, 1977. Pp. 363–84.

Clarence-Smith, F. "For Braudel: a note on the Ecole des Annales and the Historiography of Africa," *History in Africa* 4 (1977), 275–82.

Clarkson, J. "Ecology and Spatial Analysis," *Annals of the Association of American Geographers* 60 (1970), 700–16.

Claxton, R. H. and Hecht, A. D. "Climatic and Human History in Europe and Latin America," *Climatic Change* 1 (1978), 195–203.

Clayton, W. D. "The Vegetation of Katsina Province," *Journal of Ecology* 51 (1963), 345–51.

———. "Derived Savanna in Kabba Province," *Journal of Ecology* 49 (1962), 595–604.

Clough, P. "Farmers and Traders in Hausaland," *Development and Change* 12 (1981), 273–92.

Coats, A. W. "Contrary Moralities: Plebs, Paternalists and Political Economists," *Past and Present* 54 (1972), 130–33.

Cohen, R., and Brenner, L. "Bornu in the Nineteenth Century." In *History of West Africa*, vol. 2, edited by J. F. A. Ajayi and M. Crowder. New York: Columbia University Press, 1974. Pp. 93–128.

Collins, J. D. "The Clandestine Movement of Groundnuts Across the Niger-Nigeria Boundary," *Canadian Journal of African Studies* 10, 2 (1976), 259–78.

Colson, E. "In Good Years and In Bad: Food Strategies of Self Reliant Societies," *Journal of Anthropological Research* 35, 1 (1979), 18–29.

Cooper, F. "Peasants, Capitalists and Historians," *Journal of South African Studies* 17, 2 (1981), 284–314.

————. "The Problem of Slavery in African Studies," *Journal of African History* 20 (1979), 103–25.

Copans, J. "Droughts, Famines and The Evolution of Senegal (1966–1978)," *Mass Emergencies* 4 (1979), 87–93.

Coquery-Vidrovitch, C. "Recherches sur les modes de production africaines," *La Pensée* 144 (1969), 61–68. Reprinted in *The Political Economy of Contemporary Africa*, edited by P. Gutkind and I. Wallerstein. Beverly Hills: Sage, 1976. Pp. 90–111.

Corby, H. "Changes Being Brought About by the Introduction of Mixed Farming, Bomo Village (Zaria)." *Farm and Forest* 2 (1941), 106–09.

Cowen, M. "Commodity Production in Kenya's Central Province." In *Rural Development in Tropical Africa*, edited by J. Heyer, P. Roberts, and G. Williams. London: Macmillan, 1981. Pp. 121–42.

Cummings, B. "Interest and Ideology in the Study of Agrarian Politics," *Politics and Society* 10 (1981), 467–95.

Currey, B. "The Famine Syndrome: Its Definition for Preparedness and Prevention in Bangladesh," *Ecology of Food and Nutrition* 7 (1978), 87–98.

Curtin, P. "Recent Trends in African Historiography and Their Contribution to Theory in General." In *General History of Africa*, edited by J. K. Zerbo. Methodology and African Prehistory, vol. 1. London: Heinemann, 1981. Pp. 54–71.

Dahl, G. and Hjort, A. "Pastoral Change and the Role of Drought." SAREC Report no. R2, Stockholm, 1979.

D'Silva, B. and Raza, M. R. "Integrated Rural Development in Nigeria," *Food Policy* 5 (1980), 282–97.

de Crisenoy, C. "Capitalism and Agriculture," *Economy and Society* 8, 1 (1979), 9–25.

Deere, D. C., and de Janvry, A. "Demographic and Social Differentiation Among Northern Peruvian Peasants," *Journal of Peasant Studies* 8, 3 (1981), 335–36.

————. "A Conceptual Framework for the Empirical Analysis of Peasants," *American Journal of Agricultural Economics* 61 (1979), 601–11.

de Leeuw, P. N. "Livestock Development and Drought in the Northern States of Nigeria." Conference Paper no. 6, Institute for Agricultural Research, Ahmadu Bello University, Zaria, 1975.

de St. Croix, F. "Some Aspects of the Cattle Husbandry of the Nomadic Fulani," *Farm and Forest* 1 (1944), 30–31.

de Vries, J. "Measuring the Impact of Climate on History," *Journal of Interdisciplinary History* 10, 4 (1980), 599–630.

————. "Histoire du climat et économie: des faits nouveaux, une interprétation différente," *Annales* XXXII (1977), 202–07.

Donaint, P. "Les Cadres Geographiques à travers les langues du Nigeria." Etudies Nigériennes, no. 37, Institut de Récherches en Sciences Humaines, Niamey, 1975.

Dunbar, R. "African Ranches Ltd., 1914–1913," *Annals of the Association of American Geographers* 60 (1971), 102–23.

————. "Slavery and the Evolution of Nineteenth Century Damagaram." In *Slavery in Africa: Historical and Anthropological Perspectives*, edited by S. Miers and I. Kopytoff. Madison: University of Wisconsin Press, 1977. Pp. 155–177.

Elwert, G., and Wong, D. "Subsistence Production and Commodity Production in the Third World," *Review* III, 3 (1980), 501–22.

Ennew, J., Hirst, P., and Tribe, K. " 'Peasantry' as an Economic Category," *Journal of Peasant Studies* 4 (1977), 295–322.

Epstein, T. S. "Productive Efficiency and Customary Systems of Rewards in Rural South India." In *Themes in Economic Anthropology*, edited by R. Firth. London: Tavistock, 1967. Pp. 229–52.

Essang, S. M. "The Impact of Oil Production on Nigerian Agricultural Policy," *Indian Journal of Agricultural Economics* XXXII (1977), 24–32.

Etuk, E. G. "A Critical Analysis of the Approach to Agricultural Development in the Third National Development Plan 1975–1980." In *The Aftermath of the 1972–74 Drought in Nigeria*, edited by J. van Apeldoorn. Zaria: Centre for Social and Economic Research, 1978. Pp. 87–93.

Farrington, J. "A Note on Planned Versus Actual Farmer Performance Under Uncertainty in Underdeveloped Agriculture," *Journal of Agricultural Economics* 27 (1976), 257–60.

Faulkingham, R. "Ecological Constraint and Subsistence Strategies: The Impact of Drought in a Hausa Village." In *Drought in Africa 2*, edited by D. Dalby et al. London: International African Institute, 1977. Pp. 148–58.

Faulkingham, R., and Thorbahn, P. F. "Population Dynamics and Drought: A Village in Niger," *Population Studies* 29, 3 (1975), 463–77.

Faulkner, T., and Mackie, J. "The Introduction of Mixed Farming in Northern Nigeria," *Empire Journal of Experimental Agriculture* 4 (1936), 89–96.

Feder, E. "The New World Bank Program for the Self-Liquidation of the Third World Peasantry," *Journal of Peasant Studies* 3 (1976), 343–54.

Fernand Braudel Centre. "Households, Labor Force and Production Processes in the Capitalist World Economy." Working Paper of Research Group on Households and Production Processes, State University of New York, Binghampton, 1978.

Forde, D. "The North: The Hausa." In *The Native Economies of Nigeria*, vol. 1., edited by M. Perham. London: Faber, 1946. Pp. 119–79.

Forrest, T. "Agricultural Policy in Nigeria 1900–1975." In *Rural Development in Tropical Africa*, edited by G. Williams, P. Roberts, and J. Heyer. London: Macmillan, 1981. Pp. 222–58.

————. "Notes on the Political Economy of State Intervention in Nigeria," *IDS Bulletin* 9 (1977), 42–47.

Foster-Carter, A. "The Modes of Production Controversy," *New Left Review* 107 (1978), 47–77.

Freund, W. M. "Labour Migration to the Northern Nigerian Tin Mines 1903–1945," *Journal of African History* 22 (1981), 73–84.

————. "Oil Boom and Crisis in Contemporary Nigeria," *Review of African Political Economy* 13 (1978), 91–101.

Friedmann, H. "The Political Economy of Food." Research Paper no. 5, Department of Sociology, University of Toronto, 1979a.

———. "Household Production and the National Economy," *Journal of Peasant Studies* 7, 2 (1979*b*), 159–83.

———. "Simple Commodity Production and Wage Labor in the American Plains," *Journal of Peasant Studies* 6, 1 (1978*a*), 71–100.

———. "World Market, State and Family Farm: Social Basis of Household Production in an Era of Wage Labor," *Comparative Studies in Society and History* 20, 4 (1978*b*), 545–86.

Friedmann, J. "Hegelian Ecology: Between Rousseau and the World Spirit." In *Social and Ecological Systems*, edited by P. Burnham and R. Ellen. London: Academic Press, 1979. Pp. 253–70.

Fugelstad, F. "La grand famine de 1931 dans l'Ouest nigérien," *Revue Française d'Histoire d'Outre Mer* LXI (1974), 18–33.

Genovese, E. F. "The Many Faces of Moral Economy: a Contribution to a Debate," *Past and Present* 58 (1973), 161–68.

Goddard, A. "Changing Family Structures Among the Hausa," *Africa* XVIII (1973), 207–18.

———. "Are Hausa Family Structures Breaking Up," *Samaru Agricultural Newsletter* 11 (1969), 34–47.

Goddard A. D., Mortimore, M., and Norman, D. "Some Social and Economic Implications of Population Growth in Rural Hausaland." In *Population Growth and Socio-Economic Change in West Africa*, edited by J. Caldwell. New York: Columbia University Press, 1976. Pp. 321–336.

Godelier, M. "The Object and Method of Economic Anthropology." In *Relations of Production*, edited by D. Seddon. London: Cass, 1978. Pp. 49–126.

———. "The Concept of the Asiatic Mode of Production." In *Relations of Production*, edited by D. Seddon. London: Cass, 1978. Pp. 209–50.

———. "On the Definition of a Social Formation: The Example of the Incas," *Critique of Anthropology* 1 (1974), 63–73.

Gowers, W. F. "Gazetteer of Kano Province." 1926, 56 pp. Reprinted in *Gazetteers of the Northern Provinces of Nigeria*. The Hausa Emirates, vol. 1. London: Cass, 1972.

Greenberg, J. H. "Islam and Clan Organization Among the Hausa," *Southwestern Journal of Anthropology* 3, 3 (1947), 193–211.

Grossman, L. "Man-Environment Relationships in Anthropology and in Geography," *Annals of the Association of American Geographers* 67 (1977), 126–44.

Grove, A. "A Note on the Remarkably Low Rainfall of the Sudan Zone in 1913," *Savanna* 2 (1973), 133–38.

———. "Population and Agriculture in Northern Nigeria." In *Essays on African Population*, edited by K. M. Barbour and R. M. Prothero. London: Clarendon Press, 1961. Pp. 115–36.

Grove, A., and Warren, A. "Quarternary Landforms and Climate on the South Side of the Sahara," *Geographical Journal* CXXXIV (1969), 194–209.

Harlan, J. "The Origin and Domestication of Sorghum," *Economic Botany* 25 (1971), 128–35.

Harrison, M. "The Peasant Mode of Production in the Work of A. V. Chayanov," *Journal of Peasant Studies* 4, 4 (1977), 323–36.

———. "Resource Allocation and Agrarian Class Formation: The Problem of Social Mobility Among Russian Peasant Households 1880–1930," *Journal of Peasant Studies* 4 (1977a), 127–61.

———. "Chayanov and the Economics of Russian Peasantry," *Journal of Peasant Studies* 2, 4 (1975), 389–417.

Harriss, B. "Going Against the Grain," *Development and Change* 10 (1979), 363–84.

Harriss, J., and Harriss, B. "Development Studies," *Progress in Human Geography* 3, 4 (1979), 576–84.

Hartley, K. and Greenwood, M. "The Effect of Small Applications of Farmyard Manure on the Yields of Cereals in Nigeria," *Empire Journal of Experimental Agriculture* 1 (1933), 113–21.

Hays, H. "The Marketing and Storage of Food Grains in Northern Nigeria." Samaru Miscellaneous Paper no. 50, Ahmadu Bello University, Zaria, 1975.

Hazelkorn, E. "Some Problems with Marx's Theory of Capitalist Penetration into Agriculture: The Case of Ireland," *Economy and Society* 10 (1981), 284–313.

Hill, P. "From Slavery to Freedom: The Case of Farm Slavery in Nigerian Hausaland," *Comparative Studies of Society and History* 17 (1976), 395–426.

————. "Some Socio-Economic Consequences of High Population Density in Rural Areas Near Kano City." In *The Population Factor in African Studies*, edited by R. Moss and R. J. Rathbone. London: University of London Press, 1975. Pp. 198–207.

————. "Hidden Trade in Hausaland," *Man* 4 (1969), 392–409.

————. "Aspects of Socio-Economic Life in a Hausa Village in Northern Nigeria," *Rural Africana* 3 (1969a), 25–36.

————. "The Myth of the Amorphous Peasantry: A Northern Nigerian Case Study," *Nigerian Journal of Economic and Social Studies* 10 (1968), 239–60.

Hiskett, M. "The Arab Star Calendar and Planetary System in Hausa Verse," *Bulletin of SOAS* XXIX (1967), 158–76.

————. "The Song of Bagauda: A Hausa King List and Homily," *Bulletin of SOAS* XXVII (1965), 112–35.

Hobsbawm, E. J. "Scottish Reformers of the Eighteenth Century and Capitalist Agriculture." In *Peasants in History: Essays in Honour of Daniel Thorner*, edited by E. Hobsbawm et al. Calcutta: Oxford University Press, 1980. Pp. 2–29.

Hogendorn, J. "The Economics of Slave Use on Two Plantations in Zaria Emirate, Hausaland," *International Journal of African Historical Studies* 6 (1977), 369–83.

————. "Economic Initiative and African Cash Crop Farming: Precolonial Origins and Early Colonial Developments." In *Colonialism in Africa*, vol. 4, edited by L. Gann and P. Duignan. Cambridge: Cambridge University Press, 1975. Pp. 87–103.

Hopkins, A. "The Creation of a Colonial Monetary System," *African Historical Studies* 3 (1970), 101–32.

Horton, R. "Stateless Societies in the History of Africa." In *History of West Africa*, vol. 1, edited by M. Crowder and J. Ajayi. London: Longmans, 1971. Pp. 78–119.

Howard, R. "Formation and Stratification of the Peasantry in Colonial Ghana," *Journal of Peasant Studies* 8 (1980), 61–80.

Hunt, D. "Chayanov's Model of Peasant Household Resource Allocation," *Journal of Peasant Studies* 6, 3 (1979), 247–85.

Hunter, J. M. "Seasonal Hunger in a Part of the West African Savanna." Transactions and Papers of the Institute of British Geographers, no. 41, 1967. Pp. 167–85.

Jaggar, P. J. "Kano City Blacksmiths: Precolonial Distribution, Structure and Organization," *Savanna* II (1973), 1, 11–26.

Jodha, N. S., et al. "The Nature and Significance of Risk in the Semi-Arid Tropics." In *Proceedings of the International Workshop on Socioeconomic Constraints to Development of Semi-Arid Tropical Agriculture*. Hyderabad: ICRISAT, 1979. Pp. 303–16.

Jodha, N. S. "Effectiveness of Farmer's Adjustment to Risk," *Economic and Political Weekly* 13 (1978), 38–48.

———. "Famine and Famine Policies: Some Empirical Evidence," *Economic and Political Weekly* 11 (1975), 1609–23.

Joseph, R. "Affluence and Underdevelopment: The Nigerian Experience," *Journal of Modern African Studies* 16, 2 (1978), 221–39.

Kelly, K. "The Independent Mode of Production," *Review of Radical Political Economics* 11, 1 (1979), 38–48.

Keyder, C. "Credit and Peripheral Structuration: Turkey in the 1920's," *Review* III (1980), 579–97.

Kilkenny, R. "The Slave Mode of Production in Precolonial Dahomey." In *Modes of Production in Africa*, edited by C. Stewart and D. Crummey. Beverly Hills: Sage, 1981. Pp. 111–56.

King, J. "Mixed Farming in Northern Nigeria," *Empire Journal of Experimental Agriculture* 7 (1939), 271–88.

Kirk-Greene, A. "Tax and Travel Among the Hill Tribes of Northern Adamawa," *Africa* 26, 4 (1956), 369–79.

Kirkby, A. "Individual and Community Responses to Rainfall Variability in Oaxaca, Mexico." In *Natural Hazards*, edited by G. White. London: Oxford University Press, 1974. Pp. 119–28.

Klein, M. "Slavery, the Slave Trade, and Legitimate Commerce in Late 19th Century Africa," *Etudes d'Histoire Africaine* 2 (1971), 22–24.

Klein, M., and Lovejoy, P. "Slavery in West Africa." In *The Uncommon Market: Essays in the Economic History of the Atlantic Slave Trade*, edited by H. Gemery and J. Hogendorn. New York: Academic Press, 1979. Pp. 181–212.

Kowal, J. M. and Adeoye, K. B. "An Assessment of Aridity and the Severity of the 1972 Drought in Northern Nigeria and Neighbouring Countries." Samaru Research Bulletin No. 212, Institute for Agricultural Research, Samaru, 1974.

Ladurie, L. E. "Histoire et Climat," *Annales* XIV (1959), 3–34.

Lamb, G. "Marxism, Access and the State," *Development and Change* 6 (1975), 119–35.

Lamb, H. "Is the Earth's Climate Changing?" *Ecologist* 4 (1974), 10–15.

Lamb, H. and Ingram, M. "Climate and History," *Past and Present* 88 (1980), 136–41.

Langdon, S. "Multinational Firms and the State in Kenya," *IDS Bulletin* 9 (1977), 36–41.

Last, D. M. "The Presentation of Sickness in a Community of Non-Muslim Hausa." In *Social Anthropology and Medicine*, edited by J. B. Loudon. London: Academic Press, 1976. Pp. 116–19.

————. "Reform in West Africa: The Jihad Movements of the Nineteenth Century." In *The History of West Africa*, Vol. II, edited by M. Crowder and F. Ajayi. London: Longmans, 1974. Pp. 1–29.

————. "Aspects of Administration and Dissent in Hausaland 1800–1968," *Africa* XL, 4 (1970), 345–57.

Last, M. and Al-Hajj, M. A. "Attempts at Defining a Muslim in Nineteenth Century Hausaland and Borno," *Journal of the Historical Society of Nigeria* III (1965), 231–40.

Laya, D. "Interviews with Farmers and Livestock Owners in the Sahel," *African Environment* 1 (1975), 49–93.

Leys, C. "The 'Overdeveloped' Post-Colonial State: A Re-evaluation," *Review of African Political Economy* 5 (1976), 39–48.

Lipton, M. "The Theory of the Optimizing Peasant," *Journal of Development Studies* 4 (1968), 326–51.

Lofchie, M. "Political and Economic Origins of African Hunger," *Journal of Modern African Studies* 13 (1975), 551–67.

Lonsdale, J. "State and Peasantry in Colonial Africa." In *People's History and Socialist Theory*, edited by R. Samuel. London: Routledge and Kegan Paul, 1981. Pp. 106–18.

Lonsdale, J., and Berman, B. "Coping with the Contradictions," *Journal of African History* 20 (1979), 487–505.

Lovejoy, P. "Plantations in the Economy of the Sokoto Caliphate," *Journal of African History* XIX (1978), 341–68.

Lovejoy, P., and Baier, S. "The Desert Side Economy of the Central Sudan," *International Journal of African Historical Studies* 8 (1975), 1–42.

Lovejoy, P., and Hogendorn, J. "Slave Marketing in West Africa." In *The Uncommon Market: Essays in the Economic History in the Atlantic Slave Trade*, edited by J. Gemery and J. Hogendorn. New York: Academic Press, 1979. Pp. 213–38.

Low, A. "Decision Taking under Uncertainty," *Journal of Agricultural Economics* 25 (1974), 311–21.

Lubeck, P. "Islam and Resistance in Northern Nigeria." In *The World System of Capitalism: Past and Present*, edited by W. L. Goldfrank. Beverly Hills: Sage, 1979. Pp. 189–206.

———. "Labour in Kano Since the Petroleum Book," *Review of African Political Economy* 13 (1978), 37–46.

McAlpin, M. B. "Dearth, Famine and Risk: The Changing Impact of Crop Failures in Western India, 1870–1920," *Journal of Economic History XXXIX* (1979), 143–57.

McCullogh, W. "An Enquiry into the Dietaries of the Hausa and the Town Fulani," *West African Medical Journal* 3–4 (1929/30), 8–22, 62–73.

Mann, S., and Dickinson, J. "Obstacles to the Development of a Capitalist Agriculture," *Journal of Peasant Studies* 5 (1978), 466–81.

Mason, M. "Working on the Railway." In *African Labor History*, edited by P. Gutkind, R. Cohen, and J. Copans. Beverly Hills: Sage, 1978. Pp. 56–79.

Matlon, P. "The Structure of Production and Rural Incomes in Northern Nigeria: Results of Three Village Case Studies." In *The Political Economy of Income Distribution in Nigeria*, edited by H. Bienen and V. Diejomach. New York: Holmes and Meier, 1981. Pp. 323–72.

Medick, H. "The Proto-Industrial Family Economy and The Structures and Functions of Population Development under the Proto-Industrial System". In P. Kriedte et. al, *Industrialization Before Industrialization*. Cambridge: Cambridge University Press, 1981.

————. "The Proto-Industrial Family Economy: The Structural Function of Household and Family During the Transition from Peasant to Industrial Capitalism," *Social History* 1 (1976), 291–315.

Meillassoux, C. "The Economy in Agricultural Self-Sustaining Societies: A Preliminary Analysis." In *Relations of Production*, edited by D. Seddon. London: Cass, 1978. Pp. 127–58.

————. "Development or Exploitation?: Is the Sahel Famine Good Business," *Review of African Political Economy* 1 (1974), 27–33.

Merrill, M. "Cash is Good to Eat: Self Sufficiency and Exchange in the Rural Economy of the United States," *Radical History Review* 1 (1973), 42–71.

Milewski, J. "The Great Depression of the Early 1930's in a Colonial Country: A Case Study of Nigeria," *Africana Bulletin* 23 (1975), 7–46.

Morris, W. "What is a Famine?" *Economic and Political Weekly* 8 (1974), 1855–64.

Morrison, J. H. "Early Tin Production and Nigerian Labour on the Jos Plateau 1906–21," *Canadian Journal of African Studies* XI (1977), 205–16.

Mortimore, M. "Famine in Hausaland," *Savanna* 2 (1973), 102–07.

————. "Population Density and Systems of Agricultural Land Use in Northern Nigeria," *Nigerian Geographical Journal* 14 (1971), 3–15.

————. "Population Densities and Rural Economies in the Kano Close Settled Zone, Nigeria." In *Geography and a Crowding World*, edited by W. Zelinsky, L. Kosinski and R. M. Prothero. London: Oxford University Press, 1970. Pp. 380–88.

————. "Population Distribution, Settlement and Soils in Kano Province, Northern Nigeria 1931–1962." In *The Population of Tropical Africa*, edited by J. C. Caldwell and C. Okonjo. London: Oxford University Press, 1968. Pp. 298–306.

————. "Land and Population Pressure in the Kano Close Settled Zone, Northern Nigeria," *Advancement of Science* 23 (1967), 667–83.

Moscardi, E., and de Janvry, A. "Attitudes Toward Risk Among Peasants: An Econometric Approach," *American Journal of Agricultural Economics* 59 (1977), 710–16.

Mueller, S. D. "Retarded Capitalism in Tanzania," *Socialist Register* (1980), 203–336.

Muller, J. C. "Comment s'Appauvrir en se Développant: Impôts et Changement Social Chez les Rukuba (Nigéria Central)," *Canadian Journal of African Studies* 14, 1 (1980), 83–96.

Newman, J. and Pickett, R. "World Climates and Food Supply," *Science* 186 (1974), 876–77.

Nicolas, G. "Remarques sur Divers Facteurs Socio-Economiques de la Famine au Sein d'une Société Sub-Saharienne." In *Drought in Africa: 2*, edited by D. Dalby et al. London: International African Institute, 1977. Pp. 159–169.

———. "La Pratique Traditionelle du Crédit au Sein d'une Société Sub-Saharienne (Vallée de Maradi, Niger)," *Cultures et Développement* 6 (1974), 737–75.

———. "Fondements Magico-Religieux du Pouvoir Politique au Sein de la Principauté Hausa du Gobir," *Journal de la Société des Africanistes* XXXIX (1969), 199–231.

———. "Une Forme Atténuée du Potlach en Pays Hausa (République du Niger)," *Economies et Sociétés* 2 (1967), 151–214.

Nicolas, G., Magaji, H., and Mouche, M. "Etude Socio-Economique de Deux Villages Hausa: enquête en vue d'un aménagement hydro-agricole, Vallée de Maradi," *Etudes Nigeriennes*, no. 22. CNRS, Paris, 1968.

Nicholson, S. E. "The Methodology of Historical Climate Reconstruction and its Application to Africa," *Journal of African History* 20 (1979), 31–50.

———. "Comparison of Historical and Recent Rainfall Anomalies with Late Pleistocene and Early Holcene." In *Palaeoecology of Africa*, vols. 10–11, edited by E. van Zinderen Bakker and J. Coetz. Rotterdam: Balkeme, 1978. Pp. 99–123.

Norman, D. "Rationalizing Mixed Cropping Under Indigenous Conditions: Experience from Northern Nigeria," *Journal of Development Studies* 11 (1974), 3–21.

———. "Methodology and Problems of Farm Management Investigations: Experiences from Northern Nigeria." African Rural Employment Paper no. 8, Michigan State University, East Lansing, 1973.

———. "An Economic Study of Three Villages in Zaria Province: Part 1, Land and Labour Relationships." Samaru Miscellaneous Papers no. 19, Ahmadu Bello University, Zaria, 1967.

Norman, D., et al. "A Socio-Economic Survey of Three Villages in the Sokoto Close Settled Zone, Part 3, Input-Output Study, Vol. 1, Text." Samaru Miscellaneous Paper no. 64, Ahmadu Bello University, Zaria, 1976.

Norman, D., Pryor, D. H., and Gibbs, C. J. "Technical Change and the Small Farmer in Hausaland, Northern Nigeria." African Rural Economy Papers no. 21, 1979.

Noy-Meir, I. "Desert Ecosystems: Environment and Producers," *Annual Review of Ecology and Systematics* 2 (1973), 25–51.

Nzimiro, I. "Feudalism in Nigeria." In *Toward a Marxist Anthropology: Problems and Perspectives*, edited by S. Diamond. The Hague: Mouton, 1978. Pp. 337–63.

Oculi, O. "Planning the Bakalori Irrigation Project," *Food Policy* 6 (1981), 201–04.

Oguntoyinbo, J. S. "Climatic Variability and Food Crop Production in West Africa," *Geojournal* 5 (1981), 139–50.

Okediji, F. "The Cattle Industry in Northern Nigeria 1900–1939." African Studies Program, Bloomington, Ind., 1973.

O'Keefe, P., and Wisner, B. "African Drought: The State of the Game." In *The African Environment*, edited by P. Richards. London: International African Institute, 1975. Pp. 31–39.

Olinger, J. "The World Bank in Nigeria," *Review of African Political Economy* 13 (1978), 101–07.

Olofson, H. "Yawon Dendi: A Hausa Category of Migration," *Africa* 46 (1976), 66–79.

Oram, P. "Agriculture in the Semi Arid Regions." In *Proceedings of an International Symposium on Rainfed Agriculture in Semi Arid Regions*, University of California, Riverside, 1977. Pp. 2–59.

Orlove, B. "Ecological Anthropology," *Annual Review of Anthropology* 9 (1980), 235–73.

Ormerod, W. "The Ecological Effect of the Control of African Trypanosomiasis," *Science* 191 (1976), 815–21.

Osoba, S. A. "Phenomenon of Labour Migration in the Era of British Colonial Rule: A Neglected Aspect of Nigeria's Social History," *Journal of the Historical Society of Nigeria* IV (1969), 513–38.

Otterman, J. "Baring High Albedo Soils by Overgrazing: A Hypothesized Desertification Mechanism," *Science* 186 (1974), 531–33.

Oyemakinde, W. "The Pullen Marketing Scheme: A Trial in Food Price Control 1941–47," *Journal of the Historical Society of Nigeria* IV (1973), 413–24.

Paden, J. "Aspects of Emirship in Kano." In *West African Chiefs*, edited by M. Crowder and O. Okime. Ife: University of Ife Press, 1972. Pp. 163–86.

Padug, R. A. "Problems in the Theory of Slavery and Slave Society," *Science and Society* XL, 1 (1976), 3–27.

Paine, S. "Agricultural Development in Less Developed Countries," *Cambridge Journal of Economics* 1, 4 (1977), 335–39.

Palmer-Jones, R. "How Not to Learn from Pilot Irrigation Projects: The Nigerian Experience," *Water Supply and Management* 5 (1981), 81–105.

Patnaik, U. "Neopopulism and Marxism: The Chayanovian View of the Agrarian Question and Its Fundamental Fallacy," *Journal of Peasant Studies* 6 (1979), 375–420.

Patterson, O. "Slavery in Human History," *New Left Review* 117 (1979), 31–68.

Pedler, F. "A Study of Income and Expenditure in Northern Zaria," *Africa* 18 (1948), 259–71.

Pilaszewicz, S. "The Song of Poverty and Wealth: A Hausa Poem on Social Problems by Imam Imoru," *Africana Bulletin* 21 (1974), 67–117.

Piuz, A. M. "Climat, Récoltes et Vie des Hommes à Genève, XVIe–XVIIe Siècle," *Annales* XXIX (1974), 601–22.

Plange, N. K. "Opportunity Cost and Labor Migration: A Misinterpretation of Proletarianisation in Northern Ghana," *Journal of Modern African Studies* 17 (1979), 655–76.

Popkin, S. "The Rational Peasant: The Political Economy of Peasant Society," *Theory and Society* 9 (1980), 411–71.

Porter, P. "Environmental Potentials and Economic Opportunities," *American Anthropologist* 67 (1965), 409–20.

Post, K. "Peasantization and Rural Political Movements in Western Africa," *Archives Européenes de Sociologie* 13 (1972), 223–54.

Poulantzas, N. "The Capitalist State: A Reply to Milliband and Leclau," *New Left Review* 95 (1976), 63–83.

Prothero, R. "Migrant Labor from Northwestern Nigeria," *Africa* 27 (1957), 251–62.

Pullan, P. "Farmed Parkland in West Africa," *Savanna* 3 (1974), 119–51.

Ranger, T. "Growing from the Roots: Reflections on Peasant Research in Central and Southern Africa," *Journal of Southern African Studies* 5 (1978), 99–133.

———. "The People In African Resistance: A Review," *Journal of Southern African Studies* 4 (1977), 125–46.

Rapp, A. "A Review of Desertification in Africa." SIES Report no. 1, Stockholm, 1974.

Rappaport, R. "Ritual, Sanctity and Cybernetics," *American Anthropologist* 73 (1971), 59–70.

Raulin, H. "Techniques et bases socio-économiques des sociétés rurales nigèriennes," *Etudes Nigèriennes* no. 12. CRNS, Paris, 1964.

Raynault, C. "Lessons of a Crisis." In *Drought in Africa 2*, edited by D. Dalby et al. London: International African Institute, 1977. Pp. 17–29.

———. "Circulation monétaire et évolution des structures socio-économiques chez les haoussa du Niger," *Africa* 47 (1977a), 160–71.

———. "Aspects socio-économiques de la circulation de la nourriture dans un village hausa (Niger)," *Cahiers d'Etudes Africaines* 17 (1977b), 569–97.

———. "Transformation du système de production et inégalité économique: le cas d'une village haoussa (Niger)," *Canadian Journal of African Studies* X (1976), 279–306.

———. "Le Cas de la Région de Maradi, Niger." In *Sècheresse et Famine Du Sahel*, vol. 1, edited by J. Copans. Paris: Maspero, 1975. Pp. 5–42.

———. "Quelques Données de l'Horticulture dans la Vallée de Maradi." *Etudes Nigeriennes*, no. 26. CNRS, Paris, 1969.

Richards, P. Editorial in *African Environment* 1 (1975), 3.

Richards, P., and Oguntoyinbo, J. "Extent and Intensity of Drought in Nigeria." In *Drought in Africa* 2, edited by D. Dalby et al. London: International African Institute, 1977. Pp. 114–26.

Rimmer, D. "Development in Nigeria: An Overview." In *The Political Economy of Income Distribution in Nigeria*, edited by H. Bienen and V. P. Diejomach. New York: Holmes and Meier, 1981. Pp. 29–87.

Roberts, R. "Fishing for the State." In *Modes of Production in Africa*, edited by C. Stewart and D. Crummey. Beverly Hills: Sage, 1981. Pp. 175–204.

———. "The Emergence of a Grain Market in Bamako: 1881–1903," *Canadian Journal of African Studies* 14, 1 (1980), 55–81.

Robson, E. "Utilisation du concept d'adaptation en anthropologie culturelle," *Social Science Information* 17 (1978), 279–335.

Roder, W., and Dupree, J. "Coping with Drought in a Pre-industrial, Pre-literate Farming Society." In *Natural Hazards*, edited by G. White. London: Oxford University Press, 1974. Pp. 115–19.

Rognan, P., and Williams, M. A. J. "Late Quarternary Climatic Changes in Australia and North Africa," *Palaeogeography, Palaeoclimatology and Palaeoecology* 21 (1977), 285–327.

Roseberry, W. "Peasants as Proletarians," *Critiques of Anthropology* 3, 11 (1978), 3–18.

Rupley, L. A. "Revenue Sharing in the Nigerian Federation," *Journal of Modern African Studies* 19, 2 (1981), 257–78.

Ruttenberg, S. "Climate, Food and Society." In *Climate's Impact on Food Supplies*, edited by L. E. Slater and S. K. Levin. Boulder: Westview Press, 1981. Pp. 23–38.

Salamone, F. "Early Expatriate Society in Northern Nigeria: Contributions to a Refinement of a Theory of Pluralism," *African Studies Review* XXI (1978), 39–54.

Salifou, A. "When History Repeats Itself: The Famine of 1931 in Niger," *African Environment* 1, 2 (1975), 22–48.

———. "Le Damagaram ou le Sultanat de Zinder au XIXe Siècle." *Etudes Nigeriennes* no. 27. CNRSH, Niamey, 1971.

Sandford, S. "Toward a Definition of Drought." In *Symposium on Drought in Botswana*, edited by M. Hinchley. Worcester: Clark University Press, 1979. Pp. 33–40.

Sauer, C. "The Agency of Man on the Earth." In *Man's Role in Changing the Face of the Earth*, edited by W. L. Thomas. Chicago: University of Chicago Press, 1957. Pp. 49–69.

Sayer, A. "Epistemology and Conceptions of People and Nature in Geography," *Geoforum* 10 (1979), 19–43.

Schove, D. "African Drought and the Spectrum of Time." In *Drought in Africa 2*, edited by D. Dalby et al. London: International African Institute, 1977. Pp. 38–52.

———. "African Droughts and Weather History. In *Drought in Africa*, edited by D. Dalby and R. J. Harrison-Church. London: SOAS, 1973. Pp. 29–30.

Schuurmans, C. J. E. "Influence of Solar Activity on Winter Temperatures," *Climatic Change* 1 (1978), 231–37.

Scott, E. "Land Use Change in the Harsh Lands of West Africa," *African Studies Review* XXII (1979), 1–24.

Scott, J. "Some Notes on Post-Peasant Society," *Peasant Studies* 7 (1978), 267–96.

———. "Revolution in the Revolution," *Theory and Society* 4 (1977a), 1–38.

———. "Protest and Profanation," *Theory and Society* 4 (1977b), 211–46.

———. "Hegemony and the Peasantry," *Politics and Society* 7, 3 (1977c), 267–96.

———. "Patron-Client Politics and Political Change in Southeast Asia," *American Political Science Review* 66 (1972), 93–112.

Scott, J. and Kerkvliet, B. "How Traditional Rural Patrons Lose Legitimacy in Southeast Asia," *Cultures et Développement* V (1973), 501–40.

Seaman, J. and Holt, J. "Markets and Famines in the Third World," *Disasters* 4, 3 (1980), 283–97.

SEDES. "Réflexions sur l'Avenir des Systèmes Pastouraux Sahéliens et Sahélo-Soudaniens." In *Les Systèmes Pastoraux Sahéliens*. Etude FAO no. 5, Production Végétale et Protection des Plantes. Rome: FAO, 1976.

SEDES. "Project de Modernisation de la Zone Pastorale: Zone d'Intervention de Tejira: Annexes." Rapport Provisoire. Paris: SEDES, 1978.

Sen, A. "Famines," *World Development* 8, 9 (1980), 613–21.

———. "Starvation and Exchange Entitlements: A General Approach and Its Application to the Great Bengal Famine," *Cambridge Journal of Economics* 1 (1977), 33–59.

————. "Famines as Failures of Exchange Entitlements," *Economic and Political Weekly* XI (1976), 1273–80.

Shanin, T. Introduction to *Peasants and Peasant Society*, edited by T. Shanin. Harmondsworth: Penguin, 1971. Pp. 11–19.

Shaw, T. "The Prehistory of West Africa." In *The History of West Africa*, vol. 1, edited by M. Crowder and F. Ajayi. London: Longmans, 1971. Pp. 38–44.

Shenton, R., and Freund, W. "The Incorporation of Northern Nigeria into the World Capitalism Economy," *Review of African Political Economy* 13 (1978), 8–20.

Shenton, R., and Lennihan, L. "Capital and Class: Peasant Differentiation in Northern Nigeria," *Journal of Peasant Studies* 9, 1 (1981), 47–70.

Shepherd, A. "Agrarian Change in Northern Ghana: Public Investment, Capitalist Farming and Famine." In *Rural Development in Tropical Africa*, edited by J. Heyer, P. Roberts, and G. Williams. London: Macmillan, 1981. Pp. 168–192.

Simmons, E. "Calorie and Protein Intake in Three Villages of Zaria Province." Samaru Miscellaneous Paper no. 55, Ahmadu Bello University, Zaria, 1976.

————. "Rural Household Expenditures in Three Villages in Zaria Province." Samaru Miscellaneous Paper no. 56, Ahmadu Bello University, Zaria, 1976.

Slobodkin, L., and A. Rapoport. "An Optimal Strategy of Evolution," *Quarterly Review of Biology* 49 (1974), 151–200.

Smith, H. F. C. "The Early States of the Central Sudan." In *West African History*, vol. 1, edited by M. Crowder and F. Ajayi. London: Longmans, 1971. Pp. 158–201.

————. "Some Considerations Relating to the Formation of States in Hausaland," *Journal of the Historical Society of Nigeria* 3 (1970), 329–46.

Smith, M. G. "Slavery and Emancipation in Two Societies," *Social and Economic Studies* 3 (1954), 239–90.

————. "The Beginnings of Hausa Society." In *The Historian in Africa*, edited by J. Vansina, R. Mauny and L. Thomas. London: Oxford University Press, 1964. Pp. 338–45.

————. "Historical and Cultural Conditions of Political Corruption Among the Hausa," *Comparative Studies in Society and History* VI (1964a), 164–94.

————. "The Hausa of Northern Nigeria." In *Peoples in Africa*, edited by J. L. Gibbs. New York: Holt, Rinehart, and Winston, 1965. Pp. 119–25.

————. "Hausa Inheritance and Succession." In *Studies in the Laws of Succession in Nigeria*, edited by J. Derrett. London: Oxford University Press, 1966.

————. "The Jihad of Usman dan Fodio." In *Islam in Tropical Africa*, edited by I. Lewis. London: Oxford University Press, 1966a. Pp. 56–78.

————. "A Hausa Kingdom: Maradi under Dan Baskore." In *West African Kingdoms in the Nineteenth Century*, edited by D. Forde and P. Kaberry. London: Oxford University Press, 1967. Pp. 99–122.

Smith, S. "Colonialism in Economic Theory," *Journal of Development Studies* 15 (1979), 38–59.

Spittler, G. "Peasants and the State in Niger," *Peasant Studies* 8, 1 (1979), 30–47.

Spitz, P. "Silent Violence: Famine and Inequality," *International Review of Social Science* XXX, 4 (1978), 867–92.

Stebbing, E. T. "The Encroaching Sahara: The Threat to the West African Colonies," *Geographical Journal* 65 (1935), 136–57.

Stock, R. "The Impact of the Decline of the Hadjia River Floods in Hadejia Emirate." In *The Aftermath of the 1972–74 Drought in Nigeria*, edited by G. J. van Apeldoorn. Zaria: CSER, Ahmadu Bello University, 1978. Pp. 141–46.

Suret-Canale, J. "The Economic Balance Sheet of French Colonialism in West Africa." In *African Social Studies: A Radical Reader*, edited by P. Gutkind and P. Waterman. London: Heinemann, 1977c. Pp. 125–36.

————. "Les sociétés traditionelles en Afrique Tropicale et le concept de mode de production asiatiques." In *Sur le Mode de Production Asiatique*. Paris: Centre d'Etudes et Recherches Marxistes, 1969. Pp. 101–33.

Sutton, J. G. "Towards a Less Orthodox History of Hausaland," *Journal of African History* 20, 2 (1979), 179–201.

Swainson, O. S. "A Note on the Kwarre Irrigation Scheme," *Farm and Forest* V (1944), 158–60.

Swift, J. "Sahelian Pastoralists, Underdevelopment, Desertification and Famine," *Review of Anthropology* 6 (1977), 457–78.

Tambo, D. "The Sokoto Caliphate Slave Trade," *International Journal of African Historical Studies* 9, 2 (1976), 187–217.

Terray, Emmanuel. "Long Distance Exchange and the Formation of the State: The Case of the Abron Kingdom of Gyaman," *Economy and Society* 3, 3 (1974), 315–45.

Thom, D. J. "The Niger-Nigeria Boundary 1890–1906." Papers in International Studies, African Series, no. 23, Ohio University, Center for International Studies, 1975.

Thompson, E. P. "Eighteenth Century English Society: Class Struggle Without Class?" *Social History* 3, 2 (1978), 133–65.

———. "Patrician Society," *Journal of Social History* VII (1974), 382–405.

———. "Under the Same Roof Tree." In *Times Literary Supplement*, New York, May 4, 1973. Pp. 485–87.

———. "Anthropology and the Discipline of Historical Context," *Midland History* 13 (1972), 41–55.

———. "The Moral Economy of the English Crowd during the Eighteenth Century," *Past and Present* 50 (1971), 76–116.

Titow, J. "Evidence of Weather in the Account Rolls of the Bishopric of Winchester, 1209–1350," *Economic History Review* 12 (1960), 360–407.

Torry, W. "Anthropological Studies in Hazardous Environments: Past Trends and New Horizons," *Current Anthropology* 20, 3 (1979), 517–40.

Tosh, J. "Lango Agriculture During the Early Colonial Period: Land and Labor in a Cash Crop Economy," *Journal of African History* 19 (1978), 415–39.

Triulzi, A. "Decolonizing Africa History." In *People's History and Socialist Theory*, edited by R. Samuel. London: Routledge and Kegan Paul, 1981. Pp. 286–96.

Uchendu, V. "State, Land and Society in Nigeria: A Critical Assessment of the Land Use Decree (1978)," *Journal of African Studies* 6 (1979), 62–74.

Vayda, A. "Problems in the Identification of Environmental Problems." In *Subsistence and Survival*, edited by T. Bayliss-Smith and R. Feachem. London: Academic Press, 1977. Pp. 411–18.

Vayda, A., and McCay, B. "New Directions in Ecology and Ecological Anthropology," *Annual Review of Anthropology* 4 (1975), 293–306.

Vayda, A. P., and Rappaport, R. "Ecology, Cultural and Non-Cultural." In *Introduction to Cultural Anthropology*, edited by J. Clifton. Boston: Houghton Mifflin, 1967. Pp. 477–97.

Vergopoulos, K. "Capitalism and Peasant Productivity," *Journal of Peasant Studies* 5, 4 (1978), 446–65.

———. "Capitalisme difforme: le cas de l'agriculture dans le capitalisme." In *La Question Paysanne et le Capitalisme*, edited by S. Amin and K. Vergopoulos. Paris: Editions Anthropos, 1974. Pp. 48–62.

Von Freyhold, M. "The Post-Colonial State and Its Tanzanian Version," *Review of African Political Economy* 8 (1977), 75–89.

Waddell, E. "The Hazards of Scientism," *Human Ecology* 5 (1977), 69–76.

———. "How the Engae Cope with Frost," *Human Ecology* 4 (1975), 294–73.

Waldman, M. "The Fulani Jihad: A Re-Assessment," *Journal of African History* VI (1968), 333–55.

Wallace, T. "The Challenge of Food: Nigeria's Approach to Agriculture 1975–1980," *Canadian Journal of African Studies* 15 (1981), 239–58.

———. "Rural Development Through Irrigation: Studies in a Town on the Kano River Project." CSER Research Report no. 3, Ahmadu Bello University, 1979.

Wallerstein, I. "The Rise and Future Demise of the World Capitalist System: Concepts for Comparative Analysis." In *The Capitalist World Economy*, by I. Wallerstein. Cambridge: Cambridge University Press, 1979. Pp. 1–36.

Wallerstein, I., and Martin, W. "Household Structures and Production Processes." Working Paper, Fernand Braudel Centre, State University of New York, Binghamton, 1979.

White, G. "Natural Hazards Research." In *Directions in Geography*, edited by R. Chorley. London: Methuen, 1973. Pp. 193–216.

Williams, G. "The World Bank and the Peasant Problem." In *Rural Development in Tropical Africa*, edited by J. Heyer, P. Roberts, and G. Williams. London: MacMillan, 1981. Pp. 10–51.

————. "Taking the Part of Peasants: Rural Development in Nigeria and Tanzania." In *The Political Economy of Contemporary Africa*, edited by P. Gutkind and I. Wallerstein. Beverly Hills: Sage, 1976. Pp. 131–54.

Winstanley, D. "Rainfall Patterns and General Atmospheric Circulation," *Nature* 245 (1973) 190–94.

Wolf, E. "Closed Corporate Communities in Meso-America and Java," *Southwestern Journal of Anthropology* 13 (1957), 1–18.

Wolpe, H. "Capitalism and Cheap Labour Power in South Africa: From Segregation to Apartheid," *Economy and Society* 1, 4 (1972), 425–56.

Wood, G. "Class Formation and Antediluvian Capital in Bangladesh," *IDS Bulletin* 9 (1978), 39–43.

Wright, M. "The Reluctant Integration of Zimbabwe 1852–1908," *Review* III (1979), 211–28.

Zerbo, J. K. Introduction to *General History of Africa: Volume 1*, Methodology and African Prehistory, edited by J. K. Zerbo. London: Heinemann, 1981. Pp. 1–24.

INDEX

Abalu, G., 114
Abdu, P., 383, 384
Abdullahi, M., 171, 229
Adamawa, 153
Adaptation, 139, 140, 145, 463, 465; to capitalism, 10, 12, 19–25, 62, 233, 449–461, 522 n. 19; to climate, 83–84, 105, 113, 139, 418–430; colonialism affects, 152, 266; to environmental risk, 85–87, 89, 105; evolution as, 86; as pastoral strategy, 118–121
Adar, 133, 134, 143
Adas, M., 89, 107, 108, 136, 369
Adebo wage claim, 483, 508
Adeleye, R., 46, 365
Adeoye, K. B., 92, 377
Adeyeye, S. O., 247
Advance system. See Credit; Crops, mortgaged in advance
Africa: agriculture in, 5–9; colonial era of, 19, 22, 40 (see also Colonial protectorate); economy of, 10, 19, 86; food deficits in, 5, 9; food production in, 5–9; historiography of, 40. See also Nigeria
Agege, 492
Agricultural Development Council, 15
Agriculture: African, 5–9; and capital, 4, 21, 22–23, 24, 153, 176–178, 182, 183–186, 187, 452, 460–461, 466, 493–494, 495, 496, 505–506, 509, 512; in colonial protectorate, 24, 150, 176–178, 180–181, 190, 323–326, 351–357; commercialized, 267, 364; cycle of, 92, 93, 114–115, 116, 263–265, 416, 420; devel-

opment projects, 502, 505–506 (see also Nigeria, development plans of; River basin development); dry-season (see Irrigation); foreign capital in, 374, 493–494, 495, 496, 505, 512; government policy on, 488, 489–511; in Hausaland, 60–61; in Kaita, 396; landlord mode of, 157; multinationals in, 374, 491; and oil, 470–471, 483–506; v. pastoralism, 206–213; plantation, 180; productivity in, 498–505, 506; rainfall affects, 112, 114, 416, 420, 442; risk in, 147, 462–463; risk aversion in, 13, 15–17, 105, 107, 113–121; ritual in, 116–117; in Sokoto Caliphate, 60–61, 65, 68; and taxes, 70, 263–265; technology in, 27, 190, 323–326, 336, 396, 460–461, 491, 492, 493, 495–498, 500; war affects, 377. See also Farm/farming
Ahmadu, Caliph, 49
Ahmadu Bello University, 422
Ahmed, M. L., 390
Ahn, P. M., 90
Alamgir, M., 18
Alhaji Mohammed Marawa, 508
Al-Hajj, M., 53
Aliyu, A., 143
Aliyu, M., 385
Allan, W., 105
Allegiance. See Clientage
Al-Mahili, 46
Altman, L., 193
Ambrosini Company, 295
Amin, Samir, 75
Anderson, J., 74, 85

Geographies of Justice and Social Transformation

1. *Social Justice and the City*, rev. ed., by David Harvey

2. *Begging as a Path to Progress: Indigenous Women and Children and the Struggle for Ecuador's Urban Spaces*, by Kate Swanson

3. *Making the San Fernando Valley: Rural Landscapes, Urban Development, and White Privilege*, by Laura R. Barraclough

4. *Company Towns in the Americas: Landscape, Power, and Working-Class Communities*, edited by Oliver J. Dinius and Angela Vergara

5. *Tremé: Race and Place in a New Orleans Neighborhood*, by Michael E. Crutcher Jr.

6. *Bloomberg's New York: Class and Governance in the Luxury City*, by Julian Brash

7. *Roppongi Crossing: The Demise of a Tokyo Nightclub District and the Reshaping of a Global City*, by Roman Adrian Cybriwsky

8. *Fitzgerald: Geography of a Revolution*, by William Bunge

9. *Accumulating Insecurity: Violence and Dispossession in the Making of Everyday Life*, edited by Shelley Feldman, Charles Geisler, and Gayatri A. Menon

10. *They Saved the Crops: Labor, Landscape, and the Struggle over Industrial Farming in Bracero-Era California*, by Don Mitchell

11. *Faith Based: Religious Neoliberalism and the Politics of Welfare in the United States*, by Jason Hackworth

12. *Fields and Streams: Stream Restoration, Neoliberalism, and the Future of Environmental Science*, by Rebecca Lave

13. *Black, White, and Green: Farmers Markets, Race, and the Green Economy*, by Alison Hope Alkon

14. *Beyond Walls and Cages: Prisons, Borders, and Global Crisis*, edited by Jenna M. Loyd, Matt Mitchelson, and Andrew Burridge

15. *Silent Violence: Food, Famine, and Peasantry in Northern Nigeria*, by Michael J. Watts

9 780820 34